The New York Times Sports Hall of Fame

The New York Times Sports Hall of Fame

Edited by
Arleen Keylin
and
Jonathan Cohen

Introduction by Gerald Eskenazi

Arno Press • New York • 1981

A Note to the Reader

Original issues of The New York Times were not available for use in preparing this book. The best facsimile reproduction possible was obtained by utilizing photostats created from the microfilm edition of The Times. In many cases new type has been set to assure legibility.

Library of Congress Cataloging in Publication Data

Main entry under title:

The New York times sports hall of fame.

1. Athletes—Biography—Addresses, essays, lectures.
2. New York times—Addresses, essays, lectures.
3. Obituaries—New York (City)—Addresses, essays, lectures. I. Keylin, Arleen. II. Cohen, Jonathan. III. New York times.
GV697.A1N45 796.375'092'2 [B] 80-28594
ISBN 0-405-13942-X

Editorial Assistant: Daniel Lundy

Book design by Stephanie Keylin

Manufactured in the United States of America

Contents

Introduction

by Gerald Eskenazi

The obituary of a sports hero is a celebration of the life he led.

It is a rare form of writing—it gives us the opportunity to put into perspective, to reminisce about, to marvel at, the accomplishments of a man or woman who, for whatever reason, had glorious moments that made all of us happier for them.

The stories that follow also provide a fascinating look at ourselves, at how we perceive the death of an idol at that moment in time. They also give us an immediate perspective that is lacking if we merely look up isolated microfilmed stories on, say, Babe Ruth being fined for missing a baseball game. Or Jim Thorpe's olympian accomplishments at the 1912 Olympic Games. Or Peter Revson gunning his racing machine around the Monte Carlo streets.

The headlines are evocative, probably because they are so straight. They are classic *New York Times* heads. They fit the column well, they are balanced, they do not shout: "Clemente, Pirates' Star, Dies in Crash of Plane Carrying Aid to Nicaragua" or, "Gehrig, 'Iron Man' Of Baseball, Dies At The Age of 37" or, "John L. Sullivan Fatally Stricken".

These articles have special meaning for me. There are so many legends among the more than 90 here that were part of my vocabulary as a teen-ager in Brooklyn in the 1950's. We all dreamed of meeting Jackie Robinson, Joe Lapchick, Rocky Marciano. If we hadn't seen other idols, such as Ruth, and Bobby Jones and Big Bill Tilden, we certainly read about them. These were glorious figures, transcendental characters.

I have autographs from some of the people whose names are here. One day outside the Polo Grounds, where I had traveled to see my Dodgers play the Giants, I was one of a hundred youngsters who asked Jackie Robinson for his autograph. I also asked him a question.

"How come you're not stealing so many bases this year, Jackie?"

"You've got to get on base first, kid," he replied.

And I recall that same day getting an autograph from Gil Hodges, the huge quiet man, who patiently signed my program while a friend of his waited in a big Cadillac and kept repeating, "C'mon, Gillie, we gotta go."

Later, as a reporter, I met Jackie Robinson and I was surprised. I found an intense, often angry man, so out of keeping with how I had imagined he would be from what I had read in newspapers. In other words, he was more than a ballplayer. He was flesh and blood. These qualities, unfortunately, often are not transmitted to newspaper readers.

I covered Gil Hodges, too, and against my better instincts—for I now was a reporter, not a fan—told him I had once received his autograph. He smiled, and for an instant seemed embarrassed. But he quickly recovered.

"It doesn't say much for your taste," he said. We both laughed.

One day, I also would write obituaries of some of these people. I don't recall whose was the first. In my early years as a reporter for *The Times,* I spent evenings on rewrite. As soon as a famed sports personality was hospitalized for any reason, I would be asked to update his obituary. It surprises people to learn that, at *The New York Times,* we have hundreds of advance obituaries written and waiting.

But the most challenging sports writing of all is to write the life of a legend while under deadline pressure. You must avoid the cliche, get beneath the statistics. With difficulty, I wrote of the life and tragic death of Terry Sawchuk, perhaps hockey's greatest goalie. I had found him a bitter, edgy player at the end of his career when he joined the New York Rangers. I also wrote of the career of Ken Strong, a larger-than-life football hero, and I tried to evoke the time and place of which he was a part. In updating Casey Stengel's advance obituary, I was astounded at how much emphasis had to be shifted, for he had begun a new career as manager of the New York Mets while in his 70's.

It is remarkable that such an eclectic sampling has been gathered between covers. We have not only Tinker and Evers and Chance, but Sonja Henie and Thurman Munson, James J. Corbett and Willie Hoppe, Judge Kenesaw Mountain Landis and Knute Rockne. These are the people that America admired, eulogized, often raised high onto a pedestal from which, inevitably, they fell. But if we sometimes created false heroes from those whose stories follow, we also extracted the good, those parts of their character that we wanted for ourselves.

Ultimately, the myths of our sports heroes are part of our own longings for something special. And what is wrong with that?

The New York Times SUNDAY, NOVEMBER 5, 1950.

ALEXANDER IS DEAD; NOTED PITCHER, 63

Fanned Lazzeri With Three on Base to Take 1926 Series for Cards Against Yanks

SET 1.22 EARNED RUN MARK

Righthander Won 30 or More 3 Successive Years for Phillies —Also Hurled for Cubs

ST. PAUL, Neb., Nov. 4 (AP)—Grover Cleveland Alexander, one-time star major league baseball pitcher, was found dead of a heart ailment this afternoon in his room here. The 63-year-old mound master had been in failing health in recent years.

Alexander had been rooming here at the home of Mrs. Josie Nevrivy. When the Nevrivys heard no sounds from his room during the forenoon, a son investigated. Dr. E. C. Hanisch Sr. said he had been dead for several hours.

A friend reported that Alexander had planned to go to Omaha this week to visit his divorced wife, Aimee. An unfinished letter to Mrs. Alexander was found in the pitcher's typewriter.

He leaves three brothers, Charles of St. Paul, and Alvie and Warren of Grand Island.

Outstanding for Nineteen Years

Ranked among baseball's immortals, Alexander was an outstanding right-handed pitcher for nearly twenty years. Nicknamed Old Pete and Alex the Great by his admirers, he proved a thorn to major league batsmen from 1911 to 1930, and during that period compiled several pitching records.

Alexander, who had helped pitch the Phillies to their last previous pennant, in 1915, stood for three innings in the back of the mezzanine of the Yankee Stadium grandstand, unrecognized by anyone, during the recent Yankees-Phillies world series. He was attending the series through the courtesy of a friend and a Chicago radio program.

A baseball writer caught sight of him and took him into the press box where he was glad to sit down. He watched the game closely, but from time to time talked of other days, of the trouble he had pitching to Hornsby, and how he held Babe Ruth to a single in sixteen times at bat.

He was born in St. Paul, Neb., on Feb. 26, 1887, learned to play the game on the prairies and was

Grover Cleveland Alexander compiled a remarkable 1.22 earned run average in 1915.

a sensation in his first season as a major leaguer after a brief stay in the minors. Alexander was obtained by the Phillies from the Syracuse club in 1911 and won twenty-eight games that year, a remarkable achievement for a rookie.

Won 373 Games for 3 Teams

His curve ball and perfect control brought him thirty or more triumphs in successive seasons from 1915 through 1917, an accomplishment credited to only one other National League hurler, Christy Mathewson of the New York Giants, in this century. Alexander won thirty-one victories in 1915, thirty-three in 1916 and thirty in 1917.

Although he never pitched a no-hit, no-run game, he registered many amazing records. He pitched 696 contests for three teams, the Phillies, Chicago Cubs and St. Louis Cardinals, during his National League career, and won 373 of them. For six years he led the circuit in complete games pitched, and in 1915 he established a National League earned run mark of 1.22 for pitchers working in 250 innings or more.

Alexander enjoyed his most successful year in 1916 and in that campaign scored sixteen shutout triumphs. During his entire career in the majors, he blanked his rivals on ninety occasions, a feat still unequaled in National League history.

After seven years with the Phillies, Alexander was sent with his battery mate, Bill Killifer, to the Chicago Cubs for $55,000 and several players, an enormous price at the time. He twirled the opening game of the 1918 campaign for the Cubs and then became a member of the A. E. F. He saw service overseas during the first World War and was made a sergeant.

In 1919 Alexander picked up the thread of his spectacular feats with the Cubs and was an idol of Wrigley Field fans in Chicago for eight years. When he appeared to be losing his mastery, the Cubs sent him on waivers to the St. Louis Cardinals in June, 1926, but, in a sensational comeback, he became the hero of the World Series that Fall.

Beat Yanks Twice in '26 Series

Alexander proceeded to win twelve of twenty-two games during the regular campaign and then hurled the Cardinals to two victories over the New York Yankees in the World Series. His pitching in the sixth game enabled St. Louis to tie the count at three-all in the baseball classic, and excitement ran high at the Yankee Stadium as the seventh and deciding contest moved into the seventh inning with the Cardinals holding a 3-to-2 lead over the American League pennant winners.

Although denied by Alexander, the story circulated through the Stadium that afternoon that he had celebrated his previous day's triumph too well and was catching up on his sleep in the bullpen, when a teammate told him that Manager Rogers Hornsby wanted him to enter the game as relief pitcher.

When he was summoned, the bases were filled, there were two out and Tony Lazzeri, slugging second baseman of the Yankees, was at bat. Alexander trudged slowly to the mound looking dejected, but fanned Lazzeri on three pitched balls to quell the Yankee threat. He continued to tame the New Yorkers during the remaining two frames and clinched the world championship for the Cards.

Exultant St. Louis fans gave the club a roaring welcome when Alexander and his mates returned to that city after their capture of the World Series. One of the most conspicuous banners carried in the St. Louis victory parade bore the inscription, "Alexander for President."

During his last big season, in 1927, Alexander won twenty-one games and lost ten for the Cards. He scored sixteen victories the next year but lost his effectiveness thereafter and returned to the Phillies after the 1929 campaign. The Phils handed him his unconditional release on June 3, 1930, thus ending his major league career.

Later he pitched for a brief time for Dallas in the Texas League and in 1938 he was still twirling an occasional game for the House of David and other independent clubs, when he was voted into baseball's Hall of Fame at Cooperstown, N. Y. His selection made Alexander the fourth pitcher to receive that honor. The others were Mathewson, Walter Johnson and Cy Young.

Alexander, who saw action in the 1915 world series with the Phillies as well as in the 1926 and 1927 classics with the Cards, was carefree and had an utter disregard for training rules. His inclination to break training frequently got him in difficulties with his managers and in later years club owners hesitated to take a chance on him as a team leader.

Hard times resulted for Alexander and he turned to various odd jobs. One Summer he sold tickets at a Middle West race track. In recent years he was an added attraction at a sideshow on West Forty-second Street, where, in a low, soft voice, he enthralled the customers with stories concerning baseball heroes of bygone days.

Alexander survived a skull fracture in 1941 and, when it became generally known that he was in need of money, baseball fans rallied and contributed handsomely to a fund for the old-timer. During the war he was employed at a Cincinnati airplane factory. At that time he wanted it known that his physical condition was such that he would welcome a job in baseball, as a pitching coach or in some other capacity.

Apparently, no one found a need for old Pete in the game that made him famous.

The New York Times SATURDAY, SEPTEMBER 14, 1968

Tommy Armour, Golfer, Dead; Won Many Major Open Events

Special to The New York Times

LARCHMONT, N. Y., Sept. 13 — Tommy Armour, one of the best and most colorful golfers of the century, died here Wednesday after a long illness. He was 72 years old. Private funeral services were held here yesterday.

Player and Teacher

Both as an amateur and a professional, Armour was one of the most successful golfers in the 1920's and 1930's. In addition, in his later years he was known as one of the keenest students of the game and one of its most talented teachers.

In a career that started just after World War I he scored notable victories in the United States and British opens, the Professional Golfers Association championship, the French amateur and the Canadian open. He also won numerous smaller tournaments on the P. G. A. tour.

Thomas Dickson Armour was born on Sept. 24, 1895, in Edinburgh, Scotland, attended Edinburgh University and served during World War I with the Black Watch Highland Regiment. He was severely wounded in the eyes and arms. After a period of blindness that lasted six months, he regained sight in his right eye.

The fact that he was blind in his left eye did not hinder his golf game, although it may have contributed to his well-known habit of waggling his club repeatedly before executing a shot. At times, players and spectators would bet on how many preliminary moves he would make before a shot.

Although known as one of the greatest iron players that the game has produced, Armour was also an exceptional shot with woods.

He came to the United States in 1921 a few months after playing with a British amateur team that defeated an American team in a forerunner of the Walker Cup series. In 1926 he played on an American professional squad that defeated a British team.

After serving as golf secretary at the Westchester-Biltmore Country Club in Harrison, he became a professional in 1924 and achieved his first major success by winning the Florida East Coast Open in 1925.

In 1927, he won the United States Open at Oakmont, Pa., by defeating Harry Cooper, an English professional, in an 18-hole playoff. For his victory, he won $500, plus $100 for the playoff and $100 from the Oakmont Club as a gift.

He won the P. G. A. title in 1930, defeating Gene Sarazen, 1 up, in the final at the Fresh Meadow Country Club in Flushing, Queens. The next year he won the British Open at Carnoustie, Scotland, with a 72-hole score of 296.

After his competitive career, Armour designed clubs for the Crawford, McGregor and Canby Company, and served as a teacher at the Boca Raton Club in Florida where his pupils included well-known politicians and theatrical stars as well as some expert golfers.

He was a convivial man who loved to tell golfing stories over a drink or two in the clubhouse and he was known for the Scottish burr that colored his speech. In addition, he often punctuated his remarks with a "Now, lassie" or "Well, laddie."

Since 1951 he had been a member of the Winged Foot Golf Club in Mamaroneck. He was in great demand as a speaker at athletic functions because his interest in all sports was intense and his knowledge great.

He leaves his second wife, Estelle; a son, Thomas Jr., and a stepson, John. A first marriage ended in divorce.

Tommy Armour won virutally every major golf championship possible.

"All the News That's Fit to Print"

The New York Times.

LATE CITY EDITION
U. S. Weather Bureau Report (Page 95) Forecast: Variable cloudiness, mild today. Increasing cloudiness tomorrow.
Temp. range: 58—42, yesterday: 47.2—38.6

NEWS SUMMARY AND INDEX, PAGE 95

SECTION ONE

VOL. CIX..No. 37,192. NEW YORK, SUNDAY, NOV. 22, 1959. TWENTY-FIVE CENTS

CITY FILES 10 BILLS ON YOUTH CRIMES WITH LEGISLATURE

Program Is Aimed to Tighten Laws on Possession of and Dealing in Weapons

SALES RECORDS SOUGHT

Psychotherapy Leader and an Assemblyman Call for 'Boys' Towns' in State

By PAUL CROWELL

Ten bills to help the city combat juvenile delinquency have been filed with the Legislature, Mayor Wagner announced yesterday.

He said that they would be introduced immediately after the 1960 Legislature convened on Jan. 6.

The bills were drafted after the Mayor and his top advisers had conferred with the District Attorneys of the five counties in the city, Police Commissioner Stephen P. Kennedy, City Administrator Charles F. Preusse, Corporation Counsel Charles H. Tenney and the members of the Youth Board.

Another move to help stem the tide of juvenile crime was announced at the second annual meeting of the Citizens Legislative Conference at the Brooklyn Law School, 375 Pearl Street, Brooklyn.

Weapons Curbs Sought

Members of the civic group were told that an effort would be made to obtain legislation putting teeth into laws against the sale of weapons to unauthorized persons.

The program sent to Albany by the Mayor was the basis for his request last month that the ten bills be considered at a special session of the Legislature. Governor Rockefeller declined to call such a session, but indicated that the measures would be carefully studied by his newly appointed "task force" committee on juvenile delinquency.

The bills, which were filed Friday, would:

¶Reduce from 16 years to 15 the age at which youths could be tried for crimes other than murder.

¶Provide that physical possession of weapons, such as guns, knives, blackjacks or brass knuckles by anyone participating in an unlawful assembly be presumptive evidence of illegal possession by all other persons in the gathering.

¶Make it a felony for a person to carry a loaded pistol or revolver whether exposed or concealed. At present the carrying of an unconcealed weapon is only a misdemeanor.

¶Provide that illegal possession of weapons by two or more persons in an assemblage of three or more on a public highway be presumptive evidence that the assemblage is for the

Continued on Page 45, Column 1

U. S. and Panama Begin Talks in a Friendly Mood

Associated Press

Livingston T. Merchant, second from left, in Panama yesterday with For... Miguel A. Moreno Jr., at left, and Julian F. Harrington, right, the U...

Special to The New York Times.

PANAMA, Nov. 21—An atmosphere of relaxed friendliness surrounded a ninety-minute talk this morning between President Ernesto de la Guardia Jr. and Livingston T. Merchant, United States Dep-uty Under Secretary of State... Mr. Merchant ... nied by ... Ambas...

Cuba Limits Sea... Nationalization S...

By R. HART PHILLIPS

Special to The New York Times.

HAVANA, Nov. 21—The Government ... petroleum law today to reduce the size of ... ploration. The law will halt large-scale expl... by private ... open the door fo... tion of the refini... in Cuba, according... eum industry sour...

Petroleum claims, ... run into millions of ... been reduced by th... 20,000 acres for each ... or individual. A period ... years has been gran... owners for petroleum ... tion. All claims pendi... tration were canceled.

Big oil companies, the ... jority of which are Amer... Canadian and British, ... spent about $30,000,000 here ... the search for petroleum duri... the last twelve years. It is be... lieved that they will abandon their holdings and withdraw from further exploration.

Royalty Is Imposed

At the same time the law imposes a 60 per cent royalty for the Government on oil production. The Government owns all mineral rights. This is the highest royalty ever imposed anywhere, according to the petroleum industry. Oil producers also will be required to continue digging wells in accordance with the regulations fixed by the law.

The decree establishes the Cuban Petroleum Institute as a department of the industrialization division of the Agrarian Reform Institute, which controls all land. The Petroleum Institute has been given the authority to carry out exploration, refining, transportation, distribution, purchase and sale of petroleum products.

The institute also has the power to operate any petroleum company or refinery seized by the Government and to regulate oil refining and the sale of oil

Continued on Page 24, Column 1

ALAN FREED IS OUT IN 'PAYOLA' STUDY

Disk Jockey Refuses to Sign WABC Denial on Principle —Says He Took No Bribes

By RICHARD F. SHEPARD

Alan Freed, the disk jockey, was abruptly dismissed from his job at radio station WABC yesterday.

Mr. Freed had refused to sign a statement to the effect that he had never taken money or gifts to promote records. The station is requiring all its disk jockeys to sign such a statement.

Mr. Freed was reported, however, to have based his refusal on principle, and to have denied taking bribes at any time. He was said to have viewed the presentation of such a document as "an insult to my reputation for integrity."

The disk jockey, who played a major role in promoting the rock 'n' roll craze, could not be reached for comment yesterday at either his New York or Stamford, Conn., home.

Right to 'Terminate' Noted

Ben Hoberman, general manager of WABC, said that the station had a "contractual right to terminate" Mr. Freed's services at any time it thought it necessary to do so.

Mr. Hoberman said that the station's decision had nothing to do with "payola." But he declined to give a specific reason for Mr. Freed's dismissal. Payola is the practice under which some disk jockeys are paid to plug records.

Mr. Freed signed a five-year contract with WABC in June, 1958.

No regular substitution was announced to fill the gap created by Mr. Freed's dismissal. However, another WABC disk jockey, Dick Shepard, substituted for him last night. The radio broadcast is heard six days a week.

Faces TV Cancellation

It was also reported that Mr. Freed's daytime disk jockey program on WNEW-TV faced the possibility of cancellation.

In a separate development, the National Broadcasting Company announced that "Treasure Hunt," a daytime quiz show, would leave the air on Dec. 4. The program had been mentioned in the investigations into such programs.

Mr. Freed's trouble on the Channel 5 station stemmed from difficulties with the American Federation of Television and Radio Artists. The problem was apparently not connected with the "payola" situation, but was concerned with the failure to

Continued on Page 62, Column 4

U. N. BIDS WORLD HALT ATOM TESTS; URGES EARLY PACT

Assembly Vote Asks Big 3 to Speed Control Accord—France Withholds Assent

Texts of the two resolutions will be found on Page 3.

By LINDESAY PARROTT

Special to The New York Times.

UNITED NATIONS, N. Y., Nov. 21—The United Nations called on all states today to refrain from testing nuclear or thermonuclear weapons pending attempts of the atomically armed powers to reach a general agreement for the cessation of such experiments.

... Assembly took ... adopting two ... efore it by its ... The com... d both reso... e week after ...

Eisenhower Names Head Of Military Aid Program

Selects General Palmer for Pentagon Post at Chief-of-Staff Level

By FELIX BELAIR Jr.

Special to The New York Times.

AUGUSTA, Ga., Nov. 21—President Eisenhower created a new post of Chief of Staff today to direct foreign military assistance programs. He named Gen. Williston B. Palmer to fill the Pentagon position.

A White House announcement said General Palmer's official title would be Director of Military Assistance. It said "the President felt that this position should be for the military assistance program on the same level as that of the Chiefs of Staff for the three service branches and with comparable military rank."

"The President felt," said Wayne Hawks, acting White House press secretary, "that the military assistance program should be an integral part of the defense system and make the Department of Defense responsible for carrying out operating details and expediting the program, leaving to the State Department responsibility for guidance and diplomatic implications of the program."

Associated Press

Gen. Williston B. Palmer

In creating the post, President Eisenhower carried out a recommendation of his committee to study the military assistance program that supervision of all foreign military-aid funds be placed in the office of the Assistant Secretary of Defense for International Security Affairs.

Another recommendation was

Continued on Page 5, Column 1

Catholic Bishops See Trap In Russian Talk of Peace

By JOHN D. MORRIS

Special to The New York Times.

WASHINGTON, Nov. 21—The Roman Catholic Bishops of the United States challenged the Soviet Union's avowal of peaceful aims today while issuing a stern warning against appeasement of world communism.

... 'peace' the Communist ... subversion to his pro... they declared. "By ...

...of Bishops' statement ...rinted on Page 76.

... he means the ac... the part of others ... for coexistence." ... of the world, the ... "must be firm ... principle and jus... appeasement ... leads only to ... conquered." ...

U.S.-SOVIET ACCORD IN CULTURAL FIELD EXTENDED 2 YEARS

Program of Exchanges to Be Enlarged—Both Nations Express Satisfaction

PACT SIGNED IN MOSCOW

Student and Teacher Visits and Technical Studies Among Expansions

By MAX FRANKEL

Special to The New York Times.

MOSCOW, Nov. 21—The United States and the Soviet Union agreed today to extend for two years an agreement for scientific, technical, cultural, educational and sports exchanges.

The accord expands the program that has operated to mutual satisfaction in 1958 and 1959. Both sides described themselves today as satisfied and encouraged by the agreement.

[In Washington, the State Department expressed gratification at the extension of the program.]

Under the extension the Soviet Union gained a considerable increase in the number of industrial and technical delegations to be exchanged. The United States was successful in arranging for expanded exchanges of students and teachers.

The new accord envisages considerable cooperation in medical and public health research. It holds promise of interchanges of other scientific information and delegations.

Radio-TV Exchange

A new attempt is to be made to exchange noncontroversial radio and television broadcasts, a part of the old agreement never fulfilled.

Exchanges of performers and athletes are to continue as before. Tourism and mutual visits of special delegations are to be further encouraged.

The agreement remains vague on exchanges of films and political broadcasts, although both sides declare themselves ready to cooperate.

The negotiators failed to make material progress on the establishment of permanent reading rooms in Moscow and New York. There has also been little progress for establishment of direct air service between the United States and the Soviet Union.

The agreement was signed here today after two weeks of negotiation by United States Ambassador Llewellyn Thompson and Georgi A. Zhukov, chairman of the State Committee for Cultural Relations with Foreign Countries.

Both expressed appreciation of the fact that they had been able to arrange in two weeks the renewal of an agreement that had required three months

Continued on Page 27, Column 1

SOVIET LETS FOUR EMIGRATE TO U. S.

Hints Others May Get Visas to Join U. S. Kin—Yields to Appeal by Nixon

By The Associated Press.

WASHINGTON, Nov. 21—Four Soviet citizens have received permission to join relatives in the United States, Vice President Richard M. Nixon said today.

Mr. Nixon said he had received the information from the State Department. He also made public a letter from Foreign Minister Andrei A. Gromyko promising that the 'Kremlin would consider requests by other citizens who wish to be reunited with relatives in the United States.

The four were on a list Mr. Nixon submitted when he visited the Soviet Union last summer. They have been granted exit visas. They are:

Karl Aistrauts, husband of Mrs. Amilda Aistrauts of Rochester, N.Y.; Mme. Juliana Nicis, mother of Mrs. Valentine Nicis Avotins of Chicago; Mme. Natali Yarits, wife of John Yarits of Hollywood, Fla., and Miss Anne-Reet Nomm, daughter of Mrs. Armilde Nomm of Detroit.

A statement from Mr. Nixon's office said the State Department was continuing its effort to gain the release of American citizens and other relatives of American citizens who wish to

Continued on Page 4, Column 1

Max Baer, 50, Dies; Ex-Ring Champion

By The Associated Press.

HOLLYWOOD, Calif., Nov. 21—Max Baer, world heavyweight boxing champion in the Nineteen Thirties, died of a heart attack today. He was 50 years old.

Mr. Baer, who previously had suffered two mild attacks, was stricken while shaving in his room at the Hollywood Roosevelt Hotel. He died about forty-five minutes after a physician arrived. He was pronounced dead by Dr. Edward S. Koziol, house physician.

The former champion had come to Hollywood Thursday to appear in a series of television commercials.

Last Wednesday he refereed a ten-round nationally televised heavyweight bout at Phoenix, Ariz., between Zora Folley and Alonzo Johnson. After Folley

Continued on Page 88, Column 2

Sports News

FOOTBALL

Harvard crushed Yale and Pittsburgh upset Penn State yesterday. Columbia downed Rutgers. Scores of leading games:

Columbia	26	Rutgers	16
Dartmouth	12	Princeton	7
Harvard	35	Yale	6
Illinois	28	Northwest'n	0
Kentucky	20	Tennessee	0
L. S. U.	14	Tulane	6
Marquette	30	Holy Cross	12
Michigan	23	Ohio St.	14
New Mexico	28	Air Force	27
Notre Dame	20	Iowa	19
Oklahoma	35	Iowa State	12
Oregon State	15	Oregon	7
Pitt	22	Penn St.	7
Purdue	10	Indiana	6
Syracuse	46	Boston U.	0
U. C. L. A.	10	So. Calif.	3
Washington	20	Wash. State	0
Wisconsin	11	Minnesota	7

HORSE RACING

Bald Eagle set a track record in taking the $85,200 Gallant Fox Handicap at Aqueduct. Manuel Ycaza rode the Cain Hoy Stable's racer to a length-and-three-quarters victory over Whodunit. Bald Eagle ran the mile and five-eighths in 2 minutes 41 seconds and paid $4.20 for $2. Whitley ran third before a crowd of 41,076. At Pimlico, the Wheatley Stable's Progressing won the $117,320 Pimlico Futurity and paid $19.20. Progressing scored by a half of a length over Hands.

Details in Section 5.

Max Baer, 50, Dies; Ex-Ring Champion

By The Associated Press.

HOLLYWOOD, Calif., Nov. 21—Max Baer, world heavyweight boxing champion in the Nineteen Thirties, died of a heart attack today. He was 50 years old.

Mr. Baer, who previously had suffered two mild attacks, was stricken while shaving in his room at the Hollywood Roosevelt Hotel. He died about forty-five minutes after a physician arrived. He was pronounced dead by Dr. Edward S. Koziol, house physician.

The former champion had come to Hollywood Thursday to appear in a series of television commercials.

Last Wednesday he refereed a ten-round nationally televised heavyweight bout at Phoenix, Ariz., between Zora Folley and Alonzo Johnson. After Folley

Continued on Page 88, Column 2

Boy ... at River

Pushed in M... He Slithers ... Feet to Safety

By GAY TALESE

A 9-year-old boy was pushed into a sewer through an open manhole yesterday. Forty-five minutes later he was washed into the Harlem River and rescued by two policemen.

The boy, Antonio Batista, cannot swim. After toppling down a fifteen-foot shaft, he floated and slithered most of the way through 600 feet of sewer. As the water grew deeper he was finally washed into the river.

He was brought out of the river at about 2:45 P. M., dazed and incoherent. At Jewish Memorial Hospital, he was found to have suffered a broken left kneecap and a banged forehead.

"I prayed down there," he said later. "I did not think I was going to die. It was dark, and the water came up to my chest, and I floated much of the way."

Two hours before his ordeal, Antonio had been playing with a dozen other boys in High Bridge Park. They were playing "monster," running around trying to catch each other. Shortly before 2 o'clock, Antonio said, some other boys came

'I Prayed,' Lad Says —Knee Broken in 45-Minute Ordeal

me and threw me down," Antonio said.

Neither Antonio nor the police could say for sure whether the manhole had been covered before the boys began playing.

Antonio's playmates ran to get help. One of them saw a policeman on Amsterdam Avenue, and he notified others. At 2:15 policemen had arrived at the Harlem River Drive, where the sewer empties into the river.

Patrolman Anthony Taccia of the West 135th Street station and Detective Luther Evans of the Wadsworth Avenue station, both former lifeguards, took off their shoes, coats and guns. They plunged into the water.

"We jumped over the wall of the Harlem River Drive but we didn't expect we'd see the kid," Detective Evans said later from his hospital bed, resting from overexposure.

"There were rescue squads on the edge of the drive, about three or four radio cars, an emergency truck, and a police launch was in the river, too," the detective said.

"We kept watching the mouth of the sewer. Suddenly I saw him come to the top. He was along and began throwing rocks.

One large, fat boy grabbed

Continued on Page 46, Column 1

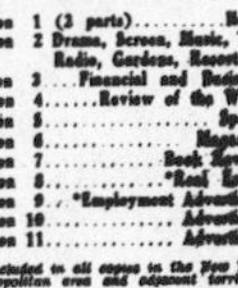

The New York Times

Antonio Batista in hospital

The New York Times Nov. 22, 1959

Where the boy fell in (1) and where he emerged (2).

L.I. Father Sees Fire Kill 5 in His Family

Special to The New York Times.

BAY SHORE, L. I., Nov. 21—Five persons died here today in a pre-dawn fire. The only survivor was a Brentwood High School teacher who tried desperately to save the victims, all members of his family.

William George Mayo, 29 years old, watched helplessly as the front porch roof he had used for climbing started to collapse as his family tried to follow.

The dead were Mr. Mayo's wife, Barbara, 24; their two children, Corinne, 1½, and William Jr., 2 months; and two visiting relatives, Mr. Mayo's mother-in-law, Mrs. Catherine White, 50, and his niece, Catherine Fiske, 11, both of Danvers, Mass.

Mr. Mayo said he awoke about 3 A. M. in his home at 150 Clinton Avenue to find most of the floor below an inferno. Mr.

Continued on Page 47, Column 1

Today's Sections

Index to Subjects

Max Baer, Ex-Boxing Champion, Dies

Continued From Page 1, Col. 3

won by a unanimous decision, the former champion waved to the crowd. Then he grasped the top rope and vaulted out of the ring.

He had eighty fights during his twelve years as a professional. He won sixty-six of them, fifty-one by knockouts.

For the last three and a half years Mr. Baer had been public relations director for a Sacramento auto agency. Before that he had been a disk jockey for a Sacramento radio station.

Clowned Way to Title

In an era when heavyweight boxing included such colorful fighters as Jack Sharkey, Max Schmeling, Jim Braddock and Primo Carnera, Max Baer clowned his way into the championship in June, 1934, and he was still laughing when he lost it a year later.

Endowed with a 6-foot-3-inch frame and 220 well-muscled pounds, he had everything a champion needed except the disposition to attend to business. Always a happy-go-lucky sort, he just could not see life as a serious affair. His outlook earned him the nickname of Madcap Maxie from the boxing writers.

He was born in Omaha, Neb., on Feb. 11, 1909, and named Maximilian Adelbert Baer. When he was a child, his parents, of Jewish, German and Scottish extraction, took the family to Livermore, Calif. There the young man followed his father into the meat business. The fighter said the hard work of lifting heavy slabs of meat had developed his arms and shoulders. This background was responsible for another ring nickname, The Livermore Larruper.

He started boxing professionally in 1929 and remained active in the ring for the next dozen years. After a wartime hitch in the Army he starred with Myrna Loy in the film "The Prizefighter and the Lady" and made numerous other movie, radio, television and night-club appearances. Invariably he addressed friends and well-wishers as "Champ."

"What a ham!" was his favorite description of himself. He won the championship from Primo Carnera on June 14, 1934, in the Long Island City Bowl. Carnera was down eleven times before Arthur Donovan, the referee, stopped the title bout in the eleventh round.

Laughed at Carnera

Hilarious as always, the challenger had no trouble in tagging his 267-pound opponent

Max Baer—World Heavyweight Champion 1934–1935.

with long right-hand swings to the chin. Once, when both were on the floor together, he cracked: "The last one up is a sissy." Again, when Carnera suddenly backed up, tripped over his own feet and fell, his opponent roared with laughter.

While Max was training for this fight, Bill Brown, a New York boxing commissioner, looked him over. As was his custom, the fighter preferred rhumba dancing in the night club circuit to serious work.

"You're a bum," Mr. Brown told him, bringing a hearty laugh from the next world champion.

After the knockout, the boxer leaned over the ropes to Mr. Brown and said:

"Well, Mr. Commissioner, what do you think of me now?"

"You're still a bum," Mr. Brown replied. After a moment he added: "And so is Carnera."

One day less than a year later, on June 13, 1935, he lost the championship to the plodding James J. Braddock in the same Long Island City Bowl, by a fifteen-round decision.

"I just clowned the title away," he said. "It was so lonesome on the way back to my dressing room I nearly caught cold from the draft. Just me and my trainer took that walk. What a difference a year made."

After losing the title, he fought Joe Louis in New York on Sept. 24, 1935, before 88,150, a million-dollar gate. He had little desire for this match and he appeared nervous before the opening bell. Toward the end of the fourth round the champion's face was battered and he was down on one knee signaling the referee that he wanted no more.

When the crowd jeered him, he said:

"He hit me eighteen times on the way down, yet they said I laid down."

Knocked Out Schmeling

On June 8, 1933, in New York, he knocked out Max Schmeling of Germany in ten rounds. The victory gave him particular satisfaction, since Schmeling was then the sports idol of Hitler's Germany.

Early in his career Max knocked out Frankie Campbell in five rounds in San Francisco on Aug. 25, 1930. Campbell died of head injuries after the fight, and Mr. Baer lost four of his next six fights.

In his last fight, on April 4, 1941, in New York, he was knocked out by Lou Nova in eight rounds. He enlisted in the Army the next year and received a medical discharge as a staff sergeant in 1945 at Kelly Field in Texas. He had suffered shoulder and neck injuries when an eighty-five-pound punching bag fell on him before he entered the service.

Mr. Baer's boxing career was managed by Ancil (Pop) Hoffman. He made the fighter put $200,000 into annuities when his earnings were large, and the fighter could have begun drawing more than $1,000 a month a year ago. However, he decided to leave the money in his account.

"Thanks to Ancil's foresight," he told friends recently, "I'll never have to worry about where my next meal is coming from. When I made it I spent it, and sometimes I spent it faster than I made it."

In 1932, Mr. Baer married Dorothy Dunbar, a movie actress. They were divorced a year later. He married Mary Ellen Sullivan of Washington in 1935. His widow lives in the family home in Sacramento, Calif., with their three children, Max, Jr., now in the Air Force; Jimmy, and Maudie. He is also survived by a brother, Buddy, who also was a heavyweight fighter.

Max Schmeling goes down in the last round, losing the 1933 bout to Max Baer.

The New York Times SATURDAY, JUNE 29, 1963.

Home Run Baker Dies at 77; Slugger in Era of the Dead Ball

3d Baseman in the Athletics' $100,000 Infield — Later Sold to the Yankees

TRAPPE, Md., June 28 (AP) — Home Run Baker, a baseball slugger of the "dead-ball" era, died today in his home at the age of 77. He suffered his second stroke in two years this month.

The former Maryland farm boy, who played third base for the Philadelphia Athletics and New York Yankees, was named to Baseball's Hall of Fame in 1955.

After his major-league days ended in 1922 he returned to Trappe to become a farmer.

Mr. Baker's first wife died in 1920, and in 1922 he married Margaret E. Mitchell. There were two children from each marriage. Survivors include his widow and the children, Mrs. Fred Hooper of Cambridge, Mrs. James Wimer of Adelphi and Mrs. Fred Wesson and J. Franklin Baker Jr. of Trappe.

An Auspicious Start

On April 24, 1909, John Franklin Baker started his first game in his first full season with the Athletics. Coming to bat in the first inning with the bases loaded, he hit a home run.

In the era of the dead ball and the wagon-tongue bat it was a feat that, according to an account published several years later, "was the talk of the circuit for several days."

The 6-foot, 175-pound third baseman went on to become the game's first slugger. He led the American League in homers four times — in 1911 with 9, in 1912 with 10, in 1913 with 12 and in 1914 with 8. His lifetime major league batting average was .307.

Mr. Baker received his nickname in the 1911 World Series with the New York Giants. His home run off Rube Marquard won the second game. The next day he belted another off Christy Mathewson, which tied the score. His single figured in the rally that brought the Athletics the victory in the 11th inning.

In his final days as a player, Baker saw his records obliterated by Babe Ruth and others. His career total of 93 home runs would now be regarded merely as a respectable two-season output for a Willie Mays or a Mickey Mantle.

The changes wrought in the game by the livelier ball, the lighter bat and the continuous quest for the long ball drew this observation from him several years ago:

"I guess it's true that the game has changed so much that we old gaffers are hardly a part of it any more. Why, I remember a few years ago when I went up to Philadelphia and was astonished to see Joe DiMaggio hit a home run over the fence in right center. That fence was unchanged from the days when I played in that park and we almost never hit it on the fly or the first bounce. But DiMaggio cleared it easily, and he didn't even seem to swing hard."

Baker used a 52-ounce bat, 20 ounces heavier than those used today. He was a left-handed batter and a right-handed thrower.

Baker was born in Trappe, where his ancestors had lived and farmed since before the American Revolution. He played in local leagues, failed a tryout with the Baltimore Orioles, and in 1908 signed with Reading, Pa., in the old Tri-State League. Late that season he received a tryout from Connie Mack, owner and manager of the Athletics, and was signed.

Home Run Baker

Baker joined what became known as the $100,000 infield, with Stuffy McInnis at first base, Eddie Collins at second and Jack Barry at shortstop. In 1910, 1911 and 1913 the Athletics won the pennant and the World Series and Baker became a hero of Philadelphia.

Sold to Yankees

The Athletics won the pennant again in 1914 but lost the Series in four games to the Boston Braves. The angry Mr. Mack broke up his team, Baker being sold to the Yankees for $37,500.

Now it was his turn to become angry. He refused to report to New York, sitting out the 1915 season. Baker joined the Yankees the next year, but soon began to speak of retiring. In 1920, after the death of his first wife, he quit the sport, but returned to play in 1921 and 1922.

With his legs weakening, he left baseball after the 1922 season, returning to Maryland to manage several farms he owned, to raise and train hunting dogs and to fish and hunt the waterfowl that sweep over the Eastern Shore each autumn.

In 1950 and 1951 Mr. Baker played in the annual Old-Timers Day game at Yankee Stadium. In 1951, pinch-hitting for his old Yankee teammate, Earl Combs, he hit a single. It was his last time at bat.

Baker following through after connecting for a home run in the 1911 World Series. His performance in that series earned him his nickname.

The New York Times SUNDAY, MAY 23, 1954.

CHIEF BENDER DIES; A FAMOUS PITCHER

He Led Philadelphia Athletics to 5 Pennants—Was Elected to Hall of Fame in 1953

PHILADELPHIA, Pa., May 22 (AP)—Chief Bender, one of baseball's great all-time pitchers and a member of the Hall of Fame, died today at the age of 71.

Bender, who had been ill for some time, died in Graduate Hospital. He had been under treatment for cancer and had recently suffered a heart attack.

Bender, in fifteen years as one of the best pitchers in baseball, never made more than $2,400 a season as an active player. He had been serving as a coach for the Philadelphia Athletics at more than double the pay he got as a pitcher.

The venerable Connie Mack, former manager and owner of the Athletics, regarded Bender as his greatest one-game pitcher. "If everything depended on one game," Mack once said, "I just used Albert." He always called the Chief by his middle name.

Was a Chippewa Indian

For a dozen seasons before World War I, Charles Albert (Chief) Bender was among the foremost pitchers in the American League. During that span from 1903-1914 he pitched for the Philadelphia Athletics and won a place in baseball history.

In 1953 Bender was elected to baseball's Hall of Fame, joining the game's other immortals in the Cooperstown, N. Y., shrine.

A full-blooded Chippewa Indian, who was born in Brainerd, Minn., on May 5, 1883, Bender was one of the most versatile men who ever participated in major league baseball. Highly educated and regarded as an expert on jewels and diamonds, Bender also was a talented trapshooter and billiard player.

In his American League debut in 1903 he faced the strong New York Highlanders and blanked them with four hits. His mound opponent that afternoon was Clark Griffith, who was the manager of the Highlanders.

During his stay with the Athletics, Bender was a powerful force in helping Connie Mack's squad capture the pennant five times. In three of those years, 1910, 1911 and 1913, the Philadelphia club went on to win the world series. The other seasons in which the team took the American League flag with Bender as one of its mainstays were 1905 and 1914.

Best Season Was 1910

The Chief's greatest year was 1910, when as a 27-year-old righthander, he won twenty-three games and lost five. With Eddie Plank and John Coombs, Bender led the Atnletics to their first world series title. That was the year of the famous $100,000 infield of Eddie Collins, Stuffy McInnis, Jack Barry and Home-run Baker. Bender's catcher for many years was Ira Thomas.

Bender registered one of the outstanding feats of his career on May 12, 1910, when he pitched a no-hit contest against Cleveland. Except for a base on balls issued to Terry Turner, Cleveland shortstop, Bender would have been credited with a perfect game. Turner, the only man to reach first, was caught off that bag inmmediately thereafter by Bender.

Another outstanding event in his career occurred in the opening game of the 1911 world series. Bender's speed ball enabled him to fan eleven Giants, but the New York club, behind their famous pitcher, Christy Mathewson, gained a 2-to-1 decision. A costly error by Eddie Collins contributed largely to Bender's defeat.

However, he topped the Giants in both the fourth and final contests of that year's six-game series.

Led League Three Years

In three seasons, 1910, 1911 and 1914, Bender was the leading American League pitcher. In 1911 he had seventeen triumphs and four defeats, and in 1914 won seventeen and lost three.

Bender's connection with the Athletics as a player was severed when Mack broke up his great team following the 1914 world series. The Chief played with Baltimore, in the Federal League, in 1915. He terminated his playing career in the major leagues as a member of the Philadelphia Nationals during 1916 and 1917.

Bender, a notable control artist, had an all-time record in the major leagues of 206 victories and 111 defeats. Of these, 41 were shut-outs. In 1914 he won 14 consecutive games.

In later years Bender hurled for several minor league clubs and also served as manager of some. He coached the Naval Academy baseball team at Annapolis for years and in 1925 was coach of the Chicago White Sox, when Collins was managing that American League club. In 1939 he returned to the Athletics as a scout of minor league talent.

Bender, a product of the Carlisle Indian school, from which Jim Thorpe also came, was rated by Mack as "the greatest money pitcher" in the history of the Athletics. The Chief was the first pitcher to win six world series games, taking two each in 1911 and 1913 against the Giants and single triumphs in 1905 against the Giants and in 1910 against the Chicago Cubs.

He was signed as a coach by Mack just before the end of 1943.

41 of Chief Bender's 206 career victories were shutouts.

Associated Press, 1950

Chief Bender

The New York Times MONDAY, SEPTEMBER 25, 1978

Lyman Bostock, Angels' Star Outfielder, Is Dead

By FRED GOODALL
Associated Press Writer

GARY, Ind. (AP)—California Angels outfielder Lyman Bostock, one of major league baseball's highest-paid players, died Sunday of a shotgun blast fired into a car in which he was riding with the wife of the man arrested for the shooting, police said.

Bostock, 27, who was visiting relatives in Gary, died about three hours after he was shot late Saturday night while riding in a car with his uncle and at least two other persons.

One of the passengers was identified by police as Barbara Smith, 26, whose husband, Leonard, 31, was arrested in the shooting.

Police said Smith, who was identified by his wife, was arrested at his home Sunday about six blocks from where the shooting occurred. Charges were not immediately filed, police said.

Gary police Sgt. Charles Highsmith said Smith and his wife apparently were getting a divorce and had quarreled earlier in the day.

Police said Bostock, Mrs. Smith and her sister were all passengers in a car driven by the ballplayer's uncle, Thomas Turner. Highsmith said it was not known why Mrs. Smith was in the car.

Highsmith quoted witnesses as saying that a car pulled alongside Turner's and that Bostock's uncle went through two red lights before stopping at a third light at the intersection of 5th Avenue and Jackson Street.

Police said Smith stopped his car, got out and approached the Turner vehicle. One shot was fired into the car, striking Bostock in the left side of the head and also injuring Mrs. Smith. The gunman then fled in a car, police said.

Bostock, who collected two hits in four at-bats in his final major league game Saturday against the Chicago White Sox, often stayed with his uncle when his team was playing in Chicago, about 35 miles west of Gary.

Angels manager Jim Fregosi reached Sunday prior to the Angels-White Sox game in Chicago, said, "I didn't have much to say to the players. I told them all I knew about it. There's not really too much you can say. Everybody on the club knew what a good guy he was."

Gene Mauch, who was Bostock's manager when he played for the Minnesota Twins, said, "I'm shocked. I'm sorry. I'm angry. I'm sick. People don't realize the strong feelings of admiration and respect that develop on a ballclub. I thought the world of that man."

Bostock, a .318 career hitter, left the Twins after last season and signed with the Angels in November as a free agent. His five-year, $2.7 million contract made him one of baseball's highest-paid players.

He was in a serious batting slump early this season, but he gradually raised his batting average to .294 with five home runs and 70 runs batted in. Because of the early-season slump, he donated his April salary to charity, saying that he felt he didn't deserve it.

A native of Birmingham, Ala., Bostock was the 26th round draft pick of the Twins in 1972 summer draft. The left-hand hitter enjoyed considerable success in the minor leagues and was promoted to the majors in 1975 and batted .282 in 98 games.

He improved his average to .323 in 1976, his first full season with the Twins, and finished second to teammate Rod Carew in the American League batting race in 1977 with a .336 mark.

When he was in a batting slump, Lyman Bostock donated one month's salary to charity because he felt he did not earn it.

The New York Times

SATURDAY, NOVEMBER 30, 1974

Braddock, Who Beat Baer for Title, Dies

NORTH BERGEN, N. J., Nov. 29 (AP)—James J. Braddock, who won the world heavyweight championship in 1935 by outpointing Max Baer in one of boxing's biggest upsets, died today at his home here. He was 68 years old.

Surviving are his widow, the former Mae Fox; two sons, Howard and Jay; a daughter, Rose Marie DeWitt; four brothers, two sisters, and six grandchildren.

Diffident Demeanor

By JOE NICHOLS

Jimmy Braddock of the soft voice, twisted smile and diffident demeanor looked more like the old-time friendly Irish cop on the beat than a prize fighter. His patient manner marked his everyday pose just as it did his way of going into the ring. To those who knew him well the nickname Plain Jim, handed to him by John Kieran was far more descriptive than the more famous sobriquet of Cinderella Man that Damon Runyon dubbed him.

And yet, there was pertinence in Runyon's name for Braddock. The fighter's professional career was a true sign of the ring, embracing as it did a promising start, a skid to oblivion and retirement, a desperate return to fighting from the relief rolls of the Depression era and, as a fairy tale climax, the winning of the heavyweight boxing championship of the world, the richest individual prize in the realm of sports.

This final achievement was as surprising in its way as the miraculous climb of the 1969 Mets in baseball greatness. For Braddock had to hurdle three heavily favored and highly rated foes at the time to get the shot at the title. And to get the title he had to fight and beat Max Baer, a mighty hitter whose strength and awesome reputation made him the favorite at odds of 10 to 1, and even more.

But on the night of June 13, 1935, in the Madison Square Garden Bowl in Long Island City, Queens, Braddock brought off the boxing miracle of the time. He boxed his way, patiently and craftily, to the unanimous decision over the baffled Baer in 15 rounds.

Again, on June 22, 1937, Braddock was the short-ender in the betting in a fight with Joe Louis, but this time Braddock lost his title by a knockout in eight rounds. Before bowing to Louis, though, Braddock had the satisfaction of knocking him down, in the fourth round. The Cinderella era having closed, Braddock had only one more regular fight after that, a 10-round decision conquest of Tommy Farr on Jan. 21, 1938.

His complete ring career embraced 84 bouts with 52 victories of which 28 were knockouts, 21 defeats including two knockouts, three draws, two no contests and six no decisions. He stood 6 feet 2½ inches tall and, for his title fight with Baer, weighed 190 pounds.

Braddock was born here on Dec. 6, 1905. When he was a child his family moved to West New York, N.J., just the other side of the Hudson River. He engaged in his first amateur bout at the age of 17, and it was not until he was 20 that he turned professional, as a middleweight (160 pounds).

He built up a good record frequently beating heavier opponents, and in 1929, having reached the light heavyweight class of 175 pounds, he met Tommy Doughran in a bid for the latter's championship of that division, but was outpointed.

Went Into Decline

He went into a decline after that, and lost frequently until, after breaking a hand in a fight with Abe Feldman on Sept. 25, 1933, he gave up the ring to become a longshoreman. Work was scarce in that line, and Braddock was forced to apply for relief to support his wife and three children. It is a frequently repeated story that, as soon as he became solvent again, Braddock repaid every cent of the $17 a week relief money to the agencies.

Early in 1934 a fighter named Corn Griffin from Georgia appeared on the heavyweight scene, and a local heavyweight "name" was sought to oppose him in a frank effort to build him up as a championship contender. Braddock was working on the docks, but his friend and manager, Joe Biegel, professionally known as Joe Gould, persuaded Mike Jacobs, the promoter to accept Braddock as a sacrificial lamb for Griffin. On June 14, in a preliminary to

James J. Braddock—World Heavyweight Champion 1935–1937.

the championship fight between Baer and the unsuccessful defender, Primo Carnero, Braddock knocked the favored Griffin out in three rounds.

After that surprise victory, Braddock successively defeated John Henry Lewis and Art Lasky, and earned the match with Baer. That triumph brought financial security to Braddock who, according to the custom of the era, profited through personal appearances and testimonials for two years before risking his title. It was in his first defense, against Joe Louis, in Chicago, that Braddock was dethroned by a knockout in eight rounds.

The New York Times SUNDAY, FEBRUARY 15, 1948.

MORDECAI BROWN, PITCHER, DIES AT 71

Star of Chance's Cubs Despite Loss of Finger in Boyhood—Dueled With Mathewson

TERRE HAUTE, Ind., Feb. 14 (AP)—Mordecai Brown, one of the all-time great pitchers in major league baseball, died in Union Hospital here today at the age of 71.

Born in near-by Nyesville, he broke into baseball in 1898 as a third baseman with a Coxville semi-pro team of miners. When their pitcher fell and injured his arm, Brown got his chance on the mound. His 9-3 victory so impressed the losers, from Brazil, Ind., that they "signed me up for much more money."

After leaving professional baseball he managed a semi-pro team for the Indian Refining Company in Lawrenceville, Ill. Later he returned to Terre Haute and opened a filling station, which he ran until three years ago.

Surviving are his widow, Sallie; two brothers and two sisters, who live in Indiana.

A funeral service will be held at 2 P. M. on Tuesday in the Thomas Funeral Home here.

Name Up For Cooperstown

Despite a boyhood accident that caused the loss of the index finger on his right hand, Mordecai Peter Centennial Brown became such a noted pitcher that he is under consideration for membership in baseball's Hall of Fame at Cooperstown, N. Y.

Known as "Three-fingered" Brown through his career, he entered the major leagues with the St. Louis club in 1903 and the next year joined the Cubs, where he remained through 1912. When the Federal League launched its baseball insurrection, Brown went with the St. Louis club of the "outlaw" league, after spending 1913 with the Cincinnati Reds.

The right-hander spent part of 1914 with the St. Louis "Feds," and finished the season with the Brooklyn club. In 1915 he was with the Chicago Federal League club, which won the "outlaw" league's pennant before peace was signed by the insurgents and the major leagues.

Brown, who completed his career with the Chicago Cubs in 1916, had a lifetime record of 480 games, of which he won 239 and lost 131, for a percentage of .646. He was famous for his pitching duels with Christy Mathewson of the Giants, beating the great Giant hurler more often than not.

Won Five Series Victories

A member of a great Chicago Cubs' pitching staff, Brown shared honors with Ed Reulbach, Orval Overall and Jack Pfeister, under the leadership of "Peerless" Frank Chance. In world series play Brown, who was also known as "Miner," bagged five victories, two of them in relief roles.

He won one of the two games taken by the Cubs in the series that the White Sox captured in 1906, 4 games to 2. Reulbach won the other. Brown took the fourth skirmish, beating Nick Altrock, 1 to 0, allowing two hits, in a game in which Altrock had three putouts and eight assists. This was the series of the famous "hitless wonders."

The next year, when the Cubs beat Hughey Jennings' Detroit Tigers four straight games after tying the first 3-all in twelve innings, Brown clinched the series with a 7-hit shutout, 2 to 0, in the fifth game. Against the Tigers again in the 1908 series, Brown hurled two victories, the Cubs beating Detroit, 4 games to 1.

Brown won the first game, at Detroit, in a two-inning relief appearance following Reulbach and Overall, five Cubs runs in the ninth inning pulling out the victory. He came back in the fourth game to shut out the Tigers, 3 to 0, on four hits.

In 1910 Brown received credit for the only game the Cubs won as Connie Mack's Philadelphia Athletics swept to victory, 4 games to 1. Replacing Leonard (King) Cole and pitching the last two innings of the fourth game, Brown received credit for a ten-inning triumph, 4 to 3.

Beat Mathewson in Vital Game

One of his most notable achievements was his victory over the Giants on Oct. 8, 1908, in the play-off for the National League pennant tie that followed Fred Merkle's failure to touch second base. Relieving Pfeister, Brown scored over Mathewson sending the Giants to defeat and the Cubs into the world series.

Brown led the National League pitchers in 1906, winning 26 games and losing 6, for an average of .813, and again in 1907, when he won 20 and lost 6, for an average of .769. He shared with his rival Mathewson, a world series record of ten fielding chances in five games, which he made in 1910. With Mathewson and George Mullin, Detroit, he shared a world series record of twelve assists for a pitcher in six games. Brown established this mark in 1906, Mullin equaled it in 1909 and Mathewson in 1912.

Another record shared by Brown is a National League season's mark of 1.000 in fielding for a pitcher. In 1908 Brown accepted 108 chances flawlessly, thirty-five putouts and seventy-three assists

"Three-Fingered" Brown won 20 or more games six seasons in a row.

The New York Times FRIDAY, JUNE 30, 1967

Primo Carnera, Ex-Boxing Champion, Dies

Heavyweight Titlist in 1933 Was Tool of Racketeers

Special to The New York Times

ROME, June 29—Primo Carnera, who won the world heavyweight boxing championship 34 years ago today, died this morning at his birthplace, Sequals, in northern Italy. He was 60 years old and had been suffering from cirrhosis of the liver.

The former boxer spent most of his life in the United States but he returned to Italy last month. His home town organized a rose festival in his honor but he was too ill to participate.

At his bedside when he died were his wife and daughter.

Target for Hustlers

Primo Carnera's strange career in the ring was glaring evidence of why professional boxing in the United States came to be known as the fight "racket." Rarely has anyone been victimized as thoroughly by criminal elements in this field as he was.

Maneuvered in an atmosphere of cynical publicity and rigged matches, this former circus giant was mulcted by underworld vultures and opportunistic hustlers of every penny of the more than a million dollars he had made with his massive fists and his ability to withstand punishment.

Barely a year after he had won the heavyweight crown, he was not only ex-champion but also broke. At his bankruptcy proceedings he made a comment that changed public ridicule to sympathy. He said:

"I don't pay any attention to money and those things."

His misfortunes attained almost classic stature as they became the subject for one of the most revealing and literate novels about boxing, Budd Schulberg's "The Harder They Fall."

Carnera was never a very good fighter. His huge, rawboned frame—he stood 6 feet, 6 inches and weighed, in his prime, 261 pounds—let him outlast inferior opponents. But he was a glass-jawed target for a superior puncher.

Although he accumulated 87 victories, including 66 knockouts, in his 100 professional bouts, many of his early triumphs were suspect.

One of his entourage, Good Time Walter Friedman, once conceded that many of Carnera's bouts were "mischievous." But Friedman insisted that when Carnera won the heavyweight title from Jack Sharkey on June 29, 1933, at the Long Island Bowl, the bout was on the level.

Primo Carnera—World Heavyweight Champion 1933–1934.

"Every once in a while Carnera could complete a perfect punch," Friedman said. "That's what happened when he caught Sharkey with that right uppercut in the sixth round."

After successfully defending the title twice in 15-round decisions over Paulino Uzcudun and Tommy Loughran, Carnera lost the crown to Max Baer on June 14, 1934, at the Long Island Bowl. Baer, laughing at the ineptness of the man nicknamed "The Ambling Alp," floored him 12 times before the referee, Arthur Donovan, pronounced Carnera defenseless on his feet in the 11th round.

In 1935 Joe Louis used Carnera as a rung on his ladder to the heavyweight title. The bout was stopped in the sixth round after Carnera had been on the canvas at Yankee Stadium three times.

Again, Carnera was not counted out. His strength and stamina were superb, even if his skill was not. In The New York Times the next day, Carnera was described as "a

(continued)

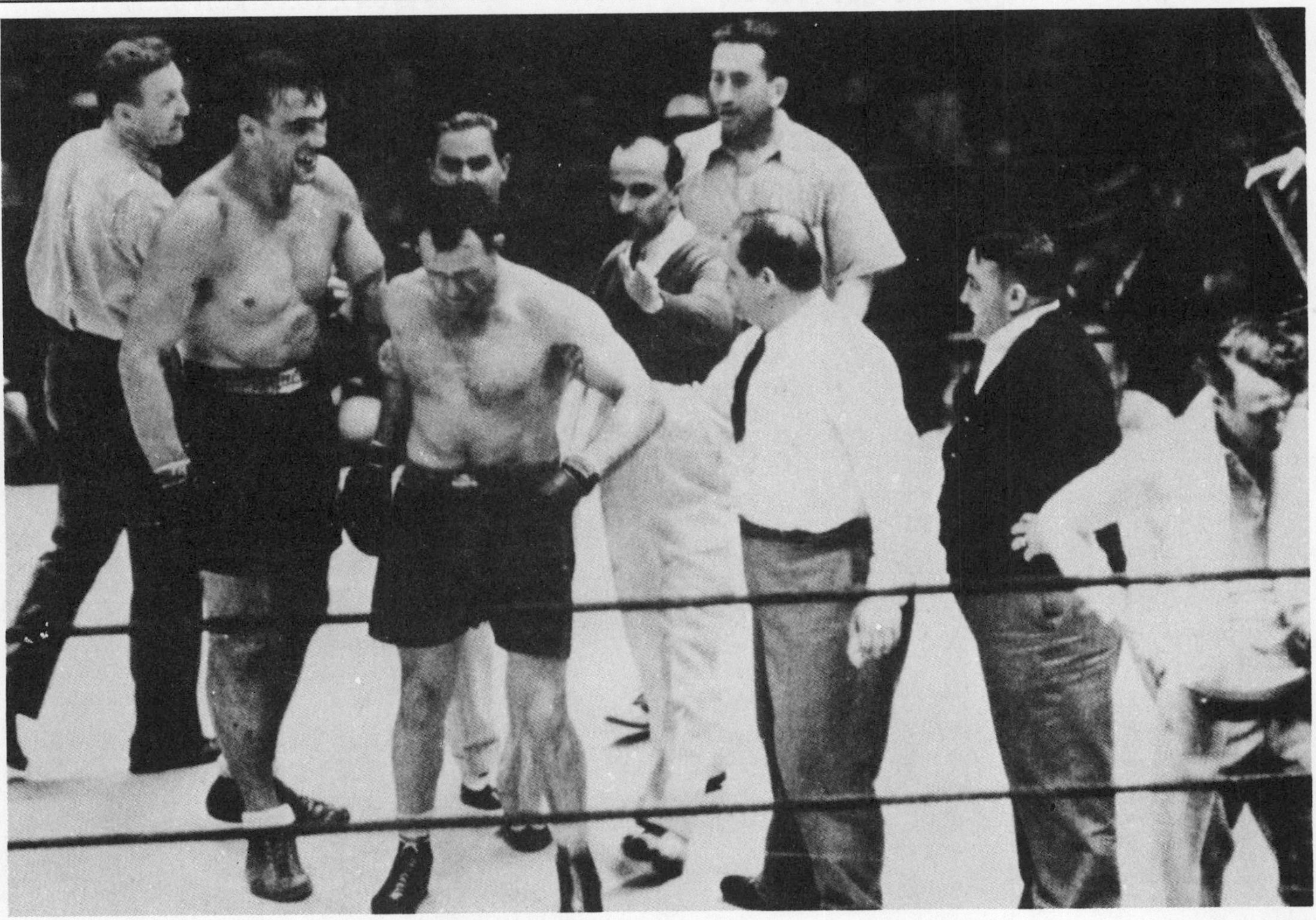

Primo Carnera (left) was declared the new heavyweight champion after knocking out Jack Sharkey in the sixth round on August 29, 1933.

figure of utter helplessness, clinging feebly but grimly to the top rope of the ring" when the referee intervened.

A Heavy Baby

Carnera was born on Oct. 25, 1906 in Sequals, Italy, not far from Venice. Although his parents were of moderate size, he is said to have weighed 22 pounds at birth.

His father was a mosaic worker. By the time Primo was 12, he had outgrown his father's old clothes. With his feet wrapped in burlap, he left home to seek his fortune. In Paris he labored as a tile-layer. One day he went to a circus. Noticing the huge teen-ager, the circus owner walked over and told him:

"You shouldn't be watching a circus, you should be in one."

He soon was, as a strongman and wrestler. His favorite stunt was to prevent two small autos, their motors racing, from moving as he, with a thick rope in each hand, held onto them. During his circus days, he weighed as much as 300 pounds. When he was 22, he began to box, but he was more a curiosity than a contender.

His manager, Leon See, accompanied him to the United States in 1930. Carnera had 16 bouts in less than four months winning all of them in early round knockouts.

An incident occurred in Los Angeles on the tour that added to the legend. Carnera, who knew only a few phrases in English at the time, visited a barber shop and decided to have a manicure.

"How do you like Los Angeles?" the girl asked.

"I knock him out in two rounds," Carnera responded.

On Feb. 10, 1933, one of Carnera's most memorable bouts took place at Madison Square Garden. He knocked out Ernie Schaaf with a soft left jab. As Schaaf sprawled on the canvas, shouts of "Fake, fake, fake!" thundered throughout the Garden. But Schaaf had to be hospitalized. Three days later, he died.

Punch Was Fatal

It was established later that Schaaf had sustained serious brain damage in a bout with Max Baer. Carnera's punch had aggravated it, fatally.

After winning the title from Sharkey, Carnera returned to Rome to defend the crown against Uzeudun. Before the Loughran bout in Miami, Carnera mentioned that he planned to use his flat feet as a weapon. The idea was to stomp on Loughran's weak arches Loughran complained of foul intent, but the local commission supported Carnera.

"Fighters must protect their feet just as they do their jaws," one of the commissioners proclaimed.

At the time, Carnera was something of a comic champion. But after his brutal bludgeonings by Baer and Louis, the comedy turned to tragedy. His money had vanished from boxing, too. He was suspended by the New York State Athletic Commission after a poor effort against Leroy Haines at Ebbets Field.

In 1938, he appeared in vaudeville in Italy. He skipped rope as dancing girls whirled about him. Spectators whistled, a form of derision there.

Accused by France

During World War II, he was charged by the French Government with having deserted from the Army. He was a citizen of France. But he had returned during the German occupation, to Sequals where he was an inspector of Italian civilian workers laboring for the Nazis.

"They paid us 15 cents a day," he once said, "and you had to sign a receipt for it, too."

When the war ended, he attempted a comeback at 39. He was knocked out in his only bout by Luigi Musina in Milan. Carnera later complained that he had been ordered at gunpoint by a spectator to enter the ring after the bout had been delayed. Earlier in his career, he used a virus and a "doping" incident as excuses for losses. But in Milan, the promoter had another explanation.

"Carnera no longer is a drawing card," the promoter said, "and he also has a glass jaw."

His jaw was not a factor in his next career, however. He began to wrestle professionally in 1946. He proved to be quite a drawing card, particularly in the United States. Somewhat wiser regarding his finances, he recouped some of the money that had disappeared when he was a boxer. He moved his wife, Pina, and two children to California wher he later operated a liquor store in Westwood.

Carnera became a naturalized United States citizen in 1953. His son, Umberto, is a graduate of the University of California, Los Angeles, and is studying medicine. His daughter, Jean Marie, is married to Philip Alderson, an engineer.

The New York Times WEDNESDAY, OCTOBER 29, 1975

Georges Carpentier, Boxer, Dies in Paris

He Fought Dempsey at Boyle's Thirty Acres in 1921

PARIS, Oct. 28 (AP)—Georges Carpentier, who lost on a fourth-round knockout to Jack Dempsey in boxing's first $1-million gate, died last night of a heart attack. He was 81 years old.

Mr. Carpentier died at the home of his daughter Jacqueline.

Mr. Carpentier's death came at a time when Mr. Dempsey, first his adversary and then a warm friend, was a patient in a hospital in New York.

By JOHN S. RADOSTA

Dempsey's Foe and Friend

As much a creature of press agentry and promotion as many American sports figures, Carpentier achieved his greatest renown in Europe, but he was best known to, and liked by, the American public for his brief encounter with Jack Dempsey on July 2, 1921, at Boyle's Thirty Acres in Jersey City.

At 168½ pounds, he was 19½ pounds lighter than Dempsey. He had a negligible left hand, but he hit hard with his right. Carpentier's nose was broken in the first round. In the second round he landed high on Dempsey's cheekbone solidly enough to daze the champion. He also broke a couple of bones in his right hand.

At a 75th-birthday party for Dempsey in 1970, where Carpentier was his guest, Dempsey said he would have been knocked out if that blow had found his chin.

Dempsey Then Took Command

Dempsey recovered in the third round and beat Carpentier pitilessly.

"Jack came out fresh for the third round," Carpentier recalled, "and he hit me with the hardest punches any human ever threw. Nobody cold hit like Dempsey that day. And he was shaking off my punches as if I was patting him with an open hand."

Carpentier was knocked down in the fourth round. In a retrospective New Yorker article some years ago. John Lardner wrote that Carpentier, "faithful to [his manager's] code of histrionics . . . stayed down for the count of nine and then, jumping up, made an artful rush at Dempsey, which carried his chin headlong into Dempsey's right hand. He was counted out in 1 minute 16 seconds of the round."

Georges Carpentier on the canvas in the fight he lost to Jack Dempsey on July 2, 1921. The bout was fought in the daytime, in the open air.

Publicity of the 1920's made it appear that Mr. Carpentier had worked as a pit boy in the coal mines near Lens, his birthplace, but later accounts dispute this.

There also is some question about his publicized birth date, Jan. 12, 1894. If the date is correct, it would suggest Mr. Carpentier was only 12 or 13 when he began fighting for money in bars and dance halls. Francois Descamps, the only manager he ever had, at first passed a hat among the spectators.

Carpentier was so handsome that George Bernard Shaw and other writers and artists described him in the most extravagant terms, "Greek god" being among the more modest. In the American press he was known as "Gorgeous George" and "The Orchid Man." American fans went to the trouble of pronouncing his name correctly, Car-PAWN-tee-air.

He was idolized in France before, during and after World War I. By the beginning of the war Carpentier had worked his way thorugh each of the eight divisions of boxing all over Europe. In the war he served as a flying artillery spotter, and Lieutenant Carpentier won the Croix de Guerre and the Medaille Militaire.

After the war Carpentier won the world light-heavyweight championship by beating Battling Levinsky on Oct. 20, 1920, in Jersey City.

Amid all kinds of publicity stunts and phoney confrontations comparable to 1975 build-ups, the promoter Tex Rickard arranged a Carpentier-Dempsey match for July 2, 1921.

The fight could not be held in New York because Gov. Nathan L. Miller prohibited it as a threat to good morals and manners. So Rickard acquired a tract of land in Jersey City known as Boyle's Thirty Acres, which now is the site of a housing project.

With the cooperation of other backers, Rickard built a wooden arena. In those days fights were conducted in the daytime, and this one started a bit after 3 P.M. It drew more than 90,000 spectators and $1.7 million.

Dempsey earned $300,000 and Carpentier $215,000.

Considerable American public opinion favored Carpentier because he was a war hero, while Dempsey was considered a slacker who avoided military service. Rickard shrewdly exploited the difference.

Gene Tunney fought in the semi-final of that day's card, knocking out Soldier Jones in seven rounds. In 1924, Carpentier lost to Tunney by a technical knockout in the 15th round at the Polo Grounds (by now boxing was welcome in New York). Tunney went on to take the title from Dempsey in 1926.

After the Tunney match, Carpentier lost his light-heavyweight title to Battling Siki. From then on his boxing was limited mostly to exhibitions until he retired from the ring in 1927. In his 105 professional fights Carpentier had scored 51 knockouts and won 30 decisions. He was elected to the Boxing Hall of Fame in 1964.

After leaving the ring Mr. Carpentier made some good money in French music halls and motion pictures, but he lost most of his fortune in the Depression.

From the 1930's until about 10 years ago Mr. Carpentier managed a bar in Paris.

Mr. Carpentier married Georgette Elsasser in 1920. They had a daughter, Jacqueline. The marriage ended in divorce. In 1956 Mr. Carpentier married Huguette Massis.

The New York Times SATURDAY, OCTOBER 29, 1949.

CERDAN ESTEEMED BY BOXING WORLD

Most Popular Post-War Sports Figure in France Had Been Middleweight Champion

A swarthy, chunky bundle of energy, Marcel Cerdan, who was killed in the plane crash in the Azores yesterday, was as amiable out of the ring as he was savage within its confines. The former middleweight champion of the world was by far the most popular post-war sports figure in France, and his magnetism and geniality were such as to enable him also to win the warm regard of the American boxing populace.

Although he was the idol of the boulevards since he won the 160-pound championship of the world from Tony Zale on Sept. 21, 1948, Cerdan was not a full Frenchman by blood. He was the son of a Spanish father, who became a citizen of France, and a French mother. The boxer was born in Sidi Bel Abbes, Algeria, on July 22, 1916, and in his childhood his family moved to Casablanca, Morocco, which was his home the rest of his life.

In his ring work, Cerdan compiled the impressive record of ninety-six victories in 100 fights. Two of his setbacks were on "fouls," one was by a decision, and the other by a knockout handed him by Jake La Motta in Detroit on June 15. It was in this battle that Cerdan lost the middleweight championship that he had held for only nine months.

Cerdan began his professional boxing career in 1935, and was successful against mediocre opposition in North Africa. He met and defeated more formidable rivals on the Continent but when the Germans swept through France he slipped through their guard to return to Casablanca.

There he enlisted as a marine in the reorganized French Navy, and took part in inter-Allied boxing competition. He become known to thousands of American soldiers by the ease with which he swept through all opposition to capture the inter-Allied middleweight championship on Feb. 20, 1944. In 1945 he captured the European 160-pound crown in Paris.

Cerdan made his first American showing on Dec. 6, 1946, when he outpointed the capable Georgie Abrams in Madison Square Garden. He alternated his appearances between this country and Europe, building up a list of victims that at length earned him a chance at the title, held by Zale. The latter was a heavy favorite for their clash, which was held in Jersey City, but Cerdan took the title by scoring a knockout in twelve rounds.

His battle with La Motta was his first in defense of the title. He was the choice to beat the Bronx fighter, but suffered a shoulder injury in the early going and was unable to come out for the tenth.

It was to prepare for a return meeting with La Motta, scheduled for Dec. 2 at Madison Square Garden, that Cerdan was making the flight to this country. He was matched for a clash with Jake at the Polo Grounds last Sept. 28, but the fight was postponed when La Motta withdrew because of a neck injury.

Marcel Cerdan (left) is rocked by a blow from Jake LaMotta during Cerdan's last fight.

ALL PARIS MOURNS CERDAN AS A HERO

Special to THE NEW YORK TIMES.

PARIS, Oct. 28—Few deaths in recent years have been felt so deeply in France as that of Marcel Cerdan, who was seeking to regain the world middleweight boxing championship when a plane crash tragically ended his life.

He was one of the most popular figures in the history of French sports, and athletes and fans alike had to go back today to Georges Carpentier, former light heavyweight champion and a great public favorite, to find his equal.

His death excluded all other topics of conversation in the cafés of Paris, and the shock that was felt was equaled perhaps only by the air of mourning that reportedly had spread through Casablanca in French Morocco, where Cerdan lived with his wife and three children.

The café the boxer, himself, owned at Casablanca was closed as soon as the news arrived, and a large crowd remained outside throughout the day. Some placed flowers around the entrance even before his death was a certainty.

When Cerdan returned to Paris after beating Tony Zale for the championship in September, 1948, he was greeted with delirious joy. His victory was regarded as a great spur to French prestige in general and French sports in particular, and all of France basked in his glory.

When he lost the title to La Motta last June the sorrow was as deep as the previous joy, but everyone here was confident—and not the least Cerdan himself—that he would regain it. He reiterated his confidence in his fitness and ability last night before boarding the plane.

Georges Carpentier said today, Cerdan's death "had plunged the nation into mourning" and he was echoed by other well known boxers, including Marcel Thil and Theo Medina.

The New York Times

TUESDAY, SEPTEMBER 16, 1924

FRANK CHANCE DIES IN COAST HOSPITAL

Suffers Sudden Relapse in Los Angeles Home and Succumbs Within Half an Hour.

CALLED PEERLESS LEADER

Won Fame as Manager of the Cubs for Eight Seasons, and Later Led Yanks and Red Sox.

Special to The New York Times.

LOS ANGELES, Sept. 15.—Frank L. Chance, for many years the manager and field captain of the old National League baseball team in Chicago, died here tonight. Death followed a long illness, which early last Spring caused Chance to give up the hope of managing the Chicago White Sox.

The famous first baseman, after several attempts to join the White Sox earlier in the season, had been given indefinite leave of absence by Charles Comiskey and had returned here, where he had lived for several years after his active campaigning on the baseball field ended.

Since his return to Los Angeles, Chance had shown some indication of regaining strength, but tonight he suffered a sudden relapse. He was rushed to the Good Samaritan Hospital where he died within half an hour.

Chance Outstanding Figure.

Frank Leroy Chance was one of the best known baseball men in the history of the national game. Born in Fresno, Cal., on Sept. 19, 1877, Chance first played baseball on the University of California team in 1894 and 1895. The following season found him playing independent baseball in Illinois, but the major leagues had heard of him and he became a member of the Chicago National League Club in 1898. It was with the Cubs, first as player and later as manager, that Chance became famous. He led the Cubs to National League pennants in 1906, 1907, 1908 and 1910.

Chance, one of the greatest first basemen the game ever has developed, gained the name of the "Peerless Leader" for his remarkable managerial ability in landing three successive pennants for the Cubs. His team became one of the famous ones of baseball and figured in half a dozen of the greatest pennant fights in the history of the parent major circuit.

In the pennant race of 1908 when the Giants were beaten for the pennant in a play-off of the game in which Fred Merkle, then first baseman of the Giants, failed to touch second, Chance was the manager of the Chicago team.

Chance became manager of the Cubs in midseason of 1905. He led the Cubs until the end of the 1912 season. He then resigned from the Cubs and in the Winter of 1913 was signed as manager of the New York Yankees, where he held the reins until September, 1914, when he was relieved of the management of the club, which then was owned by the Farrell interests. Chance then retired from baseball to take up orange growing near his old home at Fresno and remained in retirement until 1916, when he again was lured back to baseball and became manager and part owner of the Los Angeles Club of the Pacific Coast League.

He again retired in 1917 and was out of baseball until December, 1922, when he was appointed manager of the Boston Red Sox. His success with the Red Sox was considerable, but when that club was sold in the Fall of 1923 Chance was released and later signed as manager of the Chicago White Sox.

Early in the Spring of this year just before the White Sox were to have gone to their training camp, Chance became ill and had to return to California after undergoing an operation. He declared he would be fit to assume the management of the club, but was unable to go to the training camp. A few weeks later it was announced that Chance had retired as manager and in his place had been appointed Johnny Evers, who, in the old Cub days, was the pivot player of the famous combination of "Tinker to Evers to Chance," one of the greatest infield combinations in the history of the game.

Chance retired again to his home in California and it was reported some time ago that he was improving.

Frank Chance led the Chicago Cubs to four pennants and two World Series victories as their playing manager.

The "Tinker to Evers to Chance" double-play combination was immortalized in verse by columnist F. P. Adams.

The New York Times — THURSDAY, MAY 29, 1975

Ezzard Charles, 53, Dies; Held Heavyweight Title

CHICAGO, May 28 (UPI)—Ezzard Charles, the world heavyweight boxing champion from 1949 until 1951, died today at the Veterans Administration Hospital here. He was stricken in 1966 with amyotrophic lateral sclerosis, a muscle-debilitating disease, and had been confined to a wheelchair. He was 53 years old.

Surviving are his widow, Gladys, and three children, Ezzard 2d, Deborah and Leith.

Glamour Eluded Him

By THOMAS ROGERS

Although acknowledged—and often grudingly praised—as one of the finest boxers ever to hold the heavyweight title, Ezzard Mack Charles somehow was never able to capture in addition the glamour and unrestrained idolatry that often accompany boxing's most coveted goal.

Although his purses totaled $2-million while he was winning 96 of 122 bouts from 1940 to 1959, Charles had the misfortune to gain the title upon the 1949 retirement of Joe Louis, one of boxing's most popular champions.

He ended Louis's comeback in 1950 by winning a 15-round decision, but found the triumph hollow. Reporters and fans talked only of Louis's diminished talents and berated Charles for his inability to knock out the aging hero.

Throughout his ring career, Charles was criticized for lacking "the killer instinct," that highly salable knockout drive that created box-office bonanzas for Jack Dempsey, Louis and the late Rocky Marciano. It also earned them acclaim as the toughest men of their eras.

Charles was instead a cool ring tactician who was content to outpoint his opponents or to wear them down through a profusion of punches. The quick knockout was never his objective.

Yet he himself was the victim of the one-punch knockout, in July, 1951, when he lost his title to Jersey Joe Walcott in the seventh round at Pittsburgh. He had won 15-round decisions from Walcott two times earlier.

Lost Walcott Rematch

A rematch in Philadelphia the following year saw Charles take an impressive lead on points, but squander it (and the decision) through conservative tactics. He coasted through the final four rounds and lost the chance to become the first man to regain the heavyweight championship.

In the first of two losing efforts against Marciano in 1954, Charles achieved his highest moment of recognition. His finest skills of ringmanship enabled him to go 15 hard rounds at Yankee Stadium in June, but the Brockton Bomber won the decision in what he called one of his toughest fights.

A rematch three months later, when Charles had not fully recovered from his previous battering, resulted in a eight-round knockout by Marciano and an effective end to Charles's championship aspirations.

After retiring in 1956, he made brief comeback attempts in 1958 and 1959, losing to a compendium of also-rans. He gave up for good when a fighter named Alvin Green defeated him on Sept. 1, 1959.

After retiring to his hometown, Cincinnati, he announced two years later that he was penniless.

"I was saving for a rainy day, and the rainy day has come," he said after admitting that his $2-million had finally drained mysteriously away. Chuckling at his problems, he added:

"It's more than a rainy day, it's a flood."

Charles attempted to right his financial fortunes through careers as a professional wrestler, a greeter at a night-club and then as a coordinator of boxing clubs in Chicago's Commission on Youth.

During the mid-nineteen-sixties he became increasingly afflicted by lateral sclerosis, a disease that crippled his once-powerful legs and then impaired his ability to speak.

When expenses for therapy became more than he could handle, Charles was honored at a benefit in Chicago on Nov. 13, 1968. Boxing celebrities, including Marciano, Archie Moore and Muhammad Ali (then Cassius Clay), turned out to honor the former champion.

Praised by Marciano

Marciano pointed out the lack of appreciation that had dogged Charles, especially in his fight against Louis.

"Nobody gave any credit to Ezzard," he said. "It was as if he had lost."

"He gave me two of the toughest fights of my life. I finally figured it out. People just didn't want to see Louis lose. It wasn't Ezzard's fault. He had simply come along at a time when a blood-hungry public couldn't appreciate him."

Ezzard Charles—World Heavyweight Champion 1949–1951.

Charles was six-feet tall and usually weighed in the 180's. He was born July 7, 1921, in Lawrenceville, Ga. After his family moved to Cincinnati when he was a child, he became interested in boxing.

He trained himself so well that he fought 42 amateur bouts and won them all before embarking on a professional career in 1940.

Listened to 'Older Guys'

"When I first decided to get into boxing, I'd listen to all of the older guys in the game," he remarked recently. "They'd all say the same thing: if you want to be a fighter, you've got to eat it and sleep it. Square that I was, I believed every word. I'd win a fight—and the very next day, I'd be back in the gym."

Three years service in the Army during World War II interrupted his climb to the heavyweight crown, which he finally attained on June 22, 1949, winning a decision from Walcott for the vacant National Boxing Association title.

Then followed his lackluster reign and the weary road to retirement, poverty and sickness.

"Just a simple, square sort of fellow, who believed in playing the game by the rules," Charles said in self-description some years ago. "But if I had it to do over again, I wouldn't change a thing."

"All the News That's Fit to Print"

The New York Times

LATE CITY EDITION

Weather: Sunny, mild today; cold tonight. Mostly sunny tomorrow. Temp. range: today 35-50; Monday 40-60. Full U.S. report on Page 70.

VOL. CXXII . . No. 41,982 © 1973 The New York Times Company NEW YORK, TUESDAY, JANUARY 2, 1973 15 CENTS

Major Revision of State's Courts Urged

Panel Proposes Abolition of Bail System and Strict Discipline for Judges

By LESLEY OELSNER

A radical revamping of the state's courts—in which bail would be abolished, judges would be subject to strict discipline and courts would be run by administrative technicians rather than judges—was proposed yesterday by the Temporary Commission on the New York State Court System.

The goal is to rid the courts of their biggest weaknesses—the principal one of which, according to the commission, is extreme administrative inefficiency and lack of central direction— and thus put them in a position to provide what the commission calls "justice for all."

Increase in Costs

The commission plan called for restructuring the courts into a "unified" system, wi... a merger of the five... trial courts — S... Court, Family... gate's Cou... and Court o... single "Super...

It prescri... management o... a superstructur... tors with a cl... command" — a... state's ranking jud... of their present adm... powers.

The panel called ... state to finance al... costs of the courts, i... probation services an... construction. These c... now shared by the sta... municipalities.

Implementing the re... mendations, the commiss... said, would add about $3... million a year to the alread... steadily growing total cost of the court system.

The commission explained ... the $38-million-a-year added...

New York State Judicial System — PROPOSED

Court on the Judiciary — COURT OF APPEALS — APPELLATE COURT — Appellate Term — SUPERIOR COURT — Appellate Session — NYC Criminal Court — NYC Civil Court — District Court — Town Court — City Courts

NEW YORK CITY — OUTSIDE NEW YORK CITY

PRESENT — COURT OF APPEALS — Court on the Judiciary

CONGRESS FACING DRIVE FOR REFORM AS SESSION NEARS

Goals Include Restoral of Its Power and Election of Committee Leaders

By MARJORIE HUNTER
Special to The New York Times

WASHINGTON, Jan. 1—With many of the aging power brokers of the past now gone, reform-minded Democrats... Republicans will... drive this wee... gress...

Associated Press

...the enlarged Common ...y in the community.

PAUSE IN BOMBING IS ENDED BY U.S., OFFICIALS INDICATE

Aides Say Raids Below 20th Parallel Have Resumed—American Command Silent

NEW YEAR TRUCES END

49 Enemy Violations of the Cease-Fire Reported by the South Vietnamese

By FOX BUTTERFIELD
Special to The New York Times

SAIGON, South Vietnam, Tuesday, Jan. 2 — American warplanes this afternoon resumed their raids in South Vietnam and in North Vietnam below the 20th Parallel after a 36-hour pause to observe a New Year's Day cease-fire, American officials indicated.

The United States command refused to confirm the resumption, but other American sources said privately that it began at noon today (11 P.M. Monday, New York time).

The halt in the massive aerial campaign against Hanoi, Haiphong and other areas above the 20th Parallel in North Vietnam, called by President Nixon last Saturday, remained in effect.

Violations Reported

During the 24-hour New Year's cease-fire, there were 49 Communist violations, the South Vietnamese command reported, 9 more than the reported total of Communist-initiated attacks on the day before the cease-fire began.

A Saigon military spokesman said that 11 South Vietnamese, including three civilians, had been killed in the violations and 79 wounded, 10 of them civilians. Forty-four Communists were said to have been killed in the violations.

The only major fighting reported during the cease-fire occurred near devastated Quang Tri city, just south of the demilitarized zone, where the North Vietnamese were said to have ...red over 300 mortar rounds ...d artillery shells into Gov...ment paratroop positions ... several sharp ground ...s also took place.

...Comment,' U.S. Says

...erday, several American ... privately indicated to ... that United States ...d temporarily stopped ...acks over southern ...nam and South Viet... New Year's cease... United States com... to confirm the ...

...th its policy of ... information" ...resident Nix... large-scale ...d Haiphong ... command ...say only "no ...hen asked about ...pause.

Before the cease-fire began Sunday, American planes, including B-52 heavy bombers and smaller Air Force, Navy and Marine fighter-bombers, reportedly attacked targets in the North Vietnamese panhandle and South Vietnam.

199 Air Strikes

One of the few disclosures the United States command made in its daily war communiqué yesterday was that American fighters had carried out 199 tactical air strikes over South Vietnam on Sunday.

Navy A-7 pilots from the aircraft carrier Oriskany were said to have knocked out two North Vietnamese tanks 15 miles southwest of Quang Tri city and destroyed an enemy bulldozer and .51-caliber machine gun near Kontum city in the Central Highlands.

The command refused again to provide any information on the number or location of B-52 raids Sunday as it has for the last two weeks.

The command also said that

Continued on Page 8, Column 1

...rs Cool ...of Talks

North Vietnam... ...gree to recog... ...ty of South ...id he was ...eu "would ...ce settle... ...uarantee ...gnty." ...him... ...ource

...bombing; ...of course, we did not go originally to observe bombing; we went to take Christmas mail to prisoners of war and to bring back mail from them," said Telford Taylor, professor of law at Columbia University, who was chief United States counsel for the prosecution at the Nuremberg war crimes trials. He said that the group

Continued on Page 4, Column 3

...pal... ...hood as ju...

Today the Government source said that the halt in the bombing and the announcement of plans to reopen the peace talks "came as no surprise to us."

The source said he was con...

...tain ...ulted ...a conviction ...as an artillery offi... during World War II that

Continued on Page 11, Column 1

Clemente, Pirates' Star, Dies in Crash Of Plane Carrying Aid to Nicaragua

Special to The New York Times

SAN JUAN, P. R., Jan. 1—Roberto Clemente, star outfielder for the Pittsburgh Pirates, died late last night in the crash of a cargo plane carrying relief supplies to the victims of the earthquake in Managua.

Three days of national mourning for Mr. Clemente were proclaimed in his native Puerto Rico, where he was the most popular sports figure in the island's history. He is a certainty to be enshrined in Baseball's Hall of Fame. He was only the 11th man in baseball history to get 3,000 hits, and his lifetime batting average of .317 was the highest among active players.

Mr. Clemente, who was 38 years old, won the National League batting championship four times in his 18-season career, was named to the All-Star team 12 times and in 1966 was named the league's Most Valuable Player. He was also one of the finest defensive outfielders with a very strong throwing arm. He led the Pittsburgh Pirates to two world championships, in 1960 and 1971, the latter time being named the Most Valuable Player in the World Series.

Mr. Clemente was the leader of Puerto Rican efforts to aid the Nicaraguan victims and was aboard the plane because he suspected that relief supplies were falling into the hands of profiteers.

The four-engined DC-7 piston-powered plane crashed moments after takeoff from San Juan International Airport at 9:22 P.M.

The plane, carrying a crew of three and one other passenger, came down in heavy seas a mile and a half from shore.

Coast Guard planes circled the area trying to locate the plane by the light of flares. The wreckage was not found until 5 P. M. today in about 100 feet of water. There was no sign of survivors.

Airport officials said the plane crashed after making a normal left bank while climbing after the takeoff. It could not be learned if the pilot, identified as Jerry Hill, radioed that he was in difficulty.

Cristobal Colon, a friend of Mr. Clemente who was working on the committee to raise funds and collect clothing for the earthquake victims, said he had driven Mr. Clemente and his wife, Vera, to the airport. Mrs. Clemente did not board the plane.

Mrs. Clemente said she was concerned that the plane seemed old and overloaded, but her husband assured her that everything would be all right. When the pilot did not show up until late, she said he told her, "If there is one more delay, we'll leave this for tomorrow."

Mr. Colon said Mr. Clemente had insisted on going with the flight to make certain that the supplies got into the hands of the people who needed them. "He had received reports that some of the food and clothing he had sent earlier had fallen into the hands of profiteers," said Mr. Colon.

Mr. Clemente had been asked to take part in the collection of funds by Luis Vigoraux, a

Associated Press
Roberto Clemente

Continued on Page 48, Column 8

Clemente, Pira... Of Plane Carr...

Special to The New York Times

SAN JUAN, P. R., Jan. 1—Roberto Clemente, star outfielder for the Pittsburgh Pirates, died late last night in the crash of a cargo plane carrying relief supplies to the victims of the earthquake in Managua.

Three days of national mourning for Mr. Clemente were proclaimed in his native Puerto Rico, where he was the most popular sports figure in the island's history. He is a certainty to be enshrined in Baseball's Hall of Fame. He was only the 11th man in baseball history to get 3,000 hits, and his lifetime batting average of .317 was the highest among active players.

Mr. Clemente, who was 38 years old, won the National League batting championship four times in his 18-season career, was named to the All-Star team 12 times and in 1966 was named the league's Most Valuable Player. He was also one of the finest defensive outfielders with a very strong throwing arm. He led the Pittsburgh Pirates to two world championships, in 1960 and 1971, the latter time being named the Most Valuable Player in the World Series.

Mr. Clemente was the leader of Puerto Rican efforts to aid the Nicaraguan victims and

Associated Press
Roberto Clemente

was aboar... he suspecte... plies were ... hands of profi...

The four-eng... ton-powered plan... ments after take... Juan International ... 9:22 P.M.

The plane, carryi... of three and one o... senger, came down ... seas a mile and a h... shore.

Coast Guard planes ... the area trying to ... the plane by the light of fl... The wreckage was not fo... until 5 P. M. today in about

Continued on Page...

Both Sides Gird for Battle on Abo...

By TOM BUCKLEY

In 1970, when abortion on demand was legalized in New York State, its opponents, led by the Roman Catholic Church, said they had been taken by surprise.

Last spring, when the State Legislature voted to repeal the law, which was kept only by Governor Rockefeller's veto, it was the supporters of abortion who said they had been lulled into overconfidence.

This year, both sides say they are ready for the renewal of the struggle, which is expected to provide once again the most explosive issue of the legislative session that begins tomorrow.

During the weeks ahead, thousands of easily enraged partisans will prowl the corridors of the Capitol, buttonholing members of the State Senate and the Assembly, arguing, cajoling and often abusing them, on the one hand, for being responsible for the murder of hundreds of thousands of unborn infants, or, on the other, for trying to turn the clock back to a ghastly period of filthy abortion mills, abused and unwanted children and abridged civil liberties.

"Until now we have tried to keep our arguments on an intellectual plane," said Dr. Alan F. Guttmacher, the grandfatherly obstetrician who heads Planned Parenthood-World Population. "The other side waves its fetuses in bottles, but we haven't shown pictures of battered babies or frightened, pregnant 14-year-old girls, or the bodies of young women who have died in coat-hanger abortions. Now we may pull off the silk gloves and fight them with bare knuckles."

Dr. Guttmacher is one of the leaders of a loose coalition of organizations that are determined to keep the present law, which permits abortion through the 24th week of pregnancy, on the books. Other leaders are Protestant and Jewish clergymen, civil libertarians, population planners, women's liberationists, radical feminists and several city officials, including Gordon Chase, the Health Services Administrator, and Eleanor Holmes Norton, chairman of the City Commission on Human Rights.

The opposition to the law

Continued on Page 24, Column 1

...for the ...leader of the ...offense was Sam Cunningham, who scored four touchdowns to break a Rose Bowl record.

COTTON

Two touchdown runs in the second half by Alan Lowry enabled Texas to defeat Alabama, 17-13, at Dallas. The Longhorns' quarterback scored from the 3-yard line in the third period and then raced 34 yards down the left sideline late in the final quarter for the deciding touchdown.

ORANGE

Nebraska, coached by Bob Devaney for the last time, trounced Notre Dame, 40-6, at Miami. Johnny Rodgers paced the Cornhuskers' attack as the Heisman Trophy winner made four touchdowns and passed for a fifth score.

Details on Page 47

Lab Rats Sustained on Substitute Blood

By ROBERT REINHOLD
Special to The New York Times

BOSTON, Jan. 1—Several small white rats are living in apparent contentment in a laboratory here with nothing in their blood vessels to nourish and cleanse their tissue but a milky solution of fluorocarbons and industrial emulsifiers.

The animals are the experimental subjects in a project to develop a totally artificial blood substitute. After five years of testing different mixtures, the scientists here recently achieved a milestone by removing all traces of the blood of a rat, replacing it with the substitute, and having the animal survive long enough on the solution for natural blood to regenerate and take over again in about seven days.

Although other laboratories have been working on a blood substitute, this was believed to be the first successful 100 per cent blood replacement.

Already 35 rats have survived the treatment, apparently retaining normal behavior, breathing, eating, excretion and response to light, pain and sound.

The biochemist who heads the project, Dr. Robert P. Geyer of the Harvard School of Public Health, is reluctant to discuss the practical implications of the work in detail because it is still entirely experimental.

However, an effective blood substitute is likely to be of importance to basic research, and in the treatment of a number of conditions — such as leukemia, anemia and shock—as well as in organ transplants and blood transfusions for surgery.

Although the substitute has been used to achieve 80 per cent replacement in monkeys, Dr. Geyer stresses that use in humans remains a distant objective. No tests in humans are yet planned.

The John A. Hartford Foundation of New York has invested more than half a million dollars in the project since 1966 and recently awarded Dr. Geyer $122,000 more for the next two years.

The chief constituent of the substitute was drawn from a group of semiorganic compounds called fluorocarbons. These are highly inert and heat-

Continued on Page 18, Column 4

NEWS INDEX

CLEMENTE DIES IN PLANE CRASH

Continued From Page 1, Col. 3

television producer.

"He did not just lend his name to the fund-raising activities the way some famous personalities do," said Mr. Vigoraux. "He took over the entire thing, arranging for collection points, publicity and the transportation to Nicaragua."

Mr. Clemente's relief organization had collected $150,000 in cash and tons of clothing and foodstuffs. More money and clothing are still being donated.

"We sent a ship loaded with supplies during the week," said a member of the earthquake relief committee. "One of the reasons Roberto went on the plane was to get there before the ship arrived to see the supplies were distributed properly."

The baseball star was supposed to be met at the airport by Anastasio Somoza, the Nicaraguan military leader, a friend said.

Mr. Clemente's interest in Nicaragua may have been heightened by his experience in managing the Puerto Rican team that participated in the amateur world series held in Managua in late November and December. Sixteen teams participated. The Puerto Ricans took fifth place.

News of Mr. Clemente's death plunged Puerto Rico into mourning.

Gov. Louis A. Ferré decreed three days of mourning and Governor-elect Rafael Hernandez Colon, who will be sworn into office tomorrow, ordered the cancellation of an inaugural ball and all other social activities related to the inauguration.

Cross marks site of crash of plane bound for Managua.

Clemente a Player Involved On and Off the Diamond

Proud of Being Puerto Rican and Black

By LEONARD KOPPETT

The way Roberto Clemente died had more to do with the way he had lived than all the spectacular baseball statistics for which, in due course, he will be enshrined in the Hall of Fame.

Few men, if any, have played professional baseball better than Clemente did during his 18-year career with the Pittsburgh Pirates. And few players put as much passion into other aspects of life as he did.

Not halfway through his 39th year, he was mpersonally involved in a mission of mercy, trying to relieve the suffering of strangers caused by an earthquake in a country he had previously visited only briefly. Most athletes, or anyone else earning nearly $200,000 a year, as Clemente did, lend their names, financial support or even their exhortations to some worthy cause and let it go at that. But Clemente had to go in person.

This capacity for involvement characterized him as a ballplayer and helped generate some of the misunderstandings that made him a controversial personality.

But in the end—the brutally abrupt end—his baseball skills remained the achievement of his life and the reason his personality mattered to so many people.

The moody Roberto Clemente was one of the best players in National League history.

He made exactly 3,000 hits, and only 10 players in more than 100 years of major league baseball had made more. He won four National League batting championships and a most-valuable-player award. He helped his team to victory the only two times it reached the World Series. His career batting average was .317, highest of all active players with at least a few years of service.

In addition he was acknowledged as one of the greatest fielders of his day with an exceptionally strong and accurate throwing arm, and a first-rate base-runner. As the "complete player," his only peers as contemporaries were Willie Mays and Hank Aaron, each of whom got greater recognition because they hit more home runs.

Clemente was Puerto Rican and black, and fiercely proud of his identity. His status as a national hero in Puerto Rico stemmed as much from his outspoken expression of such pride as from his baseball feats. Other Puerto Ricans had won baseball glory, but few had made such explicit demands for respect and recognition.

His destiny was baseball from the start. He was born on Aug. 18, 1934, in Carolina, the San Juan suburb that remained his home. He was the youngest child in a large, financially comfortable family. His father was a foreman on a sugar plantation, and his plans for Roberto pointed toward engineering.

But while still in high school at 17, he was playing baseball so spectacularly that he was given a $500 bonus to join the Santurce team in the Puerto Rican League, in which professionals from the States also played. In his third season, the winter of 1953-54, he hit .356, and the major league scouts had no doubts.

In 1954 there was still an unspoken quota system limiting the number of black players a team would use, although Jackie Robinson had already completed seven seasons with the Brooklyn Dodgers. There was also a distinct set of prejudices about "Spanish-speaking players." And there was a "bonus rule" that forced a major league team to keep on its active roster any player to whom it had paid more than $4,000 for signing—a deterrent to giving bonuses to a player

(continued)

not ready to play in the majors immediately.

But Clemente's talent was so evident that all three deterrents were disregarded. After some bidding, the Dodgers landed him for $10,000 outright and a $5,000 salary to play for their Montreal club. That meant he could be drafted by another team for $4,000 after the 1954 season.

There are conflicting versions of what happened next. The facts are that Clemente played part-time for Montreal, batted .257 and was drafted by Pittsburgh, which had first choice because it finished last in 1953.

The Dodgers had won the pennant in 1953 by a huge margin and couldn't have signed Clemente without a bonus. They knew, they said afterward, they would lose him in the draft, but it was worth the money to keep him from signing with the New York Giants, who already had Mays. The idea of a Mays and Clemente playing side by side was too frightening for the Dodgers to allow.

Another version is that the Dodgers hoped to sneak Clemente through the draft by not playing him much (to hide his ability) and by loading the Montreal roster with other attractive draft picks. But the Pirates, under the direction of Branch Rickey, who had left Brooklyn three years before, were not fooled.

Clemente started the 1955 season with a Pittsburgh club that had lost 317 games in three years, finishing last each time. He was not yet 21 and was among a half-dozen young players who were to make Pittsburgh a World Series winner by 1960—Dick Groat, Bill Mazeroski, Roy Face, Vern Law, Don Hoak and Bill Virdon, now Pittsburgh's manager.

Clemente's bitterness about nonrecognition dates to the 1960 season. A key member of that team, he felt unjustly neglected when so much of the praise was heaped on others who had done no more. For the next decade, during which he won his four batting championships and the M.V.P. in 1966, a feeling of being unappreciated marred his satisfaction with increasing fame and wealth.

Recognition finally came in full measure in 1971. By then the acknowledged leader of the Pirates, he led them into the World Series and, as underdogs, to a dramatic seven-game victory over Baltimore. He hit .414 in that Series, but was even more dominating by his involvement in key plays and was finally hailed by the widest possible audience for what he had been all along: a player of all-round excellence second to none.

By that time he was deep into his dream of building a "Sports City" in Puerto Rico to encourage children and youngsters to play. It was a project that needed financing but could not provide profit—quite different from the usual "baseball school camp."

He had been to Nicaragua for an amateur baseball tournament. That was enough of a tie to impel him to head a relief committee after the earthquake last month, interrupting his activities with baseball for youngsters. His organization collected $160,000 and tons of supplies in a week.

He could have stayed home with his wife, Vera, and their children, Roberto Jr., 7; Luis, 5, and Ricky, 4. He almost returned to them from the airport when the takeoff was delayed several hours. But he decided to go.

He had expected to be back in time for a New Year's Eve party and a meeting today with Joe L. Brown, the Pittsburgh general manager, who was coming to him with his 1973 contract.

A Man of Two Worlds

Clemente as Deeply Pledged to Civic Concerns in Puerto Rico as to Baseball

By JOSEPH DURSO

An Appreciation

Tom Seaver sat by the Christmas tree yesterday in his home in Greenwich, Conn., and reflected on the life and times of Roberto Walker Clemente. He agreed that the key word in everything Clemente did for 38 years, nearby half of them in the big leagues, was "passion."

"Also compassion," Seaver said. "Emotional, sincere, a compassionate type of person. I could not believe what I heard on the radio, that he was gone. It was just chills, period. It's a horrible loss, not only to his family and teammates but to all of us, especially to the young players. I mean, you look up to Henry Aaron and Sandy Koufax and Roberto Clemente."

Since 1955, when he became a rookie outfielder with the Pittsburgh Pirates, Roberto Clemente lived in two worlds and they had one thing in common: passion. On the baseball field, he played 18 seasons with passion, often complaining of aches and pains as he attacked National League pitching. Off the field, he would retreat to his handsome house in Puerto Rico to spend the winter with his wife and three sons while resting those aches and pains, but then he would become involved with passion in civic projects until spring training.

"I had a rough winter," Clemente said last February as he sat exhaused in the Pirates' training camp in Bradenton, Fla., four months after he had hit .414 in the World Series at the age of 37. 'I didn't do any exercise, I kept going from one place to another and never had enough time home. My father was very ill. I lost 10 pounds and now I have stomach trouble.

"In addition to my house, I have a place in the mountains, and I said I would spend a lot of time there. I got there three times all winter.

"For a month and a half, my wife and I couldn't sleep. Our house was like a museum—people flocking down the street, ringing our bell day and night, walking through our rooms. People from the town, even tourists.

"Then I had so many things going on down there, and I just couldn't say no. Every day I was doing something different. The Governor sent for me, the park administration, civic clubs. We tried to get away to South America for a vacation and were called back because my father took sick."

Even at his peak moments on the ball field, Clemente related his baseball world to his world back home. After the Pirates had dethroned the Baltimore Orioles in the 1971 series, he was called to the microphones in the tumultuous locker room. He asked permission to include

(continued)

Clemente's lifetime batting average of .317 was highest among active players at the time of his tragic death.

a few words in Spanish to his mother and father in Puerto Rico, then said:

"On this, the proudest moment of my life, I ask your blessing."

"I thought he was great," Brooks Robinson was saying in the losers' locker room at the same time, "but now that I've seen him more than I ever had, he's greater than I thought."

"When a guy gets older, you usually see him slow up," Don Buford of the Orioles was saying. "But not Clemente."

"Very few players can win a game in as many different ways," observed Bill Mazeroski, his teammate for 17 years.

"The very special thing about Roberto physically," Tom Seaver reflected yesterday, "was his hands. So very powerful. He stood there far away from the plate with that great big, long bat, and with those strong hands he controlled it like crazy, hitting pitches on the other side of the plate.

"There was that one area out there at the knees off the outside corner. If you hit that spot with a pitch, he'd look and walk away. If you missed it, he'd hit the ball very hard."

"His weakness was so close to his strength that you were always in danger," said Jim Russo, chief scout for the Orioles. "I mean, I told our pitchers they could throw low and away. But if they made a mistake, he'd hit it out of sight to right field."

They will remember Roberto Clemente as one of the rare ones in his world of baseball: 12 All-Star games, 11 times the Golden Glove winner in right field, five times the league leader in throwing out base runners from the outfield, the best career batting average (.317) on today's scene, the 11th player in history to total 3,000 hits.

They even named a race horse after him — Roberto, winner of the 1972 English Derby and owned by John W. Galbreath, who also owns the Pittsburgh Pirates. And he doubtlessly will become the first Latin player elected to baseball's Hall of Fame.

But for all his honors on the field, it may well be that Roberto Clemente will be remembered longer and more lovingly off the field, in that "other" world back home, the world where his strong bronze face and his passion made him a folk hero, where his house was like a museum and where he couldn't say no.

Puerto Rico Goes Into Mourning

By SAM GOLDAPER

Roberto Clemente touched people from all walks of life, especially those with whom he had the closest contact—his Pittsburgh Pirate teammates, many of whom planned to fly to Puerto Rico this week to pay him tribute.

Gov. Luis A. Ferré of Puerto Rico issued a proclamation yesterday ordering three days of official mourning because of "the death of the great Puerto Rican, Roberto Clemente." The governor also joined Pirate players, Manny Sanguillen, Bob Johnson and Rennie Stennett, in a visit to Clemente's widow and three children.

In Puerto Rico, radio stations cancelled regularly scheduled programs and played somber music. His friends in North and South America planned memorial services.

Despite his individual success and ambition, Clemente was always a team player and he never lost respect for the fans he loved.

"Without the fans, there would be no baseball," he often said.

The Pittsburgh star drives a Jim Palmer pitch up the alley for a triple in the 1971 world series.

The Reactions

This was how some of his own fans, players and dignitaries spoke of Roberto Clemente yesterday:

"Roberto Clemente touched us all and we're all better players and people for having known him. I think we all learned from him," said Steve Blass, a Pittsburgh Pirate pitcher.

"Words seem futile in the face of this tragedy," said Bowie Kuhn, the baseball commissioner, "nor can they possibly do justice to this unique man. Somehow, Roberto transcended superstardom. His marvelous playing skills rank him among the truly elite. And what a wonderfully good man he was. Always concerned about others. He had about him a touch of royalty."

"He was one of the greatest persons I knew," said John Galbreath, chairman of the board of the Pittsburgh Pirates. "If you have to die, how better could your death be exemplified than by being on a mission of mercy? It was so typical of the man. Every time I was down there, someone was always saying how he contributed to the youth and needy of his island; how he was going to make that his life's work. He did these things without fanfare or anything—just what he thought was right to help somebody else."

Anastasio Somoza, Nicaraguan leader, sent a cable of condolence to Clemente's family. "He died a hero, leaving his family in order to aid humanity." Clemente was on his way to the earthquake-ravaged nation with supplies when his plane crashed.

'Greatest Player'

"It was so typical that he'd meet his death in such a fashion—helping people less fortunate," said Danny Murtaugh, who managed the Pirates to their 1960 and 1971 World Series victories. "I thought Roberto was the greatest player I've ever seen.

"It was quite an honor to manage in the major leagues," said Murtaugh, now retired, "but it was a double honor to manage a superstar like Roberto . . . . and he was a superstar."

Bill Virdon, the Pirate manager, said, "Roberto loved baseball. Baseball was his life. He gave much more to baseball than he took away from it no matter how much money he made.

"When you think of baseball and Pittsburgh, there will be a definite void. In my opinion, he will be enshrined in the Hall of Fame within five years."

"Pittsburgh lost a heck of a man," said Willie Stargell, the Pirates' outfielder, his eyes filled with tears. "Clemente's work with the relief effort was typical. Roberto was always trying to help someone."

Dick Williams, the manager of the Oakland A's, said, "Clemente was the greatest player I have ever watched." Jim Brewer, the Los Angeles Dodger pitcher, said, "Clemente was a fantastic outfielder, the best hitter in the National League and someone who constantly gave everybody fits."

For most Americans, Clemente will be remembered for his feats on the baseball field. But for those kids in the barrios of Puerto Rico who were touched by their national hero, he will be remembered for other things as well.

Many of them will be present at Hiram Bithorn Stadium in San Juan where an organized ecumenical service will be held. Clemente occasionally played winter baseball in the stadium and it was being used as a collection headquarters for Nicaraguan-bound mercy material.

Two veterans—Walter Johnson with Ty Cobb in 1925.

"All the News That's Fit to Print"

The New York Times.

LATE CITY EDITION
U. S. Weather Bureau Report Page 58) forecasts: Warm, humid, chance of showers today, tonight. Partly cloudy tomorrow.
Temp. range: 89—72; yesterday: 89—73.
Temp.-Hum. Index: near 80; yesterday: 80.

VOL. CX...No. 37,796. | © 1961 by The New York Times Company. Times Square, New York 36, N. Y. | NEW YORK, TUESDAY, JULY 18, 1961. | 10 cents beyond 50-mile zone from New York City except on Long Island. Higher in air delivery cities. | FIVE CENTS

ELECTIONS BOARD TO SEEK MACHINES FOR PRIMARY VOTE

Democrats May Get Them If Enough for 3 Parties Cannot Be Obtained

MEETING SET FOR TODAY

Sharkey Attacks the Mayor for 'Big-Lie Technique' In Judgeship Charge

By CLAYTON KNOWLES

The Board of Elections will make a new effort today to find a way for one or more political parties to use voting machines in the Sept. 7 primary.

A review of the question was ordered by James M. Power, the board president. His action followed a wave of protests over the board's decision last week to use paper ballots for all three parties because there were not enough city-owned machines for the job.

All five candidates for Mayor in the primary joined in the outcry. The Citizens Union, one of the city's most respected civic groups, insisted that the Democratic primary battle, the biggest of the lot, should be decided on voting machines.

The concern was based on fear that the election would be slowed by the use of paper ballots and on the possibility of large-scale mistakes and fraud.

Rented Machines Sought

At its meeting today, the board will explore more fully the possibility of renting the machines necessary to enable all three parties to use them in the primary. The prospect seemed dim, but the board was in communication yesterday with the Shoup Voting Machine Corporation, which said it might be able to supply enough machines.

If enough machines cannot be obtained, the board will consider whether it should reverse itself and permit the use of machines for one party, as it has the authority to do. If it should adopt this course, the other parties would use paper ballots.

The indication was that the machines would be assigned to the Democratic primary, the hottest of the contests, if such a step were taken. There was no commitment, however, and

Continued on Page 15, Column 3

THEOBALD DENIES ANY WRONGDOING

He Asks to Go Before Jury 'to Clear My Name'

By LEONARD BUDER

Dr. John J. Theobald, the Superintendent of Schools, denied yesterday that he had used school building supplies to repair his Sands Point, L. I., home or that city high school students had performed services for him there.

The denial was reported by District Attorney Frank D. O'Connor of Queens, who questioned Dr. Theobald for about an hour yesterday morning.

Later in the day Dr. Theobald met for more than an hour with District Attorney Edward S. Silver of Brooklyn, who announced afterward that he would convene a rackets grand jury next Tuesday to look into the propriety of the Superintendent's having students build a boat for him.

Theobald Request Cited

"I have no evidence that Mr. Theobald has committed a crime," Mr. Silver said. "However, he has requested that we put all the evidence before the grand jury."

Dr. Theobald, after his meeting with Mr. Silver and Assistant District Attorney Aaron E. Koota, said he had asked that the matter go before a grand jury because "I want to clear my name."

The Superintendent declared that there had been "too many inferences and innuendoes" against him recently and he wanted the subject fully aired.

"I have come here voluntarily and I know I will get fair treatment," he said. "I am looking for justice."

Dr. Theobald acknowledged

Continued on Page 17, Column 2

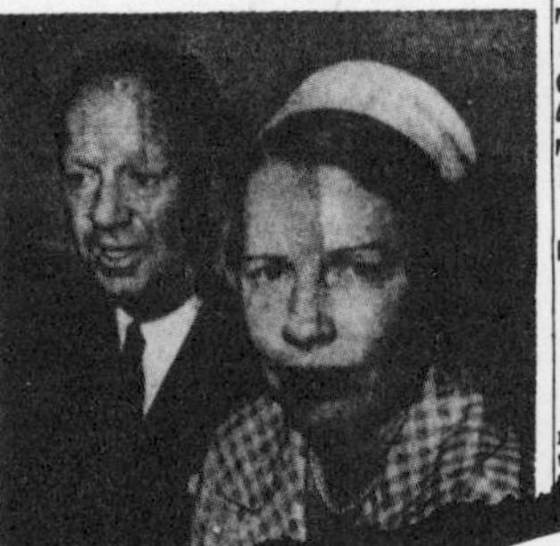

G.O... For...

The New... day designa... candidate fo...

MAYOR SE... IN SEYMOU...

Calls Charges Irre... and Attacks Au... Report as Fan...

By CHARLES G. BENN...

Mayor Wagner charged yesterday that the investigation... Whitney North Seymour... into New York City affa... "has gone out of business the way it started—in a blaze of mud."

With these words and about 600 more, Mayor Wagner retorted to criticisms made of his administration in a thirty-seven-page report issued Sunday by the Special Unit of the State Investigation Commission. Mr. Seymour headed the Special Unit.

The report charged the city administration with failing to investigate corruption or punish employes. It said corruption still existed "at every level of the city government." The Seymour unit went out of existence last Wednesday.

Mayor Sees a Challenge

Mr. Seymour issued the report on his own without consulting the parent body, the State Investigation Commission. Mayor Wagner dubbed this action "a challenge to the integrity of his [Mr. Seymour's] own state commission."

Last night Goodman A. Sarachan of the state commission said at his home in Rochester, N. Y., that the Special Unit's report was "simply the view of Mr. Seymour as a private citizen" and would "not be made part of the commission's record."

Asked how he felt about the

Continued on Page 16, Column 3

2d U. S. Space Trip Put Off by Weather

By RICHARD WITKIN
Special to The New York Times.

COCOA BEACH, Fla., July 17—The nation's second manned flight into space was postponed by unfavorable weather tonight until Wednesday morning at the earliest.

The delay was announced at 11:30 P. M., Eastern daylight time, after a sudden deterioration of the weather had spread several cloud layers over the Cape Canaveral launching area.

Forecasters saw no hope for improvement for several hours. But they anticipated that conditions would be better in another twenty-four hours or more.

The launching originally had been set for 7 A. M., daylight time tomorrow. Assigned to "fly" the two-ton Mercury cap-

Continued on Page 2, Column 3

TUNIS GIVES PARIS 24 HOURS TO AGREE TO LEAVE BIZERTE

Bourguiba Demands Answer on Evacuation of Base—Critical of Algerians

By THOMAS F. BRADY
Special to The New York Times.

TUNIS, July 17—...

Fleeing East Germans Tell Fears

Associated Press Radiophoto

...tion center yesterday in West Berlin

...having their wedding trip at Marienfelde, West Berlin's busy reception center for East German refugees. They set out on their wearisome journey last Wednesday "after party

Continued on Page 3, Column 2

Ty Cobb, Baseball Great, Dies; Still Held 16 Big League Marks

First in the Hall of Fame—Top Star, 74, Played 22 Years With Detroit

Special to The New York Times.

ATLANTA, July 17—Ty Cobb, the No. 1 player elected to baseball's Hall of Fame and probably the greatest star in the game's history, died today.

The famed Georgia Peach, a giant in baseball almost from the start of his major league career in 1905, died at the age of 74 in Emory University Hospital.

Cobb, one of the most feared players in the game because of his daring and his short-fused temper, had suffered from cancer of the prostate gland.

In addition, he had had diabetes and chronic heart disease. Physicians at the hospital said that his general condition had deteriorated rapidly during the last two weeks.

After playing twenty-two years with the Detroit Tigers and two years with the Philadelphia Athletics, Cobb was chosen in 1936 to the Hall of Fame. He beat out Babe Ruth, who was still playing at the time, by seven votes.

Ty Cobb

Sixteen of the major-league records he set still stand.

Tall, (6 feet), tough and fiery, Cobb was noted for the deadly use of his spikes on the base paths, his dramatic base-stealing and his skill at bat. His

Continued on Page 21, Column 2

Ty Cobb... Still He...

First in the Hall... Top Star, 74, Pl... Years With De...

Special to The New York T...

ATLANTA, July 17—T... the No. 1 player elected... ball's Hall of Fame and... ably the greatest star... game's history, died today.

The famed Georgia Peach, a giant in baseball almost from the start of his major league career in 1905, died at the age of 74 in Emory University Hospital.

Cobb, one of the most feared players in the game because of his daring and his short-fused temper, had suffered from cancer of the prostate gland.

In addition, he had had diabetes and chronic heart disease. Physicians at the hospital said that his general condition had deteriorated rapidly during the last two weeks.

After playing twenty-two years with the Detroit Tigers and two years with the Philadelphia Athletics, Cobb was chosen in 1936 to the Hall of Fame. He beat out Babe Ruth, who was still playing at the time, by seven votes.

Associated Press

Ty Cobb during interview

Sixteen of the major-league records he set still stand.

Tall, (6 feet), tough and fiery, Cobb was noted for the deadly use of his spikes on the base paths, his dramatic base-stealing and his skill at bat. His

Continued on Page 21, Column 2

Industry Tax Credit Voted by House Unit

By RUSSELL BAKER
Special to The New York Times.

WASHINGTON, July 17—Tax cuts to stimulate new business investment in plant and equipment were approved today by the House Ways and Means Committee.

The objective is to encourage capital investment, promote national economic growth and create jobs, although there is speculation that new incentives to retool may accelerate the trend toward automation.

The bill is expected to go to the House floor early in August, with good prospects for passage. Prospects for Senate action this year, however, remain uncertain.

The committee-approved plan is a modified version of the Ad-

Continued on Page 14, Column 4

MOSCOW BALKING ON ARMS PARLEY

...oses Multi-Nation Talks ...s U.S. Accepts Soviet ...rmula in Advance

...EYMOUR TOPPING
...to The New York Times.

...July 17 — The ... declared today ... refuse to par... multi-nation con... armament before ... ment with the ... on the main

...inistration's ...fense Policy Moves

...following is the second of three articles appraising President Kennedy's first six months in the White House.

By JAMES RESTON
Special to The New York Times.

WASHINGTON, July 17—In the first six months of the Kennedy Administration, United States foreign policy has remained basically the same as under President Eisenhower but has become more flexible and venturesome.

President Kennedy seems more willing than his predecessor to increase the range of American power, particularly in the field of conventional weapons, and to use that power in the skirmishes of the "cold war."

He intervened indirectly in the invasion of Cuba. He was prepared to intervene directly in Laos until the failure of the Cuban adventure changed his mind. There is now much more analysis of the tactics of combating Communist guerrila tactics in such places as South Vietnam, and a bolder spirit of preparation to meet the much more serious danger of war in Germany.

The changes since the Eisenhower Administration, therefore, while primarily changes of emphasis and degree, are nevertheless important, and include the following:

¶A marked willingness to risk larger budget deficits in order to provide stronger ground forces and transportation to carry them quickly to critical areas of the "cold war."

¶Greater emphasis on attacking the weakness of the Communist policies in the underdeveloped and neutral nations.

¶More confidence in the United Nations as an instrument for preserving peace and

Continued on Page 11, Column 1

NEWS INDEX

WEST TURNS DOWN KHRUSHCHEV PLAN FOR GERMAN PACT

U. S., Britain and France, in Notes to Moscow, Reject Berlin 'Free City' Proposal

ALLIES' STAND IS FIRM

They Weigh Early Meeting of 3 Foreign Ministers to Chart Policy in Crisis

By E. W. KENWORTHY
Special to The New York Times.

WASHINGTON, July 17—The United States, Britain and France presented notes to the Soviet Union today categorically rejecting Premier Khrushchev's proposals on Berlin and Germany.

The similar messages were delivered to the Soviet Foreign Ministry shortly after noon in Moscow. The three powers refused to accept the Soviet plan for a peace conference on Germany and free-city status for Berlin.

The White House announced that the text of the United States note would be made public at 10 A. M. tomorrow. It is about twelve pages long and is believed to total approximately 3,500 words. It is expected that Britain and France will make public their somewhat shorter notes at the same time.

Three-Power Parley Weighed

Meanwhile, the State Department said consideration was being given to a meeting of the Western Big Three foreign ministers—Secretary of State Dean Rusk of the United States, the Earl of Home of Britain and Maurice Couve de Murville of France—to concert policy and planning on the Berlin crisis.

Lincoln White, State Department press officer, said "no definite decisions" had yet been made on whether to have such a conference, or on the possible time and place. It became known, however, that the meeting was expected to take place in Paris early next month if the present tentative plans were carried through.

Mr. White said such a meeting would give the three foreign ministers "an opportunity for further consultations among our NATO Allies."

The United States note is a

Continued on Page 3, Column 5

BOWLES RETAINED AS AIDE TO RUSK

Kennedy Postpones Change Regarded as Inevitable

By WALLACE CARROLL
Special to The New York Times.

WASHINGTON, July 17—President Kennedy retained ...ester Bowles today as his ...der Secretary of State.

The President thus put off a ...nge in the high command of ... State Department that im...ant Administration sources believe to be inevitable.

Pierre Salinger, the White House press secretary, cleared up the question of Mr. Bowles' immediate future after the Under Secretary had lunched with President Kennedy at the White House.

Mr. Salinger told reporters that Mr. Bowles would stay as Under Secretary. Earlier, he refused to discuss published reports that Mr. Bowles would either resign or be dismissed.

Criticism at Height

According to these reports, criticism of Mr. Bowles within the White House, in Congress and in the State Department was coming to a head.

President Kennedy himself was said to be dissatisfied with the policy-making performance of the State Department and to hold Mr. Bowles, as the Under Secretary for Political Affairs, largely responsible.

Accordingly, he suggested to Mr. Bowles last week that he give up the job of Under Secretary and go abroad as an Ambassador. He was to talk to Mr. Bowles again this week, the reports said, and offer him the choice between the ambassadorship and dismissal.

These reports were privately accepted as true by members of

Continued on Page 10, Column 2

TY COBB, 74, DIES; HELD 16 RECORDS

Continued From Page 1, Col. 4

numerous records include the following:

Highest career batting average (.367); most batting championships (twelve); most stolen bases (829).

During fourteen of his years in the major leagues, he batted when the old "dead" ball was still in use and when there was virtually no limit on the tricks a pitcher could use.

Cobb started with Detroit on Aug. 30, 1905, at the age of 18. The Tigers had paid between $700 and $750 to get him from Augusta in the South Atlantic League. Cobb hit a double off Jack Chesbro in his first time at bat.

His first-year batting average was .240 for forty-one games but from then until he called it quits in 1928 he never fell below .322. Three times, he batted more than .400 in a season. He had 4,191 hits in 11,429 times at bat.

Batting left-handed and throwing right-handed the center field star played in 3,033 games, scored 2,244 runs, hit 297 triples and nine times made more than 200 hits in a season. In 1915 he stole ninety-six bases.

Nine Homers in 1909

A master of the hook and fall-away slide, Cobb raised base stealing to a height it has never regained. The league champions since Cobb's time have averaged under fifty steals a season.

Several times Cobb stole second, third and home in one inning. One manager reportedly asked his catcher:

"What do you do when Cobb breaks for second?"

The catcher replied:

"I throw to third."

Cobb was once home-run champion of his league. He hit nine in 1909, helping Detroit win its third straight American League pennant.

It was not only his ability that inspired fear and respect in his foes, but also the temper of his playing. He once said that the reason he was so tough on the diamond was that he had entered baseball in the days when a player had to be tough to survive.

Often called the "stormy petrel" of the game, as well as less printable epithets, he played every game as if it were the deciding contest in the world series.

At the height of his career he was frequently embroiled in fights with other players and with fans. In 1912 the Tigers went on strike because he was suspended for attacking a heckler who happened to be a cripple. In another famous scrap, Cobb squared off with George Moriarty, an umpire, in a bout under the stands.

Ty Cobb is considered to be the greatest baseball player ever.

In his later years Cobb became a "mellow sort of fellow," in the words of a man who knew him and was impressed with the apparent turn-about in his personality.

Where as a player he had battled with his own teammates as well as with opposing team members, and had only a few intimates, he seemed in his later years to want to atone for his long period of aggressiveness.

In a soft-spoken way he liked to make jokes about his days as a "difficult player," and it was a habit of his to attend many of the old-time affairs and reminisce.

He continued to take long hikes and to go hunting for many years, activities that in his playing years he credited with developing his endurance and quick awareness.

As a manager, as well as a player, Cobb gave the fans repeated thrills and excitement. In the off-season of 1920, he signed to manage the team on which he had starred for so long. He brought the Tigers home second in 1923, but that was his best.

In his last years as player-manager, Cobb drove fans and opposition to distraction by jogging back and forth from center field to talk to his pitcher, shift his infield, or otherwise evolve strategy. But he was still batting .339 when he resigned as manager in 1926.

Soon afterward he figured in a potential scandal that threatened to become another "Black Sox" affair. With Tris Speaker, another of baseball's old-time heroes, he was accused by Dutch Leonard, a former Tiger pitcher, of figuring in an agreement to throw a game in 1919—the year of the crooked series between Cincinnati and Chicago.

But on Jan. 27, 1927, the two stars were exonerated by Judge Kennesaw Mountain Landis, and Cobb said at once he felt "honor bound" to put in at least one more "big year."

Connie Mack signed him for the Athletics for a reported $75,000, and Cobb promptly predicted a pennant. But Mack's line-up of stars—he had signed Eddie Collins and Zach Wheat as well—lost to the Yankees that year. Cobb never had another chance to be on a pennant winner. He played in ninety-five games in 1928, batting .323, or 44 points below his career average.

Waspish as he was on the field, Cobb was a quiet man away from the diamond. Known to have invested his money wisely, he became a millionaire, largely on the investments he had made in a soft-drink stock.

After he left the game as a player he rarely went to a ball park. He insisted that the game that he had played in the era of the fast, multiple steal, the squeeze bunt and the dead ball was not matched in contemporary baseball.

In recent years Cobb had been relatively inactive. In November, 1953, he donated a reported $100,000 to establish the Cobb Educational Foundation for promising Georgia students.

Cobb, who never went to college, sought to give scholarships to students interested in higher study. His father had wanted him to become a lawyer or physician instead of a ballplayer. The foundation provided outright gifts rather than loans to the students selected.

Front Row, Left

Cobb was playing baseball when he was 9 years old. A picture of the Royston (Ga.) Midgets, taken in 1895, hardly indicated, however, that of the whole squad of unsmiling youngsters, the half-pint with the torn stockings sitting at the left end of the front row would be the only one to make the picture worth reprinting.

In the majors, Cobb's weight varied from 178 pounds to 192. But in boyhood he was a slim, jittery nobody, dwarfed by the bigger-chested, older members of the Midgets.

Cobb was one of the first major leaguers to get into military service during World War I. He became a captain with the Army's Chemical Warfare Division and served overseas.

Cobb was divorced twice. His first wife was the former Charlie Lombard of Augusta. They were divorced after thirty-nine years of marriage. They had five children.

In 1955, Cobb divorced his second wife, Mrs. Frances Cass Cobb.

Those who were with him when he died included his son, James; his daughters, Mrs. Beverly McLauren and Shirley Cobb, all of California, and his first wife.

The nickname Georgia Peach was given to Cobb by Grantland Rice, the sports writer, who was impressed with the daring, talented youngster in action with Augusta. After watching Cobb, Rice went back to his typewriter and recounted one dramatic play made by the lad he called the Georgia Peach. The name stuck.

Sports of The Times

By JOHN DREBINGER

The Cobb We Knew

IT WAS not by accident or whim of choice that when they held the first poll for baseball's Hall of Fame in 1936, the name of Tyrus Raymond Cobb led all the rest. To be on top had been the only creed by which the Georgia Peach had lived through all the years of his spectacular—and at times turbulent—career.

His one goal was to win by any means the rules allowed. That, of course, got him into no end of fights. On and off the field the Georgia firebrand conducted countless feuds.

Even mild-mannered Eddie Collins, a great second baseman in Ty's heyday as a daring base-stealer, confessed to us once that he had harbored a burning hatred for Cobb. Eddie used to go on hunting trips, but just for the exercise. He hadn't the heart to shoot a sparrow.

"But when that Cobb came sliding into me with those gleaming spikes, I saw red," said Eddie. "Throwing to first for a double play, I must have tried to nail him between the eyes with the ball 100 times. But so agile was that demon in twisting out of reach I never got him once."

They Paid Back

But Cobb didn't do all the spiking. He was sitting in a hotel room a few years after he had hung up his spikes for good when the talk got around to some of his more reckless exploits on the base paths.

"Yes," he admitted, "I guess I may have been a trifle rough. But take a look at this."

With that he rolled up his trousers and revealed a pair of shins criss-crossed with myriads of scars from ankles to knees.

"I didn't get those playing tiddlywinks," said Ty. "They gave it to me as hard as I gave it to them. The only difference was I never gave them the satisfaction of hearing me squawk. I'd sooner let them cut out my tongue than let them know I was hurt."

It was when the opposition was at its roughest and hostile crowds rode him hardest that he rose to his greatest heights as a player. Such was one memorable day at the Polo Grounds in 1920.

A few days before, the Yankees, who then made their home in the Polo Grounds, were playing the Indians. Carl Mays, a pitcher with a deceptive underhand or "submarine ball" delivery, was on the mound for the Yankees. A stray pitch struck Ray Chapman, a Cleveland infielder, in the head. He died without regaining consciousness.

The next day, Cobb, whose Tigers were playing elsewhere, was quoted as saying Mays had done it deliberately and should be driven from baseball. The New York fans and press rallied to Mays' support.

One of His Biggest Thrills

Cobb and his Tigers followed the Indians into New York and for the first game a capacity crowd packed the Polo Grounds. For more than an hour before game time they waited for Cobb. But throughout the pregame practice there was no Cobb.

Then, just as the umpires were getting ready to start the game, the clubhouse door in center field opened. Down the steps trotted the Georgia Peach. Up the middle of the field he marched, jauntily slapping his thigh with his glove, while the crowd jeered and booed with deafening noise. Unmindful of it all, Cobb strode to the press box, then in the front of the lower stands directly behind home plate. He doffed his cap with a mock bow. Then he walked to his dugout where he gave the outraged gathering a final salute of utter disdain.

This done, the game started and the great Ty all but tore it apart with bat and glove. On his final hit the crowd gave him a standing ovation. You simply had to admire the guy.

"Yes," he said years later, "I guess you could say that was one of my biggest thrills.

A Severe Taskmaster

There was, however, another side of Cobb's play that, perhaps, was not so well known and certainly not as much publicized. It was a side to which modern players could well pay close heed.

He was perhaps one of baseball's keenest students and at all times his own severest critic and taskmaster. He studied every type of batting form and mastered them all.

If any pitcher bothered him with a certain pitch, Cobb would be out early the next day wearing out his own batting-practice pitcher as he worked on that pitch over and over again. It was the same with his fielding. He had, of course, a wealth of natural talent, but he insisted on attaining perfection in all phases of the game.

"If I have any criticism of the modern player," he once said, "and I guess that could apply to my day as well, it is that so few will practice what they can't do. If a fellow can hit a long ball, that's all he tries for. He won't have any part of learning how to bunt or stroke a ball to the opposite field. My advice to young players is, work at what doesn't come easy to you."

It was a formula that kept him on top for close to a quarter of a century with an incredible lifetime batting average of .367.

Records Cobb Shares

Most years batting .400 or better —3 (also held by Rogers Hornsby and Jess Burkett).

Most consecutive years batting .400 or better—2 (also held by Honrsby and Burkett).

Most years playing 100 or more games—10 (also held by Honus Wagner and Tris Speaker).

Most times five hits in a game in one season—4 (also held by Willie Keeler and Stan Musial).

Most home runs in two consecutive games—5 (also held by six others).

How Career of Cobb Compared With Ruth's

Following is a statistical comparison of the careers of Ty Cobb and Babe Ruth, generally acknowledged as the greatest baseball players of all time:

	COBB	RUTH
Years	24	22
Games	3.033	2.502
Career average	.367	.342
Batting championships	12	1
Highest average	.420	.393
Runs scored	2.244	2.174
Hits	4,191	2,873
Home runs	118	714
Triples	297	136
Doubles	724	506
Total bases	5,863	4.693
Runs batted in, career	1.901	2.209
Most runs batted in, season	144	170
Stolen bases	892	123

PASSING OF AN ERA IS NOTED BY FRICK

Cobb Called Link Between Old and New—Mantle, Stengel Pay Tribute

The world of baseball yesterday mourned the death of Ty Cobb, hailed by many as the game's greatest star and acknowledged by all as its fiercest competitor.

From the top officials of baseball, oldtime team-mates and opponents, modern players and fans came the same phrases . . . "a great player" . . . "the best of all time" . . . "a legend in American sports" . . . "an inspiration to all."

Cobb was called by Commissioner Ford Frick a "great baseball player who was representative of a competitive spirit that must be continued if baseball is to continue."

Frick said the death of Cobb "marks the passage of one of the few remaining links between the old and the new."

"We have many baseball players," said Frick, "but very few Ty Cobbs. He belongs with the Ruths, Mathewsons, Alexanders and Johnsons of a golden era."

George Weiss, the president of the New York Mets, said:

"There was no denying that Cobb stood alone as a baseball player, undoubtedly the greatest of all.

"Baseball and the Detroit Tigers owe more to Ty Cobb than either of them ever will be able to repay, regardless of the well-deserved honors heaped upon the greatest of all Detroit players."

Dean Pays Tribute

Dizzy Dean said, "We've lost a lot of great ball players. Now we've lost the greatest."

The former pitcher said he had admired Cobb from the time they met in 1934.

"I was just a young guy then," said Dizzy, "and I remember the first time he saw me pitch. He called me over after the game and said: 'You can be great, kid. If you can win thirty games in a regular season there is no reason why you can't win thirty games every season.' "

Casey Stengel, the former New York Yankee pilot, called Ty Cobb "the most sensational of all the players I have seen in all my life."

"By sensational," Stengel elaborated, "I mean he surprised all his opponents. He would shock them with startling base-running plays and he could always outhit any oppo-

(continued)

nent, even if they were great players."

Stengel recalled once seeing Cobb tag up and score from third on an infield pop-up. "He just waited until the infielder got ready to throw to the pitcher," said Stengel.

George Sisler, the former great first baseman, recalled that Cobb was a fighter on the field, "but to me he went out of his way to be nice." Sisler played against Cobb with the old St. Louis Browns.

"He was a good friend of mine, and I consider him a fine man and gentleman," Sisler said

Mantle Recalls Visits

Mickey Mantle of the New York Yankees, in Baltimore for a twilight-night double-header against the Orioles, said:

"I'm sorry to hear it. He used to come see me in the dugout when he visited New York and give me some batting tips.

"He would say 'Come here, kid, let me show you what you're doing wrong.'

"He'd tell me I was standing too close or too far away from the plate. He must have helped me two or three times."

"Sorry to hear about Ty," said Stan Musial, the St. Louis Cardinals' star. "He was a great baseball figure, a great credit to the game. He always followed the game closely, even when he was no longer directly connected with it."

Said Roy Hamey, the general manager of the New York Yankees:

"Ty Cobb, of course, was a legend in American sports. His feats were such that nobody has seriously challenged his immortal records.

COBB OFTEN WENT TO BAT FOR COBB

At 17, He Flooded Grantland Rice With Self-Praise

When Ty Cobb was 17 years old, he played for a baseball team in Anniston, Ala. Grantland Rice was the sports columnist of The Atlanta Journal.

Rice began getting a flood of mail from many Southern towns, all with different handwriting and different names but all with the same theme:

"Watch this fellow Ty Cobb. He is going places with his hitting and fielding."

Finally, Rice ran a paragraph in his column about young Ty Cobb. Cobb confessed to Rice years later that he had written all the letters.

"I wanted to get my name in his column," Cobb told the North American Newspaper Alliance. "My father read it regularly, and he would think I was making good."

Feared on the basepaths, Cobb was a master of the hook and fall-away slides.

One spring with the Tigers, Cobb noticed a rookie who was entertaining the players with tremendous broad jumps. The youngster had been a college broad jump star. Cobb challenged the rookie and couldn't come within six inches of him. Two weeks later he challenged the youngster again and beat him.

"No punk is going to outjump me," United Press International reported Cobb as saying.

What Cobb didn't say was that he had practiced secretly for two weeks.

In an Old-Timers game at Yankee Stadium in 1947, Cobb expressed concern about swinging a bat. He hadn't touched one since 1928, he complained.

"I'm way out of practice and I sure don't want to hit you when I swing," he said solicitously to the rival catcher, Benny Bengough. "Better move back a bit so you don't get hurt."

Bengough unsuspectingly obliged. Cobb bunted the first pitch and beat it out for a single while the red-faced Bengough huffed and puffed trying to catch up with the ball.

Two years ago an old-time major league player was interviewed by a broadcaster.

"What do you think Ty Cobb would bat today under modern conditions?" the player was asked.

"Oh, about .305 or .310," was the laconic reply.

"Only .305 or .310," exclaimed the astonished announcer. "Do you really think that is all the great Cobb could bat today?"

"Well, replied the old-timer, "you have to remember that he's 72 years old."

Cobb's Career Batting Figures

Year	G.	AB.	R.	H.	SB.	Pct.
1905	41	150	19	36	2	.240
1906	97	350	44	112	23	.322
1907	150	605	97	212	49	.350
1908	150	581	88	188	39	.324
1909	156	573	116	216	76	.377
1910	140	509	106	196	65	.385
1911	146	591	147	248	83	.420
1912	140	553	119	227	61	.410
1913	122	428	70	167	52	.390
1914	97	345	69	127	35	.368
1915	156	563	144	208	96	.370
1916	145	542	113	201	68	.371
1917	152	588	107	225	55	.383
1918	111	421	83	161	34	.382
1919	124	497	92	191	28	.384
1920	112	428	86	143	14	.334
1921	128	507	124	197	22	.389
1922	137	526	99	211	9	.401
1923	145	556	103	189	9	.340
1924	155	625	115	211	23	.338
1925	121	415	97	157	13	.378
1926	79	233	48	79	9	.339
1927	134	490	104	175	22	.357
1928	95	355	54	114	5	.323
TOTAL	3,033	11,429	2,244	4,191	892	.367

Played with Detroit from 1905 through 1926 and with the Philadelphia Athletics in 1927 and 1928.

Records Held by Cobb

Highest batting percentage, ten or more seasons—.367.

Most years leading league in batting—12.

Most consecutive years leading in batting—9.

Most years batting .300 or better—23.

Most games played in major leagues—3,033.

Most times at bat—11,429.

Most runs scored—2,244.

Most hits—4,191.

Most singles—3,052.

Most years leading league in hits—8.

Most years 200 or more hits—9.

Most times five or more hits in one game—14.

Most stolen bases—892.

Most stolen bases in one season—96.

Most total bases—5,863.

Most triples—297.

The New York Times FRIDAY, JUNE 29, 1962.

Mickey Cochrane Is Dead at 59; Star Catcher for A's and Detroit

Member of Hall of Fame Had Managed Tigers 1934-39 —Won Two Pennants

LAKE FOREST, Ill., June 28 (AP) — Mickey Cochrane, one of baseball's great figures, died today in Lake Forest Hospital. He was 59 years old.

A spokesman at the hospital said death came after a long illness.

Mr. Cochrane, whose full name was Gordon Stanley Cochrane, lived with his wife in near-by Lake Bluff. He had been "in and out of our hospital several times over the last few years," George Caldwell, hospital administrator, said. Mr. Cochrane was admitted to the hospital Monday.

Also Called Black Mike

Black Mike, a nickname given Cochrane in the colorful rea of baseball in the Nineteen Thirties, became linked with the phrase "greatest catcher in the game."

Thirteen seasons as a player with the Philadelphia Athletics and as player and manager of the Detroit Tigers bore out the phrase.

During those years in the American League, from 1925 to 1937, Cochrane placed a .320 batting average in the records. He was elected to the Hall of Fame at Cooperstown, N. Y., in 1947.

Cochrane, who made his major league debut with the Athletics in 1925 was the American League's Most Valuable Player of 1928. He became the spark behind the plate on Connie Mack's great pennant-winning Philadelphia teams of 1929 through 1931.

With the A's and later with Detroit he became known for his durability by catching 100 or more games for eleven successive seasons. It was said of him that as a master of the mechanics of catching, he had no peer.

An Assist From Mack

When Mack decided to break up his championship team, he was reluctant to part with Cochrane. He did not stand in the way, however, when Cochrane was offered the managership of the Detroit Tigers after the 1933 season.

Cochrane's drive as a playing manager guided the Tigers to two successive pennants, in 1934 and 1935. In 1934 he took over a team that had not taken part in a world series since 1909 when Ty Cobb was the star. He hit 320, caught Schoolboy Rowe in his sixteen consecutive victories and was voted the Most Valuable Player in the league.

The 1934 Series ended with a victory for the Gas House Gang from St. Louis. In 1935, the Tigers defeated the Chicago Cubs.

In 1937, Cochrane's playing career, and very nearly his life, came to an end at home plate in Yankee Stadium.

Having worked Cochrane to a count of 3 and 2, New York pitcher Bump Hadley hit him in the head with a pitched ball. Later, X-rays showed skull fractures in three places.

He guided the Tigers as non-playing manager in 1938 and into 1939. In August of that year he was replaced by Del Baker.

Served in the Navy

Soon after the United States became involved in World War II, Cochrane applied for service in the Navy's health training program. Then 39 years old, he was accepted in 1942, as a lieutenant in the physical education branch under Lieut. Cmdr. Gene Tunney.

He served in the South Pacific and managed the Great Lakes Naval Training Station's baseball team.

Mickey Cochrane as he appeared when attending the funeral of Ty Cobb.

In 1947 he was voted into the Hall of Fame with three other greats—Carl Hubbell, Frank Frisch and Lefty Grove, his battery mate on the Athletics. He received mention on 136 of the 161 ballots cast.

He came back to baseball in 1949 as a coach with the Athletics. To take the job he left Billings, Mont., where he operated a ranch and an automobile sales agency.

A year later, he was elevated to the post of general manager in charge of the club's farm teams.

It was a job Cochrane was to have only a matter of months. He resigned after Mack's sons, Roy and Earle, bought out their father's share in the team.

Honors kept coming to Black Mike. He was named with Bill Dickey of the Yankees as the best catcher of the half century by the All-American Board of Baseball in 1952.

Toward the end of his career, he was a scout for the Yankees with headquarters in Detroit and afterward a scout for the Tigers. He then turned to public relations work.

Cochrane, whose first athletic prominence came as a Boston University halfback, was born in Bridgewater, Mass., on April 6, 1903.

He leaves his wife, Mary, and two daughters, Mrs. John Cobb of Denver and Mrs. Kenneth Bollman of Allentown, Pa. His only son, Gordon Stanley Jr., was killed in the Netherlands during World War II.

Cochrane put the tag on St. Louis' Ducky Medwick in the 1934 World Series.

Section 1

"All the News That's Fit to Print."

The New York Times.

Section 1

LATE CITY EDITION
WEATHER—Fair today; tomorrow rain and warmer.
Temperatures Yesterday—Max., 55; Min., 38.

VOL. LXXXII....No. 27,420. Entered as Second-Class Matter, Postoffice, New York, N. Y. NEW YORK, SUNDAY, FEBRUARY 19, 1933. F Including Rotogravure Picture, Magazine and Book Sections. TEN CENTS

CORBETT, RING IDOL, DIES AT AGE OF 66

Ex-Champion Succumbs Here to Cancer—He Believed He Had Heart Disease.

FIRST SCIENTIFIC BOXER

His Defeat of Sullivan in 1892 Started New Era—Also Was Actor and Promoter.

James J. Corbett, who won the heavyweight championship of the world from John L. Sullivan and lost it to Bob Fitzsimmons before the turn of the century, died yesterday in the little stucco house at 221-04 Edgewater Avenue, Bayside, Queens, where he had lived for more than thirty years.

He died in the belief that the pain that had wracked his body for the last few years of his life had been caused by heart disease. Actually his death was caused by cancer of the liver, according to Dr. G. Willard Dickey, his physician. Knowing that Corbett was an avid reader of the newspapers, Dr. Dickey said, he had announced that the fighter was suffering from heart trouble.

Sixty-six years old, "Gentleman Jim's" powerful body had wasted away until he weighed scarcely 140 pounds. He had been critically ill since Jan. 31 and for the last three days had been in a state bordering on coma. The end came at 1:30 P. M. so peacefully that his wife, who held him in her arms, did not know at once that he had died.

Friend Describes His Death.

John Kelleher of Boston, a friend of long standing, who with his brother, Dennis, a former sparring

Continued on Page Thirty-two.

NAVY GAME LEAVES DOUBT AIR RAIDERS COULD BOMB COAST

Carriers Protected Only by Cruisers Too Vulnerable, Mimic War Indicates.

'ENEMY' USES 175 PLANES

Black's Thrusts at San Pedro and San Francisco Largely Balked by Heavy Guns.

TEST GREATEST EVER HELD

Men of Fleet Enjoy Shore Leave—Planes Move Entire Battery in Canal Zone Manoeuvres.

By HANSON W. BALDWIN.
Special to The New York Times.

SAN FRANCISCO, Feb. 18.—Steaming past the rugged headlands of the Golden Gate, vessels of the United States fleet stood into the broad reaches of San Francisco Harbor today to give their crews a few days of rest and recreation after a week of strenuous "war."

The Black and Blue fleets, the traditional "enemies" of the navy's annual war game, anchored off the narrow streets of Chinatown, and their crews, weary of days of strain and nights of alarums, swarmed ashore, white hats cocked jauntily on close-cropped heads, legs swinging in the peculiar gait of seamen "on the beach." The "Battle of the Pacific" is over but its memories linger on.

The past problem was one of the most ambitious and, officers believe, one of the most realistic ever worked out. An air raid against the Pacific Coast, which was not very successful, was the aim of the Black "enemy." The defense of the coast against such a raid and the destruction of the Black carriers was the mission of the Blue defending fleet.

Navy Never Names the Victor.

The navy never names the victor or the vanquished after its annual problems; it draws its lessons from the thrusts and riposts of the opposing fleets. In the game just ended the Black forces launched two raids, one against San Pedro and the other against San Francisco, but the important naval and industrial centres clustering around Puget Sound were left untouched.

The bombing attacks against San Francisco and San Pedro are not believed to have been extremely effective, and in return for its attack the Black fleet was practically wiped out by the Blue battleships.

It will be for the umpires to decide and the strategists to discuss the intricate moves and countermoves of this far-flung naval war; not until a critique of the problem is held early in March at Long Beach will the brilliant feints, the lightning strokes of strategy and the mistakes be completely known and fully discussed.

But as a result of the war game there seems to be a belief that an air raid against the coast, a raid unsupported by battleships, or a fleet in force, cannot have much hope of high success. This is, of course, disputed by air enthusiasts, but it seems to be pretty well established that carriers protected by nothing more formidable than cruisers are likely to be quickly put out of action if they venture too near an "enemy" coast.

This does not mean, of course, that unsupported air raids cannot do some damage; the moot question is whether the damage that can be inflicted is worth the almost certain loss of carriers, cruisers and planes.

Two Carriers in Black Fleet.

In the problem just ended, which started at "zero hour" on midnight, Feb. 9, the Black raiding group was known to be somewhere in mid-Pacific steaming rapidly toward the western seaboard. The commander of Black—the traditional "enemy" of the navy's annual mimic wars—Vice Admiral Frank H. Clark, had under his orders the two powerful carriers Lexington and Saratoga, seven 10,000-ton eight-inch-gun cruisers, twelve destroyers and two tankers.

Admiral Clark's "flying fleet" packed in serried rank on rank on the broad flight decks of the carriers and cradled on the cruisers' catapults, numbered about 175 planes of all types.

The Blue defending forces commanded by Admiral Luke McNamee, whose four-starred flag flies from the battleship California, consisted of about 113 ships of all types, about 150 planes based on ships and ashore and a number of small naval district craft manned partly by reserves and operating out of San Francisco, Puget Sound and the San Pedro-San Diego areas.

The Pennsylvania, flagship of Admiral Richard H. Leigh, commander-in-chief of the fleet, who acted

Continued on Page Eleven.

Congressional Medal Sought As Reward for Mrs. Cross

By The Associated Press.

WASHINGTON, Feb. 18 (AP).—A Congressional Medal for the woman credited with saving the life of President-elect Roosevelt by deflecting the aim of Joseph Zangara was proposed today in the House.

Representative Green, Democrat of Florida, said that when Mrs. W. J. Cross of Mia[mi] ... Zangara's arm and ... miss his target she ... questionably heroic ac[t] ...

"She should have an[d] ... have a Congressional ... Honor," he said.

CORBETT, RING ... DIES AT AGE ...

Ex-Champion Succumbs He[re] to Cancer—He Believed He Had Heart Disease.

FIRST SCIENTIFIC BOXER

His Defeat of Sullivan in 1892 Started New Era—Also Was Actor and Promoter.

James J. Corbett, who won the heavyweight championship of the world from John L. Sullivan and lost it to Bob Fitzsimmons before the turn of the century, died yesterday in the little stucco house at 221-04 Edgewater Avenue, Bayside, Queens, where he had lived for more than thirty years.

He died in the belief that the pain that had wracked his body for the last few years of his life had been caused by heart disease. Actually his death was caused by cancer of the liver, according to Dr. G. Willard Dickey, his physician. Knowing that Corbett was an avid reader of the newspapers, Dr. Dickey said, he had announced that the fighter was suffering from heart trouble.

Sixty-six years old, "Gentleman Jim's" powerful body had wasted away until he weighed scarcely 140 pounds. He had been critically ill since Jan. 31 and for the last three days had been in a state bordering on coma. The end came at 1:30 P. M. so peacefully that his wife, who held him in her arms, did not know at once that he had died.

Friend Describes His Death.

John Kelleher of Boston, a friend of long standing, who with his brother, Dennis, a former sparring partner of Corbett, has been staying at the boxer's home, thus described his passing:

"Jim died in his wife's arms," he wished. It happened some time between 1:30 and 1:45 in the afternoon. My brother and Joe Smollen of Bayside were in the room with him. Jim had been sleeping since early this morning, when the doctor gave him a sedative. Suddenly we noticed that his lips were twitching. Mrs. Corbett put her arms around him. Then he relaxed. That was all."

Because of Corbett's refusal to have a nurse, the Kellehers have been staying at the home helping Mrs. Corbett and acting as buffers between her and the host of friends of the stage and ring who telephoned and called almost continuously during the fighter's last illness. They were overcome with grief.

The end came so suddenly that

Continued on Page Thirty-two.

REPUBLICAN WETS IN HOUSE PLEDGE 110 REPEAL VOTES

Lead...

Re... hea... Pen... Demo... Blaine... tion on...

At a ... anti-prohi... unanimou... to back t... with 110 v...

With the s... in which the ... tension over ... of ratification... adoption of the ... was a foregone ... they turned direct... obtaining ratificatio...

The drys, meanwhi... on one last effort to ... adoption Monday. Hou... were being bombarded ... dry demands and s... many of them coming f... home," and prohibition ... tions at the capital were ... overtime.

Canon Chase Warns of Sale...

Canon William Sheafe Chase, ...perintendent of the Internat... Reform Federation, sent a 1... word letter to each member of ... House today, warning of the ret... of the open saloon if the Bl... resolution were adopted.

He called particularly upon ... Democrats, suggesting that ... would be better "to refuse to b... bound by an unconstitutional caucus vote than to violate your oath to support the Constitution."

Notwithstanding this statement, even drys expected some unusual votes in the House. Rumors were numerous of a change in attitude toward the repeal resolution by a number of heretofore stalwart drys.

Still others declined to state publicly what they proposed to do, explaining that they did not want to be "bombarded" with messages from interested groups on one side or the other.

Brief Debate Expected.

The vote Monday is expected to come early and it is believed improbable that debate will be extended much beyond the forty-minute limitation fixed by the rules for the procedure under which the resolution will reach the floor. Members probably will receive several days in which to "extend" their remarks in the Congressional Record.

In the course of debate on the

Continued on Page Twenty-four.

Quito University to Be Closed; Student's Arrest Starts Revolt

Special Cable to THE NEW YORK TIMES.

GUAYAQ[UIL] ...—The ... intends ... accord... city, ...mong ...ison... for ...

Chi... Pueblo, C... Brother, ... James Spinelli, ... actor.

Louis Brindisi, fr... and minor police cha... Morteliaro and Roti... rested at the home o... just around the corne... Roma home. Both w... Clark said, and they w... with carrying concealed...

Killed by "Friends," Say...

The Smaldones, Spinelli an... disi told Clark they visited ... from 10 A. M. until after noo... day in an effort to borrow m... They left shortly after noon ... went to a motion picture ho... they said, differing, however, ... cording to Clark, on the show th... attended. They returned to ... Roma home after word got arou... that Mrs. Roma had found her husband's body at 1:45 P. M., and then voluntarily went to Police Headquarters. Police Chief Clark said they showed ticket stubs indicating they entered the theatre at 1:55 P. M.

Mrs. Roma, who at first denied her husband had visitors today, later admitted to Clark that the four men came into the house shortly before she left to visit her mother, Mrs. Mary Greco.

Clark said that Roma was killed by "friends."

The little grocer who had ruled Denver's bootlegging industry since the wiping out of the Carlino gang of Southern Colorado more than two years ago, was seated in a corner of the front room of his home. From windows he could see the streets which intersected before his home. Behind his home a vicious police dog paced the yard.

Some one came in. The door was locked, so Roma must have let them in, Police Captain David

Continued on Page Twenty-One.

ROOSEVELT TO MEET LINDSAY TOMORROW FOR TALK ON DEBTS

They Will Discuss First Steps in Negotiations—Stimson Agrees to Proposal.

NEW BRITISH VIEW A TOPIC

...Ronald Expected to Tell ...Changed Attitude on ...Bargaining' Principle.

...T SHAPING GOES ON

...Wallace Call at Home ...ice Guard of 550 ...Circle Dinner.

...nference between ...ranklin D. Roose... ...Lindsay, Brit... ...the procedure ...rting the ne... ...sion of the ...xpected to be ...Roosevelt's ...Street. ...rday that ...elephone ...enry L. ...hat, if ...ppro... ...uld ...urn ...to

Boy, 8, Killed by Auto After Saving Sister; Police Rescue Drivers From Crowd of 1,000

John Pellicone, 8 years old, and his sister, Mary, 7, attended a showing of the motion picture "Orphan Annie" at the Gloria Theatre, at Carroll and Court Streets, Brooklyn, yesterday afternoon. About 6:50 o'clock they started for their home at 359 Court Street, hand in hand. The little boy had been trained to beware of automobiles and he carefully guided his sister through the busy traffic on Court Street.

They reached the sidewalk at the northeast corner of the intersection without mishap, but just then two automobiles were in collision in the street a few feet behind them. One of the machines, a light truck driven by Nicholas Miraglio of 2,282 East Second Street, had been going north on Court Street; the other, a sedan driven by Louis Olivieri of 1,774 Seventy-third Street, had been proceeding east on Carroll Street.

The sedan caromed off as the two cars came together and, completely out of Olivieri's control, hurtled over the curb toward the two children. They heard the crash and turned to see what was happening. John grasped the situation instantly and half-shoved, half-threw his sister out of harm's way. But before he himself could jump from the path of danger the front wheels of the sedan had pinned him to the sidewalk.

His crushed body was quickly extricated by a taxicab driver, whose name the police did not obtain, who gently placed the youngster in his own car and rushed him to the Long Island College Hospital. Physicians there found that he had been killed almost instantly. An ambulance surgeon was sent to the scene, where he treated Mary for bruises on her forehead and legs.

Meanwhile, however, her wails and the shouts of spectators had attracted a large crowd to the scene, which kept growing until it was estimated at close to 1,000. Menacing words were hurled at the two drivers and a detail of six patrolmen and two detectives which had arrived from the Hamilton Avenue station had its hands full in holding back the crowd.

By assuring the throng that the boy had not been killed, the policemen managed to disperse the crowd peaceably. They said later, however, that but for the quick work of the anonymous taxicab driver in carrying away the child's body it would have been difficult to prevent violence. Both drivers were taken to the Hamilton Avenue station, where they were still being questioned late last night.

...appeal ... In ... "We ... strong ... says. ...it the ... that would make for a stronger face. People these days are inclined to be irreverent about beards, children particularly so. We want to get rid of sentimentality and substitute virility."

Dr. Albert A. David, Anglican Bishop of Liverpool, attracted wide comment at the consecration of a new cathedral for his See in 1924, one year after his appointment to it, when he invited "ministers from

...tion to the epis... ...pointment to the See ...dmundsbury and Ipswich ...e, 1921, the Bishop was headmaster of Rugby for eleven years.

The Very Rev. Dr. Hewlett Johnson, Dean of Canterbury since 1931, was formerly Dean of Manchester.

The Right Rev. Professor Hugh R. Mackintosh, Moderator of the General Assembly of the Church of Scotland since 1932, has been Professor of Systematic Theology at New College, Edinburgh, since 1904. He is regarded as an authority on the person of Christ.

MANCHUKUO SENDS ULTIMATUM TO CHINA; WARNS OF IMMINENT ATTACK IN JEHOL; SOONG TELLS TROOPS CHINA WILL FIGHT

Lloyd's to Increase War Risk Rates in the Orient; Renew Measures Taken During the Shanghai Clash

Special Cable to THE NEW YORK TIMES.

LONDON, Feb. 18.—Beginning Monday, Lloyd's and other marine insurance companies will cancel existing war risks on all open covers and contracts on voyages to the Far East.

So threatening does the situation appear to underwriters here that a higher insurance rate will be charged on all voyages "to, from, in or through" China and Japan, including Hongkong, Formosa, Korea and Manchuria and the Russian Siberian port of Vladivostok. The action was described as "purely precautionary," but indicates the state of mind of British business men in the present stage of the Manchurian dispute.

The charging of higher premiums will begin to operate Monday and will become effective after the period stated in the contracts, which generally is ten days. Thereafter the underwriters agree to restore the canceled risk "at a rate to be arranged," depending on conditions in the Far East. In the absence of specific provision to the contrary this means the current market rate.

In normal times the war risk usually is nominal although it covers the possibility not only of actual war but "strikes, riots and civil commotion." Whenever there is a chance of hostilities or other trouble, however, the underwriters give notice of cancellation, as has been done in the present instance.

A year ago, during the Shanghai fighting, when it appeared war on a big scale might develop, the underwriters gave similar notice, canceling the war risk on Far Eastern voyages. Higher war risks were charged for several weeks while the Chinese and Japanese were battling in Chapei and the International Settlement was in danger of attack. Later, when the situation became normal, war risks were placed at a nominal charge again.

COLOMBIA INVOKES LEAGUE COVENANT

Council Will Meet Tomorrow to Consider Action in Undeclared War.

...Y AS FIRST STEP

...Charges "Flagrant" ...by Peru of Treaty ...bligations.

...NCE K. STREIT. ...New York Times. ...18.—The League ...unced today that ...oking Article XV ...gainst Peru, had ...meeting of the ...il will meet ...to hear both ...at least the ...icle XV re...

...y Ameri... ...lly asked ...to keep ...covered ...The ...ing de... ...ristide ...nt of ...either ...in ...ia

LEAGUE WANTS US TO APPROVE REPORT

Any Delay Is Held Certain to Encourage Policy of the Japanese Military.

ANXIETY FELT ON RUSSIA

Her Adherence Also Is Seen as Essential—Japan Moves to Reject Recommendations.

Wireless to THE NEW YORK TIMES.

GENEVA, Feb. 18.—Anxious interest in the attitude non-League nations, notably the United States, will take toward the report on Manchuria by the Committee of Nineteen of the League of Nations, broadcast yesterday, was shown today by League delegates and officials, particularly those who worked hardest to get it to include the Stimson doctrine of non-recognition.

There are many indications that refusal by the United States to associate herself with the League stand when it adopts this report next week would have a very bad effect here both on the attitude of the great powers toward its execution and on the general attitude toward the United States.

Similarly, there is no reason to expect that any delay by the United States in associating herself with the League would have anything but a demoralizing effect in proportion to the length of the delay.

It is generally considered here that it is logically inconceivable for Washington even to delay in approving the report after the League assembly shall have done so, though no one, of course, expects non-League nations to adopt the report before the Assembly does.

Delay Is Opposed.

...is due not merely to the fact ...e United States supplied the ...keystone—non-recognition ...o to the fact, as one offi... ...ined, that "every day the ...e nations delay in back... ...gue they will be encour... ...ilitary party in Japan ...erate gamble, and that ...in the interest neither ...nor Moscow."

...non-League states ...the League mem... ...will be merged ...others as to pub... ...day they delay ...potlight will shine on Washington and Moscow, and the more conspicuous will their new approval be when it comes, and the more will it cause the Japanese to transfer the popular animosity from Geneva to Washington and Moscow, and obviously neither wants that.

Pleased by Our Policies.

League quarters are equally hopeful that the non-League States will be prepared unhesitatingly to accept an invitation to consult with the Assembly on the situation which the report's adoption over Japan's protest will create, if such an invitation is extended. They have been much encouraged by the evolution of American policy as revealed by Secretary Stimson's

Continued on Page Twenty-nine.

HAILED AT JEHOL CAPITAL

Finance Minister and Chang Set Precedent by War-Zone Visit.

SUPPLIES BEING RUSHED

Foreign Observers Believe, However, Nanking Is Too Tardy With Aid.

JAPAN SHOWS HESITANCY

Majority Party Leader and an Influential Paper Fight League Withdrawal.

By The Associated Press.

MUKDEN, Manchuria, Feb. 18.—The State of Manchukuo delivered today an ultimatum to Marshal Chang Hsiao-liang, commander-in-chief of China's Northern army, demanding withdrawal of all Chinese troops from the Province of Jehol.

This warned that failure to comply would bring an attack by the combined armies of Manchukuo and Japan.

This appeared to be the opening gun in the Jehol offensive, which has been in preparation for several weeks.

Leaders at Jehol Capital.

By HALLETT ABEND.
Wireless to THE NEW YORK TIMES.

SHANGHAI, Feb. 18.—For the first time in China's modern history government leaders ventured toward the front-line danger zones when Dr. T. V. Soong, Nanking Finance Minister, Marshal Chang Hsiao-liang and other officials and commanders arrived today at Chengteh (Jehol City), the capital of Jehol Province, from Peiping.

Chengteh was brightly decorated and greeted the national leaders tumultuously. Dr. Soong and Marshal Chang assured the enthusiastic populace that China had abandoned her non-resistance policy.

This afternoon Jehol military commanders, many of whom had traveled long distances, cheered the visitors, after which they were addressed by Dr. Soong, who said:

"As I proceeded along the highways of this interior province, I saw many posters saying 'Long Live International Justice!' Geneva, representing the world's conception of justice, will not fail China.

"The Committee of Nineteen, after long and painful hesitation, fearing to offend another member, completely and finally vindicates China. Our cause thus becomes the world's cause. For China, too, have died the ten millions of the Great War who gave up their lives to make a better world.

Would Face Adversities.

"Japanese militarism's reckless ambition believes one nation can defy the awakened consciousness of mankind. We can safely rest assured the eventual victory will be China's, but we must steel ourselves to temporary disappointments and adversities.

"Japan is going to launch a new attack upon China, is again going to visit upon us the unspeakable cruelties and nameless horrors that she inflicted upon our countrymen in Manchuria, later in Shanghai and more recently at Shanhaikwan.

"Because Tokyo published a map of the so-called Manchukuo with Jehol on it, Japan claims the title to this province. You must now color this map with your own hearts' blood to show the world that Jehol, like Manchuria, is Chinese territory.

"On behalf of the Central Government, I pledge to you that we will never give up Jehol. The enemy may blockade our ports, may capture Nanking, but there will be no one to sign the terms of surrender."

Foreign military observers marvel at the fact that Japan has given China more than two months' notice of the fact that she will open an offensive into Jehol, thus granting ample time for China to rush enormous reinforcements to the province.

It is a melancholy commentary upon China's lack of internal unity and upon her financial stringency that, despite these repeated warnings, less than 60,000 effective troops, plus possibly 90,000 certain-by ineffective irregulars, have been mobilized in Jehol to meet the cer-

Continued on Page Twenty-nine.

CORBETT, RING IDOL, DIES AT AGE OF 66

Continued from Page One.

partner of Corbett, has been staying at the boxer's home, thus described his passing:

"Jim died in his wife's arms, as he wished. It happened some time between 1:30 and 1:45 in the afternoon. My brother and Joe Smollen of Bayside were in the room with him. Jim had been sleeping since early this morning, when the doctor gave him a sedative. Suddenly we noticed that his lips were twitching. Mrs. Corbett put her arms around him. Then he relaxed. That was all."

Because of Corbett's refusal to have a nurse, the Kellehers have been staying at the home helping Mrs. Corbett and acting as buffers between her and the host of friends of the stage and ring who telephoned and called almost continuously during the fighter's last illness. They were overcome with grief.

The end came so suddenly that there was no chance to call Dr. Dickey. In a formal statement issued from Corbett's home, giving the cause of death as "carcinoma of the liver, with metastasis in adjacent organs," Dr. Dickey said:

"His unusual reserve of vitality was amazing to all. His persistent determination to fight to the end was only overcome by the seriousness of the disease."

The doctor was asked if a blow received by Corbett during his career as a fighter might have caused the disease and he replied:

"Any statement on that would be only a guess."

The body of the former champion will be taken from the home to St. Malachy's Roman Catholic Church, 241 West Forty-ninth Street, Manhattan, tomorrow morning at 11 o'clock, when a solemn high mass of requiem will be celebrated by the Rev. John Hayes, a curate of Sacred Heart Roman Catholic Church, Bayside. Father Hayes administered the last rites to Corbett two weeks ago. A friend of the former champion for several years, Father Hayes had been a daily visitor at his bedside.

James J. Corbett was the first "scientific" boxer.

Honorary Pallbearers Named.

The honorary pallbearers will include many persons prominent in the sports world and a large contingent of sports writers whom Corbett had known as friends. They are:

Gene Buck
Charles Stoneham
John J. McGraw
Jack Curley
Edward P. Mulrooney
William Slocum
Charles Dillingham
R. H. Burnside
Bill Carey
James Johnston
Harry Hershfield
Gene Tunney
Jack Dempsey
Grover Whalen
George M. Cohan
William Collier
Fred Block
Jack Hazzard
Harry Levin
Fred Hilderbrand
Patrick Cavanaugh
Dr. George W. Fish
Damon Runyon
Arthur Baer
George Phair
James P. Dawson
Colonel Bernard Thomson
George W. Daley
John Kieran
Paul Gallico
Frank Wallace
Jimmie Powers
Grant Powers
Gus Edson
W. O. McGeehan
George H. Daley
Harry Cross
Richards Vidmer
W. J. McBeth
Dan Parker
Murray Lewin
James Hurley
James Jennings
W. S. Farnsworth
Robert G. Anderson
Fred Stone
Joe Humphreys
John McKenzie
John J. McDevitt
Judge Harry McDevitt
Walter C. Kelly
James Young
Paul Nicholson
Brig. Gen. John Phelan
William Muldoon
James A. Farley
De Wolf Hopper
Dr. Carnes Weeks
Henry Medicus
Alfred E. Smith
The Rev. Charles A. Brown
John B. Kitcher Jr.
Joseph Johnson
Ring Lardner
Frank Case
J. Wilson Dayton
Douglas Van Riper
Howard Winter
Nat Fleischer
John McCormack
George F. Hoffman
Dennis Kelleher
John Kelleher
Richard Doded
O. O. McIntyre
Bill Corum
Hype Igoe
Frank Buck O'Neill
Burris Jenkins
Harry Singer
Marty Berd
Joe Vila
Grantland Rice
Wilbur Wood
Henry King
William Treanor
Joe Williams
Harry Grayson
Peter Llanuza
Tim Byrne
Jack Kofoed
Eddie Forbes
Ed Hughes
Paul Warburg
Bill Vreeland
Len Wooster
James Wood
Charles Vackner
Eddie Neal
Allan Gould
Dave Walsh
Gene Lawrence
Pat Robinson
L. M. Cameron
George Finley
Joe Connolly
George Pardy
Jack Curdy
Vince Treanor
George U. Harvey
Jack Sharkey
James J. Jeffries
Edward Frayne
Sid Mercer
Walter Trumbell
L. L. Leonard
Charles Matthewson
Joe Millard
William Granger

Telegrams of condolence were received in large numbers at the home after his death had been announced.

DEATH SADDENS TUNNEY.

Dempsey, Jeffries and Willard Also Pay Tribute to Corbett.

By Telegraph to the Editor of THE NEW YORK TIMES.

CHANDLER, Ariz., Feb. 18.—I am deeply grieved to learn of Jim Corbett's death. My great regret is in not having seen Jim again before he passed. He was gentle in manner, always frank and generous in his opinions. His was a brave spirit that had no room for pettiness or meanness; he lived by the code of the true sportsman. Besides bringing a charming personality and a gracious manner to what was considered a brutal calling, he brought the keenest and most analytical fighting brain that ever graced a prize ring. In his death the sporting world loses one of its most colorful figures, while I lose a dear friend and a boyhood idol that never let his worshipper down.

GENE TUNNEY.

LOS ANGELES, Feb. 18 (AP).—Visibly shaken by the death of Jim Corbett, Jack Dempsey, himself a former world's heavyweight boxing champion, said today "he was a champion all by himself."

"The fight game," said Dempsey, "probably never will see another

(continued)

man like 'Gentleman Jim.' As a champion he was all by himself.

"As a gentleman, there was none finer. The fight game and the world at large has lost one of its greatest men. He was a dear friend of mine, and although I never had the pleasure of seeing him fight, I am convinced there never was a greater boxer."

Special to THE NEW YORK TIMES.

LOS ANGELES, Feb. 18.—James J. Jeffries, commenting here today on the death of Corbett, said: "I am sorry to hear of Corbett's death. The finest thing you can say of him is that he was always a good loser and a good winner. He and his wife had dinner and spent the day at my home last year, and he seemed to be in good health, although he didn't have the rugged physique he had when I fought him twice years ago."

HOLLYWOOD, Feb. 18 (AP).—"There were just prizefighters before Corbett," Jess Willard, former heavyweight champion, said today.

"He put the game on a different basis—put science into box-fighting," Willard said. "He did a great deal for the game and will be missed. Naturally, I am sorry to hear of his death. He was in every sense of the word a gentleman."

BROUGHT TO BOXING A NEW TECHNIQUE

Corbett, the First Champion Under Queensberry Rules, Introduced Ring Science.

HIS STYLE ONCE RIDICULED

Defeat of Sullivan in 1892 Unpopular, but Gradually the Victor Won Acclaim.

By JAMES P. DAWSON.

James J. Corbett, the first heavyweight boxing champion of the world under Marquess of Queensberry rules, was the ring's best and first really scientific fighter, a pioneer in the sport as it is regulated today. He introduced a new era in a sport that had been outlawed in every State of the Union save Louisiana. He laid the groundwork for the development of boxers along scientific lines in preference to the knock-down-and-drag-out, bullying style that was the specialty in the London prize ring days when brute strength was paramount with the ring fighter, and savage, primitive fighting was the rule.

He introduced a mental capacity in a sport where illiteracy was an outstanding characteristic. He paved the way for the golden days that followed, and have since disappeared—the days when Jack Dempsey fought Gene Tunney in another ring exhibition which was, after all, but another demonstration of the efficacy of intelligence over brute strength, before a gate of $2,650,000 and more than 100,000 people.

Jim Corbett in the 1894 fight in which he knocked out Charlie Mitchell in three rounds.

Corbett started a new era in boxing and lived through it to enjoy the transformation he originated. He went from the ring to the stage, then to the lecture platform, and, more recently, to radio. He made a comfortable fortune in boxing, but was reckless with his money in youth and enjoyed life. Nevertheless, unlike so many other oldtimers of the ring, he never wanted for capital. To Corbett always was assured a good income from his stage, lecture and radio work.

Few men ever had more warm and loyal friends in New York than the tall, slender, blue-eyed ex-champion. For years he was one of the most popular members of the Friars and the Lambs clubs. When he joined the Lambs there were more signatures on the page endorsing his election than ever had been written for a candidate in the club's history.

Whenever he took the train from his Bayside home, friends crowded around his seat discussing sport. Once or twice a week he could be found in a box at the Polo Grounds back of the home plate, rooting for the Giants. He was a regular attendant at prize fights and he often deplored the lack of skill of contemporary boxers in using the left hand.

His illness kept him from attending the fatal fight between Primo Carnera and Ernie Schaaf at Madison Square Garden last week. In the radio broadcast of the battle, Joe Humphreys, the announcer, paid a tribute to Corbett's sportsmanship.

He never lost interest in the sport that was nearest his heart, boxing. Never a heavyweight championship bout was held, never an important battle in any one of the eight standard ring divisions was fought, that Corbett was not a conspicuous ringsider if it was physically possible for him to attend. He was conspicuous in Madison Square Garden. Indeed, through the Summer of 1932 he branched out as a promoter of boxing, holding forth at the Jamaica Arena, Jamaica, Queens, where, in a depression period, he thought he could advance the sport notwithstanding. This was more or less a hobby with Corbett, an outlet for some of his enthusiasm for boxing. He soon gave up the activity. He always took a keen interest in teaching youngsters the art of ring fighting.

Corbett was born in San Francisco, on Sept. 1, 1866, one of nine children of Patrick J. Corbett, a prosperous owner of a livery stable. Like so many other youngsters who scaled the fistic heights since his time, Corbett was attracted early in life to sport. His specialties were baseball and boxing, and his preference was for the ring sport. Not for him was the routine life of a worker in commercial, industrial or business lines. His parents, after educating him at Sacred Heart College, sent him to the Nevada Bank of San Francisco as a clerk. His penchant for sport led him to join the Olympic Club of San Francisco, and his social and athletic associations sent into the background whatever ideas his family had of making a business man of him. Until he split a finger in a ball game he was a baseball player of such ability that many thought he would go on to the big leagues. The injury to his finger, however, induced him to forsake baseball. A brother, Joe Corbett, developed into a major league pitcher.

Took Up Sport as Amateur.

Naturally attracted to boxing, Corbett took up the sport as an amateur and was unbeatable. It is told of him that he became so proficient other members of the Olympic Club refused to box with him, and he was prevailed upon eventually to turn professional. He came out of San Francisco a bank clerk, a "bombastic bluffer" in the estimation of the immortal John L. Sullivan, "Gentleman Jim" and "Pompadour Jim" to others, to enter on a career that had its climax with his knockout of Sullivan that startled the sport world.

Corbett was 18 years old when he started boxing. He stood 6 feet 1½ inches and weighed 145 pounds, a welterweight. But he waded through the ranks of available middleweights, light heavyweights and

(continued)

heavyweight in his campaign for the Sullivan match, growing in size as he matured in years and gained in experience.

Corbett first attracted attention when he fought and beat Joe Choynski of the California Athletic Club, a bitter rival of the Olympic Club. This battle started on May 30, 1889, in Fairfax, Cal., but was interrupted after four rounds by the appearance of the police. Hostilities were resumed on June 5, that year, on a barge in San Francisco Bay, Corbett winning by a knockout in the twenty-eighth round. In this battle Choynski wore ribbed driving gloves, while Corbett wore three-ounce mitts, because, as he explained later, he had a broken right thumb and needed the padding of the heavier gloves for protection.

Early in the fight Corbett broke two knuckles of his left hand, and with this important weapon of ring warfare practically useless he originated what today is known as the left hook, snapping the left at Choynski and striking in an arched blow, rather than in the straight jab of the extended arm. A month later Corbett again trounced Choynski, this time in four rounds, and became imbued with the idea that he could be world's heavyweight champion.

A straight, stand-up fighter, Corbett had a style that was peculiarly his own. His idea was to hit and get away rather than to go tearing into a rival pell-mell, slugging in an out-and-out demonstration of the survival of the fittest. Corbett's build was not that of the slugger. A student of his sport, Corbett always said that no important fighter ever came to San Francisco that he did not observe in action or against whom he did not spar. "You could always learn something, because every fellow had something different, some characteristic of fighting that set him apart from others," Corbett often said. Corbett specialized in speed of foot and hand and a trigger brain that worked in perfect harmony with his legs and feet and arms and fists. More, he concentrated on a certain psychology which, he always maintained, aided him more than physical perfection in winning from Sullivan.

After the Choynski battles Corbett gained nation-wide attention through a six-round victory over Jake Kilrain in a battle held on Feb. 18, 1890, at New Orleans. He followed this with an exhibition against Mike Donovan, and won in four rounds from Dom McCaffrey on April 14 that year in Brooklyn. It was at the time that the great Peter Jackson, Negro heavyweight, was dogging the footsteps of Sullivan, and the Boston Strong Boy was drawing the "color line," ignoring Jackson's challenges. The California A. C. was seeking a Sullivan-Jackson fight, or some one to fight the Negro when Corbett came forth with the startling proposal that he would fight Jackson. He demanded $10,000, however, and this, for a time, was regarded as an insurmountable barrier. Corbett finally convinced the club officials the fight could be held successfully, but his price was hammered down to $5,000. The fight was held on May 21, 1891, at San Francisco, and in record books is described as a draw in sixty-one rounds. It is recalled, however, that Jackson, a prohibitive favorite entering the ring, was being pounded helpless by the clever young Corbett when the referee suddenly called a halt, declared all bets off and called the bout "no contest."

Aside from the prestige this fight brought Corbett, it proved, indirectly, the first step in convincing Corbett to his own satisfaction that he could beat Sullivan. "Gentleman Jim" received only $2,500 of the $5,000 he had been promised for the Jackson fight and a benefit was arranged by the California A. C. to make up the difference. At the time John L. was on tour through the country on the way to Australia, and was prevailed upon to appear in an exhibition. He demurred at first, claiming he was out of condition, but finally consented, with the stipulation that he would box in evening clothes. Corbett agreed to box him in formal evening attire, and they entered the ring in their swallow-tails, doffing only the coat when they climbed through the ropes at the old Grand Opera House on Mission Street, San Francisco, for an exhibition of four one-minute rounds. The exhibition was held on June 26, 1891, the month after the Corbett bout with Jackson.

Corbett brought into play his wonderful store of cleverness, jabbing, feinting, slipping and side-stepping blows, and making Sullivan appear decidedly awkward. Billy Delaney was in Corbett's corner for the occasion, and when he returned to the corner after the second round Corbett turned to Delaney and said:

"I can lick this fellow. He can't hit me."

Delaney admonished him to control his enthusiasm. Then and there, however, Corbett was seized with a desire to fight Sullivan for the title. His conviction he could beat Sullivan was formed in this exhibition.

In the East William A. Brady was starring in a play he was also producing called "After Dark." Brady had been a newsboy pal of Corbett's in their boyhood days. They grew up together, and "kept company" with sisters, Corbett later marrying one of the sisters, Olive Lake. Brady "kept company" with Georgie Lake. The Choynski fights, the battle with Jackson and the exhibition with Sullivan led Brady to suggest to Corbett that he come East to spar in a concert hall scene in "After Dark." Corbett came East, and placed himself under the management of Brady. At the time Charlie Mitchell, John P. Slavin and Corbett were recognized challengers for Sullivan's crown. Sullivan, as Brady recalls the circumstances, delivered a broadside against all three, and particularly against Corbett, to whom he referred as a "bombastic bluffer," among other things. The great John L. agreed to fight the first man who could produce a $10,000 side bet, and Brady beat Mitchell and Slavin to this requirement with an initial payment of $2,500 which clinched the Sullivan-Corbett fight.

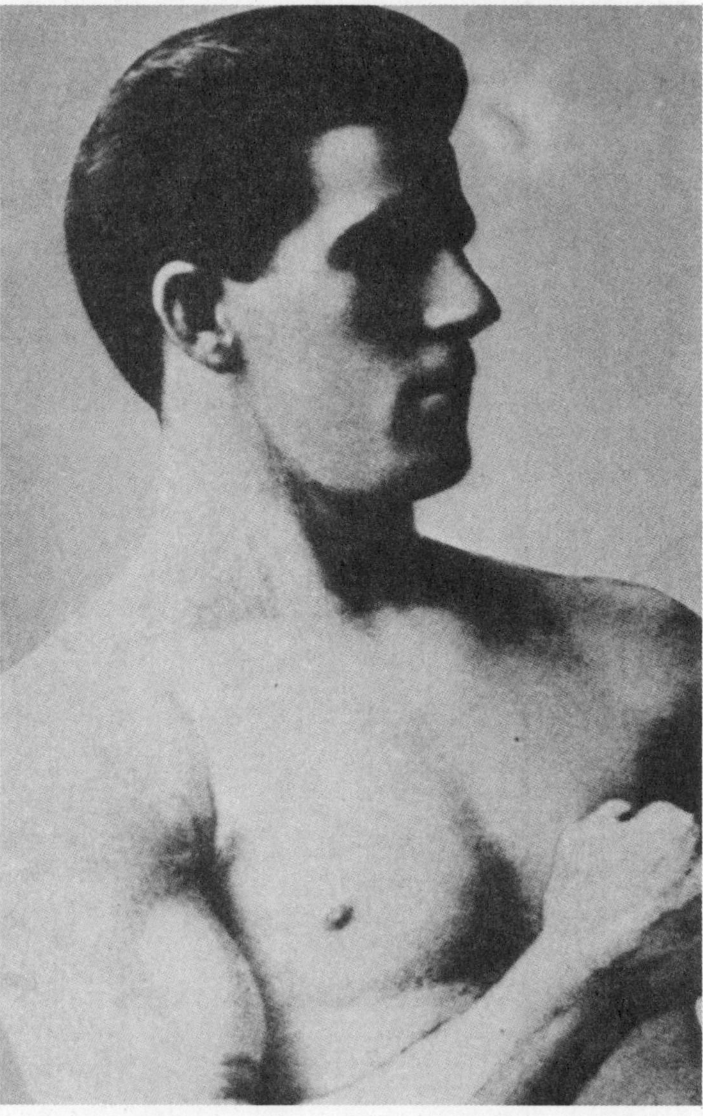

James J. Corbett—World Heavyweight Champion 1892–1897.

Corbett enjoyed in his later years recalling the strategy and psychology he employed in this memorable battle to bring about the defeat of Sullivan in twenty-one rounds.

"I knew Sullivan liked to bulldoze everybody and knew he would try bullying me," Corbett would say. "For a long time before the bout I concentrated day and night on a plan whereby I could dominate Sullivan, instead of having him dominate me. I determined to ignore his bullying and to give him a style of fighting that would enrage him to such an extent that he would be practically helpless. I was in no hurry to land a blow, but I was determined that when I did land, it would be a blow that would make Sullivan believe that I could hit as well as he could."

Corbett followed his plan expertly. They met on Sept. 7, 1892, at New Orleans, and for two rounds Corbett did nothing but box defensively while Sullivan charged with his bull-like rushes, seeking to annihilate the dancing foe who tantalized and tormented him with his elusiveness. It was a shock to those who had expected Corbett to collapse from fright. At one stage Sullivan stopped dead in his tracks and demanded that Corbett stop running away and fight. Finally in the third session Corbett thought the time had arrived to drive home his first blow. As Sullivan charged, Corbett side-stepped and, with all the force of his body back of the blow, drove a terrific right flush to Sullivan's face. The punch, aside from startling the great John L., broke his nose and infuriated him to a state almost of helplessness.

Corbett then gradually wore Sullivan down to the point of collapse with his superb boxing, defensive and offensive skill, as the Boston Strong Boy charged bullishly. At the beginning of the twenty-first round Corbett drove a terrific left hook to Sullivan's jaw and the "irresistible force and immovable object" of pugilism, whose boast it had been that he "could lick all creation," collapsed inertly to be counted out, struggling to get back on his feet. Through bruised lips John L. muttered his immortal tribute: "The old pitcher went to the well once too often, but I'm glad the championship remains in America."

Perhaps no single ring victory in modern history was as unpopular as was Corbett's triumph over Sullivan in a battle in which the great John L. entered the ring favorite to win at odds as high as 6 to 1. It is told of the Sullivan camp, which also included Jack McAulliffe, retired undefeated world's lightweight champion, that every last cent of his followers was bet on Sullivan and that every man of the party was stone broke after the battle.

Indicating the shock of Corbett's triumph, is the following extract from The World's account of the fight, printed on Sept. 11, and typical of the opinion of most sports lovers:

"He (Corbett) has robbed the country of a very striking individuality. If he had gone to Switzerland with a shovel and dug away Mont Blanc he could not have hurt the feelings of the Swiss more than he has damaged the feelings of hundreds of thousands of Americans. * * * It is unquestionably true that he is a very gentlemanly

(continued)

young man and a remarkably gentlemanly fighter, but, then, we do not want gentlemanly fighters. We want a fighter to be nothing at all on this earth but a fighter."

Corbett, though champion, faced a storm of ridicule and contemptuous indifference from sport followers that would have affected a less intelligent mind. "Gentleman Jim," however, went serenely on his way, setting a new standard for fighting champions. He received $45,000, representing a $10,000 side bet he had made with Sullivan and a $25,000 purse, arranged on a winner-take-all basis. This was Corbett's largest ring purse. It is recalled by Mr. Brady that, whereas Sullivan reveled in the noisy acclaim of the saloon, Corbett, never a drinking man, although he was not a "teetotaler," preferred rather the society of the most exclusive restaurants of the day, where he was something of a favorite with bankers, statesmen and sportsmen.

Corbett held the title for close to five years, beating Charlie Mitchell at Jacksonville, and Peter Courtney at Orange, N. J., in 1894, fighting a four-round draw with Tom Sharkey in San Francisco and a three-round exhibition with Jim McVey in this city, in 1896. He met his Waterloo on March 17, 1897, at Carson City, Nev., when Bob Fitzsimmons knocked him out in fourteen rounds with the body blow which later became famous as the "solar plexus" punch. After this defeat Corbett toured through the country in a play named "Gentleman Jack." He severed relations with Brady and, with George Considine as his partner, opened a café on Broadway between Thirty-third and Thirty-fourth Streets which was a tremendous success for a year. Brady, in the meantime, had acquired the management of James J. Jeffries, who had trained Corbett at Carson City, and a year later induced Fitzsimmons to fight the big boilermaker.

Jeffries knocked out the Cornishman in eleven rounds at Coney Island on June 9, 1899, becoming heavyweight champion. Brady then found himself beseeched by Corbett to give him another chance at the title. He consented and Jeffries and Corbett fought at Coney Island on May 11, 1900. "For sixteen rounds it looked bad for Jeff, and I had reason to regret my haste in giving Corbett a chance at my new champion," said Mr. Brady in recalling the incident. "But Jeff plodded on in the face of Corbett's clever work and knocked out Corbett in twenty-three rounds."

Corbett conquered Kid McCoy in old Madison Square Garden on Aug. 30, 1900, a bout to which some attached the stigma of "fake," over Corbett's protests, and on Aug. 14, 1903, he made another attempt to lift the crown from Jeffries. In this bout, held in San Francisco, Jeffries knocked out Corbett in ten rounds.

This bout marked the end of Corbett's ring career. He went from the ring to the legitimate stage, was a star in vaudeville, played in motion pictures, took to the lecture platform and, more recently, was active in radio work. He was for years a prominent member of the Friars Club and took part in innumerable benefit performances for charity. In 1930 he was chairman of a special committee of the Queens Emergency Employment Committee.

Recognized as an authority on boxing, his opinion was sought frequently for newspaper and magazine articles. In 1925 his autobiography was published under the title, "The Roar of the Crowd." Through his comments in the newspapers on the training of fighters who were preparing for important battles, and his prognostications on the outcome of these struggles as they approached, Corbett acquired an undeserved reputation. He became known throughout the length and breadth of the land as a man who had seldom, if ever, picked a winner. Corbett took the ridicule this reputation engendered without complaint, but in self-defense disclaimed responsibility a few years ago. "I take the slap for these poor selections without being responsible for them," he explained. "You see, my newspaper articles are written by a ghost writer who makes up his own mind as to who will win and who will lose and then proceeds to make his pick under my signature."

Corbett was married twice. His first wife was Olive Lake, an actress, whom he married in Salt Lake City on June 8, 1886. She obtained a divorce in July, 1895, and on Aug. 15 of that year he married Miss Jessie Taylor of Omaha, Neb., at Asbury Park, N. J.

OFFICIAL RECORD OF CORBETT'S CAREER

The complete ring record of James J. Corbett, as contained in T. S. Andrews's "Ring Battles of a Century":

Born Sept. 1, 1886, San Francisco, Cal. Height, 6 feet 1 inch. Weight, 187 pounds. Heavyweight. Color, white. Nationality, Irish-American.

Won—Dave Eisenman, Duncan McDonald, Captain J. H. Daly, 2 rounds; Mike Brennan, 3 rounds; John Donaldson, 4 rounds; Martin Costello, 3 rounds; Professor William Miller, 6 rounds; Frank Smith, Salt Lake City.

Year.	Opponent.	Result.	Place.	Rds.
1886—	Billy Welch	L.	San Fran.	4
1886—	Billy Welch	K.	San Fran.	1
1887—				
Aug. 27—	Jack Burke	D.	San Fran.	8
1888—				
June 30—	Frank Glover	D.	San Fran.	3
1889—				
May 30—	*Joe Choynski	Police.	Fairfax.	4
June 5—	*Joe Choynski	W.	Benecia.Cal.	28
July 15—	Joe Choynski	W.	San Fran.	4
July 29—	Dave Campbell	D.	Portland	10
1890—				
Feb. 18—	Jake Kilrain	W.	N. Orleans.	6
Mar. 20—	Mike Donovan	Exh.	New York.	3
Apr. 14—	Dom McCaffrey	W.	Brooklyn	4
1891—				
May 21—	Peter Jackson	D.	San Fran.	61
June 26—	John L. Sullivan	Exh.	San Fran.	4
Aug. 5—	Jim Hall	Exh.	Chicago	4
Oct. 8—	Ed Kinney	W.	Milwaukee.	4
1892—				
Feb. 16—	Bill Spillings	W.	New York.	1
Feb. 16—	Bob Caffrey	W.	New York.	1
Feb. 16—	Joe Lannon	No dec.	N. York.	3
Sep. 7—	John L. Sullivan.	K.	N. Orleans.	21
1894—				
Jan. 25—	Charlie Mitchell.	K.	Jacksonville.	3
Sep. 7—	Peter Courtney	K.	Orange, N.J.	6
1896—				
June 24—	Tom Sharkey	D.	San Fran.	4
Dec. 14—	Jim McVey	Exh.	New York.	3
1897—				
Mar. 17—	Bob Fitzsim'ns.	K. by.	Car. City.	14
1898—				
Nov. 22—	Tom Sharkey	L-F.	New York.	9
1900—				
May 11—	Jim Jeffries	K. by.	Coney Is.	23
Aug. 30—	Kid McCoy	K.	New York.	5
1903—				
Aug. 14—	Jim Jeffries	K. by.	San Fran.	10

*Fight May 30 was interefered with and continued June 5.

Corbett's biggest fight and largest purse fought for was when he defeated John L. Sullivan at New Orleans on Sept. 7, 1892, for a purse of $25,000 and $20,000 stake money; total, $45,000; Marquess of Queensberry rules, five-ounce gloves, for the world's championship, winning in 21 rounds.

SAN FRANCISCO, Feb. 18 (AP).—Sailor Tom Sharkey, who first gained ring fame by holding James J. Corbett to a four-round draw here in 1896, expressed his grief today at the passing of the former champion.

"He was a grand man, always a gentleman and a real credit to boxing," said Sharkey. "He was the most clever man I ever fought."

The fight with Bob Fitzsimmons at Carson City, Nevada, in which Corbett (right) lost the championship.

LONDON, Feb. 18 (AP). — Since Jim Corbett's illness became critical, the London press has been paying tribute to him, recalling his picturesque career, including his last visit to London in 1909. Tonight the news of his death was a topic of discussion in London clubs, restaurants and a few old bars in the Strand which were the centre of London life in Corbett's best days.

"Gentleman Jim" is remembered here as the man who lifted boxing from the hands of thugs and brawlers to a great sport which now features the bills at the great Albert Hall. It also was recalled that Corbett even antedated Gene Tunney as a boxer who had read a book and knew his Shakespeare. As far back as 1905 he urged Shakespearian productions in modern dress and said his ambition was to show the world an up-to-date Hamlet.

ROME, Feb. 18 (AP).—Officials of the Italian Boxing Federation tonight expressed deep regret at the death of Jim Corbett. They said the pugilistic world had lost one of its greatest and noblest fighters of all time.

BERLIN, Feb. 18 (AP).—The news of James J. Corbett's death came as a surprise here today, since he had been reported dead on Feb. 9. The newspapers emphasized the gentlemanliness of the former champion and reported his career in detail, ranking him among the world's greatest boxers.

James A. Farley, chairman of the State Athletic Commission and national chairman of the Democratic party, said:

"I am sincerely sorry to learn of the death of Jim Corbett. I always admired the man. He has been an outstanding figure in the sporting world for many years and always will be. He was a great champion and truly deserved the title of 'Gentleman Jim.' I extend my sincere sympathy to Mrs. Corbett and members of his family."

Max Schmeling, former heavyweight champion, in a cablegram to his manager, Joe Jacobs, said:

"I feel keenly the death of Jim Corbett. I had the pleasure of meeting him when I was in training at Kingston for my bout with Jack Sharkey and on several other occasions. He took the trouble to show me some of the punches that made him famous, and which he thought I might use. But none but a Corbett could perfect the punches he used. I was very fond of him and am grieved to hear of his death."

William Muldoon, 87-year-old member of New York State Athletic Commission, who trained John L. Sullivan for the Corbett fight—Want to express my most sincere regret at the loss of James J. Corbett at such an early age. He was a leader in his profession.

Bernard Gimbel, Executive of the Gimbel Stores and a boxing enthusiast—Having known Jim Corbett for more than twenty-five years, I can truthfully say that he was a credit, not only to boxing, but to athletics in general. As far as I know, he was the originator of the scientific school of fighting, and the first to make a real study of boxing, as against brute force. He had a pleasant and genial personality which endeared him to many.

The New York Times THURSDAY, AUGUST 28, 1975

Bobby Cruickshank, 80, Is Dead; 'Dour Scot' Was Early Golf Pro

DELRAY BEACH, Fla., Aug. 27 (AP)—Bobby Cruickshank, the "dour little Scot" who was one of the leading money-winners in the early days of the professional golf tour, died here today. He was 80 years old.

Mr. Cruickshank was an active member of the P.G.A. tour from 1921 to 1950, winning 20 tournaments, six of them in 1927, when he led the tour with winnings of $17,800.

Mr. Cruickshank, a member of the Golf Hall of Fame, had maintained a residence in South Florida for about 45 years. For most of that time, he served as winter club pro at the Gulfstream Golf Club.

He is survived by his widow, Lucille; a daughter, Elsie C. Hoke; a sister, and a granddaughter.

Athlete From the Start

Robert Allan Cruickshank, known as Wee Rab, was born at Grantown-on-Spey, Scotland, on Nov. 16, 1894. During his school days he was a fine athlete and, despite his short legs, set up some records in sprints and jumps.

When World War I broke out, he was a student in Edinburgh College and, like so many youths of his age then, he joined the Black Watch, the Scottish regiment. He was captured by the Germans and imprisoned, though he managed to escape and make his way back to Scotland.

When the war ended Mr. Cruickshank resumed his golf, which he had started at 4, playing with his father, and later on with Tommy Armour, one of his chief rivals as a youth.

His major achievements as an amateur were his triumphs in Edinburgh Coronation Trophy events in 1919 and 1920 and in the St. Andrews Eden tournament, in which he was runner-up in 1920. This established him as one of the most promising players in British amateur golf, but, loving the game as he did, he decided to become a professional.

In 1923, when the United States open championship was held at the Inwood Country Club on Long Island, Mr. Cruickshank tied Bobby Jones for the title, only to lose in a play-off. The shot that enabled him to tie Mr. Jones is still talked about in golf, a long iron shot to the green.

His showing then stamped Mr. Cruickshank as one of the outstanding golfers in America and he lived up to that reputation. In 1932, when the championship was played at Fresh Meadow Country Club in Queens, he tied for second, only three strokes behind the winner, Gene Sarazen, who played the last 28 holes in an even 100 strokes.

Two years later, when Olin Dutra won at the Merion Cricket Club in Philadelphia, Mr. Cruickshank was only two strokes away from a tie. He broke 70 twice in the same day at Fresh Meadow in 1932, when his last two rounds were 69 and 68.

He was a master in every part of the game, endowed with a swing he had fitted to his physique. His first professional berth was at the Shackamaxon Club in New Jersey, and after spending several years around the Metropolitan area, he went to the Country Club of Virginia at Richmond.

In 1923, "Wee" Bobby Cruickshank tied Bobby Jones in the U.S. Open only to lose in the play-off.

The New York Times THURSDAY, JULY 18, 1974

Dizzy Dean, Hall of Fame Pitcher, Dies

Dizzy Dean in his broadcasting days.

RENO, July 17 (AP)—Dizzy Dean, a farmboy who pitched his way into the Baseball Hall of Fame with a blazing fastball, died here early today in St. Mary's Hospital at the age of 63.

Mr. Dean had suffered a severe heart attack on Monday after complaining of chest pains last Thursday in South Lake Tahoe, Calif. The hospital attributed his death to heart failure.

Surviving are his widow, Patricia, and his brother, Paul.

A funeral service will be held Saturday in Wiggins, Miss., with burial in Bond, Miss., where Mr. Dean had lived as a boy.

A Modern Folk Hero

By JOSEPH DURSO

His father was an itinerant sharecropper who wandered around the South picking cotton. His mother died when he was only 3 years old. His own education ended in the second grade in a place called Chickalah, Ark., and — he confessed later — "I didn't do so good in the first grade, either."

But, despite all such handicaps and the Ozark countryboy image he carried into high places, Jay Hanna (Dizzy) Dean rose serenely and unflappably into a career as one of the best pitchers in modern baseball and as a folk hero who brought great turns of the English language to radio and television.

He could be vague about details of his early life and times. He suggested, on different occasions, that he had been born in Arkansas, Oklahoma and Mississippi. He estimated the date as 1911, or thereabouts. He even gave his formal name variously as Jay Hanna or Jerome Herman Dean. Then, when he reached the big leagues in 1930 at the age of 19, his career barely covered the decade and included only half a dozen seasons of front-rank pitching.

Enjoyed the Spotlight

But wherever he came from, and however long he held the spotlight, few personalities commanded the public's attention as joyously as Dizzy Dean.

In his first full season with the St. Louis Cardinals, he won 18 games and led the National League in strikeouts and shutouts. In the following four seasons, he won 102 games, including 30 in 1934 and 28 in 1935. He once struck out 17 Chicago Cubs in nine innings. And in the 1934 World Series, he and his younger brother, Paul (Daffy) Dean, pitched two victories apiece while the Gashouse Gang of St. Louis defeated the Detroit Tigers, four games to three.

When an injury shortened his baseball career a few years later, Dizzy switched his showmanship behind a microphone and broadcast games for the Cardinals and Browns in St. Louis and for the Yankees in New York. Then he attained new heights as an innovator of language, coining words the way Casey Stengel coined paragraphs.

"Come on, Tommy, hit that old patata," he once said with the partisanship of a full fan. "This boy looks mighty hitterish to me," he observed another time. "Boy, they was really scrummin' that ball over today, wasn't they?" he reported on another occasion. And when purists complained over his statement that a baserunner "slud into third," he would reply in self-defense: "Paul and me didn't get much education."

Teachers in Wrath

His style proved so unusual that, in the summer of 1946, a group of Missouri schoolteachers complained to the Federal Communications Commission that his broadcasts were "replete with errors in grammar and syntax" and were having "a bad effect on the pupils." But in the public debate that followed, powerful voices were raised to champion Dizzy Dean, including that of The Saturday Review of Literature.

Norman Cousins, the guiding spirit of the magazine, now titled Saturday Review/World, extended his own approval of the Dean linguistic style to the great man's pitching style in these words:

"He was supposed to be as fast as Walter Johnson, and though he couldn't curve them and mix them up like the great Matty [Christy Mathewson], his assortment was better than most. You were attracted by the graceful rhythm of his pitching motion; the long majestic sweep of his arm as he let the ball fly; the poised alertness after the pitch. That was what counted, and you knew it when batter after batter swung ineptly at pitches they couldn't even see."

The man behind the fractured syntax and the fractured batting averages was a 6-foot-2-inch giant whose playing weight of 182 pounds expanded well above 200 during the 20 years he spent as a broadcaster, public speaker, raconteur, rancher and golfer. The consensus is that he was born Jan. 16, 1911, in Lucas, Ark., and Red Smith portrayed him in The New York Times in these words:

"As a ballplayer, Dean was a natural phenomenon, like the Grand Canyon or the Great Barrier Reef. Nobody ever taught him baseball and he never had to learn. He was just doing what came naturally when a scout named Don Curtis discovered him on a Texas sandlot and gave him his first contract."

That was in the fall of 1929, and Dean later recalled that his "bonus" amounted to $300. He earned it the next season by winning 17 games at St. Joseph, Mo., plus eight more at Houston in the Texas League. The Cardinals promoted him to the majors around Labor Day and he pitched once — beating the Pittsburgh Pirates.

A Youth of Confidence

He was still a teen-ager at the time, not far removed from the 16-year-old who had enlisted in the Army, where he supposedly wore his first pair of good shoes. But he was a teen-ager with absolute confidence in his baseball ability, and he demonstrated the confidence after his debut by boasting that he could "pitch St. Louis to the pennant." The Cardinals responded by relegating him back to the minors in 1931, but he promptly demonstrated his ability there by winning 26 games.

Branch Rickey, who was running the Cardinals then, brought Dean back to St. Louis to stay in 1932 and Dizzy won 18 times with 16 complete games and 191 strikeouts. Two years later, he touted Rickey on his brother Paul and, in 1934, the Dean boys pitched 49 victories (30 by Dizzy) and pitched

(continued)

Dizzy Dean pitched and talked his way into baseball's Hall of Fame.

the Cardinals to the world championship.

Pitchers may have had better seasons than Dizzy did that year, but not many. He was suspended briefly for insubordination and held out briefly for more money in midseason, yet he finished the summer with a 30-and-7 record that included these highlights down the home stretch of the pennant race:

On Sept. 21, he pitched a three-hitter against the Brooklyn Dodgers (Paul pitched a no-hitter in the second game of the doubleheader). Two days later, Dizzy relieved in both games of a doubleheader in Cincinnati. Two days after that, he went nine innings and beat Pittsburgh, 3-2. Three days later, he stopped Cincinnati, 4-0. And two days after that, he shut out the Reds again, 9-0, to clinch the flag. Three days later, he beat Detroit in the opening game of the World Series.

Strikeouts His Goal

"I always just went out there and struck out all the fellas I could," he remembered. "I didn't worry about winnin' this number of games or that number — and I ain't a-woofin' when I say that, either."

As one of the ringleaders of the rowdy Gashouse Gang that summer, Dean had plenty of support from Frank Frisch, Rip Collins, Joe Medwick and the other Cardinals. They invaded hotel ballrooms in painters' overalls, they formed a hillbilly band, they nearly provoked a riot in the World Series. But they won, even though Dizzy was struck on the head by a thrown ball while running the bases.

Things started to unwind in 1937, when Dean was struck on the left foot by a line drive while pitching in the All-Star Game in Washington. He suffered a broken toe, but suffered more permanently when he tried to pitch despite the handicap and subsequently ruined his right arm. So in 1938, the Cardinals traded him to the Chicago Cubs for $185,000 and three players.

He did pitch in the World Series for the Cubs against the Yankees, but he was never his old fireballing self on the mound. And in May of 1941, at the age of 30, he retired as a player with a career record of 150 victories and 83 losses for a winning percentage of .644, and an earned-run average of 3.03.

Folk Legend Filmed

He was elected to baseball's Hall of Fame in 1953 (in an election in which Joe DiMaggio placed eighth). But by then, Dizzy Dean was already a folk legend that even Hollywood had tried to capture on film. It was titled "The Pride of St. Louis," starring Dan Dailey as Dizzy, and Bosley Crowther wrote in his review in The New York Times:

"The magnetic thing is the nature of a great, big lovable lug who plays baseball for a living and lives just to play — or talk — baseball. It is not Dizzy Dean, the Cardinal pitcher, the powerhouse of the old Gashouse Gang, the man who won so many games in so many seasons, that is the hero of this film. It is Dizzy Dean, the character, the whiz from the Ozark hills, the braggart, the woeful grammarian, the humbled human being."

Through it all, Dean was abetted by Patricia Nash, a department-store sales clerk he met while pitching for Houston. They were married in 1931 and later made their home in Dallas, where he played golf and did some ranching and eventually worked his vernacular into the broadcast booth.

"The players returned to their respectable bases," he once advised the radio audience. Then, when he got into television, he declared: "I'm through talking about things folks ain't seeing." And later: "The trouble with them boys is they ain't got enough spart."

When he was pressed for an explanation of that bit of Ozark inflection, Dizzy replied: "Spart is pretty much the same as fight or pep or gumption. Like the Spart of St. Louis, that plane Lindbergh flowed to Europe in."

The New York Times WEDNESDAY, AUGUST 20, 1975

Donohue, 38, Dead Of Racing Injuries

GRAZ, Austria, Aug. 19 (AP)—Mark Donohue, who ended an eight-month retirement as an auto driver last year because he couldn't keep away from racing, died tonight of injuries suffered Sunday at the Austrian Grand Prix.

The 38-year-old Donohue underwent a three-hour operation at a hospital here Sunday to remove a blood clot from his brain. He was hit on the side of his helmet with debris as his car, which had suffered a punctured tire, went out of control in prerace practice and crashed through four rows of wire catch-fences and some billboards along the Oesterreichring race course.

Donohue's death was announced by a spokesman for Roger Penske, a close personal friend and his team boss. Penske, along with Donohue's wife, Eden, and father, Mark Sr., were at Donohue's bedside.

The Penske team leader, Heinz Hofer, said Donohue had told him after the crash that the left front tire had been punctured as he was traveling about 160 m.p.h. through one of the fastest turns on the track.

One track marshal was killed by the crash and another seriousy injured.

Thinking Man's Driver

By MICHAEL KATZ

Along pit row, Mark Donohue was known as "the thinking man's driver," especially by rivals who looked at the Ivy League graduate's chubby face and couldn't figure out any other way this kid was beating them.

It was true that Donohue used his engineering education at Brown University to become one of the most expert chassis men in auto racing. But it was also true that beneath the boyish looks that made him appear years younger than he was, and despite his reputation as "Captain Nice," Mark Donohue was one of the toughest —and best—racing drivers in history.

"He was not the kind of guy you wanted to get too close to on the road," said eGorge Follmer, one of Donohue's rivals and a former teammate.

The competitive fires had not died, either, when he announced his retirement in October, 1973, after winning the final race of the season that capped his Can-Am championship. But he was 36 then, and as far as American racing was concerned, he had done it all.

He had been a national amateur champion and the

(continued)

Mark Donahue wears a winner's grin after finishing first in the 1972 Indianapolis 500.

Sports Car Club of America driver of the year in 1965. He joined Roger Penske, a former sports car rival who had set up his own team, the following year as a full-time professional. That long association resulted in the ultimate triumph for an American driver in 1972, when he won the Indianapolis 500.

In all, he won 57 major races and more than $1-million. There were victories in stock-car racing against Richard Petty, Bobby Allison and the other Southern drivers; in the Trans-Am series, where three times he captured the season title competing against the best sedans the Detroit factories could produce; in the 24 hours of Daytona, against the best international sports cars endurance pilots, and in the initital Pocono 500 in 1971 against A. J. Foyt, Bobby and Al Unser, Mario Andretti and the other stars from the United States Auto Club championship circuit.

But there was one phase of racing that he had never really taken part in, what he called his personal "missing link." This was in the Formula One cars, perhaps this dangerous sport's most dangerous, which run on the grand prix circuit. Once, Penske rented a Formula One car for Donohue and in 1971, in his first start in one of these single-seat, open-cockpit racing cars, he finished third in the Canadian Grand Prix.

When Penske decided late to enter Formula One full time, Donohue had a difficult decision to make. "I could see what was coming," he said. "I could see myself helping to develop the Formula One car, setting it up and then having some younger hot-shot driver take over. I don't think I could have handled that."

Instead, Donohue retired. He turned his "last" race, the first International Race of Champions final—in which top driver from all forms of racing competed — into an easy victory Feb. 15, 1974, and then concentrated on his new duties as president of Penske Racing.

But supervising the Penske efforts in stock car and Indianapolis-type racing did not agree with Donohue. Directing other drivers, making suggestions, helping mechanics—even sweeping up around the garage—were not enough.

Then, in March, 1974, Peter Revson, Penske's first choice as driver for the Formula One car that was to make its debut later in the season, was killed in an accident practicing for the South African Grand Prix. There was little question then that Donohue, who would test-drive the new car and help supervise its development, would come out of retirement. It became official last September.

However, the Penske Formula One car proved unsound and Donohue's best finish this year was a fifth place. Two weeks ago, however, he showed he had not lost his skill at getting a race car around a track when he set a world speed record of 221.160 miles an hour for a closed course. He did it at Talladega, Ala., in the turbocharged Porsche he drove to the 1973 Can-Am title.

In an interview then, he talked of his disappointing grand prix showing. "I can hardly wait to get back to work with our car," he said. "We think we've made a major discovery. If we're right, by next season we could be the dominant team in Formula One."

Donohue began working with cars while growing up in the nineteen-fifties in a comfortable neighborhood in Summit, N. J. "The hot-rod phenomenon came East from California and caught me up in it," he once explained.

But where other youngsters were souping up cars to impress girls, "I was only interested in the mechanics," Donohue said.

He tinkered his way all through Pingry School, Brown University and a job as a mechanical engineer with the Pulverizing Machinery Corporation in Summit.

But if his father, Mark Sr., a successful patent lawyer, never envisaged a racing career for his son, neither did young Mark. It began as a hobby in 1959 when Donohue sold his souped-up Corvette, which he used to drive around at Brown, and for $3,000 purchased his first racing car—a little Elva with an MG engine. With the Corvette money, he also bought a trailer "to hold the car" and a station wagon "to tow the trailer."

He took the lot to Lime Rock, Conn., and finished fourth in a sports car race.

"I realized then that if I wanted to do better in this business I had to spend more time on my car," he said.

He began to spend more than time. "Every dime I had I put into cars," he said. "My friends began warning me."

Racing was becoming an obsession, but in 1965, he realized: "Maybe I can make a living out of something I like to do. What can be better in life, a better ideal?"

In 1966, Penske told him: "Try it for a year, you're still a young man, and if it doesn't work out you can always go back to engineering."

The only engineering Donohue went back to concerned race cars. "I'd always thought that I'm not as good a driver as I am capable of figuring out how to make the car the quickest," he once said.

But his "thinking man's" approach to racing, while successful on the track, was difficult off. His first marriage ended in divorce and some friends blamed racing. Since his remarriage eight months ago, those same friends found Donohue relaxed and cheerful, something he had not been while retired.

"No, I never worried about the dangers of racing," he said in March, 1974, in New York while being honored at a luncheon. "I always said driving wasn't really a dangerous situation. The driver must accept the risks involved, which I did — and I spent my time in the hispital as a result."

Two weeks before his death, Mark Donahue set a world speed record of over 220 miles per hour.

Mark Donahue

The New York Times

THURSDAY, NOVEMBER 8, 1979

CHARLES EVANS DIES; WAS NOTED GOLFER

Former Leading Amateur, 89, Helped to Create Caddie Scholarship Funds

Charles (Chick) Evans, who rose from the caddie ranks to play golf with five Presidents of the United States, died late Tuesday in Augustana Hospital in Chicago. He was 89 years old.

Mr. Evans, who was born in Indianapolis on July 18, 1890, held major golf championships for 16 years. He was the first man to win the United States Open and the United States Amateur championships in the same season — 1916.

He was an outstanding amateur and had a great impact on the game. He continued playing golf for recreation into his 70's, an age when most of his contemporaries had abandoned the sport. He never turned professional.

Mr. Evans learned to play golf as a youngster and in 1907, at 17, he won his first golf trophy. Nine years later Mr. Evans captured the Open and the Amateur titles. He competed in the United States Amateur championship more than 50 times, a record, and was the only amateur to win the Western open, a prestigious tournament that attracted many top professionals and with which he became permanently identified. He was also a member of the first United States Walker Cup team.

Years of Skill in Game

In his mid-50's, Mr. Evans was still scoring in the low 70's and was still the Chicago champion. At age 68, Mr. Evans had a handicap of 6. He said then, "I haven't won any kind of national senior tournament yet, but I have fun just the same."

He and his wife, Esther, who died in 1967, were married for 40 years and lived in a house bordering the Edgewater Country Club in Chicago.

Mr. Evans attended Northwestern University, but was forced to leave after one year because of a lack of funds. In 1930 he helped to establish the Evans Scholarship Fund, which made funds available for youngsters to attend college. It was created mainly to help caddies, but over the years many other young men also were aided. The fund was started with Mr. Evans's golf earnings, which he put into an escrow account because, as an amateur, he could not accept prize money for golfing victories and still retain his amateur status.

The fund is now conducted by the Western Golf Association and has enabled more than 4,000 youngsters to attend college.

Charles "Chick" Evans was the first professional golfer to win the "Double Crown"—the U.S. Open and the U.S. Amateur Championships.

Links Companion of Presidents

Mr. Evans, a member of the Golf Hall of Fame, toured the links with five Presidents — William Howard Taft, Woodrow Wilson, Warren G. Harding, Calvin Coolidge and Dwight D. Eisenhower — during his many years in the sport.

As a competitor Mr. Evans was noted for his big, smooth swing and his crisp play from tee to green. But on the greens his deft touch deserted him. Grantland Rice noted that Mr. Evans's game had one flaw — he could not putt effectively.

"I've seen him miss shorties you could hole with a flick of your finger," Joe Williams, the sportswriter, once wrote.

The ultimate judgment on Mr. Evans's putting ability was made by his long-time friend, Jerome Travers, also a United States Amateur champion. In his will, Mr. Travers left his putter to Mr. Evans.

Mr. Evans was also a wholesale milk salesman for a Chicago dairy. Last winter, despite his age, he still commuted regularly in heavy snow and inclement weather to his downtown office.

In accordance with Mr. Evans's wishes, a private memorial service will be held later this week.

The New York Times SATURDAY, MARCH 29, 1947.

JOHNNY EVERS DIES; FAMED IN BASEBALL

Middle-Man in Double-Play Combination of Chicago Cubs With Tinker and Chance

CAUGHT MERKLE IN BONER

He Saw Giant Fail to Touch Base—Elected to Hall of Fame Last April at 64

Special to THE NEW YORK TIMES.

ALBANY, March 28—Johnny Evers, the second baseman in the famous baseball triumvirate of Tinker-to-Evers-to-Chance, died this morning in St. Peter's Hospital of a cerebral hemorrhage suffered earlier this week. He was 65 years old.

In 1942 Evers suffered a stroke which left him partially paralyzed. Notwithstanding his condition, he was frequently seen at Albany baseball games.

He leaves a widow; a son, John Joseph Evers Jr. of Albany; two sisters, Mrs. William P. McCarthy of Troy, N. Y., and Miss Ella Evers of New York, and three brothers, Edward S., Joseph F. and Michael P. Evers of Troy.

In a tribute to the baseball hero, Governor Dewey said: "The untimely passing of Johnny Evers will sadden every American who loves competitive sport. As a member of the immortal "Tinker-to-Evers-to-Chance" combination, he was one of the greatest infielders of all time. More than one generation of Americans will join in mourning his loss."

ALBANY, March 28 (AP)—Joe Tinker, the last survivor of the famous baseball combination, is in an Orlando, Fla., nursing home recovering from an operation in which his leg was amputated. On hearing of Evers' death he said baseball had lost one of its greatest players. Frank Chance, who was the first baseman in the double-play trio, died in 1924.

Middle-Man in Double Play

The playing days of Johnny Evers ended thirty years ago, but his name will remain a baseball byword long after his death because of the faithful adherence by diamond fans to the "Tinker-to-Evers-to-Chance" standard in measuring the worth of double-play combinations.

It was as the middle-man of this great infield trio of the Chicago Cubs that Evers attained enduring acclaim. Appropriately, he was immortalized jointly with Joe Tinker and Frank Chance in April, 1946, by admission to Baseball's Hall of Fame in Cooperstown, N. Y.

However, Evers was more than just the pivotal cog in a smoothly functioning machine. On his own merits he was one of the most vivid personalities the American national pastime has known.

A bantam in physique — he weighed only ninety-five pounds when he joined the Cubs in 1902 and never topped 130 during a stormy, embattled career that extended through 1917—Evers attained the stature of a giant by his dauntless spirit and quick thinking.

The most celebrated example of his resourcefulness beat the Giants out of the National League pennant in 1908 and made a national "goat" of Fred Merkle, the New York team's first baseman.

This was the situation: the Giants and Cubs, locked in a duel for the championship, were tied 1—all in the ninth inning of their final meeting at the Polo Grounds on Sept. 23. With two out, the Giants had Moose McCormick on third base and Merkle on first.

Don Bridwell, the Giant shortstop, drove a single to center field. McCormick dashed home, but Merkle headed for the clubhouse, figuring, of course, that his team had won the game, 2—1.

The crafty Evers noticed that Merkle had failed to touch second base and motioned frantically for the ball. Although the crowd already was surging on the field, it finally was relayed to him and he touched second base, whereupon Umpire Hank O'Day called Merkle "out," invalidating the run and leaving the score tied.

In the resultant confusion it was impossible to resume play. The upshot was that the game was ordered to be replayed after the close of the season. The Cubs won the play-off and the pennant by defeating Christy Mathewson, 4—2, on Oct. 8.

It later came out that this unheard-of play was not sheer inspiration. The crafty Evers knew the rule book by heart and for long had been waiting for such an opportunity. In fact, he had previously discussed it with Umpire O'Day.

A police escort was needed to get him off the field in one piece that day, for the enraged fans were ready to tear him apart. For the rest of his playing days he was persona non grata at the Polo Grounds, which didn't faze him a bit.

With the uncompromising outlook peculiar to many great athletes, Evers thrived on storm and strife. He and Tinker were bitter personal enemies off the field. They did not speak the last two years they played together and had several rough-and-tumble fights in the clubhouse. Yet they continued to sparkle as a team.

Dubbed "the Trojan" because he came to Chicago from his home-town team in Troy, N. Y., where he was born on July 28, 1881, Evers stayed with the Cubs for twelve years, during which his stellar play had much to do with their keeping at or near the top.

In 1914, he shifted to the Boston Braves, with whom he participated in another of baseball's greatest epics. Teamed with another tough little campaigner, Shortstop Rabbit Maranville, he helped set up the airtight defense that aided Boston in its celebrated drive from the cellar to a pennant and world series victory.

He stayed with the Braves for three years, then wound up his playing career in Philadelphia in 1917. Turned down by the Army when he sought to enlist, he went overseas in the first World War as director of physical activities for the Knights of Columbus.

He coached for his old diamond enemy, John J. McGraw of the Giants, in 1920. The next season he returned as assistant manager of the Cubs but lasted only until August. He went to the Chicago White Sox as a coach in 1923 and the next season managed that club.

Then he dropped out of baseball to go into business in Albany but returneda s assistant manager of the Braves in 1929. He continued with the Boston team and, then the Giants again, in various coaching and scouting capacities until 1935.

After leaving major league baseball for good, Evers was for awhile associated with the management of the Albany Eastern League team and served as superintendent of the municipal stadium there. He also operated a sporting goods business.

Although not noted as a hitter, Evers had an average of .279 in fourteen years of regular play. He achieved .341 in 1912 and, in four world series, batted .316. A daring base-runner, he led the league in stealing several times.

Johnny Evers, the pivot man of the famous "Tinker to Evers to Chance" double-play combination smiling uncharacteristically in this photo of him and his son.

The New York Times MONDAY, AUGUST 8, 1960

Luis Firpo Dead; Fought Dempsey

Special to The New York Times.

BUENOS AIRES, Aug. 7—Luis Angel Firpo, who knocked heavyweight champion Jack Dempsey out of the ring at the Polo Grounds in 1923, died here today of a heart attack. He was 65 years old.

The Wild Bull of the Pampas, as he was known, invested the earnings of his fighting years and amassed a fortune in ranches and in Buenos Aires real estate.

His widow survives.

Immortal in Defeat

Paradoxically, Luis Angel Firpo became a ring immortal in defeat rather than in victory. In the wildest type of brawl-type fighting, before he was knocked out in the second round, the hulking 216½-pound South American succeeded in knocking Jack Dempsey through the ropes.

Dempsey landed on his neck on a typewriter on the press table. Whether he was pushed back into the ring by newspapermen or climbed back himself has been disputed ever since.

Dempsey, who was defending his world championship title, said later that he was in "pitch dark" briefly from the challenger's blow and then had seen the bright lights over the ring and Firpo's dim form looming above.

The champion said he suddenly realized where he was and mumbled, "Push me back in there somebody."

Firpo's version, based on what he saw from the ring, was that so many hands were pushing Dempsey back into the ring that it looked as if he were receiving a massage.

The near defeat of Dempsey at this moment came after he had knocked Firpo down five times. Then, upon returning to the ring, Dempsey fended off his opponent successfully until the bell sounded to end the round.

In the second round, Firpo was hammered to the canvas twice more before being knocked out in the fifty-seventh second of this round.

The blazing action and drama, which still make reminiscing fans bright-eyed with excitement, created near pandemonium at the time. The fight was at the Polo Grounds here on Sept. 14, 1923.

Subsequently, although Mr. Dempsey and Señor Firpo became friends, the Argentine once told a friend visiting him in Buenos Aires that he had been deprived of the world's title four times in the fight.

"He hit me twice after the bell." Firpo said, "Once he stood over me after a knock-down and hit me when I was getting up. And he hit me once when I was talking to the referee."

However, Firpo made no formal protest and Dempsey kept his title until losing it to Gene Tunney in Philadelphia on Sept 23, 1926.

Yesterday, upon learning of Señor Firpo's death, Mr. Dempsey said the challenger was "the most dangerous man I ever fought." Expressing regret at Firpo's death, the former champion said "his punch, ruggedness and raw courage gave boxing one of its greatest boosts."

"He not only knocked me out of the ring in our fight," Mr. Dempsey said, "but he had me out on my feet. I don't remember climbing back into the ring again.

"They called him the Wild Bull of the Pampas, and that was an understatement. He came at me like a herd of wild bulls that day.

"He hit me with a right on the cheekbone early in the first round and I was woozy and numb, and I knocked him down and he got up and came at me and I knocked him down and he got up; but near the end of the round he hit me and I went out through the ropes into the press section and landed on my neck on a typewriter."

At the time, Dempsey weighed 192½ pounds.

Firpo, who arrived in New York with a few dollars, a cardboard suitcase, and a spare celluloid collar, received a sizable percentage of the gross receipts of $1,188,603, a near record then, and through careful investments and savings became a multimillionaire in Argentina.

He was the son of an Italian emigrant father and a mother of Spanish stock. Young Firpo worked as a butcher, brickmaker and drugstore clerk before turning to boxing.

Señor Firpo came to the United States in 1922 and won nine consecutive fights by knockouts, including an eight-round victory over former champion Jess Willard on July 12, 1923, which earned him the bout with Dempsey.

He fought only a few times after losing to Dempsey. He came out of retirement only once. In 1936 he accepted a bout in Buenos Aires with Arturo Godoy. He was floored seven times and was knocked out in three rounds.

Three photographs from the famous bout of September 14, 1923: Dempsey falls out of the ring (top), Firpo stands by as Dempsey climbs back into the ring (middle), and Dempsey in turn knocks down Firpo (bottom).

"All the News That's Fit to Print"

The New York Times.

LATE CITY EDITION

U.S. Weather Bureau Report (Page 54) forecasts: Cloudy, occasional rain or drizzle today, tonight and tomorrow. Temp. Range: 45—35; yesterday: 50—43.

VOL. CXV..No. 39,494. © 1966 by The New York Times Company. Times Square, New York, N. Y. 10036 | NEW YORK, SATURDAY, MARCH 12, 1966. | TEN CENTS

Sunny Jim Fitzsimmons Is Dead; Racing's Grand Old Man Was 91

Trained Gallant Fox, Omaha and Nashua in Turf Career Covering 78 Years

By The Associated Press

MIAMI, March 11—Sunny Jim Fitzsimmons, who devoted 78 years to riding and training horses, died today at the Cedars of Lebanon Hospital. He was 91 years old.

A funeral service will be held Tuesday at 9:30 A.M. at St. Mark's Roman Catholic Church in Mr. Fitzsimmons's native Brooklyn, New York. Burial will be in Holy Cross Cemetery in Brooklyn.

A more appropriate nickname than Sunny Jim could not have been devised for James E. Fitzsimmons, the grand old man of thoroughbred racing. His kindly disposition and warmth made friends for racing and for himself through a career that began on March 4, 1885, the day Grover Cleveland was inaugurated President of the United States.

He remembered the day well, for the employes of the Brannon Brothers Stable, where he had just gone to work, were, as Mr. Fitz often said, "probably all Democrats, from the way they were cheering Cleveland." It was as an errand boy and a general helper that the young Fitzsimmons embarked on a race-track career that was to make him one of the most famous trainers in thoroughbred history, with more than 250 stakes victories to his credit.

He saddled the winners of 2,275 races. His horses won $13,082,911. He had two winners of the Triple Crown series of the Kentucky Derby, the Preakness and the Belmont Stakes—Gallant Fox in 1930 and Omaha, a son of Gallant Fox, in 1935.

On his way to the top, Mr.

Continued on Page 24, Column 2

The New York Times
Sunny Jim Fitzsimmons

GILHOOLEY SCORES CITY TRANSIT PLAN AS A 'POWER GRAB'

Terms Proposals by Lindsay a 'Ripper Bill' in Hearing by Legislative Panels

WAGNER ALSO CRITICAL

Opposes Power for Mayor—Amendments to Program Predicted by Travia

By RICHARD L. MADDEN
Special to The New York Times

ALBANY, March 11—Lindsay's trans... for New York ... strong oppositi... John J. Gilhooley, member of the T... ity, and former ... F. Wagner, a Dem...

Mr. Gilhooley ... tacked Mr. Lindsay's proposals to the Legisl... "a political power grab-... per bill" that would "com... ly destroy the independence ... the Transit Authority."

In his first detailed critique of a major program of his successor, Mr. Wagner said the proposals were "really a reach for more power than is necessary or desirable."

Mr. Wagner sent his statement in writing. Mr. Gilhooley delivered his remarks in person to the Senate and Assembly Rules Committees, which completed two days of public hearings on Mr. Lindsay's transit bills.

Need for Changes Seen

After the hearing, Assembly Speaker Anthony J. Travia, Democrat of Brooklyn, said the Lindsay proposals would be amended, but he declined to give details. "I frankly feel that the bills in their present form must stand some change," Mr. Travia said.

The Democratic leader reiterated that the plan appeared to give "too much power" to one man and added that the testimony at the hearings indicated "that one man is the Mayor."

The Lindsay plan, which requires authorization by the politically divided Legislature, would give the Mayor power to remove the present members of the Transit and Triborough Bridge and Tunnel Authorities and group all city transportation operations under an administrator appointed by the Mayor.

Critics of the plan have charged that the administrator would become a "czar" and that the Mayor would have the veto power over the entire operation.

Under one proposal of the Lindsay administration, the Mayor could appoint the three new members of the Transit and Triborough Authorities. An alternate proposal would let the Mayor appoint two members

Continued on Page 10, Column 3

TEACHERS STRIKE IN NEW ORLEANS

Hundreds Stay Out to Press Bid for Bargaining Agent

By ROY REED
Special to The New York Times

NEW ORLEANS, March 11—Several hundred teachers went on strike today in the American Federation of Teachers' first major bargaining effort in the Deep South.

Officials of the union, an affiliate of the American Federation of Labor and Congress of Industrial Organizations, said about 1,000 of the Orleans Parish school district's 3,900 teachers had stayed home.

Superintendent of Schools Carl J. Dolce, who came here last year from the Harvard Education School faculty, said that fewer than 400 teachers were on strike and that school operations were almost normal.

"I anticipate that on Monday most of the teachers will be back in school," Dr. Dolce said.

The strike failed to shut down the school system, but it apparently disrupted several schools, particularly in Negro areas. Eighty per cent of the union's 1,400 members here are Negroes.

Only seven of the 56 teachers at the Green Junior High School appeared for work this morning, and the authori-

Continued on Page 25, Column 1

JA... PO...

Says ... Name ... When A...

By RICHA...

Senator Jac... closed yesterd... recommended ... say before Mr. L... fice that Sanford ... would make a "ap... lice commissioner."

Mr. Garelik's recent... tion to chief inspe... No. 1 uniformed post ... department, has been one ... focal points of the angry ... changes over alleged City H... interference with the police.

Mr. Javits said in an interview that he had submitted Mr. Garelik's name in response to a request from Mr. Lindsay back in December for recommendations for the commissionership.

Recalls Interview

The New York Republican said he had no idea what consideration Mr. Lindsay had given the recommendation.

Mr. Javits contended that, in any case, it was not the Mayor or the new Police Commissioner, Howard R. Leary, or Mr. Garelik who were "introducing a political note" into police affairs.

He said it was "the fellows criticizing them."

The Senator, recalling that Mr. Garelik was Jewish, like himself, said he had known him from community activities. But before sending his name to City Hall, he called him in for an interview and said he had his extremely favorable impression confirmed in checks with officials.

Continued on Page 9, Column 6

Two Accused of Plot To Sell Trade Secret

By The Associated Press

WILMINGTON, Del., March 11—The Federal Bureau of Investigation said today that two Cleveland men had been arrested in connection with what agents described as a scheme to sell stolen secret trade formulas and processes worth several million dollars to the E. I. du Pont de Nemours & Co. in Wilmington.

An F.B.I. spokesman said one of those arrested was alleged to have sought $42,500 from the chemical company for the secret formulas and processes he said he had.

The F.B.I. said the formulas involved a new process for synthetic rubber and belonged to the B. F. Goodrich Corporation in Akron, Ohio, and the Montecatini Corporation, a chemical manufacturer in Italy.

A spokesman for du Pont said

Continued on Page 25, Column 2

Sunny... Racing's...

Trained Gallant F... and Nashua in T... Covering 78...

By The Associated Press

MIAMI, March 11—... Jim Fitzsimmons, who d... 78 years to riding and tra... horses, died today at the Ce... of Lebanon Hospital. He wa... years old.

A funeral service will be h... Tuesday at 9:30 A.M. at ... Mark's Roman Catholic Chur... in Mr. Fitzsimmons's native Brooklyn, New York. Burial will be in Holy Cross Cemetery in Brooklyn.

A more appropriate nickname than Sunny Jim could not have been devised for James E. Fitzsimmons, the grand old man of thoroughbred racing. His kindly disposition and warmth made friends for racing and for himself through a career that began on March 4, 1885, the day Grover Cleveland was inaugurated President of the United States.

He remembered the day well, for the employes of the Brannon Brothers Stable, where he had just gone to work, were, as Mr. Fitz often said, "probably all Democrats, from the way they were cheering Cleveland." It was as an errand boy and a general helper that the young Fitzsimmons embarked on a race-track career that was to make him one of the most famous trainers in thoroughbred history, with more than 250 stakes victories to his credit.

He saddled the winners of 2,275 races. His horses won $13,082,911. He had two winners of the Triple Crown series of the Kentucky Derby, the Preakness and the Belmont Stakes—Gallant Fox in 1930 and Omaha, a son of Gallant Fox, in 1935.

On his way to the top, Mr.

Continued on Page 24, Column 2

The New York Times
Sunny Jim Fitzsimmons

HOUSE UNIT VOTES $13.1-BILLION FUND FOR VIETNAM WAR

Appropriati... Action Unan... ...ected ...ay

SUKARNO YIELDS POWERS TO ARMY TO CURB UNREST; COMMUNIST PARTY BANNED

Sukarno | Lieut. Gen. Suharto
Associated Press

TROOPS ACCLAIMED

Jakarta Is Reported Calm—President to Retain His Title

By Reuters

JAKARTA, Indonesia, Saturday, March 12—Army leaders under Lieut. Gen. Suharto staged a peaceful take-over of power in Indonesia today after all-night talks with President Sukarno lasting into the early hours.

Crack troops and paracommandos moved into the city and took up positions under cover of the predawn darkness. The moves followed days of mounting unrest by students engaged in anti-Communist demonstrations.

Early this morning the Jakarta radio announced that President Sukarno had transferred his powers to General Suharto.

The army's orders were being issued in the name of President Sukarno and he was evidently keeping the formal title of the office.

Victory Parade Held

Heavy armor and armed troops of the Indonesian Army held a massive victory parade today, wildly cheered by hundreds of thousands of students and citizens.

While the parade was going on General Suharto issued in President Sukarno's name a decree banning the Indonesian Communist party.

The ban applied to the party and its affiliates.

General Suharto ordered "immediate, precise and correct" action against the Communists. He said this was necessary because remnants of the Sept. 30 Movement, which staged the abortive coup d'etat last fall, were still active.

The order said that the Communists were conducting underground activities, including slander, aggravation, threats, rumors and armed activity, which seriously threatened the peoples' peace and security.

Grave Threat Seen

General Suharto said the party's underground activities posed a grave threat to the Indonesian Revolution in general and prevented it from continuing its course, especially in the economic field and in crushing Malaysia.

A particular target of the sweeping moves by General Suharto and the army leadership has been Foreign Minister Subandrio, who has shown strong leanings toward Communist Chinese policies.

The political fate of the un...lar Ministers, Dr. Subandrio and the Minister of Basic ...ion, Dr. Sumardjo, was ... known officially. ...cial reports said the ... army custody. ... Suharto is expected ...e a new Cabinet

... official announcement signed by General Suharto in the President's name said the

Continued on Page 6, Column 3

...des Are Cautious ...nesia Power Shift

...MAX FRANKEL
The New York Times

...rday, March 12—United States ...ared to be pleased but were cau... ...is morning as they received evi-

HUMPHREY BARS ... VIETCONG DEAL

U.S. Won't Allow Reds ...n Coalition Unless ...y Win in Vote

...New York Times

...N, March 11—... Humphrey de... that the United ...ke no settle... that gave the ...tical role they ...ree elections. ...rous defense ...inistration's ...tives, Mr. ...t for the ...ce in a ... had ...route ... National ... that the Commu... ...uld not draw the wrong ...nclusion from debate here.

He said the Vietcong had always counted upon traveling three roads to success. The first, he said, is a general uprising in South Vietnam, which "didn't work"; the second, a guerrilla war of the kind now under way, in which Mr. Humphrey predicted that they would fail; the third a coalition.

"Should there be any doubt in Hanoi," he said, "let me, as Vice President of the United States, make it once more clear: We will neither tire nor withdraw. We will remain in Vietnam until conditions permit genuinely free elections to be held."

Continued on Page 3, Column 5

...er, ...Remain

...ARRISON
The New York Times

...11—...ing body has had ... thoughts about the ouster of 1,000 Soviet technicians and teachers stationed here.

The regime, which unseated President Kwame Nkrumah in a coup Feb. 24, has denounced most Soviet and Chinese Communist projects in Ghana as wasteful and ill-managed. But some now appear too useful to scrap.

However, the Government has no intention of recalling any Chinese Communist technicians, all of whom have left the country.

According to the Foreign Ministry, the National Liberation Council, as the ruling body is formally known, has asked the 300 Russians manning Ghana's 15 large fishing trawlers to remain. Also asked to stay were nine engineers working on the reactor near Accra.

The Soviet Embassy has approved both requests. This has brought increased confidence here that Moscow intends to recognize the new regime despite the Soviet Union's past intimate identification with Mr. Nkrumah.

The regime has made no secret of its desire to win Moscow's recognition. There are two reasons for this. One is to continue a nonaligned stance in the cold war, while redressing Mr. Nkrumah's previous pro-Communist bias. The second is to further isolate Mr. Nkrumah, who still claims to be Ghana's President and has vowed to make a comeback

Continued on Page 7, Column 4

NEWS INDEX

Inquiry on 'Scandal' Ordered by Pearson

By JAY WALZ
Special to The New York Times

OTTAWA, March 11—Prime Minister Lester B. Pearson ordered today a full inquiry into an alleged security scandal during the former Conservative regime.

He said his Liberal Government would stake its future on the results of the investigation.

"If you don't like it [the investigation], you can throw us out," the Prime Minister shouted over an angry roar from the Opposition side of the House of Commons.

The case in dispute took a dramatic turn this afternoon when Real Caouette, the leader of a minority opposition party, the Social Credit Rally, put in the record names of principals and other details of the purported scandal.

This information was based

Continued on Page 8, Column 5

Sunny Jim Fitzsimmons Is Dead at 91

Continued From Page 1, Col. 4

Fitzsimmons often showed the soft, attractive qualities that earned him the sobriquet of Sunny Jim. For many years he was one of the busiest men at the race track, training as many as 50 horses a season. He followed a strict timetable, arising at 4:30 A.M. and keeping occupied through most of the day.

He was never too busy, though, to engage in a few moments' talk with anyone who demanded his time — from a famous, rich owner inquiring about the condition of his horse, to an apprentice groom asking which part of the saddle was the front end. In these activities, Mr. Fitzsimmons was sincerely attentive, cooperative, and considerate.

Sunny Jim's qualities, well known though they were, often aroused skepticism among those who had never met him. Many, who had a "this guy's too good to be true" attitude, were determined to carry on a studied hostility against him on introduction. But the Fitzsimmons charm, openness and ingenuousness dissolved these calculated searchers for the false note.

The man was not all softness however. In debate and discussion, he did not hesitate to make his point of view known with definite declaration and sound argument when necessary. And he did not tolerate slipshod work at his barns.

Mr. Fitz was also admired as a trainer because of his dedication to the sport. He had a matchless record since his start in 1893, having saddled stakes winners by the score, including Johnstown, the 1939 Kentucky Derby winner; Fenelon, Fighting Fox and Vagrancy.

He had three winners of the Kentucky Derby, five of the Belmont Stakes, six of the Dwyer, eight of the Lawrence Realization, eight of the Saratoga Cup, and successes in most of the prominent stakes events in North America. His training achievements were the most important of his race-track activities, but they were by no means his only connection with the sport. Indeed, he did just about everything, from cleaning stalls to owning horses.

He was a jockey, too, from 1889 through 1894. Most of his riding was done on the unflatteringly named "Frying Pan Circuit" that included half-mile tracks at Guttenberg, N.J., at Carnegie, Pa., and under lights at Maspeth, Queens. Mr. Fitz never rode a stakes winner, his best performance in silks being a second-place finish in the Flash Stakes at Saratoga in 1893. He had to give up riding for the usual reason, he said: "I got to having trouble with my weight."

Mr. Fitzsimmons turned to training after he outgrew the jockey ranks and applied himself to it virtually the rest of his life. He saddled his first winner, a horse named Agnes D. on Aug. 7, 1900, at Brighton Beach. For many years Mr. Fitz conducted a public stable and also raced his own horses.

Jim Fitzsimmons holds Hitting Away at Belmont on his 81st birthday.

In 1924 he took over the horses of William Woodward's Belair Stud. A year later he also took over the horses of Mr. Henry Carnegie Phipps's Wheatley Stable. Mrs. Phipps's son Ogden and grandson Ogden Mills, also became his patrons. It was for these devoted enthusiasts of the turf and their families that Mr. Fitzsimmons trained his most famous stakes winners.

The stakes winners were to include the two horses that Sunny Jim had difficulty choosing between in later years when he tried to answer the constantly repeated question, "Which was your favorite, of all the horses you ever trained?" The answer was relatively easy for him after Gallant Fox won the Kentucky Derby, the Preakness and the Belmont Stakes to sweep the Triple Crown for 3-year-olds in 1930.

But when Nashua developed into one of the greatest colts of the American turf, in 1953, his answer changed.

Nashua was defeated by Swaps in the 81st running of the Kentucky Derby, but he so impressed the trainer with his career performances that the answer became "Nashua" for a time. As the years went by, Gallant Fox again loomed large in Sunny Jim's eye, and he came around to bracketing that colt with Nashua as his favorite. Nashua was the horse of the year for 1955, won $1,288,565 in purses and was sold by the estate of William Woodward Jr. for what was then a record, $1,251,200, for breeding purposes, at an auction in December, 1955.

A third favorite horse with Mr. Fitzsimmons was Bold Ruler, the winner of horse-of-the-year honors when he was a 3-year-old in 1957. In 1958 Mr. Fitzsimmons said that Bold Ruler probably could have beaten Gallant Fox and Nashua "up to a mile and an eighth."

Mr. Fitzsimmons was born to racing on July 23, 1874. His birthplace was a farm that later became part of the Sheepshead Bay race track, and the Fitzsimmons family never moved from the section. Except for his journeys to Saratoga and to Miami, Mr. Fitz always lived in Sheepshead Bay. It was there that he reared his family of five sons and a daughter. His wife, Jenny, whom he married when he was 17 years old, died in 1950.

Two of Mr. Fitz's sons, James J. and John, became his chief assistants. The Fitzsimmons clan his thrived; a member of the clan said yesterday that Mr. Fitz had 17 grandchildren and 41 great grandchildren.

In his early days Mr. Fitzsimmons experienced more than his share of rough going, riding in races to make a single dollar, riding and falling on ice-covered tracks in below-zero temperature, and walking thoroughbreds for distances of 15 or more miles from track to track to earn money to feed his growing family. Early in life he formed a friendly attachment with a boy named George Tappan, nicknamed Fish. The pair remained associates until Mr. Tappan's death in 1951. For 40 years Mr. Tappan was the assistant trainer of the thoroughbred stock that was under Mr. Fitzsimmons's supervision.

One of his brightest days came on Oct. 13, 1956, at Belmont Park. He saw Nashua set a record in winning the two-mile Jockey Club Gold Cup and Bold Ruler win the $124,845 Juvenile.

His greatest single enjoyment, however, took place at Chicago's Washington Park in August, 1955, when Nashua beat Swaps in a $100,000 match race. More than anything, Mr. Fitz wanted to beat the horse that had beaten Nashua in the Kentucky Derby.

Sunny Jim had as a formula for his training success nothing but hard work. His early-to-rise regimen was an important part of the formula, and also a part of his approach to betting. He frequently said, in answer to those seeking inside information, that "I like to sleep in the mornings. If I had a way to beat them, I wouldn't be getting up at 4:30 every day."

When asked for the secret of his success as a trainer he usually said, "Good horses and good bosses." He frequently added: "A trainer needs a boss who will stick with him. Anybody who couldn't train for the people I work for just can't train."

Fitzsimmons called a halt, offically, to his career on June 15, 1963, when he resigned his post with the Phipps family. Mr. Fitz marked his retirement by sleeping late — as late as 6 o'clock in the morning.

Of all the race tracks that he raced at, it seemed that Mr. Fitz liked Saratoga the best. In his last full year of training, he led the list of stakes winners at the Spa.

The New York Times SATURDAY, JULY 22, 1967

Jimmy Foxx, Athletics Slugging Star in 30's, Dies

Third in Career Home Runs Behind Ruth and Mays

MIAMI, July 21 (AP)—Jimmy Foxx, the Hall of Fame baseball played who ranked third on the list of career home runs, died today at the age of 59. He became ill while visiting his brother, Sam, and died on the way to Baptist Hospital.

Foxx, who helped the old Philadelphia Athletics achieve baseball dominance in the early Nineteen - Thirties, retired in 1945 with 534 major league home runs—second only to Babe Ruth until Willie Mays passed him last year.

Trial in Majors at 17

Jimmy Foxx was born in Sudlersville, Md., on Oct. 22, 1907. He was discovered by Franklin (Home Run) Baker, who urged the late Connie Mack, manager of the Philadelphia Athletics, to give him a trial. He was 17.

The big boy came to the A's as a catcher and batted .667 in 10 games during the 1925 season. He was sent to the minors for more training and came back to the parent club in 1926 and 1927 for a few games each year.

Then in 1928 Foxx came up to stay.

He was one of the strongest right-handed batters who ever played baseball DoubleX, as sportswriters called him, once hit a ball thrown by Vernon (Lefty) Gomez of the Yankees into the upper left-field stands of the Yankee Stadium. The ball broke a seat in the next to last row just to the left of the bullpen area.

His greatest year of home run production was 1932. The 225-pound, mild-mannered player cracked 58 round trippers, just two short of Ruth's record of 60 set in 1927. Foxx hit 50 in 1938, after he had joined the Boston Red Sox.

Soon after he joined the A's, Manager Mack moved him to first base and then to third. He played most of his major league games at those positions.

Near the end of his playing days, on Aug. 20, 1945, Foxx got permission to pitch one game. At the time he was playing with the Philadelphia Phillies in the National League. He pitched six and two-thirds innings to beat the Cincinnati Reds, 4-2.

In December, 1935, he was sold by the Athletics to the Boston Red Sox in one of the biggest major league transactions. To get him, the Red Sox gave up a number of lesser players and $150,000. He was the last of Mack's great stars to be sold when the manager of the A's broke up his fine team of the early nineteen-thirties.

Foxx was one of the main reasons the A's won the pennants in 1929, 1930 and 1931 and he contributed to World Series victories in 1929 and 1930.

In the 1930 series against the St. Louis Cardinals, he turned the tide in favor of the Athletics in the fifth game. With the series tied, he slammed a two-run homer off Burleigh Grimes in the top of the ninth for a 2-0 Philadelphia triumph. The A's easily won the next game, 7-1.

Famed Strike-Out Victim

One of Foxx's claims to fame was as a strike-out victim. He was the middle man when Carl Hubbell of the New York Giants fanned five successive sluggers in the 1934 All-Star game. Ruth, Lou Gehrig, Foxx, Al Simmons and Joe Cronin went down before the screwball hurler. Foxx had some consolation out of the incident. He was the only one of the five batters to hit a foul ball.

When Mays hit his 535th home run, breaking Foxx's record as the most proficient right-handed power hitter in baseball, Foxx said:

"I hope Mays hits 600. For 25 years, they thought only left-handers could hit the long ones. "They even teach right-handed youngsters to hit left."

When he requested his release from the Phillies in the fall of 1945 he had a lifetime total of 534 home runs. This stood second to Ruth's total of 714. Mays now has 555.

Foxx turned to radio sports announcing after his major league career and briefly to managing the Bridgeport, Conn., Bees in the Colonial League.

In January, 1951, he was elected to the Baseball Hall of Fame, along with Mel Ott, the former New York Giants star.

In 1958, Foxx, who had earned more than $250,000 as a player, was without a job and unable to pay his rent. After this was revealed by the Boston chapter of the Baseball Writers Association he was offered jobs throughout the country.

Foxx always said that he had never gone after the homers.

"But if I had broken Ruth's record," he said, "it wouldn't have made any difference. Oh, it might have put a few more dollars in my pocket, but there was only one Ruth." Besides his brother and son, Foxx is survived by a daughter, Nancy

Jimmy Foxx during his rookie year with the A's in 1925. He batted an incredible .667 in just 10 games that year.

Slugger Foxx after he had been traded to the Boston Red Sox.

The New York Times TUESDAY, MARCH 13, 1973

Frankie Frisch, 74, Dead; Baseball's Fordham Flash

By JOSEPH DURSO

Frankie Frisch, who went from the Fordham campus to the Baseball Hall of Fame as one of the game's greatest second basemen, died yesterday in Wilmington, Del., a month after he was critically injured in an automobile accident. He was 74 years old.

Death was attributed to cardiac arrest. Frisch died at the Wilmington Medical Center, where he had been taken when his car struck an embankment near Elkton, Md., after a rear-tire blowout.

"Then there was Mr. Frisch, which went to a university and could run fast, besides," Casey Stengel once remembered. "He was the first second baseman that didn't pedal backwards when they hit the ball down the line. He'd put his head down and commence running like in a race, and he'd beat the ball there."

The old Fordham Flash—Frank Francis Frisch—commenced running fast from the time he stepped off the campus in 1919 and joined the New York Giants of John McGraw. For the next 19 years, he was one of the most versatile and tempestuous performers in baseball, manager of the storied Gashouse Gang of St. Louis and an early member of the Hall of Fame.

Talent for 'Needling'

He was also a remarkable study in contrasts, a hellcat in a baseball suit but a devotee of classical music and gardening at his home in New Rochelle. To the public in the nineteen-twenties and thirties, he was an accomplished infielder with a strong arm and strong features, speedy though slightly bowlegged, a strong batter who compiled a .316 career average as a switch-hitter.

Frisch's talents for trouble, mimicry and umpire-baiting were just as solid. As a player, he once disappeared after a tongue-lashing from McGraw and soon thereafter was traded to the Cardinals for Rogers Hornsby. As a manager, he once was ejected from a game for arguing and drew a five-day suspension the next afternoon for arguing again.

Even in his twilight, at the age of 53, he led the National League in "thumbs" by being thrown out by umpires six times in one summer. The following year, he found Johnny Vander Meer sunning himself in Arizona instead of running laps around the ball park. He unconditionally released the pitcher, whose achievements included consecutive no-hit games.

In one of his earlier capers, Frisch was put out of a game in the Polo Grounds and headed for the clubhouse in center field by a circuitous route, to annoy the umpires. He accidentally stepped through the wrong door, wandered beneath the stands and found himself standing on Eighth Avenue—locked out of the park in his uniform. He drew a crowd of autograph-seekers until a policeman rescued him.

Baited Dean of Umpires

Another time, he was confronted by Bill Klem, the authoritarian dean of umpires, who often drew a line in the dirt with his spikes and said: "Don't you dare cross that line." Few would, but Frisch kept circling Klem while the umpire kept drawing lines until Frisch chortled: "Hey, Bill, you're all fenced in."

Red Smith, the columnist, once walked into Frisch's room in the Ben Franklin Hotel in Philadelphia and asked teasingly if the manager had sent his check for a fine to the league president, Ford Frick. He was astonished when Frisch whipped out a check, signed it and wrote in a note:

"Dear Ford: Here is my check for $25 to pay for the fine. Please use it for a good cause—like buying your umpires new caps. They now look like Civil War veterans."

"Rampaging, dictatorial managers have vanished with the bunny hug and the hip flask," Frisch lamented in 1954. "Gone are the feuds, fines, profanity and fun. This is an era of love and kisses, of sciences and psychology."

"I love to get the Dutchman riled," once said Leo Durocher, the manager and a past master of riling competition. "He lets go with a full fireworks display. It's like the Fourth of July."

Yet, for all his skyrockets on the field, Frankie Frisch somehow became a gentle, genial and becalmed squire off the field, a man who liked to sit in his yard gazing at his flowers, magnolias, maples and azalea bushes. He had a large collection of musical records and particularly favored Arthur Schnabel, the pianist.

He also liked to sit on a bench in his garden and watch a pair of cardinals, which he had named "Musial" and "Slaughter."

He was nevertheless, a complete athlete, one of the few in the early years of the century to graduate from college baseball to the big leagues.

He was born in New York on Sept. 9, 1898, the son of Franz Frisch, and 22 years later he took the long stride to McGraw's Giants. They were then the toast of the town and Frisch was the toast of the Fordham campus: the captain of the baseball, football and basketball teams.

Daredevil Baserunner

Inside two seasons, he was recognized as a pro, the sort of daredevil baserunner and all-out player cast in McGraw's own image. Starting in 1921, the Giants won four straight National League pennants while Frisch batted .341, then .327, then .348 and .328. His headlong style carried over into the World Series, which the Giants won from the Yankees in 1921 and 1922 before losing to them in 1923 and to the Washington Senators in 1924.

Two years later, after his run-in with McGraw, he was abruptly traded to St. Louis. The move came as a shock to the Polo Grounds fans, who had assumed that Frisch would eventually succeed McGraw as manager. The two men's fiery dispositions collided, and they parted.

With the Cardinals, though, Frisch became just as popular. He played second base, third base and shortstop, and helped the Redbirds win pennants in 1928, 1930 and 1931. In 11 seasons with two clubs, he had played on seven pennant winners, with more victories to come.

In 1933, he was still an active player when he was named manager of the Cardinals, who made sporting lore the next season as the rough-and-tumble Gashouse Gang. They were led by Paul and Dizzy Dean, Joe Medwick, Pepper Martin, Durocher and Frisch, and they barreled to the pennant and then to a tumultuous World Series victory over the Detroit Tigers.

By 1937, Frisch was still the playing manager of the troupe—until he decided one day that his famous legs had lost their speed. He was on second base with Terry Moore on first when another Cardinal drove a hit between two outfielders. The 40-year-old Frisch huffed his way home sliding safely across the plate with Moore sliding in just behind him.

"When they start to climb up the back of the old Flash," he said clinically, "I know it's time to quit."

And he did, though he con-

(continued)

Frankie Frisch and Eddie Collins

tinued as manager through 1938. Then he led the Pittsburgh Pirates from 1940 through 1946 and finally, after a break, the Chicago Cubs for 2½ years until July, 1951. Meanwhile, he also worked as a coach with the Giants and emerged as a play-by-play radio announcer, whose oft-repeated "Oh, those bases on balls" became part of baseball lore.

He conducted a post-game show on early television, too, and in 1953 a critic in The New York Times wrote:

"The best post-game show on the air locally is that of Frankie Frisch, who appears over WPIX after each Giant game at the Polo Grounds. Most baseball players are not looked upon as performing talent except on the diamond but, as a former player and manager, Mr. Frisch knows how to talk in front of a camera.

"Oddly enough, and fortunately enough, he never even seems to know it's there. He's as calm as if he were at the plate with the count of 3 and 0."

Stricken With Heart Attack

Following a game between the Giants and the Philadelphia Phillies in 1956, Frisch, who was 58, completed his TV program and was stricken with a heart attack. He spent five weeks in New Rochelle Hospital. Later on he moved to Westerly, R. I., where he lived more quietly though he remained a spirited raconteur of baseball.

Frankie Frisch and Dizzy Dean celebrate after the St. Louis Cardinals won the 1934 World Series.

Arthur Daley

Fond Farewell to the Fordham Flash

ST. PETERSBURG, Fla., March 12—After five weeks of battling against insuperable odds, tough-fibered Frank Frisch finally succumbed today to the crippling injuries of his automobile smashup. The world of sports has to be desolated by the news, and I am more deeply grieved than most because the old Fordham Flash was not only my first sports idol but also my close personal friend. I placed him on a pedestal even before I knew him, and the better I got to know him the higher that pedestal kept mounting. He may have been a short-tempered firebrand on the ball field, but off it he was an utter delight, a genuine funnyman with an outrageous sense of humor. When I was a small boy in short pants, I had many opportunities to introduce myself to the great Frank Frisch. I didn't have the nerve. I was too awed by him. I thought of that episode about a dozen or so years ago when my young daughter, Kathy, answered the phone at home. She looked a little bewildered as she handed it to me.

Sports of The Times

"It's for you," she said, "and the man on the other end is talking in a heavy German accent. I think I recognize the voice. I think it's Uncle Frank."

It was the old Dutchman, of course, putting on an act. But what struck me was that my daughter already had as an adopted uncle a man I once didn't have the nerve to approach.

Without Any Flaws

As a sports writer I naturally got to know him. But even before that my admiration for the man kept increasing. The Hall of Fame hadn't even been invented when he started playing but he was destined for it anyway, as one of the greatest second basemen. No one ever paid him higher praise than did Joe McCarthy, a man chary of praise. The Yankee manager was talking about great ballplayers one day, mentioning that almost every one had some little flaw that made each critique say, He was great, but. . . .

"Was there ever anything that Frisch couldn't do?" he said simply. It was the perfect description. Frisch could run, hit, throw. He could do it all. He had an inner fire as steady as a pilot light, and it burst into consuming flame when needed. It is possible that baseball never had a more dangerous clutch hitter or a man who could rise to the occasion more spectacularly than the Fordham Flash.

Flash he was. No one was faster than Frank in his prime. A favorite story is about when the Giants were traveling by train and a stranger came into the club car. He placed an odd-looking valise at his feet. He introduced himself as a man who had traveled around the country giving lectures on snakes. He reached into the bag and drew forth a squirming, tan snake.

"This one," he said proudly, "is the fastest thing on the continent. As fast as you young men are, none of you ever could catch this snake."

"Frisch could," said Ross Youngs.

"I doubt it," said the snake fancier condescendingly. "After all, you've never seen this snake on the loose."

"Maybe not," said the stubborn Youngs, "but I've seen Frisch."

He was unbelievably fast and was mighty proud of his nickname. Any time I'd get a letter or a Christmas card from him, he always would sign it "The Old Flash."

The Advancing Years

Seventeen years after he left the Fordham campus to become a big leaguer, Frank was playing manager of the St. Louis Cardinals. He was the baserunner on second, with Terry Moore, young swift and eager, the runner on first. The batter doubled and Frank cranked up the old soupbones and started for third. Moore just flew.

"Yu hurree, Frong!" screamed Mike Gonzales, the third-base coach, in his quaint Cuban patois.

Poor Frank was struggling because he could feel Moore breathing down his back. The throw home was true. Frisch slid safely into the plate from one side and Moore slid safely from the other.

"When they start climbing up the back of the Old Flash," he announced slowly, "it's time to quit. I'll never play again." He never did.

It was as player and manager that this blithe spirit inspired the Cardinals' famed Gas House Gang to a world championship in 1934. He had the damnedest collection of uninhibited screwballs ever to drive a manager nuts. But he was their match, funnier than any of them and just as flamboyant. Although he had the reputation of being an umpire-baiter, all the umpires loved him. He never blew the whistle on any of them at league headquarters and he never carried a grudge from one day to the other.

He was a great ballplayer, a great man and a great friend. I shed a tear for one of my most cherished heroes, the Old Flash, who was also known in my household as Uncle Frank.

The New York Times MONDAY, JULY 23, 1979

Tony Galento, Brawling Heavyweight, Dies

By THOMAS ROGERS

Tony (Two-Ton) Galento, a brawling heavyweight boxer of the 1930's who knocked Joe Louis down in a losing championship bout, died yesterday morning at St. Barnabas Hospital in Livingston, N.J., of a heart attack. He was 69 years old.

Mr. Galento won fame during his prime for his motto, "I'll moider da bum." He offered that boastful prediction to the boxing community before each of his 114 heavyweight fights from 1929 until 1944. He often made the pronouncement with a bottle of beer in one hand and a long cigar in the other.

The 5-foot-9-inch puncher, whose fighting weight ranged from 200 to 240 pounds, was powerful enough to make good on his prediction 82 times. In that total of victories, 52 were by knockouts. He lost 26 fights and had six draws. There was one constant: His opponent was always "da bum," even Mr. Louis, from whom he tried to wrest the crown before a crowd of 34,852 at Yankee Stadium on June 28, 1939.

Good Show Against Champion

Although he took a streak of 11 knockout victories into the fight, Mr. Galento was given only a small chance against the champion, who was making the seventh defense of the title he won two years earlier. Mr. Louis had scored first-round knockouts against his three previous opponents.

But Mr. Galento, wading in with left hooks, his favorite punches, shook up the champion in the second round, then floored him in the next round. It was his greatest moment, the title was nearly his, but he could not follow up and finish his foe.

Mr. Louis quickly regained his feet, avoided more lethal lefts and began a relentless assault on the tubby challenger, who weighed 233 pounds, 33 more than Mr. Louis. With Mr. Galento bleeding profusely and reeling about the ring, Referee Arthur Donovan stopped the bout at 2 minutes 29 seconds of the fourth round.

Mr. Galento richly enjoyed fighting, inside or out of a ring. He honed his pugilistic talents in many a back-alley brawl, always on the attack, using his elbows and skull to accomplish what his powerful fists did not. Early in his career, he worked between bouts as a bouncer in a saloon for $25 a week.

A Face of Many Scars

His heavily jowled face bore many reminders of his bare-knuckle skirmishes: gashes over both eyes, a scar on his lip where a tooth had penetrated and another scar on the chin, where he had been hit by a beer bottle.

In the ring he cared little for the niceties or the rules. "Who is this guy, Queensbury?" he once asked a member of the New Jersey Boxing Commission. "I don't see anything wrong in sticking your thumb into any guy's eye. Just a little."

He even fought exhibitions with animals. He claimed to have defeated a kangaroo and a bear and to have choked an octopus to death.

Anthony Galento was born in Orange, N.J., on March 12, 1910, one of four children of Italian immigrants. His schooling ended after the sixth grade and he went to work, mainly as an iceman.

He made his debut as an amateur boxer at 16, knocking out his opponent in the first round at the Orange Y.M.C.A. He lost only one amateur fight in two years and turned professional on Jan. 15, 1929. He began with a third-round knockout of a fighter named Babe Farmer at Laurel Garden in Newark.

Fighting mainly in New Jersey the next seven years, he enjoyed moderate success, but could never move into the front rank of heavyweights. In 1936 he opened a tavern on Dey Street in Orange and briefly contemplated retirement from the ring.

But he was taken over by Joe Jacobs, his seventh manager, and began a string of successes that led eventually to the title shot against Mr. Louis.

In the prefight ballyhoo Mr. Galento was often photographed in bizarre poses at training camp: doing roadwork with a cigar in his mouth, devouring enormous portions of spaghetti or steak and, inevitably, washing everything down with 12 bottles of beer.

His personal physician, Dr. Joseph E. Higi of Orange, was quoted as having said at the time: "Tony is a throwback. He is the thick-boned, hyposensitive type which does not readily register pain. I doubt if any of the thousands of blows he has stopped really has ever hurt him. He has no nerve or brain injury because he never has been stunned."

But he was to be stunned by Mr. Louis and others. In one of the dirtiest fights Max Baer stopped him in eight rounds in 1940, and Buddy Baer, Max's younger brother, stopped him in seven a year later.

From Ring to Mat

He finished his ring career with seven knockouts against undistinguished opposition in 1943 and 1944, then took out a license as a professional wrestler.

Citing the acting experience he had gained as a wrestler, he obtained small parts in several movies in the 1950's and 1960's — "On the Waterfront," "Wind Across the Everglades," "Guys and Dolls" and "The Best Things in Life Are Free."

He married Mary Grasso of Orange in 1935 and they had a son, Anthony, in 1938. The couple separated in 1948.

A diabetic with circulatory problems, Mr. Galento suffered a blackout at a boxing reunion in 1976 and had to spend two weeks in a hospital before he was permitted to return to a senior citizens' apartment complex in Orange. In June 1977 he underwent surgery to remove his left leg at midcalf and was fitted with an artificial limb. Last week his right leg was amputated.

In addition to his wife and son, he leaves a brother, Russell, and two sisters, Jenny Aiello Pino and Lena Petrillo. A funeral service will be held Wednesday morning at Our Lady of Mount Carmel Church in Orange.

Tony Galento stands over Joe Louis after knocking him down in the fight that took place on June 28, 1939. Louis went on to win in the fourth round.

"All the News That's Fit to Print."

The New York Times.

LATE CITY EDITION
Mostly cloudy and mild today. Tomorrow cloudy, cooler with intermittent rain.
Temperatures Yesterday—Max., 72; Min., 57

Copyright, 1941, by The New York Times Company.

VOL. XC..No. 30,446. Entered as Second-Class matter, Postoffice, New York, N. Y. NEW YORK, TUESDAY, JUNE 3, 1941. THREE CENTS NEW YORK CITY and Vicinity

GEHRIG, 'IRON MAN' OF BASEBALL, DIES AT THE AGE OF 37

Rare Disease Forced Famous Batter to Retire in 1939—Played 2,130 Games in Row

SET MANY HITTING MARKS

Native of New York, He Became Star of Yankees—Idol of Fans Throughout Nation

Lou Gehrig, former first baseman of the New York Yankees and one of the outstanding batsmen baseball has known, died at his home, 5204 Delafield Avenue, in the Fieldston section of the Bronx, last night. Death came to the erstwhile 'Iron Man' at 10:10 o'clock. He would have been 38 years old on June 19.

Regarded by some observers as the greatest player ever to grace the diamond, Gehrig, after playing in 2,130 consecutive championship contests, was forced to end his career in 1939 when an ailment that had been hindering his efforts was diagnosed as a form of paralysis. The disease was chronic, and for the last month Gehrig had been confined to his home. He lost weight steadily during the final weeks and was reported twenty-five pounds under weight shortly before he died.

Member of Parole Board

Until his illness became more serious Gehrig went to his office regularly to perform his duties as a member of the New York City Parole Commission, a post he had held for a year and a half following his retirement from baseball. Ever hopeful that he would be able to conquer the rare disease—amyotrophic lateral sclerosis, a hardening of the spinal cord—although the ailment was considered incurable by many, Gehrig stopped going to his desk about a month ago to conserve his strength.

HUGHES, 79, RETIRES FROM HIGH COURT; 2 VACANCIES

PRESIDENT ACCEPTS

Tells Chief Justice His Decision Is a 'Great Shock' to Nation

JURIST CITES HEALTH, AGE

He Found Duties Increasingly Difficult—Wide Speculation as to Successor

By FRANK L. KLUCKHOHN
Special to THE NEW YORK TIMES.

HYDE PARK, N. Y., June 2—Charles Evans Hughes announced his retirement, effective July 1, as Chief Justice of the United States in a letter sent to President Roosevelt today. He gave as his reasons "health and age." The President, in accepting his retirement by telegraph, expressed deep distress, and added that he was sure the announcement would come as a shock to the country.

The Chief Justice offered his retirement under the law permitting members of the nation's highest court to retire on full pay after they pass the age of 70, which was the outcome of the Supreme Court battle in Congress in 1937. His letter was dated today and the Executive's telegram of reply accepting the resignation was transmitted immediately.

The text of the two messages read as follows:

Hughes to the President

Supreme Court of the United States, June 2, 1941.
My dear Mr. President:

Considerations of health and age make it necessary that I should be relieved of the duties which I have been discharging with increased difficulty. For that reason I avail myself of the right and privilege granted by the Act of March 1, 1937, 28 United States Code, Section 375a, and retire from regular active service on the bench as Chief Justice of the United States, this retirement to be effective on and after July 1, 1941.

I have the honor to remain,
Respectfully yours,
CHARLES EVANS HUGHES.

The President's Reply

June 2, 1941.
The Honorable The Chief Justice of the United States,
2223 R Street, N. W.,
Washington, D. C.
My dear Mr. Chief Justice:

I am deeply distressed by your letter of June 2 telling me of your retirement on July 1 from active service as Chief Justice of the United States. This comes to me, as I know it will to the whole nation, as a great shock for all of us had counted on your continuing your splendid service for many years to come.

My every inclination is to beg you to remain; but my deep concern for your health and strength must be paramount. I shall hope to see you this coming week in Washington.

Sincerely and affectionately yours,
FRANKLIN D. ROOSEVELT.

The resignation of Mr. Hughes, who has been ill a great deal this Winter and absent from high court sessions for long periods, came as no surprise, since it had been generally understood that he would retire at the termination of this session of the Supreme Court.

Speculation immediately developed as to who would succeed him. Among those mentioned were Robert H. Jackson, of New York, Mr. Roosevelt's Attorney General, who this Spring accompanied the Executive as a guest on a fishing cruise in Florida waters; Associate Justice Harlan F. Stone, Associate Justice Frank Murphy and Associate Justice Stanley Reed and Secretary Hull.

Jackson Rumored as Possibility

Special to THE NEW YORK TIMES.

WASHINGTON, June 2—The retirement of Chief Justice Hughes gives President Roosevelt the opportunity to appoint two new members of the highest court, making his total larger than any other Executive except George Washington.

With the resignation of Mr. Hughes there are now two vacancies. For months the supposition has been that Robert H. Jackson, now Attorney General, would be an appointee if Mr. Hughes resigned and would be named not only to the bench but to the Chief Justiceship by President Roosevelt.

Mr. Roosevelt has not yet appointed a successor to Associate Justice James C. McReynolds, who left the bench in February. It is presumed that Senator James F.

Continued on Page Nineteen

WASHINGTON ... in chronological ... changes in ... since President ... office on March ...

Willis Van ... June 2, 1937; succeeded by ... L. Black.

George Sutherland ... 18, 1938; succeeded by ... Reed.

Benjamin N. Cardozo di... 9, 1938; succeeded by Felix ... furter.

Louis D. Brandeis retired ... 13, 1939; succeeded by W... O. Douglas.

Pierce Butler died Nov. 16, 1... succeeded by Frank Murphy.

James C. McReynolds retired Feb. 1, 1941; vacancy unfilled.

Charles Evans Hughes retired effective July 1, 1941.

ORDERS REARGUING OF CONTEMPT CASES

Supreme Court Acts on Bridges and Los Angeles Times 'Free Speech' Stand

By LEWIS WOOD
Special to THE NEW YORK TIMES.

WASHINGTON, June 2—After more than seven and one-half months of consideration the Supreme Court gave orders today that the contempt cases of Harry Bridges and The Los Angeles Times should be reargued in October, to which date the tribunal took a recess.

The "free speech" issue was invoked by the defendants in these cases after they had been convicted of contempt of court for comment on cases before the court prior to final judgement.

Rarely has so long a period intervened between an argument and an order as in these cases which were heard last October. In the absence of definite information the general opinion is that the eight justices are hopelessly split and must await the appointment of a ninth before making a final decision. Both defendants are accused of contempt of the California courts.

Gov. Phillips Loses Case

In one of the four opinions handed down on the last day of the term the court rejected the efforts of Governor Phillips of Oklahoma to stop work on the government dam, to cost $54,000,000, across the Red River between Texas and Oklahoma near Denison, Texas. Through a ruling by Justice Douglas, the court extended the power of flood control to include tributaries of navigable streams and held constitutional the construction of the dam.

Governor Phillips had protested that 100,000 acres of Oklahoma would be inundated, much of it being valuable oil and farm land; that Oklahoma's boundary would be obliterated for forty miles and that State subdivisions would lose $40,000 in annual taxes. The court in quoting a recent decision regarding the regulatory power of the Federal Government over navigable streams, remarked:

"We now add that the power of flood control extends to the tributaries of navigable streams. For just as control over the non-navigable parts of a river may be essential or desirable in the interests of the navigable portions, so may the key to flood control on a navigable stream be found in whole or in part in flood control on its tributaries.

"We are of the view that the Denison Dam and Reservoir project is a valid exercise of the commerce powers of Congress."

Rules Against Kansas

Dividing four to three, the court sustained an injunction preventing Kansas City, Kan., and the Union Pacific Railroad from making payments to induce produce merchants of Kansas City, Mo., to move into a new food market in Kansas. Justice Reed wrote the majority opinion, while Justices Roberts submitted a dissent in which Justices Black and Douglas joined. Justice Murphy did not participate.

The majority held that the action of Kansas City, Kan., in "giving cash and rental credits" and other inducements, violated the Elkins act prohibiting rebates, concessions and discriminations respecting railroad transportation of property in interstate commerce.

Justice Roberts scouted this conclusion, saying the Elkins law was never intended to cover such a case and that members of Congress would be surprised to know that

Continued on Page Fifteen

... weight ... weeks and ... pounds under ... he died.

Member of ...

Until his illness ... serious Gehrig went ... regularly to perform ... a member of the N... Parole Commission, ... held for a year and a h... his retirement from bas... hopeful that he would ... conquer the rare dise... trophic lateral sclerosis, ... ing of the spinal cord—althou... ailment was considered incu... by many, Gehrig stopped goin... his desk about a month ago to c... serve his strength.

Two weeks ago he was confin... to his bed, and from that time unt... his death his condition grew stead... ily worse. He was conscious until just before the end. At the bedside when he died were his wife, the former Eleanor Twitchell of Chicago; his parents, Mr. and Mrs. Henry Gehrig; his wife's mother, Mrs. Nellie Twitchell, and Dr. Caldwell B. Esselstyn.

It was said last night that funeral services would be private and would be held tomorrow morning at 10 o'clock in the Christ Episcopal Church in Riverdale. The Rev. Gerald V. Barry will officiate.

The body was taken this morning to the E. Willis Scott Funeral Parlor at 4 West Seventy-sixth Street.

Record Spanned Fifteen Years

When Gehrig stepped into the batter's box as a pinch hitter for the Yankees on June 1, 1925, he started a record that many believe will never be equaled in baseball. From that day on he never missed a championship game until April 30, 1939—fifteen seasons of Yankee box scores with the name of Gehrig always in the line-up. He announced on May 2, 1939, that he would not play that day, and thus his streak came to an end.

But as brilliant as was his career, Lou will be remembered for more than his endurance record. He was a superb batter in his heyday and a prodigious clouter of home runs. The record book is liberally strewn with his feats at the plate.

Only in his first season, 1925, and in his last full campaign, 1938, did he fail to go over the .300 mark. Once he led the American League in hitting with .363, but on three occasions he went over that with-

Continued on Page Twenty-six

Mr. Thomas ... who had a ... with a well-kn... tion" had been ... portant gun posi... cock, but was ... "less strategic" ... Tilden.

Known Communis... were employed in the ... Fort Monmouth, he s... protection against sabo... the laboratory appeared to ... safeguards against outsiders ... the premises for po... sabotage were inadequate.

Although a civilian employ... Fort Monmouth was discov... sending vital defense informatio... in code to a Communist leader, Mr. Thomas said, he had not been discharged, presumably because of "red tape" in the War Department and the Civil Service Commission.

He recommended that the Army be authorized to discharge civilian personnel without regard to any ruling of the Civil Service Commission.

At Fort Dix, Mr. Thomas said, there was a "deplorable state" in that there was no reserve supply of ammunition and not enough small arms ammunition to deal with an internal disorder. He charged that

Continued on Page Ten

Roosevelt Signs Mandatory Priorities Bill; Will Confer With Winant on Britain Today

Special to THE NEW YORK TIMES.

HYDE PARK, N. Y., June 2—President Roosevelt prepared today for conferences in Washington tomorrow which likely will be of far-reaching importance.

Meanwhile he signed two defense measures, one imposing mandatory priorities of wartime scope on industry. The other permits Canadian ships to carry ore between American Great Lakes ports during the 1941 transportation season and is intended to assure an adequate supply of steel.

Mr. Roosevelt will confer tomorrow with John G. Winant, Ambassador to Great Britain; Secretary Hull and, probably, his military and naval staff chiefs. He spent much time today in telephone conversation with Washington, according to William D. Hassett, Presidential secretary.

"No comment," said Mr. Hassett when reporters told him of rumors that Adolf Hitler and Benito Mussolini had discussed possible peace negotiations in their meeting at the Brenner Pass today. Speculation that the Axis leaders had considered countering any moves by the United States met with silence.

Before the new Priorities Law became effective with the President's signature, the government could give mandatory priorities only to contracts placed by the Army or Navy. Now the government also has authority to establish the order in which materials and machines are to be delivered for all planes, tanks, ships and other war equipment being produced under the Lease-Lend Act for Britain and other countries resisting the Axis.

Thus the government acquired the right to decide in all cases what production should come first, whether in the armaments or domestic civilian supply field.

The President already had delegated the priority power to the priority division of the Office of Production Management, which is headed by Edward R. Stettinius Jr., for-

Continued on Page Eight

GOVERNMENT BACKS A BILL FOR SEIZING DEFENSE PROPERTY

Sweeping Power Requested of Congress to Take Any Private Holdings in Emergency

ON FULL WORLD WAR LINES

President in Message Asks for $125,000,000 to Build Roads Into Military Areas

By TURNER CATLEDGE
Special to THE NEW YORK TIMES.

WASHINGTON, June 2—Follow... the proclamation of an un... national emergency by ... Roosevelt Tuesday night, ... ministration asked Congress ... authority to requisition, ... compensation, any private ... or personal, which ... in the interest of ... emergency.

... interest therein ... compensation the ... as the President s... to be fair and just.

If any such person ... entitled to receive th... ing to accept as full and ... compensation for such ... the sum so determined ... President, such person or ... shall be paid 75 percentum ... sue the United States for such a... ditional sum as when added to the sum already received shall be determined as fair and just compensation for such property in the manner provided for by Section 24, paragraph 20, and Section 145 of the Judicial Code (U. S. Code, Title 28, Section 41, paragraph 20, and Section 250), but no recovery shall be allowed against the United States in any such action unless the action be brought within two years after the date on which notice shall have been given of the determination by the President of the amount to be paid as compensation.

Section 3—Appropriations available for the acquisition of prop-

Continued on Page Eight

HITLER AND MUSSOLINI CHART WAR MOVES IN 5-HOUR TALK; BRITISH MASS AROUND SYRIA

The International Situation

TUESDAY, JUNE 3, 1941

Reichsfuehrer Hitler and Premier Mussolini met at Brenner Pass yesterday for another of their secret war councils that in the past have usually preceded new moves in Axis war operations. The dictators were accompanied this time not only by their Foreign Ministers and chiefs of staff, but also by an unusually large number of other military and political advisers. They conferred for more than five hours and it was generally believed that they discussed future operations in the Eastern Mediterranean, the Middle East and Africa, and the position of the United States in the light of President Roosevelt's recent speech. [Page 1, Column 8.]

The conquest of Crete was described by Reich Marshal Goering, in a special order of the day praising the work of the Luftwaffe, as proof that there was "no unconquerable island" so far as Germany was concerned. The German High Command, meanwhile, increased to 13,000 the number of Allied prisoners it claimed had been captured in Crete, and said that another British destroyer had been sunk. [Page 1, Column 6.]

In Iraq the German air-borne units that had been landed at Mosul were reported to have quit that oil center, although it was not determined whether other German forces remained at Kirkuk, the Iraqi terminal of the ... to Haifa. British pres... the Arabs was re... the administra... Rashid Ali el Gailani's ... Iran. [Page 4, Column ...

... in Iraq and Palestine. Hundreds of German technicians have arrived in Syria, food supplies have been shipped there, and Nazi agents are stirring up trouble between the Moslem and Christian population, according to Ankara reports. [Page 1, Column 7; Map, Page 4.]

General Weygand, Commander-in-Chief of France's colonial empire, flew to Vichy and had a two-hour talk with Marshal Pétain, presumably on the swiftly developing situation affecting French interests in the Near East and Africa. No official explanation was made, however, concerning the surprise visit. [Page 4, Column 3.]

Italy's High Command hinted that the next major move might be an Axis attempt to drive the British out of besieged Tobruk on the Libyan coast, and said that German and Italian dive bombers had made heavy attacks on Tobruk's defenses. The British reported evidences of new activity by Axis forces at the Libyan-Egyptian border. [Page 4, Column 6.]

Berlin was attacked by British bombers last night and civilians were killed and injured, Nazi spokesmen reported early today. They claimed the destruction of three of the raiders. The British reported attacks on industrial targets in the Ruhr. London disclosed, meanwhile, that the English city blasted by Nazi raiders Sunday night was Manchester, where great devastation and many casualties were indicated. [Page 2, Column 2.]

In Washington the Administration placed before Congress a far-reaching proposal for the requisitioning by the President for defense purposes of private property of any kind and amount—from housewives' pots and pans to railroads and public utilities systems. The bill would authorize the President to fix compensation for the requisitioned property. [Page 1, Column 5.]

BRITISH SET LINES FOR SYRIAN MOVE

...ised for Drive to Checkmate ...rmans in French Area—...azi Landing Reported

By ... L. SULZBERGER

... Turkey, June 2—Brit... reported to be con... positions in West... Northern Palestine to... East in general ... responsible ... on both sides ... concurred ... necessary for ... French ...

... to the hills. The German radio reported that a state of siege had been declared for Eastern Syria, but The United Press said Vichy had no confirmation of this.]

The exiled Mufti of Jerusalem, who had sought to abet Premier Rashid Ali el Gailani's cause in Iraq, has fled from Baghdad and is rumored to have crossed the Syrian frontier, where presumably he will attempt to spread more anti-British sentiment among the Arabs.

[Rashid Ali's arrival in Teheran, Iran, was reported by The United Press.]

It is clear from the latest information received here that the Germans have established formidable

Continued on Page Four

... from our ... dumb; the enemy fled from fortified positions, and British warships and merchantmen that tried to bring aid were sunk or burned.

"In an old comradeship of arms from the great days of Narvik, aviators and mountain troops conquered the island and thereby threw England out of an important position in the Eastern Mediterranean.

"Comrades! The entire German people feels the deepest wonder and

Continued on Page Three

U. S. BELIEVED TOPIC

Brenner Meeting Seen Laying Plans to Offset Our Expected Entry

ATLANTIC IS ONE PROBLEM

Nazis Stress Military Aspect of Parley—Mediterranean Drive Forecast in Rome

By CAMILLE M. CIANFARRA
By Telephone to THE NEW YORK TIMES.

ROME, June 2—With the Axis forces in possession of Crete, Reichsfuehrer Hitler and Premier Mussolini met today at the Brenner Pass for five hours to decide upon their next military and political moves.

A communiqué issued after the conference said that the two dictators and their Foreign Ministers had discussed "the political situation" for several hours. The conversation, it was stated, was held "in the spirit of the most cordial friendship and ended in complete agreement."

While it is impossible at present to have even an inkling of what the two dictators discussed specifically—the utmost reserve is being kept in Italian and German official quarters — the general opinion among the Italians is that the discussion touched on the three closely interlocked main problems facing the Axis. These are United States intervention in the war, which, after President Roosevelt's most recent speech, every one here believes to be only a matter of weeks; the Battle of the Mediterranean and the Battle of the Atlantic.

Longer War Is a Problem

In event of United States intervention, neutral diplomatic quarters say, the Axis, despite its chain of military successes, will be faced with a prolongation of the war for a period that not even Signor Mussolini and Herr Hitler are in a position to estimate. The two leaders, it is stressed, must therefore devise means to minimize as far as possible the weight of armed United States assistance to Britain and win positions that will enable them to cope for an indefinite period with a new strategic and political situation.

It is a safe guess, it is held, that the Axis will aim at transforming Europe and North Africa into a veritable fortress, making them impregnable, as far as possible, against Anglo-American attack, both militarily and economically.

To do this, it is generally believed, some countries that are still outside the direct influence of the Axis will be "induced" in one way or another to "collaborate." Italy's assistance on this point of the program is necessary, since one of the future Axis moves will, according to today's press, take place in the Mediterranean, where the Italian Navy and mercantile fleet will be useful.

"The result and the consequences of the new Axis victory in Crete," writes Virginio Gayda, "will soon be seen in the new developments in the Mediterranean war."

Role of Russia Is a Factor

In this connection Axis spokesmen have been saying for some time that a clarification of German-Russian relations will have to take place soon. Russia is said to be needed not only because her economic resources are valuable to the Axis, but also because of her political influence over Turkey. If Russia were "induced" to fight ... the Axis, Turkey, it is held ... would have to conform and ... Axis drive to the Middle East ... be immeasurably facilitated. ... however, while the operations in ... Eastern Mediterranean will probably be intensified, the situation in the Western Mediterranean is held by the Italians to be no less important to the Axis, since it is closely connected with the Battle of the Atlantic. It is insisted that the war will be won in the Atlantic.

Signor Mussolini and Herr Hitler cannot, therefore, have failed to discuss what they can expect from France and Spain, since those two Mediterranean countries have a geographical position as well as African possessions that would be extremely valuable to the Axis.

The announcement of the Hitler-Mussolini meeting came as a distinct surprise in both diplomatic and journalistic quarters here. Arrangements for it were made in the strictest secrecy and only a few per-

Continued on Page Six

Lou Gehrig, "The Iron Man."

GEHRIG, 'IRON MAN' OF BASEBALL, DIES

Continued From Page One

Two weeks ago he was confined to his bed, and from that time until his death his condition grew steadily worse. He was conscious until just before the end. At the bedside when he died were his wife, the former Eleanor Twitchell of Chicago; his parents, Mr. and Mrs. Henry Gehrig; his wife's mother, Mrs. Nellie Twitchell, and Dr. Caldwell B. Esselstyn.

It was said last night that funeral services would be private and would be held tomorrow morning at 10 o'clock in the Christ Episcopal Church in Riverdale. The Rev. Gerald V. Barry will officiate.

The body was taken this morning to the E. Willis Scott Funeral Parlor at 4 West Seventy-sixth Street.

Record Spanned Fifteen Years

When Gehrig stepped into the batter's box as a pinch hitter for the Yankees on June 1, 1925, he started a record that many believe will never be equaled in baseball. From that day on he never missed a championship game until April 30, 1939—fifteen seasons of Yankee box scores with the name of Gehrig always in the line-up. He announced on May 2, 1939, that he would not play that day, and thus his streak came to an end.

But as brilliant as was his career, Lou will be remembered for more than his endurance record. He was a superb batter in his heyday and a prodigious clouter of home runs. The record book is liberally strewn with his feats at the plate.

Only in his first season, 1925, and in his last full campaign, 1938, did he fail to go over the .300 mark. Once he led the American League in hitting with .363, but on three occasions he went over that without winning the batting crown—.373, .374 and .379.

But baseball has had other great hitters before and other great all-around players. It was the durability of Gehrig combined with his other qualities that lifted him above the ordinary players and in a class all his own.

An odd little incident gave Gehrig his start and an even stranger disease, one almost totally unknown for a robust athlete, brought it to an end. Columbia Lou's string of consecutive games began, innocently enough, when the late Miller Huggins sent him up to bat for Peewee Wanninger on June 1, 1925. The husky 22-year old promptly singled.

Huggins was impressed by the way Gehrig had delivered, but according to the tale that is told he had no notion of using him as a first baseman. The Yankees had a star at the initial sack in those days, Wally Pipp. But Pipp was troubled with frequent headaches.

On June 2 he was bothered by pains in his head.

"Has any one an aspirin tablet?" asked Pipp.

Huggins overheard him and, on a sheer hunch, decided to use the "kid"—Gehrig—at first base. He never left the line-up again until his voluntary resignation fourteen years later. Perhaps that story is not cut from the whole cloth. Gehrig has denied it, but Pipp insists just as vehemently that it is true. At any rate, it is an interesting sidelight on how a spectacular career was begun.

Slipped in 1938

The beginning of the Gehrig playing days was abrupt but the ending was a much slower process. In 1937 the Iron Horse batted .351, his twelfth successive season over the .300 mark. But in 1938 the Yankee captain slipped to .295, the same figure he had established in his 1925 campaign.

Not only his hitting but his fielding had lost much of its crispness. Batted balls that the Gehrig of old had gobbled up easily skidded past him for base hits. In fact, the situation had developed to such an extent that there was continual talk in Spring training in 1939 that the endurance record was approaching its completion.

This became even more obvious in the early games of the campaign. Yankee followers were amazed to see how badly Gehrig had fallen from the peak. He was anchored firmly near first base and only the fielding wizardry of Joe Gordon to his right saved Gehrig from looking very bad. The second sacker overshifted to cover the hole between him and his captain. Lou couldn't go to his right any more.

At bat Gehrig was not even a pale shadow of his former self. Once he had the outfielders backing up to the fences when he stepped to the plate. But this time he could hardly raise the ball out of the infield. On one occasion when he caromed a looping single to left—a certain double for even a slow runner—Gehrig was thrown out at second, standing up.

Last Game Against Senators

That day he saw the handwriting on the wall. And on April 30, 1939, he played his last big league game against the Washington Senators. The Bombers lost and Gehrig realized that he was a detriment to his team. When the Yanks took to the field again in Detroit on May 2, Gehrig—his batting average down to .143—withdrew from the line-up, his first missed game after 2,130 straight.

He acted as nonplaying captain from that point on. On June 12, when the Yankees engaged in an exhibition game in Kansas City, Lou played the last three innings, did nothing and promptly left for the Mayo Clinic. He was there a week, determined to discover just what was the matter with him. That something was wrong he was certain.

On June 21 the diagnosis was made. It was that he had a mild attack of paralysis. His career thus was brought to an abrupt conclusion. And an amazing career it had been.

Tribute by 61,808 at Retirement

The public's reaction to Gehrig's swift retirement gave rise to one of the most inspiring and dramatic episodes in sport when on July 4, in ceremonies preceding the afternoon's holiday double-header, a crowd of 61,808 joined in the Lou Gehrig Appreciation Day exercises at the Yankee Stadium and thundered a "hail and farewell' to baseball's stricken Iron Horse.

Players, officials, writers and employes at the park showered Lou with gifts, the climax of the spectacle coming when the Yankees themselves paraded on the field their world championship team of 1927. From far and wide these diamond stalwarts had returned to join in the tribute to their former team-mate, who had managed to carry on long after their own retirement from the game.

The group included such Yankee immortals as Babe Ruth, Waite Hoyt, Bob Meusel, Herb Pennock, Joe Dugan, Tony Lazzeri, Mark Koenig, Benny Bengough, Wally Schang, Everett Scott, Wally Pipp, George Pipgras and Bob Shawkey.

Overcome by this spontaneous reception, Gehrig finally mastered his emotions, and, in perhaps the most remarkable valedictory ever delivered in a sport arena, literally poured his heart out to his great throng of listeners, thanking them for their appreciation and assuring them, with characteristic pluck, that he still considered himself "the luckiest fellow on earth, with much to live for."

From then until the end of the season Gehrig stuck by his guns as retired field captain, and spent every day on the bench. He accompanied the club on all its road trips, and at the finish sat through all four of the 1939 world series games in which his colleagues crushed another National League rival.

With the close of the campaign, Lou retired himself within a small circle of close friends, spent much time in fishing, a sport second only to baseball in its fascination for him, and on Oct. 11 figured in another surprise move when Mayor La Guardia announced his appointment to a ten-year term as a member of the three-man Municipal Parole Commission at a salary of $5,700 a year. He tackled with considerable enthusiasm this newest job that was to launch him upon a new chapter in his astounding career.

In Spotlight Again

Although anxious to go quietly about his new task and remain as much as possible in complete retirement, Gehrig was catapulted prominently into the spotlight again in mid-August of the 1940 pennant campaign when a New York newspaper, in a featured article, intimated that the extraordinary collapse of the four-time world champion Yankees might be attributable to the possibility that some of the players may have become infected with Gehrig's disease.

The story brought vehement protests from the Yankee players, who insisted they were suffering from no physical ailments and then, as if in final rebuttal to the charge, the Yanks, within a few days after publication of the article, launched their spectacular drive which was to lift them from fifth place into the thick of the flag race throughout the month of September.

In the meantime, Gehrig had papers served for a $1,000,000 libel action, while the publication printed an apology to Gehrig, stating that thorough investigation revealed that Lou's ailment was not communicable. No legal action was taken after this.

Gehrig was born in New York on June 19, 1903.

His career began unobtrusively enough when, as a husky youngster, he reported for the High School of Commerce nine in New York. He was tried in the outfield, where he was no Joe DiMaggio at catching fly balls. He was tried as pitcher but was as wild. He was tried as a first baseman and clicked. In later years Lou explained that, with his ever ready grin, by saying "We were mighty short on infielders in those days."

In his first season on the Commerce team he batted .170. Then he started hitting until he cracked the headlines with a crash in 1920. Commerce, the New York schoolboy champions, played Lane Tech of Chicago in a scholastic "world series." The single game was played at Wrigley Field and Gehrig was awed by his surroundings. But he was not too awed. In the ninth inning with Commerce one run behind and the bases full he drove a home run over the right field fence.

Columbia All-Around Player

Buster Gehrig was beginning to take shape. He matriculated at Columbia, pitching, outfielding and playing first base. He was a good enough college pitcher but did have the knack of hitting home runs. For one year there he also tried football, but that sport did not have the same appeal that baseball bore.

The diamond game carried such a zest for him that he quit before he had been long at Morningside Heights, joining the Yankees in 1923. He played thirteen games before Huggins decided that he was not yet ready for major league ball. Farmed out to Hartford in the Eastern League, he batted .304 for the rest of the season. Back with the Yanks the next campaign he followed the identical procedure. He took part in ten games and then it was a return trip to Hartford, where he began to belabor the fences in the circuit, hitting .369. That figure was an eye-opener to Huggins, who recalled him the following season.

That was in 1925. Gehrig batted .295 in 126 games and then he began to rocket through the baseball firmament. His first full season showed him with .313, but after that his successive batting averages were .373, .374, .300, .379, .341, .349, .334, .363, .329, .354, .351 and finally he was back to .295 in his last full campaign. The .363 average gave him the batting championship in 1934, but signal honors had come to him before that. In 1927, his second full campaign with the Yankees, he was voted the most valuable player in the American League.

Seven times he participated in world series and, oddly enough, was a star on the Yankees of 1926-27-28 and with the all-star contingent of 1936-37-38. Each of these groups has its supporters as the greatest baseball team of all time. Ruth-Gehrig-Meusel, the famed "Murderers' Row," or DiMaggio-Gehrig-Dickey? Those were the batting fulcrums around which the teams revolved. Columbia Lou was the lone tie between the two.

His series deeds have been awe-inspiring. His lifetime average in world series games was .361—his full regular average .340—and twice he hit over the fantastic mark of .500, with .545 in 1928 and .529 in 1932. Babe Ruth, however, holds the series record of .625 in 1928.

That is an oddity in itself, Gehrig with two terrific averages but still behind the Babe. Yet for the better part of his career the Iron Horse was to be in the shadow of Ruth. Lou entered baseball when the Babe was riding high, straddling the sport such as no man has straddled it before or since.

Gehrig never left that shadow. His all-time home run production was 494, a figure topped by only two men, Ruth and Jimmy Foxx who at the end of 1940 had reached a 500 total. For many years Lou gave the Babe his closest pursuit in the home-run derby, but he never caught him until the Babe's last year as a Yankee. Only when the King was on the decline did the Crown Prince win the home-run championship of the league, 49 in 1934.

(continued)

Lou Gehrig was hailed by thousands on Lou Gehrig Appreciation Day, July 4, 1939.

For one thing, Gehrig did not have the flamboyant Ruth personality. They were team-mates but far apart, one quiet, reserved and efficient and the other boisterous, friendly and efficient. Let it not be deduced that the Iron Horse was not of the friendly type. He was pleasant at all times, but unlike Ruth he never considered the world at large as his particular friend. Whereas the Babe would greet all and sundry with a booming "Hiya, kid?" Lou's was a more personalized welcome.

They were sharp contrasts, those two, both hulking men but as far apart as the two poles. Ruth was Gehrig's boyhood idol, and with the passing years Lou never lost that respect for the Home Run King. And in spite of his own tremendous record, Gehrig was always subordinated to Ruth.

What a pair they made at the plate, coming up to bat in order! Each was likely to drive the ball out of the park. Frequently either or both did just that. In fact, one of the many records that Lou set was that of hitting the most home runs with the bases filled, a startling twenty-three. Another was of four homers in one game.

The Ruthian association affected Gehrig's salary in two respects. In one way the heavy blow that Ruth struck at the payroll kept Lou from getting a compensation as close to the Babe's as their relative batting averages would indicate. Yet, on the other hand, the Bambino lifted the scale so high that Gehrig probably received more than he would have had there been no Ruth to blaze the trail.

Made Fortune in Game

Like most payrolls, the Yankee one is not open to the public gaze, but is more public property than an ordinary business. So the amount of money that Gehrig received each season is part guess and part accurate knowledge, especially in the more recent years when the Federal income tax rolls ceased being secret.

The general estimate is that the Iron Horse received a total of $361,500 in salary from the Yankees. Since he participated in seven world series where the share always was heavy his total income from baseball is estimated at $400,000.

Gehrig received $3,750 in his first season, $6,500 in his second year. This advanced $1,000 in 1927 and then the Iron Horse moved into the big-money class. He never dropped out of five figures for the rest of his career.

For the next five years he received $25,000 and then he dropped to $23,000 for 1933 and 1934, after which he received $31,000 in 1935 and 1936, $36,750 in 1937, $39,000 in 1938 and $35,000 for 1939, a campaign in which he played only eight games.

Baseball contracts are peculiar things, strictly one way. The club has the upper hand at all times and can sever any contract at will. Had they so desired the Yanks could have dropped Gehrig the day the report from the Mayo Clinic arrived. But he was kept on full salary for the remainder of the year.

So firm was his place in the Yankee scheme of things that Manager Joe McCarthy refused to break the Gehrig string even when there was a clamor to the effect that the Iron Horse himself would benefit from it. Marse Joe shook his head to that. "Gehrig plays as long as he wants to play," he said. Not many ball players would be granted such a privilege.

But in this respect McCarthy knew his man and knew him well. He realized that once Lou discovered his form had departed and that he was hindering the progress of the team he would call it quits. And that is what happened.

Had it not been for the attack of paralysis Gehrig might have continued as a part-time performer. Ball players do not go as fast as he went. The disintegration always is gradual enough for managers and club owners to make preparations. But the Yankees were caught without an adequate substitute for him, only the light-hitting but surefielding Babe Dahlgren.

Previously, being Gehrig's replacement had been the height of frustration. There was just no hope that he ever would give way to any one else. In their thorough fashion the Yankees had had several first basemen on their farm teams. All of them pleaded to be sold or traded elsewhere so that they would be able to play regularly.

One was Buddy Hassett, now at first base for the Boston Braves. Another was George McQuinn, hard-hitting initial sacker for the St. Louis Browns. Many others have paraded into the Yankee orbit and out again, balked of their desire by the stalwart figure of Lou Gehrig.

The day before he entered the Mayo Clinic for the examination baseball celebrated its centennial at Cooperstown and the Hall of Fame was dedicated. Ruth already had been elected to it and within a short time another bronze plaque joined the Babe's as Henry Louis Gehrig took his proper place among the all-time greats that this sport had produced.

For though Baseball's Hall of Fame committee decided to hold no elections for new candidates in 1939, it chose, upon recommendation of the Baseball Writers Association of America, to make an exception and name Gehrig as the lone Hall of Fame award for the year.

Gehrig's Impressive Records

The major records that Gehrig made:

REGULAR SEASON

Most consecutive games—2,130.

Most consecutive years, 100 games or more—14.

Most years, 150 games or more—12.

Most years, 100 runs or more—13.

Most consecutive years, 100 runs or more—13.

Most years, 100 or more runs batted in—13 (tied with Ruth).

Most years, 150 or more runs batted in—7.

Most consecutive years, 100 or more runs batted in—13.

Most runs batted in, one season—184 (American League).

Most times, four long hits in one game—5.

Most years, 400 or more total bases—5.

Most years, 300 or more total bases—13.

Most home runs with bases filled—23.

Most consecutive home runs in one game—4 (modern record).

Most total bases, one game (modern record)—16, (tied with Ruth and Klein).

Most years, leading league, runs batted in—5 (tied with Ruth).

Most years, leading league games played, season—8.

First baseman participating in most double plays, season—157.

WORLD SERIES

Highest batting percentage, total series—.361 (7 series).

Most runs, one series—9 (tied with Ruth).

Most runs batted in, total series—35.

Most runs batted in, one series—9.

Most home runs, one four-game series—4.

Most home runs, 3 consecutive games—4.

Most extra bases on long hits, one series—13.

The New York Times *FRIDAY, MAY 23, 1975*

Lefty Grove, Hall of Fame Pitcher, Dies

Robert Moses (Lefty) Grove, a member of Baseball's Hall of Fame who as a star pitcher with Connie Mack's Philadelphia Athletics in the nineteen-twenties and thirties won 300 major-league games, died last night, apparently of a heart attack, in Norwalk, Ohio. He was 75 years old.

Mr. Grove died at the home of his daughter-in-law, Mrs. Robert C. Grove.

A funeral service will be held Monday in Lonaconing, Md.

The fiery left-hander chalked up a phenomenal winning percentage of .682 with the Athletics and later the Boston Red Sox. There were eight seasons in which he won 20 or more games—once registering 31 victories, this during the 1931 season. That year was generally considered his best—he lost only four games.

In a 17-year major league career, Mr. Grove recorded 2,266 strikeouts and posted a life-time earned-run average of 3.06.

He joined the Athletics in 1925 after four outstanding seasons with Baltimore of the International League.

He started a string of seven consecutive 20-victory seasons in 1972, reaching 28 wins and 5 losses in 1930. Coupled with his outstanding performance in 1931, his 59-9 won-loss record for two consecutive seasons is an achievement never since equaled.

Mr. Grove tied the American League record of 16 consecutive victories in the summer of 1931 and shares the league's record with Walter Johnson, Joe Wood and Linwood (Schoolboy) Rowe.

Known for His Temper

Lefty Grove pitched only to win and when he didn't win he could make life hard for team-mates and others. He had one of the hottest tempers in the major leagues.

However, one of the biggest blows he suffered did not make him angry. Uncharacteristically, he was left speechless.

That blow fell Dec. 9, 1941, when he received his unconditional release from the Boston Red Sox and the other 15 major league clubs waived on the 40-year-old hurler.

Actually, the Grove pitching story ended on July 25, 1941, when he struggled to a 10-6 victory over the Cleveland Indians. This was the pitcher's 300th and last major league triumph.

Grove tried time and again before he posted his 300th.

Born March 6, 1900, Mr. Grove never cared much about baseball until he was asked to play for a company team in his home town of Lonaconing, Md. He was noticed by a scout and signed in 1920 to play professional ball for the Blue Ridge League.

In 1925, Connie Mack, owner and manager of the Philadelphia Athletics, purchased him for $100,600. At the time it was a record price.

According to stories of the time, the price was made $600 higher than the price the Yanks paid for Babe Ruth just for the sake of a record.

Mr. Grove was sold to the Red Sox for $125,000 in 1934.

It was Mr. Mack who had the best success in handling the hot-tempered pitcher. Once after he had lost a 1-0 decision to the St. Louis Browns he got angry at his team-mates, who had three hits. Later that night, Mr. Mack said to him, "Robert, didn't Coffman [Brown's pitcher] pitch a wonderful game? We made only three hits and we wouldn't have scored a run if we'd been still playing."

Mr. Grove came around to his manager's way of thinking and calmed down in his attitude toward his team-mates.

He had his own ideas of what were his best performances and liked to recall some. Among his favorite accomplishments was the time he struck out Lou Gehrig, Babe Ruth and Bob Meusel on nine pitches in a game in which the Yankees had the tying run on third in the ninth inning. Another feat was his striking out of Ruth, Gehrig and Tony Lazzeri on 10 pitches, with bases loaded.

Mr. Grove, who was voted to Baseball's Hall of Fame in 1947, finished his 17-year major league career with 300 victories and 141 defeats.

Hall of Fame member Robert "Lefty" Grove won exactly 300 games and posted a lifetime winning percentage of .682.

The New York Times TUESDAY, OCTOBER 7, 1969

Walter Hagen, Leading Professional Golfer, Dead

TRAVERSE CITY, Mich., Oct. 6 (AP)—Walter Hagen, one of the greatest shotmakers in the history of golf, died of cancer last night at the age of 76.

First stricken in 1964, when a cancerous larynx was removed, Mr. Hagen underwent two other operations, the last in January of 1967. He died on his estate here.

He was divorced twice. A son, Walter Jr., survives.

Burial will be on Thursday at Southfield, following a funeral service at 11 A.M. at Birmingham.

He Set the Pace

By ALDEN WHITMAN

In the nineteen-twenties, the "golden era of sports," Walter Charles Hagen was a giant in professional golf, a man mentioned in the same breath as Bobby Jones, the king of the amateurs.

A fabulous player, an elegant dresser and a truly impressive bon vivant, The Haig (as Mr. Hagen was generally known) captivated the public imagination as much for his resplendent personality as for his prowess with mashie and putter.

He elevated the professional golfer from his role as a country club hireling to the status of a friend of royalty and a man of means. Former King Edward VIII of England was "Eddie" to Mr. Hagen, and, as the Prince of Wales, he delighted in being ordered to hold the flag for a Hagen putt.

Mr. Hagen made one of his last public appearances in August 1967 at a testimonial sponsored by his local friends. Arnold Palmer, in a moving tribute to a man he idolized, said: "If it were not for you, Walter, this dinner tonight would be downstairs in the pro shop and not in the ballroom."

Mr. Hagen earned a lot of money—he put it at $1-million—and he spent it as easily as he made it.

From 1914, when he won his first championship, the United States Open, until 1929, when he retired from competition, Mr. Hagen won 17 major golf titles, gathered laurels and entranced galleries in every country in which the game was played. He appeared in more than 2,500 exhibitions, made thousands of friends and led a life that was the envy of and the pattern for his fellow professionals.

Haunted by Thought of 80

"He is in golf to live, not to make a living," Chick Evans, one of Mr. Hagen's contemporaries, once observed. But there was pride, too, for Mr. Hagen retired, he said, because "I couldn't stand the thought of possibly shooting an 80."

Walter Hagen won his first championship in 1914 at the age of 21.

Mr. Hagen's major championships were two United States Opens (1914 and 1919); five Professional Golf Association titles (1921, 1924, 1925, 1926 and 1927; four British Opens (1922, 1924, 1928 and 1929); five Western Opens; and one Canadian Open. He also was captain of the American Ryder Cup teams in 1927, 1929, 1931, 1933, 1935 and 1937, and was the nonplaying captain in 1948.

Of all Mr. Hagen's victories, the most satisfying was a one-sided triumph over Jones in a special 72-hole match in Florida in 1926.

"Everybody was saying Jones was the greatest golfer in the world and I was second best," Mr. Hagen recalled later. "It rankled me a bit, so I got a friend to arrange the match—36 holes over Bob's course at Sarasota and 36 over mine at St. Petersburg.

"I had an eight-hole lead leaving Sarasota and went on to win, 11 and 10. It was my greatest thrill in golf."

But Mr. Hagen did not let his victory obscure his esteem for Mr. Jones's golf. When a sportswriters' poll in 1950 picked Mr. Jones as the greatest golfer of the half-century (Mr. Hagen was third and Ben Hogan second), Mr. Hagen remarked:

"I would have voted for Jones myself. He was marvelous."

Mr. Hagen was an immaculate dresser and his attire helped to revolutionize wearing apparel on the golf course. He is credited with introducing plus-fours — knickerbockers for men—to golfing. He also made the camel's hair coat standard equipment for the well-dressed golfer.

A 6-footer and trim about the waist and jowls in his prime, Mr. Hagen looked handsome in a dress suit. His sleek black hair added to the suave impression that he gave at dances and at parties. Some of these lasted all night, and Mr. Hagen, not one to go to bed while the fun was on, sometimes showed up for a morning golf engagement in a dress shirt. His game on such occasions was not noticeably affected.

Mr. Hagen was renowned for his devastating mashie shots and his marvelous putting skill. He was frequently in trouble off the tee, so that his talent with the irons was essential. A serene disposition, an almost faultless aplomb and a knowledge of psychology were also a part of his wizardry.

Used Gamesmanship

An example of his guile was the P.G.A. final at Salisbury, L.I., in 1926. Mr. Hagen began by conceding six-and eight-foot putts to his opponent, Leo Diegel. Then, late in the match, when pressure had mounted, Mr. Diegel had a simple 25-incher. He glanced at Mr. Hagen for another concession, but the Haig turned away.

"There must a hidden roll," Mr. Diegel said nervously. He missed his putt, and Mr. Hagen went on to win 5 and 3.

On another occasion Mr. Hagen's ball was 15 feet from the cup while his opponent's was half that distance. Mr. Hagen broke into a grin.

"What's the joke?" his opponent asked.

"I was just thinking how much harder your putt will look after I make mine," Mr. Hagen replied.

Mr. Hagen went on to sink his putt with ease. His opponent missed.

He unnerved his opponents still more by the way he played. He would ponder an easy shot, creating the impression that it was difficult and thereby eliciting whoops of joy from the gallery when he made it. "Impossible" shots Mr. Hagen made with debonair ease, and this, too, threw his adversaries off.

Mr. Hagen had, moreover, a Babe Ruthian confidence in

(continued)

himself. To win the British Open in 1924 he had to get a 4 on the last hole to nose out E. R. Whitcombe. It was a rainy day and the greens were slippery. He wound up by having to drop a six-foot putt to carry off the cup.

With scarcely a glance at the flag, Mr. Hagen hit the ball and, without waiting to see where it went, tossed his club to the caddy and started off the green. He didn't actually know what had happened to the ball until the crowd's roar told him that it had gone into the hole.

He had, too, an unmatched insouciance. Members at one golf club bet him $3,000 he couldn't equal the course mark of 68. He reached the final green, needing only a 12-foot putt to make good.

"Step up, suckers, and pay me," he sang out. Then he holed the putt.

Mr. Hagen was often late for golf appointments. One such occasion, a match in Tokyo with Prince Konoye, gave rise to a celebrated remark. Mr. Hagen arrived two hours late, and a nervous aide to the Prince said, "The Prince has been waiting since 10 o'clock."

"Well, he wasn't going anywhere, was he?" Mr. Hagen shot back.

The Prince wasn't, and the two played amiably.

Excellent Competitor

Mr. Hagen was a splendid competitor, even when he wasn't at the top of his form. His last P.G.A. championship at Dallas in 1927 was one example. He had at first no intention of defending the title he had won three times in succession. He was, in fact, on a fishing expedition in Wisconsin and hadn't touched a club for weeks when he decided to compete.

"Well, I just got to thinking that if I didn't play," he explained, "much of the credit would be taken away from the man who won. People would say, 'It would have been different if Hagen had played.' I didn't think I had one chance in a million to win for the fourth consecutive time."

When Mr. Hagen appeared in Dallas, it was just in time to play the quaifying round. He not only qualified, despite his rustiness, but he also went on to defeat Al Espinosa and Joe Turnesa for the title.

To win four times in a row meant that Mr. Hagen took 24 consecutive matches. Actually, he did better than that, for after losing to his archrival, Gene Sarazen, in the final round of the 1923 P.G.A. event he did not suffer defeat until he bowed to Mr. Diegel in the third round of the 1928 play.

Mr. Hagen disdained thrift. He once collected $3,000 on a Canadian tour and just before leaving Winnipeg for home he telephoned the hotel where he was stopping and told the manager, "Fill the bathtub with ale and champagne and break out your best Scotch. The party's on me."

When he returned to the United States he had less money than when he began the tour.

Mr. Hagen got $500 as his first British Open prize and gave it all to his caddy. His tips were rarely less than $20, and it was not all for showmanship. He was genuinely open-handed and carefree.

Mr. Hagen did a great deal to break down the caste barriers behind which golf professionals had been herded. In many country clubs here and abroad the professionals had to use the servants' entrance, and they were not permitted in the dining room or the bar.

His triumphs obliged the snobbish to seek him out, and for his friendship he insisted upon his social due. He got it, and so did professionals that followed him.

Mr. Hagen left his imprint in another way, too, in that he was a model for such caddies as Mr. Sarazen and Johnny Farrell, who rose to fame.

Caddying was how Mr. Hagen got his start. He was born in Rochester, N. Y., Dec. 21, 1892, the son of William and Louise Balko Hagen. His father was a blacksmith.

Starting Playing Golf at 5

When he was 5 years old, he began playing with a discarded golf club left at his home by a local professional. He started caddying at 9, and spent a lot of his spare time in the pro shop of the Rochester Country Club, where he swept the floor and polished clubs. He practiced whenever he could, and when he was 11 years old he broke 80.

He had a chance to play baseball for the Philadelphia Phillies, but decided against it after high school. He made his competitive golf debut at 20 at the United States Open in Brookline, Mass., and he finished only three strokes away from making it a four-way tie for the championship.

From that time until he retired Mr. Hagen was not often out of the money, or out of the sports headlines. When he was not playing for titles, he was engaged in exhibition matches.

Joe Kirkwood, an Australian trick-shot artist, was a frequent companion in these matches, which contributed greatly to popularizing golf as a game for everyone, not just the wealthy and idle.

Worked for Wilson Company

After his retirement Mr. Hagen kept only a business attachment to golf as head of the Walter Hagen Division of the Wilson Sporting Goods Company.

Living near Detroit he renewed his interest in baseball as a fan of the Detroit Tigers. He did some hunting and fishing and wrote a book, "The Walter Hagen Story," that Simon & Schuster published in 1956.

He was elected to the Golf Hall of Fame. In 1961 he was given the Walter Hagen Award of the Golf Writers Association of America. The following year the Metropolitan Golf Writers Association bestowed its Gold Tee Award on him at a dinner in New York.

Although he was obliged to give up even friendly golf because of a heart condition, Mr. Hagen often turned up in the clubhouse at big tournaments. Older, more fleshy and scarcely able to talk, he nonetheless liked to chat about the game and to meet those who had followed in his footsteps.

Even in semi-retirement, Walter Hagen still drew a gallery.

The New York Times MONDAY, OCTOBER 13, 1969

Sonja Henie, Skating Star, Dies

Olympic Winner Made Fortune in Movies

OSLO, Oct. 12 (AP)—Sonja Henie, ice-skating queen and film star, died tonight on an ambulance plane flying from Paris to Oslo. She was 57 years old.

Miss Henie had been suffering from leukemia for the last nine months. In Paris yesterday her condition worsened, and it was decided to fly her home.

Her husband, Neils Onstad, a Norwegian shipowner, said she "just slept away" halfway through the two-hour flight.

Champion and Star

Three times the Olympic figure-skating champion, Miss Henie won most of the major world skating titles from 1927 to 1936, when she turned professional.

A petite, glamorous woman with a taste for luxury and a shrewd business sense, she was immensely successful next with a series of her own ice revues, and prospered as a motion picture star.

After her marriage to Mr. Onstad, a childhood sweetheart, in 1956, she became interested in modern art. The Onstads gave Norway an art museum and 250 of their paintings in August 1968.

Two earlier marriages to Americans, Daniel Reid Topping and Winthrop Gardiner Jr., ended in devorces in 1946 and 1956. She had become an American citizen in 1941.
had a home in the Holmby Hills section of Los Angeles, an apartment in Lausanne, Switzerland, and an estate overlooking the Oslo fjord.

Skated as 6-year-old

Born in Oslo on April 8, 1912, Miss Henié received her first skates from her father, a Norwegian fur wholesaler, on the Christmas after her sixth birthday. She had already delighted in dancing, and—with her brother Leif giving her her first lessons—enjoyed skating even more.

While improving her skating, in the next few years, she also studied ballet with a former teacher of Anna Pavlova, and eventually she combined the two forms on ice.

She won the children's figure skating championship of Oslo when she was 8, and two years later, in 1923, she won the figure skating championship of Norway.

She entered her first Olympic Winter Games the next year, primarily for experience, and took third place in the free skating competition.

Practicing as much as seven hours a day, she studied with teachers in Germany, England, Switzerland and Austria. With her well-to-do father's backing, she studied ballet in London, and began applying choreography to her routines. Her mother traveled with her constantly, as she did throughout Miss Henie's career.

She won the first of 10 consecutive world skating titles at Oslo in 1927, captivating the crowd with her ballet style, a white silk and ermine costume and short skirt and a dimpled smile.

Over the next decade Miss Henie won Olympic titles at St. Moritz, Switzerland (1928), at Lake Placid (1932), and at Garmisch-Partenkirchen in Bavaria (1936).

She announced then that she was turning professional, and toured the United States in an ice show. She said her greatest hope was to become a movie star, and she soon did.

"I want to do with skates (in the movies) what Fred Astaire is doing with dancing," she said.

She signed with Darryl F. Zanuck and 20th Century-Fox, and her first skating film, "One in a Million," was released at the end of 1936.

It was a box-office smash, as were others she made in the following dozen years. The pictures were reported to have grossed $25-million.

She herself earned over $200,000 from her film work alone in 1937.

She also began staging and appearing in ice shows, in association with Arthur Wirtz, her business manager, and these, too, were very successful — with lavish costumes and spectacular routines.

These shows, the "Hollywood Ice Revues," were major attractions at Madison Square Garden for many years, up to 1952.

Miss Henie was an exacting star. She once called Eddie Pec, the only person she permitted to sharpen her skates, in New York, to ask him to come to Chicago, where her show was to open.

He hopped on a train, reached Chicago the next day, rushed to her hotel, and sharpened the skates with a hand stone—a few minutes work.

"Anything else?" he asked.

"No, thank you," she said sweetly. "That's all."

And back he went to New York.

She broke with her manager in 1951, and began producing shows on her own, but gave them up after a block of seats at a Baltimore armory collapsed before a show in March, 1952, injuring more than 250 people.

Although later cleared of any responsibility for the accident, she did not stage any more arena-type shows. She appeared on several television shows in the next few years, including a one-hour special of her own.

Sonja Henie in *Second Fiddle*, one of the musicals she starred in.

Between the years 1927 and 1936, Sonja Henie won ten world skating titles.

The New York Times MONDAY, DECEMBER 1, 1975

Graham Hill, 46, Retired Racer, In Fatal Crash Piloting His Plane

LONDON, Nov. 30 (UPI)—The auto racing world mourned today the death of Graham Hill, twice the world drivers' champion and five members of his racing team.

The 46-year-old Englishman, who cheated death on Grand Prix circuits round the world for nearly two decades until his retirement last July was killed yesterday when his Piper Aztec plane, which he was piloting, crashed and burned as he was coming in for a landing at Elstree Airport, 12 miles north of London.

In Monte Carlo, where Hill won the Grand Prix a record five times, Prince Rainier of Monaco said: "It's a very big loss for the automobile sport because Hill was an excellent technician and equally a leader in the sports world."

Another former world champion and close friend, Jackie Stewart said: "My love for Graham was more as a man than anything else.

"I think he projected the image of Britain that was correct—of the typical Britisher, cool, calm and collected, never getting ruffled."

Among those who died with Hill was Tony Brise, his 23-year-old English protege, who survived a crash Friday while the team was testing at the track at Le Castellet, near Marseilles. The team was returning from these practice sessions in France when it crashed.

Friends said the others aboard the plane, which crashed in thick fog on a golf course near Hill's home, were Ray Brimble, the Embassy Hill team manager; Andy Smallman, designer of the car, and Terry Richards and Tony Alcock, the mechanics.

The police said the air controller at Elstree, who knew Hill well, said he had given the go-ahead to land, and Hill had radioed that he was making his final approach. The plane, however, went down on the second tee of Arkley golf course, about two miles short of the airport runway.

Hill's body was identified from dental records. The police said identification of the other victims was more difficult.

Hill was England's most successful racing driver. He was the only man to achieve the "triple crown" of auto racing, winning the world Formula One drivers' championship in 1962 and 1968, the Indianapolis 500 in 1966 and the Le Mans 24-hour sports car classic in 1972.

Dennis Hulme of New Zealand, president of the Grand Prix Drivers Association—a position once held by Hill—said: "We have lost one of the last of the great Grand Prix drivers."

A Profile of Courage

By MICHAEL KATZ

He walked into the bar of the Hotel de Paris at Monte Carlo on two canes one evening in 1970, his legs bowed by shattering accident eight months earlier. The doctors had said that Graham Hill would never drive again, but this was the night before the Grand Prix of Monaco, the most glamorous automo-

(continued)

Graham Hill (left) and Henri Pescarolo hoist champagne after their victory in the 1972 Le Mans endurance classic. After learning that one of his friends, Jo Bonnier, had been killed in the race, Hill said, "This is one of the saddest days of my life."

Hill crosses the finish line with a flair to win the 1964 U.S. Grand Prix.

bile race in the world, and Graham was a fixture at Monte Carlo.

He had raced, almost miraculously, two months earlier in the Grand Prix of South Africa, where he had to be lifted into and out of his single-seat Formula One racing car. So when he walked into the Hotel de Paris bar, just across the square from the Casino and the "in" spot for the "in" people at the Grand Prix, almost everyone in the room stood up in tribute to the courage of the man who had both legs broken in the 1969 Grand Prix of the United States at Watkins Glen, N. Y., the preceding fall.

Hill spotted some friends at the bar and made his way through the back-slapping admirers to join them. Friends go up off their stools to offer the crippled Englishman a seat. Hill politely refused.

And so he stood at the bar for a half-hour, his broken legs wobbly beneath him. But Graham Hill would not accept a seat that night.

In the world of auto racing, where Graham Hill had already earned a reputation for "guts," this was one of his finest performances. He didn't go on to win the 1970 Grand Prix of Monaco — although he did win the most prestigious event on the international calendar a record five times — but there were many other victories.

Graham Hill, who did not learn how to drive until he was 23 years old and who began his racing career the following year while he was collecting wefare benefits, was the only man to win the world drivers' championship, the Indianapolis 500 and the 24 Hours of Le Mans. Only Jackie Stewart, with 360, earned more world championship points than Hill, who had 289.

For his services to auto racing, he was made an officer of the Order of the British Empire in 1968 by Queen Elizabeth.

Norman Graham Hill was born Feb. 15, 1929, to middle-class parents in London. He attended engineering school, and became a rowing champion for the London Rowing Club—his familiar dark blue racing helmet with white stripes was in the colors of the club. It was after the 1953 rowing season, searching for something else to do with his spare time, that he bought his first car, a 1934 Morris 8. He said later his main reason was that a car "was better than a motor bike for taking girls out."

But he enjoyed driving so much that he took advantage of a newspaper advertisement offering drivers four laps around England's famed Brands Hatch racing circuit south of London for $2.80. Soon after, he was working for the racing school that had made the offer as a mechanic, paid not in cash but in free laps around the track.

He managed to get on the British unemployment list and began what at first was a frustrating racing career in 1954. For a long while, he was hindered by mediocre machinery.

He made his debut in Grand Prix racing—the élite international circuit of races throughout the world—in 1958 and spanned the eras from Juan Manuel Fangio through Jimmy Clark to Jackie Stewart and Emerson Fittipaldi.

When he retired last July he was the oldest driver on the circuit and had driven in more Grand Prix races than anyone in history—176. Last season, he managed the Graham Hill Embassy Formula One team, but with little success.

Hill won two world championships, in 1962 with B.R.M. and in 1968 with Lotus. In 1966, driving a Lola-Ford for John W. Mecom, a wealthy Texan, Hill became the first "rookie" (or first-time starter in the race) to win the Indianapolis 500 since 1927, driving through a first-lap pile-up that eliminated many of the favored cars.

But although he won the United States Grand Prix three times, Hill was best known abroad, where his straight mustache—which later became a handle-bar—beneath a large nose were as recognizable as his helmet.

In Britain, Hill became a celebrity, his wit and cool humor helping make him a familiar participant in television talk shows. He was fond of responding to what he believed were silly questions with straight-faced put-ons. After having won the 1964 United States Grand Prix while wearing a brace for a stiff neck, he was asked why he had the collar.

"Confidentially," he replied, "motor racing gives me a pain in the neck."

Hill was known as a cautious, precise driver, but one who never gave up. In his last years, although much slower than in his peak, he was still a tough man to pass. He was active in the struggle for better safeguards in racing, and ironically his worst accident — at 150 miles an hour in the 1969 United States Grand Prix — came when a rear tire blew out and he was not wearing his seat belt.

He was lucky to escape with his life, but he was not the same driver again. In 1972, co-driving with Henri Pescarolo of France, he won the Le Mans endurance classic in a Matra. Afterward he learned that one of his closest friends, Jo Bonnier of Sweden, had been killed in that race. It was Hill's last great victory, but he said: "This is one of the saddest days of my life."

Hill is survived by his wife, Bette, who was a familiar figure in racing paddocks and pits throughout the world, and his children, Brigitte, Damon and Samantha.

"All the News That's Fit to Print"

The New York Times

LATE CITY EDITION

Weather: Partly sunny today; cloudy tonight. Chance of rain tomorrow. Temp. range: today 38-50; Sunday 39-54. Full U.S. report on Page 74.

VOL. CXXI . . . No. 41,708 | © 1972 The New York Times Company | NEW YORK, MONDAY, APRIL 3, 1972 | 15 CENTS

HALF OF PROVINCE IN SOUTH VIETNAM LOST TO INVADERS

Saigon's Troops Pull Back From Northern Quangtri —A Few Posts Hang On

B-52'S FLY SIX MISSIONS

They Bomb Through Clouds in the Mountains West of the Contested Area

By CRAIG R. WHITNEY
Special to The New York Times

SAIGON, South Vietnam, Monday, April 3—South Vietnamese forces abandoned the northern half of Quangtri Pr[ov]ince yesterday to a ... Vietnamese force, esti[mated at] 12,000 to 15,000 men ... still advancing south ... hind tanks and inte[nse artil]lery barrages. But w... cloud cover that has th... effective air support ... South Vietnamese rem... United States B-52's dro[pped] hundreds of tons of bo[mbs] through it yesterday.

The only South Vietname[se] positions still holding in the northern part of the province last night were at Dongha city, Quangtri city, and the Quangtri combat base, all reported under heavy attack.

After the combat base was struck by more than a thousand 122-mm. rockets and long-range 130-mm. artillery shells, Brig. Gen. Vu Van Giai, commander of the South Vietnamese Third Infantry Division, moved his staff three miles south to the citadel at Quangtri city, which is believed to be the objective of the North Vietnamese drive.

Tank Battle Reported

The combat base was the headquarters of an American infantry division until last summer and since then had been the Third Division's command post.

Another base a few miles south of Quangtri at Lavang also came under rocket and mortar attack yesterday, but late reports said that neither had been attacked by ground forces.

North of Dongha, South Vietnamese tanks engaged in a battle with North Vietnamese armor and the Saigon command said that 19 enemy tanks were destroyed late yesterday afternoon by low-flying, propeller-driven fighters of the South Vietnamese Air Force. Ground fighting was said to be heavy north of the base late last night.

The B-52's, in six missions of as many as three planes each, dropped their bombs through the cloud cover yesterday over suspected Communist troop concentrations in the mountains in a semicircle west of Quangtri. The clouds had blocked effective air support since Thursday.

Five North Vietnamese sur-

Continued on Page 2, Column 4

La... Re... to...

By ...
Special ...

MILWA[UKEE] ... ator Georg[e] ... day that th... phone and ... tion paid n... taxes for the ... and accused ... $400,000 gift to ... National Conven[tion] ... ness expense" in ... with the Securiti[es and Ex]change Commission ...

Within minutes aft[er] ... the charges in a ... televised interview, the ... said he had made "an ... mistake" in saying tha[t] ... $400,000 appeared in the se[curi]ties commission report. ... was followed within an ... by a press release from ... headquarters reiterating the ... mission of a "mistake" a[nd] scaling down from five to thre[e] the number of years that International Telephone had allegedly not paid income taxes.

The accusation dominated the day's developments in Tuesday's Wisconsin Democratic Presidential primary. The polls will close at 8 P.M., Central standard time.

A spokesman for International Telephone in New York denied that the company had not paid corporate income taxes. He said that Federal taxes from the company's consolidated operations were paid

Continued on Page 22, Column 1

...A. Burns and Lee Romero and United Press International

...tion of Easter ...d and Secular

... MONTGOMERY

... were well attended, and Coney Island had a full house for its season opening.

Elsewhere, Pope Paul VI in [h]is Easter message called for [a] new ecumenical commitment [am]ong Christians. A crowd of ...0,000 filled St. Peter's Square [to] hear the Pontiff. In Jeru[sale]m, the Vatican's represent[ative] in the Holy Land cele[brated] mass at the Church of [the Hol]y Sepulcher. President ... [an]d his family attended ... Gettysburg, Pa.

... focus of the morn[ing] ... worship. At the ... [Chu]rch of St. John ... the Right Rev. ...negan gave his ...on before re... ...al Bishop of ...e Council of ... Easter dawn ... City Music ... Wyatt Tee ...

... Column 2

STATE STRIKE ENDS AS WORKERS WIN RAISE AND BONUS

5.5% Money Pact Follows Work Snarls at Prisons and Mental Institutions

COST PUT AT $82-MILLION

Governor Says Borrowing or New Aid Will Be Needed —Legal Sanctions Hinted

By JAMES F. CLARITY
Special to The New York Times

ALBANY, April 2—The Civil Service Employes Association today called off its strike, which had disrupted work at state prisons and mental institutions for more than a day and a half.

The union, which represents 140,000 of the state's 185,000 employes, said it was canceling the strike after accepting a tentative settlement offer that included a 4 per cent raise, effective immediately, and a 1.5 per cent bonus, payable next April.

Governor Rockefeller said the $60-million cost of the pay increase would be financed through borrowing or additional Federal aid. The $22-million cost of the bonus was to be met through savings from increased productivity.

Court Order Ignored

The strike began at 12:01 yesterday after the union ignored a court order forbidding such action.

By 6 P.M. today, two hours after the union called an end to the strike, state officials reported that picket lines had been withdrawn from mental institutions and prisons and that evening-shift employes were reporting for work.

Because the strike began on the weekend, its impact was not felt at scores of state offices, particularly in Albany and New York City. The state said the situation had never become "critical" at the mental institutions, where meals and other services were delayed, and at state prisons, where guards refused to cross picket lines.

The state sent a total of about 30 troopers to work at the prisons at Auburn, Attica and Elmira, principally to maintain watch towers.

The state refused to promise amnesty for strikers, though neither the state nor the union estimated how many people actually had gone on strike.

Union Denies Breaking Law

The union maintained that it had not struck illegally because a court order forbidding the [st]rike had been improperly [ser]ved Friday night. State of[ficials] insisted the strike was ... and Governor Rockefel[ler's of]fice said this afternoon ...e will comply with the ... Law."

... the Taylor Law, [which f]orbids strikes by public [e]mployes, the union leaders may be jailed, the unions fined and union members docked two days' pay for each day they strike.

It could not be determined

Continued on Page 43, Column 1

Hodges, Manager of Mets, Dies of Heart Attack at 47

Special to The New York Times

WEST PALM BEACH, Fla., April 2—Gil Hodges, popular first baseman of the old Brooklyn Dodgers who later manipulated the New York Mets to their surprising baseball championship, died of a heart attack today after playing 27 holes of golf.

Hodges, who would have been 48 years old Tuesday, collapsed while walking to his room at the Ramada Inn on the Palm Beach Lakes golf course. He was rushed to Good Samaritan Hospital but was pronounced dead 20 minutes after being admitted.

The Mets' manager, who played with the Dodgers for 15 seasons and with the Mets for parts of two more, suffered a mild heart attack near the end of the 1968 season but returned the following year and managed the so-called Miracle Mets to the National League pennant and a World Series triumph over Baltimore.

He played golf instead of managing today because the team's scheduled exhibition game with the Montreal Expos had been canceled as a result of the player strike.

The three Met coaches who played with him—Joe Pignatano, Eddie Yost and Rube Walker—reported he wanted to play 27 holes instead of 18 because he felt so good.

As they were returning to

Continued on Page 52, Column 3

The New York Times

Gil Hodges

...more, suffered a ... attack near the end [of] the 1968 season but returned the following year and managed the so-called Miracle Mets to the National League pennant and a World Series triumph over Baltimore.

He played golf instead of managing today because the team's scheduled exhibition game with the Montreal Expos had been canceled as a result of the player strike.

The three Met coaches who played with him—Joe Pignatano, Eddie Yost and Rube Walker—reported he wanted to play 27 holes instead of 18 because he felt so good.

As they were returning to

Continued on Page 52, Column 3

The New York Times

Gil Hodges

Solzhenitsyn Tells of Struggle to...

By HEDRICK SMITH
Special to The New York Times

MOSCOW, April 2—Aleksandr I. Solzhenitsyn opened the apartment door, but only a few inches. His eyes, dark and penetrating, peered out intently, his rust-brown beard partly visible. He kept the door chain latched while he checked who was calling.

Satisfied, he unlatched the door quickly to permit entry

Excerpts from discussion are printed on Page 10.

and just as quickly he shut it again. Inside, his greeting was warm.

Then for four hours, in his first on-the-record talk with any Western newsman in nearly a decade, the controversial 53-year-old Russian novelist provided a vivid and poignant picture of his defiant struggle to continue writing under the stigma of official ostracism and under the pressure of what he called an official campaign "to suffocate me."

With the kind of compelling detail that made his anti-Stalinist novels world famous in the nineteen-sixties and won him the 1970 Nobel Prize for Literature, he described how he was barred from access to Government archives necessary for his new set of historical novels on World War I, how elderly survivors of the war "shut up" out of fear of talking to him, how he was prevented from hiring research assistants and how he must rely on haphazard voluntary help.

He told how his mail was checked, his living quarters bugged, his friends shadowed "like state criminals" and his second wife dismissed from her job when the director of the institute where she worked discovered her connection with Mr. Solzhenitsyn.

"A kind of forbidden, contaminated zone has been created around my family," he explained. "You Westerners cannot imagine my situation. I live in my own country, I write a novel about Russia. But it is as hard for me to gather material as it would be if I were writing about Polynesia."

More than once during the

Continued on Page 10, Column 1

The New York Times

Aleksandr I. Solzhenitsyn with wife, Natalya Dmitreeva, and son, Yermolai, in Moscow

Those Rising Beef Prices: Some Surprising Answers

By RICHARD D. LYONS
Special to The New York Times

WASHINGTON, April 2 — Which of the following statements about beef are true?

Steak prices in New York City are the highest in the nation.

The cost of beef is at a record.

High prices have given producers a bigger share of the beef dollar.

Answer: None.

The perhaps surprising answer serves to underscore the statistical complexities and common misconceptions surrounding who gets what share of the beef dollar.

"Trying to make sense out of beef statistics gets to be a bucket of eels very quickly," said Donald B. Agnew of the Marketing Economics Division of the Agriculture Department.

Mr. Agnew, together with specialists both within and outside the beef industry who have been interviewed, were unanimous in contending that the consumer is really getting his money's worth for the amount he spends on beef.

In New York City, meanwhile, the United States Bureau of Labor Statistics released a report showing that food prices in metropolitan area stores, particularly for meat and vegetables, rose "sharply" in February. [Details on Page 30.]

Mr. Agnew and the other specialists say that the reason the consumer is getting his money's worth on beef is that

Continued on Page 31, Column 1

NEWS INDEX

Gil Hodges, Mets' Manager, Dies of a Heart Attack at 47

Piloted New York to World Series Title in 1969

Continued From Page 1, Col. 6

their rooms at the motel, Pignatano asked, "Gillie, what time should we meet for dinner?"

Hodges turned around and said, "7:30". Then he toppled backward and collapsed.

While Pignatano and Walker rushed to help Hodges, Yost ran to a telephone and called the police, a fire emergency unit and an ambulance. All arrived within three minutes with a policeman getting there first and working on him for about a minute until the ambulance arrived.

Treated by Obstetrician

Dr. James Smith, an obstetrician who happened to be at the hospital, treated the stricken manager, inserting a tube in his throat and a needle in his heart.

However, a cardiogram showed a complete arrest of Hodges's heart, and the pupils of his eyes were dilated. He was pronounced dead at 5:45 P.M. by Dr. William Donovan, a local doctor who was called by Jack Sanford, former Philadelphia pitcher who is the pro at the Palm Beach Lakes course.

The news of Hodges's collapse spread quickly. Telephone calls poured into the hospital and several baseball officials in the area—in addition to executives of the Mets—arrived shortly afterward.

Hodges's wife, Joan, was home in Brooklyn. His son, Gil Jr., is a player in the Mets' farm system. Also surviving are three daughters, Irene, Cynthia and Barbara.

A Met spokesman said Hodges's body would be returned on the charter flight that will bring officials and several players of the Mets and Yankees to New York tomorrow.

Funeral arrangements are being handled by the Torregrossa Funeral Home in Brooklyn.

The Hero of Flatbush

One warm Sunday in May of 1953, a parish priest in Brooklyn told his congregation: "It's too hot for a sermon. Keep the Commandments and say a prayer for Gil Hodges."

Gil Hodges when he played for the Brooklyn Dodgers. He set a National League record of 14 grand-slam home runs.

Gilbert Ray Hodges, the first baseman and power hitter for the Brooklyn Dodgers, was in the throes of a particularly fretful batting slump that day. But by the time the season had ended, he had hit .302 with 122 runs batted in and 31 home runs.

He also had appeared in the All-Star Game and the World Series, and had fastened his grip on the public affection to a degree that rarely was rivaled in modern baseball.

Some years later, though, in 1969, Hodges reached even greater heights of esteem when he managed the New York Mets to the first pennant in their eight-year history and a World Series triumph over the potent Baltimore Orioles.

That feat, coming with a team that only a few seasons before had been one of the most laughed at in baseball history, stood as a tribute to Hodges's managerial ability, an ability that equaled his prowess as a player.

Unusual Type of Athlete

A 6-foot-2-inch, 210-pounder with a brute's physique, he was that unusual type of professional athlete—the gentle giant in private, the executioner in a baseball suit.

For 16 seasons, he was one of the most graceful first basemen in the major leagues, and one of the most feared hitters. He started with the Dodgers in 1947, then played 2,006 games with them and 65 with the New York Mets. He hit .273 with 1,274 runs batted in and 370 home runs — 14 of them with the bases loaded.

He also appeared in seven World Series and six All-Star Games, and then settled into a career as manager with the Washington Senators and the Mets.

But, for all his success with the cudgels of the game, Gil Hodges became best known as the "nice guy" who finished first, the hero of Flatbush, the devoted family man, the good Marine—the man for whom a congregation would say prayers.

Father a Coal Miner

Although he worked for years at Ebbets Field and lived for more years five miles farther down Bedford Avenue, Hodges really was a Midwesterner who adopted Brooklyn as his home.

He was born April 4, 1924, in Princeton, Ind., a town of about 8,000 persons in the mining and farm region in the southwestern part of the state. He was the second son of Irene and Charles Hodges, a coal miner who lost several toes and his right eye in a mining accident.

The family moved to Petersburg, Ind., where Gil won seven varsity letters in track, basketball and baseball. He also played American Legion ball for two summers and was offered a minor league contract by the Detroit Tigers. But he declined, followed his brother Bob to St. Joseph's College nearby, and decided on a coaching career.

But in 1943, while he was a full-time drill-press operator and part-time baseball player for a company team, he was signed by the Brooklyn Dodgers.

However, except for one game at third base that summer, Hodges did not become a regular member of the Dodger carnival until 1947. He spent most of the intervening time in the Marines, where the Hodges legend quietly took form.

He served in the Pacific at

(continued)

Pearl Harbor, Okinawa and Tinian until he was discharged as a sergeant early in 1946. Don Hoak, who became his teammate with the Dodgers later, remembered that "we kept hearing stories about this big guy from Indiana who killed Japs with his bare hands."

Strong, Silent Man

Hodges was generally silent about his adventures as a jungle fighter, but once he returned to baseball his reputation grew as the strong, silent man with pale blue eyes who could hit balls with remarkable right-handed power.

He spent the 1946 season at Newport News, Va., in the Piedmont League as a catcher. Then in 1947 he joined the Dodgers, caught 28 games, gradually yielded his spot to Roy Campanella and in 1948 took over at first base.

The switch was arranged by Leo Durocher in one of his final tactical moves as manager of the Dodgers, and Hodges rapidly established himself as one of the surest fielders in baseball history.

He hit 23 home runs the next year, then 32 in 1950 and 40 in 1951. For seven straight years he hit more than 20 home runs.

On Aug. 31, 1950, Hodges hit four home runs and a single in one game. The same season he took part in 159 double plays at first base, and a year later he took part in 171. He hit 14 grand slam home runs for a National League career record. He finished with 1,921 hits, about 40 per cent of them for extra bases.

Hodges was part of the pride of Flatbush, the flamboyantly potent Dodger teams of Campanella, Duke Snider, Pee Wee Reese, Jackie Robinson, Pete Reiser, Carl Furillo, Cookie Lavagetto and later of Don Drysdale and the young Sandy Koufax.

Hodges suffered from some unusual lapses, but even these seemed to endear him to the public as human failings of a superman.

1953 a Big Season

He sometimes had trouble hitting curveballs. He had a fast-footwork style at first base that brought complaints that "he never touched the bag." He even tied a record by going to bat 21 times without a hit in the 1952 World Series.

But Hodges always seemed to possess the serenity and the strength to be a winner. In 1953, when his World Series slump extended into the regular season, he was flooded with letters of encouragement, good-will messages, charms and prayers. At midseason, he started to rally, finished the season with 32 home runs and then hit .364 in the Series with eight hits, including a home run.

Hodges surpassed even that performance in 1954, when he hit .304 with 42 homers and 130 runs batted in, and the next year he helped the Dodgers win their first world championship in a seven-game series against the Yankees.

When the Dodgers migrated to Los Angeles after the 1957 season, Hodges went with them. But his family moved back to Brooklyn after one year and re-established its home in Flatbush. Then, when the Mets were organized in 1962, they bought Hodges for $75,000 and for part of two seasons he helped them revive memories of the Dodgers and the good old days of National League baseball in New York.

His last season was 1963. He played in only 11 games, then on May 22 started his career as a manager by taking charge of the Washington Senators. He had never played in the American League and had never managed anywhere. But in five seasons he guided the Senators from last place to sixth, and then returned to the Mets in 1968 as manager where he had started—in the National League in New York.

"It's a good thing he's a nice guy," Pee Wee Reese said once, reviewing Hodges's role as a mild-mannered Tarzan. "With his strength, he had to be a peacemaker."

Reese recalled a fight he once had with Dee Fondy of the Chicago Cubs, and remembered most of all how it ended. Hodges moved quietly toward the husky Fondy, grasped him by the front of his uniform shirt, lifted him easily off the ground, and said:

"I don't know where you're going, Dee, but you're not going near Pee Wee."

"He's a gentle father," said his daughter Irene. "One word from him, though, can mean an awful lot."

Hodges married Joan Lombardi of Brooklyn in 1948, just as he was becoming a kind of institution in Brooklyn. They lived at first with Joan's parents on Hawthorne Street, then moved to Foster and Ocean Avenue, then to 32d Street and Avenue K, and finally into a house on Bedford Avenue in a residential neighborhood of Flatbush.

Hodges spent an occasional afternoon at the racetrack or an evening at the trotting track. But most of his free time was given to his family and to the Gil Hodges Lanes—a 48-lane bowling center in Brooklyn complete with four grandstand seats salvaged from Ebbets Field.

Suitably Impressed

The Hodges's four children were suitably impressed with their father. But they still tied

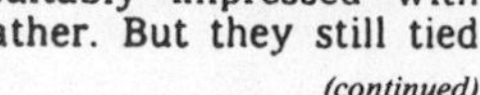

(continued)

The man who guided the New York Mets to their first World Championship.

up the family telephone so persistently that Hodges was forced to change the number several times.

"He's a devoted man," his wife said when he became manager of the Mets. "Devoted to his family, his work, his religion. There's only one thing he can do with the Mets—his best."

Hodges, in his first season with the Mets, quickly renewed all the old public esteem from the Dodger days.

Even though they wound up ninth, the Mets began to play a more business-like brand of baseball, won more games than any team in Met history and developed some of the best young pitchers in the game.

Hodges's adoring public was shocked on Sept. 24 of that season when he suffered a heart attack during the second inning of a game in Atlanta. But the manager recovered, and one year to the day later, the Mets clinched the National League's Eastern Division championship.

Within a few weeks, the Mets had added the pennant and the World Series to their collection of sudden riches—riches that earned the gentle giant an even more deeply imbedded spot in the hearts of New York baseball fans.

JOSEPH DURSO.

Transformer of Mets

Quiet but Forceful Hodges Changed Club Into Champions in 2 Seasons

By JOSEPH DURSO

"It was a colossal thing that they did," Gil Hodges said that October afternoon in 1969, while New York Mets poured champagne and danced with Pearl Bailey in their chaotic clubhouse in Shea Stadium. "These young men showed that you can realize the most impossible dream of all." As he spoke, he had been manager of the Mets for two seasons and had led them from last place in the National League to first—a team that had lost 101 games the year before he arrived and then had swept spectacularly to the top two months after man first walked on the moon. And his own contribution to that coup, a longtime baseball man said last night, was simple: "He took the clown out of the Mets."

An Appraisal

That is, Gilbert Ray Hodges deliberately set out to erase the "mystique" that had made the Mets rich, famous and cuddled as a sort of national joke — and that had drawn two million customers into their ball park.

He talked less than Casey Stengel, sermonized less than Wes Westrum and tolerated less than either. He gambled that the boys could become men and survive in the public's affection, and he won the gamble because the boys responded with the only result that could have survived the change: success.

Middle-Aged Eagle Scout

He took over the mammoth job of redirecting the Mets in the spring of 1968. He had powerful muscles and a gentle voice, he helped old ladies cross the street and young pitchers cross the infield. He was reverent, friendly, strong and silent. He had a reputation for shooting straight, and he kept his hands in his back pockets when arguing with umpires. He was a kind of middle-aged Eagle Scout.

He also had the problem of following one of the great acts on the public stage—Stengel's. And he knew that Stengel had had an absolutely clear view of his mission as master of the Mets: Not so much to build up the stamina of the team as to build up the stamina of the public for the team.

It was something that the interregnum of Westrum did not change from 1965 through 1967, and it was there when Hodges took over that spring day with the terse announcement to the circle of players: "My name is Hodges."

In pursuit of his own philosophy as manager of the lovable clowns of baseball, Hodges immediately laid down the law, quietly but absolutely. The curfew was midnight, the hotel bar was off limits, golf was permitted in spring training but not swimming, and everybody was expected in uniform by 9:30 in the morning.

That was an hour after he had arrived, and, during the regular season, the early bird players who got to the park by 4:30 for a night game found the Eagle Scout already in uniform, sitting in the swivel chair in the manager's office, planning the "platoon" moves that he followed on the field.

He enforced his quiet revolution through his coaches, three of whom accompanied him to New York from Washington, where he had worked small miracles with the Senators—Rube Walker, Eddie Yost and Joe Pignatano. He rarely stopped in the players' part of the clubhouse to chat, he levied fines but refused to discuss them publicly and, Tom Seaver once said, "He probably hasn't talked to me directly about pitching more than three times in three years."

He was, in short, an organization man, raised on the type of organization that had surrounded him with the Brooklyn Dodgers, especially under another strong and silent manager, Walter Alston.

To most of his players, his style added up to a "lack of communication." But after he suffered his first heart attack in September, 1968, they closed ranks around him and charged to their 1969 pennant while denying that any "conspiracy of silence" had been formed in the clubhouse to protect him.

This spring, Hodges appeared healthy and relaxed as the Mets won 15 of 23 games in Florida despite an agonizing series of injuries. He resumed smoking cigarettes, he drank coffee again, he hit grounders (one of which broke Jim Fregosi's thumb), he played golf a few times — and he had just played golf with his coaches yesterday when he collapsed in West Palm Beach.

True, he was surrounded by trouble. The team had finished third two years in a row. His key players were still injured, and all his players were on strike over pensions with the season's opening in doubt. But he was still the quiet man of baseball who had taken the clown out of the Mets and had steered them to the impossible dream of 1969.

STENGEL MOURNS A PERSONAL LOSS

GLENDALE, Calif., April 2 (UPI)—Casey Stengel, the first manager of the New York Mets, expressed his sorrow today over the death of Gil Hodges, who had played for him before becoming a manager.

"It's a personal loss to me, the club and to baseball," the retired Stengel said. "I was very close to him. I just got back from several weeks in Florida, where I spent most of my time with the Mets."

As a player, Stengel compared Hodges with Hal Chase whom he called the most graceful first baseman he had ever seen. But Stengel said what was remarkable about Hodges was that he became so great a first baseman as a right-hander and at a position other than the one in which he started—catching.

"The best remark he ever made, if anybody said anything about him was, 'My goodness, a man has a right to his opinion.' He had a terrific respect for standing up for the rights of himself and others."

Alston Recalls Help

LOS ANGELES, April 2 (UPI) — Walter Alston of the Los Angeles Dodgers, dean of major league managers, recalled today that Gil Hodges was one of the experienced players who helped make his job easier when Alston first took over the Brooklyn Dodgers in 1954 as a rookie manager.

Alston said: "Gil was that type of man. He never gave anyone any trouble; he was a great man on the field and off of it.

"We were quite close, and all I can say is that there was never a finer man in baseball than this gentleman. Baseball has lost a real big man."

Kuhn Calls Him Inspiration

Commissioner Bowie Kuhn praised Gil Hodges last night as a "thorough champion," saying:

"His unique decency and class inspired us all, and I thank God they will continue to do so in our memories of him."

Loss to Management

Special to The New York Times

WEST PALM BEACH, Fla., April 2—M. Donald Grant, chairman of the Mets' board of directors, said tonight: "On behalf of our entire organization and all of those who knew and loved Gil, I cannot adequately express our sorrow at this moment of great shock. Our hearts go out to his family, which is our primary concern now."

Bob Scheffing, Mets' vice president and general manager, added:

"Gil's loss will be felt by anyone and everyone who's been associated with baseball. I've lost someone whose friendship I can't possibly evaluate in words."

"All the News That's Fit to Print"

The New York Times.

LATE CITY EDITION
U. S. Weather Bureau Report (Page 47) forecasts: Fair and cold today and tonight. Some cloudiness and milder tomorrow.
Temp. range: 30—9. Yesterday: 24.3—13.9

VOL. CVIII . . No. 36,899. NEW YORK, MONDAY, FEBRUARY 2, 1959. FIVE CENTS
10 cents beyond 50-mile zone from New York City except on Long Island. Higher in air delivery cities.

BONN IS HOPEFUL VISIT BY DULLES WILL HEAL RIFTS

Expects Him to Try to Unify Western Allied Policies on the German Question

SMALLER NATIONS WARY

Looking to Re-examination of Basic NATO Stand on the Principal Issues

By SYDNEY GRUSON
Special to The New York Times.

BONN, Germany, Feb. 1—Diplomats and officials here expressed the view tonight that Secretary of State Dulles would seek on his European trip this week to patch up Western differences over how to proceed on the German question.

The Secretary has given no indication of what is on his mind, according to information available here. He simply requested that United States representatives in London, Paris and Bonn inquire whether a quick visit would be convenient.

Mr. Dulles is not believed to be bringing new proposals to deal with the problems raised by the Soviet demand that Western forces be withdrawn from Berlin. Rather, it is felt here, Washington has suddenly become alarmed over Allied differences that are beginning to show through the agreement achieved to meet the Soviet stand.

Assessment of Soviet Plan

The belief here, based on an assessment of the position disclosed at the Soviet Communist party congress, is that the West must reckon on the Russians' carrying out their threat to transfer their responsibilities in Berlin to the East German Communists.

With two of the six months' of grace allowed in the original proposal, made by Premier Nikita S. Khrushchev Nov. 27, already gone by, there still is no agreement on what should be done if the East Germans try to assume control of Allied communications to the city.

London has made it clear that it does not share Washington's belief in the necessity of using force on the land route to Berlin if the East Germans take over. Bonn believes this fundamental difference must be cleared up before the Allies can go on to other decisions concerning the possibility of a conference with the Russians.

The Allies are not even agreed on the value of a conference. But there is no inclination here to oppose one even though

Continued on Page 2, Column 5

MERCURY HITS 9, LOW FOR WINTER

Cold Expected to Last Here Today—Nation Gripped

The temperature dropped sharply early today to 9 degrees, the lowest reading of the winter.

The season's low was reached at 3 o'clock this morning. The previous low for the season, 12.5 degrees, was recorded on Dec. 22.

The mercury dropped more than 12 degrees in about nine hours. It was 24.3 degrees at 3:40 P. M. and dipped steadily through the evening. At midnight the temperature was down to 13.9 degrees.

The record low for a Feb. 2 in New York is 1 degree above zero, set in 1881.

The Weather Bureau said the cold was expected to continue through today. The highest temperature may be near 30, but northerly winds up to 20 miles an hour may make it seem colder.

The Weather Bureau also said there was a chance of rain or snow tomorrow.

A vast inflow of Arctic air gripped much of the nation yesterday. Freezing rain fell as far south as Texas and New Mexico.

The nation's low reading yesterday was 40 below zero at Bemidji, Minn. It was 33 below in Lone Rock, Wis., and 30 below in Williston, N. D.

Snow extended into the Texas Panhandle. It was a foot deep between Wichita, Kan., and northern Oklahoma. The weather caused ten traffic deaths in Texas.

U. S. Priest Prays in Moscow for Russia's Conversion

The Rev. Louis F. Dion, Ameri… ducting mass yesterday in t…

By The Associated Press.

MOSCOW, Feb. 1—An American Roman Catholic priest prayed in Moscow today for the conversion of Russia. The Rev. Louis F. Dion of Worcester, Mass., said low mass in a temporary …

1957 Bid for Sov… Laid to 'Anti-Part…

By The Associated Press.

MOSCOW, Feb. 1—Pravda gave new … the Kremlin's campaign against its so-called … ponents. The Communist party newspaper s… planned to tak… Soviet Governme… 18, 1957.

Quoting from a sp… the current Commun… congress by Alexei I. … ko, a Presidium membe… Premier Nikita S. Khr… Pravda said the anti-par… was quashed by a quick m… of the party's Central Com… tee only four days before … take-over date.

An earlier summary of … Kirichenko's speech, issued y… terday by Tass, Soviet pr… agency, did not go into detai… but said he had denounced th… anti-party group.

Members of the Group

The group includes former Premiers Nikolai A. Bulganin and Georgi M. Malenkov, former Foreign Ministers Vyacheslav M. Molotov and Dmitri T. Shepilov and Lazar M. Kaganovich, former economic boss. All have been moved to jobs in remote places. [Mikhail G. Pervukhin and Maksim Z. Saburov, leading economic officials, were added to the list last week.]

Mr. Kirichenko, who formerly served as party chief in the Soviet Premier's native Ukraine, now is a full member of the Presidium. He gave a chronology that began with the return of Mr. Khrushchev and Marshal Bulganin from a trip to Finland on June 14, 1957.

The Central Committee formally began its meeting June 22 and ended June 29. Then came the announcement of the disgrace of the four leaders.

Continued on Page 2, Column 2

FRANCO FOES JOIN IN A NEW PARTY

Spaniards of Widely Varying Views Unite in Movement Forbidden by Regime

By The Associated Press.

MADRID, Feb. 1—A group of liberal and Rightist Spaniards announced today the formation of a political party opposed to the regime of Generalissimo Francisco Franco.

The party, called Union Española (Spanish Union), is illegal because all political parties except the Falange, on which the regime is based, are forbidden by law.

The new party was formed at a dinner Thursday at which Joaquin Satrustegui Fernandez, a liberal monarchist and member of a wealthy family of Basque industrialists, made a strong speech against the regime.

He declared that General Franco had seized power illegally and had stayed in office by force.

General Franco seized power from the Spanish Republic in the civil war of 1936-39.

Madrid Awaits Reaction

The dinner, held publicly in a hotel in the heart of Madrid, was attended by nearly 100 army generals and other officers, bankers, lawyers, university professors and others.

Madrid now is awaiting the Government's reaction. Political sources said that if the Government did not act against the three speakers at the meeting, this would be an admission of weakness.

The new group includes a wide range of opinion, from the extreme Right, represented by José Maria Gil Robles, a Roman Catholic monarchist, to the Left.

Four left-of-center groups are not participating. They are the Socialists, the Anarchists, the Left-Wing Christian Democrats, headed by Manuel Gimenez Fernandez, a wealthy landowner who was Minister of Agriculture in the Spanish Republic, and the Social Democrats, headed by Dionisio Ridruejo.

Sources close to the Union Española said they believed a compromise on doctrine would be worked out to permit the participation of Señors Ridruejo and Gimenez Fernandez and possibly even the Anarchists.

Socialist representatives in

Continued on Page 2, Column 3

Willie Hoppe Dead; Master of Billiards

By United Press International.

MIAMI, Fla., Feb. 1—Willie Hoppe, a legend in the billiards world, died in a hospital here today after a long illness. He was 71 years old.

Hospitalized here last Sept. 18 after a heart attack, Mr. Hoppe succumbed at 4:40 P. M. apparently of a gastric hemorrhage, according to hospital authorities.

Mr. Hoppe, the only billiard player to give an exhibition at the White House, played before President William Howard Taft in 1911.

He won fifty-one world titles, the first in Paris in January 1906, when he was 18 years old, and the last in San Francisco in March, 1952.

During his years in retirement, Mr. Hoppe looked back with sorrow on the slow death of the sport.

"There's almost nobody left

Continued on Page 25, Column 4

s… la… Co… tha… signa…

The… weak… Copenh… Danish… Company… toft.

Resc…

The Uma… nals had b… trained oper… weak and ir… The Umanak's… that it appeared… tor was trying t… tress signals or a h…

Two radio stat… Greenland coast s… first signals had b… about 5 P. M. yester… New York time). T… were heard again between 10 and 11 P. M. and then disappeared.

The rescue center of the Royal Canadian Air Force at Halifax, N. S., reached by telephone early today said that none of its receiving centers, vessels or aircraft had heard the signals reported by the Danes. However, ships and planes in the search were advised of the Danish report, the center said.

The plight of the Hedtoft had plunged Denmark into a state of virtual mourning.

Denmark's state radio service canceled all light programs, special prayers were said in all churches and there was talk of dropping the winter shipping service to Greenland.

United States Coast Guard headquarters in New York said the search would continue. The Coast Guard cutter Campbell and three other vessels continued the hunt all day yesterday without finding any trace of lifeboats or wreckage of the passenger-cargo ship, which carried ninety-five persons.

Four C-54 aircraft of the United States Air Force scanned thousands of square miles of

Continued on Page 3, Column 2

CRIME RISE IN CITY IS SHOWN FOR '58; JUVENILE RATE UP

Major Offenses Climb 5.2%, Lesser Ones 3.4, Police Say—Higher for Youth

Major crimes in the city last year increased 5.2 per cent over 1957 and misdemeanors were up 3.4 per cent.

The Police Department's annual crime figures, made public yesterday, showed an even greater increase in youth arrests. In the under-16 category 11,570 arrests were made for juvenile delinquency, compared with 9,886 in the year before. This was a rise of 17 per cent.

In the 16-to-20 age group there were 1?,750 arrests, against … 1957, or an increase … cent.

…s showed a juvenile …se in murder, felo… …, rape, burglary, …eft and carrying …pons, but there …bery and grand …

…Homicide

… group in… …d in every … both age …of arrests … declined. …were ar… …d non… … three …s year. … there …com… …57. … re…

2 Virginia School Systems Begin Integration Today

Four Negroes Will Enter 7th Grade at Arlington —Violence Doubted

By ANTHONY LEWIS
Special to The New York Times.

ARLINGTON, Va., Feb. 1—Arlington County officials expect quiet acceptance tomorrow of Virginia's first school integration.

Four Negro seventh-graders will enter Stratford Junior High School along with 1,700 white children.

While the expectation is for a peaceful transition, officials are taking no chances. They have taken extraordinary precautions against violence around the school or recalcitrant students inside.

More than fifty policemen will be stationed around Stratford, along with many radio cars. Traffic will be blocked off on some near-by streets and parking banned on many. No one but students, teachers and other school employes will be allowed on the school grounds.

The school board has issued this warning:

"Any student creating a disturbance will automatically be

Continued on Page 9, Column 2

Norfolk Will Admit 17 at Institutions Closed by Almond in Fall

By HOMER BIGART
Special to The New York Times.

NORFOLK, Va., Feb. 1—Norfolk is awaiting with an air of studied casualness the first integration of its public schools tomorrow.

At 9 A. M., six previously all-white secondary schools, closed by the state last September to avoid integration, will open to receive seventeen Negro students.

The schools had an enrollment of 10,000 white students when they were shut, but only about 7,500 are expected to answer roll-call tomorrow.

No one knows how many will stay away in protest against integration. But hundreds that were sent to distant cities for schooling are unlikely to return for this semester.

Other hundreds, who simply dislike schools, will take advantage of the repeal yesterday of the state's compulsory attendance law.

With Little Rock in mind, officials plan to make tomorrow's reopening as normal as

Continued on Page 8, Column 3

Jewish Body Sees Segregation Here, Bids Schools Act

The New York Metropolitan Council of the American Jewish Congress charged yesterday that racial discrimination existed in the city's public schools.

"Tens of thousands" of Negro …nd Puerto Rican children, the …uncil declared, are receiving …ferior education in "segregat… …schools. The group asserted … a recent statement by Su… …endent of Schools John J. …ld, denying that discrimi… …xisted, "was contradict… …ve separate reports of … of Education's own …n on Integration."

…tion Charged

…r to the Board of …e council called for …ion to end "de … in fact rather …regation in the …The statement … Howard M. …n of the coun… …n Law and … … that the …on many …s made …Commis… which … was …iver, …ard, …hur …of

…Disputed; …n Corn Experiment

…'s Power to Produce Color in Kernel Vanishes After a Combining Test

By JOHN W. FINNEY
Special to The New York Times.

WASHINGTON, Feb. 1—One of the basic axioms of modern genetics—the "individuality" of the gene—has been challenged in research sponsored by the National Science Foundation.

For the first time in a half century of genetics research, a case has been discovered where the gene, an element of the germ plasm, did not follow the rule of "individuality" in passing on its characteristics to succeeding generations.

The foundation said that "this discovery may well turn out to be among the most significant basic discoveries in genetics."

It may now become necessary, the foundation said, to discover a new mechanism to explain genetic mutations, which are responsible for evolutionary changes.

The foundation described the results of the research into the "individuality of genes" in its latest annual report. The research was performed by Prof. R. Alexander Brink at the University of Wisconsin under grants from the foundation.

Associated Press
Prof. R. Alexander Brink

The concept of the individuality of the gene dates to the birth of modern genetics nearly a century ago with Gregor J. Mendel, Austrian botanist. It has been a basic tenet of genetic theory.

The individuality theory

Continued on Page 28, Column 3

CARLINO SCUTTLES CITY BETTING PLAN

Assembly Leader Declares 'Responsible Republicans' Oppose Off-Track Tax

By DOUGLAS DALES

Majority Leader Joseph F. Carlino of the State Assembly apparently exploded yesterday any hope of the Wagner Administration that legalized off-track betting might rescue the city from its financial dilemma.

The Long Beach Republican declared that he not only opposed immediate legalization of off-track betting, but opposed also the alternate proposal to submit the question to a referendum.

Mayor Wagner has proposed the legalization of off-track betting as the principal source of revenue to close a $145,000,000 gap in the city's expense budget for the fiscal year starting July 1. The Administration has estimated that the tax would yield between $80,000,000 and $160,000,000.

Interviewed on a radio broadcast, Mr. Carlino said his views were shared generally by "those in positions of responsibility" among the Republicans in the Legislature.

'A Dangerous Concept'

Terming off-track betting a "dangerous concept," he said:

"I think it would create many …ore problems than it would …lve. I have grave doubts as … the amount of money to be …aised by off-track betting, but I have no doubts as to the tremendous damage that it would do to the security, financial stability and even the welfare of the average middle-income or lower-income family."

Mr. Carlino said he did not favor referendums to decide every question that came along and predicted that the Legislature would not authorize one for off-track betting.

"People who are elected to positions of responsibility," he said, "should not turn over every serious question for a determination in a referendum.

Rockefeller Gain Seen

"There are certain areas where referendums are very useful instruments, but I think we are elected to provide the leadership and mold the thinking of people, particularly in areas where the results might be damaging and might not be fully understood by those who innocently may advocate a course of this kind."

In a defense of Governor Rockefeller's proposals for new state taxes, which will be submitted to the Legislature today, Mr. Carlino said he believed the public would accept the necessity for the increases when all the facts had been presented.

Asked whether the tax program had tarnished some of the Governor's pre-election luster, the Assembly leader replied:

"I wouldn't think so. I think that in the final analysis a public official who takes a strong

Continued on Page 7, Column 1

ROCKEFELLER ASKS RECORD TAX RISE IN BUDGET TODAY

275 Million in New Levies Listed in State's First 2-Billion Program

GOVERNOR TO BE ON TV

Shows Deep Concern About Opposition—Wagner Plan for New Impost Due Soon

By LEO EGAN
Special to The New York Times.

ALBANY, Feb. 1—The Legislature was bracing itself tonight against the expected shock of receiving tomorrow the largest budget and tax program in the state's history.

Governor Rockefeller's budget and tax program are scheduled for submission to the Legislature at a special midday session.

Later in the week Mayor Wagner is expected to submit his request for a broadening of New York City's taxing powers.

Advance indications have been that Mr. Rockefeller will ask for $275,000,000 in new state taxes to balance the first $2,000,000,000 budget in the state's history. This would be the largest increase in state taxes ever requested by a Governor at one time.

Twenty years ago the total expenditures of the state were only $46,000,000.

New York to Seek Aid

Mayor Wagner's program reportedly involves a request to the Legislature to authorize New York City to levy $145,000,000 more in non-property taxes. Since the city is already levying the maximum real estate tax permitted by the State Constituton it cannot get any more money from this source.

Governor Rockefeller has indicated deep concern about possible opposition to his tax program. For this reason he has scheduled a special state-wide television program for tomorrow night to explain and justify his tax requests to the public.

The telecast has already been recorded on tape. It will originate in New York City and will be carried over station WRCA-TV, Channel 4, from 6:15 to 6:30 P. M.

Joseph H. Murphy of Syracuse, new chairman of the State Tax Commission, and Dr. T. Norman Hurd, the State Budget Director, are reported to be the main architects of the tax program Mr. Rockefeller will submit to the Legislature.

Both are old hands at draft-

Continued on Page 6, Column 5

MAYOR SEEKS PACT IN TUGBOAT STRIKE

City Hall Meetings Follow Union Rejection of Offer

By WERNER BAMBERGER

Striking tugboat workers voted by the narrow margin of 1,100 to 916 yesterday to continue a walkout that had begun at midnight. Mayor Wagner immediately called the disputants to City Hall in an effort to end the strike.

A joint meeting was held, and Mayor Wagner said after it that the union and the employers would try to resume negotiations tomorrow. The meeting, which lasted fifty minutes, ended at 9:05 P. M.

The Mayor also announced that the employers—the Marine Towing and Transportation Employers Association—would meet with its members today and would ask them to schedule a meeting with the union negotiating committee tomorrow.

The union, he said, had indicated its readiness to attend such a meeting, which would be held under the auspices of Federal and city mediators.

Mr. Wagner added that he had been assured that the fuel supply in New York City was "much better than normal."

Shortly before the City Hall meeting ended, a spokesman for the five heating-oil associations in the metropolitan area issued a statement describing supplies as ample.

Mayor Wagner explained that he had called the meeting to impress upon the parties the "grave responsibility to find a

Continued on Page 12, Column 6

Willie Hoppe Dead; Master of Billiards

By United Press International.

MIAMI, Fla., Feb. 1—Willie Hoppe, a legend in the billiards world, died in a hospital here today after a long illness. He was 71 years old.

Hospitalized here last Sept. 18 after a heart attack, Mr. Hoppe succumbed at 4:40 P. M. apparently of a gastric hemorrhage, according to hospital authorities.

Mr. Hoppe, the only billiard player to give an exhibition at the White House, played before President William Howard Taft in 1911.

He won fifty-one world titles, the first in Paris in January 1906, when he was 18 years old, and the last in San Francisco in March, 1952.

During his years in retirement, Mr. Hoppe looked back with sorrow on the slow death of the sport.

"There's almost nobody left

Continued on Page 25, Column 4

Willie Hoppe, 71, Dies in South; Billiards Master Half Century

Continued From Page 1, Col. 3

now to stimulate interest in the game," he said recently. "They're all dead and an old-timer like myself can't do it alone. I guess the youngsters have more important things to do nowadays than to play billiards."

Mr. Hoppe always opposed those who maintained that pool halls helped to breed juvenile delinquents.

"The pool hall is a great leveler," he often said. "In my day, shoe-shine boys mingled and played against millionaires and each benefited from the association. And juvenile delinquency was nothing more than a minor problem then."

Won 51 World Titles

At first a "boy wonder," Mr. Hoppe was the acknowledged and repeatedly proved grand master of billiards for nearly half a century.

As early as 1899, when the top of his head came barely level to the top of the table, Mr. Hoppe was hailed as a lad of "brilliant promise" with excellent prospects of becoming the world's best billiard player. He had to stand on a crate to make his shots.

Mr. Hoppe's long career began in the small town of Cornwall-Landing-on-Hudson, N. Y., where his father kept a small hotel and barber shop. A battered billiard table helped to amuse travelers who had stopped.

For William Frederick Hoppe and his older brother, Frank, there were no other games. They stayed indoors and practiced billiards.

"Father was one tough taskmaster," Mr. Hoppe recalled. "He trained my brother Frank and me so we could trim all the visiting drummers."

A Grand Master

In the spring of 1895, when Mr. Hoppe was 8 and his brother was 10, their father took them on a barnstorming tour of upstate towns. It led, finally, to an exhibition at the famous Maurice Daly Academy at Broadway and Thirty-first Street.

Willie struck Daly's fancy by scrambling onto the table for a difficult shot, then flopping onto the floor to get out of the way of the cue ball.

The tour paid better than barbering and hotel-keeping; the boys' father sold his business and took his skilled children on longer rounds of smoky pool halls and lavish billiard academies.

Mr. Hoppe was to spend nearly the rest of his life on the road—in championship play, cross-country marathon matches, exhibitions and international competitions. His suave manner, flawless grooming and rock-calm play made him a favorite with spectators.

It was a drizzly night in January, 1906, when the 18-year-old Mr. Hoppe met the great Maurice Vignaux of France in the ballroom of the Grand Hotel in Paris for the world 18.1 balkline championship.

The boy was nervous and missed some plays at the start, but he kept control. When the match was over, the score was 500 to 323, and Mr. Hoppe was the champion of the world.

When he took up three-cushion billiards, some thought it posed a threat to his mastery of the older version of the game. In 1936, Mr. Hoppe said he thought he would give up three-cushion competition. But he was tempted from "retirement," and it was in three-cushion play that he won his greatest victory.

This occurred in the world tournament in Chicago in 1940. In a field of eleven players, Mr. Hoppe won every one of twenty games. Thereafter, he dominated the three-cushion field, winning the championship in eleven of thirteen seasons.

Parallel Lines Drawn

In balkline billiards, parallel lines are drawn either eighteen or fourteen inches from each cushion. The cue ball must make a carom with two object balls, but varying restrictions are made as to hitting balls in the corner or side areas of the table.

In three-cushion billiards, the cue ball must touch the cushions three times before making a carom.

Both balkline and three-cushion are played on pocketless tables. They are generally regarded as experts' games. In the United States, pocket billiards—common garden variety pool—is the most popular game. The object here is to call the pockets and put the balls in without sinking the cue ball.

Mr. Hoppe had great competitive drive. He was hospitalized with a fever of 106 degrees just before the 1941 world's three-cushion championship tournament in Chicago. The tournament was well under way before he fought off a threat of pneumonia and induced physicians to release him. Then he caught up by playing a match every day, winning sixteen of seventeen in an eighteen-player field to retain the title.

Ten years later Mr. Hoppe still had the same determination. At the end of the 1950 world three-cushion meet on Chicago's Navy Pier, he was tied with Joe Chamaco of Mexico City. There also was a tie in the pocket billiards division.

In the interests of showmanship, management and players agreed on a play-off after only a twenty-minute rest. At that time Mr. Hoppe was 62 years old.

He sprawled on a cot, with his tuxedo and shoes beside him, got up at the summons to action and beat Chamaco, 50 to 28. Mr. Hoppe said the twenty-minute wait was the worst part.

Mr. Hoppe quit tournament play as a champion in 1952 after a successful defense of the world's three-cushion title in San Francisco. He appeared in exhibition matches after his retirement to Miami.

Surviving are a son, William F. Jr. of Sonora, Calif.; a daughter, Alice of Los Angeles; three sisters, and a brother, Albert Hoppe of Miami. Mr. Hoppe's elder brother, Frank, died many years ago.

The legendary Willie Hoppe—one of the greatest billiards players of all time.

The New York Times MONDAY, JANUARY 7, 1963.

Hornsby, in Death, Acclaimed for Great Hitting

CHICAGO, Jan. 6 (AP)—The frankness and bluntness that characterized the great Rogers Hornsby in life were there at the end—rather symbolized in a succinct request of "no flowers, please."

"He didn't like flowers and his desire was that none be sent," said his stepdaughter, Mary Beth Porter. "He wanted any such money to go to the National Heart Fund instead."

She and her mother, his third wife, were at the bedside of baseball's famed Rajah when he died yesterday morning in Wesley Memorial Hospital at the age of 66.

An autopsy revealed that death came from a heart condition known as myocardial infraction in which the blood supply to heart muscles is blocked and the muscles die.

The man for whom baseball

Rogers Hornsby

was the breath of life had undergone a cataract operation Dec. 10. He had suffered a small stroke Dec. 14.

His condition was reported improving until late Friday night when he developed a high temperature and lung congestion.

Funeral services will be Tuesday at 3 P.M. (Eastern standard time) at Drake and Son Funeral Home, 5300 Northwestern Ave., Chicago. Burial will be Thursday from the family home in Bend, Tex., near Austin.

Hornsby, shy and retiring despite his outspoken nature, was elected to baseball's Hall of Fame in 1942.

At least three other members of the Hall of Fame — Ray Schalk, Ted Lyons, and Gabby Hartnett—will be honorary pallbearers along with Rip Collins, Lou Boudreau, Johnny Mostil, Frank Parenti and Glen Miller.

The Rajah was hired and fired as manager by five major league clubs.

He was considered by many as the greatest right-handed hitter in baseball history with a lifetime batting average of .358.

He batted over .400 in successive years, a modern record of .424 in 1924 with the St. Louis Cardinals and .403 in 1925.

Hornsby was a rugged individualist and a man who walked alone. He shunned social gatherings, music, books, and even the company of other ballplayers.

One of his most remarkable achievements was winning the National League's Most Valuable Player award in 1920 with the Cardinals when the great second baseman went through the season with a painfully injured heel. He kept it a secret from everyone except his manager and trainer.

When it at last became known, Hornsby, in a typical candor, said: "There wasn't any use telling the world about my sore foot. The ball club needed me and it was up to me to get around the best way possible."

Rogers Hornsby, winner of seven league batting titles, would stand as far away from the plate as he could.

The New York Times MONDAY, DECEMBER 15, 1980

Elston Howard, Yank Star for Many Years, Dies at 51

By THOMAS ROGERS

Elston Howard, the first black to play for the New York Yankees, who was named the American League's most valuable player in 1963, died early yesterday of cardiac arrest at Columbia Presbyterian Medical Center, where he had been a patient since Dec. 2. He was 51 years old.

Since February 1979, Howard had suffered with myocardinitis, an inflammation of the muscles around the heart.

He had coached at first base and worked with catchers for the Yankees since his retirement as a player after the 1968 season. He was not active in baseball last year, but returned to the Yankees this year as an administrative assistant to George Steinbrenner, the club's principal owner.

In 1955, eight years after Jackie Robinson had become the first black to play in the majors as a member of the Brooklyn Dodgers, Howard joined the Yankees. An outfielder who had been converted in the Yankee minor league system to catcher, Howard first was used as a backup to Yogi Berra, the regular catcher. Then Manager Casey Stengel made use of his fielding versatility and potent bat by playing him in the outfield, at first base and more and more as catcher.

A Dependable Hitter

Whatever his position, Howard, who batted and threw right-handed, was one of the Yankees' most dependable hitters, averaging .274 with 167 home runs over 14 seasons. He gradually took over the catching job and won Gold Glove awards at that posiition in 1963 and 1964.

In 1963 he won the honor as the league's most valuable player after batting .287 with 28 home runs and 85 runs batted in.

He appeared in 10 World Series and was a member of four world championship teams. In 1958 he was given the Babe Ruth Award as the outstanding player in the Series. Over 54 Series games, he batted .246 with five home runs.

He was also named to the American League All-Star team nine times.

"Ellie was a permanent fixture in the Yankee picture," Cedric Tallis, the team's executive vice president, said yesterday. "He was one of the most popular Yankees of all time. He represented the team at many functions, giving speeches and meeting people. He also helped coach minor league players, especially catchers, during spring training. And he was always helpful in evaluating players during consultations on trades. He was a humble and unique man."

Steinbrenner said:

"We have lost a dear friend and a vital part of the organization. If indeed humility is a trademark of many great men, with that as a measure, Ellie was one of the truly great Yankees."

Traded to Red Sox in 1967

In 1967, near the end of his 13th season with the Yankees, he was traded to the Boston Red Sox and helped them to win the pennant. After batting only .241 with Boston in 1968, he retired as a player and returned to the Yankees as the first black coach in the American League.

During the 1970's he was often mentioned as a candidate for managerial positions, but was never selected to run a major league team.

Elston Gene Howard was born in St. Louis on Feb. 23, 1929. In high school he starred in football, basketball and baseball. He turned down many offers of college athletic scholarships and entered professional baseball, initially with the Kansas City Monarchs of the Negro League. Soon he attracted the Yankees' attention.

After two years of service in the Army, he played with Kansas City of the American Association in 1953, showing promise. He went to Toronto of the International League in 1954, when he batted .330 with 22 home runs.

The Yankees assigned Bill Dickey, one of their great catchers, to teach Howard the fine points of the position. He quickly mastered the basic fielding skills and the knack of handling pitchers, but had to wait a long while before taking over the starting job from Berra.

His career bloomed in 1961, when he batted .348 and cracked 21 home runs. He was then the starting Yankee catcher, remaining so until being traded to Boston in 1967.

"Elston exemplified the Yankee class of the 1950's and 1960's," said Dick Howser, the former Yankee manager who knew Howard as a teammate and a fellow coach since 1967. "Class was the way to describe the guy. He epitomized the Yankee tradition. Everybody in baseball respected the guy."

Elston Howard in his coaching days.

"All the News That's Fit to Print."

The New York Times.

Copyright, 1929, by The New York Times Company.

THE WEATHER
Fair today; tomorrow showers and cooler.

VOL. LXXIX....No. 26,178. NEW YORK, THURSDAY, SEPTEMBER 26, 1929. TWO CENTS

MILLER HUGGINS DIES; MANY PAY TRIBUTE

Manager of Yankees' Baseball Team for 12 Seasons Is a Victim of Blood Poisoning.

LEAGUE'S GAMES TODAY OFF

Group He Led to Three World Championships Will Attend the Funeral Here Tomorrow.

Miller J. Huggins, for twelve seasons manager of the New York Yankees and one of the most noted figures in baseball, died yesterday afternoon at 3:15 o'clock in St. Vincent's Hospital. The man who had won fame with the Yankees, which under his guidance captured six pennants and three world's championships, was a victim of blood poisoning brought on by an infection beneath his left eye.

Huggins, who was 50 years old, became unconscious early yesterday morning, and the battle which he had waged since last Friday was virtually over, for Dr. Edward H. King, his physician, said then that his patient had only hours to live.

When the end came there were close by, his sister, who had been for years his constant companion; his brother, Arthur Huggins; his friend of many years' standing and his business partner, Bob Connery; Charles McManus, superintendent of the Yankee Stadium; Dr. King and several nurses.

Toward the end Huggins was able to fight his illness with courage alone, for the once wiry strength that he had combined with remarkable skill to make himself into one of the brilliant second basemen of a decade or more ago had long since left him.

Sorrow Is Widespread.

Sorrow was felt all over the baseball world when news of his death became known. Colonel Jacob Ruppert, owner of the Yankees, who looked upon his manager more as a

Continued on Page Twenty-two.

MACDONALD MAY ASK RUM TREATY CHANGE ON HIS VISIT HERE

Capital Reports Say I'm Alone Case Will Figure in Talks With Hoover.

POSSIBILITIES DISCUSSED

Prohibition of Extreme Measures Against Fleeing Craft Might Be Considered.

CANADIAN OWNERS MOVE

Outline Their Position in Arbitration of I'm Alone Case With Their Government.

Lincoln's Bed for MacDonald During His White House Visit

MRS. HOOVER HERE FOR GIRL SCOUT FUND

She Opens Art Exhibition to Help Raise $3,000,000 for Development Program.

ANNOUNCES $500,000 GIFT

Girls, Leaders and Money Are Needed, She Says—Visits the Theatre—To Shop Today.

...Carry 400 Passengers; ...Hull and Rest on Water

HURRICANE MOVES SLOWLY ON FLORIDA; COAST IS PREPARED

Cities, Utilities and Red Cross Mobilize for Emergency and Take Precautions.

BLOW DUE AFTER DAYLIGHT

People in Everglades Go to High Ground as Lake Waters Rise and Barometer Falls.

CUBA SENDS A WARNING

Great Storm From Bahamas Will Hit Between Palm Beach and Miami, It Says.

Storm Cuts Bahaman Radio; 'Something Wrong at Nassau'

Hoover to Visit Rhode Island; May Open Mt. Hope Bridge

Special to The New York Times.

WASHINGTON, Sept. 25.—President Hoover today told Senator Hebert of Rhode Island he plans to visit Rhode Island some time between the present time and next Summer.

Senator Hebert called to ask the President to press an electric button from the White House on Oct. 10 marking the opening of the new Mount Hope Bridge which spans Mount Hope Bay, connecting the Newport and Bristol (R. I.) roads. The President is understood to have indicated that he would probably do so.

The President also was invited by the Senator to attend the dedication of a soldiers' memorial at Providence on Armistice Day.

ROTHSTEIN INQUIRY PLEDGED BY CRAIN

Tammany Candidate, in Line With Rival, Indicates He Will Investigate Fully.

DIFFERS WITH BANTON

Praises Him, but Holds That It Is Prosecutor's Duty to Sift as Well as Try Cases.

'BRITISH DOCUMENT' WILL BE DISCLOSED IN CALLING SHEARER

Senate Committee to Reveal Contents While Examining Him Monday.

SAID TO SHOW HOSTILITY

And Suggest to Lloyd George United States of Europe Aimed at America.

SHEARER SPENT BIG SUMS

They Ran Into "Six Figures," He Says in Letter—Pay Agent Is a Witness.

Prince of Wales Has Never Been in Love And Won't Wed Until He Is, Book Says

...Eternal Calendar ...Orders Day Off in Five for Workers

MILLER J. HUGGINS DIES HERE, AGED 50

Continued from Page 1, Column 4.

son that an employee, was grief-stricken. So was Ed Barrow, business manager of the club, who had fought beside Huggins through the many years that the latter was constructing what came to be known as one of the great teams of all times.

Hundreds of telephone calls and telegrams from baseball fans had poured into the club offices since it became known last Sunday that Huggins had been taken ill and removed to the hospital. Late yesterday afternoon telephone and telegraph messages flooded the offices, expressing sympathy and condolences.

Today all games in the American League are called off by order of President Ernest Barnard. Tomorrow the Yankee players will pay a final tribute to their departed dead. The Yankee-Washington game at Washington will be postponed and the players brought on to New York to attend the funeral services. The simple services will be held at the Little Church Around the Corner at 2 o'clock tomorrow afternoon. Dr. J.E. Price of the Washington Heights Methodist Episcopal Church, a life-long friend, will officiate.

The services will be brief and two hours later the body will be placed upon a Pennsylvania Railroad train bound for Cincinnati, where Huggins was born and where he will be buried beside his mother and his father.

Death Came Quickly

The death of Huggins came with shocking swiftness. A week ago today he was suffering apparently only from a slight infection beneath his eye. On that day he made an engagement with a friend among the baseball writers to play a round of golf last Sunday, but on Sunday he was fighting the fight of his life, and although he gained on that day and blood transfusions helped temporarily, the poison spread throughout his system. Desperate efforts were made by Dr. King and more blood transfusions were given. Monday he rallied somewhat, but apparently he knew his own fate better than those friends who gathered about his bedside, for he called in his pastor and his lawyer.

Shortly afterward he lapsed into unconsciousness, never again to revive completely, although he muttered the names of friends and dear ones. Yesterday morning, after a night that saw his temperature rise slowly to the danger point, he slipped off into a coma from which he never emerged. He had suffered greatly before he became unconscious, but never complained and smiled wanly throughout.

Born in Cincinatti.

Miller Huggins was born in the famous old Fourth Ward of Cincinnati, then known as one of the roughest in the Ohio city, on April 19, 1879, according to the family records, though the baseball records give the date as March 27, 1880. Huggins grew up in a neighborhood where he had to learn to fight his own battles. And this he always did. He was handicapped by his size—he was 5 feet 4 inches tall and never weighed more than 145 pounds. Yet despite that he took his place alongside of big men and held his own as a player and almost performed miracles as a manager.

Huggins came to the Yankees in the war year of 1918 after Colonel Ruppert and Colonel T.L. Huston, then half owner of the club, had had three failures in the years since

Miller Huggins with "Colonel" Jacob Ruppert, owner of the New York Yankees. Huggins was manager of the 1927 Yankees — probably the greatest team in baseball history.

they bought the club from the old Farrell regime. The New York club was the weak link in the American League, and President Ban Johnson, who had known Huggins and had followed his career, first as a player at St. Paul, Cincinnati and then at St. Louis and the Cardinals and as the manager of the Cardinals from 1913 to 1917, introduced Huggins to Colonel Ruppert and recommended him for the job.

Ruppert signed Huggins, who took charge in 1918. The Yankees had finished last in 1917. Huggins, commanding no particular respect for his past achievements and with material that was good only in spots, brought his team to the finish line in fourth place in 1918, which in itself was an achievement. And through eleven more seasnos Huggins's men finished worse than third only once—in 1925, when they wound up the season in seventh place.

The signing of Huggins did not bring about complete harmony between the two owners of the Yankees. Colonel Huston, who aspired to own a pennant winner as quickly as possible, did not quite agree with the painstaking methods of Huggins, so that the new manager had trouble from within and trouble from without. With the advent of Babe Ruth in 1920 as one his players, more troubles piled upon his frail frame Ruth was hard to manage in those days and in the years that followed when Huggins was forced to discipline Ruth by heavy fines and suspensions. Huggins lost the backing of fans. But only for a time.

When the disciplined Ruth burst forth as a still greater star and when youngsters schooled by Huggins began to blossom forth as stars and when the first pennant came to Huggins in 1921 things began to change and the criticism that had been directed at him subsided. It became apparent that New York had a real manager. In time that belief became complete and permanent. Huggins won pennants in 1921, 1922 and 1923, and in the latter year his first world's championship, cementing his hold on the New York public, which continued to stand by him in 1924 and 1925 when the team failed, finishing second in 1924 and seventh in 1925. In 1926 Huggins came back to win his fourth pennant. This was followed with pennants in 1927 and 1928. In those last two years he won two world's championships, beating the Pirates four straight games in 1927 and the Cardinals four in a row last year, which set a record never before approached.

This year luck was against him. Ruth was ill for a long while in the early part of the season and other ill and injured players hampered the progress of the club. Huggins's worry regarding the collapse of his one-time world's champions preyed on his mind and, it is believed, hastened his end. This worry added to the illness that had followed him for years—a series of misfortunes which cluminated in an attack of influenza a year ago last Spring and kept him in bed for three weeks at one stretch and two weeks at another—left him in weak physical condition.

For years he had been a highly nervous man, his condition aggravated by bad teeth, a poor digestion and an inability to rest.

The courage which carried Huggins through the past six years also had enabled him to become a great baseball player in his late teens. At that time he played second base on the Shamrocks, a fast semi-pro team in Cincinnati. In 1899 he played with a team organized by the late Colonel Julius Fleishman of Cincinnati, who was Mayor of that city for many years and also a stockholder in the Cincinnati Reds.

Fleishman, himself a great lover of baseball and a player in his younger days, first realized the skill of Huggins. It was Fleishman who sent Huggins to Mansfield, Ohio, for his first professional engagement, and who engineered his sale to the St. Paul club of the American Associatio in 1900 and his acquisition as a member of the Reds in 1904.

That started Huggins on his major league career as a player that was not to end until 1916. During that time Huggins became one of the most accomplished of fielders, and a batter who ammassed an all-time major league average of .265 and often went above .300 despite the handicap of size. As a lead-off man he had few equals.

He was traded to the Cardinals in the Winter of 1909. He became manager of the Cards in 1913, and remained as the pilot until the end of the 1917 season when his release was negotiated so that he could join the Yankees.

While a member of the Cincinnati Reds Huggins found time to study law, and for three years applied himself to the task, finally graduating from the Cincinnati Law School. He never practiced the profession, however, although he found his knowledge of law a big help in his business enterprises, especially those connected with his real estate ventures in St. Petersburg, Fla., where he had made his Winter home in recent years.

NEWS HALTS YANKEES' GAME.

Special to The New York Times.

BOSTON, Sept. 25—The news of the death of Miller Huggins, manager of the New York Yankees, occasioned a temporary break today in the game between the Yankess and the Boston Red Sox, during which the two rival teams and the 7,000 spectators in Fenway Park united at the end of the fifth inning in a tribute of silence.

For exactly one minute by Umpire McGowan's watch an impressive stillness settled over the field, while the two teams and three umpires assembled at home plate and stood with heads bared and bowed. In the stands the 7,000 spectators rose.

The stillness was broken only by noises from the traffic on the streets outside and by the voice of an announcer megaphoning to every section of the stands word of Huggin's death.

During the one-minute pause the flag in centre field was lowered to half staff. The Yankees, most of whom did not know of their manager's death until the word came for them to assemble at the end of the fifth inning, looked crushed. It was as if the news had come to them without warning. Until the news flash came over the wires to Fenway park they had not given up hope even though they knew the seriousness of their leader's fight, even though their earnest and repeated inquires of the past three days and nights had brought them nothing but discouragement, even though they knew hope had been abandoned by the bedside watches.

For sixty seconds they stood at the home plate, a few fidgeting with their toes in the dust some with their shoulders or heads quivering but most of them stonily immovable.

Then they turned and trudged back to their dugout on the third-base flank of the grand stand. The scene became a ball game again, with only the flag flapping at half staff in centre field to mark Huggins's death.

The Yankees won the game by a score of 11 to 10 in eleven innings.

The New York Times THURSDAY, DECEMBER 6, 1951

JOE JACKSON DIES; FIGURE IN BASEBALL

'Shoeless Joe' Was One of Stars on 1919 White Sox Involved in World Series Scandal

GREENVILLE, S. C., Dec. 5 (UP) "Shoeless Joe" Jackson, a prominent figure in the 1919 White Sox world series scandal, died of a heart attack here tonight.

Along with seven other White Sox players, he was barred for life from organized baseball by the late Judge Kenesaw Mountain Landis. Involved with Mr. Jackson in the scandals were Oscar Felsch, Arnold Gandil, George Weaver, Charles Risberg, Fred McMullin, Eddie Cicotte and Claude Williams.

Mr. Jackson hit .375 in the 1919 White Sox-Cincinnati series, which the Reds won, five games to three. The exiled players were accused of accepting bribes to "throw" the series games.

The story is told of a youngster who, when the scandal broke, tugged tearfully at Mr. Jackson's sleeve, begging the great outfielder to "say it ain't so, Joe."

He received the nickname "Shoeless Joe" because he was supposed to have once played the outfield without shoes in the minors because of a sore heel. But Joe was no clown on the diamond. He was one of the game's most feared and respected hitters. He also was fast on the bases, stealing 202 of them in the majors with a high of forty-one in 1911.

Lauded by Ty Cobb

"Shoeless Joe" Jackson, one of the best remembered of the players who rocked baseball with its great scandal more than thirty years ago, was one of the great outfielders of the game. As expert an observer of baseball talent as Ty Cobb, once said he was the finest natural hitter in the game.

"He batted against spitballs, shineballs, emeryballs and all the other trick deiveries now outlawed. He never figured anything out or studied anything with the same scientific approach I gave it," said Mr. Cobb. "He just swung. If he'd have had any knowledge of batting his average would have been truly phenomenal."

One of the game's tragic characters, even without that knowledge, he was a tremendous hitter, nevertheless. One year he batted .408, only to lose the batting championship to Cobb, who hit .420.

"Shoeless Joe" was born in Brandonville, S. C., adjoining Greenville, on June 19, 1888, and lived in or near Greenville for most of his sixty-three yars. He always maintained his innocense of any wrongdoing in connection with the scandal. In 1933, he applied to Judge Landis for reinstatement, but the judge refused, saying:

"Several others have asked for reinstatement in the past and they, too, have been turned down."

Last February the South Carolina House of Representatives passed a resolution asking baseball to reinstate him.

Kept in Touch With Game

After he was banished, Jackson kept in contact with textile and sandlot baseball and was a respected figure in his community. The fans in the area believed him innocent of all charges. He took part in unorganized games.

In 1948 he suffered a heart attack, and later he said in an interview:

"I can't play any more on account of my heart, but I can watch ball games for the rest of my life."

He made his livelihood from a retail liquor store he owned in Greenville for several years and became a member of the protest board of the Western Carolina League, a textile organization.

"Shoeless Joe" Jackson compiled an impressive .356 batting average over 13 seasons in the major leagues.

"All the News That's Fit to Print"

The New York Times.

LATE CITY EDITION
Showers, windy and warmer today. Mostly fair and cooler tomorrow.
Temperature Range Today—Max., 54; Min., 30
Temperatures Yesterday—Max., 42; Min., 32
Full U. S. Weather Bureau Report, Page 31

VOL. CII . No. 34,738. Entered as Second-Class Matter, Post Office, New York, N. Y. NEW YORK, WEDNESDAY, MARCH 4, 1953. Times Square, New York 36, N. Y. Telephone Lackawanna 4-1000 FIVE CENTS

STALIN GRAVELY ILL AFTER A STROKE; PARTLY PARALYZED AND UNCONSCIOUS; MOSCOW DISCLOSES CONCERN FOR HIM

USE OF LIMBS LOST

Premier Also Is Deprived of Power of Speech by Brain Hemorrhage

IS STRICKEN AT AGE OF 73

Party Bulletin Calls on Nation to Maintain Unity While Ministers Take Control

By HARRISON E. SALISBURY

Special to The New York Times.

MOSCOW, Wednesday, March 4—The Government announced shortly before 8 A. M. today [Tuesday midnight, Eastern standard time] that Premier Stalin had suffered a brain hemorrhage Sunday night with paralysis of the right hand and leg, loss of speech and loss of consciousness.

The Government's announcement described the illness of the 73-year-old chief of the Soviet state as "heavy" and said daily bulletins would be issued on the progress of the illness. The announcement was made jointly in the name of the Council of Ministers and the Central Committee of the Communist party.

The announcement said Mr. Stalin had suffered a hemorrhage of the brain Sunday night in Moscow, affecting important areas of the brain. The hemorrhage occurred while he was in his quarters in Moscow. In addition to losing consciousness and suffering partial paralysis, Mr. Stalin also suffered severe impairment of the heart and breathing functions.

Ten Physicians on Case

His breathing rate rose to thirty-six times a minute, with irregularity of function, and his pulse rose to 120 beats a minute. Blood pressure was 220 over 120 and temperature 38.2 degrees Centigrade [100.76 Fahrenheit].

The announcement, by the Government and the Central Committee of the Communist party, said that because of the gravity of Mr. Stalin's illness daily bulletins would be issued on the progress of the illness. The medical bulletin on Mr. Stalin's illness was signed by ten physicians headed by the new Minister of Health, A. F. Tretyakov, and including the chief Kremlin doctor, I. Kuperin, and P. E. Lukomsky, N. V. Konovalov, A. L. Myasnikov, E. M. Tareyev, I. N. Filimonov, I. S. Glazunov, R. A. Tkachev and V. I. Ivanov-Neznamov.

The Moscow newspapers were delayed until after 8 A. M. to carry the announcement, which occupied the top of three left-hand columns under the heading, "Government Announcement About Illness of Chairman of Council of Ministers of U. S. S. R. and Secretary of Central Committee of the Communist Party, Comrade Joseph Vissarionovich Stalin."

The first indication that the unusual news would be forthcoming was the delay in the appearance of Pravda and Izvestia when they

Continued on Page 3, Column 2

: President Eisenhower presents to Gen. James A. Van Fleet, former Army, a third oak leaf cluster for his Distinguished Service Medal.

Associated Press Wirephoto

RENT BILL IS FILED; 1,000,000 IN STATE FACE A RISE OF 15%

800,000 Subject to Increase Here—Legislature Receives 2-Year Control Extension

OWNERS TO GET 6% RETURN

Measure Empowers Cities and Counties to Decontrol Areas —Democrats Are Critical

Texts of statements on proposed rent control bill, Page 18.

By LEO EGAN

Special to The New York Times.

ALBANY, March 3—Joseph D. McGoldrick, State Rent Administrator, estimated today that 1,000,000 of the 2,300,000 residential tenants in New York State would have to pay 15 per cent rent increases under the administration's rent control bill, which was introduced in the Legislature today.

Drafted and approved by the majority members of the Temporary State Commission on Rents and Rental Conditions, the bill extends state controls for two more years with a provision making all tenants automatically subject to rent increases to bring their rents 15 per cent above those in effect on March 1, 1943.

Any rent increases put into effect since March 1, 1943, could be subtracted from the 15 per cent automatic rise authorized by the bill, D. Mallory Stephens, chairman of the commission, said. This means that most of those who agreed to 15 per cent voluntary increases within this period would not be affected at all, he added.

Mr. McGoldrick estimated 1,300,000 of the state's residential tenants either had agreed to 15 per cent increases or had been required to pay them under Federal or state orders. The Federal Government supervised rent control in New York from March 1, 1943, to May 1, 1950, and the State Government from the latter date to the present.

800,000 in New York City

The State Rent Administrator estimated that 35,000 tenants whose rents had been increased by 15 per cent since 1943 would be subject to another rise, up to a maximum of 15 per cent, under another provision of the bill that gives property owners the right to a 6 per cent return on the assessed value of rental property in place of the 4 per cent return provided by existing law.

Of the 1,000,000 tenants who will be subject to the flat 15 per cent increase under the administration bill, 800,000 to 850,000 live in New York City, Mr. McGoldrick estimated.

The new bill also would:

¶Decontrol vacancies as they occurred in one and two family houses only.

¶Require landlords to notify the Rent Administrator of first rentals after a dwelling unit had been decontrolled.

¶Authorize landlords to pass on to tenants, subject to the approval of the Rent Administrator, any increases in real estate taxes occurring after Jan. 1, 1953.

¶Remove the 15 per cent limitation on rent increases that could be put into effect in one year for landlords who owned four or less dwelling units within the state only.

¶Empower city governing boards in the case of cities and county boards of supervisors for areas

Continued on Page 18, Column 3

'Voice' Aide Sees McCarthy Aiming at 'My Public Neck'

Reed Harris Assails Methods of Inquiry—New Test Indicated on Congress' Right to See Security Files on Employes

By C. P. TRUSSELL

Special to The New York Times.

WASHINGTON, March 3—Through hours of bristling and at times explosive exchanges—many of them on television—Reed Harris, deputy director of the State Department's International Information Administration, today accused Senator Joseph R. McCarthy, Wisconsin Republican and chairman of a subcommittee investigating the Voice of America, of "trying to wring my public neck."

Mr. Harris contended that the inquiry was putting questions to him and drawing from his answers "innuendos" and "aspersions." He charged, in effect, that the investigating subcommittee, and especially its chairman, was refusing to concede that a person responsible for emotional outbursts as a youth in the confused period of a depression a score of years ago could develop into maturity and [illegible] sorry for what he had said [illegible] written then.

It appeared that all members [illegible] the Senate permanent subcommit[illegible]tee on investigations had not been convinced that Mr. Harris, now 43 years old, had cut entirely loose from the views he expressed at 21. Mr. Harris was instructed to employ what time he could spare from continued investigation to produce documentary evidence that, since about 1934, he had used writings, speeches or performance to prove public repudiation of his youthful position.

Mr. Harris shouted angrily that since his Government service began years ago he had been investigated six or seven times, twice in full inquiries by the Federal Bureau of Investigation, [illegible] ways had been cleared o[illegible] counts.

Senator [illegible] this [illegible]

Quill Pay Rise [illegible] To City Fiscal C[illegible]

Special to The New York [illegible]

ALBANY, March 3—Michael J. Qui[illegible] of the Transport Workers Union, C. I. O. [illegible] have added a new complication to the prob[illegible] and city o[illegible] ing a long-r[illegible] York City's [illegible]

In a letter [illegible] C. Moore, wh[illegible] terday's secret[illegible] and city officials [illegible] notice that his un[illegible] on a further roun[illegible] creases and other[illegible] when its present ag[illegible] the city covering tran[illegible] expires on Dec. 31.

Mr. Moore and State [illegible] J. Raymond McGovern, [illegible] been representing the s[illegible] ministration in negotiatio[illegible] Mayor Impellitteri and oth[illegible] officials, have been insisting [illegible] the city's present transit oper[illegible] deficit, estimated at $45,000[illegible] for the current year, be redu[illegible] before any consideration is giv[illegible] to other measures the city h[illegible] been requesting.

[When he returned to New York yesterday from his Albany fiscal conference, Mayor Impellitteri insisted that no rise in the 10-cent transit fare was in prospect for New Yorkers. He said he and the Board of Estimate were "absolutely adhering" to the principle of the 10-cent fare.

[The city-state conferences are scheduled to be renewed in New York today or tomorrow. Staff explorations preceding

Continued on Page 19, Column 4

TAFT BLOC UPSETS YALTA RESOLUTION EISENHOWER ASKED

Senate Unit Attaches Rider Stating Congress Does Not Act on Validity of Pact

DEMOCRATS ASSAIL STEP

Say It Puts Doubt on Status of U. S. in Berlin—Map a Fight for President's Idea

By WILLIAM S. WHITE

Special to The New York Times.

WASHINGTON, Ma[illegible] ator Robert A. T[illegible] Republican [illegible] defea[illegible]

[illegible] the[illegible] att[illegible] fere[illegible] ander [illegible] Jersey, [illegible] vanced [illegible] ator Taf[illegible]

"Resol[illegible] this reso[illegible] any dete[illegible] to the va[illegible]

Continu[illegible]

BRONX FIRE KILLS 7, INJURES 15 IN PLANT

Two Women Among Dead as Dust Blasts Sweep Factory —Blaze Started by Torch

Seven persons lost their lives and fifteen others were injured yesterday as one of the most deadly fires in recent city history swept a Bronx factory building and sent billows of dense, acrid smoke skyward over lower West Bronx.

The dead, five men and two women, all employes of the Utility Products Company, 570 River Avenue, were trapped in the building as dust explosions propelled a flash fire through the two-story structure with jet speed.

Thirteen of the injured were firemen. One of them, Fireman Rudolfo Gonzalez of Engine Company 41, was taken to Morrisania Hospital suffering smoke poisoning. Twelve other firemen were treated at the scene.

The two other injured were employes of the company, which makes aluminum summer furniture. They also were taken to Morrisania Hospital. They are Peter Caton, 27, of 1704 St. Marks Avenue, Brooklyn, and Alden Bunn, 28, of 11 Mount Morris Park West. Mr. Bunn and Fireman Gonzalez were sent home after treatment. Mr. Caton's condition is critical.

Investigations Are Started

As the dead were counted in a temporary morgue set up on an outdoor loading platform in a corner of the Bronx Terminal Market across the street, the Police Department, the Fire Department, the Bronx District Attorney's office and the Department of Housing and Buildings began investigations into the smoky, stubborn blaze.

The fire made up in swelling billows what it lacked in flame and raged for two hours before it was brought under control by 100 firemen and more than twenty-five pieces of equipment. Four alarms were turned in in the hour beginning at 9:30 A. M.

Late yesterday, after scores of persons were questioned by fire officials and Assistant District Attorney Wilfred Waltemade, Assistant Fire Marshal Thomas Washington announced that the fire was caused by sparks from an acetylene torch used by an iron worker at work on the sidewalk cutting away a grating on the building.

The iron worker was identified by Mr. Waltemade as Harry Awner, 34, of 1995 Sedgwick Avenue, the Bronx, who was working with Emil Fichter, 44, of 57 South Prospect Terrace, Teaneck, N. J. Both are employed by the Barnett Smith Iron Works Company of 314 West 118th Street.

Assistant Fire Marshal Wash-

Continued on Page 36, Column 6

Washington Jolted by News, Fears Rise of Red Extremists

By JAMES RESTON

Special to The New York Times.

[WA]SHINGTON, Wednesday, March 4—United States offi[cials] early today that the news of Premier Stalin's paralytic [illness w]as an event of such momentous importance that they [mad]e no official comment [pending re]ceipt of further infor[mation].

[illegible]ion in well-informed [illegible]was that if the So[illegible]d he would prob[illegible] by one of three [illegible] M. Malenkov, [illegible] or Vyacheslav [illegible]

[illegible] White House [illegible] early this [illegible] whether [illegible] President [illegible] Depart[illegible] State [illegible]nd told [illegible] sug[illegible] dis[illegible]

[illegible] world. [illegible] illness oc[illegible] control over the new [Com]munist satellite empire had been completed and at a time when there was evidence of considerable uneasiness within that empire.

Satellites Arouse Speculation

Accordingly, there was immediate speculation here about the possibility of increased opposition within Poland, Czechoslovakia and other parts of central and eastern Europe against Soviet rule.

Mr. Stalin's illness also occurred while his ally Mao Tse-tung in Communist China was engaged in open warfare against the United States and the coalition of other United Nations members.

Here again the state of Mr. Stalin's health raised questions about the relationship in the future between Communist China and the Soviet Union. These two countries have been cooperating in the war against the West in Korea, but historically their interests have been in conflict, especially over the industrial and transportation facilities in Manchuria. While Mr. Mao and Mr. Stalin have managed to prevent any open break in the period of the Korean war, officials here will be watching to see whether Mr. Mao will be willing to subordinate himself to Moscow in the future.

Comparatively speaking, Mr. Stalin has been regarded by Soviet experts in this capital as a more moderate influence on Soviet policy than some of his associates in the Politburo.

It was Mr. Stalin who intervened at the end of the war to make concessions that enabled the United Nations organization to be

Continued on Page 3, Column 4

MOSSADEGH FORCES CRUSH REDS' RALLY

Clubs and Guns Subdue Tudeh —Premier Arrests 15 More as Backing Court Intrigue

Special to The New York Times.

TEHERAN, Iran, March 3—Soldiers and policemen broke up a Communist demonstration today, before it could get started, in the fourth day of reaction since the feuding between Shah Mohammed Riza Pahlevi and Premier Mohammed Mossadegh broke into the open. With a firm hold on the situation, the Premier again demanded that intrigues against him be ended and promised to go to the people, if necessary, to accomplish this.

Making free use of clubs and rifle butts, the Government forces dispersed small groups moving toward Parliament Square, where a mass meeting had been scheduled at 3 o'clock to show the strength of the outlawed Tudeh (Communist) party. Minor fracases also occurred in other parts of the city, but the "demonstration" was over by 6 o'clock, when the streets were cleared and stores reopened.

It was the Government's strong-

Continued on Page 8, Column 1

Mrs. Luce Is Sworn In a[illegible]

Mrs. Clare Boothe Luce being sworn in yesterday as Ambassador to Italy by Chief Justice Fred M. Vinson. Ceremony was held in the office of Secretary of State John Foster Dulles, center.

The New York Times

Special to The New York Times.

WASHINGTON, March 3—Mrs. Clare Boothe Luce took the oath of office today as Ambassador to Italy. The former Republican Representative and playwright was sworn in by Fred M. Vinson, Chief Justice of the United States, in the office of John Foster Dulles, Secretary of State.

Mr. Dulles, confronting a battery of photographers, reporters, newsreel and television camera men, and an audience of officials and well-wishers estimated at about a hundred, observed that Mrs. Luce would be the first woman in the United States diplomatic corps to hold a post of such responsibility.

"The President and all who

Continued on Page 17, Column 5

Germans Urge U. S. Army Airlift To Speed Refugees Out of Berlin

Special to The New York Times.

BERLIN, March 3—United States authorities here are considering the re-establishment of a "little airlift" of military planes to help ferry refugees from Berlin to West Germany.

Such a plan had been proposed by German refugee officials on the ground that the commercial airlines had failed to keep up with the influx of refugees from East Germany.

In recent days this influx has risen to new heights. More than 7,200 refugees arrived in the first three days of this month.

The West German Refugee Ministry said today it had sought the transportation of two large groups of refugees from Berlin to West Germany in Allied military planes. One group would consist of 3,100 refugees and the other 5,000 to 10,000.

Evacuees from Berlin are being held in West German refugee camps until plans for their resettlement in West Germany or elsewhere can be effected.

United Nations refugee experts have proposed housing projects to settle the refugees near West German industrial centers. Dr. Konrad Adenauer, West German Chancellor, recently outlined a plan to lend some of the farmers among them to Canada. This is being discussed with the Canadian Ambassador in Bonn.

Otto Bach, head of West Berlin's Welfare Department, which is dealing with the refugee crisis, said at a press conference, that even if the flow stopped tomorrow it would take the city a full year to straighten out the situation.

He added that the type of refugees had altered gradually in recent weeks. Almost none of those entering the city now are fleeing because of immediate danger to themselves, he said. Likewise far

Continued on Page 12, Column 3

James J. Jeffries Dies On Coast at Age of 77

By The Associated Press

BURBANK, Calif., March 3—James J. Jeffries, former world heavyweight boxing champion, died tonight at the age of 77. Mr. Jeffries suffered a stroke recently. He had been in ill health for several years.

Mr. Jeffries won the championship from Bob Fitzsimmons at Coney Island, N. Y., in 1899 by a knockout in the eleventh round. He retired undefeated in 1905, but was persuaded to enter the ring again for a comeback against Jack Johnson in 1910. Johnson stopped him in the fifteenth round at Reno, Nev. It was the only time in his career that Jeffries had been knocked off his feet.

Jeffries' career shows twenty-three fights, eleven of which he won by knockouts, and he gained seven decisions, two draw decisions, had one technical knockout against him, and two exhibitions.

He was the last of the old line

Continued on Page 27, Column 2

James J. Jeffries Dies On Coast at Age of 77

By The Associated Press

BURBANK, Calif., March 3—James J. Jeffries, former world heavyweight boxing champion, died tonight at the age of 77. Mr. Jeffries suffered a stroke recently. He had been in ill health for several years.

Mr. Jeffries won the championship from Bob Fitzsimmons at Coney Island, N. Y., in 1899 by a knockout in the eleventh round. He retired undefeated in 1905, but was persuaded to enter the ring again for a comeback against Jack Johnson in 1910. Johnson stopped him in the fifteenth round at Reno, Nev. It was the only time in his career that Jeffries had been knocked off his feet.

Jeffries' career shows twenty-three fights, eleven of which he won by knockouts, and he gained seven decisions, two draw decisions, had one technical knockout against him, and two exhibitions.

He was the last of the old line

Continued on Page 27, Column 2

James J. Jeffries Dies on Coast; Ex-Heavyweight Champion, 77

James J. Jeffries—World Heavyweight Champion 1899–1904.

Continued From Page 1

of heavyweight champions—John L. Sullivan, James J. Corbett and Fitzsimmons. He was reared in Los Angeles, one of four sons of a Free Methodist preacher, and started life as a boilermaker.

His Popularity World-Wide

About the time that brown derbies, whatnots and mustache cups were losing favor in the land, the United States — indeed, all the world—worshiped big Jim Jeffries as the mightiest heavyweight boxer in history.

Some there were, of course, who disputed his right to the title. They argued that big Jim lacked one great fighter ingredien —natural viciousness, a thirst for blood.

He always admitted that, but laughed it off. Between championship bouts with the brawny maulers of his day he loved to get down on all fours and romp with his brothers' children.

Dogs loved him on sight. Strays would pick him out of a crowd to lap at his hamlike fists. Out on his Los Angeles ranch in the Arroyo Seco he never sallied forth without a half-dozen dogs at his heels.

He came of God-fearing parents. His father, a Free Methodist preacher who exhorted street-corner crowds in Los Angeles, rather frowned on his brawny son making a living at fisticuffs, but came to boast of it, in a mild sort of way.

"The Jeffries," said the Man of God, "have always been a quiet, peace-lovin' people who never allowed themselves to be whipped."

Even Mrs. Jeffries, mother of ten sons and daughters, became somewhat reconciled to the world acclaim won by her Jim in the ring, though she'd frowned on it at first.

Out of her girlhood memories she drew the almost-forgotten fact that Jim's maternal Grandpaw Boyer was one of the lustiest men in old Schuylkill Valley; a righteous Christian but a mean hand with a wagon-tongue when roused to wrath.

From a Family of Big Men

Big Jim's folks, on the father's side, were of old English stock; his mother's, Holland Dutch. All their sons were of giant mold, but Jim was the biggest—and at the same time the gentlest; slow to anger.

James J. Jeffries was born in Carroll, Fairfield County, not far from Toledo, Ohio, on April 15, 1875. He was "rising 7," as his father put it later, when the family moved to California.

As a lad he romped the California hills, played with his pets, and was something of a mama's boy. At school, his mother recalled, a boy hit him in the face twice before he decided to do something about it. Then Jim almost drove him through a bar wall with one punch.

Not far from the Jeffries home was an old mine where most of the neighborhood lads, if they were big enough, worked for a living. At 15 Jim was acknowledged champion wrestler of that rough crowd.

At 16 he worked in the Lacey Manufacturing Company, a boiler works near Los Angeles, and he came to be known throughout his fighting career both as "Big Jim" and as "The Boilermaker."

There have been several legends about his first professional fight. The true version seems to be that he was forced into it through no design of his own by Hank Griffin, a Negro, who was chief bully in the tough Lacey crew.

Griffin walked into a saloon one afternoon in 1893, so the story went, threw a handful of gold coins on the bar and bellowed that he could whip any man in the works for the full amount or for any part of it.

Big Jim had been taught from the Scriptures that boastfulness and false pride are sinful. He did not particularly want to fight, but felt that it might do Griffin some moral good if he got his comeuppance.

Word got around and some ambitious local boy arranged the bout. The bellowing Griffin got his, with extra measure. At the end of the fourteenth round a crushing body blow put him out for the night.

Retired Undefeated in 1905

That launched the "Big Feller." His career was comparatively brief —less than twenty-five fights in a little under eight years—but in that period he mowed them down like ripe wheat. He retired, undefeated, in 1905.

He liked to recall, later, that until the famous comeback failure, when he was battered down in Reno by the Negro, Jack (Li'l Arthur) Johnson, no opponent ever knocked him down, or even made him back up.

The historic Jeffries crouch, in which the giant converted himself into a solid arc to protect his stomach and jaw, found many imitators. With Jeff, though, it was a bitterly learned trick.

After he had knocked out Hank Griffin, three years passed before he took on Dan Long of Denver in a match for $1,000. He broke Mr. Long's nose in the second round. A ferocious bruiser yclept Eddie (Slaughter House) Baker was the next victim; out in nine rounds at San Francisco.

Jeffries' admirers thought he was invincible and were for putting him against the rugged Goliaths of the distant East without further experience, but he needed one more lesson, and he got it from Johnny Brink, a Los Angeles business man.

Brink knew that the genial Boilermaker was a bit crude. He undertook to teach him a few tricks, and they'd work out together in a Los Angeles gymnasium. One day Brink ripped in a body blow that almost blew Jeffries's liver and lights.

The blow crippled him, but it taught him that, strong as he was, there was a limit to the punishment he could absorb. He had to perfect a stance to cover the vulnerable spot that the shrewd Brink had touched; the stance was the famous crouch.

Harry Corbett, brother of Gentleman Jim, heard of the lusty Boilermaker and sent him out to Carson City to help Jim Corbett train for one of his fights. Jeff took plenty of punishment there, but learned a lot.

Back East the sports writers beban to take notice of the Genial Giant. They were amazed when he slugged toe to toe with the cunning veteran, Joe Choynski. In that fight, he often said later, he got the hardest single blow of his career—a right to the jaw that almost snapped his head off at the stem.

At Coney Island, one blistering hot night in June, 1899, the Boilermaker, dripping perspiration, faced lanky Bob Fitzsimmons. The Cornishman, older and cooler, had the best of everything for nine rounds. In the eleventh his nose furrowed the resin three times. Then he could not get up before the bell. Jeffries was champion.

Five months later, again at Coney Island, Jeffries beat Tom Sharkey. In 1902 he took Fitzsimmons on a second time, and again, in the first eight rounds Foxy Fitz slashed Jeffries' face, and had a big advantage. Then down he went, almost blown apart by a crusher to the midriff.

Just before the fight Fitzsimmons had said: "The bigger 'e is, the 'arder 'e'll fall." But that finishing punch ended his ring career. He told sportsmen that Jeffries' strength was superhuman, that he'd never been hit so hard in his embattled life.

Jim Corbett, the soul of caution, made the mistake, in his fight with his former sparring partner, of trying to slug it out with big Jeff. The fight had gone twenty-two rounds, with Corbett leading on points, but the fans, howling for blood, were shrieking:

"Get in there, Corbett, and fight!"

Corbett made the fatal mistake in the twenty-third round of casting caution aside. George Considine, his manager, begged him to ignore the roaring fanatics, to keep on boxing, but Corbett was seeing red—while he saw at all. He went in, punching, and went down, bruised and battered. The Boilermaker ruined him that night.

Glorified in Art

By this time Jeffries' name was a household word. Wherever he walked, men and boys—even the bolder women of that era of unemancipated females — clustered around him; worshiped his brute strength.

Those were not the golden days

(continued)

Former champion James J. Jeffries returned to the ring at 35 in an attempt to defeat Jack Johnson. Johnson won in 15 rounds.

Jeffries in semi-retirement. One year later, in 1910, he lost to Jack Johnson—the first fight in which he was knocked down.

of prizefighting, though—not financially; he was lucky to get as much as $5,000, even for his big bouts. Still, he was a man of simple tastes and was able, when he retired, to buy himself a nice stock ranch in Burbank, Calif. No more mountain climbing, no more long hikes on fishing trips. He went abroad; met princes and kings—and began to go soft.

He owned blooded dogs, basked in the flattering admiration of fellow-townsmen and of visitors, and was well on the way to becoming merely another big, fat man—he was 6 feet 1½ inches in height and fought at 220 pounds—when canny promoters hauled him out of retirement with the plea that the world needed "a white hope" to beat the new Negro champion, Jack Johnson.

Ballyhoo without end finally did the trick—that and the promise of a $101,000 purse, a sum unheard of in Jeff's early fighting days. He trained with old Joe Choynski as his adviser and at 35 years of age, on July 4, 1910, faced the powerful Johnson under a burning Nevada sun in Reno. There was no radio in those days, but late in the afternoon the humming telegraph wires brought the news that shocked the Jeffries worshipers. He was knocked out in the fifteenth round.

The Turn of the Tide

Praise turned to abuse. At crossroads stores, around the cracker barrel; in rich barrooms and clubrooms draped with dusty red plush, the disappointed fight fans heaped anathema on "Big Jeff." Their idol had let them down. Then grew the legend that Jeffries had been "doped" before the fight, but he admitted, since he was a fair and honest man, that the "dope" and the poison stories were so much rot.

He went back to Burbank, brokenhearted, an old man at 35. He was moody. Friends said he aged ten years after that defeat; that he felt he had betrayed the whole white race. Finally, though, that passed, and even the bitterest fans saw the injustice of their anger. They accepted the credo, "They never come back," and spoke fondly again of the Jeffries that was.

Meanwhile, he went on with his stock farming. His genial smile and good nature mellowed in the California sun. He had ups and downs in his business ventures.

He was in the news for a paragraph or two in 1940 when, after reading that Jack Dempsey had challenged Gene Tunney to box for the Red Cross, he offered to take on the winner—"provided either can go over four rounds." He was 65 at the time.

In 1941 his wife, Frieda, 60, was killed when struck by an automobile. They had been married thirty-seven years. Jeffries met her in New York when he was on tour as champion.

During the war Jeffries kept in condition by cultivating a victory garden. He conducted amateur boxing shows and assisted in putting on sports shows for service men.

"All the News That's Fit to Print"

The New York Times.

LATE CITY EDITION

Copyright, 1946, by The New York Times Company.

VOL. XCV—No. 32,280. Entered as Second-Class Matter. Postoffice, New York, N. Y. NEW YORK, TUESDAY, JUNE 11, 1946. THREE CENTS IN NEW YORK CITY

HIGH COURT HOLDS 'BIG THREE' A TRUST IN CIGARETTE FIELD

Justices, 6 to 0, Back Fining of R. J. Reynolds, American and Liggett & Myers

'POWER' TO EXCLUDE FOUND

Need Not Show Actual Forcing Out of Competition, Burton Says in Main Opinion

Special to THE NEW YORK TIMES.

WASHINGTON, June 10—In an opinion holding that monopoly may be proved even when there is no actual exclusion of competitors, the Supreme Court affirmed today the conviction of the three leading tobacco companies of this country for violation of the Anti-Trust Act.

The court's decision, in which six justices participated, was unanimous. It upheld fines aggregating $255,000 against the R. J. Reynolds Tobacco Company, the Liggett & Myers Tobacco Company and the American Tobacco Company and its subsidiary, American Suppliers, Inc. These were levied on conviction on four counts: Conspiracy in restraint of trade, monopolization, attempt to monopolize and conspiracy to monopolize.

In a separate concurring opinion, Justice Rutledge, saying that the sole issue before the court was "whether actual exclusion of competitors is necessary to the crime of monopolization," declared that on this point he had no hesitation in agreeing with his colleagues.

Punishment an Open Question

On the issue of "multiple punishments," of which the companies had complained, he observed that these presented "a different question which can be determined only by the manner in which the particular application has been made."

Justice Frankfurter expressed a belief that the court should have gone into the matter of whether errors were made in selecting the trial jury.

The principal opinion, delivered by Justice Burton, noted that the precise question before it had not previously been decided, although he recalled that a similar issue had been raised in the case of the Aluminum Company of America, and thus summed up:

"The authorities support the view that the material consideration in determining whether a monopoly exists is not that prices are raised and that competition is actually excluded, but that power exists to raise prices or to exclude competition when it is desired to do so."

The companies argued that the Sherman Act should be interpreted as requiring proof of an actual exclusion of competitors before "monopolization" could be shown, and contended also that any other finding would lay them open to double jeopardy.

The court found that while the total domestic production of American, Liggett and Reynolds fell from 90.7 per cent of the national production in 1931 to 68 per cent in 1939, their combined volume rose from 106,000,000,000 cigarettes in 1931 to 123,000,000,000 in 1939.

Thus, it added, "without adverse criticism on it, comparative size on this great scale inevitably increased the power of these three to dominate all phases of their industry."

Justices Reed and Jackson took no part in the cases.

End of Six-Year Legal Battle

WASHINGTON, June 10 (UP)—The Justice Department won its six-year "trust-busting" fight against the big three of the tobacco industry today.

The unanimous decision of the Supreme Court holding that the American, Liggett & Myers and R. J. Reynolds companies formed a monopoly in violation of the Sherman Anti-Trust Act ended a prolonged legal battle which began in 1940 when the Justice Department filed suit against the big three, accusing them of such practices as buying up unneeded tobacco to prevent its use by competitors, and agreeing on the maximum prices they would pay at tobacco auctions.

The companies said in their appeal that the intense rivalry existing in the tobacco business disproved the monopoly charge.

The following are the defendants who were convicted of anti-trust law violation:

American Tobacco Company, New York City; American Suppliers, Inc., a wholly owned subsidiary of American Tobacco, New

Continued on Page 2, Column 6

Woman Considered For Judge in Jersey

By The Associated Press.

TRENTON, N. J., June 10—Gov. Walter E. Edge may name the first woman judge in New Jersey history when he sends a long list of appointments for confirmation to a special session of the State Senate on Wednesday.

He finished the list he will propose today, and it appeared that Mrs. Libby E. Sachar, Plainfield lawyer, would be named to the bench of the Union County Juvenile and Domestic Relations Court. Long active in Republican circles, Mrs. Sachar worked with State Senator Herbert J. Pascoe in support of Alfred E. Driscoll, victor in the primary for the Republican nomination for Governor.

Another nomination regarded likely by sources close to the Governor was that of George Page, Trenton City Commissioner, to succeed John L. O'Hara as principal keeper of the State prison.

PRESIDENT WILL ACT ON CASE BILL TODAY

Congress Prepares for Veto, Although Leaders Insist They Remain in Dark

By C[...]

WAS[...] dent Tru[...] at the [...] Case L[...] row. Co[...] for a veto [...] finality.

Bitterly opp[...] rallying their [...] test of wheth[...] membership ex[...] could be overr[...] thirds vote of both [...] be sustained. Nose-c[...] cated a close call [...] Doubt persisted that eit[...] could muster an overr[...] jority.

These preparations w[...] based upon definite word [...] President had decided to [...] his veto power on this lon[...] troverted measure, or upon [...] that he would not.

Leaders See President

Congressional leaders, after conferring with the President and being authorized to announce officially that his message would be sent to the Capitol at noon tomorrow, said they did not know what his message would say, whether it would veto or approve. Their demeanor indicated that they had neither sought nor wanted the information in advance.

In Senate and House planning went forward for means through which the President might, after all, take the Case Bill, or some permanent legislation resembling it, without waiting for conclusions drawn from a six months' study of labor-management problems such as he recommended when he asked recently for enactment of his Emergency Strike Control Bill.

It was believed that if the President did invoke his veto he would ask again for the pre-legislating study of the fundamentals of industrial disputes. It also was believed that, in the light of the intense controversy over this permanent control legislation, the President would not use a veto without explaining why he would not approve this provision or that, and possibly indicating what he would accept if Congress had prepared the measure in a different way.

In such an event, it was hinted

Continued on Page 4, Column 2

CONCILIATORS URGE A BONUS TO AVERT MARITIME STRIKE

Labor Department Suggests a Cash Payment Instead of Cutting 56-Hour Week

PROPOSAL SEEMS DOOMED

Spokesmen for Seven Unions, Operators Hold Little Hope for Stopping Walkout

By LOUIS STARK

Special to THE NEW YORK TIMES.

WASHINGTON, June 10—Direct negotiations between seven maritime unions and three ship operators' associations having failed to reach an agreement to avert a strike on June 15, the Department of Labor today pressed for joint acceptance of a proposal whereby seamen would be paid a cash bonus for hours worked over a fixed li[...] within the present fifty[...] week.

Although nei[...] of Industri[...] tional M[...] eral [...]

[...] deci[...] setti[...] Conci[...] seek [...] result [...] committ[...]

Chairm[...] committee [...] and Mr. Cu[...] the committe[...] morrow. The [...] be heard subse[...]

Owners Ho[...]

Representative[...] he and his assoc[...] at a solution of t[...] time labor dispute, [...] erally one of the mo[...] labor problems that ha[...] the Administration for y[...]

Last week Mr. Kelley h[...] liminary hearing, but, at [...] quest of the Labor Departm[...] cided to wait for a few days [...] if the Conciliation Service w[...] succeed in its mediation effor[...]

Philip Murray, president of CIO, conferred today with [...] Bridges, Mr. Curran and H[...] Bryson, vice president of the M[...] rine Cooks and Stewards. Th[...]

Continued on Page 4, Column 7

U. S. Aide, Briton Accused As Mikhailovitch Case Opens

Prosecution Says Chetnik Met Nazi Officer While American Colonel Looked On—Order to Kill Reds Laid to Briton

By The Associated Press.

BELGRADE, Yugoslavia, June 10—The Yugoslav Government's indictment of Gen. Draja Mikhailovitch charged today that the Chetnik leader had been told by a British officer in 1943 to "liquidate the Communists" in Yugoslavia, and that in 1944 an American officer had taken part in conferences between General Mikhailovitch and a German commander.

Referring to another British message, purportedly sent from the British Command in Cairo in 1941 and relayed by a British liaison officer, the indictment said Mikhailovitch had been told "that Yugoslavs are to fight for Yugoslavia and not transform the [...] into a rebellion [...] behalf of Sov[...]

The indic[...] openi[...]

packed with more than 1,000 spectators.

Observers noted that the prosecutor did not mention the death penalty, but said he "will expect the court to pass severe and just sentence over these traitors and criminals." The prosecution asked the court to "pronounce such verdict as each accused deserves, according to the gravity of his criminal acts; severe and just punish[...] ment—for those w[...] cruel crimes."

Drawn [...] Govern[...]

[...] ary Vin[...]

[...]odernize Congress[...] [ma]chinery, raise the pay [...] members to $15,000 and provide a pension system for Congressmen was passed by the Senate. A proposal to appoint Capitol employes by merit was stricken out in favor of the traditional patronage system. [1:6.]

Current meat shortages were attributed by Stabilization Director Bowles to deliberate withholding of livestock in anticipation of the end of price control. He said the Senate OPA bill would result in an immediate jump of 40 to 50 per cent in meat prices. [26:4.]

Unless Congress extends stringent price control, a new wave of strikes will set in about Labor Day, Assistant Secretary of Labor Gibson and other speakers declared at the Michigan CIO convention. [4:1.]

President Truman will send to Congress today his decision on the Case strike-control bill. A veto is expected. [1:2.] It appeared that nothing short of a Presidential fact-finding board could avert the nation-wide maritime strike called for Saturday. A Labor Department suggestion for a cash bonus for overtime

[...]lion of [...]half of Soviet Rus[...]

[R]ussia, having "experimented with distrust," was advised by Professor Laski, retiring chairman of the British Labor party, "to experiment in friendship" with Britain. He condemned British-American secrecy on the atomic bomb. [6:3.]

Although Italy became a de facto republic when the Court of Cassation announced the plebiscite results, King Humbert retained his throne pending a decision on vote irregularities. [1:5.]

France dismissed a high official of the detective service after Britain had inquired how the Grand Mufti of Jerusalem had been able to escape. Although reported to be in the Near East, no one acknowledged having seen him. [1:4.]

India's independence moved a step nearer when the Chamber of Princes approved the British mission's proposals. [15:3.]

The United Nations Security Council will not meet today, Britain has not yet informed her representative what position to take on the Franco subcommittee's report. [10:2.] Secretary General Lie declared in Detroit that there was no British-American bloc in the United Nations. He limited his optimism about another war by saying it was not likely "in the nearest future." [11:1.]

SENATE VOTES, 49-16, CONGRESS PAY RISE, REORGANIZATION

Bill Would Raise Salaries to $15,000, Provide Pensions, Increase Expert Aides

SPEEDIER SYSTEM IS GOAL

Cuts Standing Committees to 15, Merges Functions—Move to End Patronage Beaten

By [JO]HN D. MORRIS

[Special to] THE NEW YORK TIMES.

[WASHINGT]ON, June 10—The [...] bill to modernize [...]achinery, provide [...] Senators and [...]aise their sal[...] to $15,000.

[...] by a vote of [...]d only after a [...]outhern Demo[...] the right to retain [...]onage in the [...] employes.

[...] against [...] Congres[...]ctor of [...]egisla[...]

[...] including [...] Barkley and Senator [...] White Jr. of Maine, mi[nori]ty leader, joined others in opposing the amendment. They said that Federal judges and Army and Navy personnel received pensions without making contributions which would be required of members of Congress.

Another Byrd amendment, approved by voice vote, eliminated

Continued on Page 3, Column 2

Russia to Help Tito Build Arms Plants

By Wireless to THE NEW YORK TIMES.

LONDON, June 10—The Soviet Union will supply the Yugoslav Army with munitions, arms and equipment and will help to build up the Yugoslav armament industry under a new Russian-Yugoslav agreement ratified Saturday, the Belgrade radio said tonight.

Yugoslavia will also get from the Soviet Union supplies of raw materials for other industries.

The announcement of the new agreement came simultaneously with a report by the Moscow radio that Marshal Tito, who arrived in the Soviet Union May 27, left Moscow yesterday with other members of the Yugoslav delegation.

PAPER MILLS HEAD SLAIN IN HIS OFFICE

W. A. Whitcomb, 73, Shot at Boston by Visitor Saying He Is Treasury Agent

Special to THE NEW YORK TIMES.

BOSTON, June 10—William A. Whitcomb, 73, president of the Great Northern Paper Company, was shot dead in his eighth-floor office at 201 Devonshire Street just before 11 A. M. today by a man who had represented himself to be a Treasury Department agent.

The man, after waiting in the [ou]ter office, was received by Mr. [Wh]itcomb. He was in the private [...] for seven minutes, then he [...]tered out, walked down the [...] flights of stairs instead of [...] an elevator and disappeared [in d]owntown crowds.

[Edwa]rd W. Fallon, deputy su[perinten]dent of police, said that [...] had a revolver in his [...] he came out of Mr. [...] office and that sev[...] [i]n the outer office [...]re too terrified to [...] outcry.

[...]ding Shot

[...] Mr. Whitcomb's [...] the private of[...] [b]ody doubled [...] immediately [...] building at [...]d, but the [...] Mr. Whit[...] bullets [...]

[...] killed him [...] for possible clues [...]igned copies of a [...]rawn and crudely worded contract calling for a life job with the company at $25,000 a year. The contracts were found on Mr. Whitcomb's desk.

The name on the three copies is "George E. Hardy." Company officials asserted that they had never heard of such a person.

The company has had dealings with a Robert Hardy, an elderly and highly respected man in paper circles, who was known to employes, but who bears not the slightest resemblance to the killer. On one of the copies of the con-

Continued on Page 46, Column 5

JACKSON ATTACKS BLACK FOR JUDGING EX-PARTNER'S CASE

Justice Says in Germany He Was Threatened With 'War' Unless He Covered Up Facts

FEUD BREAKS INTO OPEN

Jackson Cables Report to Congress—Asserts He Will Not Be 'a Stealthy Assassin'

The text of Justice Jackson's statement is on Page 2.

By The Associated Press.

NUREMBERG, Germany, June 10—In an unprecedented attack on a colleague of the United States Supreme Court, Justice Robert H. Jackson asserted tonight that Justice Hugo Black participated in decisions affecting a former law partner, and that the practice, if continued, would bring America's highest court into "disrepute."

Mr. Jackson, on leave from the court to serve as chief American prosecutor at the war crimes trial here, said in a statement issued at a news conference that a "feud" existed between Mr. Black and him.

The feud, he said in the statement, which was cabled to the House and Senate Judiciary Committees, "has been so long publicized that Congress has a right to know the facts and issues involved."

Saying that Mr. Black threatened him with "war" unless he "covered up facts" in a case in which Mr. Black's law partner was involved, Mr. Jackson said:

"If war is declared on me, I propose to wage it with weapons of an open warrior, not those of a stealthy assassin."

Warns of Peril to Court

"There may be those who think it quite harmless to encourage employment of justices' ex-law partners to argue close cases by smothering objections which the bar makes to this practice.

"But in my view such an attitude soon would bring the court into disrepute. However innocent a coincidence these two victories at successive terms by Justice Black's former law partner, I wanted that practice stopped.

"If it is ever repeated while I am on the bench I will make my Jewell Ridge opinion look like a letter of recommendation by comparison."

Mr. Jackson refused to elaborate on his statement except to tell reporters that the feuding existed among justices appointed by President Roosevelt.

"[...] and they called us rubber [stam]ps," he added.

His cable to the two committees, Mr. Jackson stated, was in answer to what he termed unjustified attacks in the press and intimated Mr. Black was behind these attacks.

He referred to a Washington Star column by Doris Fleeson on May 16, 1946, which, he said, quoted Mr. Black as complaining against a decision by Mr. Jackson in the Jewell Ridge coal case as an "open and gratuitous insult" and a "slur upon his (Mr. Black's) personal and judicial honor."

The column purportedly related to the "inside story" of the case as laid before President Truman.

[In Washington, Justice Black refused to comment on Justice Jackson's charges. The United Press reported: "I haven't made a statement of any kind to the press since coming up here," Justice Black said. "I don't expect to make any now."]

The Supreme Court decision in the Jewell Ridge coal case held that soft coal miners were entitled to portal-to-portal pay. In the 5-to-4 decision handed down on May 7, 1945, Justice Murphy wrote the majority opinion and Mr. Jackson a dissenting opinion.

Jackson Praises Vinson

"I want it understood," Mr. Jackson said, "that nothing in this statement is to be construed as the slightest reflection upon Fred Vinson," who has been nominated by Mr. Truman to be the Chief Justice of the United States. Mr. Vinson's appointment has not been confirmed by the Senate.

"It is desirable to get the controversy all back of us now so that he (Mr. Vinson) can take up his task without the cloud hanging over the court."

Describing Mr. Vinson as "an upright, fearless and well-qualified man" for the Chief Justice post,

Continued on Page 2, Column 7

Tube Head Calls Fare Rise Vital; Prospects for Ending Strike Dim

By A. H. RASKIN

Prospects for settlement of the twelve-day-old Hudson & Manhattan tube strike appeared dimmer than ever last night despite completion by the company of its presentation of direct testimony before the emergency fact-finding board appointed by President Truman.

Robert A. W. Carleton, H. & M. president, interviewed by reporters at the board's hearing in the Hotel Victoria, indicated there was a strong likelihood that the line would refuse to put into effect any wage increase recommended by the panel unless it was accompanied by assurances of a simultaneous increase in passenger fares.

While avoiding any definite commitment on what the company would do, Mr. Carleton emphasized that any increase in wages without an increase in fares would add to the line's operating deficit and that it was his duty, as principal officer of the corporation, not to follow a spending policy that seemed likely to lead to bankruptcy.

He conceded that the Truman fact-finding panel had no authority to adjust fares and that it might take a full year before the Interstate Commerce Commission completed action on an application for higher rates. He said it was impossible to say in advance whether the company would decide to pay any higher wages recommended by the board while awaiting authorization to raise its fares.

The striking unions, the Brotherhood of Locomotive Engineers and the Brotherhood of Railroad Trainmen, stood firm in their determination to boycott the activities of the Truman panel and to refuse to return to work until the line granted the pay increase of 18½ cents an

Continued on Page 4, Column 3

Jack Johnson Dies in Auto Crash; Ex-Heavyweight Champion Was 68

By The Associated Press.

RALEIGH, N. C., June 10—Jack Johnson, former heavyweight champion of the world, died at St. Agnes Hospital here of injuries he suffered in an automobile accident near Franklinton early this afternoon.

Dr. W. D. Allison said that the 68-year-old Negro died from internal injuries and shock.

The accident occurred just south of the Franklinton line, which is about twenty miles north of Raleigh on U. S. Highway No. 1.

Johnson was reported to have lost control of the big automobile which he was driving, causing it to crash into a light pole and overturn. Fred L. Scott, who was riding with him, was slightly injured.

Scott said he was accompanying Johnson to New York from Texas, where the former champion had concluded a personal appearance tour. He explained that for several years such appearances had been Johnson's sole occupation.

Both Johnson and Scott were thrown out of the car, which was demolished. They were taken to the hospital, where Johnson died at 6:10 P. M.

Johnson's wife, Mrs. Irene Johnson, has been notified of her husband's death and is coming to Raleigh, Scott said. Funeral arrangements have not been made.

Death ended a strange career when it took Jack Johnson—a mad-cap existence that touched the heights, hit the depths and lingered at intermediate points in the scale.

One of the craftiest boxers known to the ring, recognized by many as one of the five outstanding heavyweight champions of all time, Jack Johnson lived in the lap of luxury, abused the fame and

Continued on Page 46, Column 2

Jack Johnson Dies in Auto Crash; Ex-Heavyweight Champion Was 68

By The Associated Press.

RALEIGH, N. C., June 10—Jack Johnson, former heavyweight champion of the world, died at St. Agnes Hospital here of injuries he suffered in an automobile accident near Franklinton early this afternoon.

Dr. W. D. Allison said that the 68-year-old Negro died from internal injuries and shock.

The accident occurred just south of the Franklinton line, which is about twenty miles north of Raleigh on U. S. Highway No. 1.

Johnson was reported to have lost control of the big automobile which he was driving, causing it to crash into a light pole and overturn. Fred L. Scott, who was riding with him, was slightly injured.

Scott said he was accompanying Johnson to New York from Texas, where the former champion had concluded a personal appearance tour. He explained that for several years such appearances had been Johnson's sole occupation.

Both Johnson and Scott were thrown out of the car, which was demolished. They were taken to the hospital, where Johnson died at 6:10 P. M.

Johnson's wife, Mrs. Irene Johnson, has been notified of her husband's death and is coming to Raleigh, Scott said. Funeral arrangements have not been made.

Death ended a strange career when it took Jack Johnson—a mad-cap existence that touched the heights, hit the depths and lingered at intermediate points in the scale.

One of the craftiest boxers known to the ring, recognized by many as one of the five outstanding heavyweight champions of all time, Jack Johnson lived in the lap of luxury, abused the fame and

Continued on Page 46, Column 2

Jack Johnson Dies in Auto Crash; Ex-Heavyweight Champion Was 68

Continued From Page 1

fortune that came to him, and died bereft of riches.

Since 1937 he had lectured at Hubert's Museum, 228 West Forty-second Street, once a year or oftener, disregarding gibes that he was competing with the flea circus, and finished his last engagement there only three weeks ago.

Friends who saw him recently said that he drove his own car, was well dressed, had an apartment in Chicago and had tried unsuccessfully to find one in New York.

At the height of his career Johnson wore diamonds. His "golden smile" revealed a mouth full of gold. He had at one time as many as half a dozen automobiles when they were a luxury. He shook hands with royalty as he traveled the world over with a retinue of servants.

He was involved in a sensational court trial which ended in his conviction on a charge of violation of the Mann Act. He fled justice, roamed the world, a man without a country, until his fortune was gone. He confessed "faking" a fight, a battle in which he admitted he let his title pass to Jess Willard in Havana in 1915.

Got $120,000 in 1910

Among the distinctions that came to him was that of having collected the largest purse ever paid a boxer until the golden era of the Jack Dempsey days—$120,000 he received in 1910 when he knocked out James J. Jeffries in fourteen rounds at Reno, Nev. For this bout Johnson collected 60 per cent of the purse of $101,000, $10,000 as a bonus and $50,000 for his share of motion pictures.

He was the cause of the "white hope" craze that swept the country after the Reno débâcle when Jeffries succumbed to his craft after being brought out of retirement "to bring the title back to the white race."

The result of that fight brought a ban on interstate commerce of motion pictures of fights. Also on the result came riots in different sections of the country which resulted in eight deaths and injuries to many.

Johnson was arrested many times for minor law violations. He exhausted his supply of money while a fugitive in foreign lands.

He came back after seven years and ser ed a one-year jail sentence for his Mann Act violation, tried fighting again and failed, made a precarious living as evangelist, spear-carrier in opera and a maker of personal appearances at museums and carnivals.

Out of the wealth of his ring experience he predicted that Max Schmeling would knock out Joe Louis and Schmeling won by a knockout.

John Arthur Johnson was his name. He was also known as "Li'l Arthur." He was born in Galveston, Tex., March 31, 1878. He was one of the craftiest boxers known to the ring. He boasted a right-hand uppercut that was his greatest weapon of attack and defense.

None has been seen like it in a heavyweight since his day. With Johnson, too, the art of feinting, parrying, leading an opponent into mechanical mistakes, drawing a foe out—all this passed, as it was known to the ring of another day and age.

Usually supposed to have been discovered by Sam Fitzpatrick, who had managed Peter Jackson and Kid Lavigne, Johnson was discovered instead by Leo Posner, leader of the Galveston Athletic Club, quite by accident.

It was later in his career that Fitzpatrick signed as manager of Johnson, and as heavyweight champion the Galveston Negro led his manager many a merry chase.

Charley Brooks, who spent much time in Galveston gymnasiums, introduced Johnson to Posner at a time when ring talent was scarce in Galveston. The test of the newcomer was made by Brooks, who was looking for an easy foe. Brooks was knocked out in the trial, for which Johnson received about $10, and there and then Johnson's ring career was launched.

Won Six Fights in 1901

In 1901 he won six bouts, one of them a two-round knockout of Brooks, and fought a draw, until he undertook a clash with Joe Choynski, known in ring history as a great boxer. Choynski knocked out Johnson in three rounds, but the setback was temporary.

Choynski took an interest in Johnson when they were jailed as a consequence of the battle, and undertook a course of instruction which started in the jail yard and formed the foundation of the ring development of Johnson.

In 1902 Johnson started a campaign in which he lost only three bouts in six years. He lost a twenty-round decision to Hank Griffin in 1902, another to Marvin Hart in 1905 and in the same year lost on a foul to Joe Jeanette in two rounds.

He was fighting all over the country, against whatever opposition was presented, and his engagements included bouts with Sam McVey, Sandy Ferguson, Sam Langford, as well as Jeanette.

It is recorded that in an early round of their bout in Boston in 1906 Langford, hardly more than a welterweight, knocked Johnson down with a left hook early in the fight and Johnson, profiting by a count that was none too accurate, survived by calling upon all his consummate defensive boxing skill. They never fought again.

Johnson's 1907 victories included a two-round knockout of Bob Fitzsimmons, but the Cornishman at the time was at the end of his pugilistic career.

This consistent campaign established Johnson as a title threat at a time when Tommy Burns was recognized as a champion. Burns shied away from a meeting, but Johnson pressed his challenge until he finally got a match with Burns in Sydney, Australia, and there pounded Burns to such an extent that police stopped the fight in the fourteenth round, giving Johnson claim to the title.

Johnson's next battle of note, aside from a six-round no-decision affair with Philadelphia Jack O'Brien, was a twelve-round knockout of Stanley Ketchel, world mid-

(continued)

Jack "Li'l Arthur" Johnson—World Heavyweight Champion 1908-1915.

Jack Johnson (right) in his historic battle with Jess Willard.

dleweight champion, at Colma, Calif., in 1909.

This was an ill-fated undertaking by the smaller Ketchel, who nevertheless pressed Johnson hard at times before being knocked out. It was also the last bout for Johnson before he knocked out Jeffries in the fifteenth round on July 4, 1910, in Reno, a contest promoted by Tex Rickard and Jack Gleason that drew an unprecedented $270,775 in receipts.

Beset By Difficulties

After that bout, his claim to the title undisputed since he had knocked out the man who had gone into retirement as champion, Johnson came upon difficulties. He married two white women. One of them committed suicide in a room above his Cafe de Champion in Chicago.

The other he married while she was being interrogated as the Government's chief witness in prosecution of charges that Johnson violated the Mann Act in transporting her from Pittsburgh to Chicago.

The champion was found guilty, was released from jail, pending sentence, on $30,000 bond, was sentenced to a year in jail, and released on bond of $15,000 pending appeal, and went to Canada as a member of a Negro baseball team, leaving Chicago after a game. He sailed from Montreal and arrived in Havre on the morning of July 10, 1913, as a fugitive.

For seven years Johnson fought on foreign soil. Barred from music halls of London, he subsequently was expelled from the country. He fought three bouts in Paris in 1913, beating Frank Moran, Al Sproul and Jim Johnson.

In 1915 he went to Havana, where he was knocked out in twenty-six rounds by Willard, a bout for which Johnson later said he was promised, but never collected, $50,000 for "laying down."

Gradually Johnson disappeared from the picture thereafter, fighting in Spain for the most part until in 1919 he went to Mexico City to win a fight from Capt. Bob Roper.

In 1920 he arranged for his surrender to Federal marshals who awaited him as he stepped across the border. Old and fleshy when he emerged from Leavenworth prison, Johnson intermittently undertook a ring come-back thereafter, with indifferent success, until in May, 1926, Bob Lawson knocked him out in seven rounds of a scheduled twelve-round bout at Juarez, Mexico.

He finally retired from the ring in 1928 after a six-round bout with Bill Hartwell in Kansas City.

The New York Times WEDNESDAY, DECEMBER 11, 1946.

WALTER JOHNSON DIES IN CAPITAL, 59

Pitching Star for Washington Senators 21 Years Held Many Baseball Records

WASHINGTON, Dec. 10 (AP)—Walter Johnson, former strikeout king of the American League and a member of baseball's official hall of fame, died late tonight of a brain tumor. His age was 59.

Members of Johnson's family were at the bedside when the end came.

Johnson's wife, Hazel, died in 1930, leaving five children, three of them boys.

Attained Great Popularity

There has not been a pitcher in recent years who had a greater hold on the American baseball public than Walter Johnson. Following the immortal Christy Mathewson, "Big Barney" attained popularity among the fans of the country equal virtually to that of "Big Six."

In more ways than one they were alike. Both were great pitchers, both were sterling characters and both were idols of young America. In 1936 Johnson was one of the first five men named to baseball's Hall of Fame at Cooperstown, N. Y., the others being Babe Ruth, Ty Cobb, Honus Wagner and Mathewson.

Johnson, coming to the big leagues several years after Mathewson, but contemporary with him when Christy was fading and the youngster was at his peak, had a longer time to wait for his triumph. Destined to be with a second division club, Johnson waited seventeen long seasons before he played in his first world's series.

When the chance came, however, he made good, and his feat of winning for the Senators in the deciding game with the Giants in 1924, a twelve-inning classic, earned for him a place secure in the baseball hall of fame.

When he retired as a player in 1927, after twenty-one consecutive years with one club—a record in itself—he went for a time to the minors as a manager and then returned to Washington to become the leader of the team with which he had started as a major leaguer in 1907. He was manager of the Senators for 1929, 1930, 1931 and 1932.

He retired in 1932, willing to go back to his Maryland farm, but in midsummer of 1933 returned to the big leagues to become manager of the Cleveland team. "The Big Train," as he was also called, piloted the Indians until he resigned early in August, 1935.

Walter Johnson was one of the original five members of baseball's Hall of Fame, and was known for his blazing fastball.

Johnson received much publicity on Feb. 22 of the following year when he hurled two silver dollars across the Rappahannock River—a span of 272 feet—in connection with the annual Washington's Birthday celebration at Fredericksburg, Va. He thus duplicated a feat said to have been performed by George Washington in the latter's boyhood days.

The Presidential campaign of 1936 found Johnson taking an active interest in politics and his Maryland farm was the scene of a Republican rally for Alf Landon, Governor of Kansas and his party's candidate for President.

In 1938 Johnson was the lone Republican elected to the Board of Commissioners in Montgomery County, Md., adjoining the District of Columbia. Two years later he was the Republican nominee to represent Maryland's Sixth Congressional District, but was defeated by his Democratic opponent.

On his fiftieth birthday, Nov. 6, 1937, Johnson was acclaimed by 450 admirers at a dinner given in his honor at the Mayflower Hotel in Washington. He was president of the Association of Professional Baseball Players for several years and also served as a radio announcer for baseball games.

Between games of a Yankee-Washington double-header at Yankee Stadium on Aug. 23, 1942, Johnson and George Herman (Babe) Ruth came out of retirement to thrill 69,136 fans in a benefit program which enriched the Army-Navy Relief Fund by more than $80,000.

The assemblage gave a tremendous ovation as Johnson walked out to the mound and the Sultan of Swat stepped to the plate. Benny Bengough was behind the plate, with Billy Evans umpiring. Then the Big Train tossed them up, perhaps not so fast, but with the same effortless motion, while Ruth swung with all his old-time fervor.

The story of Johnson's entrance into the American League is one of the most interesting ever told. If ever there was a story-book career, Johnson's was it. In 1926, when Johnson celebrated his twentieth year with the Washington club, at which time a Walter Johnson Day was held in Washington on Aug. 2 and at which a letter from President Coolidge was read, Clark Griffith told how Johnson came into major league baseball. It is well worth repeating, especially if the Coolidge letter first is read to bring into highlight the success that Big Barney attained.

Here is what President Coolidge wrote:

"I am sure that I speak for all when I say that he (Walter Johnson) has been a wholesome influence in clean living and clean sport."

Looking over his record, one finds it a veritable mine of wonderful feats. He held the world's shut-out record, having registered 113 shut-outs since 1907 He also struck out more batters than any other pitcher. His total, including his last season as a hurler, 1927, when he was ill and unable to pitch very many times, was 3,497 for 802 games. Next to Rube Waddell, who struck out 343 in 1904, he fanned more men in one season than any other hurler in history. That mark was 313, made in 1910.

These are only a few of forty-five records. His twenty-one years with one club and his pitching 802 games for Washington constitute another. He led the American League in most complete games for the greatest number of years, six, in 1911, 1913, 1914, 1915, 1916 and 1918. He led his league in earned-run averages for six years.

In addition to his 3,497 strike-out record, he held the big league record for the greatest number of consecutive scoreless innings, fifty-six, and he scored three consecutive shut-outs in four playing days. On April 15, 1911, he struck out four men in one inning.

Not until 1920 did Johnson pitch his way into the baseball hall of fame reserved for no-hit, no-run games. On July 1 of that year he turned the trick against the Boston Red Sox. In his major league career he won 414 games and lost 276. His best season was in 1913, when he won thirty-six games and lost only seven. He led the American League in games won for six years. His longest winning streak was sixteen, in 1912. He was voted the most valuable player in the American League in 1924.

"All the News That's Fit to Print"

The New York Times

LATE CITY EDITION

Weather: Possible light snow today; cloudy tonight. Warmer tomorrow. Temp. range: today 17-31; Saturday 25-38. Full U.S. report on Page 71.

SECTION ONE

VOL. CXXI . No. 41,602 © 1971 The New York Times Company NEW YORK, SUNDAY, DECEMBER 19, 1971 75¢ beyond 50-mile zone from New York City, except Long Island. Higher in air delivery cities. NJ 50 CENTS

10-NATION MONETARY AGREEMENT REACHED; DOLLAR IS DEVALUED 8.57%; SURCHARGE OFF

Pakistan Calls Bhutto to Form Regime With New Charter

YAHYA DENOUNCED

Approval by President of Cease-Fire Spurs Demonstrations

By MALCOLM W. BROW[NE]

Special to The New York Times

RAWALPINDI, Pakistan, [Dec.] 18—President Agha Mohamm[ed] Yahya Khan today asked Zu[lfi]kar Ali Bhutto, the Depu[ty] Prime Minister and Foreign Minister, to return immediately from the United States to form a new government.

"On the arrival of Mr. Bhutto, power will be transferred to a representative government formed under the new constitution," an official statement said.

The announcement did not say what form the new constitution and government would take. Last night the President issued an outline of a new constitution and then withdrew it a few minutes later. The document had been written as if East Pakistan were still an integral part of the nation.

There were continuing indications today of political turmoil in West Pakistan, all related to the announcement yesterday that President Yahya Khan had accepted an Indian cease-fire offer.

Editorials Assail Him

The President was denounced at angry demonstrations in various cities, by newspaper editorials and even by politicians who owe the little authority they have to him.

A particularly bitter statement was issued by a coalition of minor right-wing parties headed by Nurul Amin, the aging Bengali whom President Yahya Khan on Dec. 8 designated as Prime Minister.

Mr. Nurul Amin said later that he would not take office.

The statement by his party demanded President Yahya Khan's immediate resignation and said:

"The tragedy of East Pakistan, the intolerable and humiliating manner in which the national army was forced to surrender its arms and the order of cease-fire against the sentiments of the people are the logical results of the policies Agha Mohammed Yahya Khan has been following over the last three years."

"Internally," the statement

Continued on Page 22, Column 6

NIXON HAILS PACT

He Makes a Surprise Appearance—Gold Goes to $38

By EDWIN L. DALE Jr.

Special to The New York Times

WASHINGTON, Dec. 18—The world's 10 leading non-Communist industrial nations reached agreement tonight on a new pattern of currency exchange rates, including a devaluation of the United States dollar by 8.57 per cent.

Speaking to reporters as the negotiations ended, President Nixon said, "It is my great

Text of President's remarks and communiqué, Page 56.

privilege to announce, on behalf of the finance ministers and the other representatives of the 10 countries involved, the conclusion of the most significant monetary agreement in the history of the world."

The new United States 10 per cent import surcharge will be removed next week. The surcharge was imposed, and the entire recent monetary turmoil began, with President Nixon's dramatic domestic and international economic measures of August 15.

Yen to Go Up

Several other currencies, led by the Japanese yen, will be revalued upward.

Treasury Secretary John B. Connally said that the over-all effect would be an effective devaluation of the dollar by 12 per cent. This figure is arrived at by allowing for United States trade with each of the countries. The Canadian dollar, which will continue to float in daily trading, was left out of the calculation.

A communiqué issued by the Group of 10, said that most foreign exchange markets would be closed on Monday, but Mr. Connally said the United States market would be open.

The dollar devaluation figure of 8.57 per cent used by Mr. Connally results from a proposed increase in the official price of gold from $35 to $38 an ounce. Congress, however, will not be asked to approve the necessary legislation to increase the gold price until the [U]nited States wins concessions [fr]om Japan, the European Com[mo]n Market and Canada on [tra]de matters.

[Ho]wever, foreign exchange [...]hat is, the actual ex[change] rate of the dollar [...]he other currencies—[will] be conducted at levels as if the new gold price were already in effect.

As in all cases of changes in a currency's exchange rate, the

Continued on Page 56, Column 3

[...]king at the Smithsonian Insti[tution] [...] Minister of West Germany.

Associated Press

[...]s Accord [...]ious Impact

[...]LORAN

[...]mier Eisaku Sato of [...]aluation of the yen [...]tion's economy but

[...] ENCOURAGES [...] EXPERTS

[...]ic Climate [...]nfidence [...]or U.S.

[...] relief to bank[ers and] businessmen everywhere. It will ease future plan-

Continued on Page 56, Column 4

REDISTRICTIN[G]

REPO[RT] Pakist[an]

Pres[...] Of [...]

WASHINGTON, [...] President Nixon [...] Pakistan's Deputy [...] ister and Foreign [...] Zulfikar Ali Bhutto, [...] power cooperation wo[uld be] needed to prevent furth[er out]breaks of war on the [sub]continent.

Mr. Bhutto, who is lea[ving] shortly for Pakistan to hel[p in] the formation of a new civi[lian] government, met with [the] President for about 25 minu[tes] at the White House. Earlier, he had met for 45 minutes with Secretary of State William P. Rogers.

Ronald L. Ziegler, the White House press secretary, said that Mr. Nixon had told Mr. Bhutto that the "first requirement" in the wake of the war between India and Pakistan was to "establish confidence that the people there can live in security."

"This will require the cooperation of major powers as well as with those in the region," Mr. Nixon was reported to have said.

This was a reference to the Administration's concern over the failure of the Soviet Union to join with the United States in seeking to head off an Indian attack on East Pakistan on Nov. 1, which, the Administration charges, led to the actual war.

Mr. Ziegler said that he expected Mr. Nixon to make this matter a principal subject in his meetings with Soviet leaders next May.

The Administration indicated yesterday that Mr. Nixon had

Sta[...] On[...]

Across th[e] [...]tible swing [...] from what [...] consider a [...] environmental [...] resentation of [...] ests on state b[...] with pollution.

In the last ye[ar] New York Times su[...] a score of states ha[ve] plan to take steps [...] or reduce such po[...] flicts of interest fr[...] tory panels.

The number of sta[...] air or water pollution [...] reflecting pollution i[...]

[...] misfea[...] boards, many [...] officials, conservationists and laymen share a conviction that the pattern of "foxes guarding the henhouse" at best does not expedite pollution abatement.

The boards' defenders insist it is necessary to include members with links to pollution sources in order both to draw on their expertise and to achieve balance of a sort between clean-environment advocates and major economic interests.

But conservationists reply that expertise is available elsewhere; that environmental cleanliness and economic prosperity are complementary

Continued on Page 38, Column 1

Index to Subjects

125 Slain in Dacca Area Believed Elite of Benga[l]

Following is the text of a pool report received in Washington from the American press corps in Dacca:

DACCA, Pakistan, Dec. 18—At least 125 persons, believed to be physicians, professors, writers and teachers, were found murdered today in a field outside Dacca.

All the victims' hands were tied behind their backs and they had been bayoneted, garrotted or shot. They were among an estimated 300 Bengali intellectuals who had been seized by West Pakistani soldiers and locally recruited supporters.

Razakar (pro-Pakistani) irregulars had apparently held the victims as "hostages" for fair surrender terms. They appeared to have been killed just before Pakistani commanders in the East surrendered two days ago.

Nearby residents said that many other Bengalis had been killed in a neighboring factory and thrown into pits. The razakars were reported still holding out in the factory and they took part in a fight with an Indian patrol.

Two of the razakars who were captured were said to have admitted killing some of the intellectuals, and they were then reportedly beaten

Continued on Page 22, Column 1

[...] lawyer by profession, who competed only as an amateur, had suffered from a progressive disease of the spinal cord since 1948. By the middle of last December he was no longer able to go to the offices of his firm, Jones, Bird & Howell, although he tried to continue working at home. Death came from an aneurysm in his chest.

Surviving are his widow, the former Mary Malone; a son, Robert T. 3d of Nashville; two daughters, Mrs. Carl Hood Jr. and Mrs. Clara J. Black, and seven grandchildren.

Star of a Golden Age

By FRANK LITSKY

In the decade following World War I, America luxuriated in the Golden Era of Sports and its greatest collection of super-athletes: Babe Ruth and Ty Cobb in baseball, Jack Dempsey and Gene Tunney in boxing,

Continued on Page 60, Column 5

Bobby Jones in 1930

Organized Crime Selling Official (Forged) Papers

By NICHOLAS GAGE

Organized crime members are going into the business of selling a vast variety of official identification documents according to law enforcement officials.

The documents include birth certificates, driver's licenses, car registrations, high school diplomas, armed forces discharges, Social Security cards and even passports.

Some of these documents are counterfeit, but most are the real thing stolen from government offices or printing houses, according to Edward J. McLaughlin, chief counsel of the State Joint Legislative Committee on Crime.

Mr. McLaughlin, whose committee is looking into the racket, said the documents were put to a number of practical uses.

Con men use identification cards to cash bad checks and commit other frauds. Car-theft rings use driver's licenses and car registrations to dispose of stolen cars easily and quickly.

But the largest market for some of these documents are individuals with no criminal connections. Many driver's licenses, for example, are bought by non-English-speaking persons who are not able to

Continued on Page 21, Column 1

Bobby Jones, Golf Master, Dies; Only Player to Win Grand Slam

Special to The New York Times

ATLANTA, Dec. 18—Bobby Jones, the master golfer who scored an unparalleled grand slam by winning the United States and British Open and Amateur Tournaments in 1930, died today at his home. His age was 69.

Mr. Jones, a lawyer by profession, who competed only as an amateur, had suffered from a progressive disease of the spinal cord since 1948. By the middle of last December he was no longer able to go to the offices of his firm, Jones, Bird & Howell, although he tried to continue working at home. Death came from an aneurysm in his chest.

Surviving are his widow, the former Mary Malone; a son, Robert T. 3d of Nashville; two daughters, Mrs. Carl Hood Jr. and Mrs. Clara J. Black, and seven grandchildren.

Star of a Golden Age

By FRANK LITSKY

In the decade following World War I, America luxuriated in the Golden Era of Sports and its greatest collection of super-athletes: Babe Ruth and Ty Cobb in baseball, Jack Dempsey and Gene Tunney in boxing,

Continued on Page 60, Column 5

Bobby Jones in 1930

Bobby Jones, Only Golfer to Win Grand Slam, Dies

Continued From Page 1, Col. 6

Bill Tilden in tennis, Red Grange in football and Bobby Jones in golf.

Many of their records have been broken now, and others are destined to be broken. But one, sports experts agree, may outlast them — Bobby Jones's grand slam of 1930.

Jones, an intense, unspoiled young man, started early on the road to success. At the age of 10, he shot a 90 for 18 holes. At 11 he was down to 80, and at 12 he shot a 70. At 9 he played against men, at 14 he won a major men's tournament and at 21 he was United States Open champion.

At 28 he achieved the grand slam—victories in one year in the United States Open, British Open, United States Amateur and British Amateur championships. At that point, he retired from tournament golf.

A nation that idolized him for his success grew to respect him even more for his decision to treat golf as a game rather than a way of life. This respect grew with the years.

"First come my wife and children," he once explained. "Next comes my profession—the law. Finally, and never as a life in itself, comes golf."

His record, aside from the grand slam, was magnificent. He won the United States Open championship four times (1923, 1926, 1929 and 1930), the British Open three times (1926, 1927 and 1930), and the United States Amateur five times (1924, 1925, 1927, 1928 and 1930).

"Jones is as truly the supreme artist of golf as Paderewski is the supreme artist of the piano," George H. Greenfield wrote in The New York Times in 1930.

Felt the Tension

Success did not come easily. Though Jones was cool and calculating outwardly, he seethed inside. He could never eat properly during a major tournament. The best his stomach would hold was dry toast and tea.

The pressure of tournament competition manifested itself in other ways, too. Everyone expected Jones to win every time he played, including Atlanta friends who often bet heavily on him. He escaped the unending pressure by retiring from competition.

"Why should I punish myself like this over a golf tournament?," he once asked. "Sometimes I'd pass my mother and dad on the course, look at them and not even see them because I was so concentrated on the game. Afterward, it made a fellow feel a little silly."

Intense concentration shows on the face of Bobby Jones shown here competing in the U.S. Amateur event in 1927.

The quality of the man projected itself, too. He was worshiped as a national hero in Scotland, the birthplace of golf. Scots would come for miles around to watch him play.

In 1936, on a visit, he made an unannounced trip to the Royal and Ancient Golf Club at St. Andrews for a quiet morning round with friends. There were 5,000 spectators at the first tee and 7,000 at the 18th. Businesses closed as word spread that "Our Bobby is back."

In 1927, when he tapped in his final putt to win the British Open there, an old Scot stood by the green and muttered: "The man canna be human."

Off the course, Jones was convivial in a quiet way. He was a good friend and always the gentleman, though he had full command of strong language when desired. He had a fine sense of humor, and he laughed easily. He smoked cigarettes and drank bourbon.

He was besieged by people who wanted to play a social round of golf with him. When they talked with him, it was always golf. He managed to tolerate their one-sided approach to life. He also learned to put up with the name of Bobby, which he hated (he preferred Bob).

He was not always so serene. As a youngster, he had a reputation for throwing clubs when everything was not going right. When Jim Barnes, the 1921 United States Open champion, watched him let off steam, he said:

"Never mind that club-throwing and the beatings he's taking. Defeat will make him great. He's not satisfied now with a pretty good shot. He has to be perfect. That's the way a good artist must feel."

The defeats Barnes spoke of were frequent in the early years. For young Jones, though he had the game of a man, had the emotions of a growing boy. He never won the big tournaments until he got his temper under control.

At 18, he learned that his greatest opponent was himself. He was playing at Toledo one day with Harry Vardon, the great English professional, and was his usual brash self. They were about even when Jones dribbled a shot into a bunker. Hoping to ease his embarrassment, he turned to Vardon and asked:

"Did you ever see a worse shot?"

"No," replied the crusty Vardon. It was the only word he spoke to Jones all day.

Jones matured, so much so that O. B. Keeler, an Atlanta sports writer and his long-time Boswell, once wrote:

"He has more character than any champion in our history."

He also had the dream of every golfer—a picture swing. No one taught it to him, for he never took a golf lesson in his life. He learned the swing by watching Stewart Maiden, a Scottish professional at the Atlanta Athletic Club course. He would follow Maiden for a few holes, then run home and mimic the swing.

His putting was famous. So was his putter, a rusty, goose-necked club known as Calamity Jane. His strength was driving, putting and an ability to get out of trouble. He was an imaginative player, and he never hesitated to take a chance. In fact, he seldom hesitated on any shot, and he earned an unfair reputation as a mechanical golfer. The game often baffled him. "There are times," he once said, "when I feel that I know less about what I'm doing on a golf course than anyone else in the world."

When he was an infant, doctors were not sure that he would survive, let alone play golf. He had a serious digestive ailment until he was 5, and he stayed home while other children played. In his

(continued)

Bobby Jones

later years, he was crippled by syringomyelia, a chronic disease of the spinal cord, and he had circulation and heart trouble.

Robert Tyre Jones Jr. (named for his grandfather) was born on St. Patrick's Day, 1902, in Atlanta. His father was a star outfielder at the University of Georgia, and the youngster's first love was baseball. He also tried tennis. At the age of 9 he settled down to golf.

His parents had taken up the game after moving to a cottage near the East Lake course of the Atlanta Athletic Club. Young Bobby would walk around the course, watch the older folk play and learn by example. He was only 6 years old, a scrubby youngster with skinny arms and legs, when he won a six-hole tournament. At 9 he was the club's junior champion.

In Philadelphia Tourney

He was 14 when he journeyed to the Merion Cricket Club near Philadelphia for his first United States Amateur championship. He was a chunky lad of 5 feet 4 inches and 165 pounds and somewhat knock-kneed. He was wearing his first pair of long trousers.

After qualifying for match play, he defeated Eben M. Byers, a former champion, in the first round. He beat Frank Dyer, a noted player at the time, in the second round, after losing five of the first six holes. Then he lost to Robert A. Gardner, the defending champion, 5 and 3.

In 1922 he reached the semifinals of the United States Amateur before losing. That ended what he called his seven lean years. Next came what Keeler called "the eight fat years" as Jones finally achieved the heights.

All this time, golf was a sidelight to education. Jones wanted to be an engineer, and he earned bachelor's and master's degrees in engineering at Georgia Tech. Then he decided to become a lawyer. He went to Harvard and earned another bachelor's degree, than to Emory University in Atlanta for a Bachelor of Laws degree. In 1928, he joined his father's law firm in Atlanta.

In 1924, Jones decided that he was worrying too much about his opponent in match-play (man against man) competition. He vowed to play for pars and forget about his opponent.

This was a turning point in his career. He started to win match-play competition. That year, at Merion, Pa., he won the United States Amateur for the first time. In the final, he defeated George Von Elm by the overwhelming score of 9 and 8.

Also in 1924, he married Mary Malone, his high school sweetheart.

In 1929 Jones had a close call in the United States Open at the Winged Foot Golf Club, Mamaroneck, N. Y. He sank a 12-foot sloping, sidehill putt on the last green to tie Al Espinosa. The next day, Jones won their 36-hole title playoff by 23 strokes.

Then came 1930 and the grand slam. Lloyds of London quoted odds of 50 to 1 that Jones wouldn't win the world's four major tournaments that year. He won them.

First came the British Amateur. He started his opening match by shooting 3, 4, 3 and 2. In the final he beat Roger Wethered, 7 and 6. Next was the British Open at Hoylake, England, and his 72-hole score of 291 won that championship.

Back home, Jones got his sternest test of the year in the United States Open at Interlachen near Minneapolis. There were 15,000 spectators in the gallery as he played the par-4 18th hole. He got a birdie 3 by sinking a 40-foot undulating putt, and his 287 won by two strokes.

He had become the first man to win three of the four major titles in one year. The last of the grand-slam tournaments, the United States Amateur at Merion, was almost anticlimactic.

No one doubted for the moment that Jones would win. He captured the qualifying medal. He routed Jess Sweetser, 9 and 8, in the semifinal round, and in the final he defeated Gene Homans, 8 and 7. The crowd surged around him so wildly that it took a detachment of United States Marines to get him out safely.

Soon after, he retired from tournament play and made a series of golf motion pictures,

(continued)

Two immortals of golf—Bobby Jones and Francis Ouimet.

the only time he ever made money from the game. Later, he became a vice president of A. G. Spalding & Bros., the sporting goods manufacturer. He became a wealthy lawyer and soft-drink bottler and a business and social leader in Atlanta.

He never played serious tournament golf again. He didn't seem to mind.

"Golf is like eating peanuts," he said. "You can play too much or too little. I've become reconciled to the fact that I'll never play as well as I used to."

A few years later, Jones and the late architect, Alister Mackensie, designed the Augusta National Golf Course in Georgia. In 1934 the Masters tournament was started there, and in Jones's lifetime many golf people considered it the most important tournament of all.

Jones played in the first Masters and in several thereafter, but he was never among the leaders. He always wore his green jacket, signifying club membership, at victory ceremonies, and he served as club president.

He became strong enough to rip a pack of playing cards across the middle, but his health deteriorated. He underwent spinal surgery in 1948 and 1950. He was forced to use one cane, then two canes and then a wheelchair, and his weight dropped to less than 100 pounds. He last saw the Masters in 1967.

He was a close friend of Dwight D. Eisenhower, and the President often used his cottage adjacent to the Augusta National course for golfing vacations. During his first term in office, the President painted a 40-by-32-inch oil portrait of Jones at the peak of his game. On the back was printed by hand:

"Bob — from his friend D.D.E. 1953."

In January of 1953, three months after a heart attack, Jones was honored at Golf House, the United States Golf Association headquarters in Manhattan. Augusta National members, including General Eisenhower, had donated another oil portrait to be hung at Golf House. A highlight of the ceremony was the reading of a letter from the President.

"Those who have been fortunate enough to know him," the letter said, "realize that his fame as a golfer is transcended by his inestimable qualities as a human being . . . His gift to his friends is the warmth that comes from unselfishness, superb judgment, nobility of character, unwavering loyalty to principle."

Bobby Jones listened and cried.

JONES IS MOURNED AT SCOTTISH LINKS

Royal and Ancient Club Flag Is Lowered in Memory

ST. ANDREWS, Scotland, Dec. 18 (AP)—The town of St. Andrews and the Royal and Ancient Golf Club, headquarters of the game, mourned the great Bobby Jones today.

Golfers stopped on the Old Course when the news of his death reached them. The flag on the clubhouse was lowered to half staff.

It was on the St. Andrews course that Jones won the British Amateur as part of his grand slam in 1930. Three years earlier he had won the British Open here.

An Honorary Freeman

Later Jones was made an honorary freeman (citizen) of the old town.

The Royal and Ancient Club cabled a message of sympathy to the great golfer's widow.

Keith MacKenzie, secretary of the club, said: "Bobby Jones was an honorary member of this club and his death is a tremendous personal loss to us. We are cabling Mrs. Jones in the name of the captain and members expressing our deepest sorrow."

Mayor Feels His Loss

David Niven, the provost, or mayor, of St. Andrews, said: "What can one say about Bobby Jones? He was a great golfer and the game is poorer for his death. But he was a freeman of St. Andrews, too, and in common with all Scots we are saddened by the news.

"He was held in great affection by the citizens of St. Andrews."

Arthur Havers, British Open champion in 1923 and an opponent of Jones in many tournaments, said: "He was a wonderful man, and all professional golfers held him in esteem. He was always a possible winner in any event he entered. Because of his build he had an unusual style, but it was certainly effective and he was a beautiful putter."

Havers, now 73 years old, once defeated Jones, 2 and 1, in a 36-hole exhibition match.

Palmer: Deeds Will Live On

LATROBE, Pa., Dec. 18 (UPI) — Arnold Palmer said today that Bobby Jones's accomplishments "will live on forever."

Palmer, a four-time winner of the Masters tournament that Jones helped establish, issued the following statement from his home here:

"In the passing of Bob Jones, the world of golf has suffered a great loss. What he established with the grand slam and the Masters tournament will live on forever in the minds of golfers and sportsmen everywhere.

"In the Masters, its fine club, and great golf course, we have a living memorial to Bob Jones. As his health failed in recent years, you had to admire the courage of this man, who was almost totally immobilized, and how he maintained to the end his high interest in the game.

In 1930, when Bobby Jones was on his way to winning golf's grand slam, Lloyds of London quoted 50 to 1 odds that he would not do it.

Jones's Route to the Grand Slam

ATLANTA, Dec. 18 (AP)— Bobby Jones won golf's only grand slam, in 1930. Here is how he did it:

BRITISH AMATEUR

(At St. Andrews, Scotland)

First round: defeated S. S. Roper, 3 and 2.

Second round: Defeated Cowan Shankland, 5 and 3.

Third round: Defeated G. O. Watt, 7 and 6.

Fourth round: Defeated H. R. Johnston, 1 up.

Fifth round: Defeated Eric Fiddian, 4 and 3.

Semifinals: Defeated George Voigt, 1 up.

Championship: 36 holes: Defeated Roger Wethered, 7 and 6.

BRITISH OPEN

(At Hoylake, England)

Jones won with rounds of 70-72-74-75—291, defeating Leo Diegel and Macdonald Smith by two strokes.

U.S. OPEN

(At Interlachen, Minn.)

Jones won with rounds of 71 73-68-75—287, defeating Macdonald Smith by two strokes.

U.S. AMATEUR

(At Merion, Pa.)

Jones led qualifiers with 69-73—142, tying record.

First round: Defeated Ross Somerville, 5 and 4.

Second round: Defeated F. G. Hoblitzel, 5 and 4.

Third round: 36 holes: Defeated Fay Coleman, 6 and 5.

Semifinals: 36 holes: Defeated Jess W. Sweetser, 9 and 8.

Championship: Defeated Gene Homans, 8 and 7.

The New York Times TUESDAY, JANUARY 2, 1923

WILLIE KEELER DIES OF HEART DISEASE

Famous Oldtime Baseball Player Succumbs to Malady at His Brooklyn Home.

William H. ("Wee Willie") Keeler, one of the most famous of old-time baseball players, died yesterday at his home, 1,010 Gates Avenue, Brooklyn. He had been a sufferer from heart disease for more than two years.

Keeler had expressed a desire to live until the beginning of the new year, and on Sunday he remarked to his brother, Thomas F. Keeler, that he was fighting a losing fight but would live to see 1923 ushered in. On New Year's Eve several members of his family and some friends visited him at his home. Just before midnight all the members of the party left the room where Keeler was lying and stepped outside to hear the bells. They came back a few minutes later to find the sick man sitting up in bed ringing in the new year with a bell he had for the purpose of calling his attendant. He was playing the game of life as he played the game of baseball—until the last man was out in the ninth.

Keeler was one of the greatest batsmen of all time. He first became noted as a great hitter while playing in the outfield with the famous Baltimore Orioles in the nineties. Several of the records he set while with that organization, thrice a pennant winner of the old National League, remain unbroken. Some of his nineteen years in the majors were spent with the Giants and Brooklyn Nationals and the New York Yankees.

He was not a batsman of the slugging type, such as Ed Delehanty and the late Pop Anson, but was a pioneer in the art of place hitting, the philosophy of which he explained in the simple and now famous utterance, "Hit 'em where they ain't."

While with Baltimore, Keeler twice led the National League in batting, in 1897 with .432, a mark second only to Hugh Duffy's .438 in baseball annals, and in 1898 with .379. His greatest year was 1897, his feats that season including six hits in one game and records of 199 one-base blows and hitting safely in 44 consecutive games, both of which still stand as major league high marks. His total hits that year, 243, also stood as a National League record until the past season, when Rogers Hornsby, great second baseman of the St. Louis Cardinals, established a new standard with 250. The nearest approach to his consecutive game hitting was made last season by George Sisler of the St. Louis Browns, who reached 41 before going hitless.

Over a stretch of eight seasons, from 1894 to 1901, Keeler hung up two other unique marks, scoring more than 100 runs and rapping out more than 200 hits in each of these seasons. By gathering 211 safe blows last season Ty Cobb equaled Keeler's hitting mark, but the Detroit star's record was not made in consecutive seasons.

National League records show Keeler's life-time batting mark, for nineteen years, to be .305, but for fourteen seasons, from 1893 to 1906, inclusive, when he was at his best, his average was close to .350.

Keeler was born in Brooklyn, March 3, 1872. He played his first major league game Sept. 30, 1892, with the Giants, who secured him from Binghamton, N. Y. The following year he played with the Giants and Brooklyn. From 1894 to 1898 he patrolled right field with Baltimore, a team on which other stars were John McGraw, Wilbert Robinson, Hugh Jennings and Joe Kelley. He returned to Brooklyn in 1899, the Dodgers winning pennants that year and the next. He was with the New York Yankees from 1903 to 1909 and signed in 1910 with the Giants, who released him the same year to Toronto. That year marked the end of his major league career.

Ill health coupled with financial misfortune some years later, brought Keeler's circumstances to a low ebb and in 1921 he was aided by a joint gift of $5,500 from the National and American Leagues.

"Wee Willie" Keeler was one of the greatest batsmen of his day. His 44-game hitting streak stood as a record until Joe DiMaggio broke it 43 years later.

BASEBALL MEN PAY TRIBUTE TO KEELER

McGraw and Heydler Are Among Those Who Praise Famous Old-Time Player.

"The best place hitter I ever saw" was the tribute paid by John J. McGraw yesterday to Willie Keeler, one of the greatest batsmen of all time, who died Monday afternoon at his home, 1,010 Gates Avenue, Brooklyn. For five years McGraw and Keeler were teammates on the famous Baltimore Orioles. Later, for part of one season, "Wee Willie" was under McGraw on the Giants—the last major league club he played for actively.

"What a wonderful hitter Keeler was!" said McGraw. "He could place hits better than any other batter I ever saw. He was also the fastest man going down to first base that I ever watched on a ball field. That was in his prime, when it was child's play for him to beat out bunts and infield grounders. He was one of the best fielders baseball has ever seen, and a tremendous influence on the club—aggressive, smart, dauntless. I am sorry to see him go."

Scores of other tributes came to the Keeler home yesterday. Messages of condolence were received from prominent men in baseball, including Keeler's old teammates at Baltimore and many other old-time players who remembered Willie when he was the most scientific batter in baseball.

President John A. Heydler of the National League made this statement to newspaper men:

"In an age when roughness—and sometimes rowdyism—was almost a virtue in baseball, Willie Keeler was always a gentleman. That strikes me as the most remarkable of his many fine traits. He was a fighter, a never-say-die player, a man who had the will to win ingrained deeply in him. But whatever he did was always done in a clean, gentlemanly manner. He was not an umpire baiter, although he wanted always to win. Keeler's impress on baseball was great."

Funeral services will be held at the Keeler home tomorrow morning, with a requiem mass afterward at the Church of Our Lady of Good Counsel, Putnam and Ralph Avenues, Brooklyn. The mass will be celebrated by Father McGowan, for many years a close friend of Keeler. Interment will be in Calvary Cemetery. The Yankees, Giants and Brooklyn Robins, three of Keeler's old teams, and the National and American Leagues will be represented at the services.

The New York Times — SUNDAY, FEBRUARY 8, 1959.

Napoleon Lajoie Is Dead at 83; Baseball Hall of Fame Member

One of First 9 Elected in '37 —Hit .422 in 1901, Still the American League Record

DAYTONA BEACH, Fla., Feb. 7 (AP)—Napoleon Lajoie, a charter member of the Baseball Hall of Fame, died at a hospital here today. His age was 83.

Mr. Lajoie was stricken with pneumonia in January. He was believed to have recovered and was due to be discharged from the hospital this week but suffered a relapse yesterday.

A second baseman, he was elected to the Hall of Fame in 1937 along with Christy Mathewson, Ty Cobb, Walter Johnson, Babe Ruth, Hans Wagner, Cy Young, Tris Speaker and Grover Cleveland Alexander. Of the original nine members, only Cobb survives.

Mr. Lajoie in playing days

Lajoie in 1901, the year he hit .422 to win the American League's first batting championship.

The "Most Graceful"

In the Hall of Fame at Cooperstown, N. Y., there is only one bronze tablet bearing the words "most graceful." It is the tablet for Mr. Lajoie (pronounced Lah-joe-way).

Nap, as most of his friends called him, was an outfielder early in his career and finished as a first baseman but it is as a second baseman that he will be remembered. He indisputably was the top player in the American League until Ty Cobb came along. Then both battled for top honors during the years their careers overlapped.

In a twenty-one-year span—with the Philadelphia Athletics and the Cleveland Indians—Lajoie, who was a right-handed batter, compiled a lifetime average of .339 in 2,475 games.

In 1901, while with the Athletics, he won the American League's first batting championship with an average of .422, which is still the league record. Lajoie led the league on two other occasions. In 1903 and 1904, with Cleveland, he hit .355 and .381.

He was denied credit for his .422 average for years because of a typographical error. His 1901 average was correctly recorded as .422, based on 229 hits. But somewhere along the line the hits became listed as 220. An eagle-eyed statistician noted this, with the result that the average was "corrected" to .405.

Not until 1954 was this injustice erased and Lajoie restored to his leadership. Until then Cobb and George Sisler had been the accredited joint leaders with averages of .420.

Lajoie's major league total of 3,251 hits is topped by only four others—Cobb with 4,191, Tris Speaker, 3,515; Honus Wagner, 3,430, and Eddie Collins, 3,313.

Nap staged a duel with Cobb for the batting title in 1909 but lost, .3848 to .3841, despite his getting eight hits in eight times at bat on the season's final day.

Those eight hits stirred a bit of a scandal, because six of them were bunts and obvious gifts from the opposing club, the St. Louis Browns.

The Browns' third baseman was Johnny (Red) Corriden, then a rookie. His manager ordered him to "play back on the edge of the grass" for Lajoie. Young Corriden obeyed his manager. Later, when Ban Johnson, the American League president, investigated, Corriden was absolved. But the manager, Jack O'Connor, and his pitcher-coach, Harry Howell, were dismissed.

This little plot had been designed because most players disliked Cobb and wanted Lajoie to capture the batting title.

Napoleon Lajoie, of French-Canadian descent, was born in Woonsocket, R. I., Sept. 5, 1875. As a young man he drove a hack and played baseball in his spare time.

He signed his first contract with Fall River of the New England League and was a star from the start, batting .429 to lead his team to a pennant.

On Aug. 12, 1896, Lajoie reached the big leagues when he signed with the Phillies. One tale, perhaps apocryphal, had it that the Phils really wanted a player named Phil Geier and took Lajoie as a minor part of the transaction.

Jumped to Athletics

Lajoie jumped to the Athletics in 1901 when the American League invaded Philadelphia. When an injunction was obtained forbidding him to play in Pennsylvània, the Athletics traded him to Cleveland. There he spent thirteen productive years. They even named the club the "Naps" in his honor shortly after he joined it. That nickname held until 1915, when the present name, the Indians, was adopted.

Lajoie managed the Indians from 1905 to 1909.

His grace, both at bat and in the field, was legendary. He had extraordinary ability, supreme confidence and was never hesitant or indecisive.

Nap became a fine golfer. On one eighteen-hole round in St. Petersburg, Fla., about thirty years ago, the big fellow stepped up to putt after putt, ranging from eight to fifteen feet, and sank the ball without a pause to line it up or address it. He did miss one 15-footer, demonstrating that he was human.

"Why fool around?" he said. "There's the ball, there's the hole. What else is there but to tap it in?"

The New York Times SUNDAY, NOVEMBER 26, 1944.

JUDGE LANDIS DIES; BASEBALL CZAR, 78

Commissioner for 24 Years Barred Eight Players for Throwing' 1919 Series

FREED 'SLAVE' ATHLETES

On Bench, Fined Standard Oil $29,240,000—Presided in Haywood, Berger Cases

CHICAGO, Nov. 25 (AP)—Kenesaw Mountain Landis, ruler of baseball for twenty-four years, died here early today in St. Luke's Hospital after a long illness. His age was 78. The immediate cause of death was coronary thrombosis. Members of his family were at the bedside.

Judge Landis entered the hospital on Oct. 2 suffering from a severe cold. On the same day his wife fell and fractured her right wrist, and they occupied adjoining hospital rooms.

His death left the major leagues without a guiding genius and placed tremendous importance on the National and American League winter meeting here on Dec. 11, 12 and 13, when a successor probably will be named. Until the meetings, at least, the commissioner's office will be conducted by his secretary, Leslie M. O'Connor, who also was at the bedside.

Just a week ago, when the commissioner was fretting over what he protested was an overly long hospital stay, a joint committee of the two leagues recommended that Landis be re-elected for another seven-year term when his term expired Jan. 12, 1946.

Cheered by Confidence Vote

Ostensibly cheered by that vote of confidence, the commissioner chided his physician for warnings that his condition was delicate. But he suffered a setback Sunday and early this morning was placed under an oxygen tent a little more than an hour before he died.

In compliance with his wishes, there will be no funeral service. Cremation will take place privately.

Only recently Judge Landis, after living in a hotel for twenty-seven years, purchased a home in suburban Glencoe and worked so diligently in his victory garden that he overtaxed his heart.

He missed his first world series this fall since he took office in 1920 as baseball commissioner. The office of commissioner replaced the old national commission of three, composed of the late Ban Johnson, president of the American League; John A. Heydler, president of the National League, and the late Garry Hermann, president of the Cincinnati Reds.

Judge Kenesaw Mountain Landis

Besides his widow, Judge Landis leaves a son, Reed G. Landis, ranked as America's second aviation ace in the first World War, and a daughter, Mrs. Richard W. Phillips.

Baseball Involved in 1919 Scandal

The year 1920 found professional baseball suffering from a most unsightly black eye. The fans had developed a deep-rooted suspicion that the victory of the Cincinnati Reds over the Chicago White Sox in the 1919 world series had not resulted entirely from superior brawn and skill, and the financiers of the game, which is as much a business as it is a sport, were more than a little worried.

At that time Judge Landis was presiding in spectacular fashion over a United States District Court in Chicago. In his capacity as a judge he had made the acquaintance of the leaders of baseball six years previously, during the Federal League "war," when those would-be invaders of the field alleged that organized baseball was a trust in violation of the Sherman Act and sought equal status with the National and American Leagues as a major organization.

Judge Landis had taken his time about deciding the case and in the interim the Federal League compromised and dissolved.

The club managers and owners discovered during the trial that he knew a great deal about their business and baseball. It was then he was first mentioned as chairman of the National Commission.

Finally, in November, 1920, a delegation of baseball financiers waited on Judge Landis in his chambers to offer him the high commissionership of baseball at a salary of $50,000 a year. He accepted the offer, but cut the proffered salary by $7,500, the amount he received as a Federal judge.

Barred Eight Chicago Players

Then he began to clean house. He issued an order barring eight members of the Chicago White Sox from future participation in big league baseball. The eight had been tried and acquitted on indictments charging them with having accepted bribes from gamblers to "throw" the 1919 world series to the Cincinnati team, but Judge Landis held they had forfeited their right to play.

The strict discipline that Judge Landis imposed on clubs and players had a sensational test in 1921. At that time he fined George Herman (Babe) Ruth, Bob Meusel and Bill Piercey, members of the New York Yankees, American League champions, their full share of the world series bonuses because they had defied his rule against barnstorming tours. He also suspended them for the first month of the succeeding season.

In his later years Judge Landis was sometimes resentfully referred to by the club owners as "Abraham Lincoln" Landis because he freed so many baseball "slaves." In 1938 he freed 100 St. Louis Cardinals farm-hands, imposed fines on the Dodgers and the Tigers for concealing player contracts a year later and then in 1940 made free ninety-two Detroit athletes whose value was estimated at $500,000.

But for all of his unbending qualities, Judge Landis was recognized by the New York Chapter of the Baseball Writers Association in 1938 as a fitting recipient of its "meritorious service" plaque which annually goes to a man who has contributed much to the sport throughout the years.

President Backs Game

Bronchial pneumonia confined Judge Landis to Little Traverse Hospital in Petoskey, Mich., for several weeks during the autumn of 1941, but he recovered sufficiently to attend the major league meetings in Chicago in December of that year.

At these sessions, held a few days after the United States had become involved in the present World War, Judge Landis joined with the heads of the National and American circuits in stating that while baseball contemplated no immediate changes in its affairs, it would stand ready to cooperate with the Government and military authorities.

A month later Judge Landis addressed a letter to President Franklin D. Roosevelt asking the Chief Executive if he thought professional baseball should be played in wartime. Landis emphasized he was not raising the question of continuance with the baseball clubs of individual players who might be called up for service.

The country's baseball executives were delighted witn President Roosevelt's prompt reply to Landis' query. The President endorsed the sport, saying that he felt professional baseball should be continued during the war to provide relaxation for a hard-working populace, and suggesting more night games.

Judge Landis first achieved national prominence in 1907, two years after the late President Theodore Roosevelt appointed him to the Federal Bench in the Northern District of Illinois, when he imposed a fine of $29,240,000 on the Standard Oil Company, which then was extremely unpopular. The imposition of the fine—greater than the company's total capitalization at the time—won the young judge popular acclaim, but it never was collected because the higher courts set it aside.

Forced Rockefeller to Testify

The fine was imposed after a trial of a freight rebate case which lasted six weeks. In the course of the trial Judge Landis forced the

(continued)

Judge Landis throws out the ball in 1923.

elder John D. Rockefeller to come to Chicago to testify. The Standard Oil Company had been indicted on 1,462 counts, each charging that it had accepted a rebate from the Chicago & Alton Railroad on the shipment of oil from Whiting, Ind., to East St. Louis, Ill. The oil, at $450 a car, was valued at about $650,000 and the rebates totaled $223,000. The Judge assessed a fine of $20,000 on each of the counts, the maximum penalty allowed under the Elkins law.

During the First World War Judge Landis presided at the trial of William D. Haywood, secretary-treasurer of the I. W. W., and 103 of his followers. He also presided at the trial of Victor Berger, Social Representative from Wisconson, and six other Socialist leaders. In both cases the defendants were charged with obstructing the country's war program.

Haywood and ninety-three of his fellow-defendants were convicted, and when the United States Supreme Court upheld the convictions the I. W. W. leader fled to Russia, where he died. Berger and his fellow-defendants also were convicted before Judge Landis, but the Supreme Court granted them new trials. Shortly after the I. W. W. trials a bomb wrecked the north entrance to the Federal Building in Chicago, killing several persons, but Judge Landis in his chambers on the sixth floor was unharmed.

The threat of violence was no novelty to him. In 1911, during his hearing of Black Hand trials, he received many threats by telephone and mail, and again in 1919 he was one of thirty persons to whom bombs were mailed on May Day. A strong advocate of prohibition, even before it became the law of the land, he closed 600 Chicago saloons by injunctions after the Eighteenth Amendment was adopted.

His courtroom procedure was unorthodox and shocking to the sticklers for legal forms. A favorite expression when he had pronounced sentence was:

"Take this man up to Mabel's room."

Resigned From Federal Bench

The picturesque jurist was criticized widely for retaining his Federal job after taking his position as Commissioner of Baseball, and in March, 1922, after seventeen years on the bench, he stepped down.

Judge Landis was born at Millville, Ohio, on Nov. 20, 1866, son of Abraham H. and Mary Landis, who named him after the mountain near Atlanta, where his father, a Federal soldier in the Civil War, was wounded. The family later moved to Logansport, Ind., where the son received his early training in the public school.

Emerging from the Logansport school, young Landis took up shorthand and having mastered it obtained a job as official reporter of the Crown Point court.

He made his way through the Law School of Cincinnati and the Union Law School of Chicago and, graduating, plunged into the practice of law. Then his father's old commander, Col. Walter Quinton Gresham, was called to Grover Cleveland's Cabinet as Secretary of State.

When Secretary Gresham went to Washington he took young Landis with him as his private secretary. When Mr. Gresham died his secretary returned to Chicago and the practice of law.

Judge Landis married Miss Winifred Reed of Ottawa, Ill., on July 25, 1895.

LANDIS IS PRAISED BY HIS COLLEAGUES

Officials of Baseball Leagues Throughout Country Recall Judge's Help to Game

Baseball leaders throughout the United States and part of Canada paid tribute yesterday to Judge Kenesaw Mountain Landis, commissioner of organized baseball, who died in a Chicago hospital.

Will Harridge, president of the American League, said: "Baseball has lost not only a great executive and leader but a real friend who had the best interests of the game always at heart. Deeply devoted to the sport, Judge Landis brought to baseball a fine mind, always alive to every problem. His guidance throughout the years added a great chapter to baseball history, and baseball forever will be indebted to its first commissioner, Judge Landis.

"His passing comes as a great personal loss to me."

Ford Frick, president of the National League, declared that Judge Landis' passing "is a terrific loss to baseball. He contributed more to the game than any other man. I feel a deep personal loss, for through our years of close association I developed for him an intense personal affection."

Heydler Lauds "Integrity"

John A. Heydler, president of the National League from 1918 to .934 and last survivor of baseball's three-man commission which ruled the game before the selection of Judge Landis, said: "The passing of Judge Landis brings a sense of loss to everyone, and sincere sorrow to those of us in baseball who have been closely associated with him.

"Chosen to his post of great power as a representative of the public, Judge Landis was always independent and impartial in motive and action. He was a man of unswerving integrity. His long and honorable record as a leader of our national game, together with his outstanding success in preserving peace between the always keenly-competitive elements of organized baseball will forever live as his memorial."

William G. Bramham, president of the National Association of Professional Baseball Leagues, commented in Durham, N. C.: "The hearts of all in baseball will bow down in the presence of this great sorrow. We shall not see his like again. None knew better than I the warmth and constance of his friendship; the unswerving integrity and uprightness of his nature. To know him was to know truth, honesty and integrity."

Personal Loss to Barrow

Ed Barrow, president of the New York Yankees, described Judge Landis' death as "a terrible personal shock, and an irreparable loss to baseball. I feel that I have lost one of my finest friends."

Horace Stoneham, president of the New York Giants, called Judge Landis' death "baseball's greatest loss."

Branch Rickey, president of the Brooklyn Dodgers, asserted that baseball faced a major task in finding a man "as rigid and strong" as Judge Landis.

In Buffalo, Joe McCarthy, manager of the Yankees, said "baseball has lost a great man, and I have lost a very good friend."

Tributes also came from owners, managers and representatives of major and minor league teams throughout the country. Among other baseball leaders who offered comment were Frank Shaughnessy, president of the International League; Thomas H. Richardson, president of the Eastern League, and Billy Evans, president of the Southern Baseball Association.

The New York Times   *TUESDAY, AUGUST 11, 1970*

Joe Lapchick, St. John's and Knick Coach, Dies

Star of Basketball's Original Celtics Won Renown Leading Teams Here

MONTICELLO, N. Y., Aug. 10 (AP) — Joe Lapchick, one of basketball's Original Celtics, who spent 50 years in the sport as a player and coach, died today at Hamilton Avenue Hospital, where he was taken last week after having suffered a heart attack. He was 70 years old.

Since his retirement from coaching five years ago, Mr. Lapchick served as sports coordinator at Kutsher's Country Club.

He is survived by his widow, Bobbie; two sons, Joseph Jr. and Richard, and a daughter, Barbara.

A funeral mass will be offered Thursday at 10 A.M. at St. Denis Roman Catholic Church, 470 Van Cortlandt Park Avenue, Yonkers.

Enduring Figure in Sport

By GEORGE VECSEY

Joe Lapchick began his career in the dance-hall days of basketball, a gangly young man with a grade-school education who was trying to keep away from the factories.

He ended his career as a respected educator, a basketball coach at St. John's University who supervised his players' study habits and warned them of the dangers of associating with gamblers.

Lapchick, a gentle man, honest and smart, had a nervous stomach and jangled nerves, souvenirs of too many close games. Yet he endured in basketball and retired in 1965 only because of a mandatory retirement rule at St. John's.

Joseph Bohomiel Lapchick was born on April 12, 1900, to a Czechoslovak immigrant family in Yonkers. The family was poor and young Joe helped out by collecting coal from the railroad tracks.

Basketball was just working its way down from Springfield, Mass., where it had been invented in 1890 by Dr. James Naismith of Springfield College. Young Lapchick, already 6 feet, 2 inches tall at the age of 12, was playing on a number of club teams, in a uniform his mother had made.

One day Mrs. Lapchick hung out the uniform on the clothesline of their tenement. When her husband came home, he spotted the skimpy outfit.

"What is that?" Mr. Lapchick roared.

"That's my basketball uniform, Dad," the young man replied.

"You mean you get in front of people dressed like that?" shouted the father.

A Profitable Alternative

At 14, after graduation from Public School 20 in Yonkers, young Lapchick went to work, first as a golf caddy, later in a factory, working a 10-hour day for about $15 a week.

But he found it more profitable to hang around the information booth at Grand Central Terminal juggling offers from the Holyoke Reds, the Brooklyn Visitations and other clubs. A good negotiator, he worked his way up to $75 a game.

Finally, Lapchick got to play against the best team in the area, the New York Celtics, and their experienced center, Horse Haggerty. When Haggerty wore out in the early 1920's, Lapchick joined the Celtics.

They were the finest team of that day, not big by today's standards, but rough and smart.

Lapchick when he was coach of the St. John's University Basketball team.

Nat Holman, Dutch Dehnerg, Chris Leonard, Pete Barry, Johnny Beckman and the 6-foot, 5-inch Lapchick toured the East.

The tour was a succession of one-night stands, automobile rides and third-rate accommodations. There was no such thing as medical aid. If a man was hurt, his teammates treated him.

Once Lapchick had a nasty cut on his wrist that became infected from the green dye of the uniforms. Johnny Beckman, the leading medical authority of the Celtics, knotted a towel, rubbed off the scab and poured whisky on the wound. The whisky killed the infection; Lapchick survived.

The Celtics dominated the American Basketball League until the other teams insisted they disband. Lapchick was assigned to Cleveland, where he helped win two straight championships before the Depression ended the league.

From 1930 to 1935, Lapchick pulled his old teammates together and toured as "The Original Celtics," backed by Kate Smith, the singer.

Fainted During Game

In 1936 Lapchick took the coaching job at St. John's College of Brooklyn. He was nervous about facing young men with better educations than his own. For a while he merely let them shoot baskets in practice, but eventually he paced off the old Celtic plays, showing how Nat Holman used to work the "give-and-go."

St. John's soon became a prominent team, winning the National Invitation Tournament in 1943 and 1944. In the 1944 finals, Lapchick fainted early in the second half but woke up to see his players holding a 12-point lead just before the final buzzer.

After the 1947 season, Lapchick accepted the coaching job of the New York Knickerbockers in the National Basketball Association. Pro ball had grown up considerably in Lapchick's absence, but there was still a 70-game grind, one-night stands, strange travel connections and constant pressure.

Lapchick was a peaceful man, enjoying his home and three children, working in his flower garden. Pro basketball made a nervous wreck of him.

Sometimes he would rip off his jacket, pull the sleeves inside out and stomp on it. Once he threw a water tray in the air and it fell on his head, drenching him. Another time he smashed a chair against a wall. Sometimes he feared that his team would not score a single point that night.

"The trouble with you," a doctor told him, "is that day after day, you're suffering what the average person suffers once or twice in a lifetime."

One thing Lapchick particularly hated was cutting a player from the squad. Once he had to give the bad news to young Tommy Byrne, just out of Seton Hall College. A few minutes later, Lapchick collapsed on the floor. He spent a week in the hospital before his system calmed down.

In Finals Three Times.

For all his suffering, Lapchick was a good coach, patient and knowledgeable. The Knicks did not have a superstar, but they worked together and in three straight years — 1951-52-53 — they reached the finals of the playoffs, only to lose.

When the Knicks began to fade, Lapchick began to feel pressure from his boss, Ned Irish, and in 1956 he resigned. At the age of 56 he started all over again at St. John's.

This time Lapchick knew the right words and the techniques of coaching. But the angular, bald man was more than a coach. He lectured his young players on the value of a college degree, sometimes looming over them in study hall.

The coach had another mes-

(continued)

sage for his players. He had kept newspaper clippings about several basketball gambling scandals and pasted them in a scrapbook. Before each season, he made each player read the clippings—and sign his name after reading it.

The young players responded well to the coach. Perhaps Lapchick's greatest asset was his ability to inspire his players. They may have laughed at his speeches—but then they ran out on the court and "gave 110 per cent," just as he had asked.

The players knew he was being forced to retire after the 1964-65 season because of the university rule, so they dedicated themselves to "win for the coach."

They responded by clawing past a superior Michigan team, with Cazzie Russell, to win the Holiday Festival in December, 1964. Then in March of 1965 they beat Villanova, 55-51, in the finals of the N.I.T.

"What a way to go," Lapchick shouted as his players hoisted him on their shoulders.

Joe Lapchick as a member of the original Celtics. He joined the team in 1923 and helped them dominate the old American Basketball League.

Lapchick Rated a Place With Rockne, McGraw

An Appreciation

Pride was the mainspring of Joe Lapchick's character and philosophy. That he had a philosophy, in the most unpretentious way, was the aspect of his personality that made the most lasting impression on the thousands of people who had direct dealings with him through the half-century he lived in the sports limelight. He preached pride —pride in oneself, pride in accomplishment, pride in being a true professional who delivers all the effort he is paid for, pride in being able to win without gloating and to lose without whining.

As a basketball coach, he never presented himself as a tactical genius or master technician. He taught attitudes rather than mechanics, and he had one of the rarest and least definable qualities a leader can have: the capacity for bringing out the best in the men who played for him, not "for the coach," but out of the sense of obligation he could make them feel toward themselves.

His career went through four stages, all marked by success. In his 20's, he became one of the best professional basketball players in his day. In his mid-30's with no college education and no teaching experience, he became coach of St. John's and took a key role in the process that built basketball from a localized to a national mass spectator sport.

In his mid-40's, he returned to the pros as coach of the newly formed New York Knickerbockers, and played a vital part in building the stability and success of the National Basketball Association.

Finally, approaching 60, he returned to St. John's, to a college basketball world in which recruiting competition was far more extensive than any he had faced. Once again he produced championship teams whose main characteristic was fighting spirit. When he retired five years ago, he remained a familiar and gregarious figure on the basketball scene, an elder statesman whose advice was always sought and freely given.

In each stage, he had an important effect on the basketball world. As a player, he was a "giant" at 6 feet 5 inches in a day of few 6-footers, skinny and tough. He won most fame as a member of the Original Celtics, the team that dominated the sport so thoroughly in the 1920's that no effective league could be formed around it.

His more famous teammate, Nat Holman, was already coaching City College and was accepted as the greatest player. But Lapchick, even then had started to learn and to prove the basic fact of basketball's future: The overwhelming importance of getting the ball, and therefore the inescapable supremacy of the big man.

In his first tour at St. John's, college basketball blossomed through the Madison Square Garden doubleheaders, and four coaches and their teams took the lead in selling the game to the public: Lapchick, Holman, Clair Bee at Long Island University and Howard Cann of New York University.

Cann was basically shy, reserved; Holman aloof; Bee and Lapchick were the gregarious ones, but Bee was busier and more erratic. In educating the press and public in basketball's inner dramas, Lapchick was of supreme importance.

When he went to the Knicks, he performed the same function for the N.B.A. His reputation made him the most sought after figure connected with the league, and he used his position to promote pride, dignity (despite lost battles with himself about referee-baiting) and maximum honest effort.

It's not a coincidence that so many of his players became coaches. He can be compared, in this way, to Knute Rockne in football and to John McGraw in baseball. When he returned to St. John's, he cemented the bonds between college and professional basketball, helping to make them, in the minds of the public, more than ever two parts of one attractive sport.

His legacy, and his philosophy, were often expressed in one sentence: "Anyone can walk with kings if he walks straight." Belief in yourself, he felt, was what mattered — and one had to try to behave so that the belief would be justified.

You might fail, and the exceedingly human Lapchick did at times, but you had to try. Few major sports figures went through so long a career generating so much affection in so many places, and that's something no statistic can match.

LEONARD KOPPETT.

The New York Times SUNDAY, JULY 1, 1973

Elmer Layden Dead; Fullback Of Notre Dame's 4 Horsemen

CHICAGO, June 30 (UPI)—Elmer Layden, the 160-pound fullback in the storied 1924 "Four Horsemen" backfield at the University of Notre Dame and former commissioner of the National Football League, died this evening at a hospital here. He was 70 years old.

Mr. Layden was head football coach and athletic director at Notre Dame from 1934 to 1940 and was N.F.L. commissioner from 1941 until 1946. He later became an executive of a Chicago area transportation firm.

He married the former Edythe Davis and the couple had four children, Joanne, Elmer Jr., Pat and Mike.

Pierced Opposition

One of football's most glamorous pages was written by the "Four Horsemen" of Notre Dame. In that quartet, Elmer Layden was the fullback, 160 pounds of flashing speed, the first of the "rapier" fullbacks who could pierce, rather than crush, opposition lines.

Remaining in football after his college days, Mr. Layden became one of the game's foremost coaches and subsequently the first "czar" of the professional gridiron. Somber - eyed, stoop - shouldered, he was marked by a nervous energy that gave him little time for idleness. His frame never really filled out, and sportswriters referred to him as the "Thin Man of Notre Dame."

Yet in spite of the high voltage that drove him and a worrying disposition that caused him to lose considerable weight during football campaigns, Mr. Layden was rarely known to lose his temper. To players and acquaintances he was always calm and courteous. In his coaching he chose reason, rather than sentiment, to stir his teams.

A disciple of Knute Rockne, Mr. Layden learned well the lessons of the master. At both Duquesne University and Notre Dame—where he later served as coach—he turned out well-rounded football machines. He gave Duquesne some of its best elevens, and at Notre Dame he raised Irish from the low estate into which they had fallen in 1933 to their former high place in the football world. When he finally left his alma mater, its football receipts were almost twice as large as when he had taken command.

All Round Athlete

Mr. Layden was born in Davenport, Iowa, May 4, 1903. An outstanding, all round schoolboy athlete, he entered Notre Dame in 1921. During his freshman year he alternated with Harry Stuhldreher at quarterback. An injury to Paul Castner the next season gave him his big chance.

1952
Elmer Layden

As a junior, Mr. Layden filled the regular fullback assignment and won national recognition. With Jim Crowley, Don Miller and Stuhldreher, Mr. Layden helped to begin the saga of the Four Horsemen. Notre Dame went without a defeat that season until its final meeting—with the University of Nebraska.

By 1924 the Four Horsemen had developed into one of the most polished scoring units in football. Notre Dame emerged from that campaign undefeated and recognized as the national champion.

After graduation in 1925, Mr. Layden played a season of professional ball with an all-star aggregation. The next year he coached at Loras College in Dubuque, Iowa, and in 1927 he moved to Duquesne. His success with the Pittsburgh team won him acclaim.

During the 1933 season Duquesne rolled up nine victories in ten games and amassed 173 points to only twenty-six for the opposition. Then came the call to Notre Dame. Mr. Layden returned to his alma mater as football coach and athletic director.

He was credited with giving the Hoosier institution one of the finest gridiron schedules in its history. His teams registered forty-seven victories, thirteen defeats and three ties. The 1938 campaign, in which Notre Dame won eight of nine games, was the most successful since the death of Rockne in 1931.

In 1941, the National Professional Football League decided to appoint a supreme authority, and Mr. Layden was selected. Although reluctant to leave Notre Dame, to which he said he "owed everything," he saw an opportunity to work for the greater welfare of the game.

The owners of the 10 teams in the league gave him a contract to run for five years. In addition, they gave him powers as sweeping, if not more so, than those enjoyed by the commissioner of baseball.

It was within Mr. Layden's province to settle all disputes between players and clubs, levy and collect fines, govern conduct of club owners and all their employes in any activity connected with the sport and have complete control of the league's finances.

In January, 1946, however, he dropped a bombshell at a meeting by suddenly resigning. A contract was offered to him to serve in an advisory capacity for an indefinite period. His salary was to be $20,000, the same he had received as commissioner.

However, the former Notre Dame star turned down the offer. He revealed that he had accepted a position as president of the Shippers Car Line Corporation in New York. Later he entered the railroad equipment business and, in 1957, he was in the employ of the General American Transportation Corporation of Chicago.

The Four Horsemen's 25 year reunion. From left to right, fullback Elmer Layden, Jim Crowley, Harry Stuhldreher and Don Miller.

The New York Times FRIDAY, JUNE 22, 1973

Frank Leahy, Notre Dame Coach, Dead

PORTLAND, Ore., June 21 (AP)—Frank Leahy, coach of many of the University of Notre Dame's winning football teams, died shortly after noon today at Good Samaritan Hospital. He was 64 years old.

A Winner From Winner

By STEVE CADY

When Francis William Leahy was only a few months old, his family moved from O'Neill, Neb., to Winner, S. D.

Considering young Frank's future success as a football coach, his parents couldn't have picked a town with a more appropriate name. In his 13-year career as head football coach at Boston College and Notre Dame, Leahy was a winner with a capital W.

In two seasons at Boston College, he directed the Eagles to 19 victories in 20 games, capped by a 19-13 upset over undefeated Tennessee in the 1941 Sugar Bowl. His Notre Dame elevens won 87 games, lost 11 and tied nine, giving him a career coaching record of 106-12-9.

Leahy's rapid rise in his profession had a Cinderella quality. Ten years after being graduated from Notre Dame, where in 1930 he played on the last team coached by the celebrated Knute Rockne, Leahy returned to his alma mater as head football coach and director of athletics.

Only 24 hours before receiving the call to Notre Dame, he had signed a new five-year contract with Boston College. He previously had turned down three flattering offers from other colleges, one of which, it was said, would have guaranteed him financial independence for life.

Leahy's switch to Notre Dame ruffled feathers at Boston College, but he was released from his contract at the New England school. In his first year at South Bond, he promptly turned out the first Fighting Irish eleven to go through a season without defeat since 1930—Rockne's last team. Leahy, the rookie tactician, was chosen coach of the year in a poll of his colleagues.

He remained as Notre Dame's head coach until January, 1954, when he resigned. He said he was acting on the advice of physicians, who had based their findings on his state of health then as well as on a severe pancreatic attack he had suffered during the Notre Dame-Georgia Tech game the previous year.

Kept on Sidelines

A knee injury that kept him on the sidelines throughout the final season of his varsity career turned out to be the foundation on which Leahy's coaching brilliance was built. He would have been the starting left tackle. Instead, he sat on the bench with Rockne and soaked up knowledge from the master. Later, Leahy would come to be known as The Master.

Frank Leahy

At the end of the 1930 season, Rockne went to the Mayo Clinic in Rochester, Minn., for treatment of a leg ailment. He took Leahy along "for company" and to have an operation performed on Leahy's torn knee cartilage. For two weeks, the teacher and the pupil lay in adjoining beds in the hospital and talked football.

When Leahy was graduated in 1931, Rockne gave him his pick of a half-dozen jobs for which the coach had been asked to recommend candidates. Leahy accepted a job as line coach at Georgetown University.

During their stay at the Mayo Clinic, Rockne had told a friend he wanted him to meet a young man named Frankie Leahy. Rockne was quoted as telling the friend, "The reason I want you to meet him is that someday he will be recognized as the greatest football coach of all time."

When the friend asked what was so exceptional about young Leahy, Rockne replied: "That kid has the greatest football brain I have ever come in contact with. He is just simply a genius when it come to planning ways and means of getting that ball across the goal line and smothering the play of the opponents; take it from me, he is a superstrategist already."

Leahy's college coaching innovations included the double quarterback, having his teams run from an erect stance, optional blocking assignments for linemen on the same running play and a pass defense against Georgia Tech in 1941 that was employed at the time by most professional teams.

Despite his genius, it was not until February, 1970, that Leahy was elected to the National Football Foundation and Hall of Fame. Many observers considered the honor long overdue.

Like Rockne, Leahy was a perfectionist, a stickler for detail. And like Rockne (who in 13 seasons at Notre Dame produced a record of 105-12-3), Leahy won football games. But that was about the only similarity between them.

Rockne was an extrovert, a robust charmer whose wit and graciousness could make a defeated rival feel almost cheerful. Leahy was an introvert, a shy, diffident, overly modest man of such sincerity that at times he seemed insincere.

Whereas Rockne was always ready with a wisecrack, Leahy talked in a stilted language filled with platitudees. He used to say he'd be "the happiest Irishman in America" if Notre Dame could win by one point. When his team went out and won by 40 points, the rival coach Leahy had hoped to beat by one point would boil.

Once, Ziggy Czarobski, the all-America tackle, was rumored to be overweight after a summer of idleness. Reporters went to Leahy and received the unsmiling comment: "If Zigmont does not return to the campus in perfect condition, we shall be obliged to ask him to disassociate himself from our group."

The reporters weren't surprised. That's the way Leahy talked. Ziggy was never Ziggy to the coach, because the player's first name was Zigmont. Lujack was never Johnny. He was John.

Leahy's fearful pregame statements often caused his detractors to regard him as a hypocrite. His admirers saw it as good psychological warfare.

Two games when he was at Boston College illustrate the point. When the Eagles left by train for New Orleans for a game with Tulane, he moaned, "Here we are idling around on the train, getting stiff, while that big Tulane bunch is working out and improving!"

Later in the same season, the Idaho eleven headed East by train for a game with the Eagles. Told that the visitors would be easy pickings, Leahy hollered, "How can I help worrying with them resting up on a leisurely train ride East while we wear ourselves out at practice?"

On the field, Leahy worked his men hard, but they respected his authority and knowledge. And they appreciated his concern for their physical wellbeing. Perhaps because of his own knee injury, suffered during a scrimmage, he was a fanatic in finding ways to safeguard his players from injury.

His rapid rise in the coaching profession began at Georgetown when he caught the attention of Jim Crowley, then head coach of Michigan State. Crowley was so impressed by the

(continued)

Georgetown line's work against Michigan State that he signed Leahy to join his staff in 1932.

In 1933, Crowley went to Fordham as head coach, and there Leahy helped to turn out the Seven Blocks of Granite, the line that was the chief strength of teams that went through the seasons of 1935, 1936 and 1937 with only two defeats.

Then came the step up into the head-coaching ranks in 1939 at Boston College, and Leahy was on his way. After his two seasons directing the Eagles, Leahy was nationally known.

His coaching tenure at Notre Dame was interrupted in the spring of 1944, when he entered the Navy. He became a lieutenant commander in charge of recreation programs for submarine crews. Because of his wartime service, he missed two football seasons at South Bend.

When he returned in 1946, Notre Dame again was ranked the best team in the country. The Irish went undefeated through four consecutive seasons. As they rolled through 1948 and 1949 still undefeated, Leahy turned down offers to coach professional football teams. However, he did drop the burden of director of athletics to devote himself strictly to football.

In 1950, Notre Dame lost to Purdue, ending a 39-game unbeaten streak, and wound up the season with a record of 4-4-1. It also had a mediocre record in 1951.

Though he predicted it would be five years before Notre Dame once again had what he often termed "a representative team," Leahy surprised the football world in 1952 by sending out a squad that scored a series of upsets. With a record of seven victories, two losses and a tie, it was rated among the nation's top teams.

At the time Leahy was stricken by the pancreatic attack on Oct. 24, 1953, his Notre Dame eleven was undefeated, and ranked as the best in the country.

When he accepted the post of general manager of the Los Angeles Chargers of the embryonic American Football League in October, 1959, it marked his return to football after a six-year absence. However the pro job was short-lived. He had to give it up in July, 1960, because of poor health.

Before that, he conducted radio and television shows on which he gave football forecasts; became associated with Louis Wolfson, the financier, and was elected in 1955 vice president for trade relations for the Merritt-Chapman & Scott Corporation, a marine construction and salvage concern.

He was also connected with the Hamilton Oil and Gas Company of Denver. In April, 1960, government lawyers filed a brief with the Securities and Exchange Commission saying Leahy had used false and misleading information to sell oil stock to friends and acquaintances. He denied the charge.

As a retired Notre Dame coach, The Master occasionally angered the authorities at South Bend and even some of the alumni by sniping at coaches who had followed him in the football job there: Terry Brennan, his immediate successor, Joe Kuharich and Hugh Devore.

After one loss, Leahy complained bitterly, "The spirit of Notre Dame doesn't exist today." When Notre Dame lost a game to Iowa, 40-0, Leahy moaned, "This was the first Fighting Irish football team I've seen without any fight."

Frank Leahy with Edward "Moose" Krause, Notre Dame line coach.

The New York Times MONDAY, JULY 4, 1938.

SUZANNE LENGLEN, TENNIS STAR, DIES

One of Greatest Players of Her Sex, Long a Champion, Victim of Anemia in Paris

WON FIRST TITLE AT 14

Gained Wimbledon Crown in 1919 and Led Amateurs Till She Turned Pro in 1926

PARIS, Monday, July 4 (AP).—Suzanne Lenglen, noted French tennis player, died at her home at 6:50 A. M. today (1:50 A. M., Monday, New York time). She had been critically ill the last week of pernicious anemia.

A blood transfusion was administered after she became ill last Wednesday. She appeared to be resting comfortably, but her condition became worse on Friday. Her age was 39.

Won First Title at 14

That Suzanne Lenglen was the greatest of all women tennis players and one of the greatest of all feminine athletes might possibly be disputed, although a demurrer to these statements unquestionably would prove difficult to sustain. That she was the most colorful, temperamental and tempestuous quite definitely cannot be challenged.

Born in Compiègna, France, on May 24, 1899, Mlle. Lenglen launched her brilliant career on the courts at the age of 14, when she won the singles championship of Picardy. By the following year the stardom predicted for her was an accomplished fact, as on the very eve of the World War she captured the world's hard-court singles and doubles titles at Paris.

Her rise to international fame was temporarily checked by the war, but she utilized the time to good advantage in perfecting her game, so that after the armistice she quickly established herself at the top of her field. She swept triumphantly through her first Wimbledon tournament in 1919, capturing the singles, doubles and mixed doubles titles.

Lost One Match in Six Years

From that year to 1926, when she quit the amateur ranks, Mlle. Lenglen's name was synonymous with tennis perfection and she ruled supreme. She repeated her Wimbledon singles triumph in 1920, 1921, 1922, 1923 and 1925, missing the 1924 tournament because of illness, and in 1920 carried off all the gold medals at the Antwerp Olympic Games.

Through all these years, she dropped only one match. However, that lone defeat proved to be more of a cause célèbre by the manner of its sufferance than perhaps any other incident in the turbulent career of this stormy petrel of the courts.

Trailing her arch-rival, Mrs. Molla Bjurstedt Mallory, the American champion, at the end of the first set of their second-round match in the 1921 American championships at Forest Hills, Mlle. Lenglen dramatically stalked off the court, saying that she was too ill to continue.

That incident and others of a similar stripe in later years—such as her refusal to play in a scheduled match at Wimbledon in 1926, when Queen Mary was among the disappointed audience, and her subsequent withdrawal from that tournament because of "illness"—had a dimming effect on her personal popularity in America and England, but there was no gainsaying her consummate ability.

In 1922 she gained revenge at Mrs. Mallory's expense for the Forest Hills fiasco in 1922 by humiliating the American champion, 6–2, 6–0, at Wimbledon.

Victor Over Helen Wills

Another celebrated triumph for Mlle. Lenglen was that over Miss Helen Wills, whom she defeated, 6–3, 8–6, at Cannes in 1926. Preceded by months of fanfare, her victory was front-page news the world over. After the Wimbledon débâcle of that same year, which was so much of an international incident that the French Government apologized to the Queen for Mlle. Lenglen's conduct, the volatile Suzanne dropped another bombshell into tennis ranks by announcing she had accepted a professional contract.

Under the auspices of Charles C. Pyle, Mlle. Lenglen toured the United States for a series of exhibition matches in all the major cities. Large crowds turned out for many of her appearances, including a gathering of 13,000 at Madison Square Garden for her debut. After the conclusion of her tour in 1927, she returned to France and, with the gates of amateur competition closed and no great enthusiasm for professional tennis in Europe, faded rapidly out of the spotlight.

A genius of the courts, Mlle. Lenglen had all the temperament of a great artiste. Her public life was a tale of foot-stampings, defiances and tears—a veritable comic opera in a tennis setting. Except as to her game itself, Suzanne was consistently inconsistent.

From the mechanical point of view, no player of her sex has ever matched Mlle. Lenglen's tennis equipment. She backed her flawless ground strokes with sound strategical technique, but above all her chief assets were her fiery aggressiveness and flashing speed, unparalleled before or since by any woman player.

Recipe for Success

To interviewers who sought an explanation for her success. Mlle. Lenglen said, with a deprecating shrug: "My method? I don't think I have any. I just throw dignity to the winds and think of nothing but the game. I try to hit the ball with all my force and send it where my opponent is not. I say to myself, let the other one do the running about but run as fast as you can yourself if you have to. Voila, messieurs."

At the height of her career, the proposal often was made that Mlle. Lenglen try her hand against a leading male player. She conceded the superiority of the other sex, but, nevertheless, when news of a practice match in which William T. Tilden had decisively beaten her leaked out, she hotly and indignantly denied that she had been trying to make it a contest. Mlle. Lenglen was an arrogant champion, intensely proud of her ability.

She was possessed of exceptional charm and physical grace. Once, when interviewed with regard to an article expressing fears lest the strain of tennis tournaments wear away the good looks and youthful bloom of feminine participators, Suzanne protested "But, monsieur, surely it is not for me to express an opinion about that?"

Between tournaments, Mlle. Lenglen often wrote on tennis for newspapers, including THE NEW YORK TIMES, to which she contributed a series of articles on her celebrated visit of 1921. She also wrote several books on the subject and made several motion picture shorts here and on the continent.

Suzanne Lenglen, who was Wimbledon champion for five consecutive years, is considered by many to be the greatest woman tennis player of all time.

The New York Times THURSDAY, JANUARY 7, 1971

Sonny Liston, Ex-Heavyweight Champion, Is Dead

LAS VEGAS, Nev., Jan. 6 (UPI) — Sonny Liston, former world heavyweight boxing champion, was found dead in his home last night by his wife, Geraldine.

Newspapers dating from Dec. 29 were stacked on the front porch, and a deputy coroner estimated that the boxer had been dead about a week.

Narcotics were discovered at the scene, but the initial autopsy gave no clues as to the cause of death.

The police said that Liston apparently had been undressing for bed when he fell over backward with such force that he broke the rail of a bench at the foot of his bed. There was no indication of foul play.

Last Thanksgiving Day, the former champion was injured in an automobile accident. He had complained of chest pains recently.

'Bad Guy' of Ring

By STEVE CADY

Discussing his plans for the future a few years ago, Charles (Sonny) Liston struck a lyrical note that hardly matched his image as everybody's bad guy.

"What I'd like," he told an interviewer in his $50,000 Las Vegas home, "I'd like to get me a farm somewhere . . . Denver maybe . . . where it nice and clean . . . with some cows, horses . . . some pigs . . . that kind of thing . . . I use to live on a farm."

Asked if his first farm had those things, the ex-convict who slugged his way to the world heavyweight boxing championship glowered. "Naw! We didn't have any cows and horses and pigs. We had *cotton*."

Liston also had 23 older brothers and sisters, a mother he described as "helpless" and a father "who didn't care about any of us." There was little to eat, few clothes and no shoes.

Liston never did learn to read, or to write more than his name, but in rare moments of reflection he would say, "You know what I often wonder about? Where were all these people who work with kids when I was growing up?"

Without guidance, Liston quickly developed into a juvenile delinquent, filled with hatred, insecurity and distrust. Later, he graduated to an anti-labor goon-for-hire, a strong-arm man, an armed robber and an alleged rapist.

By the age of 18, he had been convicted of six muggings, and was on his way to Missouri State Penitentiary to serve 19 months for robbing a gas station in St. Louis. It was the first of two prison sentences. The second, in 1957, is reflected by the notation "Inactive" under that year's heading in his official ring record. He had become a professional boxer four years earlier.

Nino Valdes was pounded to the ground by Sonny Liston in his 18th consecutive victory.

In the ring, Liston was able to channel his aggressions into a controlled ferocity that eventually gained him $3,847,272 in purses from title bouts. He was a hulking, menacing figure (6 feet 1, 200 pounds) with size 13 fists and a baleful glare that intimidated many an opponent even before a bout started.

'I Don't Get Beat'

Bull-shouldered and brutish, he was a sledgehammer puncher with either hand. In the words of one of his managers, his left was "death," his right "destruction." Stalking an opponent, Liston looked like the meanest bouncer in the world's roughest nightclub. He didn't mind being the bad guy.

"A boxing match is like a cowboy movie," he once said. "There's got to be good guys and there's got to be bad guys. That's what people pay for—to see the bad guys get beat. So I'm the bad guy. But I change things. I don't get beat."

Directed toward boxing by a Roman Catholic chaplain during his first prison term, Liston began his pro career on Sept. 2, 1953, with a one-round knockout of Don Smith in St.

(continued)

Louis. He won his next six fights before suffering a broken jaw in the fourth round of an eight-round bout with Marty Marshall in Detroit. Despite the pain, Liston finished the fight, but lost it on a decision.

That was his only loss in 34 bouts before he won the heavyweight title by knocking out Floyd Patterson in the first round on Sept. 25, 1962, in Chicago.

The National Association for the Advancement of Colored People had urged Patterson not to defend against Liston, fearing the latter would hurt the cause of the Negro. Liston never forgot the N.A.A.C.P. attitude, and later included black militants along with student protesters and others on his list of those he felt "should get run over by a truck."

If the N.A.A.C.P. had been wary, the boxing world and most of the country went into a state of shock when the ex-convict took the heavyweight title. A number of state legislators introduced bills to outlaw boxing, and New York State refused to license the new champion to fight here.

In its refusal, the Boxing Commission described Liston as "a child of circumstance, without schooling and without direction or leadership . . . he has been the victim of those with whom he has surrounded himself."

It had taken Liston 10 years to smash his way to the title. It took him only 17 months to lose it. And the manner in which he lost it (to Cassius Clay, now Muhammad Ali) tarnished his image as an invincible slugger.

Clay, the brash newcomer, ridiculed the champion as "The Ugly Bear," and predicted he would knock him out in eight rounds. Liston said, "Cassius can't lick a popsicle. He should be arrested for impersonating a fighter. I expect he'll run for a couple of rounds, and I'll chase him; then it will be all over."

The Feb. 25, 1964, bout in Miami Beach lasted six rounds. When Liston remained on his ring stool before the seventh round, unable to answer the bell, Clay was awarded a seventh-round technical knockout.

Liston said his left shoulder had been injured and he couldn't lift his arm, a contention later supported by medical evidence. But there were accusations that Liston had thrown the bout in a fix engineered by his alleged underground associations. Others accused him of having quit under fire.

Fifteen months later, on May 25, 1965, in Lewiston, Me., what remained of the Liston image was shattered. In the shortest heavyweight title bout on record, Clay knocked him out after 1 minute 42 seconds of the first round.

There were charges that Liston had gone down from a phantom right-hand punch. But the consensus was that the blow destroyed a fighter who had gone over the hill physically and mentally.

Liston began a comeback in 1966, and won 14 bouts in a row before being knocked out by Leotis Martin in the ninth round of a fight at Las Vegas on Dec. 6, 1969. He had fought only once since then, scoring a ninth-round knockout over Chuck Wepner in a small, smoke-filled arena at Jersey City last June 29.

In recent years, Liston had played bit parts in various movies. Invariably, the characters he portrayed were bad guys, mean and surly and tough. They fit the image.

To his wife, Geraldine, however, he was "a nice thoughtful man." She called him Charles. To others, he was intimidating in presence, a crude-mouthed "put-down artist" fast to trump another man's statement with a piece of so-called jailhouse wit.

Nevertheless, Liston was able to communicate well with two kinds of people—the very young and the very old. While he completely shunned the civil-rights battle, he spoke often of the need for youth programs.

Family of 25 Children

His concern for youth undoubtedly stemmed from his own impoverished childhood on a worn-out cotton farm 18 miles outside Little Rock, Ark. His father was married twice, and there were 25 children in all. Sonny was No. 24.

His birth date is listed as May 8, 1932, but Ring Magazine always refused to verify any date, citing reports that he could be 44.

Liston's scrapes with the law continued through his life. The most recent run-in came on a drunken-driving charge. He resented questions by the press about his prison record and his alleged associations with underworld figures such as Frankie Carbo and Blinky Palermo.

"These newspapermen can ask dumb questions," he would say. "They'll look up at the sun and ask you if the sun is shining."

On many occasions, however, Liston's responses were limited to a grunted "yes" or "no." Liston's career record was 50 victories (39 by knockout) and 4 losses.

In addition to his 1962 victory over Patterson for the championship, Liston defended his crown in 1963, once again knocking out Patterson in the first round. Then he lost the title to Clay, and failed to regain it in the controversial Lewiston bout.

If anything, his philosophy was best summed up in this remark: "Ever since I was born, I've been fighting for my life."

The 1961 Westphal-Liston bout that took place before the coming of Cassius Clay.

"All the News That's Fit to Print"

The New York Times

LATE CITY EDITION

Weather: Showers and thunderstorms likely today, tonight. Sunny tomorrow. Temp. range: today 82-70; Thurs. 77-64. Full U.S. report on Page 56.

VOL. CXIX...No. 41,131 © 1970 The New York Times Company. NEW YORK, FRIDAY, SEPTEMBER 4, 1970 15 CENTS

Delegates Welcome Governor at A.F.L.-C.I.O. Parley

Governor Rockefeller—and hi...

ARMS TALKS CLOSE AS VOTE SUPPORTS TREATY ON SEABED

U.S.-Soviet Plan Forbidding Atom Weapons Is Said to Win in Geneva, 24-1

By THOMAS J. HAMILTON
Special to The New York Times

GENEVA, Sept. 3—The disarmament conference ended its 1970 session today after achi... ing near unanimity on... treaty to prohib... ment of...

Bruce and Thuy Meet at Paris Talks for the First Time

Associated Press

...of North Vietnam ends boycott

U.S. BIDS SOVIET AND EGYPT AVOID NEW VIOLATIONS

Asks Immediate Resumption of Peace Talks at U.N. to Preserve Cease-Fire

ISRAEL IS DISSATISFIED

She Is Believed Distressed Over Reported Failure to Get Additional Arms

By TAD SZULC
Special to The New York Times

WASHINGTON, Sept. 3—The U... States appealed to the S... Union and the United Arab Republic today to refrain from further violations of the tenuous cease-fire in the Middle East and urged an immediate resumption of the peace talks at the United Nations.

But Israel immediately made it clear to the Nixon Administration that despite a new American pledge to guarantee her military security, her negotiators would not return to the peace talks until Egypt removed the newly introduced antiaircraft missiles from the Suez Canal cease-fire zone.

The talks were initiated on Aug. 25 by Dr. Gunnar V. Jarring, Secretary General Thant's special representative for the Middle East.

Israeli Unhappiness Noted

Israel was also said to have conveyed her unhappiness over the reported refusal of the United States to increase the current shipment of arms, including deliveries of replacements for Phantom fighter-bombers lost in action before the cease-fire.

In recent pronouncements, Administration leaders, notably Secretary of Defense Melvin R. Laird, have given the impression that the United States would not allow the balance of power in the Middle East to be tipped against Israel.

The announcement of the appeal for the observance of the ...ce and the resumption of the ...e talks, as well as the lat... military assurances to Is... were contained in a brief ...ent issued by the State ...ment, which also ac...ed officially for the ... that the cease-fire ... violated by the ... of Soviet-made mis-

...ads Statement

...nt read by Rob... ...ey, the depart... ...an, said:

...vidence con... ...ave been vio... ...cease-fire-stand... ...greement. We are not going into details. We are taking up this matter both with the United Arab Republic and Soviet Union through diplomatic channels.

"We are continuing to watch the balance closely and, as we previously stated, have no intention of permitting Israel's security to be adversely affected. In the meantime, we believe it is of the utmost importance that the talks between the parties under Ambassador

Continued on Page 6, Column 7

Labor C... Roc...

KIA...SHA LAK... York State A.F.L.-C.I... Rockefeller for re-ele...

Cheering for...

The cheering, wh... pounding welcome... Rockefeller as he e... convention hall of the... Hotel here foreshadow... victory, though Goldberg... porters insisted before th... ing that the Governor's stre... was exaggerated.

The Goldberg supporters c... tended that no one really kn... how the votes would add u... until lists of delegates and thei... respective voting strengths—based on per-capita dues payments for their unions—were made available.

The battle was described by veterans of federation conventions as the most bitter and angry in the history of the organization. The heckling and shouting by rival sides was strident and sometimes personal. Speakers were often drowned out by shouts and boos.

At one point as he sought to speak, Jerry Wurf, presi-

Continued on Page 14, Column 1

M'CORMACK A... IS GIVEN 2½ YE...

Sweig Also Gets $2,000 Fin... for Perjury in Testimony on Use of Influence

By CRAIG R. WHITNEY

Dr. Martin Sweig, who was the principal aide of Speaker of the House John W. McCormack until Sweig was charged last year with defrauding the Government, was sentenced yesterday to two and a half years in prison and a $2,000 fine for lying to a grand jury.

Sweig was convicted July 9, after a three-week trial, of perjury in denying that he knew or had interceded with Government agencies on behalf of Gary Roth, a Long Island serviceman who wanted a hardship discharge from the Army.

Before Federal Judge Marvin E. Frankel sentenced him yesterday, Sweig stood up in the oak-paneled courtroom above Foley Square and said:

"I am bewildered by all this. I never had occasion to be before a grand jury before in my life. If I have done wrong I certainly did not mean to, or to cause harm to anyone."

Judge Frankel then told him: "I am of the view that I would be derelict if I did not impose a substantial prison sentence in this case, and I will." He was doing so, he said, because Sweig's actions presented "a picture of corruption of a very profound kind."

United States Attorney Whitney North Seymour Jr., who prosecuted the case with Richard Ben-Veniste, told the court: "We do not have the com-

Continued on Page 34, Column 5

...essing U.S. ...gypt's Gains

...ROSE ...Times

...Secretary General ...special representative ...Middle East. ...e Minister Moshe ...confirmed his concur... ...he compromise, saying ...interview that "what ...ded today will not ...eave the Govern-...

...ical rever... ...greeted Attorney ...n N. Mitchell's an... ...ment last summer— ...e rescinded—that 100 lawyers would be sent into the South at the opening of school to monitor the progress of desegregation.

Last week the Justice De-

...their chil... ...at assigned them to formerly all-black schools in the district.

District Judge H. Hobart Grooms ordered nine of the parents to appear in his court in Birmingham tomorrow to show cause why they should not be enjoined from further interference with the plan.

In an affidavit filed by the

Continued on Page 11, Column 1

West Point Cadet Loses Fight In Court for Objector Discharge

A West Point senior who had been denied a discharge from the Army as a conscientious objector failed yesterday to get a court order directing the Army to release him, as he wished.

With the rejection of his suit, the cadet, 20-year-old Cary E. Donham of New Baden, Ill., faces one of three prospects: He can resign from the United States Military Academy, be dismissed for lack of military aptitude, or appeal to a higher court.

The academy has said it would accept his resignation, but whether it does that or dismisses him, Cadet Donham would be liable to further military service as an enlisted man in the Army Reserve.

His lawyers, Rabinowitz, Boudin & Standard, said yesterday that they were not sure what they would do next. Two weeks ago Federal Judge Marvin E. Frankel, who decided against Cadet Donham yesterday, ordered the Army to give the youth enough time to resign before it tried to do anything else with him.

The cadet is believed to be the first student at West Point who has ever filed for conscientious-objector status, although Lieut. Louis P. Font, a West Point graduate, did it six months ago and was turned down.

Cadet Donham's application was denied last July 21 by an Army conscientious objector review board, which found that he lacked the requisite "depth of sincerity."

He then tried to get a Fed-

Continued on Page 4, Column 7

Robert Riger

Vince Lombardi discussing play. He once said, "Coaches who can outline plays on a blackboard are a dime a dozen. The ones who win get inside their players and motivate them."

By WILLIAM N. WALLACE

Vince Lombardi, the professional football coach who symbolized toughness and dedication in sports, died of intestinal cancer yesterday in Georgetown Hospital in Washington. His age was 57.

His wife of 30 years, Marie, and his son, Vincent, were at the bedside.

Lombardi, who guided the Green Bay Packers to the premier position in the National Football League in the nineteen-sixties was seeking to do the same with the Washington Redskins in the nineteen-seventies.

The Redskins had long been losers. But Vincent Thomas Lombardi had never associated with losers in his 31 years as a football coach.

Last year, his first in Washington, the Redskins had their first winning record in 14 seasons.

"Winning isn't everything," Lombardi once insisted. "It is the only thing."

Under his direction the Green Bay Packers won six division titles and five national Football League championships in nine seasons between 1959 and 1967. This was professional football's best winning record and Lombardi was acclaimed as the sport's best coach.

He retired from coaching after the 1967 season, when he was 53 years old. But his wife and his close friends wondered how long he could stay away from the sidelines. The answer: one year. Most pro football games are played on Sunday afternoons and during the season that Lombardi confined himself to the duties of the Packers' general manager he said, "I miss the fire on

Continued on Page 24, Column 1

Lawyer Teams to Observe Demonstrations Here

By DAVID BURNHAM

An experimental group of neutral observers has been organized by the Association of the Bar of the City of New York in an effort to reduce violence at mass demonstrations.

Edwin J. Wesely, chairman of the special eight-man committee established by the association to initiate the experimental observer program, said yesterday, "We contemplate having from two to 12 specially trained lawyers at all demonstrations at which there might be trouble."

"Our men will not be there as marshals or demonstrators, but just to observe and report," Mr. Wesely continued. "We will try to report on all aspects of a demonstration—the demonstrators, the counter-demonstrators, the Police Department and the bystanders."

The existence of the legal observer experiment, requested by Mayor Lindsay the day after the May 15 demonstrations by construction workers got out of hand at City Hall, became known yesterday in a brief Police Department order sent to all major commands.

The New York Civil Liberties Union and the Police Department's Civilian Complaint Review Board both have strongly recommended the establishment of a regular team of trained observers at demonstrations. The review board made its suggestion in a report several months ago that said a failure of police leadership was an important factor in the violence at Columbia University in the spring of 1968.

Aryeh Neier, executive director of the New York Civil Liberties Union, said last night that the presence of neutral observers would reduce violence at demonstrations by making the police "conscious that they are to be accountable for their actions" and by giving demonstrators "confidence that if there is abuse directed against them it will not pass unrecorded."

The observers probably would not deter provocateurs among the demonstrators, but provocations would be "less likely to attract the support of other demonstrators" with

Continued on Page 12, Column 6

NEWS INDEX

Vince Lombardi, Football Coach, Dies

Robert Riger

Vince Lombardi discussing play. He once said, "Coaches who can outline plays on a blackboard are a dime a dozen. The ones who win get inside their players and motivate them."

By WILLIAM N. WALLACE

Vince Lombardi, the professional football coach who symbolized toughness and dedication in sports, died of intestinal cancer yesterday in Georgetown Hospital in Washington. His age was 57.

His wife of 30 years, Marie, and his son, Vincent, were at the bedside.

Lombardi, who guided the Green Bay Packers to the premier position in the National Football League in the nineteen-sixties was seeking to do the same with the Washington Redskins in the nineteen-seventies.

The Redskins had long been losers. But Vincent Thomas Lombardi had never associated with losers in his 31 years as a football coach.

Last year, his first in Washington, the Redskins had their first winning record in 14 seasons.

"Winning isn't everything," Lombardi once insisted. "It is the only thing."

Under his direction the Green Bay Packers won six division titles and five national Football League championships in nine seasons between 1959 and 1967. This was professional football's best winning record and Lombardi was acclaimed as the sport's best coach.

He retired from coaching after the 1967 season, when he was 53 years old. But his wife and his close friends wondered how long he could stay away from the sidelines. The answer: one year. Most pro football games are played on Sunday afternoons and during the season that Lombardi confined himself to the duties of the Packers' general manager he said, "I miss the fire on

Continued on Page 24, Column 1

Vince Lombardi, Pro Football Coach, Is Dead at 57

Continued From Page 1, Col.

Sunday." Edward Bennett Willianms, president of the Redskins,early in 1969 offered Lombardi a position as coach, general manager and owner of 5 per cent of the team's stock, and the offer was quickly accepted.

"Everyone wants to own something sometime. Isn't that right?" asked Lombardi in explaining why he resigned the Packer post with five years remaining on his contract.

Lombardi was a symbol of authority.

"When he says 'Sit down,' I don't even bother to look for a chair," one of the Packer players explained.

"He's fair. He treats us all the same—like dogs," said Henry Jordan, another Packer.

"He coaches through fear," said Bill Curry, a sensitive player Lombardi let go.

Most of his athletes accepted his demanding ways and biting criticisms. His primary target was a player named Marvin Fleming, who said in reflection, "I didn't mind. When I came to him I didn't have anything. He taught me how to be a winner."

Another Packer, Jerry Kramer, said, "His whippings, his cussings and his driving all fade; his good qualities endure."

'It's for Them'

Lombardi admitted that his scoldings sometimes were merely for effect. During his last season at Green Bay, when he was goading an aging team to another championship, he said, "I have to go on that field every day and whip people. It's for them, not just me. I'm getting to be an animal."

Lombardi was always a hard man when it came to football. In college, at Fordham where he graduated with honors in 1937, he played guard on a famous line called the Seven Blocks of Granite. He was the smallest of the group at 5 feet 8 inches and 175 pounds. "But he hit like 250," a teammate said.

The son of an immigrant Italian butcher, Lombardi was born June 11, 1913, and grew up in the Sheepshead Bay section of Brooklyn. He went to Cathedral High School and St. Francis Preparatory School before Fordham. He had ambitions to study for the Roman Catholic priesthood for a while, but after graduation he went to law school for a year.

He supported himself by playing for a minor league football team, the Brooklyn Eagles, and serving as an insurance investigator. But a coaching career was calling and in 1939 he joined the faculty at St. Cecelia High School in Englewood, N. J. For an annual salary of $1,700 he was an assistant football coach and a teacher of physics, chemistry, algebra and Latin.

36 Victories in Row

Lombardi stayed at St. Cecilia for seven years. He soon was head coach of the football, basketball and baseball squads. His football teams won six state championships and had a string of 36 victories in a row.

He returned to Fordham to coach the freshmen in 1947 and served as an assistant in 1948. When Ed Danowski was reappointed head coach for the 1949 season, Lombardi left and joined Col. Earl Blaik's staff at the United States Military Academy.

Life at West Point suited Lombardi and he was strongly influenced by Colonel Blaik, who had his own hero, Gen. Douglas MacArthur. Lombardi, too, became a disciple of General MacArthur and in ensuing years he attempted to inspire his teams by quoting one or the other of the military men with sayings such as, "If you can walk, you can run."

Pro football beckoned in 1954

(continued)

Vernon J. Biever

Lombardi, on the shoulders of Jerry Kramer (right) and Forrest Gregg, enjoying a Packer victory.

Vernon J. Biever

Vince Lombardi

when the New York Giants put together a new coaching staff under Jim Lee Howell, who delegated the offense to Lombardi.

"Vince didn't understand our game," said Frank Gifford, one of his stars. "At first we players were showing him. But by the end of the season he was showing us."

Green Bay's Offer

Lombardi's opportunity to be a head coach did not come until 1959, when he was 46, which is considered old in that line of work. The Green Bay Packers, a community-owned team in a city of only 70,000, were losers and troubled financially.

The directors offered Lombardi the job as coach and general manager. He insisted upon full authority and they gave it to him. The prior coach, Ray McLean, had a team that won only one game in 12. With a nucleus of the same players, Lombardi's first Packer team won seven of 12 games and tied for third place in the western division of the N.F.L.

The next season they were first but lost the league championship to the Philadelphia Eagles. Then the parade began, with league titles in 1961, 1962, 1965, 1966 and 1967, plus Super Bowl victories over the American League champion in 1967 and 1968.

During his span of nine seasons as head coach, Lombardi saw his teams win 141 games, lose 39 and tie four. He insisted that the Packers never lost. Time merely ran out on them.

Avenue Named for Him

Green Bay, the smallest city in the league, became nationally known, and the citizens adulated Lombardi. They named the street outside the stadium Lombardi Avenue.

One year when the Los Angeles Rams were striving to woo him away, the directors gave Lombardi 320 acres of apple orchards in nearby Door County.

Under the rules of their incorporation, the Packers could not pay their 1,700 stockholders any dividends. The money piled up and Lombardi spent it in enlarging the stadium and building a magnificent field house. After the winning of the first championship, he bought the players' wives mink stoles.

To keep a touted rookie from Texas, Donny Anderson, from signing with the rival American League, Lombardi agreed to pay the young man the highest bonus in pro football's history, $600,000.

Lombardi, who had a keen appreciation for money, related winning to business success in pro football. "The teams that

Vernon J. Biever

Lombardi's coaching record with the Packers speaks for itself—141-39-4.

win the most make the most money," he said.

Although the Packers had annual profits as high as $800,000, Lombardi insisted upon keeping players' salaries "in line." Jim Ringo, a center who once played a game for Lombardi with 14 painful boils, held out for more money one season. He was traded the next.

The Packer fullback star, Jim Taylor, exercised the option clause in his contract and became a free agent so he could sign for more money with another team. The other running star, Paul Hornung, retired the same year. "We'll miss Hornung," Lombardi said. "The other fellow we'll replace."

Hornung, like Gifford, was a favorite of the coach. Lombardi was deeply hurt when Hornung was suspended for the 1963 season for gambling in violation of his contract, but Lombardi quickly forgave him.

The Catholic and military influences upon Lombardi were strong. After the assassination of Senator Robert F. Kennedy, whom he knew, Lombardi said, "What's the matter with the world? There has been a complete breakdown of mental discipline."

In speaking before an audience of businessmen, Lombardi said, "There is an abuse of freedom in our society—freedom without responsibility."

He deplored the long hair, the sideburns and mustaches of youth. He told a Redskin rookie, Trenton Jackson, "You could run faster if you didn't have that thing on your lip." Jackson shaved off the mustache at lunchtime.

Lombardi maintained there was no mystery to the Packer success. "Coaches who can outline plays on a blackboard are a dime a dozen," he once said. "The ones who win get inside their players and motivate them."

Perhaps there was no mystery. But the Packers had a losing record the first season after he retired as coach.

Lombardi believed in attacking strength. "Hit them at their strongest point," he said. Before their first regular season game in his first year at Green Bay, Lombardi told the Packers in the locker room, "Go through that door and bring back victory."

Bill Forester, a tackle, said, "I jumped up and hit my arm on my locker. It was the worst injury I had all year."

Lombardi loved to laugh, and his friends delighted in his company. But he put off strangers, and the public regarded him with both awe and fear.

René Carpenter, the former wife of the astronaut Scott Carpenter, described a reception held for Lombardi when he first came to Washington. "All of a sudden my skirt was too short and my back too bare," she said. "We were reduced to feeling like children."

Underwent Surgery Twice

Although the seriousness of Lombardi's condition had been known to close friends, no public announcement on his condition was made until Wednesday when Mrs. Lombardi authorized a statement describing him as suffering from "an extraordinarily virulent form of cancer."

He underwent two operations. After the first, on June 27, he appeared to be recovering and was released on July 14. However, his condition deteriorated and he had to be operated on a second time, on July 27.

President Leads Tributes

Many notables paid tribute yesterday to Vince Lombardi, the pro football coach. Following are some of the comments:

PRESIDENT NIXON — When I think of Vince Lombardi, I think of him standing at the side of a football field, his attention focused sharply on his team. He was an imposing figure—and an inspiring one. On the field and off, his very presence was commanding. As I think of him that way, I know that he will always hold a commanding place in the memory of this nation.

Like the power sweep which became his trademark, the power of Vince Lombardi's personality swept the world of sports and made a lasting impact on the life of all it touched. He asked a great deal of his players and his associates. But he never asked more of any man than he asked of himself. The lesson all Americans can learn from Coach Lombardi is that a man can become a star when, above all, he becomes an apostle of teamwork.

GOVERNOR ROCKEFELLER—Vince was more than a giant in the world of athletics. He was a leader in every sense of the word. His unrelenting demands on himself and on his players for the best efforts always are a matter of record and legand.

PETE ROZELLE, pro football commissioner—The death of Vince Lombardi is a deep, personal loss to all in professional football, but those who will miss him the most are those who still had yet to play for him, who might have been taught by him, led by him, and counseled by him. Vince Lombardi was a very rare person, a citizen whose achievements and principles were recognized and honored far beyond the framework of his role in society.

GEORGE HALAS, owner of the Chicago Bears—All too few men are around to match his forceful leadership and competitive qualities. I regret that I really came close to Vince only within the last five years—all too short a time to enjoy and admire his unforgettable personality. We understood each other. I loved him as a friend and a man. I am sure Vince would have been a leader in any field and in any era.

THE REV. MICHAEL P. WALSH, S. J., president of Fordham University—Vince Lombardi's players often said, "He made us better than we were." Many of us at Fordham who knew him as a magna cum laude undergraduate, as a brilliant assistant football coach, as a loyal alumnus and devoted trustee, could say much the same thing. His education, self-discipline, and love of God and his fellow man inspired many of us when our spirits flagged. The public side of Vince Lombardi was well publicized. But there was another—the private side—that his innate shyness often offered. This was a gentle, compassionate family man with deep religious convictions and steadfast loyalty to his alma mater and to his friends.

"All the News That's Fit to Print."

The New York Times.

LATE CITY EDITION

WEATHER—Colder today, probably snow; tomorrow fair, warmer. Temperatures Yesterday—Max., 21; min., 9.

VOL. LXXXIII....No. 27,792. Entered as Second-Class Matter, Postoffice, New York, N. Y. NEW YORK, MONDAY, FEBRUARY 26, 1934. P TWO CENTS in New York City. | THREE CENTS Within 200 Miles | FOUR CENTS Elsewhere Except in 7th and 8th Postal Zones

GALE AND SNOW HIT CITY; ALL NORTH STORM-BOUND; 23 KILLED IN TORNADOES

NO LET UP LIKELY HERE

Streets Treacherous as New Fall, Driven by Wind, Hides Ice.

REMOVAL FORCES READY

Renewed Suffering Is Feared in Outlying Districts—Northport Alarmed.

GALE SWEEPS FROM WEST

Illinois Roads Blocked—Heavy Fall in West Virginia—Two Women Freeze to Death.

Another snowstorm which threatens to bring a repetition of conditions that prevailed early last week swept over the eastern seaboard yesterday after having blanketed the northern part of the United States from Nebraska to the Atlantic.

The large star-shaped flakes that began to fall in New York and outlying communities about noon soon changed to a dry barrage of fine particles, driven by a northeast gale which piled it into drifts.

By 10 P. M. when the Weather Bureau closed, the official depth was estimated at 3.2 inches with a prospect of at least five inches, and perhaps six or seven, before the present fall is expected to end—sometime today.

In the afternoon the outlook became so grave that Commissioner E. P. Goodrich of the Department of Sanitation issued a warning over the municipal broadcasting station, asking pedestrians and automobile drivers to exert the utmost care on the streets. The new snowfall, covering the already ice-glazed streets, presents a hidden danger, he pointed out.

Street Cleaners Ready.

The city's facilities for handling the situation, the commissioner said, are sufficient to clear an additional six-inch fall with only ordinary difficulty. The department has a force of 21,500 men at its disposal, 108 crosswalk plows, 270 big plows, 69 loaders and 200 trucks, with additional trucks and cranes operated by contractors.

The temperature yesterday was not greatly different from that of Saturday. The average was 15, compared to Saturday's 12, and 18 degrees colder than the normal average for Feb. 25. The minimum was 9 at 8 A. M. and the maximum 21 at 1:30 P. M.

Yesterday's hourly temperatures follow:

Midnight	10	2 P. M.	19
1 A. M.	10	3 P. M.	20
2 A. M.	10	4 P. M.	19
3 A. M.	10	5 P. M.	18
4 A. M.	9	6 P. M.	17
5 A. M.	9	7 P. M.	18
6 A. M.	10	8 P. M.	19
7 A. M.	9	9 P. M.	17
8 A. M.	9	10 P. M.	14
9 A. M.	11	11 P. M.	*15
10 A. M.	13	Midnight	*15
11 A. M.	14	1 A. M.	*15
Noon	15	2 A. M.	*15
1 P. M.	17	3 A. M.	*15

*Unofficial street temperature at Times Square, which usually is 4 degrees above the official reading.

The temperatures for today are expected to be little lower, but the weather will probably be a great deal more unpleasant because of a rising wind. This, said Burton Salisbury, night observer of the weather bureau, will cause trouble in rural districts, where the new snow, falling on the uncleared snow of last week, is likely to be driven into high drifts.

At midnight all the principal railroads feeding New York reported no serious impairment in service. The Pennsylvania and Long Island trains were running on schedule with only a few minor delays and the traffic manager's office said no serious trouble was expected. The New York, New Haven & Hartford reported minor delays but added that the general service had not been appreciably affected.

Representatives of the Erie Railroad declared that the service up to midnight had been "100 per cent perfect," and the Lackawanna, New York Central and Baltimore & Ohio reported no delays of importance.

The subway lines reported that the snowstorm had not affected their service, but surface-car lines in the metropolitan area continued to employ snow-plows and crews which went on earlier in the day.

The snow-removal forces of the Department of Sanitation in Brooklyn began clearing the streets last night, putting into operation 260 pieces of equipment, including

Continued on Page Two.

Storms Cripple Air Mail Except in the Far West

Adverse weather conditions continued yesterday to beset the army's operations of the air-mail service, crippling it, as far as is known, in every section of the country east of the Rockies after noon. Only four planes operated in and out of Roosevelt and Mitchel Fields and there were no flights after 1 P. M. All mail and commercial flights from the Newark Airport were also canceled.

In Washington and Philadelphia air-mail service was suspended at dawn. The last ...

TO... 3...

13 Repo... 8 in M...

6 IN A FAM...

Storm's V... Pastor—Delu... Atlanta in Ta...

By The Assoc...

BIRMINGHAM, ... Tornadoes cut an ... destruction across ... States tonight, leav... wake more than a ... and dozens of injured...

...

Two occupants of an ... were injured when the ... crashed near Ashland, Fla., in ... storm.

The storms struck first in ... Western Mississippi near Meridi...

Six members of the family ... Mr. and Mrs. Carl Calvert at Cent... Hill, Miss., were killed when the twister tore their home apart.

The Calverts' eldest daughter miraculously escaped the falling timbers that killed the others of the family.

Alabama Pastor Is Killed.

Two were killed at Kewanee, near Centre Hill. More than a dozen were injured and the storm was felt far down into Mississippi.

From there, the storm apparently veered eastward, following the "tornado belt" through Alabama where more than 300 lost their lives in March, 1932, as storms cut through the State.

Twelve deaths were reported to the Sheriff's office at Ashland, Ala., in Clay County and there were stories of homes blown to bits, trees uprooted, highways blocked and lack of medical supplies and attendants for victims. Scores were injured.

One death was reported in another section.

One of the first to tell of the devastation about Ashland was an unidentified man who walked there

Continued on Page Two.

ALGER OFFERS PLAN FOR MORTGAGE AID; LEHMAN BACKS IT

Two Non-Profit Corporations Urged, One of Them to Get a $100,000,000 Federal Loan.

GOVERNOR TO ACT AT ONCE

He Will Call Conferences This Week—Sees Help by Banks as Public Duty.

Alger report to Gov. Lehman on mortgages, Page 13.

One non-profit co...

...

The sec... protection ... gages and ... standing, wo... Article 12 o... with nominal ... the certificat... court or other...

Continued o...

John J. McGraw Is Dead at 60; Called Baseball's Greatest Figure

Sports World Mourns Veteran, Giants' Manager for 30 Years, Who Won Ten Pennants and Three World Championships —Funeral Wednesday in St. Patrick's Cathedral.

John J. McGraw died yesterday in the New Rochelle Hospital. The "Little Napoleon" of the baseball diamond, who led the New York Giants through thirty successful years, passed away at 11:50 A. M. in his sixty-first year.

Death resulted from an internal hemorrhage caused by uremia. Mr. McGraw had entered the hospital on Feb. 16 after an illness of two weeks. He responded to treatmen... and until Saturday night, ... lapsed into a coma, it w... he would recover.

With the whol...

streets and sidewalks in front of the house, where Mrs. McGraw was in a state of nervous collapse.

A list of honorary pallbearers will be announced today at the Giants' headquarters, and it was announced that Bill Terry, who succeeded Mr. McGraw as manager of the New York team in 1932, would return from Florida for the funeral.

With the fa... fessional ...

John J. McGraw Is Dead at 60; Called Baseball's Greatest Figure

Sports World Mourns Veteran, Giants' Manager for 30 Years, Who Won Ten Pennants and Three World Championships —Funeral Wednesday in St. Patrick's Cathedral.

John J. McGraw died yesterday in the New Rochelle Hospital. The "Little Napoleon" of the baseball diamond, who led the New York Giants through thirty successful years, passed away at 11:50 A. M. in his sixty-first year.

Death resulted from an internal hemorrhage caused by uremia. Mr. McGraw had entered the hospital on Feb. 16 after an illness of two weeks. He responded to treatment and until Saturday night, when he lapsed into a coma, it was believed he would recover.

With the whole baseball and sporting world united in expressions of sorrow at the passing of the grand old baseball leader, it was announced that funeral services would be held on Wednesday at 10 A. M. in St. Patrick's Cathedral. Burial will be in Cathedral Cemetery, Baltimore.

Until the day of the funeral the body will remain at the McGraw home, 620 Ely Avenue, Pelham Manor. Anticipating many callers, the Pelham Manor authorities sent laborers to clear the snow from the streets and sidewalks in front of the house, where Mrs. McGraw was in a state of nervous collapse.

A list of honorary pallbearers will be announced today at the Giants' headquarters, and it was announced that Bill Terry, who succeeded Mr. McGraw as manager of the New York team in 1932, would return from Florida for the funeral.

With the famous veteran of professional baseball when he died, besides his wife and the attending physicians, were several friends and relatives. They included Charles A. Stoneham, president of the Giants; Mrs. Stephen Van Lill, sister of Mrs. McGraw; Frank Belcher, actor and lifelong friend, and Mrs. Belcher; Mrs. Peter Cregar, sister of Mrs. Christy Mathewson, and Mrs. John O'Brien.

Just before Mr. McGraw died Mrs. Van Lill sent her chauffeur for the Rev. Vincent de Paul Mulry of St. Catherine's Roman Catholic Church of Pelham Manor. He arrived at the hospital with the Rev. Joseph

Continued on Page Twenty-three.

... without ... rather than May ... the final date for payment without penalty of the Federal income tax is March 15; and the final date for payment without penalty of the State income tax, April 15; the limit of April 30 for payment of the city taxes will bring all three within a period of about six weeks.

To many of the taxpayers the new rates will mean the payment of approximately the same amount of taxes that they paid to the city during the prosperous days of 1927, 1928 and 1929. Assessments on a great number of houses were cut last year by Tammany, in anticipation of the Mayoralty campaign. However, that procedure makes the jump from last year's payments to those that will have to be made this year all the greater.

Aldermen Must Act.

The figures for both the basic tax rate and the borough tax rate are officially fixed by the Board of Al-

Continued on Page Thirteen.

... traffic duty were ... "specials," reserves drawn ... civilian life, in flat-topped ... caps like those once worn by New York policemen.

Although there were dozens of opportunities for trouble during the afternoon the police and the marchers behaved with perfect good temper. The only casualties were caused when a gang of toughs tried to overturn an automobile at one end of the crowd. The mounted police cleared the road and in the ensuing crush three onlookers fainted.

Orderly "Like a Wedding."

"It all went off like a wedding," said one police inspector afterward.

Professor Harold Laski, chairman of a committee formed to watch the actions of the police, said tonight the restraint on both sides had been "admirable."

Sir Oswald Mosley's Black Shirts, whose presence certainly would have caused a riot, were nowhere to be seen. The only uniforms in evidence apart from the police belonged to a well-drilled contingent of Green Shirts, advocates of Major S. H. Douglas's social credit program. They mingled on the friendliest terms with the Communists and when the demonstrators left

Continued on Page Four.

MISSING AIRLINER FOUND ON A PEAK; ALL 8 ABOARD DEAD

Plane Crashed Near Summit of Mountain 18 Miles From Salt Lake City Airport.

CRAFT IS BADLY SMASHED

...With Terrific Force ...ter Take-Off Friday ...d by Sister Ship.

...New York Times.

...CITY, Utah, Feb. ... occupants of the ... plane which left ... Rock Springs ... Friday at 2 ... death about ... The big dual- ... crashed into ... about 8,000 ... the summit ... Mountain ... by air line ...

... plane started out Friday, facing a low ceiling and in the rain. When the liner failed to reach

Continued on Page Four.

9 DARTMOUTH STUDENTS DIE IN FRATERNITY HOUSE FROM MONOXIDE POISONING

Mussolini's Paper Hails Stock Exchange Bill

By The Associated Press.

MILAN, Feb. 25.—Premier Mussolini's newspaper Popolo d'Italia declared today that proposed legislation for Federal supervision of stock exchanges in the United States would spell the end of the last vestige of "rugged individualism" in America.

The paper found in the idea justification for the Fascist theory that the State must guarantee the collective good, even to the detriment of individual initiative.

It said that the measure would put the money exchanges under the control of the government for protection of the savings of the working public.

3 SEIZED IN BATTLE IN LOBBY OF HOTEL

Shot Is Fired, Guests Flee as One of Two Murder Suspects Fights Policeman for Pistol.

NONCHALANT BRIDE TAKEN

...others Are Linked to Raid ...and Killings in Needham, Mass., Bank on Feb. 2.

... murder suspect, traced through ... charging of a storage battery ... a check-up of garages, ... a revolver from a detective ... cornered yesterday in ... lobby of the Hotel Lincoln, ... Fourth Street and Eighth ... and while a dozen startled ... and as many employes ..., attempted to fight off

... ran for the street, bell... shelter behind pillars, and ... behind counters as ... Merton Millen, 24 years ... wrestled with Detective ... Fitzsimmons of the ... precinct for the ... swinging the gun around, ... toward the detective's ... one shot, adding to ... persons in the lobby.

... Patrolman Pas... of the West Forty-... station rushed ... Millen on the ... back. The blow ... efforts to regain ... the aim of the ... downward. ... the right ... detective, grazing ... singed by ...

... man Amo... arrested. ... daughter ... also was ... lobby. ... of the ... detective ... there

... of ... prisoner in Boston, which ... believe solve the hold-up ... the Needham Trust Company near Boston on Feb. 2, resulted from the discovery of the stolen car the robbers had used on a lonely Norwood road. Cowing the bank staff with a machine gun, the robbers killed two policemen and

Continued on Page Three.

ALL THETA CHI MEMBERS

Gas From Poorly Banked Fire Traps the Victims in Their Beds.

JANITOR DISCOVERS BODIES

Some One Unfamiliar With It Had Fixed the Furnace, Says Examiner.

2 SONS OF PASTOR HERE

Only Residents Who Escaped Were Eight Who Were Away for Week-End.

Special to THE NEW YORK TIMES.

HANOVER, N. H., Feb. 25.—Nine Dartmouth students were found dead in their beds in the Theta Chi fraternity house at 33 North Main Street here late this afternoon. They had been killed during the night by carbon monoxide poisoning resulting from an improperly banked furnace.

Gas accumulated within the furnace until it exploded, blowing the door from its hinges and disconnecting the pipe leading from the rear of the furnace to the chimney. One of the boys living in the house is believed to have heard the explosion and replaced the door, but apparently he failed to notice the open pipe at the rear.

No one who was in the house last night escaped the deadly fumes. Eight other residents had gone out of town for the week-end. The dead included four seniors, three juniors and two sophomores.

THE DEAD.

The list of dead follows:

Seniors.

FULLERTON, WILLIAM F., 20 years old, of Cleveland Heights, Ohio.

MOLDENKE, EDWARD F., 21, of 130 East Fifty-fourth Street, New York City.

SMITH, WILLIAM M. JR., 21, Box 54, Manhasset, L. I.

WENTWORTH, EDWARD N., Jr., 21, of Chicago.

Juniors.

DE MASI, AMERICO S., 20, of 4,308 Clinton Avenue, Little Neck, L. I.

WATSON, HAROLD D., 21, of Wilton, Me.

SCHOOLEY, WILMOT H., 20, of 13 Prospect Avenue, Middletown, N. Y.

Sophomores.

GRIFFIN, JOHN J., 19, of 40 Williams Street, Wallingford, Conn.

MOLDENKE, ALFRED, 20, brother of Edward Moldenke.

The tragedy was discovered at 4:30 o'clock this afternoon by the janitor of the house, M. B. Little, when he arrived to make the beds. He had twice visited the house earlier in the day, at 6:30 A. M. when he fixed the furnace fire, and at 1:30 P. M., when he cleaned and straightened up the lower floor, without suspecting that anything was wrong.

The students all seemed to be asleep in natural postures, but, when Little was unable to waken them, he realized that something was wrong. He tried to telephone a doctor who was out. Then he called Chief of Police Dennis J. Hallasey, who met Dr. John Boardman on his way to the fraternity house and took him along.

Dr. Boardman found that all those in the house were dead, as was a pet dog which had been asleep in one of the bedrooms. He called Dr. R. E. Miller, medical referee of Grafton County, who made an investigation, in the course of which he was joined by County Solicitor Norris Cotton.

Finding of Medical Referee.

Dr. Miller gave out the following statement tonight as the result of his inquiry:

"At 4:40 P. M. Feb. 25, 1934, the bodies of nine Dartmouth students were found by Dr. John Boardman in the Theta Chi house at 33 North Main Street. An investigation not completed indicates that the students died while asleep. Medical examination indicates that the cause of death was carbon monoxide poisoning.

"The statement of the janitor, Mr. M. B. Little, indicates that the students retired some time after 12:30 A. M. and that the smoke pipe of the forced-draught coal-burning furnace had been blown off some time after 10:30 P. M., Feb. 24.

"The smoke pipe was replaced by the janitor at 6:45 A. M., Feb. 25, when he came to fix the fire at the usual hour. At that time the fire was burning brightly and the condition of the flue clean-out door indicated that some one had presum-

Continued on Page Five.

'Pacified' Moroccan Tribes Renew ... French Foreign Legion Loses Five ...

By The Associated Press.

AGADIR, Morocco, Feb. 25.—Opening a "mopping up" drive against rebel Berbers in the storm-swept deserts of the almost unknown Bani mountain regions, the French Foreign Legion today lost five men. Seven were wounded.

The opening battle was fought in storms of sand and rain. Guerrilla bands fiercely attacked a force under the command of General Catroux, inflicting the casualties. Two of those slain were officers.

The Foreign Legion is fighting against heavy natural odds in the desert. Two armies have been sent on a campaign to conquer the remainder of the vast Moroccan territory.

Heavily armed hostile tribesmen, dispatches said, headed by two sworn enemies of the French, Belkacem N'Gadi and Merebbi Rebbo, find an easy refuge in almost impenetrable forests.

Drinking water is scarce, and the Legionaires are forced to build their own motor trails to advance slowly into the unmapped territory, aided only by reconnoitring airplanes.

Pacification of Morocco was supposed to have been completed last year, after twenty-five years of warfare in desert and hills. With the surrender of Zaid ou Skounti on Koucer Peak last September it was thought the remainder of the job would be mere police duty. But the fierce tribesmen, it developed, had not been conquered, and they resumed guerrilla warfare.

This year's operations, in charge of Generals Giraud and Catroux, will centre southwest of Tiznit, between the Spanish colony of Rio de Oro and the enclave of Ifni. It will extend to the south of the Atlas mountain chain, known as Jebel Bani.

NRA to Investigate Ford Edgewater Row; Company Hit on Refusal to Attend Hearing

Special to THE NEW YORK TIMES.

WASHINGTON, Feb. 25.—The National Recovery Administration suddenly reopened its long-standing controversy with the Ford Motor Company today by serving public notice that it would make a "detailed investigation of the company's alleged refusal to bargain collectively with employes of its Edgewater, N. J., plant."

The notice, given by William H. Davis, National Compliance Director, was a sequel to the refusal of the Ford Company to send representatives to a hearing here Friday, where representatives of employes of that plant charged 511 striking workers had been "blacklisted."

He notified Edsel Ford of this decision in a letter written yesterday.

At the same time the NRA made public correspondence exchanged between Mr. Davis and B. J. Craig, secretary of the Ford Company, including one from Mr. Craig dated Feb. 20 and "respectfully informing" Mr. Davis that the Ford Company would not be represented at the hearing Friday.

The trouble at the Edgewater plant began on Sept. 29, when employes were alleged to have staged a walkout in an effort to obtain better working conditions.

The employes participating complained they were dismissed, and their spokesmen charged that the Ford officials refused to "bargain" on the employes' demands, violating Section 7a of the code for the automobile industry. The Ford Company has never signed this code.

Mr. Davis forwarded the complaints to the Ford Motor Company and received, on Feb. 2, a reply from Mr. Craig some 3,000 words long. In this Mr. Craig said he felt the "brief of facts" submitted by the strikers without a sworn complaint involved no obligation to reply but that he did so "out of respect for your honorable body."

JOHN M'GRAW DIES IN HOSPITAL AT 60

Continued From Page One.

Mahoney of St. Gabriel's Church of New Rochelle. Father Mulry will be the celebrant at the solemn requiem mass on Wednesday.

Since Feb. 16 Mr. McGraw had been under the care of Dr. Louis B. Chapman, Dr. E. L. Keyes and Dr. E. L. Kellogg. The doctors considered a blood transfusion after Saturday night's hemorrhage, but abandoned the idea in the belief that the shock of the operation might prove fatal. Oxygen was used yesterday morning to prolong the patient's life.

Attended League Meeting.

Dr. Chapman, who was Mr. McGraw's personal physician, said the first intimation of illness came when the retired manager of the Giants complained of a sore throat and gave up his plan to attend the annual dinner of the Baseball Writers Association on Feb. 4.

Two days later, however, he attended a National League meeting at which the baseball schedule for 1934 was adopted. He went to the Giants' victory dinner that evening, when the National League club owners celebrated their winning of the pennant.

He remained at the dinner only about an hour. His condition kept him at home afterward, although he insisted on performing his duties as vice president of the Giants. Until a week ago last Friday, when Dr. Chapman ordered him to the hospital, there had been nothing alarming about Mr. McGraw's condition.

CAREER OF M'GRAW UNIQUE IN SPORTS

His Ten Pennant Victories and Three World's Championships Form Unrivaled Record.

John McGraw when he was still a player with the Giants.

From the early Nineties John Joseph McGraw was one of the greatest figures in organized baseball. In his playing days a brilliant third baseman, whose efforts were not confined to the mere mechanics of the sport, but a player who brought a keen, incisive mind to the national game, a fighter of the old school whose aggressiveness inspired his team-mates of the famous old Baltimore Orioles, McGraw became the most successful figure, perhaps, in all baseball history. His record—ten pennant winners and three world's titles—speaks eloquently of McGraw, the molder of championship clubs, a stickler for discipline and a martinet who saw that his orders were rigidly enforced both on and off the field.

Baseball history does not reveal any record that approaches the achievement of McGraw in capturing ten pennants with his Giants. Connie Mack, veteran pilot of the Athletics, and Miller Huggins, late manager of the Yankees, are the only other leaders whose accomplishments are in any way comparable with those of the fiery McGraw. Mack has won nine flags. Huggins was the Yankee pilot six times for league honors.

McGraw was born in the rural community of Truxton, N. Y., on April 7, 1873, and gained his first knowledge of the game on the sand lots of that tiny village of up-State New York. There were not many boys in the little hamlet of some 300 persons, and decidedly few of any special baseball-playing ability. So it was significant of McGraw's persistency and close application to the task in hand that he was able to attain so much proficiency as a player that in 1890, at the age of 17, he obtained an engagement with the Olean (N. Y.) club, then a member of the original New York and Pennsylvania League.

The next season, 1891, found McGraw transplanted to a far distant field. He had journeyed westward to Iowa, where he signed a contract with the Cedar Rapids (Iowa) club of the Illinois-Iowa League.

Reports of McGraw's rapid-fire fielding, his speed on the bases and his solid hitting reached the ears of the officials of the Baltimore club of the old American Association, and in midsummer of that year, Aug. 26, to be exact, McGraw, following his purchase, donned the uniform of the famous old Orioles.

McGraw played in thirty-one games during the remainder of the season and showed enough ability to warrant retention. The next year Baltimore became a member of the twelve-club National League. The Orioles had been going badly and Ed Hanlon, who had shown an exceptional faculty for organization and leadership as well as playing ability, was obtained to manage the team.

Hanlon made a number of player deals during the Winter, and in one of them he acquired a youth whose name was to be linked inseparably with McGraw ever thereafter. The new acquisition was a red-headed youngster from Louisville, the late Hughey Jennings.

Jennings and McGraw met on the Orioles' Spring training trip of 1893. The conditioning campaign took the Baltimore club to New Orleans. The year before the Orioles had descended to last place in the twelve-club circuit and Hanlon was determined to lift the club out of the rut. He set to work with the fixed idea of weeding out some of the slipping veterans and replacing them with new blood. McGraw and Jennings got the chance to show what they could do at third base and short and came through with flying colors and clinched these positions.

Robinson a Team-Mate.

The Orioles of that period included many exceptional players, men like Wilbert Robinson, former manager and president of the Brooklyn club, then rated as one of the finest catchers in baseball. His battery mate was the noted pitcher John (Sadie) McMahon. Joe Kelley roamed the outfield.

Hanlon, the George Stallings of another generation, welded the club into a formidable and close-knit unit in the season of 1894 and brought it home in front of the rest of the field, a remarkable performance. By this time, however, the wily pilot had obtained Willie Keeler, Walter Brodie, Kid Gleason and others to supplement the nucleus remaining.

McGraw and Jennings in the Winter previous to the Orioles' first pennant-winning achievement had advanced themselves along another line of endeavor. In one of their long and frank talks they came to the conclusion that their education had largely been neglected and they resolved to overcome the deficiency.

Trade Experience for Schooling.

McGraw proposed taking a course at St. Bonaventure College at Allegany, N. Y., not far from his home and the scene of his first professional baseball experience, and Jennings quickly fell in line with the idea. They were not in a position financially to afford much of an outlay for the education they sought, but with real business acumen arranged with the college authorities to exchange their knowledge of baseball in a coaching capacity for an academic education.

The Orioles from 1894 to 1899 were one of the most formidable and widely discussed clubs in baseball history. Under Hanlon's magic guidance this dashing, aggressive combination captured three National League pennants in succession, then finished second two years in a row and in 1899, the last year of Baltimore's connection with the older major circuit, the club, many of whose famed veteran players had been replaced by that time, dropped to fourth.

Four times the Orioles played for the Temple Cup, the premier trophy of baseballdom of that period, which was annually contended for by the first and second place clubs in the National League. Twice McGraw and his mates captured the annual classic, and their bitter battles with Patsy Tebeau's crack Cleveland club are still vividly remembered by old-time fans.

McGraw gained his first managerial experience in 1899, taking the helm for part of the season, Wilbert Robinson succeeding him. The end of that season witnessed the sale of these two stars to the St. Louis National League Club. However, they preferred to cast their lot with the American League, then in the process of organization.

McGraw and Robinson took over the Baltimore franchise in the new circuit. Then the war between the two major circuits broke out and McGraw became involved in a controversy with Ban Johnson, then president of the American League. The late Andrew Freedman, then president of the New York Giants, had taken a fancy to McGraw and offered him the post of manager. The Giants had been going from bad to worse under several different régimes and Freedman believed that McGraw was the man to put the club on its feet.

Took Charge of the Giants.

On July 19, 1902, McGraw, then a rather stocky, black-haired little fellow, 29 years old, walked out on

(continued)

Wilbert Robinson, John McGraw and Christy Mathewson—three greats of a bygone era.

the old Polo Grounds to take command of the hapless, disorganized Giants. This date is a significant one in the annals of the diamond, and in 1927 was enthusiastically celebrated by a great army of fans and baseball and city officials on the occasion of the twenty-fifth anniversary of McGraw's leadership of the New York National League club.

McGraw undertook the reconstruction of the club, and the success of his efforts is evidenced by the fact that in 1903, his first full year at the helm, the Giants finished in second place. McGraw brought Joe McGinnity, Dan McGann and Roger Bresnahan, three bright young stars, with him from the Baltimore club. He signed Arthur Devlin as his third baseman, Billy Gilbert as his secondsacker. The immortal Christy Mathewson already had joined the club from Bucknell University.

Attendance Rose Quickly.

He was remarkably successful in the development of Mathewson, George Wiltse, Leon Ames and Dummy Taylor to aid McGinnity and the Giants were made. The attendance figures increased tremendously, and the advent of the New York Highlanders, an opposition club placed in the metropolis by the American League, was scarcely noticed.

In 1904 McGraw's Giants swept through the league, bowling over all opposition and rolling up the huge total of 106 victories, a mark that has been exceeded only twice in the history of the National League. McGraw was hailed as the "Little Napoleon" of organized baseball and baseball followers heaped encomiums on his head as the organizer of one of baseball's most powerful machines.

The previous year the Pittsburgh club, champion of the National League, and the Boston club, title winner in the junior circuit, had met in the first series for the world's championship. But, much to the disappointment of fandom, John T. Brush, who had succeeded Freedman as president of the Giants, stubbornly refused to let his club meet the Boston club, which had captured another pennant. He had been one of the stanch supporters of the National League and could not see that anything was to be gained by recognizing and playing against the champion team of a rival circuit.

The following year the Giants repeated and this year Brush finally consented to allow his club to contend against the champions of the American League, the Philadelphia Athletics. The most brilliantly pitched world's series of all time ensued.

Personnel of Famous Team.

McGraw lined up his team for the opening clash as follows: Mathewson, pitcher; Bresnahan, catcher; McGann, first base; Gilbert, second base; Devlin, third base; Dahlen, shortstop; Mertes, left field; Donlin, centre field, and Browne, right field. It was one of the finest combinations New York fans had ever seen in action.

Connie Mack's Athletics also were formidable, but were no match for the Giants with Mathewson and McGinnity pitching all five games for the National Leaguers. Mathewson established a record for all time of shutting out the opposition in three of the battles. McGinnity blanked the Athletics in another contest and in the other battle, the only one which Philadelphia won, Chief Bender shut out the Giants. All five games were shut-outs, another record for the annual classic.

The Giants then finished second to Frank Chance's sensational Cubs for the next three years, dropping to third in 1909 but rising to second in 1910. McGraw made many bold moves to strengthen his club and invariably had his nine in the running. In 1908 the Giants came within an ace of taking the flag, losing it through defeat in a playoff with the Cubs. The blunder by Fred Merkle in not touching second base and thus giving the Cubs another chance to win out ultimately was one of the most discussed diamond happenings of that decade.

Forgave Merkle for Blunder.

McGraw forgave Merkle and instead of censuring him condoned the fatal oversight, and, moreover, raised his salary for the sake of encouraging the downcast player. Merkle repaid his boss by playing stellar ball for years thereafter and was ranked as one of the most mentally alert players in the game.

In 1911 McGraw finally passed the fighting Cubs and brought his third flag to the metropolis. In that year he had Herzog, Fletcher, Doyle and Merkle in his infield; Devore, Snodgrass and Murray in the outfield; Meyers behind the bat and Mathewson, Ames and Wiltse, sole survivors of the 1905 champions, and Marquard and Crandall in the box. The Athletics boasted their "$100,000 infield," whose valuation would have been increased tenfold just a few years later, and Frank Baker's bat, more than any other factor, laid the Giants low in four out of six games.

The Giants repeated in 1912 and this year encountered the Boston Red Sox in the annual classic. The series went to the limit of seven games before Snodgrass made his fatal muff in the tenth inning and Boston pulled out the series.

The Giants captured their third straight pennant in 1913 and again faced Connie Mack's great Athletics. The latter were too much for the Giants once more and took four out of five games. The Giants still had Mathewson, and Big Six pitched the only game the New Yorkers won, but McGraw's hitters could not cope with the brilliant pitching of Coombs, Bender, Plank and Bush.

McGraw built over again, and in 1917, the Giants' next pennant-winning year, many new players were members of the combination that faced the White Sox. Burns, Kauff and Robertson roamed the outer gardens, Zimmerman, Herzog, Fletcher and Holke held down infield berths, McCarthy and Rariden were behind the bat and Sallee, Schupp, Anderson, Perritt, Tesreau and Rube Benton attended to the pitching duties. Again the Giants were doomed to defeat, the White Sox taking four contests of the six-game series.

The jinx that persistently pursued the Giants in world series was put to rout in 1921, the next year McGraw's club finished on top, and Miller Huggins's Yankees, with Babe Ruth cast in the heavy slugging rôle, could not stop the Giants' dashing, crushing attack.

Giants' Stars of 1921 Triumph.

Dave Bancroft, Frank Frisch, George Kelly, Pep Young, Emil Meusel, George Burns, Johnnie Rawlings, Frank Snyder, Phil Douglas, Arthur Nehf, Earl Smith, Fred Toney and Jess Barnes were members of the McGraw combination of that year. Practically the same players, to whom Heine Groh, Casey Stengel, Bill Cunningham, Jack Scott, Hugh McQuillan and a few others of lesser importance had been added, routed the Yankees, again winners of the American League flag, in five games, the one game the clan of McGraw did not capture being a tie.

For the third consecutive year the two New York clubs clashed in 1923, and this time the Yankees, thanks to a savage batting attack, came out on top, winning the world title by scoring four victories in six starts.

McGraw set a world's record by leading his club to its fourth consecutive pennant in 1924. That year the Giants engaged in an exciting and hard-fought struggle with Bucky Harris's Washington club, whose pitching mainstay was the redoubtable Walter Johnson. There was little to choose between the two clubs, but the Senators finally emerged triumphant, winning the odd game of seven, Johnson stemming the Giants' attack in the late innings of the crucial contest.

Fred Lindstrom, Bill Terry, Hack Wilson, Hank Gowdy, Jack Bentley, Billy Southworth and Rosy Ryan had been added to the pennant-winning ensemble of the previous year.

Victory Under McGraw.

That year, 1924, marked the Giants' last surge to the top in the National League under McGraw's leadership. In 1925 the club finished second after a hard battle with the Pittsburgh Pirates, and again in 1927 McGraw's team, after a slow start, finished with a burst of speed that nearly carried it into another championship, the Giants finally finishing two games rearward of the champion Pirates.

Again rebuilding after falling to fifth place in 1926 and finishing third in 1927, McGraw almost scaled the heights in 1928. Building around Bill Terry, Melvin Ott and Fred Lindstrom as hitters, with Frank Hogan also aiding, and with a pitching staff led by Larry Benton, the Giants carried the fight almost to the last day of the season, only to finish two games behind the St. Louis Cardinals.

In fact, with the season ending on Sunday, Sept. 30, it took defeats at the hands of the Cubs on Friday

(continued)

and Saturday, with a victory by St. Louis on Saturday, to decide the race. McGraw drove his team with all his old-time skill, winning ten and losing five in his last home stand. In 1929 he finished third because Benton failed and in 1930 he was in the same place, practically for the same reason.

The last real effort came in 1931, when he finished second, but far behind the Cardinals, who that year had a superteam, the one which beat the Athletics for the world's championship. The Giants won eighty-seven games, good enough in some years for pennants, but the Cardinals went over the 100 mark.

Then came 1932. McGraw made a few changes, and in the training season in California seemed again to have exercised his magic. On the Coast and on the way East his men could not lose, compiling one of the best pre-season records ever made. But when the games came that counted they could not win. Through April and May they went, luckless.

Their failure weighed on their leader, and illnesses that he had laughed off and fought off in former years brought him down. He was a sick man, sicker than most people ever knew, when he electrified the baseball world by resigning on June 3 and turning the club over to Bill Terry, whom he had recommended to the officials of the club.

Since his resignation he had acted in an advisory capacity in the selection of young players, something at which his wide acquaintance with baseball club owners and managers had made him invaluable, and gave much counsel to Terry in the campaign which resulted in last year's pennant and world title.

Turbulent Chapters in Career.

There were turbulent chapters in McGraw's career. Several times he became embroiled in altercations with the umpire and once lost an impromptu bout to an arbiter following a heated dispute over the umpire's decision.

A few years ago McGraw was charged with engaging in fisticuffs at the Lambs Club, of which he was a member. John C. Slavin, a comedian, and Wilton Lackaye and William H. Boyd, actors, both received hospital attention and McGraw was expelled from membership in the organization. Later the club reinstated him following the circulation of a petition to which the names of several hundred members were appended. McGraw was indicted on a charge of having liquor in his possession at the time an alleged fight occurred. The Federal court acquitted the Giants' manager.

McGraw also was a baseball missionary to foreign lands, spreading the gospel of baseball to many countries abroad. In 1913, after the Giants and Athletics had met for the world series, McGraw and Charles Comiskey, owner of the White Sox, led two teams on a world tour, embarking at San Francisco and terminating their long journey in New York. The two clubs toured Japan, China, Australia, Egypt, Italy, France and England, playing their final contest before the King and 35,000 other Britons at London.

Again Led Team Overseas.

In 1924 at the close of the regular season McGraw and Comiskey again took two teams abroad, visiting England and France. Interest in America's national game was kindled anew and many nines were organized abroad as the direct result of this second invasion. The trip, however, was said to have been a financial failure to the extent of some $20,000.

McGraw always said that he did not object to incurring the financial losses his tours abroad cost him provided the journeys had added to the general interest in baseball.

McGraw, grown plump and prosperous with success, liked to startle people with his pet margay.

Besides directing the playing of the Giants, since 1919 he had been associated in the business management and ownership of the club. In that year Harry Hempstead sold his interests to Charles A. Stoneham, Judge Francis X. McQuade and McGraw, and the Giants' pilot became vice president of the club. While the club was owned by the late John T. Brush McGraw was reputed to be drawing a salary of $30,000 a year. When he became an official it was generally accepted that he was drawing $65,000. In the early part of the 1928 season McGraw agreed to continue in his managerial capacity for the next two years. This dispelled rumors that he was planning to retire at the end of the 1928 campaign.

During his long management of the Giants McGraw was often accused of buying pennants, meaning that he purchased stars of other clubs to strengthen the Giants and aid them in their pennant fights. The club, however, was in a financial position to acquire players developed by other teams who readily parted with their stars for needed cash.

Always Strong for Fair Play.

McGraw always played the game fairly and his integrity was shown by his prompt dismissal of players who were found to have been involved in sharp practices, no matter how much this weakened the club.

His silver jubilee at the Polo Grounds in 1927 brought back many memories of his long and successful career. The general feeling of admiration and respect was in Mayor Walker's voice when he presented a huge silver loving cup to baseball's Little Napoleon. Commander Richard E. Byrd and Clarence D. Chamberlin, transatlantic airmen, stood by the Mayor's side as he eulogized the veteran silver-haired leader.

McGraw's playing days undoubtedly would have been extended had it not been for a bad spike wound he suffered as a member of the Orioles. He played only ten years and during this time compiled a grand batting average of .334, while he scored 1,016 runs and stole 443 bases, an excellent offensive record.

Hornsby Episode Recalled.

The Hornsby episode is still fresh in the minds of fandom. McGraw brought the celebrated Rajah to New York in the Spring of 1927 and he played brilliantly for the Giants, only to be traded to the Braves at the close of the season. Rumor had it that enmity had arisen between Hornsby and McGraw, but the claim was never substantiated.

Hornsby himself said after he had been traded that he still esteemed McGraw highly and considered him the greatest manager in the major leagues. McGraw denied there was anything but the most cordial relations between him and the slugging infielder. Later President Stoneham assumed full responsibility for the disposal of the star player, asserting he had been traded "for the good of the club."

When McGraw took his Giants to Olean for an exhibition contest against St. Bonaventure in the Summer of 1927 he was enthusiastically greeted after thirty-seven years' absence from that town. McGraw's homecoming was one of the biggest events that ever happened in the little city and flags waved from almost every building, while the whole population turned out with several bands to greet him. It was a happy moment for McGraw, who years before had trudged disconsolately through the streets to the railway station after committing those alleged nine errors.

M'GRAW A SYMBOL OF THE OLDEN DAYS

His Active Career Covered the Time When Stealing Bases Was Way to Pennant.

NOTED FOR HIS FAIRNESS

Refused to Punish His Men for Poor Plays—Generous With Old-Time Friends.

By JOHN N. WHEELER.

When John J. McGraw finally hung up his spangles a lot of color faded out of big league baseball. For a few years afterward he fidgeted on the bench and managed his Giants from there, but the McGraw in civilian clothes was not the same as the doughty little warrior bustling to the plate to bawl out an umpire or bait an opponent.

Then in 1932 he quit altogether as an active manager and turned the team over to Bill Terry. Today he is dead.

McGraw did not seem to be at home in the modern game. It had changed greatly since the days of the old Baltimore Orioles—perhaps for the better—but it was not McGraw's baseball. No more did a team win pennants by stealing bases as his 1911 Giants did, no more did the hit-and-run or the bunt or the unexpected play of a master settle ball games and pennants. Every big-leaguer was grabbing his bat at the end of the handle and swinging for it—not the science

(continued)

Highlights in McGraw's Career

Played his first professional game with Olean April, 1890.

Played his first big-league game with Baltimore Orioles Aug. 26, 1891.

Played his last game with the Giants Sept. 12, 1906.

Member of three pennant-winning teams in Baltimore, where he played from 1891 until 1899.

Retired with a lifetime batting average of .334, going over .300 for nine consecutive seasons and reaching .390 in 1899.

Became manager of the Giants in July, 1902, reorganizing an eighth-place club so that he finished second the next year (1903).

Won three world's championships —1905, 1921 and 1922—and ten league pennants.

Set record for consecutive pennants when he won in 1921, 1922, 1923 and 1924—four in a row.

Took teams on foreign tours in 1914 and 1924. The 1914 journey was around the world.

Developed Christy Mathewson and considered him the greatest pitcher of all time.

Retired as manager of the Giants on June 3, 1932.

of Willie Keeler, who "hit 'em where they ain't," or Ty Cobb, who called his shots and was a flash on the bases.

Noted for Generosity.

The game also had become more gentlemanly and, if you will take the word of an old-timer like the writer, less colorful. Not that there is any implication that John J. McGraw was not a gentleman, but when he went to the wars he went to win. Probably there never was a more generous man in the big leagues when it came to looking after old-time ball players who were down and out. Recently an intimate friend of McGraw's estimated he had given away to the old-timers at least $100,000.

My acquaintance with McGraw dates back to 1908, when I first began writing baseball and trouping with the Giants. That year McGraw lost a pennant on a technicality, the failure of Merkle to touch second base, which resulted in a tie with Frank Chance's Cubs at the end of the season. This play cost a pennant, but McGraw, notwithstanding his reputation for being rough with his ball players, never bawled out Merkle.

McGraw had the reputation of being a strict disciplinarian, and he was, but you won't find a ball player—or rather I never found one who worked for him—who did not think he was fair. His men also knew he would fight for their rights, and it was inspiring to see him rushing at an umpire, after what he thought was an unfair decision.

Probably two of the bitterest rivals in the history of the big leagues were Frank Chance and John McGraw. Chance was the man who made it a rule to lick every ball player as soon as he joined his club, so there would be no doubt about who was boss. Mac seldom fought with his players.

Admirer of Mathewson.

McGraw probably admired Christy Mathewson more than any other ball player he ever knew for his brains, conduct and pitching ability. Yet there was one thing he disliked about the habits of "Big Six" and that was playing golf. The Giant boss subscribed to the theory that it was an old man's game.

In the earlier days of baseball, the clubs put up at second-rate hotels and ate in hot-dog wagons. McGraw changed all that. The Giants stopped at the best and could eat what they liked at the expense of the management.

They say Babe Ruth did a lot for baseball, and they are right. Old Mac would agree. But when the final record is written, unbiased observers will have to give McGraw credit for doing as much. He was a great human being with the frailties which go with greatness. No one he liked ever went to him for a tip on a horse race or a loan or anything McGraw could give him that he didn't get. Big league baseball some day will build a monument to him.

McGraw Mourned by All on Giants' Team; Stars Tell How He Taught Them the Game

By JOHN DREBINGER.

Special to THE NEW YORK TIMES.

MIAMI BEACH, Fla., Feb. 25.—The death of John McGraw cast a pall today over the training camp of the world's champion Giants.

News of the passing of their former manager reached the players just as they were about to leave the clubhouse after their workout at Flamingo Park. All were deeply affected, especially the older players who had fought under McGraw's command in many of the turbulent pennant campaigns prior to his retirement as their pilot in 1932.

Memphis Bill Terry, who succeeded McGraw as manager, was visibly moved. He will leave here tomorrow to attend the funeral.

"At times he appeared to be pretty harsh and severe with us," Terry said, "but as I now look back on those days I realize he was moved in this by only a single purpose, namely, to drive us on to do our level best. There was never a question of his judgment. His much discussed system, covering all phases of baseball, from the training season through the pennant race, was always sound and based fundamentally on common sense and his vast experience."

Henry Fabian, veteran groundkeeper of the Polo Grounds, wept. Henry's acquaintance with McGraw began on April 7 (McGraw's birthday), 1891, in Cedar Rapids, when both were rookies on the same team. Fabian then was a young first baseman.

McGraw was just breaking in as a third baseman and it was at Henry's behest that McGraw cast his lot with the Baltimore Orioles, with whom he was to win his first renown. They became fast friends and during the following years seldom were separated.

Frank Snyder, now a coach under Terry but a catcher under McGraw in the four successive pennant-winning years from 1921 to 1924, said that in all his associations with the game he had never met a man who took his baseball more seriously.

Old Tom Clark, a veteran catcher, who was engaged by McGraw as coach, said:

"McGraw will never be forgotten as long as baseball is played, but by me he will be best remembered for his loyalty to me and thousands of other old ball players."

Carl Hubbell, ace southpaw of the Giant forces who was developed by McGraw in 1927, attributed all his success as a pitcher to the teachings of McGraw.

Much of McGraws vaunted severity with his players appeared to be something of a myth to Harold Schumacher, one of the last pitching stars uncovered by McGraw before his retirement.

"The first day I came to McGraw he had never seen me pitch a ball, yet he said to me: 'Schumacher, I have every reason to believe you are going to make a great pitcher. So just take things easy for a time and we'll get along all right.' In all my time with the Giants while McGraw was on the bench I never heard him speak a harsh word to me or any other young player."

In this Schumacher was heartily seconded by Travis Jackson, captain of the Giants.

The Giants will cancel all practice on the day of the funeral.

M'GRAW IS PRAISED AS GREAT LEADER

His Loyalty Stressed in Mass of Telegrams Received at Pelham Manor Home.

FARLEY SENDS SYMPATHY

Heydler Expresses Sentiment of National League—Old Associates Mourn.

Men well known in politics and sports joined yesterday in expressions of sorrow at the death of John J. McGraw. Messages of sympathy were received by the hundred at the McGraw home, 620 Ely Avenue, Pelham Manor.

Among those who telegraphed their sympathy were James A. Farley, Postmaster General; Joseph McCarthy, manager of the New York Yankees; John F. Curry, leader of Tammany Hall; Judge Emil Fuchs, president of the Boston National League team; John A. Heydler, president of the National League; Roger Bresnahan, the player; Eddie Collins, manager of the Boston Red Sox, and Freddie Lindstrom, one of McGraw's former players who is now with the Pittsburgh Pirates.

A joint telegram was sent to Mrs. McGraw by Travis Jackson, Carl Hubbell and Fred Fitzsimmons, star players of the New York Giants. It said:

"In your great sorrow you have our deepest sympathy."

Stoneham Among Callers.

Charles A. Stoneham, president of the Giants, upon arriving at the McGraw home said:

"Of course, I've always been a Giant rooter since I was a kid, and since I've been associating with John J. McGraw I've never known a finer man. Every one regrets his death, but none any more than I do."

Leo Bondy, treasurer of the Giants, another caller, said:

"The outstanding characteristic of Mr. McGraw was his determination. When he started out for anything he always got it. When people talk about baseball managers they must put McGraw in one group and all of the rest in another. He was liberal to a fault. I never knew of a man who could get a check from a waiter before McGraw had paid it.

"He was popular in Japan, and had met kings and princes in his efforts to extend the popularity of baseball."

Edward Burke, part owner of the Havre de Grace race track in Maryland, said:

"I knew Mr. McGraw for forty years and always thought he was the best in his business. He was the greatest handler of men that I ever met."

Tributes Paid to Ability.

Other tributes to Mr. McGraw follow:

BILL TERRY, Manager of the Giants—He was by far and away the greatest baseball manager of all time, and I doubt whether his records, achievements and personality ever can be equaled by any other. I always considered him the foremost authority on the game. His many triumphs lay chiefly in the fact that he always kept himself abreast of the times and usually was several jumps ahead. I attribute much of my own success last year to the solid groundwork of baseball which I learned under him. Baseball will never know another John McGraw.

JAMES TIERNEY, Secretary of the Club—I always respected him and held him in the highest regard because of his unbending loyalty to his friends and to the Giants, which he alone made famous. He was the greatest single figure baseball ever produced.

HENRY FABIAN, Veteran Ground Keeper of the Polo Grounds—The records of McGraw's greatness as a player and manager speak for themselves, but to me his true greatness lay in his unflinching loyalty and generosity to his friends. His hand, heart and pocket were always open to any one down on his luck. He was a greater philanthropist than the world ever knew.

FRANK SNYDER, Coach of the Club, who was a catcher during the pennant-winning years from 1921 to 1924—Young players learned more from him in one season than they could elsewhere in an entire career. He had a baseball mind that was in a class by itself.

Gerry Nugent's Comment.

By The Associated Press.

PHILADELPHIA, Feb. 25.—Gerry Nugent, president of the Phillies, said tonight baseball "has suffered a great loss with the death of John McGraw."

"He was one of the outstanding characters of baseball and a wonderful man to know," Nugent stated.

RECORD OF M'GRAW AS PILOT OF GIANTS

Year.	Position.	Year.	Position.
1903	Second	1918	Second
1904	First	1919	Second
*1905	First	1920	Second
1906	Second	*1921	First
1907	Second	*1922	First
1908	Second	1923	First
1909	Third	1924	First
1910	Second	1925	Second
1911	First	1926	Fifth
1912	First	1927	Third
1913	First	1928	Second
1914	Second	1929	Third
1915	Eighth	1930	Third
1916	Fourth	1931	Second
1917	First		

*World's championships—three.

Recapitulation—First, ten times. Second, twelve times. Third, four times. Fourth, once. Fifth, once. Eighth, once.

WORLD SERIES RESULTS.

1904—No series with Boston Red Sox, American League champions.
1905—Giants 4 games, Athletics 1.
1911—Athletics 4 games, Giants 2.
1912—Red Sox 4 games, Giants 3, tied 1.
1913—Athletics 4 games, Giants 1.
1917—White Sox 4 games, Giants 2.
1921—Giants 5 games, Yankees 3.
1922—Giants 4 games, Yankees 0, tied 1.
1923—Yankees 4 games, Giants 2.
1924—Senators 4 games, Giants 3.

Won three world's championships, ten league championships.

Won 26, lost 28, tied 2 in world series games.

"All the News That's Fit to Print"

The New York Times.

LATE CITY EDITION
Condensation of U. S. Weather Bureau forecast: Rain this afternoon, ending late tonight. Cooler tomorrow.
Temp. range today: 47-39; yesterday: 49.7-34.1
Full U. S. Weather Bureau Report, Page 63

VOL. CV..No. 35,810. Entered as Second-Class Matter, Post Office, New York, N. Y. NEW YORK, THURSDAY, FEBRUARY 9, 1956. Times Square, New York 36, N. Y. Telephone Lackawanna 4-1000 FIVE CENTS

Connie Mack, Mr. Baseball, Dies In Philadelphia at the Age of 93

Athletics' Owner-Manager 50 Years—Won 9 Pennants and 5 World Series

Special to The New York Times.

PHILADELPHIA, Feb. 8—Connie Mack, the grand old man of baseball, died at 3:20 P. M. today at the home of a daughter, Mrs. Frank Cunningham, in the Germantown section here. Mr. Baseball, as he was known the world over, had celebrated his ninety-third birthday last Dec. 23.

Mr. Mack's eldest son, Roy, said his father died "very peacefully" about three hours after a Roman Catholic priest had administered the sacrament of extreme unction.

Last Saturday, Mr. Mack was taken to his daughter's home from Roy Mack's home. He took a turn for the worse this morning and all members of the family were called to Mrs. Cunningham's home.

Roy Mack said Dr. Illarion I. Gopadze, long-time friend and for years physician for Mr. Mack's old team, the former Philadelphia Athletics, had visited his father this morning but was not present when he died.

Mr. Mack survived by about fifteen months the loss of the A's, the American League club he founded and guided for half a century. Control of the club was vested in his sons Roy and Earle when it was transferred to Kansas City, Mo., before the 1955 season.

Mr. Mack had been in poor health since his right hip was fractured in a fall from his bed last Oct. 1. The hip was set during an operation by Dr. Go-

Continued on Page 31, Column 2

The New York Times, 1954
Connie Mack

EISENHOWER GIVES PLEDGE TO GUARD PEACE IN MIDEAST

Says He Will Do Everything Constitutionally Possible to Prevent Outbreak

ALLIED PARLEY BEGINS

President Indicates Any Step to Avert War Will Not Infringe on Congress

By DANA ADAMS SCHMIDT
Special to The New York Times.

WASHINGTON, Feb. 8—President Eisenhower said today that everything he could "constitutionally do" to prevent outbreak of hostil... Middle East would b...

He announced tha... begun among Uni... British and French ...tives here to see "what ... we could apply, either severally ourselves or th... the United Nations."

These studies were starte... the State Department this af...noon by Under Secretary Robe... D. Murphy and Sir Roge... Makins and Maurice Couve de Murville, the British and French Ambassadors.

The President spoke at his news conference in reply to a request for his assessment of the possibility of stopping or averting further conflict in the Middle East by joint Western action or through the United Nations.

He ventured no assessment, but in mentioning what he could "constitutionally do" and possible action by the Western powers outside the United Nations, he touched upon two of the key problems in giving effect to the conclusions he and Prime Minister Eden reached at their meetings here last week.

Aim Is to Counter Force

They said they would, together with the French, try to determine the "nature of the action which we should take" in the event of "the use of force, or the threat of force or of preparations to violate the frontiers or armistice lines in the Middle East."

Such action could involve political pressure or economic pressure, but in a crisis it might mean using armed force.

In his news conference comments, high Administration sources explained later, the President meant to say that he was not going to do anything that could mean war. That is, he meant to be very careful not to infringe upon the constitutional prerogative of Congress to declare war.

The President, it was recalled, has at all times been anxious to exercise his powers within the limits of the authority given him by the Constitution.

That is one of the main reasons why he went to Congress for "stand-by authority" when there seemed to be danger that

Continued on Page 2, Column 3

PAKISTAN ACCEPTS SOVIET TRADE BID

Cabinet Agrees to Enter Talk in April Over a Pact

By JOHN P. CALLAHAN
Special to The New York Times.

KARACHI, Pakistan, Feb. 8—Pakistan's Cabinet approved today a recommendation of the Ministry of Economic Affairs that the Government begin formal negotiations for a trade pact with the Soviet Union.

To prepare the way for negotiations, the commercial attaché of the Soviet Embassy had discussed the issue "informally" with officials of the Ministry of Economic Affairs.

A Pakistani trade delegation probably will visit Moscow early in April after ministry representatives return from Tokyo. Trade talks with the Japanese Government will be held there next month.

The Government's concern over the effect that trade relations with the Soviet Union may have on negotiations for additional economic assistance from the United States and other Western countries was reflected in indecision as to whether the Foreign Minister or the Minister for Commerce and Industry should announce the Cabinet's action. The issue was resolved by the absence of official comment by either Minister. The

Continued on Page 3, Column 2

Malayan Dominion Status Is Slated by August, 1957

Text of Gener... statement i...

General of the A... MacArthur made ... reply yesterday to thos... of the memoirs of H... Truman dealing with the K... war and the general's ... Commander in Chief ... and Korea.

The memoirs are bein... lished in The New York Ti...

In a 5,000-word comment General MacArthur described the former President's account as "... labyrinth of fancy and fiction" and said his "narration does such violence to the truth that to remain silent would be a disservice to the nation." The general charged Mr. Truman with "twisting the facts to serve his own ends."

Harshly censuring the former President's foreign-policy views, General MacArthur asserted that Mr. Truman, by concentrating ... Europe and compromising with Communist forces in Asia, "failed abysmally to comprehend Soviet strategy."

Appeasement Charged

Describing his concept of this strategy, General MacArthur said the Soviet viewed the world struggle as taking place in three great areas with Europe as the center and Asia and Africa as the northern and southern flanks.

He charged that failure of Mr. Truman to pursue the war against Communist China to victory was "appeasement" and a manifestation of the mistaken belief that Europe was the area of supreme interest.

He said this preoccupation with Europe had enabled Moscow to turn the north flank in Asia and start the envelopment of the southern flank by recent maneuvers in the Middle East.

The general maintained that the Soviet, while deceiving the West with propaganda threats of aggression in Europe, was interested there only in defense. He emphasized the main Soviet objectives at present were Asia and Africa.

One of the highlights of General MacArthur's statement was his contention that a spy ring in Washington had obtained quick access to his top-secret messages from Japan. He said that his removal from command by Mr. Truman might have been triggered by his recommendation that a treason trial be initiated to break up the espionage net. He indicated that the British diplomats Guy Burgess and Donald Maclean were central figures in this ring.

General MacArthur rejected all the complaints against his actions and judgments related by Mr. Truman in his memoirs. Re-

Continued on Page 25, Column 6

... had been ... for the power ... most twenty ye... tation is from t... printed Jan. 26.)

In February of ... MacArthur reported ... Secretary of the Ar... C. Royall, and to ... Security Council th... and combat read... South Korean troo...

Continued on Page 24, ...

President Disput... Aide on Missile...

By ANTHONY LEVIER...
Special to The New York Times.

WASHINGTON, Feb. 8—Trevor Gardner announced his resignation today in protest against the slow rate of progress on ballistic missile production.

As the Assistant Secretary of the Air Force explained his views at a news conference, he was obviously in conflict not only with the highest officials of the Defense Department but also with President Eisenhower.

The President had told his own news conference earlier that positive orders had been issued several times to give the guided missile program "priority over any other in the Defense Department."

Mr. Gardner said that the essential point of dispute was his inability to get an appropriation of $200,000,000 more for general acceleration of re-

Continued on Page 16, Column 3

BALLOON FLIGHTS STOPPED BY U. S. TO SATISFY SOVIET

Weather Devices Grounded in Germany and Turkey After Reply to Moscow

Text of State Departm... is printe...

U. S. Acts to Carry Lakes-Europe Cargo

By JACQUES NEVARD
Special to The New York Times.

WASHINGTON, Feb. 8—The Federal Maritime Administration moved today to open the Great Lakes to American ships carrying international cargo between this country and Western Europe.

Clarence G. Morse ... time Administ... the ...

...ied "very peace-... ...t three hours after a Roman Catholic priest had administered the sacrament of extreme unction.

Last Saturday, Mr. Mack was taken to his daughter's home from Roy Mack's home. He took a turn for the worse this morning and all members of the family were called to Mrs. Cunningham's home.

Roy Mack said Dr. Illarion I. Gopadze, long-time friend and for years physician for Mr. Mack's old team, the former Philadelphia Athletics, had visited his father this morning but was not present when he died.

Mr. Mack survived by about fifteen months the loss of the A's, the American League club

Connie Mack

he founded and guided for half a century. Control of the club was vested in his sons Roy and Earle when it was transferred to Kansas City, Mo., before the 1955 season.

Mr. Mack had been in poor health since his right hip was fractured in a fall from his bed last Oct. 1. The hip was set during an operation by Dr. Go-

Continued on Page 31, Column 2

PRESIDENT URGES WIDE LAW CHANGE TO AID IMMIGRANTS

Message Calls for Raising Quota to 220,000 a Year in Liberalizing Act

Text of Eisenhower's message will be found on Page 14.

By ANTHONY LEWIS

...Prosecution

By JACK ROTH

The Court of Special Sessions ruled yesterday that unless willfulness was proved, a defendant could not be criminally convicted for failure to file a state income tax return.

The decision was said to be the first of its kind in a state court, Assistant District Attorney Eugene Leiman said an appeal was under consideration.

The case involved John J. (Ike) Gannon, 62 years old, of Lincolndale, N. Y., a former official of the International Longshoremen's Association. In a two-count information voted by a grand jury in April, 1953, he was accused of failure to file a state tax return for 1951 and 1952.

The prosecution contended that during those two years Mr. Gannon's income was $26,204. Under the law any married person with a gross in-

Continued on Page 25, Column 6

EISENHOWER SAYS HE MAY ANNOUNCE PLANS BY MARCH 1

DISCUSSES RACE

Bars Aid to Warren—Nixon Position Now Appears Best

Transcript and summary of the news conference, Page 18.

Associated Press Wirephoto
President Eisenhower mounts ...teps to building where he ...ld his news conference.

By WILLIAM S. WHITE
Special to The New York Times.

WASHINGTON, Feb. 8—President Eisenhower indicated today that he would tell the country before this month was out whether he would seek re-election.

Amid strong signs that this decision was turning toward the negative, he brushed aside any suggestion of White House ambitions by his brother, Dr. Milton S. Eisenhower.

He made it plain moreover that he would have no part in any attempt to draft Chief Justice Earl Warren as the Republican candidate, nor would he ask Mr. Warren to consent to run.

The situation tonight seemed to be that Vice President Richard M. Nixon was in a commanding position in any thoughts the President might have on a possible successor.

Though Mr. Nixon's name was not mentioned by the President at his news conference today he remained the only Presidential possibility to have been saluted without qualification by the President.

Warren Chances Dimmed

As to Mr. Warren, the effect of the President's observations was to make remote any prospect that the Chief Justice might be induced to leave the Supreme Court.

The Chief Justice had stated last April an "irrevocable" purpose not to step down from the high bench. Not many politicians in either party had believed he would do so under any circumstances.

A handful had believed he might consider such an action in response to a direct appeal from General Eisenhower.

In saying with a tone of finality that it would not be "appropriate" to make any such request of the Chief Justice, the President expressed reasonable confidence that he would be able to disclose his own plans by March 1.

In reply to a question whether he would announce his decision before the end of the month, General Eisenhower said:

"Well, I have always avoided ...fixed date for saying exactly ...t I would do. But it would ... to me that I ought to have ...uch information by the end

...inued on Page 18, Column 3

...ENHOWER FIGHTS ...D FARM PROPS

...Restoration of Such ... Would 'Defeat ...t' of Soil Bank

...that it was principally for this reason that he had proposed creation of a soil bank, which has as a main goal the retirement of much land from unnecessary production. He added:

"Of course, these price-depressing surpluses themselves are largely the result of high rigid price supports of wartime, too long continued in peace.

"It would be inconsistent to enact a soil bank program and, at the same time, re-establish production incentives that would again fill Government warehouses, again depress prices and thus defeat the main object of the soil bank.

"I realize that there is always room for varying opinions on how best to resolve public problems. Nevertheless, in this instance, I must say that I should be gravely concerned if the soil bank should be coupled with the production incentives certain to nullify the great benefits that the bank can bring."

The Senate committee plans to finish its work on the farm

Continued on Page 17, Column 6

...S. CONSIDERING ...TO TRUST SUIT

...cerned Over Power ... Big 3, Barnes Says

By MURRAY ILLSON

The possibility of antitrust action against the country's major automobile manufacturers was hinted at here yesterday by a top official of the Department of Justice.

Stanley N. Barnes, assistant attorney general in charge of the department's Antitrust Division, asserted that an undue concentration of economic power was developing in the automotive industry. He indicated that the Federal Government would not permit this to continue.

Mr. Barnes told the manufacturers' session of the National Wholesale Dry Goods Association's annual convention that he was "here representing the Attorney General of the United States." Attorney General Herbert Brownell Jr. is vacationing in Puerto Rico.

In 1949 three major automobile manufacturers produced more than 85 per cent of the cars, while the smaller concerns produced the rest, Mr. Barnes told his listeners in the Statler Hotel. Five years later, he said, the output of the three major producers had jumped to almost 95.5 per cent of the total.

"In 1954," he declared, "most

Continued on Page 24, Column 1

Connie Mack Dies in Philadelphia at 93

Continued From Page 1

padse at Presbyterian Hospital here.

Also surviving Mr. Mack are his widow, the former Katherine Hallahan, whom he married as a widower in 1910; another son, Connie Mack Jr., three other daughters, Mrs. Rita Breedlove, Mrs. Mary Schurr and Mrs. Elizabeth A. Nolan; nineteen grandchildren and five great-grandchildren.

A solemn mass of requiem will be offered at 11 A. M. Saturday at St. Bridget's Roman Catholic Church, Midvale Avenue, in suburban East Falls. Burial will be in Holy Sepulchre Cemetery.

Honorary pallbearers named today were Ford Frick, Commissioner of Baseball; Will Harridge and Warren Giles, presidents of the American and National Leagues, respectively; George Trautman, president of the National Association of Professional Baseball Leagues (the minors), and the presidents of all the major league ball clubs.

Master Builder of Teams

Connie Mack was the master builder of baseball teams.

No other manager in the history of the game ever handled more young players and brought more of them to stardom and on to fortune. But it is probable that he will be best remembered for his sensational scrapping of championship machines, the tearing apart of teams that other men would have been eager to lead.

No man in the history of organized baseball served as a manager longer than Mr. Mack—he began as a team leader in 1894—and no manager ever directed one team as long. He assumed the leadership of the Philadelphia Athletics in 1901 and held it until 1950. With them he won nine American League pennants and five world championships.

His famous scorecard waving to and fro as he stood in the dugout directing his team's attack and defense is well remembered by the fans; but it is not generally known that he kept an accurate score and used it to remind his men of lapses after the battle was won or lost.

It was more than a white plume of Navarre in the battlefront, as more than one pitcher or infielder or outfielder discovered after the dust of battle had settled. The manager knew what ball the batsman had hit that the hurler should not have thrown and the direction of every hit that had escaped a fielder who should have been in position to field it. It was this constant drilling of small details that made his teams mechanically perfect.

Through the years, Mr. Mack was one of the most respected men in baseball. He received many honors and, as he aged, was considered one of the pillars of the sport. His exit from the game was tinged with pathos as he signed the Athletics away to Arnold Johnson of Chicago, who transferred the club to Kansas City, Mo. Mr. Mack put his signature on the agreement from a sickbed.

"Mr. Baseball"—Connie Mack

Baptized Cornelius McGillicuddy—his name was shortened in his playing days so that it would "set" in the printed box scores of that period—on Dec. 23, 1862, in East Brookfield, Mass., Mr. Mack learned to play baseball while working in a shoe factory to help support a widowed mother. He became a catcher and first attracted notice in 1883, when East Brookfield won the championship of Central Massachusetts.

The next season he became a professional with the Meriden, Conn., club and played in that city and in Hartford until the Washington club of the old National League bought his release on Sept. 9, 1886.

Known as Smart Catcher

By that time he had become known as a smart catcher and a reliable batsman in the pinches, though he never was a heavy hitter. He was in Washington three years, left to join the outlaw Players (Brotherhood) League in Buffalo, where he played one year, and then joined Pittsburgh, where he remained for six years, becoming manager in 1894.

He was a new type of manager. The old-time leaders ruled by force, often thrashing players who disobeyed orders or committed blunders on the field or broke club rules off the field. One of the kindliest and most softspoken of men, he always insisted that he could get better results by kindness. He never humiliated a player by public criticism. No one ever heard him scold a man in the most trying times of his many pennant fights.

From Pittsburgh he went to the Milwaukee club of the Western Association. In 1901, when the late Byron Bancroft Johnson organized the American League, Mr. Mack became manager and a part owner of the Philadelphia franchise. He had given up catching by this time, and did not even appear on the coaching lines. He was well over six feet tall and thin, and he said that he realized he was not an impressive figure in a baseball uniform.

But he knew good ball players, and he quickly assembled a team of stars, at the same time devoting much of his time, apart from the actual directing of games, to learning the business phases of baseball.

He won his first pennant in 1902. There was no world series that year, for the National League refused to recognize the American. But in 1905 Mr. Mack won again, and his team faced the Giants under John J. McGraw in what was the first official series.

Lost to Mathewson's Art

Mr. Mack had three brilliant pitchers, Chief Bender, Eddie Plank and Rube Waddell. The last one deserted him and did not play in the series, and the Athletics were beaten, four games to one, chiefly because of the wonderful pitching of Christy Mathewson. He beat the Athletics three times, all shutouts. Bender won the only game for Philadelphia, 3—1.

Mr. Mack began his first rebuilding job after this defeat. He kept Bender and Plank, his veteran pitchers, but assembled youngsters in the field. One of them was Eddie Collins. Another was Frank Baker, a powerful hitter.

In 1910 the Athletics won the American League pennant again and faced the Chicago Cubs, under Frank Chance.

The Cubs had won the National League championship in 1906, 1907 and 1908 and were the favorites in the series, but the Mack youngsters won in one of the biggest upsets ever scored in the classic, four games to one.

The Athletics won again in 1911 and Mr. Mack had his revenge, for his team defeated the McGraw Giants, four games to two, Mathewson being beaten twice, though he defeated Bender in the opening game.

The same teams came together in 1913, and the Athletics won again. When they captured another American League pennant in 1914 and were slated to face the Braves, it seemed that the Mackmen could not lose.

They did, however, in four straight games, a crushing setback. And here Mr. Mack electrified the baseball world by scrapping the championship array, selling Collins, Baker and Barry of his famous $100,000 infield, and keeping only Stuffy McInnis, the star first baseman. In less than two seasons his team was at the bottom of the American League and he was starting all over again with a group of youngsters. He was at the bottom eight years in one stretch.

It was a long, hard struggle. He spent six seasons building and spoiling—and then building again. Then came the rush of the Yankees and Babe Ruth, and it seemed harder than ever to reach the top. He made a master stroke when he obtained Robert Moses Grove, one of the greatest left-handers of all time—almost as powerful, Mr. Mack always said, as Waddell in his prime—and in 1927 he finished second.

In 1928 he was second again. By this time he had Al Simmons

(continued)

Connie Mack with Joe Dimaggio in 1938.

1911: During his heyday with the Philadelphia Athletics

and Jimmy Foxx, powerful hitters; Cochrane, a superb catcher, Dykes, Boley and Bishop, skillful infielders—a combination considered almost as great as the Baker - Barry - Collins - McInnis machine of fifteen years before.

Then came 1929, and the Athletics made a run-away of the American League race. They beat the Cubs in the world series. In 1930 they won again and defeated the Cardinals. Grove and Earnshaw, Mr. Mack's star hurlers, performed in stunning fashion.

In 1931 the Mackmen won the ninth pennant for their manager, but were balked in the attempt to place a sixth world's championship at his feet. The Cardinals won, four games to two. The Athletics finished second to the Yankees in 1932 and third in 1933.

Being third did not suit Mr. Mack. At 71, and after thirty years of toiling with one club, he again shocked the fans by demolishing his machine.

He kept one of his stars, Foxx, first baseman and home-run leader of the previous season, but the following year sold him also to the Red Sox, with Marcum, a pitcher, for $150,000 and two players. Then he began rebuilding, making a specialty of reaching into the colleges for pitching talent.

With the arrival of the centennial year of baseball, 1939, and the Hall of Fame at Cooperstown, N. Y., Mr. Mack's name was voted among the first thirteen pioneers of the game for preservation in its archives.

When the time came for the celebration on June 12, Mr. Mack was the only one of the pioneers living.

The man who won his first American League pennant before New York ever dreamed of playing host to such a thing as a "subway world series" acquired financial control of the Athletics in December, 1940. His purchase of stock from Mrs. Ethyl M. Shibe gave him a majority interest in the club.

"My greatest thrill," he recalled on his seventy-ninth birthday, "was starting Howard Ehmke as surprise pitcher against the Cubs in the first game of the 1929 world series. My biggest disappointment was the 1914 team that lost four in a row to the Braves in the world series."

A bust of Mr. Mack has been enshrined in Cooperstown, N. Y., commemorating his long service to baseball. The bust was entitled "Mr. Baseball."

EISENHOWER PAYS TRIBUTE TO MACK

President Hails Inspiration to Youth—Giles, Frick, Harridge Mourn Loss

Among the tributes paid yesterday to Mr. Mack were the following compiled by The Associated Press and The United Press:

President Eisenhower, commenting on the death of Connie Mack yesterday afternoon, issued this statement:

"For decades Connie Mack has typified to the American people sportsmanship of the highest order.

"He will long be remembered by us all for the inspiration he gave American youth as a leader in the most American of sports."

Baseball Commissioner Ford Frick called the death of Mr. Mack a "terrific shock to baseball and a great personal shock."

Mr. Frick said:

"This is a great loss to the game. Mr. Mack was practically Mr. Baseball himself. He always will be remembered for the gentleness, kindliness, leadership and continuity he gave to our great national game."

Will Harridge, American League president, expressed regret and said Mr. Mack "was a a kindly, gracious, truly fine man."

"To me the name of Connie Mack always has been synonymous with baseball," he said, "standing for everything that is best for the game he loved. One of the founders of the American League, he held an unmatched record of service to the league and all baseball as player, manager and outstanding executive."

"All the News That's Fit to Print"

The New York Times

LATE CITY EDITION

Weather: Showers and thunderstorms likely today, tonight. Sunny tomorrow. Temp. range: today 82-70; Thurs. 77-64. Full U.S. report on Page 56.

VOL. CXVIII . No. 40,763 · NEW YORK, MONDAY, SEPTEMBER 1, 1969 · 10 CENTS

Labor Day 1969: Affluence and Quiet

Young Unionists Often Eschew Liberal Goals

By WILLIAM BORDERS

Special to The New York Times

FLINT, Mich., Aug. 31—The Labor Day weekend is passing quietly in Flint this year, with no speeches and no parades.

There used to be plenty ... both, as workers from the ... eral Motors plant ...

This quiet little city ... northwest of Detroit ... very much a union town ... one out of every four ... a member of the United ... mobile Workers of America.

But in Flint, as in many ... American cities where unions have flourished, organized labor these days has gone into a second generation, and old attitudes have changed.

The American Federation of Labor and Congress of Industrial Organizations has found that 46 per cent of the nation's union members earn between $7,500 and $15,000 a year. Of the union members under 40, about 75 per cent now live in the suburbs.

Nearly half of the union members are 39 or younger—too young to remember the days before the sitdown strikes and, as Mr. Metiva puts it, "the youngsters don't care what we cared about."

As union leaders all over America are discovering, there ...

EXACT BUS FARES BEGIN SMOOTHLY

$6 Robbery of Driver Mars First Day of New System —Big Test Tomorrow

By SYLVAN FOX

An exact-fare system designed to forestall robberies went into effect on the city's 4,285 buses and many private lines yesterday, but within hours a bus driver was held up and robbed of $6 in Brooklyn.

The Transit Authority reported that the transition to the new exact fare system was otherwise smooth and without problems.

"We've been having no problems at all," a Transit Authority spokesman said. "Apparently our advance publicity, which we disseminated far and wide, has paid off."

Under the new system, bus drivers no longer handle any passenger's money. Fares are deposited in a sealed, robbery-proof coin box bolted to the floor of the bus.

Two Men Board Bus

At 3:55 P.M., with the new system in effect less than 16 hours, two men boarded an empty bus waiting to begin a Brooklyn-Maspeth run at Kent Avenue and Broadway in Brooklyn.

One of the men pointed a gun at the driver, Norman Simington, 41 years old, of Elmhurst, Queens, and demanded money from him. Mr. Simington explained that he could not get at the fares in the sealed coin box, handed over $6 of his own money and the bandits fled.

The primary purpose of the exact fare system was to attempt to stem a rising tide of bus robberies.

The robbery of Mr. Simington was the 357th holdup of a bus driver this year, according to Transit Authority figures. There were 241 robberies in 1968, 97 in 1967 and 56 in 1966.

Passengers who rode buses yesterday confirmed the Transit Authority's observation that the transition to the new exact fare

Continued on Page 16, Column 6

Visitors ...

By STEVEN V. ROBERTS

Special to The New York Times

YOSEMITE NATIONAL PARK, Calif., Aug. 31—They came in cars and trucks, in buses and campers and trailers, lumbering through the foothills of the Sierra Nevada, toward a Labor Day weekend away from the agonies of city life. But by Thursday evening they read this sign at the park entrance: "All campsites are full."

That warning has been sounded with increasing frequency this year, not only at the national parks and forests but also at thousands of other recreation areas across the country.

Facilities are staggering under a crush of humanity. Attendance at the national parks has been rising at least 7 per cent a year. One study indicates that even if population growth is discounted, four times as many people are visit-

TAKING TIME OUT FROM THE CARES OF OFFICE: Governor and Mrs. Rockefeller feeding swans at Lake Broadmoor in Colorado Springs yesterday. Mr. Rockefeller was in the resort city to attend three-day National Governors' Conference, which begins today. Details about gathering are on Page 15.

United Press International

CAMPUS VIOLENCE ... NEW LAWS ... THE NATION

Rocky Marciano Is Killed With Two in Plane Crash

Undefeated Heavyweight Champion, 46, Was on Visit to Des Moines

By Reuters.

DES MOINES, Iowa, Aug. 31—Rocky Marciano, former undefeated world heavyweight boxing champion, was killed tonight in a plane crash with two companions about 30 miles east of here.

Marciano held the title from Sept. 23, 1952, to his retirement on April 27, 1956.

He was on his way to Des Moines to visit friends when the single engined plane in which he was travelling crashed near Newton Airport, officials said.

The crash took place about 10 P.M., Eastern daylight time, in a wooded area about two miles southeast of the Newton Airport where the aircraft was about to land, officials said.

Marciano, who would have been 46 tomorrow, was identified by the Jasper County Medical Examiner, Dr. Johnson Maughan.

The two men in the plane with him were tentatively identified as Frank Farrell, 28, an insurance executive and Glenn Bells, a building contractor, both of Des Moines.

The pilot, thought to be Mr. Bells, had radioed the Des Moines air traffic controller that he was going to land at Newton Airport. The aircraft was not heard from again until the wreckage was discovered.

Details surrounding the accident were sketchy and investigators from the Federal Aviation Administration were at the scene, officials said.

Rocky Marciano

Wanted to Play Basball

Rocky Marciano wanted to be a baseball player. He once reported as a catcher to the Chicago Cubs, who let him go because he couldn't make the throw from the plate to second with accuracy.

The champion's correct name was Rocco Marchegiano. He was born in Brockton, Mass., on Sept. 1, 1923, the

Continued on Page 17, Column 1

... 3 Women ... 6 Israelis

... statement did not ... time for the departure ... impression here ... women would be ... first plane available.

... have been ... University ... Friday.

... Italian ... asked the ... on behalf ... Government ... for ... Israelis.

... for a ... naked young ... cavorting in a lake near the site of the Texas International Pop Festival. But the police chief of Lewisville said of the 40,000 youths, "I'd have them back in Lewisville any time, they are so well-mannered."

That was very much what the law-enforcement authorities said about the crowd that jammed fields and roads for the Woodstock Music and Art Fair the weekend of Aug. 17. Policemen patrolling the 130-acre site of the rock festival on the Isle of Wight yesterday said they had no complaints about the behavior of the audience of about 150,000 who came to hear a program featuring Bob Dylan, the American singer.

In Prairieville, Sheriff Hickley Waguespack — who had

Continued on Page 12, Column 1

BRAZILIAN LEADER SUFFERS STROKE; MILITARY RULING

Ministers of Army, Navy and Air Force Say Take-Over Will Not Be Permanent

VICE PRESIDENT BARRED

Condition of Costa E Silva Is Held Satisfactory—Banks and Markets Closed

By JOSEPH NOVITSKI

Special to The New York Times

RIO DE JANEIRO, Aug. 31—President Arthur da Costa e Silva has suffered a stroke, and a triumvirate of Brazil's top military commanders announced tonight that they had assumed control of the country until he recovers.

In a statement read by a single announcer over a nationwide chain of radio and television stations, the Ministers of the Army, the Navy and the Air Force reaffirmed military domination over Latin America's largest nation.

They specifically disallowed the constitutional provision that the Vice President, Pedro Aleixo, a civilian law professor and career politician, should succeed to the Presidency in the event of incapacity.

Suffers 'Embolism'

President Costa e Silva, a 66-year-old career Army officer who retired with the rank of marshal to assume the Presidency in March, 1967, suffered yesterday what authoritative military and medical sources called "a cerebral embolism." An embolism occurs when a foreign or abnormal particle such as an air bubble or blood clot, lodges in a blood vessel too small to permit its passage.

The announcement tonight was the first official news for Brazilians, who had heard persistent rumors of the President's death during the day.

The 8-minute announcement included a medical bulletin signed by four physicians, two of them neurologists, who asserted that Marshal Costa e Silva's general condition after "a circulatory crisis" was "satisfactory."

The announcement also specifically stated that the President would resume his functions "when the impediment ceases." Estimates of the length of time needed for the President to recover ranged ... 30 days to three months.

... Announcement

... announcement was ... Gen. Aurélio de Lyra ... Minister of War; Adm. ... Rademacker Grünewald, Minister of the Navy, ... Marcio de Souza ... Air Force.

... accompanied by a ... resolution closing ... bank and stock ... the first ... elaborately ... before ... Day.

... ex- ... week ... amendments to the ... that would have ... stage for reconvening the Brazilian Congress, which he dismissed last Dec. 13 by decree. The military chiefs who have replaced him cited that decree, and the proclamation that granted Marshal Costa e Silva unlimited powers over all phases of national life in December, in their announcement to the nation.

Political observers interpreted the insistence on the December decrees as meaning that any political reform would be held in abeyance until the President's recovery was assured.

"The nation can have confidence in the patriotism of its

Continued on Page 6, Column 2

NEWS INDEX

Rocky Marciano Is Killed With Two in Plane Crash

Undefeated Heavyweight Champion, 46, Was on Visit to Des Moines

By Reuters.

DES MOINES, Iowa, Aug. 31—Rocky Marciano, former undefeated world heavyweight boxing champion, was killed tonight in a plane crash with two companions about 30 miles east of here.

Marciano held the title from Sept. 23, 1952, to his retirement on April 27, 1956.

He was on his way to Des Moines to visit friends when the single engined plane in which he was travelling crashed near Newton Airport, officials said.

The crash took place about 10 P.M., Eastern daylight time, in a wooded area about two miles southeast of the Newton Airport where the aircraft was about to land, officials said.

Marciano, who would have been 46 tomorrow, was identified by the Jasper County Medical Examiner, Dr. Johnson Maughan.

The two men in the plane with him were tentatively identified as Frank Farrell, 28, an insurance executive and Glenn Bells, a building contractor, both of Des Moines.

The pilot, thought to be Mr. Bells, had radioed the Des Moines air traffic controller that he was going to land at Newton Airport. The aircraft was not heard from again until the wreckage was discovered.

Details surrounding the accident were sketchy and investigators from the Federal Aviation Administration were at the scene, officials said.

Rocky Marciano

Wanted to Play Basball

Rocky Marciano wanted to be a baseball player. He once reported as a catcher to the Chicago Cubs, who let him go because he couldn't make the throw from the plate to second with accuracy.

The champion's correct name was Rocco Marchegiano. He was born in Brockton, Mass., on Sept. 1, 1923, the

Continued on Page 17, Column 1

ROCKY MARCIANO KILLED IN CRASH

Continued From Page 1, Col. 7

son of Piero Marchegiano, an Italian immigrant who worked in the Brockton shoe factories while Rocky was growing up.

Rocky's boyhood was the typical sports-loving one of almost any American with his main interests centered on baseball and football. Boxing was not one of his enthusiasms until he began serving as a private in the United States Army.

As a high school student, he showed so much ability as a center on the football team that he might have made a bid for an athletic scholarship at Harvard or Holy Cross.

While in the Army, Marciano participated in a number of boxing matches and won several tournaments. This sucess caused him to consider boxing as his career, and when he left the Army he went into the amateur ranks and did well, losing only one fight.

Turning professional in 1947, Rocky won his first bout by a knockout. The next year he scored twelve knockouts in a row, and in 1949 he knocked out four more rivals. A fighter named Don Mogard interrupted this string by staying 10r ounds, although Marciano won the decision.

After his clash with Mogard, Marciano's opposition became progressively stronger, and on March 24, 1950, he had his first "big" chance.

This was a clash with Roland LaStarza of the Bronx, in Madison Square Garden. Marciano gained a split decision. The setback was the first suffered by LaStarza.

Rocky went on to defeat all opposition, some of his victims being Red Applegate, Freddie Beshore and Rex Layne. His manager, Al Weill, considered him "ready" when he signed him to fight Joe Louis, the former heavyweight champion of the world, for a clash in Madison Square Garden on Oct. 26, 1951. Rocky stopped the ex-Brown Bomber in eight rounds.

In the next year Marciano registered knockout victories over Lee Savoild, Gino Buonvino, Bernie Reynolds and Harry Matthews.

It was the triumph over Matthews, a highly regarded light heavyweight from Seattle, that earned Rocky a fight with heavyweight champion, Jersey Joe Wolcott. This fight took place in Philadelphia on Sept. 23, 1952, Rocky won by a knockout in the thirteenth round.

A return clash with Walcott in May, 1953, resulted in a one-round knockout for Marciano. In September, 1953, Rocky knocked out LaStarza. Rocky also had two title fights against the ex-champion, Ezzard Charles.

Rocky took the decision in the first one and knocked out Charles in eight rounds in the return bout.

Marciano's record of forty-nine victories in forty-nine professional fights has never been equaled by any of his heavyweight championship predecessors.

He retired as undefeated world heavyweight champion at the age of 31 on April 27, 1956, saying he wanted to devote more time to his family, and vowing never to try a comeback.

"I thought it was a mistake when Joe Louis tried a comeback," he said then. "No man can say what he will do in the future, but barring poverty, the ring has seen the last of me. I am comfortably fixed, and I am not afraid of the future."

He retired with a perfect ring record: 49 victories in 49 professional bouts, 43 of them by knockouts.

He was elected to Madison Square Garden's Hall of Fame in boxing in June, 1967, along with Jack Dempsey, Sugar Ray Robinson, the late Benny Leonard, and Henry Armstrong.

Long active in a wide range of charitable causes since his retirement, Rocky appeared in the ring at the new Garden in February, 1968, in a burlesque boxing bout with Bob Hope, billed as "Chicken Delight."

The bout, part of the evening's benefit for the United Service Organizations, wound up as a waltz, with Marciano and Hope dancing arm in arm around the ring.

Rocky Marciano delivers a right uppercut to the head of Ezzard Charles. Marciano achieved a points win over the former champion on September 17, 1954.

"All the News That's Fit to Print."

The New York Times.

THE WEATHER
Fair today; probably showers tomorrow; continued cool.
Temperature yesterday—Max. 61, min. 50.
For weather report see Page 54.

VOL. LXXV....No. 24,720 — NEW YORK, THURSDAY, OCTOBER 8, 1925. — TWO CENTS In Greater New York | THREE CENTS Within 200 Miles | FOUR CENTS Elsewhere in the U. S.

WASHINGTON BEATS PITTSBURGH, 4 TO 1; JOHNSON IS MASTER

Veteran Strikes Out Ten, Yields Only 5 Hits, Pitching Champions to Victory.

JOE HARRIS GETS A HOMER

Rice's Single in Fifth Inning Off Meadows, Netting Two Runs, Is Crux of Game.

46,000 SEE FIRST GAME

Holiday Mood Pervades Pittsburgh —Traynor's Circuit Drive Only Pirate Tally.

By HARRY CROSS.

Don't Ask by Phone About The World's Series Games

THE TIMES requests its readers not to ask it by telephone today for information about the result of the world's series. It will be readily understood that to heed the overwhelming number of such inquiries would suspend other business.

Pictures of yesterday's game, brought from Pittsburgh by airplane, on Page 20.

CHRISTY MATHEWSON DIES UNEXPECTEDLY

COOLIDGE SPEECH DIRECTED AT KLAN; 'KEYNOTE' FOR 1926

President's Advisers Hail 'Tolerance' as the Slogan for Next Year's Elections.

Twenty Monkeys for Study of Evolution Are Coming to Johns Hopkins From Asia

LABOR CHIEF SPURNS PLEA TO AID SOVIET; FEDERATION CHEERS

Delegates Shout Approval as Green Denounces Communism in Reply to Purcell.

"UNIONISM FOR LIBERTY"

Willing to Help All Labor, but Not at Such a Sacrifice, He Says.

AID FOR CATHEDRAL HERE

Memorial for St. John's Proposed—To Extend Organization of "White Collar" Workers.

Ex-Soldier's Song in Street Gets Him Job in Chauve Souris

MUSSOLINI GRASPS FOR SUPREME POWER

Fascist Council Adopts Plan Ending Old Form of Constitutional Government.

PARTY SYSTEM ABOLISHED

Workers and Employers' Unions to Control Legislative Machinery of State.

BRIAND AND LUTHER TRY NEW PEACE MOVE IN A PRIVATE TALK

Quit Locarno Meetings and Go to Secluded Village for Quiet Conference.

COMPACT PROGRESS MADE

Clause Objected To by Germans, Referring to World War, Is to Be Deleted.

CLAMOR RAISED IN REICH

Nationalists Try to Sabotage Conference and Berlin Hears Poles Also Work Against It.

By EDWIN L. JAMES.

Wanamaker's Opens Airplane Department; First $25,000 Craft Due at Store Today

CHRISTY MATHEWSON DIES UNEXPECTEDLY

End Comes at Saranac Lake From Tuberculous Pneumonia —Had Long Previous Illness.

IDOL OF BASEBALL WORLD

Served With Distinction in the World War—Tribute Is Planned at Series.

SARANAC LAKE, N. Y., Oct. 7 (AP).—Christy Mathewson is dead. Baseball's "Big Six" lost his fight against tuberculosis at 11 o'clock tonight just as the game's great climax, the world series, in which he played an all-important part in 1905, had got under way at Pittsburgh.

Until several days ago Mathewson was in excellent condition, his friends here were told, and his death was unexpected.

More than five years ago the great pitcher, loved and honored wherever the game is played, began what was to be a losing struggle. Gassed in the World War in France, where he served with distinction, Mathewson returned from overseas to coach with the Giants, the club with which he won his fame, but the illness which was finally to take his life forced him to retire for recuperation in 1920.

For three years Mathewson fought the fight, and it was believed he had won. He returned to baseball as President and part owner of the Boston Club of the National League, and it was in the line of duty with that club that "Big Six" suffered a set-back which compelled his return here once more to wage a plucky but losing fight through the Summer and early Fall. On the training trip South last Spring with the Braves, Mathewson took cold and he never fully recovered. He had been in

Continued on Page Eighteen.

Christy Mathewson

CHRISTY MATHEWSON DIES UNEXPECTEDLY

Continued from Page 1, Column 2.

bed at his home ever since, Mrs. Mathewson being in constant attendance.

Loved Baseball and Checkers.

As recently as last September it was believed that baseball's great idol would eventually recover. At that time his personal physician, Dr. Edward N. Packard, introduced in Supreme Court at Norwich an affidavit declaring that Mathewson was so ill "that his recovery depends on freedom from cares and worries and any excitement would jeopardize his health." But the physician later said that he was "all right" but that he was not able to make the trip to Norwich, where he had been made defendant in an action growing out of an automobile accident.

Death, according to his physician, was due to tuberculous pneumonia. A son, Christy Mathewson Jr., who is at college, was not at the bedside when his father died.

In this village Mathewson led a quiet life. His chief diversion, outside of following baseball in the newspapers, was checkers and motoring. He loved checkers almost as dearly as he loved baseball, and many were the games he had with experts from all over the country who came to play with him.

Occasionally Mathewson appeared in public either to make an address or to talk with friends who came from afar to visit him. But his chief occupation was that of the invalid, a life which required constant rest and relaxation.

Last Fall he went to New York City to attend the world series between the Giants and the Senators. Through one of the most thrilling series in the history of baseball, the great pitcher, who was also a keen student of the game, wrote a daily article for a newspaper syndicate.

Funeral services will be held in Lewistown, Pa., Saturday morning, it was announced. The body will be taken from the home here tomorrow night.

Christy Mathewson, idol of the nation's baseball fandom over a span of more than two decades, and one of the greatest pitchers the game has ever known, was a symbol of the highest type of American sportsmanship.

Running the full gamut of baseball fame, first as a playing star, later as a coach and manager, Mathewson left the game to answer a greater call during the World War; subsequently fought and won a battle for his life, threatened by after effects of his service, and then capped the climax of his diamond career by returning as part owner and President of a major league club.

But after all the remarkable achievements of Mathewson's career are recounted, the greatest tribute of all will be paid to his wonderful pitching skill. For on the mound he was a master craftsman, the most consummate and brilliant artist of all time, in the opinion of many of the game's closest students.

"Big Six"—a sobriquet contracted from "Big Six Footer"—started his major league career with the New York Giants in 1901, and it was during his seventeen seasons with that club that he carved a lasting niche for himself in the twirling hall of fame. Later he became manager for two and a half years of the Cincinnati Reds, served as a Captain in the chemical warfare arm of the American Expeditionary Force during the World War, returned from the service to rejoin his old teammates, the Giants, as a coach, and retired from the game temporarily in 1920, when his health was dangerously impaired. He came back, again hale and hearty, in February, 1923, to accept the Presidency and part ownership of the Boston Nationals.

A graduate of Bucknell College, where he was both a football and baseball

Christy Mathewson was respected as were few ballplayers of his day.

star, Mathewson broke into the professional game with the Taunton (Mass.) club of the New England League in 1899, receiving a salary of $80 a month for his first season. He lost his first start by a score of 6 to 5 to the Manchester (N. H.) club. During the season he won but two and lost nine games, lack of control—a fault he did not overcome for several years—handicapping his effectiveness.

Mathewson, however, was not long in attracting major league attention. Playing with Norfolk, in the Virginia League in 1900 he won 21 out of 23 games, and was obtained by the Giants, who turned him back, after a brief try-out, for more seasoning with the Southern club. Later the same year he was drafted by Cincinnati, but soon afterward was sent to the Giants in a deal by which the Reds secured Amos Rusie.

Matty's first major league appearance was in the rôle of relief pitcher in a game lost by the Giants to Brooklyn. He had but indifferent success as a pitcher and utility player until 1902, when John McGraw succeeded Horace Fogel as manager of the Giants. "Big Six" was playing first base at the time, but McGraw quickly recognized his pitching ability, and took him in hand. His strides toward greatness dated from that period.

Feats of pitching brilliance too numerous to catalogue filled Matty's record during the dozen years in which he ranked consistently among the most effective twirlers in the major leagues.

He was a prominent factor in the pennant victories of the Giants in 1904, 1905, 1911, 1912 and 1913; he twirled two no-hit games, one against the St. Louis Cardinals, in 1901, and the second against the Chicago Cubs, in 1905. He held jointly with Cy Young and Grover Cleveland Alexander a major league record of winning more than thirty games three seasons in a row; but his greatest achievement was in the world's series of 1905, when he pitched three shutout victories against the Philadelphia Athletics.

McGraw ranks Mathewson's feat in the 1905 series as the greatest in his memory. All five games in that series were shutouts, Joe McGinnity twirling the fourth victory for the Giants, while Chief Bender blanked the Giants for the only triumph scored by the Mackmen.

Mathewson had the misfortune to lose two of the most important games of his career, the play-off contest with the Chicago Cubs for the pennant in 1908 and the deciding game of the world's series with the Boston Red Sox in 1912. Breaks of the game played a big part in both defeats. Misjudgment of a fly by Cy Seymour, Giant outfielder, was blamed for the defeat by the Cubs, while a costly error by Fred Snodgrass turned the tide against the Giants and Matty in the struggle with the Red Sox.

Mordecai (Three-Fingered) Brown of the Cubs was Matty's greatest rival on the mound and the two had many stirring duels. Brown was Matty's opponent when the latter pitched his no-hit game against the Cubs in 1905, but conquered his New York rival in the famous 1908 play-off game. It was related that one season when the Giants and Cubs were battling for first place, President Taft, an ardent fan, had his private car attached to the train bearing the New York team to Chicago in order to see Mathewson and Brown oppose each other in the opening game of a series.

Oddly enough, both of these great pitchers closed their major league careers as players by opposing each other in a game on Sept. 4, 1916. Mathewson then was manager of Cincinnati, and the Reds won, 10 to 8, both "old masters" being hit freely.

Mathewson suffered a shoulder injury in 1914 which virtually ended his career as a regular on the mound. He pitched infrequently thereafter and persuaded McGraw to let him go to Cincinnati during the middle of 1916 to fulfill his managerial ambition. In the deal by which Matty went to the Reds the Giants also gave Eddie Roush and William McKechnie, now manager of the Pirates, in exchange for Buck Herzog, retiring Cincinnati leader, and Wade Killifer.

The Reds finished last in 1916, but improved rapidly under Matty's leadership, landing fourth place in 1917 and third place the following year, his last with the club.

Mathewson responded to the call to war at the close of the abbreviated season of 1918 and served with distinction overseas. He returned to become a coach with the Giants, holding that post until 1920, when he became seriously ill from the effects of being "gassed" during the war, and faced a battle for his life with tuberculosis.

Displaying the courage which won him many diamond victories, Matty fought and won the battle for his health during nearly three years of treatment at Saranac Lake, N. Y. Pronounced practically cured, he returned to New York in the Fall of 1922 to witness the world's series triumph of his old teammates, the Giants, over the New York Yankees.

Restored in health, Mathewson was eager to get back into the game, and when early in 1923 an old friend and admirer, Emil E. Fuchs, prominent New York attorney, engineered a deal by which a New York syndicate obtained control of the Boston Braves from George W. Grant, "Big Six" was persuaded to take the club Presidency.

Mathewson thus took his place among the few playing stars who rose to executive power in the game, a list which included Charles Comiskey of the Chicago White Sox, Clark Griffith of Washington, Branch Rickey of the St. Louis Cardinals, John McGraw of the New York Giants, Jimmy McAleer, A. G. Spalding and John M. Ward.

Mathewson, baseball experts agreed, possessed all the attributes of a brilliant moundsman as well as those of a great athlete—natural skill, keen knowledge of the sport, generalship and coolness under fire. One of the most popular figures in the history of the game, among players and fans alike, "Big Six" also was a hero and idol to the army of youthful followers of the national pastime.

"Matty was without a peer, either before or since the days he was at the height of his greatness," declared McGraw at one time in paying tribute to the pitcher.

"He had a greater variety of stuff than any pitcher I ever knew or handled," he continued. "His fast ball was the equal of Walter Johnson's or Amos Rusie's; his curve rivaled Nap Rucker's; he had the 'fadeaway' down to perfection, and he utilized his knowledge of batsmen with greater effect than any twirler in the game. He possessed wonderful control, remarkable fielding ability and was one of the finest sportsmen the game has ever known."

BASEBALL WORLD SORROWS.

Matty's Death Casts Gloom Over Series' Players and Leaders.

PITTSBURGH, Oct. 7 (AP).—The passing of Christy Mathewson brought a heavy touch of gloom late tonight to baseball men gathered here for the World's Series, and expressions of sympathy were given by Commissioner Landis and Presidents Heydler and Johnson as well as the players, who first knew "Matty" as a fellow-player, then as a manager and latterly as President of the Boston Braves. The news of Mathewson's death was unexpected, as the last word received here by his friends was that he was holding his own.

There will be no postponement of the world series game tomorrow, but Commissioner Landis directed that appropriate action be taken to honor the man and ball player whose name ranks with the leading pitchers of all time.

"I am stunned by this word," said Commissioner Landis, himself one of the most ardent admirers of Big Six when he was informed of it by The Associated Press. "It is especially sad at this time. It comes too suddenly for me to express my thoughts adequately but you can say that we will arrange appropriate tribute to Matty's memory—possibly in some manner before tomorrow's game at Forbes Field."

President Heydler, with whom Mathewson of late years has sat in the councils of the National League, also was deeply shocked and characterized Mathewson's passing as a "great loss to the game," adding that it was a source of deep personal grief to himself.

President Johnson of the American League said: "I am very sorry to hear of Mathewson's untimely death. He was a great pitcher and a credit to the game."

"All the News That's Fit to Print"

The New York Times

LATE CITY EDITION

Weather: Sunny, hot, humid today; Cloudy tonight. Sunshine tomorrow. Temperature range: today 76-92; yesterday 77-90. Details on page A13.

VOL.CXXVIII . . . No.44,298 | NEW YORK, FRIDAY, AUGUST 3, 1979 | 20 CENTS

25 cents beyond 50-mile zone from New York City. Higher in air delivery cities.

G.M. Chairman Strongly Opposes Special U.S. Aid Asked by Chrysler

Instead, He Urges Review of Federal Rules That Raise Industry Costs

By REGINALD STUART

Special to The New York Times

DETROIT, Aug. 2 — Thomas A. Murphy, chairman of the General Motors Corporation, said today that he was firmly opposed to the Government's providing special financial aid to its ailing competitor, the Chrysler Corporation. He urged instead a complete review of Federal regulations that have forced heavy spending by the automobile industry.

The 63-year-old G.M. chief executive said that Chrysler's request for up to $1 billion in Federal aid "presents a basic challenge to the philosophy of America," the free enterprise system.

"If you say, 'O.K., if somebody fails in the competitive race, then we're going to bail them out someway,' I don't think that's in accordance with what really made this country great," Mr. Murphy said. "It removes and compromises that discipline in the marketplace."

Wide-Ranging Interview

In an interview in his office at the company's headquarters here, Mr. Murphy also said that G.M., the nation's largest car maker, had dramatically lowered its passenger car sales forecasts for the industry.

He also gave President ... able marks" on h... economic and ene... he remained opp... controls. Howeve... a Federal tax cut ...

The New York Times/Andrew Sacks

Thomas A. Murphy in Detroit

the economy became weaker than expected.

At Chrysler, the board of directors voted today to omit the common-stock dividend for the third quarter, a move widely expected following the record losses it reported for the second quarter. [Page D1.]

Mr. Murphy, peering through his thick glasses, gave a personal assessment ... Chrysler's troubles.

"When we sort ...

3 SENATORS DEMAND PLEDGE FROM CARTER ON ARMS-FUND RISE

Nunn, Jackson and Tower Call Pact Flawed Without Such Vow — Kissinger Repeats Stand

By CHARLES MOHR

Special to The New York Times

WASHINGTON, Aug. 2 — Three Senators demanded today that President Carter furnish a detailed and prompt accounting of his intentions on defense spending before the Senate considers the nuclear arms treaty with the Soviet Union.

Former Secretary of State Henry A. Kissinger, meanwhile, firmly reiterated an earlier statement that he, too, favored delaying action on the treaty until a new military program had been placed before Congress and that he would recommend rejection of the treaty if this and oth... conditions were not met by Mr. C...

Mr. Kissinger and Senator ... Democrat of Georgia ... those ...

... this sort came

... Page A10, Column 1

... elaborate. But other officials have said the Administration is debating more frequent deployment of carrier task forces from the Western Pacific into the

Continued on Page A5, Column 1

KOCH SHUFFLES HIGHEST AIDES; 3 DEPUTIES TO LEAVE, 2 SHIFTED; BADILLO IS AMONG THOSE OUT

LEVENTHAL ELEVATED

He Will Be the Deputy for Operations in Move to Streamline City Hall

By RONALD SMOTHERS

Mayor Koch, saying it was time to "pare down and streamline" his government, yesterday announced a major shake-up at the highest level.

The move will mean the departure by the end of the year of three of his seven Deputy Mayors, including

Text of Mayor's remarks, page B4

Herman Badillo, the city's highest-ranking Hispanic official, who had given up his seat in Congress to join the Koch administration. It will also mean the shifting of two others to lower-level posts and the appointment of his Housing Commissioner as Deputy Mayor for Operations with broad powers.

The scope of the changes stunned many ... City Hall, who had been awaiting only ... routine news conference to announce ... expected appointment of a new ... Mayor for Operations.

... Mayor Koch said he would appoint Na... Leventhal, currently Commissioner ... Housing Preservation and Develop... the operations post, with respon... of coordination and manage... the daily business of city govern... commissioners, Mr. Koch said, ... directly to Mr. Leventhal and ... arly with him.

Three Who Are Leaving

... marked a major change in ... approach to government. ... Koch had said his seven ... status.

... yors who Mr. Koch said ... ministration by the end ... Mr. Badillo (Policy), ... (Intergovernmental ... L. Toia (Finance). ... Mayor said, the reor... Ronay Menschel ... Herbert Sturz ... would relinquish their ... and assume other ... ion.

... he Mayor said at ... the structure ... meet the prob... city in Janu... to deal with ... I believe ... more effi... and hope... for the peo...

... Not Clear

... changes were said to be the first steps in a major reorganization and it was not immediately clear what the final structure of the Koch administration would be. No legislative approval of the changes is needed.

With the departures — and with the appointment of Mr. Leventhal and the retaining of Peter J. Solomon as Deputy

Continued on Page B4, Column 3

Yankees' ... Piloting H...

Thurman Munson, the ... catcher and team captain o... York Yankees, was killed ... when the plane he was pilotin... short of the runway while tryin... at the Akron-Canton Airport in O...

Two passengers who were fly... him were taken to local hospitals... they were reported in fair condition.

Mr. Munson's Cessna Citation twi... gine jet crashed outside the perimete... the airport and came to rest 200 feet nor... of runway 19 at 3:02 P.M., Eastern day... light time, according to the Akron police.

Federal Aviation Administration officials said that the plane had lost its wings and burst into flames after the crash, resulting in injuries to two occupants and the death of the third.

Anthony Cardarelli, sheriff of Summit County, confirmed that Mr. Munson was the one who was killed.

One of the two passengers, David Hall, 32, of Canton, who first taught Mr. Munson to fly, was reported in fair condition with burns on his arms and hands at the Akron Regional Burn Center at Chil-

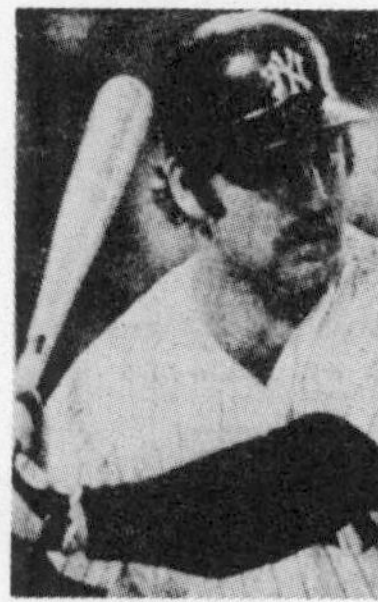

The New York Times/Sara Krulwich

Thurman Munson

H... here... ther... here, ... belief ... crisis, ... And, incr... to punish h...

That is th... people like ... this industrial ... stands slackly ... flares bloom in ... Standard Oil Con...

"Right now, I fe... coach with the ho... and a guy trying ... they are not respond... chak Sr., a 58-year-o... "Those new people in... are they going to do? ...

... sis of ... the inter... that there was, initially, ... philosophical agreement

Yankees' Thurman Munson Killed Piloting His Own Small Jet in Ohio

By JIM NAUGHTON

Thurman Munson, the 32-year-old catcher and team captain of the New York Yankees, was killed yesterday when the plane he was piloting crashed short of the runway while trying to land at the Akron-Canton Airport in Ohio.

Two passengers who were flying with him were taken to local hospitals where they were reported in fair condition.

Mr. Munson's Cessna Citation twin-engine jet crashed outside the perimeter of the airport and came to rest 200 feet north of runway 19 at 3:02 P.M., Eastern daylight time, according to the Akron police.

Federal Aviation Administration officials said that the plane had lost its wings and burst into flames after the crash, resulting in injuries to two occupants and the death of the third.

Anthony Cardarelli, sheriff of Summit County, confirmed that Mr. Munson was the one who was killed.

One of the two passengers, David Hall, 32, of Canton, who first taught Mr. Munson to fly, was reported in fair condition with burns on his arms and hands at the Akron Regional Burn Center at Children's Hospital. The other passenger, Jerry D. Anderson, also of Canton, was reported in fair condition with burns of the face, arms, and neck at Timken Mercy Hospital in Canton.

The F.A.A. authorities said the cause of the crash was unknown. Detective William Evans, who arrived at the scene five minutes after the crash said witnesses told him the jet began clipping trees as it approached the runway. It touched down just north of Greensburg Road, he said. Motorists had to "break for the plane,"

Continued on Page A15, Column 1

Nixon Dr... Purchase of Co-op Following Residents' Complaints

By TONY SCHWARTZ

Former President Richard M. Nixon withdrew his application yesterday to purchase a nine-room penthouse apartment at 19 East 72d Street. His application had been opposed by many of the residents in the building.

Owners of other apartments in the building received a letter late yesterday signed by Minot Milliken, president of the cooperative's board, regarding the apartment that Mr. Nixon was to have purchased from Robert A. Becker. It said: "Please be advised that former President Nixon and Mr. Becker have agreed to cancel the contract relating to Mr. Becker's apartment. Mr. Becker's apartment is once again on the market."

Mr. Nixon's decision came after the seven-member board of the cooperative met Wednesday evening to reconsider Mr. Nixon's application. The application had been unofficially approved more than a week ago by a majority of the board in a telephone poll conducted by Mr. Milliken.

The board took no official action to approve or disapprove Mr. Nixon's application at the Wednesday meeting. A letter that had been delivered to the board was signed by 14 residents expressing their opposition to Mr. Nixon's application. In addition, according to one resident, a lawyer representing several of the residents who opposed Mr. Nixon had been in contact on several occasions with a lawyer for the former President, to let Mr. Nixon know that he faced opposition.

"What was discussed at the meeting is confidential," said William Frankenhoff, a member of the board. "I learned today that Mr. Nixon had withdrawn his application. You'll have to call him for an explanation."

Calls to Mr. Nixon's office in San Clemente, Calif., were not returned. A secretary there explained that Jack Brennan, Mr. Nixon's top aide, was not taking any calls from newsmen.

Some residents of the building began expressing dismay about Mr. Nixon's

Continued on Page B3, Column 2

INSIDE

New Britain Officials Arrested

Six top New Britain, Conn., officials were arrested in an investigation into charges that city workers must pay bribes to get jobs. Page B3.

Bomb on Brooklyn Bridge

The police disarmed a radio-controlled device found atop a Brooklyn Bridge tower. They said the bomb could have exploded "at any moment." Page B1.

Philip L. Toia | Phillip R. Trimble | Herman Badillo

Ronay Menschel | Herbert Sturz | Haskell G. Ward | Peter J. Solomon

The New York Times / Aug. 3, 1979

Munson Killed in Accident

Continued From Page A1

he added. "It's a miracle people weren't injured during that time of the rush hour."

Mr. Evans said Mr. Hall was in the co-pilot seat, but "Munson had the plane to himself."

"Both victims tried valiantly to get Munson out," Mr. Evans added. He said the two men had about 30 seconds to try to free the Yankee star before the plane "went up in flames." One victim kicked out the emergency door while the other tried to pull Mr. Munson free. They succeeded in removing him from the pilot's seat, investigators said. However, Mr. Evans said that when the door opened "fuel, which was stored in the wing, ignited and engulfed the plane."

The two men tried to free Mr. Munson again, Mr. Evans said, "but the fire got so bad they had to get out. I think some of their clothes were on fire."

Carl Santelli, a friend of Munson's in Canton, said the Yankee star had come in from Chicago at 3 A.M. yesterday. "He said his plane wasn't acting right," said Mr. Santelli, "and he was going out to find out what was wrong with it."

A Cessna spokesman said the plane, which was lettered NY15, corresponding to its owner's Yankee jersey number, was the first Citation in the country to be involved in an accident.

Neal Callahan of the F.A.A.'s Chicago office said the plane "had been engaged in some touch-and-go practice takeoffs and landings" when the crash occurred.

Munson, a native of Akron, often flew home during home stands and road trips to be with his family. A Yankee coach, Elston Howard, said Munson told him he was interested in running a commercial commuter airline and was studying for a special license.

The coach said Mr. Munson wanted to stay as close to his family as possible. "That's why he told me he was flying home on his own plane on off days. He just said, 'Ellie, I want to see my family.' That's what he told me."

Munson, who batted over .300 five times and played on three Yankee pennant winners and two world championship teams, was the first Yankee captain since Lou Gehrig.

In his autobiography, written in 1978, he had described his love of flying. "I have a new love to make things somewhat more pleasant for me this year — airplanes. I studied for my pilot's license and received it during the winter.

Thurman Lee Munson

Now...it's possible to fly from New York to Canton in about an hour and I frequently go home even during home stands."

The police were at his home in Canton, where Mr. Munson's wife, Diane, and the couple's three children, Tracy Lynn, 9; Kelly, 7, and Michael 4, received news of the crash.

John Habermann, a flight instructor at Teterboro Airport in Bergen County, N.J., said he considered Mr. Munson "a fine pilot."

"He would study his airplane well," Mr. Habermann said. "He took it very seriously and was a very dedicated pilot."

News of the death shocked the baseball world.

The Yankees' principal owner, George Steinbrenner, said in a statement: "There's very little I could say to adequately express my feelings at this moment. I've lost a dear friend, a pal and one of the greatest competitors I've ever known. We spent many hours together talking baseball, and business. He loved his family. He was our leader. The great sport that made him so famous seems so very small and unimportant now."

Martin 'Loved Him'

Billy Martin, the Yankee manager, said: "For those who never knew him and didn't like him, I feel sorry for them. He was a great man, for his family, friends and all the people who knew and loved him, my deepest sympathy. We not only lost a great competitor, but a leader and a husband and devoted family man. He was a close friend, I loved him."

Commissioner Bowie Kuhn called the crash "an almost indescribable loss."

"He was a wonderful enormously likable guy and a truly great ballplayer," the commissioner said. "As tough a competitor as he was on the field he was a warm friend of baseball people and a loving family man. Baseball sends its heartfelt sympathy to his wife and children."

Gabe Paul, the former Yankee president, said he was shocked. "I coveted

(continued)

him as a player. That goes without saying. I just keep thinking to myself how much he wanted to play here and how close he would have been to home." Cleveland is about 45 miles from Canton.

Munson was an all-America catcher at Kent State in 1968. He came to the Yankees in 1969 and was rookie of the year in 1970. He won a Gold Glove Award in 1973, 1974 and 1975. He won the American League Most Valuable Player Award in 1976 and was named captain of the Yankees that year.

The Yankees have scheduled a team meeting today to decide what action to take. The funeral will be held in Canton. Arrangements are indefinite.

Thurman Munson Was Proud Captain of the Yankees

By MURRAY CHASS

Thurman Munson, the 32-year-old New York Yankee catcher killed in an airplane crash yesterday in Canton, Ohio, was the American League rookie of the year in 1970 and the league's most valuable player in his seventh season, in 1976. No member of the New York Yankees ever had won both awards.

Many Yankees, however, had gained entrance to the Baseball Hall of Fame, and one of Munson's goals was to play at least 10 years so he, too, could be eligible for the Hall.

This was the catcher's 10th season in the majors and he was considering making it his last.

"He hadn't decided anything," said Richard Moss, the lawyer who negotiated his last contract with the Yankees, "but he was seriously thinking about retiring at the end of the season. This was before his knees started acting up and giving him so much trouble. He was thinking that he might have had enough with playing. It was getting tougher and it was less rewarding for him. And he felt he had been away from his family long enough."

His Family Most Important

Munson's family — his wife, Diane, and their three young children — was by far the most important part of his life. He was noted as one of the best defensive and hitting catchers in baseball, and he enjoyed that status. But he enjoyed his family more.

That was the primary reason that flying his plane became the second most important part of his life, because it enabled him to spend more time during the season with his family.

Munson, as sensitive privately as he was abrasive publicly, had been flying for slightly more than two years. For the last two seasons, he had been flying his plane between New York and his home in Canton, and between other American League cities and Canton.

"He was like a little boy about flying," said Moss. "It was just the greatest thing he'd ever done. He talked about getting up in the air alone, being with nature, able to think. And of course, he was able to get home to his family. It was a marvelous, marvelous thing to him."

Flew Home Between Games

Munson flew home so often between games, leaving after one and returning in time for the next, that he did not even have a permanent residence for the season in the New York area. When someone would ask him for a telephone number where he could be reached in New York, he would say, "get me in Canton."

But Munson's plane trips took him beyond Canton. On the Yankees' trip to the West Coast last month, for example, he flew his plane rather than travel with the team. His wife joined him in Anaheim, Calif., the last stop before the All-Star Game break, and they flew home to Canton together.

Munson's desire to spend more time with Diane and their children, Tracy, 9, Kelly, 7, and Michael, 4, prompted the catcher to ask, at various times, to be traded. Following the 1977 season, he threatened not to return to the Yankees in 1978 if he was not traded. Munson, however, was too much of a competitor not to come back.

Thurman Lee Munson, whose 5-foot-11-inch, 195-pound figure prompted his teammates to call him, among other names, "Squatty Body," was born in Akron, Ohio, June 7, 1947. After he was an all-America catcher at Kent State University, the Yankees selected him in the first round of the amateur draft in June 1968. He played in the minor leagues for one season and part of another before the Yankees promoted him to the job he would hold until his death yesterday.

Adroit Handler of Pitchers

In 1971, the year after he was the league's top rookie, Munson committed

(continued)

Munson's Career Record

THURMAN LEE MUNSON

Born June 7, 1947, at Akron, O.
Height, 5.11 Weight, 190
Throws and bats righthanded
Attended Kent State University, Kent O

Led American League catchers in double plays with 14 in 1975 and tied for lead with 11 in 1973.
Named Most Valuable Player in American league, 1976
Selected by the Baseball Writers' Association as American League Rookie of the Year, 1970.
Named catcher on THE SPORTING NEWS American League All-Star Team, 1973, 1974, 1975 and 1976
Named catcher on THE SPORTING NEWS American League All-Star fielding team, 1973, 1974 and 1975.
Named American League Player of the Year by THE SPORTING NEWS, 1976
Received $75,000 bonus to sign with New York Yankees, 1968.

Year	Club	League	Pos.	G.	AB.	R.	H.	2B	3B.	HR.	RBI.	B.A.	PO.	A.	E.	F.A.
1968	Binghamton	East.	C	71	226	28	68	12	3	6	37	.301	327	53	9	.977
1969	Syracuse	Int	C-2-3	28	102	13	37	9	1	2	17	.363	81	13	6	.940
1969	New York	Amer.	C	26	86	6	22	1	2	1	9	.256	119	18	2	.986
1970	New York	Amer	C	132	453	59	137	25	4	6	53	.302	631	80	8	.989
1971	New York	Amer.	C-OF	125	451	71	113	15	4	10	42	.251	547	67	1	.998
1972	New York	Amer.	C	140	511	54	143	16	3	7	46	.280	575	71	15	.977
1973	New York	Amer	C	147	519	80	156	29	4	20	74	.301	673	80	12	.984
1974	New York	Amer	C	144	517	64	135	19	2	13	60	.261	743	75	22	.974
1975	New York	Amer	C-1-O-3	157	597	83	190	24	3	12	102	.318	725	95	23	.973
1976	New York	Amer.	C-OF	152	616	79	186	27	1	17	105	.302	546	78	14	.978
1977	New York	Amer	C	149	595	85	183	28	5	18	100	.308	657	73	12	.984
1978	New York	Amer	C-OF	154	617	73	183	27	1	6	71	.297	698	61	11	.986
Major League Totals				1326	4962	654	1448	211	29	110	662	.292	5914	698	120	.982

ALL-STAR GAME RECORD

Year	League	Pos.	AB.	R.	H.	2B.	3B.	HR.	RBI.	B.A.	PO.	A.	E.	F.A.
1971	American	C	0	0	0	0	0	0	0	.000	1	0	0	1.000
1973	American	C	2	0	0	0	0	0	0	.000	5	1	0	1.000
1974	American	C	3	1	1	1	0	0	0	.333	7	0	1	.875
1975	American	C	2	0	1	0	0	0	0	.500	1	1	0	1.000
1976	American	C	2	0	0	0	0	0	0	.000	4	0	0	1.000
1977	American	PH	1	0	0	0	0	0	0	.000	0	0	0	.000
All-Star Game Totals			10	1	2	1	0	0	0	.200	18	2	1	.952

Named to American League All-Star Team for 1978 game; replaced due to injury by Darrell Porter.

CHAMPIONSHIP SERIES RECORD

Established Championship Series record for most one-base hits, five-game Series (8), 1976
Tied Championship Series record for most at bats, five-game Series (23), 1976.
Tied American League Championship Series record for most at bats, four-game Series, (18), 1978.

Year	Club	League	Pos.	G.	AB.	R.	H.	2B.	3B.	HR.	RBI.	B.A.	PO.	A.	E.	F.A.
1976	New York	Amer.	C	5	23	3	10	2	0	0	3	.435	18	6	2	.923
1977	New York	Amer.	C	5	21	3	6	1	0	1	5	.286	24	4	0	1.000
1978	New York	Amer.	C	4	18	2	5	1	0	1	2	.278	22	4	0	1.000
Championship Series Totals				14	62	8	21	4	0	2	10	.339	64	14	2	.975

WORLD SERIES RECORD

Established World Series records for most singles, Series (9), 1976; most assists by catcher, four-game Series (7), 1976; most players caught stealing, four-game Series (5), 1976; most consecutive hits, two consecutive Series (7), 1976-77.

Tied World Series records for most hits, two consecutive games, one Series (7), October 19 and 21, 1976; most consecutive hits, one Series (6), 1976, most hits, game (4), October 21, 1976; most singles, game (4), October 21, 1976; one or more hits, each game, four-game Series, 1976; one or more hits, each game, six-game Series, 1977.

Year	Club	League	Pos.	G.	AB.	R.	H.	2B.	3B.	HR.	RBI.	B.A.	PO.	A.	E.	F.A.
1976	New York	Amer.	C	4	17	2	9	0	0	0	2	.529	21	7	0	1.000
1977	New York	Amer.	C	6	25	4	8	2	0	1	3	.320	40	5	0	1.000
1978	New York	Amer.	C	6	25	5	8	3	0	0	7	.320	33	5	0	1.000
World Series Totals				16	67	11	25	5	0	1	12	.373	94	17	0	1.000

only one error. His throwing was to become erratic in later seasons, but he was considered a master at handling pitchers and helping them surpass previous achievements.

It was in 1975, when he batted a career-high .318, that he began securing his position as perhaps the best all-round catcher in the league.

Then came the 1976 season. After being named the first Yankee team captain since Lou Gehrig, he batted .302 and drove in 105 runs as the Yankees won their first pennant in 12 years. For his effort, he was named the league's most valuable player.

Not long after receiving that honor, though, Munson engaged in a contract battle with George Steinbrenner, the team owner and also an Ohioan, who had named the catcher the team captain.

Salary Disputes

When Munson signed a four-year contract in the spring of 1976, he said the team's principal owner had promised that no player other than Catfish Hunter would earn more money than he. However, after the Yankees signed Reggie Jackson as a free agent in November 1976, Munson asked to have his salary raised to Jackson's level and Steinbrenner denied having made the promise.

Their battle lasted for more than a year, finally being resolved in the last week of spring training in 1978. An integral part of the negotiations concerned Munson's flying.

"Thurman wanted it to be up-front that he flew and that it was very important to him," Moss related. "I think George understood that it was important to Thurman."

Most guaranteed contracts that exist in baseball today have clauses absolving the team of paying the remainder of the contract if the player is killed while flying a plane himself. Munson's contract, which averaged $420,000 a year and had two more years to run after this one, had no such restricting clause.

Munson placed no restrictions on his style of play. He was aggressive in all phases of the game, and he seldom let injuries (he suffered many) force him out of the lineup. His teammates admired him so much that they were offended when Jackson, upon his arrival with the Yankees, was quoted as saying: "I'm the straw that stirs the drink. Munson thinks he can be the straw that stirs the drink, but he can only stir it bad."

Munson, who also was involved in real estate investment in Ohio, had a paradoxical personality. He often would complain about a lack of recognition, especially in comparison with Carlton Fisk, the Boston Red Sox catcher, but he often went out of his way to avoid talking to newsmen.

His relationship with them reached its low point in August 1977, when he grew a beard in defiance of Steinbrenner's rules on personal appearance. Newsmen speculated that Munson had grown the beard as a way of antagonizing the owner and getting him angry enough so that he might trade Munson to Cleveland, which is only one hour from his home.

On the day he finally shaved, several newsmen approached him in the club house in Syracuse, where the Yankees were playing an exhibition game.

"I ain't talking to one writer the rest of the year," he stated.

When his visitors persisted, Munson turned to Manager Billy Martin and said, "Billy, will you get these guys away from me?"

Munson tried to keep his life in perspective. "You're an individual before you're a baseball player," he said. "If you forget that, you're in trouble."

In the three World Series in which he played, Thurman Munson batted .373 and fielded at a percentage of 1.000.

The New York Times TUESDAY, NOVEMBER 28, 1939.

DR. J. A. NAISMITH IS DEAD IN KANSAS

Originator of Basketball Was Professor Emeritus of Physical Education

INTRODUCED SPORT IN 1891

Devised Game at Y. M. C. A. College in Springfield, Mass. —Played Only Twice

LAWRENCE, Kan. (Tuesday), Nov. 28 (AP)—Dr. James A. Naismith, inventor of basketball, died at 1:50 A. M. (Central standard time) today of a heart ailment following a cerebral hemorrhage. His age was 78.

Dr. Naismith was professor emeritus of physical education at Kansas University.

Game Played by 20,000,000

The "father of basketball," Dr. James A. Naismith had the distinction of originating the only major sport created in the United States, with the possible exception of baseball, about which there is much controversy. There is no controversy about the identity of the father of basketball, a sport introduced by Dr. Naismith in 1891 and now played yearly by more than 20,000,000 persons.

The game, called Naismith ball when he devised it at Springfield (Mass.) Y. M. C. A. College for the delectation of Gay Nineties youths, has been streamlined and speeded up through the years so that it appears to be quite different from the original sport whose main physical properties were two peach baskets and a soccer ball. However, the fast, sprightly, colorful basketball of today, enjoyed in many lands by the young of both sexes in college, school, club, association and society gymnasiums and on professional courts, bears at least the same resemblance to the early game as that of a modern airliner to the Wright brothers' first "flying machine."

He Played Game Only Twice

An athlete who had played many other sports, Dr. Naismith played basketball only twice, in 1892 and 1898. Years later he explained that he "just didn't get around to playing." He committed many fouls, he said, adding:

"I guess my early training in wrestling, boxing and football was too much for me. My reflexes made me hold my opponents. Once I even used a grapevine wrestling clamp on a man who was too big for me to handle. So I have sympathy for boys who make inadvertent fouls, but I cannot stand deliberate ones."

Dr. Naismith was born in Almonte, Ont., Nov. 6, 1861, the son of John and Margaret Young Naismith, received an A. B. degree from McGill University in 1887, graduated from Presbyterian College, Montreal, in 1890 and from the Springfield Y. M. C. A. College in 1891. He received an M. D. degree from the University College in 1898 and an M. P. E. degree from Springfield in 1910.

In 1887-90 he was director of physical education at McGill, and in 1890-95 he held the same post at Springfield College. Physical director of the Y. M. C. A. at Denver, Col., in 1895-98, he became physical director at the University of Kansas in 1898.

Went to France for Y. M. C. A.

Dr. Naismith remained on the Kansas faculty until 1937, when he became Professor Emeritus of Physical Education. He did military service with the First Kansas Regiment for four months in 1916 and served the Y. M. C. A. in France in 1917-19.

It was with basketball that the public always identified his name. In 1891, when he was on the staff of the Y. M. C. A. College at Springfield, Dr. Naismith was asked by Dr. Luther Gulick, head of the physical training department, to develop something to employ the energy of the young men of the college who found dumbbells and Indian clubs too tame between the football and baseball seasons.

Dr. Naismith recalled that he had played "duck on the rock" as a boy and remembered the comparative value of the tossed rock that was fairly likely to hit the "duck" and the hurled rock that, if it did hit, sent the "duck" farther. He decided that the tossed missile was the better and so established that as one of the principles of his new game. To guard against injuries, he decided it would be wise for the holder of the ball to throw or pass it instead of carrying it.

Thirteen Rules Established

The placing of the players as forwards and guards was suggested by lacrosse, with which he, an American citizen of Canadian birth, was familiar. Soccer, English rugby and other sports contributed to the game. Thirteen rules were formulated by Dr. Naismith and the elaborate regulations now governing the sport still conform in essence to the present twelve of the thirteen original rules.

The original rules were typed and handed to young Springfield students, who at first considered the new game as "just another sport," but after a time grew very fond of it and played well. The first game was played at Springfield College, with peach baskets tacked up in the gymnasium and with a soccer ball as the missile. It was played either in December, 1891, or January, 1892, according to accounts, which differ slightly. The three most popular dates are Dec. 21, 1891, Jan. 15, 1892, and Jan. 20, 1892.

In the United States intercollegiate leagues were formed, professional teams won popular applause. In 1936, basketball received a place at the Olympic Games. The rules changed. At first it was not unusual for from forty to fifty to play on a side, and for a time seven, eight and nine men composed a team. Now, under American men's rules, five men are on a team, with a girls' team numbering six. Girls' rules differ in some other ways from men's.

In 1894 Dr. Naismith married Miss Maude E. Sherman. Five children were born to them. His first wife died in 1937. He married Mrs. Florance Kincaid last Spring.

Basketball has come a long way since it was invented by Dr. James A. Naismith (center) in 1891.

"All the News That's Fit to Print"

The New York Times

LATE CITY EDITION

Weather: Rain ending early today; fair and mild tonight, tomorrow. Temp. range: today 63-76; Tuesday 59-73. Additional details on Page 88.

VOL. CXXIII ... No. 42,256 © 1973 The New York Times Company NEW YORK, WEDNESDAY, OCTOBER 3, 1973 15 CENTS

White House Adopts Plan For Heating Oil Allocation

Control Would Be the First in Peacetime —Details Announced on Mandatory Program for Propane Supplies

By EDWARD COWAN
Special to The New York Times

WASHINGTON, Oct. 2—After months of indecision, the White House committed itself today to Federal supply-management of heating oil for the coming winter, the first such peacetime regulation in the country's history.

Acknowledging that a heating shortage could not be avoided, Interior Secretary Rogers C. B. Morton said its severity will be dependent on "old man winter."

The White House also announced the details of its previously promised mandatory supply-allocation program for propane, a fuel used heavily in agriculture—for grain drying, for example—and to heat rural homes.

John A. Love, director of the Energy Policy Office, said at a White House news briefing that the reason for both supply-management programs was "to insure a more equal distribution of our fuels so that no one area of the country will suffer undue shortages."

"To the fullest extent possible, we want to insure that no home or hospital go... out adequate ... farm is ... propane ...

John A. Love spe... Washington yeste...

SENATE, 54 TO 42, VOTES $1.2-BILLION FOR FOREIGN AID

Amount Authorized Is Less Than in House Version—Compromise Is Due

By DAVID BINDER
Special to The New York Times

WASHINGTON, Oct. 2—The Senate approved a $1.2-billion foreign assistance bill today by a vote of 54 to 42 after resisting two attempts to trim the authorization sharply.

The measure provides considerably less aid than is fo... seen in an authorization ... by the House of Repr... July 26. The Hou... $1.6-bill... lion ...

Nurmi, Star Runner of the '20's, Dies

Special to The New York Times

HELSINKI, Finland, Oct. 2—Paavo Nurmi, the celebrated long-distance runner of the nineteen-twenties, died here today. He was 76 years old and had been in declining health for several years.

Set Scores of Records

By ALDEN WHITMAN

An incomparable long-distance runner, Paavo Nurmi dominated his category of foot-racing by a combination of fleetness, endurance and a certain cold flamboyance. "The Flying Finn" or "The Phantom Finn," as he was called, set 12 world records and captured nine gold medals in the Olympiads of 1920, 1924 and 1928—a total not yet exceeded. And in other events, until his retirement in 1932, he established a score more records.

It was not only his speed and endurance—he took both the 1,500-and the 5,000-meter crowns within 90 minutes of each other on a blazing hot day in Paris in 1924—that gained Nurmi his international renown, but it was also his flowing running style. To watch him was an esthetic experience that spectators savored for many years.

Tall, lean, dark-haired and unsmiling, Nurmi ran with high, long strides on his toes, hands, slightly clenched, held against his chest. His pace never seemed to vary; he never seemed to worry; he passed less durable runners with magical ease, and when he had broken the tape he appeared almost phlegmatic in victory.

Nurmi's performance at the Paris Olympics of 1924 touched the phenomenal with a quadruple victory for which he earned six gold medals. The races were the 1,500-meter, the 3,000-meter, the 5,000-meter and the cross-country. The last two were also team events, and

Continued on Page 48, Column 2

Associated Press
Paavo Nurmi

United Press International
Nurmi winning three-mile race in 1929 Penn Relays.

AUSTRIAN REJECTS MRS. MEIR'S PLEAS ON TRANSIT ROUTES

Kreisky Says Individuals but Not Groups of Emigrants May Go 'Shortest' Way

CENTER WILL BE CLOSED

Israeli Premier, After the Meeting, Cancels News Parley and Flies Home

By TERENCE SMITH
Special to The New York Times

VIENNA, Oct. 2 — Premier Golda Meir of Israel and Chancellor Bruno Kreisky of Austria conferred for nearly two hours today, but were unable to reach any agreement on facilities for the continued transit of Soviet Jews through Austria.

Dr. Kreisky said at a news conference later that the atmosphere in the meeting had been "very serious," and that both sides had "outlined their differences."

"I made it clear to her that the special facilities we have been granting for the transiting Soviet Jews in the past will no longer be available in the future," he said brusquely.

Meeting a Disappointment

Dr. Kreisky added that Schönau Castle, the Jewish Agency's transit facility, would have to be closed, but that individual Soviet Jews could still pass through Austria "by the shortest route and with the shortest possible stop."

The meeting was obviously a major disappointment to Mrs. Meir, who had said on the way here from Strasbourg, France, that she hoped to reach a compromise under which Schönau Castle would remain open and the large-scale transit of Soviet emi...rants would continue.

Dr. Kreisky announced early ...turday that the transiting ...ough Austria of groups of ...et Jews would cease and ... Schönau Castle would be ... ...ceded to the demands ... Palestinian terrorists ...ded a train carrying ...grants from Moscow ...ok four hostages— ...and an Austrian —and threatened ...nless Vienna ...on the transit ...

...nference

...canceled a ...e before ... outside the ...'s ornate, chande... office in the Ballhaus, a Baroque palace that housed the Congress of Vienna in 1815.

Without a word to anyone, the Premier's party headed in limousines for Vienna's Schwechat Airport and took off for Israel immediately, carrying with them about 90 Soviet Jews who had arrived at Schönau Castle during the last 24 hours. Itzhak Patish, the Israeli Ambassador to Austria who accompanied Mrs. Meir in the meeting and to the airport, said that she was "very tired but not morose."

Earlier Mrs. Meir had made it clear that the issue of continued immigration of Soviet Jews through Austria was vital to Israel. If the Arab guerrillas succeeded in forcing Austria to close her transit facilities at the point of a gun, she said, "they'll try the same thing in other countries."

Kreisky Is Blunt

As Mrs. Meir was on the way to the airport this evening, Dr. Kreisky called a news conference. He was blunt, uncompromising and at times sarcastic as he answered questions in English and German from more than 100 Austrian and foreign newsmen.

"I cannot speak for Mrs. Meir, who is not here to express her point of view," he

Continued on Page 13, Column 1

...el yesterday in Vienna
United Press International

...ny Rooney ...7th Term

...n Democratic or... John J. Rooney, ...one of the most ...

...ROVES ...TTACK

...s, It ...

... two- ...75 from ... seven-seater ...agon, to $4,350 from ...99.

By comparison, the suggest-

Continued on Page 69, Column 1

...Rooney had ... whether he in... ...eek another term, ... had pledged to be loyal to the organization that had nurtured him and supported him in Congressional races since 1944. Mr. Rooney, for his part, had given the organization increased patronage, in terms of jobs, service to constituents an

Continued on Page 89, Column 4

...ancellor Bruno ... of Austria for deciding ... close the special transit facilities in exchange for the lives of the four hostages.

Egypt's President, Anwar el-Sadat, is sending a personal envoy, Minister of Tourism Ismail Fahmy, to Vienna tomorrow with a message of thanks to the Austrian leader.

For many Arabs the events in Austria touch on a fundamental issue in the Arab-Israeli conflict.

Emigration to Israel from

Continued on Page 11, Column 1

Agnew Co... To Seek In...

By BEN A. ...
Special to The N...

BALTIMORE, Oct. 2—Vice ... will meet with Federal District ... in secret tomorrow in a reported ... into ... abou... tion, ... familia...

The law... prepared t... man's perm... witnesses un... news leaks.

The witnesses ... might include the ... Department officials ... attacked in a spee... Angeles last Saturda... he called such "flagra... fessional and outrageou... dling of his case tha... entire system of justice is ... attack."

The contention that ... Agnew has been the victim ... "malicious" Justice Departme... news leaks is a main eleme... of the Vice President's defense. In the Los Angeles speech he called himself the intended "trophy" of Justice Department lawyers who he said were trying to regain reputations

Continued on Page 30, Column 3

... fie... ment... mornin...

Contin...

SIX DRUG JUSTICES NOT OF TOP RATING

Screening Panel Governor Named Has Reservations About Qualifications

By MARY BREASTED

Six of the 16 new Court of Claims appointees who will be sitting in the new narcotics courts as acting Supreme Court Justices did not receive the highest rating of "qualified" from Governor Rockefeller's new State Judicial Screening Committee, but instead were listed as "qualified with reservations."

The committee, appointed by the Governor, considered 32 candidates for the new Court of Claims positions, rating them as "qualified," "qualified with reservations" and "not qualified."

When Mr. Rockefeller announced the members of the panel last August, he said he was appointing a screening panel of "distinguished citizens, including lawyers and nonlawyers, to help insure that the best qualified people are appointed to the bench under the recently enacted legislation."

Bar Not Consulted

Yesterday, Michael Whiteman, the Governor's counsel, said that when Mr. Rockefeller appointed the panel he did not "abdicate his responsibility to make his own judgments" about the Court of Claims appointees and that the factors that went into his appointment of candidates—other than their legal qualifications—were "balance, political, social and geographic."

Paul De Witt, executive secretary of the Association of the Bar of the City of New York, said during a recent interview that association members were unhappy that the Governor had not submitted the names of the Court of Claims candidates to the association for rating by its judiciary committee. Several Bar Association sources, who asked not to be named, said they felt that Governor Rockefeller had established his own screening panel to avoid having

Continued on Page 89, Column 1

Nurmi, Star Run...

Special to The New York Times

HELSINKI, Finland, Oct. 2—Paavo Nurmi, the celebrated long-distance runner of the nineteen-twenties, died here today. He was 76 years old and had been in declining health for several years.

Set Scores of Records

By ALDEN WHITMAN

An incomparable long-distance runner, Paavo Nurmi dominated his category of foot-racing by a combination of fleetness, endurance and a certain cold flamboyance. "The Flying Finn" or "The Phantom Finn," as he was called, set 12 world records and captured nine gold medals in the Olympiads of 1920, 1924 and 1928—a total not yet exceeded. And in other events, until his retirement in 1932, he established a score more records.

It was not only his speed and endurance—he took both the 1,500-and the 5,000-meter crowns within 90 minutes of each other on a blazing hot day in Paris in 1924—that gained Nurmi his international renown, but it was also his flowing running style. To watch him was an esthetic experience that spectators savored for many years.

Tall, lean, dark-haired and unsmiling, Nurmi ran with high, long strides on his toes, hands, slightly clenched, held against his chest. His pace never seemed to vary; he never seemed to worry; he passed less durable runners with magical ease, and when he had broken the tape he appeared almost phlegmatic in victory.

Nurmi's performance at the Paris Olympics of 1924 touched the phenomenal with a quadruple victory for which he earned six gold medals. The races were the 1,500-meter, the 3,000-meter, the 5,000-meter and the cross-country. The last two were also team events, and

Continued on Page 48, Column 2

Associated Press
Paavo Nurmi

United Press International
Nurmi winning three-mile race in 1929 Penn Relays.

Ex-City Official Says He's Homosexual

By MARCIA CHAMBERS

Dr. Howard J. Brown, the Lindsay administration's first Health Services Administrator, openly acknowledged his homosexuality in an interview yesterday—in an effort, he said, to end the prejudice homosexuals face in obtaining employment.

"I know of homosexual priests, clergymen, dentists, politicians," he said. "When I served in Mayor Lindsay's cabinet as H. S. A. and Health Commissioner, there were other homosexual Commissioners known to me."

Dr. Brown will make the same statement, he said, in an address today to 600 physicians at a symposium on human sexuality at the Carrier Clinic in Belle Mead, N. J.

Dr. Brown disclosed that he was a homosexual three weeks ago before the board of directors of the Public Health Association, a professional organization in the city.

The 49-year-old physician said it was a "tribute to the board" that following his declaration he was appointed chairman of a committee to combat discrimination against homosexuals in the health community.

Dr. Brown, who left the Lindsay administration in 1967 after 18 months as director of the city's health-services program, is now on the faculty of the New York University School of Medicine, where he is a professor of public administration of health services.

His decision to disclose his homosexuality was based in part on what he sees as a sharp decline in public hostility toward homosexuals. "And times have changed," he said.

Moreover, he said, "you get to a point in your life where you want to leave a legacy—in a sense this can help free the generation that comes after us from the dreadful agony of secrecy, the constant need to hide."

Beyond that, Dr. Brown said, he was prompted by the actions of the Gay Activists Alliance, which for two years has unsuccessfully sought a City Council bill to ban discrimination against homosexuals in housing, employment and public accommodations.

As chairman of the Public Health Association's new committee, Dr. Brown said he

Continued on Page 42, Column 3

NEWS INDEX

Paavo Nurmi, Star Runner of '20's, Dies

Continued From Page 1, Col. 3

in both Nurmi led the Finns across the finish line.

Finland had great runners before Nurmi, notably Hannes Kolehmaine, the star of the 1912 Olympics, and several after him, including Taisto Maki, his protégé; but Nurmi was the greatest, even though virtually all his records have been surpassed. Certainly, Nurmi drew the crowds and the plaudits as none others have, and he ranked with such legendary sports figures as Jack Dempsey, Babe Ruth, Bill Tilden and Helen Wills Moody.

"I'll never forget how impressed I was," said Art Letz, former executive director of the United States Olympic Committee, yesterday. "I saw him run in Milwaukee on his 1925 tour, when I was just a kid."

"I thought of him as an old man then [he was 28] and I said I had never seen an old man who could run so fast."

In the winter and spring of 1925, Nurmi was the idol of the American sports public as he broke records almost to order from coast to coast, sometimes two and three a night. His newspaper coverage was comparable to that of visiting royalty; his reflexes, heart action, diet and the trick of pacing himself with a stop-watch were discussed endlessly. In 68 races in four months he set 11 records and lost only twice.

Only the aloof Nurmi was unimpressed. He was a shy man who disliked the limelight, could not comprehend Americans' interest in records and was happiest with the countrymen he met in various cities.

Paavo Nurmi (left) takes the lead in the 1924 Olympic Games.

Broke 2-Mile Record

Many of his records on this tour were at odd distances—1¾ miles, 1⅞ miles, 2¼ miles—but there was one with which none quibbled—his 8:58.2 for two miles in a New York Athletic Club meeting at the old Madison Square Garden. It was the first time that distance had been run in under 9 minutes, and the mark stood until 1941.

He also ran the indoor mile at 4:12, a slow speed by today's standards, but then it was dizzying, like his outdoor mile of 4:10.4 on a cinder track.

Nurmi's other feats included a series of races on successive nights, during which he established three world records in New York, another in Chicago and then a final one in New York. He was beaten, twice, most memorably in a 5,000-meter race; but even as a loser he dominated the news.

In 1925 and afterward, Nurmi's financial dealings got him into trouble. He was accused of taking money under the table by submitting inflated expense accounts; and for this he was barred from 1932 Olympics at Los Angeles. He blamed his predicament on sports writers, who, he said, had disclosed his violations of the amateur code to the International Amateur Athletic Federation. The complaint was that many athletes received extra money, but that he alone had been caught.

Whatever the merits of the dispute, Nurmi was a hero in Finland, where a bronze statue of him running in the nude was put up outside the Helsinki Olympic Stadium, an uncommon tribute to even the greatest athletes. As late as last summer, tour groups were taken to the statue and told of the runner's accomplishment.

Went to Work as Boy

His beginnings were much humbler. The son of a carpenter, Paavo Johannes Nurmi was born in Turku on June 13, 1897. When he was 12, his father died. At 15 he went to support died. At 15 he went to work in a foundry to support his mother, brother and two sister. When he was 17 he began to develop his stamina and technique with solitary practice of 50 miles a week. This training, carried on through his active years, enabled him to reel off lap after lap inexorably and with graceful strides. He had learned the importance of steadiness in training by carrying a stop-watch so that he could time each lap. Sometimes, in a race, he also carried the watch to time his laps.

Nurmi was 23 when his name became a headline word for his then-startling performances at the Antwerp Olympics of 1920, He gained gold medals for the 10,000-meter race and the marathon, and a silver medal for the 5,000-meter event. After his spectacular feats in 1924, his activities in the 1928 Olympics at Amsterdam seemed tame, for he won only one gold medal—that for the 10,000-meter event. There were also two silver medals for shorter distances.

Nurmi returned to the United States in 1929 for another exhibition tour, still a splendid runner, still a magnet for track enthusiasts.

After his retirement, Nurmi entered the construction business in Helsinki and also operated a men's shop. He coached runners for the Berlin Olympics of 1936 so successfully that his protegés won both the 10,000-meter and the 5,000-meter races as well as the 3,000-meter steeplechase.

Nurmi's last sports appearance was at the 1952 Olympics in Helsinki, where he startled spectators at the opening ceremonies by appearing suddenly to run the final lap with the Olympic torch. His flowing stride was unmistakable, even in the far reaches of the stadium, so that when he came into view applause quickly rose to a mighty thundering crescéndo. And the national teams broke ranks and dashed to the edge of the track to get a glimpse of him.

In recent years, the taciturn Nurmi was a recluse. He suffered a massive coronary seven years ago, and others more recently. He had eye trouble and other enfeeblements, so that he got about only with a cane in his apartment overlooking Sibelius Park His countrymen thought him a sour fellow and miser, an impression he did little to dispel.

Asked a few ago if he had run to bring renown to Finland, he said:

"No, I ran for myself, not for Finland."

"Not even in the Olympics?" his interviewer inquired.

"Not even then. Above all, not then. At the Olympics Paavo Nurmi mattered more than ever."

His marriage of a year in the early thirties ended in divorce. He leaves a son, Matti.

The New York Times FRIDAY, AUGUST 10, 1979

Walter F. O'Malley, Leader of Dodgers' Move to Los Angeles, Dies at 75

Walter F. O'Malley, the man who took the Dodgers out of Brooklyn and opened the West Coast to major league baseball, died yesterday in Rochester, Minn. He was 75 years old.

Mr. O'Malley, board chairman of the Los Angeles Dodgers, had been under treatment for cancer in Methodist Hospital of the Mayo Clinic since June 28. The cause of death was given as congestive heart failure. His wife, Kay, a childhood sweetheart, died at the family home in Los Angeles a month ago.

Mr. O'Malley is survived by a son, Peter, president of the Dodgers; a daughter, Mrs. Terry Seidler of San Marino, Calif., and 12 grandchildren.

Mr. O'Malley, known as a hard-headed businessman, became probably the most influential owner in baseball after moving the Dodgers from Brooklyn to Los Angeles after the 1957 season. He also persuaded Horace Stoneham to move the New York Giants to San Franciso at the same time, leaving the New York area with only one big league team, the Yankees, instead of three.

Unqualified Success

The sudden exodus stunned the baseball world, stirring bitter protests by New York and Brooklyn fans who had considered it unthinkable that either team would ever abandon the metropolitan area. Yet the source of Mr. O'Malley's subsequent power was the phenomenal financial success of the relocated Dodgers. In 21 seasons on the West Coast, including an initial four-year operation at the Los Angeles Coliseum, the Dodgers have averaged more than two million paying customers a season.

Last year, at Dodger Stadium in Chavez Ravine, they drew 3.3 million fans, becoming the first team in baseball history to reach the three-million mark.

News of Mr. O'Malley's death brought tributes from throughout the baseball world. Bowie Kuhn, the commissioner of baseball, called him "as great an executive talent" as he had ever seen.

"His unique ability, charm and wit are not replaceable," said Mr. Kuhn.

Roy Campanella, whose catching career with the Dodgers was ended by an auto accident in 1958 that left him paralyzed, recalled that Mr. O'Malley had personally taken care of his medical bills and brought him to Los Angeles as director of community relations with the club.

"And when Bobby Thomson hit that homer off Ralph Branca," Mr. Campanella said, "the one that cost us the pennant in 1951, Mr. O'Malley went over to Ralph in the clubhouse, patted him on the shoulder and told him everything was all right. Baseball has lost a tremendous person."

A Wise Move West

Mr. O'Malley's behind-the-scenes power in baseball came largely from the admiration his colleagues had for his financial wizardry.

Dodger Stadium holds 56,000, compared with the 32,000 capacity of Ebbets Field in Brooklyn, which Mr. O'Malley had tried unsuccessfully to replace. Baseball men considered the owner a business genius after his gold-rush accomplishments in California . For example, he was able to purchase the Chavez Ravine property at a bargain price and the stadium was built at moderate cost. The facilities include such features as parking for 16,000 cars on 21 terraced lots adjacent to various seating levels.

Dodger Stadium, built for $16 million, opened in April 1962. It was the first baseball park constructed privately since Yankee Stadium in 1923. The present Dodger franchise, including stadium and property, is estimated to be worth $50 million now, two or three times as much as the average baseball franchise would bring.

Mr. O'Malley became president of the Dodgers in Brooklyn in 1950, increasing his holdings at that time to 67 percent. After moving to Los Angeles, he took sole control.

At the time of the controversial shift, the Dodgers were a prosperous franchise that attracted more than a million fans to Ebbets Field in 1957.

Mr. O'Malley already had earned a reputation as something of a penny-

(continued)

Brooklyn's Ebbets Field was the home of the Dodgers until Walter O'Malley moved the team to Los Angeles.

pincher. As one former employee stated, "He was a brilliant sports promoter, but he should not have been confused with a philanthropist when it came to largesse."

Mr. O'Malley's decision to take Brooklyn's beloved "Bums" to California enraged residents of the borough. The owner, however, always insisted he had wanted to keep the club in Brooklyn and that he was forced out by politics.

There was some truth to the claim. Mr. O'Malley already had picked out a spot in West Brooklyn, near the Long Island Rail Road's Atlantic Avenue station, for a new park. He wanted somebody to condemn the land and sell it to him cheap, after which he would build the new park. He lobbied in Albany for a bill to set up a commission for this.

The bill passed and Gov. W. Averell Harriman signed it, but local political squabbling over the site and the price held up the deal. The frustrated Mr. O'Malley began shopping for greener pastures.

Walter O'Malley and his wife Kay.

Queens or California

Flushing Meadows, where Shea Stadium stands now, was offered as an alternative, but Mr. O'Malley was not impressed by the possibilities there. He also felt that if the team was going to leave Brooklyn, it might as well move to California as to Queens.

"We tried for 10 long years to acquire land," he later said, "but when a high-ranking official in Brooklyn told us we didn't have a chance, I told him goodbye."

Mr. O'Malley became a director of the Dodgers in 1932, and in 1943 replaced Wendell L. Willkie as the team's legal representative. With Branch Rickey he formed a syndicate that purchased the Dodgers from Larry MacPhail. In 1950, Mr. Rickey sold his stock and Mr. O'Malley became the president. He held that position until 1970, when he passed it on to his son, Peter, and became chairman of the board.

Under Mr. O'Malley's direction, the team prospered financially in both Brooklyn and Los Angeles. On the field, it won National League pennants in Brooklyn four times and in Los Angeles seven times. In 1955, 1959, 1963 and 1965, the Dodgers won the World Series.

For seven of the last nine pennants that the Dodgers won, the manager was Walter Alston. Mr. O'Malley gave the job to Mr. Alston after the 1953 season because Chuck Dressen refused to continue as manager under a one-year contract. Mr. Alston had no problem working under that condition and did so throughout his 23-year association with the Dodgers.

Born in the Bronx

Walter Francis O'Malley was born Oct. 9, 1903, in the Bronx. The son of a commissioner of public markets, he attended Jamaica High School in Queens and Culver Military Academy in Indiana, where he played on the baseball team until a broken nose finished his playing career.

He was graduated from the University of Pennsylvania as president of his class in 1926 and earned a degree from the Fordham Law School, attending classes at night while working as an assistant engineer for the Riley Drilling Company during the day.

He practiced law for 20 years until his responsibilities with the Dodgers became too pressing.

He married the former Kay Hanson on Sept. 5, 1931. Mrs. O'Malley had an operation for cancer of the larynx before they were married and never regained the use of her voice. When Mr. O'Malley's father suggested the wedding be called off, the son replied, "No, she's the same girl I fell in love with."

A heavyset man with a gruff exterior and a gravelly voice, the 5-foot-11-inch owner referred to himself sometimes as "Fatso." He enjoyed dining at gourmet restaurants and smoked more than a dozen expensive cigars a day.

Dodger spokesmen said a private funeral mass would be celebrated for family members only and that the time and place would not be announced.

"All the News That's Fit to Print"

The New York Times.

LATE CITY EDITION
U. S. Weather Bureau Report (Page 43) forecasts: Mostly cloudy today; mostly fair and cool tonight and tomorrow. Temp. range: 44—38. Yesterday: 49.6—43.

VOL. CVIII..No. 36,827. © 1958, by The New York Times Company. Times Square, New York 36, N. Y. NEW YORK, SATURDAY, NOVEMBER 22, 1958. 10c beyond 100-mile zone from New York City. Higher in air delivery cities. FIVE CENTS

Mel Ott, 49, Dies Of Crash Injuries

Associated Press

Mel Ott

Special to The New York Times

NEW ORLEANS, Nov. 21—Mel Ott, former New York Giants' baseball star and manager, died here today of injuries received in an automobile collision a week ago. He was 49 years old.

Death came to Mr. Ott at 12:35 P.M. Central Standard time, in the operating room of Touro Infirmary, where a team

Continued on Page 18, Column 2

SOVIET AND EAST GERMANY MAP TRANSFER OF BERLIN; U. S. VOWS TO STAND FIRM

PRESIDENT STANCH

Stresses Washington Will Not Retreat From Its Policy

By FELIX BELAIR Jr.
Special to The New York Times.

AUGUSTA, Ga., Nov. 21—President Eisenhower made it clear today that the United States would make no retreat "from its firm intentions in West Berlin."

The President authorized his press secretary, James C. Hagerty, to announce that the United States Government would continue "to maintain the integrity" of the area regardless of the Soviet Union's threat to turn over its occupation functions in the eastern sector of Berlin to East Germany.

It was further made clear on the President's behalf that his statement of United States policy was issued only after the fullest discussion of the situation with Britain and France, which share the control of West Berlin with the United States.

[In Washington more high officials were favoring a tough policy, including the use of armed convoys, in the Berlin crisis.]

Background of Statement

Mr. Hagerty declined to spell ... his statement that "our ... intentions in West Berlin ... ain unchanged." However, ... Department officials said ... day that these would in- ... the right of continued ... to Western Berlin by ... l and air.

... atement for President ... er, made to newsmen ... ing the Presidential ... owed Moscow dis- ... the Soviet Govern- ... pected in forty- ... deliver notes to ... Allies contending ... elonged to Com- ... many.

... erence at the ... use room in ... ere, report- ... y to eluci- ... hat "I can ... U. S. Gov- ... r firm in- ... n remain ...

Smirnov Sees Shift In Berlin in Month

By ARTHUR J. OLSEN
Special to The New York Times.

BONN, Germany, Nov. 21—The Soviet Ambassador to Bonn said tonight that he expected the Berlin question to be settled by Christmas.

The envoy, Andrei A. Smirnov, interviewed at an Indonesian diplomatic reception, said he hoped the crisis over control of the city would be over by Christmas by means of a "peaceful" turnover of the city to the "German" authorities.

"We will give Berlin back to the Germans," he added. "I hope it will go quickly. The quicker the better. I believe the Germans will be able to celebrate a peaceful Christmas."

The Soviet Ambassador did not elaborate his reference to

Continued on Page 3, Column 4

KEY MEETING HELD

Russians Take Step to Implement Threat of Withdrawal

By SYDNEY GRUSON
Special to The New York Times.

BERLIN, Nov. 21—The Soviet Union made its first move here today to implement its threat to withdraw from the Big Four occupation of Berlin.

A Soviet-East German commission of six met in East Berlin to discuss the transfer of Soviet controls in the divided city to the Communist East German Government.

The commission was established in May, 1957, to regulate the status of the Soviet Army forces in East Germany. A communiqué issued tonight by A. D. N., the East German press agency, said only that the commission had reached unanimous agreement on a number of questions.

The major question remaining was just when the Russians would turn over their functions here. There was no clue in the communiqué as to the timing. But the conviction tonight was that the crisis for the West was fast approaching.

Effect of a Withdrawal

In effect a withdrawal by the Soviet Union would challenge the Western Allies' presence in Berlin and their right to air, road and rail access between the city and West Germany. East German soldiers would then be in control of the Allies' communications, a control the Allies have indicated they would not accept.

The May, 1957, agreement was signed for the Soviet Union by Foreign Minister Andrei A. Gromyko and Marshal Georgi K. Zhukov, who has since been deposed as Soviet Defense Minister.

It was designed to give the East Germans a theoretical measure of control over the number and movement of Soviet forces in East Germany.

Similar treaties were reached between the Soviet Union and other East European Communist countries to help quiet anti-Soviet feeling after the Polish and Hungarian upheavals of 1956.

Isolation Is Emphasized

Berlin's isolation was pointed up tonight by the failure of West Germany's Foreign Minister, Dr. Heinrich von Brentano, to reach the city for consultations on the crisis with Mayor Willy Brandt and the three Western commandants.

The plane carrying the Foreign Minister was unable to land because of fog and had to turn back to Bonn. If the Western Allies refuse to accept East German control of their rail and road communications, they will be forced to depend on their air corridors to Berlin to supply the garrisons here.

Earlier today a flash of alarm swept Berlin when Soviet troops were erroneously reported to be withdrawing.

The report was started by East Berliners who said they had seen the Russians emptying their headquarters compound in the East Berlin district of Karlshorst this morning.

Transfers Held Normal

Yuri Beburov, the Soviet Embassy's press attaché in East Berlin, said that some persons housed in the compound were leaving for Moscow. But he emphasized that these were normal transfers unrelated to the Soviet proposal to end the city's four-power status.

The Soviet commandant, Maj. Gen. Matvei V. Zakharov, was reported to be still in Berlin tonight and Soviet soldiers were still manning the rail and road checkpoints.

There was some expectation among West Berlin officials that the Soviet proposals on Berlin's status would be delivered to the Allies this week-end. The question being asked here was whether Premier Nikita S. Khrushchev would await the Allies' reply before taking action.

The Soviet and East German press has said that Allied con-

Continued on Page 3, Column 3

U.S. SAYS HUNGARY MUST HEED PACTS TO ACHIEVE AMITY

Note to Budapest Charges Moscow, Not Washington, Interferes in Affairs

Text of U. S. note to Hungary appears on Page 6.

Special to The New York Times.

... DAPEST, Hungary, Nov. ... he United States has told ... ry that improvement in ... ations between their Gov- ... s is up to the Hun- ...

... e to the Ministry of ... ffairs, made public ... United States Gov- ... d it considered that ... ovement depended ... nd basically upon ... n Government's ... willingness to live ... national obliga- ... United Nations ... e Treaty of ...

... Government ... ited States ... accusing ... rference ... affairs ... e two ... nor- ...

GEROSA'S CHARGE TERMED 'FICTION' BY SCHOOL BOARD

Members Assert His Report on Waste in Construction Used 'Dubious' Cases

WARN AGAINST POLITICS

Controller Finds 'Untruth' in Statement—Both Sides Promise More Details

The text of reply to Gerosa is printed on Page 12.

By IRA HENRY FREEMAN

The Board of Education yesterday characterized Controller Lawrence E. Gerosa's charge of waste in school construction as an "amazing mathematical fiction."

The nine members of the board and John J. Theobald, Superintendent of Schools, joined unanimously in "summary" replies to the Controller's accusations.

Mr. Gerosa declared last Monday, in a long analysis by his engineers, that $100,000,000 of a $500,000,000 school-building program had been wasted in "frills" and "extravagance" in the last seven years.

The board promised detailed answers later. It referred by innuendo to the Controller's rumored wish to become the next Mayor when it expressed "hopes that neither personal ambitions nor desire for political preferment will be interjected into the situation."

Reply by Gerosa

"A preliminary examination of the Board of Education's statement," Mr. Gerosa said last night, "indicates a wide area of untruth and misinformation, which I will answer in detail at the earliest opportunity."

The board declared it would "welcome any fair inquiry into its affairs," but it made no mention of the impending investigation by the State Commission of Investigation.

Controller Gerosa's estimate of $100,000,000 waste was "apparently arrived at by taking isolated examples of dubious validity," the board said. These examples were then applied to the total $500,000,000 building program over a "not too clearly stated period," it continued.

The Controller's report in-

Continued on Page 12, Column 5

PATROL OF METERS BY WOMEN URGED

Parking Force of 100 Asked —Motorcycle Men Added

By JOSEPH C. INGRAHAM

A program to hire civilians to handle parking enforcement is being drafted for Mayor Wagner's approval. The initial plan calls for 100 "meter maids" who would work with the city's Traffic Department.

The decision to shift responsibility for parking violations from the undermanned Police Department was taken yesterday by the Mayor's Interdepartmental Traffic Council. The action came twenty-four hours after the group had made known that it still was trying to reach a conclusion on whether persons outside the police force were necessary to solve the parking problem.

Under the "meter maid" proposal, the women workers would perform a variety of traffic-violation duties in addition to checking meters. It was proposed that widows of policemen and firemen get preference for the posts if they qualified.

The traffic council acted in the wake of another move by Police Commissioner Stephen P. Kennedy to stem parking abuses. He announced the assignment of "flying squads" of motorcycle men to the midtown's most congested area—Thirty-fourth to Sixtieth Street from Third to Ninth Avenue, inclusive.

The Commissioner said he was bringing in twenty-six motorcycle men from parkway policing to the heart of Manhattan. They will have the dual function of cutting parking violations and chasing down "red light jumpers."

The extra motorcycle men

Continued on Page 13, Column 2

ON STRIKE: Employes ... continent International A...

ALL T.W.A. FLIGHT... HALTED BY STRIKE

Union of Mechanics Rejects Offer Made 3 Minutes Before Walkout Time

By The Associated Press

KANSAS CITY, Mo., Nov. 21—The 7,000 union mechanics of Trans World Airlines went on strike today. T. W. A. immediately canceled all flights.

The International Association of Machinists posted pickets at T. W. A. stations across the United States. Flights in progress continued to their destinations but no new flights were started.

For several hours after the machinists had struck at 11 A. M. there were reports that the strike might be short-lived. Cliff Miller, chairman of I. A. M.'s District 142, said that he had received an offer from company negotiators just three minutes before the strike deadline. Charles Thomas, T. W. A.'s president, announced in mid-afternoon that the union had rejected the offer.

No Pact for a Year

In a letter to employes, Mr. Thomas said:

"The company withdraws the offers which it has made, and any future negotiations will start at present wage levels and will not include any previous offers of retroactive pay."

The union's contract with T. W. A. expired Oct. 1, 1957.

Informed of Mr. Thomas' statement, Mr. Miller said that "inasmuch as Mr. Thomas' letter covers an item not presently in the dispute, I am sincerely convinced that a clear understanding of the issues on the part of T. W. A. will lead to an early and satisfactory settlement of the dispute."

He declined to specify the

Continued on Page 22, Column 3

Mel Ott, 49, Dies Of Crash Injuries

Associated Press

Mel Ott

Special to The New York Times.

NEW ORLEANS, Nov. 21—Mel Ott, former New York Giants' baseball star and manager, died here today of injuries received in an automobile collision a week ago. He was 49 years old.

Death came to Mr. Ott at 12:35 P. M. Central Standard time, in the operating room of Touro Infirmary, where a team

Continued on Page 18, Column 2

... privat... type ... by the ... posal w... Atomic ... with a... plant w... nificant ... toward ... goal ... power.

The proposal, ... likely to revive ... argument over ... versus private devel... construction of lar... power plants.

The gas-cooled type ... involved in today's pro... become the focal point ... argument. The oppone... Democrats on the Joi... gressional Committee on ... Energy on one side an... Atomic Energy Commission ... the private utility industry ... the other.

Congress Set Deadline

Committee Democrats ha... been pressing for two years f... Government construction of ... gas-cooled reactor on the ground that it was needed to fill a gap in the nation's atomic power development program.

As a compromise with the Administration, Congress this year authorized Government construction of the plant if private industry did not come forward with a proposal. Today's proposal was submitted on the eve of the deadline imposed by Congress and was the only one received by the commission.

The proposal was submitted by the Philadelphia Electric Company, principal sponsor of the project, in collaboration with a newly formed nonprofit corporation known as High Temperature Reactor Development Associates, Inc. Within the corporation are more than fifty private utilities from all sections of the country. It is the largest group of utility concerns that has thus far combined to sponsor a nuclear power project.

Plant to Be 'Short Cut'

The group proposed to build the plant within the commission's power demonstration program. Under that plan private industry bears the responsibility of developing and constructing atomic power plants but receives Government research and development assistance. As proposed the utilities would put up $24,500,000 for construction of the plant and the Government would furnish $14,500,000 in research and development assistance. It would also waive nuclear fuel charges for a five-year period.

The reactor, conceived by General Atomic Division of General Dynamics Corporation, would use thorium and a small proportion of highly enriched uranium as nuclear fuel with graphite as a moderator. It would be cooled by helium gas. The plant would produce 30,000 kilowatts of electricity in its original version and then be improved to turn out 40,000 kilowatts.

The moderate-size plant, scheduled to be completed late in 1962 or early in 1963, would be built within the utility sys-

Continued on Page 10, Column 4

... ects.

Tho... increas... paying ... the feder... aided pro...

Continued ...

ALGERIANS PRESS FREEDOM DEMAND

Rebels Say People Endorse War Until France Grants Full Independence

By HENRY TANNER
Special to The New York Times.

TUNIS, Nov. 21—Members of the Algerian rebel government held secret meetings with Moslems deep in Algeria last month. They returned with what they consider to be a popular mandate to reject any French offer short of full independence and if necessary to continue the war regardless of cost.

They gave the impression that a negotiated agreement was far more remote than it appeared a few weeks ago, in spite of continued talk on both sides about negotiations.

Abdel Hafid Boussouf, Minister of Communications, said he crossed the Algerian border early in October and met with Moslem men and women as French guns were pounding near-by hills.

The villagers told him they had nothing against negotiation with the French provided it led to independence, he said. But they also told him that an agreement settling for less than independence would be treason, he added.

The Moslems he interrogated

Continued on Page 2, Column 5

Quee... ...ial Balance

Whites Re... Sales of H... Negroes M...

By PETER KI...

A city agency is help... homeowners who are ... maintain a racially ... community in an a... which Negroes are movin... the agency and the res... want to avoid any slide int... ghetto patterns that have ... curred elsewhere.

The Commission on Int... group Relations for the last six weeks has been starting block discussions and helping to create a Neighborhood Relations Committee in the Springfield Gardens section of southeast Queens.

One result has been the appearance in the last fortnight of the following sign in the windows of a least forty homes owned by whites who are resisting panic sales:

"Not for sale. We believe in democracy."

These white residents and others have welcomed the new Negro families.

Mrs. Evelyn Klavens, a parent-teacher representative of 137-22 Southgate Street, has stressed how well the neighborhood schools have got along over the years with integrated student bodies drawn from areas as far away as St. Albans.

Of Southgate Street's twenty-four homes, five are occupied by Negro families. Thurston

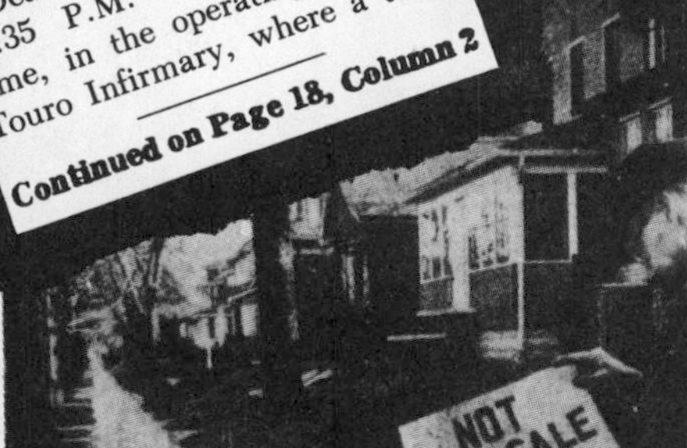

The New York Times

This sign has appeared in several homes on Southgate Street in Springfield Gardens section of southeast Queens, where homeowners are seeking racially balanced neighborhood.

Street, the next one south, received two Negro families last summer among its twenty-one. Each block-long street has about ten staying-here signs.

The one-and-a-quarter-square-mile area from a few blocks west of Farmers Boulevard eastward to Cross Island Parkway, between Merrick Road and 130th Avenue, has about 20,000 residents. Bernard Berlly, a lawyer and co-chairman of the new committee, says perhaps 10 per cent are Negroes, many clustered in specific blocks west

Continued on Page 44, Column 2

Mel Ott Dies of Auto Crash Injuries

Continued From Page 1, Col. 3

of seven surgeons prepared to operate for the second time in twenty-four hours.

Funeral services will be held at 2 P. M. tomorrow from the P. J. McMahon & Sons funeral home here. Interment will be in Metairie Cemetery.

Mr. Ott was transferred to New Orleans yesterday by ambulance from Memorial Hospital, Gulfport, Miss., where last Saturday he underwent preliminary surgery. The transfer came about as a result of a kidney malfunction.

A hospital spokesman said Mr. Ott died of uremia and the effects of a combination of injuries that resulted in "a massive failure."

In addition to uremia, Mr. Ott had kidney damage, multiple fractures, shock, six broken ribs, broken legs, a broken arm, head injuries and "other complications," the hospital spokesman added.

On his arrival at Touro Infirmary Mr. Ott underwent a seven-and-one-half-hour operation.

His wife, Mildred, also 49, was also seriously injured in the accident. She was scheduled to be transferred to a New Orleans hospital for possible surgery.

The accident occurred last Friday night on U. S. Highway 90 near Bay St. Louis, Miss. The Ott automobile had just pulled away from a highway restaurant and collided with another car. The driver of the other car, Lester F. Curry, was killed in the crash.

In addition to his widow, Mr. Ott is survived by two daughters, Mrs. Philip Loria and Miss Barbara Ott; his mother, Mrs. Charles Ott Sr.; a brother, Charles Ott; a sister, Mrs. Louis Rhodes, and a grandson. All are from the metropolitan New Orleans area.

Blazed Way to Glory

Mel Ott blazed his way to baseball glory by hitting home runs. Only two men — Babe Ruth and Jimmy Foxx—ever hit more.

Ruth and Foxx were American Leaguers through most of their careers. No one else in the National League ever came close to Ott. When his playing days were over, in 1947, the Giant right fielder had held more batting records than any other National League player. In three world series, he hit four home runs and batted .295.

He set the National League lifetime records for home runs, runs scored, runs batted in, total bases, bases on balls, extra-base hits and others.

For nearly six years, from 1942 through the middle of 1948, Ott managed the Giants. World War II took so many younger men from baseball dugouts that he was able to stretch his playing days by several years.

But in 1946, in thirty-one games, he hit only one ball out of the park. The next year he went to bat four times as a pinch-hitter, had no hits and decided to surrender his place on the players' roster.

Only four years earlier, in 1942, he had hit thirty home runs. Then he was the Ott the fans will long remember.

Exactly 511 times in his twenty-one years' service with the Giants, an opposing outfielder would race to the fence, turn, brace himself a second and then go limp as the ball sailed overhead and out of reach, and Ott had another home run.

Many of the four-baggers were made in the Polo Grounds, the discount house of baseball. At the foul-pole, the right-field fence was 257 feet from the batter's box. And Ott, a left-handed hitter, could pull the ball sharply down the line.

In home-run output Ruth leads all the rest, with 714. Foxx is second with 534. Ott's 511 was third, Lou Gehrig, with 494, and Ted Williams, with 482, come next.

Oddly, all these men outstripped him in stature. Ott generated his power from a compact frame. He stood 5 feet 9 inches and never weighed more than about 170 pounds.

Ott's signature at bat was an unorthodox, high-stepping stride with his right foot just before he brought his bat around. He looked as if he were stepping over a stovepipe, and any high school coach could have told him it was dreadful form. But the next thing a pitcher knew, the ball was in the bleachers.

John J. McGraw, manager of the Giants, was captivated by the smooth, rhythmic, level swing of Ott's bat when the youth was sent to him in 1925 at the age of 16.

A New Orleans lumberman, Harry Williams, and a close friend of McGraw's was the actual discoverer of this "diamond gem." It was Williams

(continued)

Mel Ott carried his bat low and his front foot high as he stepped into a pitch.

who gave Mel the fare to New York.

Ott always got a chuckle out of the fact that actually it was a penny post card that was his passport to fame. He received it in the summer of 1925, at a time when he was playing semi-pro ball with the Paterson Grays, a team that Williams operated as a hobby. The card read: "Report to McGraw, Polo Grounds, New York." It was signed: John J. McGraw.

But Ott thought somebody was pulling a joke on him and paid no attention to it. It wasn't until several weeks later that Williams, returning to New Orleans from a trip, tracked down Ott and virtually chased the youngster to New York with a bat.

Ott said he was a catcher. But McGraw, spotting his heavy legs, knew they would tie up in muscular knots from the crouching grind of catching. He made him an outfielder.

Remained With Team

Because McGraw wanted no one to tamper with that flawless swing, or even with that strange, goose-step stride, Ott was permitted not even a game of minor league seasoning. He stayed with the Giants through his entire playing career.

In his first season with the Giants, in 1926, Ott appeared in thirty-five games, came to bat sixty times and had twenty-three hits for a .383 average. But he hit no home runs. The next year he batted .282 and got one home run in 163 at bats.

Then, in 1928, Ott found the range. He hit eighteen home runs. In 1929, he swatted forty-two—a mark he never matched again in sixteen home-run hitting seasons.

Ott's open secret was steady production, not sensational spurts. He led the league only three times in total home runs. But over the years, he was dozens ahead.

His lifetime batting average was .304. His best year, outside of his short first season, was in 1930, when he hit .349. His worst, outside of the last two seasons, was 1943. He hit .234.

Ott was quiet, deliberative and gentlemanly. He was soft-spoken with a sort of shy humor. As a manager he was no disciple of the legendary McGraw, who threw wild tantrums and won the nickname "Little Napoleon."

However, there were occasions, rare perhaps, when, as manager, he gave vent to outbursts of McGravian temper. Once, during the war years, a Giant pitcher, Bill Voiselle, with the count two strikes and no balls on the batter, grooved the next pitch. Johnny Hopp of the Cardinals whacked it for a ninth-inning triple, a blow that cost the Giants the game. And it cost Voiselle a $1,000 fine.

As a player, even tractable Ott was not exempt from McGraw fines. Once the Old Man ruled there was to be no card playing in the clubhouse in the forenoon of a ball game. One morning, though, it rained and as it did not look as if there possibly could be a game, Ott thought there would be no harm in sitting in on a few hands with several other players. But McGraw walked into the room and it cost each player $50.

Although Ott achieved his greatest fame as a home run slugger, he also ranked for many years as one of the outstanding defensive outfielders of his time. Despite short, stocky legs and heavily muscled thighs, which almost always had to be taped before a game to fend off Charley horses, Melvin was able to cover an amazing lot of ground in the outfield.

McGraw once said of him, "This kid can just about play anywhere on a ball field, except maybe pitch." In 1937 Ott gave a practical demonstration of his rare versatility. Bill Terry, then manager of the Giants, was sorely pressed for a third baseman and finally called on Ott to help him out. Mel jumped into the position and played it to the manner born. It helped the Giants win the pennant that year for their second in a row.

Apart from his heavy legs, Mel had one other physical defect. He was nearsighted. In his later years it began to show in his play and may have hastened his retirement as a player.

Called 'Master Melvin'

A sports writer dubbed Ott "Master Melvin" at the very outset, and the title stuck with him all the way, like a piece of gum on the shoe.

As a manager, Ott got off to a satisfactory start. He brought the team in third after three straight seasons in the second division under Bill Terry. That was in 1942. After that the going was rough.

In July, 1948, he was relieved of field duties and moved into the Giants' front office in favor of the flamboyant Leo Durocher of Dodger fame.

Later, he went to Oakland in the Pacific Coast League as manager. In 1953, he said he was quitting baseball to become an executive in the construction business.

By that time he had been voted into the Baseball Hall of Fame by the Baseball Writers' Association.

In recent years, he worked as a baseball broadcaster in Detroit.

Ott's Record With Giants

	G.	AB.	H.	HR.	RBI.	PC.
1926	35	60	23	0	4	.383
1927	82	163	46	1	19	.282
1928	124	435	140	18	77	.322
1929	150	545	179	42	151	.328
1930	148	521	182	25	119	.349
1931	138	497	145	29	115	.292
1932	154	566	180	38	123	.318
1933	152	580	164	23	103	.283
1934	153	582	190	35	135	.326
1935	152	593	191	31	114	.322
1936	150	534	175	33	135	.328
1937	151	545	160	31	95	.294
1938	150	527	164	36	116	.311
1939	125	396	122	27	80	.308
1940	151	536	155	19	79	.289
1941	148	525	150	27	90	.286
1942	152	549	162	30	93	.295
1943	125	380	89	18	47	.234
1944	120	399	115	26	82	.288
1945	135	451	139	21	79	.308
1946	31	68	5	1	4	.074
1947	4	4	0	0	0	.000
Total ..	2,730	9,456	2,876	511	1,860	.304

League Records Held by Ott

Mel Ott set the following National League records:

Most home runs	511
Most runs batted in	1,860
Most total bases	5,041
Most bases on balls	1,708
Most extra-base hits	1,071
Most extra bases on long hits	3,165
Most times hitting two or more home runs in one game	49
Most years thirty or more home runs	8
Most years leading league in bases on balls	6
Most years 100 or more bases on balls	10
Most years playing 150 or more games	10
Most consecutive years playing 100 or more game with one club	18
Most years scoring 100 or more runs .... (tie)	9
Service with one club .... (years)	22

Mel Ott crosses the plate in a 1935 game against the Cubs. Ott led the National League in home runs six times between 1932 and 1942.

The New York Times SUNDAY, SEPTEMBER 3, 1967

Francis Ouimet, Golfer, Is Dead; First Amateur to Win U.S. Open

Gardener's Son Who Won in 1913 Showed Sport Wasn't Only for the Affluent

NEWTON, Mass., Sept. 2 (UPI)—Francis D. Ouimet, who amazed the sports world 54 years ago by upsetting Britain's two greatest golfers to win the United States Open, died today. He was 74 years old.

Mr. Ouimet is survived by two daughters, Mrs. Janice Salvi of Wellesley and Mrs. Barbara McLean of Closter, N. J. Funeral arrangements were incomplete.

An Amateur Sensation

The United States Golf Association's 1963 Open championship was placed at the Country Club in Brookline, Mass., in honor of Mr. Ouimet. It marked the golden anniversary of his triumph in the 1913 Open when he defeated Harry Vardon and Ted Ray, over the same course, in a playoff.

That victory by a slim 20-year-old amateur furnished front-page news for newspapers throughout the world. Overnight Ouimet (wee-met) became a new sports hero as he brought attention to a game that had previously created little international interest.

Until the gardener's son, who lived across the road from the country club, captured the Open, golf had been considered a pastime chiefly for the affluent. British professionals had dominated earlier championships and Ouimet became the first amateur to win the title.

First Round at 13

Ouimet often cut across fairways of the country club on the way to school. With his brother, Wilfred, using cast-off clubs and old golf balls, he played on a three-hole course they had set up in a pasture back of their home. He became a club caddie and played his first round at the age of 13 at a public course.

He won the Greater Boston interscholastic championship in 1909. He entered the national amateur when it was played at the Country Club in 1910. However, to become eligible he had to be a member of an accredited club. He borrowed $25 from his mother to obtain a junior membership at the Woodland Club in Newton.

During the summer, he worked in a Boston dry goods store to repay his mother's loan. Although he failed to qualify in 1911 and 1912, just as he did on his first attempt, by one stroke, he succeeded in 1913 and went to the second round before losing to the defending champion, Jerome Travers, at Garden City, L. I.

Although Ouimet's Open victory became a historic event, he maintained his goal had always been to win the amateur, not the Open. His first national amateur success came in 1914 when he defeated Travers in the final over the Ekwanok course in Manchester, Vt., 6 and 5. Then, 17 years later, he became the amateur champion again by defeating Jack Westland, also by 6 and 5, in the 1931 final at the Beverly course, outside Chicago.

During the 14 championships that intervened, Ouimet qualified 13 times and reached the semifinals six times.

Ouimet was a playing member of eight Walker Cup teams in the biennial series between United States and British amateurs, from 1922 through 1934. He was nonplaying captain of four series from 1936 through 1949 before he asked to retire. He won four singles, lost two and halved two in cup competition. In the foursome matches, his pair won five and lost three. Later he became an executive member of the United States Golf Association.

Won First Jones Trophy

In 1955 when the U.S.G.A. made its first award of the Bob Jones trophy for "distinguished sportsmanship," Ouimet was the recipient. He was honored by many golf associations but he was regarded as a patron saint of caddies when he lent his name to a scholarship fund, organized by the Massachusetts Golf Association, to send caddies to college.

Another occasion he cherished was his 70th birthday gathering, shortly before the anniversary Open, at the Country Club.

Ouimet became the first American to be named a captain of the Royal and Ancient Golf Club of St. Andrews, Scotland. In 1961, following the tradition, he "played himself in" by driving from the first tee of the Old Course at St. Andrews. That evening, the festivities continued as Ouimet, wearing the customary R. and A. long, red jacket, presided. An oil portrait of Ouimet in this colorful garb was subsequently hung in Golf House in New York.

He was a member of a brokerage firm in Boston.

Francis Ouimet returned to the scene and won his second U.S. Amateur Championship—17 years after his first amateur victory.

"All the News That's Fit to Print"

The New York Times

LATE CITY EDITION

Weather: Mostly sunny today; mostly fair tonight. Mostly sunny tomorrow. Temperature range: today 37-53; yesterday 35-47. Details on page C10.

VOL.CXXIX . No. 44,540 | Copyright © 1980 The New York Times | NEW YORK, TUESDAY, APRIL 1, 1980 | 30 cents beyond 50-mile zone from New York City. Higher in air delivery cities. | 25 CENTS

TRANSIT WORKERS STRIKE SUBWAYS AND BUSES AS WAGE TALKS FAIL; L.I.R.R. PARLEY CONTINUES

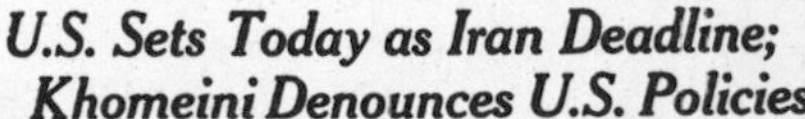

U.S. Sets Today as Iran Deadline; Khomeini Denounces U.S. Policies

Carter Plans to Retaliate if Regime Does Not Act to Take Over Hostages

By BERNARD GWERTZMAN

Special to The New York Times

WASHINGTON, March 31 — President Carter gave Iranian leaders until tomorrow to announce steps to remove the American hostages from the control of Is- lamic militants or face ... economic and ... moves, Ad... today.

At about ... portedly re... ran that o... transferring ... tants to the Go... asked the Unite... imposition of polit... tions for 24 hours.

Factor in U.

The message descri... als the Iranian Govern... ering to effect the del... tages to the Revolutiona...

Transmitted through... the message was report... the United States' decisi... sanctions.

There was cautious anti... White House that Presiden... Bani-Sadr of Iran would ... major speech tomorrow, tha... Revolutionary Council had de... take charge of the 50 America... have been held hostage in the Am... Embassy for 149 days.

But because expectations have ...

Continued on Page A12, Column

Ayatollah Repeats That Fate of Captives Is Still in Hands of Parliament

By JOHN KIFNER

Special to The New York Times

TEHERAN, Iran, ... Ayatollah ... harshl...

A Mysterious A... As a Go-Betwee...

By PHILIP TA...

Special to The New Yo...

WASHINGTON, March 31 — In the absence of normal diplomatic communication between the United States and Iran, Administration sources say that Washington has turned to a small group of foreign lawyers to carry messages to Teheran — a practice that came to light over the weekend during a flurry of reports about official and unofficial messages.

One of them, according to officials, is Héctor Villalón, a politically active lawyer from Argentina now living in Paris. Mr. Villalón, a long-time associate of the late Argentine ruler, Juan Domingo Perón, is known in his homeland as a shadowy figure with a reputation for operating close to the margin of the law at times, according to several Argentine politicians now living in the United States.

A senior Administration official said Mr. Villalón has acted as a go-between with Teheran "more than once."

The exact role being played by Mr. Villalón and others remains unclear, shielded by the Administration as it ex- plo... effor...

But... Villalo... mediar... diploma... unproductiv...

Conti...

MILLIONS FACE DELAYS

Walkout Called Two Hours After Deadline — Court Injunction Ignored

By DAMON STETSON

New York City's 33,000 bus and subway workers struck early this morning, forcing a transportation shutdown that affects millions of riders.

The strike was announced at 2:05 A.M. by Walter Gellhorn, a Columbia University professor and the chairman of the mediation panel in the dispute. "There is a strike," Mr. Gellhorn told reporters at the Sheraton Centre hotel, the site of the talks.

John E. Lawe, the president of Local 100 of the Transport Workers Union, followed Mr. Gellhorn to the microphone after the union's executive board and negotiating committee rejected a proposal for a settlement put forward by the three-member mediation panel.

"That's it," Mr. Lawe said. "The strike is on."

Five Million Rides a Day

Asked if it would be a long strike, Mr. Lawe said, "If we get a decent contract we can live with, we'll go back to work tomorrow."

At a news conference at the hotel around 3 A.M., Richard Ravitch, the chairman of the Metropolitan Transportation Authority, appeared, looking weary, while Governor Carey and Mayor Koch stood behind him.

Mr. Ravitch said, "We will do our best to bring this disupte to an end, but only on reasonable grounds." He added that a resolution of the dispute was "up to the union." He said the union leaders would ...come "a long way down from ...tain."

... Carey took a stern position. ...ey General will enforce all ...s of the Taylor Law," he ...g to the state law that pro- ...by public employees. Mr. ..."There is no requirement ... National Guard at this ...

...which came despite a ...gned yesterday, wipes ...ay transportation that ... rides a day and will ...e city's business and ...

...otiations that also ...es last night, the ... negotiations be- ...il Road and its ...ttlement was ... and Nassau ...6.] ...adline drew

...umn 1

How to Get There

A guide to commuting during ...e strike, pages B6 and B7.

Jesse Owens Dies of Cancer at 66; Hero of the 1936 Berlin Olympics

By FRANK LITSKY

Jesse Owens, whose four gold medals at the 1936 Olympic Games in Berlin made him perhaps the greatest and most famous athlete in track and field history, died of lung cancer yesterday in Tucson, Ariz. He was 66 years old.

In Berlin, Mr. Owens, who was black, scored a triumph that would come to be regarded as not only athletic but also political. Adolf Hitler had intended the Berlin Games to be a showcase for the Nazi doctrine of Aryan supremacy.

A member of what the Nazis mockingly called America's "black auxiliaries," Mr. Owens achieved a feat unmatched in modern times in Olympic track competition. The year before, with a wrenched back so painful that he could not dress or undress without help, he broke five world records and equaled a sixth, all within 45 minutes.

But the Jesse Owens best remembered by many Americans was a public speaker with the ringing, inspirational delivery of an evangelist. Later in his life, he traveled 200,000 miles a year making two or three speeches a week, mostly to sales meetings and conventions, and primarily to white audiences. With his own public relations and marketing concern, he earned more than $100,000 a year.

Mr. Owens, a pack-a-day cigarette smoker for 35 years, had been hospitalized on and off since last Dec. 12. Doctors

Continued on Page D17, Column 1

Associated Press

Jesse Owens saluting the flag after winning one of his four gold medals at Berlin's Olympic Games in 1936.

...at 66; ...erlin Olympics

By FRANK LITSKY

...se Owens, whose four gold medals at the 1936 Olympic Games in Berlin made him perhaps the greatest and most famous athlete in track and field history, died of lung cancer yesterday in Tucson, Ariz. He was 66 years old.

In Berlin, Mr. Owens, who was black, scored a triumph that would come to be regarded as not only athletic but also political. Adolf Hitler had intended the Berlin Games to be a showcase for the Nazi doctrine of Aryan supremacy.

A member of what the Nazis mockingly called America's "black auxiliaries," Mr. Owens achieved a feat unmatched in modern times in Olympic track competition. The year before, with a wrenched back so painful that he could not dress or undress without help, he broke five world records and equaled a sixth, all within 45 minutes.

But the Jesse Owens best remembered by many Americans was a public speaker with the ringing, inspirational delivery of an evangelist. Later in his life, he traveled 200,000 miles a year making two or three speeches a week, mostly to sales meetings and conventions, and primarily to white audiences. With his own public relations and marketing concern, he earned more than $100,000 a year.

Mr. Owens, a pack-a-day cigarette smoker for 35 years, had been hospitalized on and off since last Dec. 12. Doctors

Continued on Page D17, Column 1

Associated Press

Jesse Owens saluting the flag after winning one of his four gold medals at Berlin's Olympic Games in 1936.

United Press International

THIS YEAR, IN CAIRO: Eliahu Ben-Elissar, left, Israel's new Ambassador to Cairo, at the seder, the Passover meal commemorating the deliverance of the Jews from slavery in Egypt. The weeklong holiday began at sundown. Page B2.

INSIDE

Carter Submits His Budget

President Carter, proposing cuts in Government services and benefits, sent Congress a revised, balanced budget for fiscal year 1981. Page B12.

Campaign in Wisconsin

Senator Edward M. Kennedy drew enthusiastic crowds across Wisconsin as he criticized President Carter on the eve of that state's primary. Page B11.

Tate Loses, Holmes Wins

John Tate lost his heavyweight championship on a knockout by Mike Weaver, but Larry Holmes retained the other heavyweight title. Page B13.

Far-Reaching Banking Legislation Signed by President

By CLYDE H. FARNSWORTH

Special to The New York Times

WASHINGTON, March 31 — President Carter signed a new banking law today that is being described as the most far-reaching financial legislation in decades.

Among its main provisions, the new law gradually raises the ceilings on the interest paid to small savers and substantially enhances the monetary control powers of the nation's central bank, the Federal Reserve System.

The legislation, known as the Depository Institutions Deregulation and Monetary Control Bill, will "help control inflation, strengthen our financial institutions and help small savers," the President said at the White House signing ceremonies.

For the consumer, the statute phases out over six years the interest ceilings on passbook accounts; increases from $40,000 to $100,000 the amount of Federal insurance on bank savings, and authorizes the payment of interest on checking accounts, currently permitted only in New England, New York and New Jersey.

The law also permanently overrides state-imposed ceilings on mortgage rates unless states act within three years to re-enact them, wipes out for three years interest rate limits on agricultural and business loans of more than $25,000, and

Continued on Page D10, Column 4

Jesse Owens Dies of Lung Cancer at 66

Continued From Page A1

said the cancer was inoperable, and since January he had received radiation and chemotherapy treatment at hospitals in Phoenix and Tucson.

He re-entered the University of Arizona Health Sciences Center in Tucson a week ago. He lapsed into a coma Saturday night and died at 3:40 A.M., Tucson time, yesterday without having regained consciousness. His wife, Ruth, and other family members were at his bedside.

No Response to Drugs

Dr. Stephen E. Jones of the university hospital, who headed the medical team treating Mr. Owens, said his patient had remained "remarkably optimistic and hopeful that he was going to survive." However, Dr. Jones said, there was no positive response to experimental drugs tried on Mr. Owens.

The White House issued a statement yesterday in which President Carter said, "Perhaps no athlete better symbolized the human struggle against tyranny, poverty and racial bigotry."

In Vienna, Simon Wiesenthal, who has spent years tracking former Nazis, proposed that an avenue leading to the Olympic Stadium, now in West Berlin, be renamed for Mr. Owens. Mr. Weisenthal said that when he made similar suggestions in the past, he was told that streets could not be named for living persons.

In Phoenix, which had become his hometown, Mr. Owens's body will lie in state tomorrow in the Capitol Rotunda. His burial will be in Chicago, but details were still pending late yesterday.

Father Was a Sharecropper

James Cleveland Owens was born Sept. 12, 1913, in Danville, Ala., the son of a sharecropper and the grandson of slaves. The youngster picked cotton until he and his family moved to Cleveland when he was 9. There, a schoolteacher asked the youth his name.

"J.C." he replied.

She thought he had said "Jesse," and he had a new name.

He ran his first race at age 13. He became a nationally known sprinter at East Technical High School in Cleveland, slim and lithe at 163 pounds. He ran with fluid grace. There were no starting blocks then; sprinters merely dug holes at the starting line in tracks of cinder or dirt.

After high school, he went to Ohio State University, paying his way as a $100-a-month night elevator operator because he had no athletic scholarship. As a sophomore, in his first Big Ten championships, he achieved a harvest of records even greater than the Olympic glory he would attain a year later.

A week before the Big Ten meet, which was held in Ann Arbor, Mich., Mr. Owens and a fraternity brother were wrestling playfully when they tumbled down a flight of stairs. Mr. Owens's back hurt so much that he could not work out all week.

Associated Press

Jesse Owens in 1976

Owens takes the baton from Frank Wykoff during the 1936 Olympic Games in Germany.

Coach Larry Snyder and teammates had to help him in and out of the car that drove him to the track for the meet.

There, in a vain attempt to lessen the back pain, he sat for half an hour in a hot tub. He did not warm up or even stretch. At the last minute, he rejected suggestions that he withdraw from the meet and said he would try, event by event.

He tried, and the results are in the record book. On May 25, 1935, from 3:15 to 4 P.M., Jesse Owens successively equaled the world record for the 100-yard dash (9.4 seconds), broke the world record for the broad jump, now called the long jump, with his only attempt (26 feet 8¼ inches, which remained the record for 25 years), broke the world record for the 220-yard dash (20.3 seconds, which also bettered the record for 200 meters) and broke the world record for the 220-yard low hurdles (22.6 seconds, which also bettered the record for the 200-meter low hurdles).

Kenneth L. (Tug) Wilson, the Big Ten commissioner, watched in awe and said: "He is a floating wonder, just like he had wings."

The next year, with the Italians occupying Ethiopia, the Japanese in Manchuria, the Germans moving into the Rhineland and a civil war starting in Spain, the Olympic Games were held in Berlin. Despite pleas that the United States boycott the Olympics to protest Nazi racial policies, American officials voted to participate.

The United States Olympic track team, of 66 athletes, included 10 blacks. The Nazis derided the Americans for relying on what the Nazis called an inferior race, but of the 11 individual gold medals in track won by the American men, six were won by blacks.

The hero was Mr. Owens. He won the 100-meter dash in 10.3 seconds, the 200-meter dash in 20.7 seconds and the broad jump at 26 feet 5½ inches, and he led off for the United States team that won the 400-meter relay in 39.8 seconds.

His individual performances broke two Olympic records and, except for an excessive following wind, would have broken the third. The relay team broke the world record. His 100-meter and 200-meter times would have won Olympic medals through 1964, his broad-jump performance through 1968.

Actually, Mr. Owens had not been scheduled to run in the relay. Marty Glickman and Sam Stoller were, but American Olympic officials, led by Avery Brundage, wanted to avoid offending the Nazis. They replaced Mr. Glickman and Mr. Stoller, both Jews, with Mr. Owens and Ralph Metcalfe, both blacks.

Hitler did not congratulate any of the American black winners, a subject to which Mr. Owens addressed himself for the rest of his life.

"It was all right with me," he said years later. "I didn't go to Berlin to shake hands with him, anyway. All I know is that I'm here now, and Hitler isn't.

"When I came back, after all those stories about Hitler and his snub, I came back to my native country, and I couldn't ride in the front of the bus. I had to go to the back door. I couldn't live where I wanted. Now what's the difference?"

Having returned from Berlin, he received no telephone call from President Franklin D. Roosevelt, was not asked to visit the White House. Official recognition from his own country did not come until 1976, when President Gerald R. Ford presented him the Presidential Medal of Freedom. Three years later, President Carter gave him the Living Legends Award.

Nor were there any lucrative contracts for an Olympic hero after the 1936 Games. Mr. Owens became a playground janitor because he could not find a better job. He ended his career as an amateur runner and accepted money to race against cars, trucks, motorcycles, horses and dogs. He toured with the Harlem Globetrotters basketball team.

"Sure, it bothered me," he said later. "But at least it was an honest living. I had to eat."

In time, the four gold medals changed his life.

"They have kept me alive over the years," he once said. "Time has stood still for me. That golden moment dies hard."

He became a disk jockey, then ran his public relations and marketing concern, first in Chicago and then in Phoenix.

Celebrated as a Speaker

He also became celebrated as a speaker, using about five basic speeches with interchangeable parts. Each speech praised the virtues of patriotism, clean living and fair play. His delivery was old-fashioned spellbinding, a far cry from the days when he stuttered. Even in casual conversations, he spoke in sweeping tones.

"When he enters a room," wrote Jon Hendershott in Track and Field News, "he doesn't so much take it over as envelop it."

William Oscar Johnson, writing in Sports Illustrated, described him as "a kind of all-round super combination of 19th-century spellbinder and 20th-century plastic p.r. man, full-time banquet guest, eternal glad-hander, evangelistic small-talker . . . what you might call a professional good example."

Not everyone agreed. During the 1968 Olympics in Mexico City, when Mr. Owens attempted to mediate with militant American black athletes on behalf of the United States Olympic Committee, critics called him "Uncle Tom." He wrote a 1970 book, "Blackthink," decrying racial militancy, and a 1972 book, "I Have Changed," saying the ideas in his first book were wrong.

In his later years, Mr. Owens walked two miles every morning and swam and lifted weights at the Phoenix Y.M.C.A. He weighed 180 pounds.

"I don't jog," he said, "because I can't run flat-footed. And at 60 years old you're crazy to be out there running."

An Owens Sampler

On American black athletes who question the value of their gold medals: Any black who strives to achieve in this country should think in terms of not only himself but also how he can reach down and grab another black child and pull him to the top of the mountain where he is. This is what a gold medal does to you.

•

On dignity: Regardless of his color, a man who becomes a recognized athlete has to learn to walk 10 feet tall. But he must have his dignity off the athletic field.

•

On material rewards: Material reward is not all there is. How many meals can a man eat? How many cars can he drive? In how many beds can he sleep? All of life's wonders are not reflected in material wealth.

•

On the value of sport: We all have dreams. But in order to make dreams into reality, it takes an awful lot of determination, dedication, self-discipline and effort. These things apply to everyday life. You learn not only the sport but things like respect of others, ethics in life, how you are going to live, how you treat your fellow man, how you live with your fellow man.

•

On the moment before Olympic competition: You think about the number of years you have worked to the point where you are able to stand on that day to represent your nation. It's a nervous, a terrible feeling. You feel, as you stand there, as if your legs can't carry the weight of your body. Your stomach isn't there, and your mouth is dry, and your hands are wet with perspiration. And you begin to think in terms of all those years that you have worked. In my particular case, the 100 meters, as you look down the field 109 yards 2 feet away, and recognizing that after eight years of hard work that this is the point that I had reached and that all was going to be over in 10 seconds. Those are great moments in the lives of individuals.

The New York Times WEDNESDAY, JUNE 17, 1970

Brian Piccolo Is Dead at 26; Halfback on the Chicago Bears

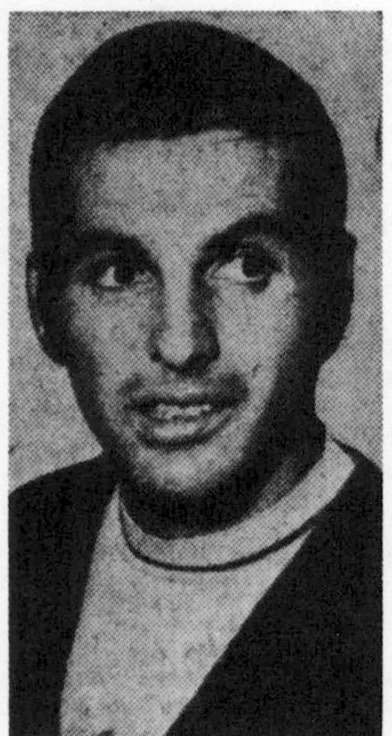

Associated Press

Brian Piccolo

Brian Piccolo, a halfback for the Chicago Bears football team died here yesterday in Memorial Hospital for Cancer and Allied Diseases. The 26-year-old athlete's death was attributed to cancer.

Piccolo played in the shadow of one of professional football's greatest stars, Gale Sayers of the Chicago Bears. Yet Sayers payed tribute to Piccolo's fight against cancer during the last eight months.

Sayers was voted an award as pro football's most courageous athlete in 1969 for the manner in which he returned to action after a knee operation. In receiving the award at a banquet here on May 25, Sayers said, "Brian is the one who should get this award. He is the one who knows about courage."

The next day Sayers gave the trophy to Piccolo in Memorial Hospital.

Louis Brian Piccolo, who was born in Pittsfield, Mass., subsequently moved to Florida, where he graduated from St. Thomas Aquinas High School in Fort Lauderdale. He attended Wake Forest College, Winston Salem, N.C. and in his senior year there was voted an all-American player. He led all the major college players in yards gained rushing and in scoring. To his surprise, however, he was not drafted by the professional teams. At 6 feet, 205 pounds, the scouts considered him to be too small.

The Bears, however, took a chance and signed him as a free agent for a modest bonus. He was hurt and did not make the team in his first season of 1965, but became a squad member the next year.

He seldomly played until Sayers hurt his knee late in the 1968 season. Piccolo stepped into the regular halfback slot for the last five games, carried the ball 76 times for 269 yards and caught 15 passes for 155 yards.

He chalked up 450 yards rushing in 1968 on 123 tries, and caught 28 passes for 291 yards.

Last season he was a part-time player again until just before Thanksgiving when he was hospitalized for treatment of a cough. There was a tumorous growth in his chest and three operations followed.

"Ah, he was a tough one," said George Halas Sr., the long-time owner of the Bears. "He was so young to die with a future that held so much for him."

In the off-season, Mr. Piccolo was a stock and bond salesman for a Chicago brokerage firm.

Survivors include his widow, Joy, and three daughters.

Brian Piccolo of the 1967 Chicago Bears breaks tackle against the Vikings and goes for yardage.

The New York Times

SATURDAY, MARCH 23, 1974

Revson Killed in Crash in South Africa

Special to The New York Times

JOHANNESBURG, March 22—Peter Revson, America's top road-racing driver, was killed today when his car crashed and burst into flames during a practice run for the South Africa Grand Prix on March 30.

Revson, a 35-year-old New Yorker, was at the wheel of a sleek black Ford UOP Shadow when it careened off the track at Barbecue Bend on the Kyalami course. The Formula One car stood on end and wrapped itself around the metal safety barrier.

Witnesses said a steering component apparently failed. The accident occured during unofficial practice as Revson, who had been having trouble with the suspension on his British-based, American sponsored car took the Shadow out for another few laps.

Revson's younger half-brother, Doug, was killed in a 1967 racing crash in Spain.

Throughout his 14-year career, "Revvie" Revson, as the older brother was called, complained of being described as the "heir" to the Revlon cosmetics fortune. It was an erroneous tag he never managed to shake.

I'm the poor relation," Revson used to say. "I think I'm about 11th in line."

His uncle, Charles Revson, founded the Revlon empire. His father, Martin Revson, owns Dell Laboratories of New York.

Only a few spectators were seated around the Kyalami circuit during this afternoon's practice. Some of them, sitting high in the main-straight stands, saw the crash. They stood up and screamed, "Fire!" to alert the fire crew and ambulance driver.

A thick cloud of black smoke climbed into the sky as spectators scrambled through thick grass toward the spot. Race officials said Revson was killed on impact in the 160-mile-an-hour crash. Graham Hill, a two-time world driving champion, helped pull Revson's body from the wreckage.

Later, the British driver returned to the site of the crash and said: "Why does it have to happen like this? There was nothing going against him. This was supposed to be jut an ordinary day's practice."

Some of the drivers entered in the race gathered in an angry cluster after the crash, criticizing the fire precautions at the Kyalami track. The fire wagon on the scene expended its supply of extinguishers without success, and had to go back for more.

Marks on the track suggested that Revson had gone into a violent skid before slamming up against the metal barrier. Eddie Keizan, a Formula One driver from South Africa, was some distance behind Revson's car. He brought his racer skidding to a halt and helped in the futile rescue attempt. Keizan refused to speak about the accident.

"This is something we keep to ourselves," he said.

Revson's parents objected to his decision to race cars, and his mother saw him in action only once—in his debut at Kahuku Point, Hawaii, in 1960. According to Revson, his mother stood on a sandy point near an abandoned air strip and kept saying to friends "Look at that damn fool!"

Later when he reached the big time, Revson took pride in telling interviewers, "I'm a professional race driver. That's where I make my money."

By then, there was never any doubt about Revson's ability to make money on his own. In 1971, the year he won the pole position for the Indianapolis 500 and then finished second in the race, his earnings came to about $300,000.

In the cliff's-edge world of auto racing, Revson evoked the kind of glamorous image associated more with fiction than with fact. He was dashing, handsome, affluent and single, a dark-haired bachelor.

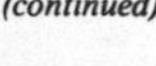
(continued)

Peter Revson, 1971

Revson on the winner's rostrum after finishing the 1973 John Player Grand Prix in London.

whose liaisons with beautiful women sometimes overshadowed his 200-mile-an-hour routine on the race course.

"He liked his women," said one racing observer. "And women liked him."

His most recent steady girlfriend was Marjorie Wallace of Indianapolis, the first American to win the Miss World beauty pageant. Miss Wallace was forced to give up the title earlier this year because of "unfavorable publicity."

Yet, Revson, more subdued and introspective than most people realized, tried hard to shake the Jet-Set image. On the racing circuit, he was not exceptionally close to any of the other drivers.

"I'm a Jet-Set wreck," he once said, referring to the extensive traveling he had to do to to compete internationally.

In New York City, Revson stayed at his father's Park Avenue penthouse apartment. He also maintained a bachelor "pad" in Redondo Beach, Calif.

Though he spent time at Columbia, Cornell and the University of Hawaii, Revson never graduated from college. He made his debut in the Indianapolis 500 in 1969, and finished fifth after starting from last place in a field of 33 cars.

"I was so far back," he said, "I couldn't hear the man say, 'Start your engines.'"

Disappointment on Award

Despite the fifth-place finish, he lost the rookie-of-the-year award to seventh place Mark Donohue because of what he called "politics."

In 1971, Revson won the Indy 500 pole position with a record qualifying speed of 178.696 miles an hour. He earned $103,198 as runner-up to Al Unser.

Last year, driving for the McLaren team, he became only the fifth American to win a Formula One Grand Prix race. He won two of them—the British and the Canadian. Colleagues considered him quick and smooth on the race course, at his best when the equipment was working properly.

He was regarded as a gifted driver who was never blessed with really good equipment until 1971. The major knock against his driving was that he sometimes had difficulty adjusting when things went wrong mechanically, and would tend to slow down instead of understeering or oversteering. But colleagues said he was not the kind of driver who made mistakes.

Revson left the McLaren team at the end of last season and signed with Shadow for the Formula One and Can-Am series. He had committed himself to drive for Roger Penske in this year's Indy 500.

At sunset tonight, the wreckage of his car was still smoking. All that was distinguishable from what had once been a proud racing car were the Shadow's number, 16, and a jagged piece of metal on which was inscribed the name—Peter Revson.

Follmer Says, 'It Hurts'

Special to The New York Times

HAMPTON, Ga., March 22—George Follmer, the man who drove Peter Revson's ill-fated UOP Shadow last year reacted to the driver's death today with the comment: "Lord, it hurts."

Follmer, preparing here for Sunday's Atlanta 500 stock-car race, was considered Revson's closest friend on the racing circuit.

"He was kind of a loner," said Follmer, "but he took racing very seriously. It was the most important thing in his life. I know he didn't crash because he made a mistake. He just didn't make mistakes."

Peter Revson (center) poses with Mark Donahue (left) and Bobby Unser a week before the 1972 Indianapolis 500. Revson was unable to complete the race due to mechanical trouble.

"All the News That's Fit to Print"

The New York Times.

LATE CITY EDITION

U.S. Weather Bureau Report (Page 93) forecasts: Cloudy, becoming fair today; fair, cool tonight and tomorrow. Temp. Range: 48—37; yesterday: 47—33.

VOL. CXV..No. 39,402. © 1965 by The New York Times Company. Times Square, New York, N. Y. 10036 NEW YORK, FRIDAY, DECEMBER 10, 1965. TEN CENTS

QUILL CALLS OFF DEC. 15 WALKOUT; 3 WILL MEDIATE

Kheel, Garrett, Feinsinger Chosen for Labor Panel—T.W.U. Lauds Selection

BARGAINING TO RESUME

Wagner and Lindsay Team Up to Press Peace Effort —Joint Statement Issued

By HOMER BIGART

Michael J. Quill called off last night the Christmas season transit strike he had threatened for 5 A.M. on Dec. 15.

The crusty 60-year-old leader of the Transport Workers Union relented after Mayor Wagner and Mayor-elect John V. Lindsay had persuaded Theodore W. Kheel to join a three-man mediation panel.

Mr. Kheel, who previously said he wanted "no part" of the mediation effort, telephoned his acceptance at about 6:20 P.M. His presence on the panel was especially desired by Mr. Quill, although the labor leader had said he would settle for "any one man or woman who understands the subway system."

2 Others Appointed

Other members of the three-man panel, announced by the Mayor at a special news conference at City Hall, are Sylvester Garrett of Pittsburgh, permanent arbitrator for the United Steelworkers Union and the United States Steel Corporation, and Nathan Feinsinger, professor of law at the University of Wisconsin and arbitrator for General Motors and the United Auto Workers Union.

The Mayor said he was reading a statement written by himself and Mayor-elect Lindsay.

He said that all three panelists had asked for informal meetings with the Mayor and the Mayor-elect.

"We are pleased to extend an invitation to do so," the Mayor said.

All three said they must clear prior commitments before taking the job, the Mayor said, but he added: "We do not anticipate that any of these matters are likely to keep them from serving."

Ringed about the Mayor's reception room were 50 burly leaders of the Transport Workers Union, who applauded warmly

Continued on Page 43, Column 2

BRANCH RICKEY, 83, DIES IN MISSOURI

A Leading Baseball Figure—Helped Break Color Bar

By United Press International

COLUMBIA, Mo. Dec. 9—Branch Rickey, a dominant figure in baseball for half a century, died tonight in Boone County Memorial Hospital at the age of 83.

He broke the color barrier in the major leagues and developed the farm system.

Mr. Rickey had remained unconscious in the hospital since he collapsed with a heart attack the night of Nov. 13 while being inducted into the Missouri Sports Hall of Fame.

Mr. Rickey, who developed baseball dynasties with the St. Louis Cardinals and Brooklyn Dodgers, had left a St. Louis hospital Nov. 13 so he could attend the Missouri-Oklahoma football game and make his acceptance speech at the Sports Hall of Fame banquet that night.

Collapsed During Speech

He was scheduled to go back to the hospital after the ceremonies. But he collapsed shortly after he had started to talk.

"I don't believe I'm going to be able to speak any longer," Mr. Rickey said as he slumped over before the stunned audience.

The cigar-chomping Mr. Rickey, who throughout his career declined to attend Sunday baseball games because of a promise to his mother and who was seldom known to say anything stronger than his famous "Judas Priest," remained in the hospital's intensive-care ward until his death, continuously receiving oxygen.

Mr. Rickey's wife, Mrs. Jane

Continued on Page 55, Column 1

Hartford Proposes Cafe Plan Changes; Lindsay Is Still Cool

By SAMUEL KAPLAN

Huntington Hartford has offered to modify drastically his plan for a sidewalk [...] Central Park to ma[...]ceptable to Mayor-elec[...] V. Lindsay, who has op[...] it. Mr. Hartford has [...] the city $862,500 toward[...] cost of the cafe.

Mr. Lindsay and his [...]coming Park Commissione[...] Thomas P. F. Hoving, wer[...] told of the proposed change[...] at a private meeting with M[...] Hartford on Monday night.

They replied that they were "not excited" by the offer but that they would consider it.

They then asked Mr. Hartford if he would consider a list of projects he could sponsor with his gift instead of the sidewalk cafe. These suggestions included vest-pocket parks in Harlem and on the Lower East Side and small kiosks for eating in Central Park.

Mr. Hartford said in an interview yesterday, using Mr.

Continued on Page 43, Column 7

LINDSAY STUDYING MOSES' CITY POST

Removal From His Highway Job or Bargaining With Him Seen as Choices

By RICHARD WITKIN

Mayor-elect John V. Lindsay has begun grappling with one of the more delicate issues he will face in City Hall—what his relationship will be with Robert Moses.

Mr. Lindsay is reliably reported to have put researchers to work to determine if he has the legal right to oust Mr. Moses as coordinator of Federal, state and city highways.

Initial indications are that he can. It is not yet clear how determined he is to do so. His motives would be his strong differences with Mr. Moses on a number of specific city projects and his concern over what he has been said to consider arbitrary methods employed by Mr. Moses in performing his duties.

The choice for Mr. Lindsay appears to be this: Should he simply seek to remove Mr. Moses from the highway job or bargain with him on the matter?

Toll Surpluses for Transit?

Reliable informants say Mr. Lindsay might offer to leave Mr. Moses in the post in return for possible concessions on proposals for using surpluses produced by bridge and tunnel tolls to help meet city transit expenses.

Mr. Moses—who will be 77 years old next week and has held many city and state posts, often several at a time—has been head of the Triborough Bridge and Tunnel Authority since 1934.

A proposal to seek $20 million a year from the authority to help pay for other transportation facilities was made 11 days ago by the City Planning Commission.

But the blunt Mr. Moses quickly rejected this, as he had

Continued on Page 40, Column 3

JOHNSON APPEALS FOR LABOR'S HELP TO BAR INFLATION

[...] "not excited" [...]

[...] "We must [...] we can, avoid [...] wage spiral [...] blames business [...] and steps up [...] to counter them [...] blames labor's [...] for rising costs [...] prices to go up," [...] said.

"I believe that [...] do your part," the [...] the delegates.

"In the last two [...] said, "the labor co[...] of output has rem[...]tively stable, and [...] responsibly, you have [...] wage gains that m[...] gains in purchasing p[...]ture progress will d[...] future responsibility."

The President's appe[...] labor was similar to one [...] he made to the business [...]munity last week in a teleph[...] call to the Business Council, [...] group of leading corporatio[...] executives who perform an informal advisory role for the Government.

Inflation Fears Rising

The two telephone calls followed a recent speech in which Secretary of the Treasury Henry H. Fowler asserted that the Johnson Administration would "blow the whistle impartially" on labor and management in any future actions that would imperil wage-price stability.

Mr. Johnson's appeals have come amid growing concern that the business boom is heating up the economy to the point where inflation may be imminent.

The Administration denies there is a current threat of inflation, but the Federal Reserve Board last weekend raised interest rates "to reinforce efforts to maintain price stability."

Secretary of Labor W. Willard Wirtz suggested in a convention speech here today that the board had been led to take the step because of a mistaken impression that unemployment

Continued on Page 28, Column 3

Tass via Associated Press Cablephoto

[...] Supreme [...]rny, new [...]nastas I. Mikoyan, whom he succeeded; Premier Aleksei N. Kosygin and Leonid I. Brezhnev, First Secretary of Communist party, whose influence was thought to have increased.

[...] *Vows to Explore* [...]*am Peace Moves*

Rusk Says China Must Decide

Excerpts from Rusk's news conference, Page 13.

By MAX FRANKEL

Special to The New York Times

WASHINGTON, Dec. 9 — Secretary of State Dean Rusk said today that Communist China would have to decide whether to wage war against the United States, because the [J]ohnson Administration would [d]o everything necessary to pre[ve]nt a Communist take-over in [Sou]th Vietnam.

"We are going to meet our [com]mitment in South Vietnam," [he s]aid, emphasizing that the [...] of a "confrontation" with [...] depended upon what [...] "is going to do about [...]

[Mr.] Rusk did not predict a [...]tation, nor would he [...]e about China's capac[...] intervene. He said there [...] some recent increases [...] support of and ship[...] North Vietnam but "qualitatively different [...]t month."

[...] at a news confer[...]ecretary said North [...]esponsible for the [...]ctive discussions [...]s for a settle[...]tly because it [...]g on attempts [...]ary victory. [...]m an authorita[...]e Hanoi news[...] to support his [...]Vietnam's con[...]

[...]13, Column 2

MIKOYAN RESIGNS; PODGORNY NAMED SOVIET PRESIDENT

Shelepin Ousted From Two Government Posts but Not From Party Hierarchy

GAIN BY BREZHNEV SEEN

Kosygin Position as Premier Unchanged—Retiring Head of State, 70, Is Praised

By PETER GROSE

Special to The New York Times

MOSCOW, Dec. 9—Anastas I. Mikoyan, who is among the last of the Old Bolsheviks, stepped down today as the Soviet chief of state. His resignation led to the most significant Kremlin shuffle since the downfall of Nikita S. Khrushchev 14 months ago.

Succeeding the 70-year-old Mr. Mikoyan as chairman of the Presidium of the Supreme Soviet or Parliament is Nikolai V. Podgorny, 62, a top party leader. A product of Mr. Khrushchev's Ukrainian party machine, he is considered a moderate in the Kremlin's political spectrum.

A controversial younger member of the party hierarchy, Aleksandr N. Shelepin, 47, was formally ousted from his posts in the Government.

Until today, he was a Deputy Premier. He was also chairman of the now-defunct Party-State Control Committee, which supervised the internal security machinery.

Shelepin Still in Presidium

Mr. Shelepin apparently retained his powerful job in the Communist party Presidium and Secretariat of the Central Committee, from which he could still operate to enlarge personal power.

But the weight of evidence as interpreted by Western analysts is that Mr. Shelepin, who has sounded a tough note on both foreign and domestic issues, has suffered a check to his ambitions.

The position of Aleksei N. Kosygin as Premier is unchanged, but today's shift suggests that the influence of Leonid I. Brezhnev, First Secretary or chief of the party, has been solidified as the nation's ultimate policy-maker.

The shuffle is judged more significant in terms of internal policy than of foreign affairs.

Retirement Is No Surprise

It comes at a time when Soviet foreign policy is being stated in fresher terms than have been heard all this year but when domestic issues are being regularly decided in favor of the so-called liberals. They favor a relaxation of controls over the national society.

The retirement of Mr. Mikoyan came as no surprise. In a weak and trembling voice, he told the Supreme Soviet:

"Not everyone knows that three years ago I had an operation and was seriously ill.

"I feel this now, and it has an effect on my work. Now I find it difficult to carry out a big job."

Mr. Mikoyan, who turned 70 Nov. 25 and who had joined the Bolshevik party 50 years ago, spoke no more than three

Continued on Page 3, Column 1

U.S. PRESSES RAIDS ON NORTH VIETNAM

Bombings Heaviest of War —Regiments of 2 Sides Battle On in Quangtin

By R. W. APPLE Jr.

Special to The New York Times

SAIGON, South Vietnam, Dec. 9—United States pilots subjected North Vietnam yesterday and early today to the most intensive bombardment of the war.

Qualified sources said the vast attack opened a drive to cut down the infiltration of North Vietnamese troops into South Vietnam. Secretary of Defense Robert S. McNamara hinted last week that such a campaign would begin soon.

The new wave of bombings involved 150 United States planes—115 Air Force F-105 Thunderchiefs and F-4C Phantoms and 35 Navy craft from the carriers Bon Homme Richard and Kitty Hawk, in the Gulf of Tonkin. The pilots reported having cut transport routes at 117 points.

Marines in Quangtin Fight

In the ground war, meanwhile, South Vietnamese Government and Vietcong regiments fought on in a confused and furious battle in Quangtin Province, about halfway between the United States' coastal enclaves at Chulai and Danang.

An American military spokesman said late in the afternoon that the fighting was still intense.

The forces engaged have been of more than regimental size on both sides—2,000 men in a Vietcong regiment—and the South Vietnamese casualties have been heavy.

[United States Marines were subsequently thrown into the battle from Danang, The Associated Press reported. Page 14.]

A correspondent at the scene said that Government infantrymen and Ranger units had run into a wall of fire from Vietcong mortar and machine-gun emplacements as they tried to sweep through the enemy positions.

One South Vietnamese battalion, sent to reinforce the units that made the initial con-

[C]ontinued on Page 14, Column 1

[...]BACK [...]OLICY

[...]tition [...]ate

[...] "We must [...] [...]rising [...] his [...] Mr[...] in a s[...] messa[...] The ca[...] 980 de[...] opening [...] vention [...] tion of La[...] Industrial [...] Civic Audit[...]

[...]sid[...] Di[...] lea[...] diss[...] their [...] traordi[...] reach o[...] other c[...] governm[...] the exec[...] procedur[...] necessar[...] stitution[...] tential [...] among [...] state go[...] Justice [...]curred with [...] dissent.

The reappo[...] in New York [...] other states has [...]

[...]y pro[...]rvard, [...]gland [...]an[...]rt [...]

Continued on Page [...]

New City Investigator to Replace Most [...]

Fraiman Seeking 'Brightest Young' Wall St. Lawyers

By TERENCE SMITH

Arnold G. Fraiman, who has been designated Investigation Commissioner in the Lindsay administration, is planning a wholesale replacement of the professional staff in the present department.

In the last three days, Mr. Fraiman has interviewed the 28 examining lawyers in the department and told most of them they will be replaced. Some of the men involved have been members of the staff for more than 20 years.

Interviews with the 12 special investigators in the department will be started today or Monday by the new commissioner.

Mr. Fraiman, a former assistant United States attorney, was selected by Mayor-elect John V. Lindsay to succeed Leon A. Fishel 11 days ago. Mr. Fraiman asked for and received the personnel files of the department four days after the announcement that he would be appointed.

Yesterday he acknowledged that he planned to replace most of the examining attorneys, whose salaries range from $6,250 to $11,000 a year.

The New York Times

Arnold G. Fraiman

Fishel Says App[...] *Right to Make* [...]

"By and large I'm [...] bring in my own staff, [...] in a telephone inter[...] want the brightest youn[...]yers in the Wall Street [...]

"I've been interviewing a[...] professional people on the [...]ent staff. In fact, I just fi[...] this afternoon. I've told [...] of them they will probab[...] replaced. I told them I'd [...] them knew in the near futu[...]

For the last several days, [...]ports of Mr. Fraiman's plann[...] sweep have been circulatin[...] among city employes.

"I was wondering when th[...] was going to get to the news[...]papers," the Commissioner designate said. "But let me make it clear that I don't want to turn anybody out on the street. We'll give 'em a chance to relocate."

The outgoing commissioner, Mr. Fishel, said yesterday that the grumblings of some of the

Continued on Page 48, Column 1

[...] cover the allocations for December January and February, which would otherwise have been made month by month.

Although the new authorization will not actually increase the amount of grain, such a step could be taken later. The

Continued on Page 8, Column 4

[Continu]ed on Page 16, Column 4

NEWS INDEX

[So]viet Says Atom Role for Bonn [W]ould End Hope for Arms Pact

Special to The New York Times

[MOSC]OW, Dec. 9—The Soviet [...]arned today that the [...]alliance must abandon [...]n of sharing nuclear [...]ith West Germany if [...]o be any East-West [...] leading to disarma[...]

[...]ul declaration by the [For]eign Minister, Andrei [Grom]yko, was apparently [...]shing any lingering [...]West that a choice [...]ided between two [...] policy: that of reaching a treaty to prevent the spread of nuclear weapons, and that of including West Germany in an Atlantic nuclear community.

Mr. Gromyko emphasized the explosive dangers of the war in Vietnam, and insisted that the Soviet Union stands firmly behind the refusal of North Vietnam to enter peace talks except on its own terms.

It seemed the Russians were trying to crush the belief spreading among Western diplomats that Moscow is weakening in its support for the Hanoi Government.

Mr. Gromyko's wide-ranging speech, to the 1,400 members of the Supreme Soviet, the country's highest representative body, was the strongest and bluntest in a series of defiant foreign policy statements.

The present campaign appears to be aimed at influencing the high-level meetings of Western leaders at which the future defense strategy of the North Atlantic Treaty Organization will be mapped out.

"People cannot be deluded by references to effective controls, guarantees, systems of locks and keys," Mr. Gromyko said. "The United States must give a clear answer: where is it going?

"Since the goal of nonproliferation of nuclear weapons, and nuclear access for West Germany's Bundeswehr are incompatible, the Soviet Govern-

Continued on Page 15, Column 1

BRANCH RICKEY, 83, DIES IN MISSOURI

A Leading Baseball Figure—Helped Break Color Bar

By United Press International

COLUMBIA, Mo. Dec. 9—Branch Rickey, a dominant figure in baseball for half a century, died tonight in Boone County Memorial Hospital at the age of 83.

He broke the color barrier in the major leagues and developed the farm system.

Mr. Rickey had remained unconscious in the hospital since he collapsed with a heart attack the night of Nov. 13 while being inducted into the Missouri Sports Hall of Fame.

Mr. Rickey, who developed baseball dynasties with the St. Louis Cardinals and Brooklyn Dodgers, had left a St. Louis hospital Nov. 13 so he could attend the Missouri-Oklahoma football game and make his acceptance speech at the Sports Hall of Fame banquet that night.

Collapsed During Speech

He was scheduled to go back to the hospital after the ceremonies. But he collapsed shortly after he had started to talk.

"I don't believe I'm going to be able to speak any longer," Mr. Rickey said as he slumped over before the stunned audience.

The cigar-chomping Mr. Rickey, who throughout his career declined to attend Sunday baseball games because of a promise to his mother and who was seldom known to say anything stronger than his famous "Judas Priest," remained in the hospital's intensive-care ward until his death, continuously receiving oxygen.

Mr. Rickey's wife, Mrs. Jane

Continued on Page 55, Column 1

Branch Rickey, Leading Figure In Baseball for 50 Years, Dies

Continued From Page 1, Col. 1

Moulton Rickey, and a daughter, Mrs. Stephen S. Adams Jr. of St. Louis, were with him when he died.

He leaves four other daughters, Mrs. John Eckler of Columbus, Ohio; Mrs. Robert Jones of Elmira, N. Y.; Mrs. Edward Jakle of Los Altos, Calif., and Mrs. Lindsay Wolfe of Swarthmore, Pa. Also among his survivors are many grandchildren and several great-grandchildren.

A son, Branch Jr., died several years ago.

Mr. Rickey's body was taken to the Lupton Chapel in St. Louis.

A Teller of Folksy Tales

Branch Rickey was an owlish, rumpled man who gave flowery speeches in answer to simple questions. He had, by his own count, more than a thousand folksy stories to illustrate his points and most of these had been told to him by his mother.

One of them summed up his philosophy of life:

"My father was 86 when he died. As an old man he was still planting peach and apple trees on our farm near Portsmouth, Ohio. When I asked who would take in the fruit he said, 'That's not important. I just want to live every day as if I were going to live forever'."

Jackie Robinson, picked to become the first Negro in the major leagues, recalled his first meeting with Mr. Rickey:

"The hand holding mine was hard, gnarled, with the often broken fingers of an ex-baseball catcher. His hair was thick, deep brown. Heavy, bushy eyebrows flapped like twin crows from side to side as he talked."

This description was included in a Reader's Digest article by Mr. Robinson in 1961. He wrote of Mr. Rickey:

"He was taking off his coat, rolling up his sleeves. His mobile face had suddenly taken on a droll, cunning look.

" 'Let's say I'm a hotel clerk. You come in with the rest of your team. I look up from the register and snarl, "We don't let niggers sleep here." What do you do then?'

"Again, before I could answer, the smudgy cigar shot toward my chin, and he was an umpire waving his huge fist too close under my nose, banishing me from the game. As a race-baiting fan he hurled pop bottles and insults. When the performance was over his shirt was soggy with sweat, his hair matted.

"His curtain line explained everything. It was the most dramatic I have ever heard, before or since:

" 'Jackie, this talk of organizing a Negro team in Brooklyn was only a cover-up for my real plans. I want you to be the first Negro player in the major leagues. I've been trying to give you some idea of the kind of punishment you'll have to absorb. Can you take it?' "

Mr. Rickey brought the young Robinson to Montreal in the International League in 1946 and then to the Dodgers the following season, opening the way for numerous Negro stars who followed him into the major leagues.

Mr. Rickey had been a farm boy, teacher, college athletic director, college trustee, college board member, prohibitionist, ballplayer, manager, general manager, club president, part owner and even president of a baseball league.

The sport is indebted to him for the "knothole gang" idea, which helped promote the interest of youngsters in baseball. With this movement he developed the fans who would in the future pay the salaries of the players. Blackboard talks, sliding pits, plays developed exclusively to catch runners off base these were innovations by Mr. Rickey.

Mr. Rickey, who was never known to play, direct or attend a ball game on Sunday, came from a devout Methodist family. In his later years he was an inveterate cigar smoker, but he never drank or used profane language. He had a reputation as a lay preacher and sometimes spoke at religious meetings.

Notable players whose development was made possible by Mr. Rickey, or with whose success he was associated, included the Dean brothers, Dizzy and Paul, whose place in St. Louis baseball will long be remembered, and Joe Medwick, a star of the "Gas House Gang" era.

Mr. Rickey, who was known as the "master trader" of his time, used shrewd judgment in trading many top stars, often when they had passed their

(continued)

Branch Rickey never attended baseball games on Sunday because of a promise to his mother.

peak as performers but could still draw a high price.

His most famous deal was probably the sale of Dizzy Dean to the Chicago Cubs in 1937. In exchange for the once-great pitcher who was suffering from a sore arm, he obtained the pitchers Curt Davis and Clyde Shoun in addition to a sum reported to have been $185,000.

He even traded the incomparable Rogers Hornsby, who had been the playing manager of the Cardinals.

Mr. Rickey always looked for what he called the"young, hungry player with the basic attributes of youth and speed plus strength of arm." The result was a Rickey dynasty of great young players who repeatedly won pennants for the Cardinals and later the Dodgers.

Born on Ohio Farm

Branch Wesley Rickey was born on a farm at Stockdale, Ohio, on Dec. 20, 1881, the second of three sons, to Jacob Franklin and Emily Rickey, who were known for their piety.

After receiving an elementary school education, Mr. Rickey became a country school teacher. He taught himself Latin, higher mathematics and other subjects, and was able to enter Ohio Wesleyan University. Later he obtained a law degree from the University of Michigan.

The young Rickey earned his way through Ohio Wesleyan by playing both baseball and football. His baseball position was always catcher, which he went on to play in his major-league career.

As a big-league player, Mr. Rickey did not amount to much. In a game against Washington in 1907, when he was catching for New York, there were 13 stolen bases charged against him. In 11 games he was charged with nine errors.

Work Brought on Illness

He entered the big leagues in 1903 with the Cincinnati Reds, but was released because of his scruples against playing on Sundays. He returned the next year from Dallas to the St. Louis Bronws, by way of the Chicago White Sox. Meanwhile, he received an A.B. degree at Ohio Wesleyan in 1905, the year in which he married Jane Moulton, after having proposed "more than a hundred times," as he later recounted.

In the off-season of 1908, he toured as a prohibiton advocate, the same year he entered the University of Michigan, where he served as baseball coach while getting his law degree.

The strain of work, play and study had its effect, and a touch of tuberculosis sent him to Saranac Lake, N.Y. His health regained, Mr. Rickey went to Boise, Idaho, to practice law. However, in 1913, he accepted the invitation of Robert Lee Hedges, president of the St. Louis Browns, to become a scout for the club.

Among other innovations, Rickey originated the idea of "farm" teams in 1919 when he was with the St. Louis Cardinals.

Mr. Rickey later became club secretary and then field manager. He had Burt Shotton manage the club on Sundays. He was vice president and general manager by 1917, when he was hired as president of the poverty-stricken St. Louis Cardinals. Under the terms of his contract, he was the highest-paid executive in baseball.

After a hitch as a major in the Chemical Warfare Service, he returned to the Cardinals in 1918. Mr. Rickey assumed the field management and started the "farm" idea. It had its origin in 1919, when the Cardinals bought an 18 percent interest in the Houston club of the Texas League.

In 1920 Sam Breadon replaced Mr. Rickey as president, but Mr. Rickey continued to develop his chain-store idea until at one time he controlled the players of two minor leagues and had interest in, or agreements with, a number of others.

Violently opposed to the Rickey idea from the outset, Judge Kenesaw Mountain Landis, the commisioner of baseball shook the Cardinal farm structure with a decree that limited the club to only one affiliation in each minor league.

The reign of Mr. Rickey as manager of the Cardinals ended in 1925, when Mr. Breadon replaced him with Rogers Hornsby. Mr. Rickey was retained as vice president and busines manager. This arrangement continued until 1942, when, after the Cardinals had won the World Series, reports of a rift between the executives brought an announcement by Mr. Breadon that Mr. Rickey's contract would not be renewed.

Mr. Rickey had taken the Cardinals when the club was $175,000 in debt and, by spending only enough for a railroad ticket at times, had developed players who brought the club the National League pennant in 1926, 1928, 1930, 1931, 1934 and 1942, along with World Series victories in four of those years.

Chosen to Head Dodgers

Shortly after leaving the Cardinals, Mr. Rickey was engaged as president of the Dodgers.

A storm ensued in Brooklyn when Mr. Rickey sold Dolph Camilli and Joe Medwick, Dodger favorites. It did not diminish when there were recurrent reports of friction between him and his club manager, Leo Durocher.

He rehired Durocher as his manager shortly before spring training of 1948, thus ending much wild speculation on that score. But he drew more resentment from the fans when he traded the beloved Dixie Walker to Pittsburgh and later, when the Dodgers were in spring training, he traded Eddie Stanky the Dodgers' sparkplug second baseman, to Boston.

Mr. Rickey's biggest baseball deal after coming to Brooklyn was the sale of Kirby Higbe and others to Frank McKinney, the new president and part owner of the Pirates. It was revealed long after the deal was made that Mr. McKinney had parted with almost $300,000 in the deal.

In November, 1950, Mr. Rickey signed a five-year contract as executive vice president and general manager of the Pirates. When he left Brooklyn, he was reported to have sold his Dodger stock for $1,000,000.

Although he resigned as chairman in 1959, his rebuilding program paid off in 1960. The Pirates, under field manager Danny Murtaugh, won the National League pennant and went on to take the World Series from the New York Yankees.

After leaving the Pirates, Mr. Rickey was appointed president of the newly formed Continental League. An hour after his appointment, he was conducting the league's first meeting. The eight teams constituting the league were New York, Buffalo, Toronto, Minneapolis-St. paul, Houston, Dallas-Fort Worth, Atlanta and Denver.

For nearly two years, it appeared that Mr. Rickey's "dream" would be realized, but he was never able to get the league out of the dugout. The final blow was struck by the two existing major leagues.

At the end of 1960, the American League issued franchises to the Los Angeles (now the California) Angels and a new Washington Senator club (the old one moved and became the Minnesota Twins), while the National League made plans to become a 10-team league in 1962 with the admission of the New York Mets and the Houston Colt 45s (now the Astros).

Mr. Rickey returned to the Cardinals late in 1962 as a "consultant on player personnel." He held that position for two years, leaving after a shake-up of the club's executives. The aging, ailing Mr. Rickey was critical of Manager Johnny Keane and other Cardinal executives.

The Rickey influence wrought revolutions in baseball—notably his developing the farm system and breaking the color barrier—that profoundly changed the game.

"All the News That's Fit to Print"

The New York Times

LATE CITY EDITION

Weather: Mostly sunny, cool today; clear, cool tonight. Fair tomorrow. Temp. range: today 51-62; Tuesday 58-74. Full U.S. report on Page 93.

VOL. CXXII ... No. 41,913 — NEW YORK, WEDNESDAY, OCTOBER 25, 1972 — 15 CENTS

PARENTS SCUFFLE AT SCHOOL DOORS BARRED TO BLACKS

Canarsie Protesters Seek to Register 29 Pupils in Defiance of Edict

SCRIBNER IS CRITICIZED

His Reversal of Decision on Tilden House Youths Is Termed a 'Sellout'

By RONALD SMOTHERS

The parents of 29 black children unsuccessfully tried to push their way past policemen and barricades yesterday to register their children at Canarsie's John Wilson Junior High School 211 in defiance of an order by Chancellor Harvey B. Schribner, who reversed an earlier directive and barred the students from entry.

The parents demonstrated outside the Brooklyn school for two hours, embittered by the Chancellor's reversal Monday of an Oct. 11 order that they be admitted to John Wilson School and further angered by the issuance of a new directive assigning the stud... to Isaac Bilderse... School 68...

Denou... and char... was a "sel... to white p... cupied the sc... protest of the... black parents, ... in Brownsville's ... den Houses, rejec... assignments.

Parents Give ...

The white parent... that the school, with... ment of 70 per cent w... 30 per cent blacks, wa... rally" integrated and th... no need to bring in ... from outside its area.

The protest yesterday a... Wilson school, at Avenue J ... East 100th Street, was ... latest in the five-week contr... versy over integration of th... Tilden Houses Pupils into thre... predominantly white schools of District 18 in the Canarsie and East Flatbush sections.

The black pupils assigned to Wilson have not attended school at all this year. The dispute has led to demonstrations by black parents, the three-day occupation last week of Wilson by white parents and the assignment of the black youths to two—and with this new order —finally a third school in the district.

Students are Screened

Parents of the Tilden pupils, insisting that they would not send their children to the 97 per cent white Bildersee School, alternately tried to push past four policemen who stood in the narrow gateway to Wilson or tried to sneak their children past the assistant principals screening every student entering the school.

Dr. Scribner's new order caused a wave of criticism and reaction among educators, civil rights leaders and educational associations around the city as well as in other parts of the district.

Parents and staff members

Continued on Page 25, Column 1

A scene outside John Wilson Junior High School yesterday...

3 Teachers and 3 ...
Held Up in ...

... yard... Brookl... gene... place.

The d... unrelated ... hension o... lieutenant, ... a Staten Is...

Last night... a high-speed ... streets of the Ba... when the form... tried to outrun ... cars, according ... official.

The official, Dep... Commissioner Willia... Carthy, head of the ... partment's Organized... Control Bureau, describ... former lieutenant's arres... unusual news conference ... 68th Precinct station at ... this morning.

Commissioner McCarthy iden... tified the arrested former officer as James E. McDermott, 52 years old, who retired from the force Aug. 3, 1971.

His last assignment, Mr.

Continued on Page 29, Column 3

THIEU ASSAILS PEACE-PLAN TERMS, ASKS GUARANTEE, HANOI PULLOUT; U.S. LIMITS NORTH VIETNAM RAIDS

SIGNAL TO ENEMY

Bombing Curb Called Act of Appreciation for Concessions

By WILLIAM BEE...
Special to The New Y...
WASHIN...

Associated Press
...on with Henry ...ls, Page 16.

...ining ...rmy

...rmy ...my ...cit

...10 ...has been ...estions from call-

In this morning's interview on the Columbia Broadcasting System's "Morning News" show, Senator McGovern declared that the terms under which the Nixon Administration might be able to settle the war now "appear to be exactly the same terms that the war could have been ended on four years ago."

"It appears to me," he went on, "that if the Presdent should end the war before we count the votes here on Nov. 7, he has run it for another four years purely to avoid criticism from the right-wing war

...now to ...d recoil-

...They cannot maintain their

...umn 3 Continued on Page 16, Column 2

Continued on Page 32, Column 4

SPEECH IN SAIGON

Cease-Fire Obstacles Seen, but President Expects Agreement

By CRAIG R. WHITNEY
Special to The New York Times

SAIGON, South Vietnam, Oct. 24 — President Nguyen Van Thieu said tonight that all the peace proposals discussed by Henry A. Kissinger and the North Vietnamese in Paris so far were unacceptable, and, in an ambiguous statement, he asserted that there were great difficulties in the way of a cease-fire.

In a nationwide broadcast, President Thieu said on the other hand that a cease-fire could come "very soon" but

Excerpts from Thieu's speech will be found on Page 17.

emphasized that the South Vietnamese could not agree to the Communist proposal for a cease-fire in place before a political settlement.

A cease-fire would be acceptable, he added, only if it was Indochina-wide, guaranteed and involved the withdrawal from the South of all North Vietnamese troops.

Stand Termed Unshakable

"Whether there is a cease-fire ...ow, before the United States ...lection, or one month, two ...onths, three months, or four ... five months after the elec...n, our position will remain ...same," he said.

...hat he appeared to do in ...eech was to leave the ...ns in the position of ...e to offer only an un...ease-fire with no guar... they could convince ...Vietnamese to accept ...ise political settle...ething the North ...t least in public, ...must accompany ...the guns.

...ts could only ...ally betrays ... Mr. Thieu ...main ally will ...betray us. He has invested so much blood and money."

In detailing his objections to several aspects of the current Communist proposals, Mr. Thieu asserted: "I have always said we are not afraid of a cease-fire, but our stance is that if there is a cease-fire it must go along with a political settlement."

"Our position," he added, "has been put forward with the purpose of guaranteeing a just and lasting peace. But this stance is that if they want U. S. troops to withdraw they must also withdraw their troops back to the North."

Geneva Accords Recalled

At another point he said: "Today I would like to reaffirm our standpoint in this way: To restore peace we first must use the 1954 Geneva accords as a basis. This means that North Vietnam is North Vietnam and South Vietnam is South Vietnam. For the time being one must accept the two Vietnams, and neither side can invade the other."

"I say that a cease-fire will have a chance to be augured soon," he added, "if such a cease-fire is guaranteed and internationally supervised as proposed by our Government and our American allies."

Mr. Thieu's broadcast was not announced until just after he arrived at the studio at 7:30 P.M. United States Embassy officials declined to comment un-

Continued on Page 16, Column 7

Jackie Robinson, First Black in Major Leagues, Dies

By DAVE ANDERSON

Jackie Robinson, who made history in 1947 by becoming the first black baseball player in the major leagues, suffered a heart attack in his home in Stamford, Conn., yesterday morning and died at Stamford Hospital at 7:10 A.M. He was 53 years old.

As an all-round athlete in college and later the star infielder of the Brooklyn Dodgers, he became the pioneer for a generation of blacks in the major professional sports after World War II.

Mr. Robinson, who was honored at the World Series in Cincinnati a week ago Sunday, had been in failing health for several years. He recovered from a heart attack in 1968 but then lost the sight of one eye and the partial sight of the other as a result of diabetes.

He remained active, though, in national campaigns against drug addiction—from which his son, Jackie Jr., had been recovering before he was killed in 1971 in an automobile accident. In fact, Mr. Robinson planned to attend a drug symposium yesterday sponsored by the business community in Washington.

When he was stricken at home, an emergency call was made to the Stamford police by his wife, Rachel, who is an associate professor of psychiatric nursing at the Yale School of Medicine. They applied external massage and oxygen before a Fire Department ambulance took him to the hospital.

For sociological impact, Jack Roosevelt Robinson was perhaps America's most significant athlete.

As the first black player in major-league baseball, he was a pioneer. His skill and accom-

Continued on Page 56, Column 1

Nima Yakubu/Nancy Palmer Agency
Jackie Robinson in New Jersey office last week.

The New York Times
Robinson stealing home against the Cubs in 1952 with the bases loaded. He excelled in the daring plays.

...k in Major Leagues, Dies

...rld Series in Cincinnati a week ago Sunday, had ...in ...uffered a ...his home in ...Conn., yesterday morning and died at Stamford Hospital at 7:10 A.M. He was 53 years old.

As an all-round athlete in college and later the star infielder of the Brooklyn Dodgers, he became the pioneer for a generation of blacks in the major professional sports after World War II.

Mr. Robinson, who was hon- been in failing health for several years. He recovered from a heart attack in 1968 but then lost the sight of one eye and the partial sight of the other as a result of diabetes.

He remained active, though, in national campaigns against drug addiction—from which his son, Jackie Jr., had been recovering before he was killed in 1971 in an automobile accident. In fact, Mr. Robinson planned to attend a drug symposium yesterday sponsored by the business community in Washington.

When he was stricken at home, an emergency call was made to the Stamford police by his wife, Rachel, who is an associate professor of psychiatric nursing at the Yale School of Medicine. They applied external massage and oxygen before a Fire Department ambulance took him to the hospital.

For sociological impact, Jack Roosevelt Robinson was perhaps America's most significant athlete.

As the first black player in major-league baseball, he was a pioneer. His skill and accom-

Continued on Page 56, Column 1

Nima Yakubu/Nancy Palmer Agency
Jackie Robinson in New Jersey office last week.

The New York Times
Robinson stealing home against the Cubs in 1952 with the bases loaded. He excelled in the daring plays.

Grand Jury Finds No Evidence In Its Inquiry on Newark Official

By RICHARD PHALON
Special to The New York Times

NEWARK, Oct. 24—An Essex County grand jury found "without substance" today allegations that the appointment of Robert Notte as executive director of the Newark Housing Authority had been supported by organized crime.

Superior Court Judge James R. Giuliano, who released the presentment today, also freed Peter J. Bridge, a former reporter for The Evening News of Newark, who was serving his 20th day in the Essex County Jail.

Mr. Bridge was sentenced for contempt for the life of the grand jury, which is expected to come to its formal end tomorrow, after refusing to go beyond the details of a story that appeared in the now-defunct newspaper last May 2.

The article quoted Mrs. Pearl Beatty, a member of the Housing Commission, as having said that she had been offered $10,000 by an unidentified man for control of her vote on the appointment of a new executive director of the authority.

In a 30-page presentment, the grand jury found no cause for indictment in allegations that Mr. Notte's appointment had been marked by attempted bribery, intimidation, harassment and the prospect of political payoffs held out by Mayor Kenneth A. Gibson to Assemblyman Anthony Imperiale.

Most of the allegations were

Continued on Page 51, Column 7

Nixon Outlay Tops McGovern by 2 to 1

By BEN A. FRANKLIN
Special to The New York Times

WASHINGTON, Oct. 24—President Nixon's main national campaign organization has outspent Senator George McGovern's by about 2 to 1 in the Presidential campaign, official campaign financial statements disclosed today.

The comparison does not include the period of the Democratic primary campaigns but does include that of the Republican primaries, in which Mr. Nixon did not participate.

In the reporting period from Sept. 1 to Oct. 16, for which mandatory financial disclosures were made today by both parties, the principal Nixon campaign committees reported

Continued on Page 33, Column 1

NEWS INDEX

Jackie Robinson, First Black Major Leaguer, Dies at 53

Dodger Star, in Hall of Fame, Began in '47

Continued From Page 1, Col. 4

plishments resulted in the acceptance of blacks in other major sports, notably professional football and professional basketball. In later years, while a prosperous New York businessman, he emerged as an influential member of the Republican party.

His dominant characteristic, as an athlete and as a black man, was a competitive flame. Outspoken, controversial, combative, he created critics as well as loyalists. But he never deviated from his opinions.

Commented on Debut

In his autobiography, "I Never Had It Made," to be published next month by G. P. Putnam's, he recalled the scene in 1947 when he stood for the National Anthem at his debut with the Brooklyn Dodgers. He wrote:

". . . but as I write these words now I cannot stand and sing the National Anthem. I have learned that I remain a black in a white world."

Describing his struggle, he wrote:

"I had to fight hard against loneliness, abuse and the knowledge that any mistake I made would be magnified because I was the only black man out there. Many people resented my impatience and honesty, but I never cared about acceptance as much as I cared about respect."

His belligerence flared throughout his career in baseball, business and politics.

"I was told that it would cost me some awards," he said last year. "But if I had to keep quiet to get an award, it wasn't worth it. Awards are great, but if I got one for being a nice kid, what good is it?"

To other black ballplayers, though, he was most often saluted as the first to run the gantlet. Monte Irvin, who played for the New York Giants while Robinson was with the Dodgers and who now is an assistant to the commissioner of baseball, said yesterday:

"Jackie Robinson opened the door of baseball to all men. He was the first to get the opportunity, but if he had not done such a great job, the path would have been so much more difficult.

Jackie Robinson

"Bill Russell says if it hadn't been for Jackie, he might not ever have become a professional basketball player. Jack was the trail-blazer, and we are all deeply grateful. We say, thank you, Jackie; it was a job well done."

"He meant everything to a black ballplayer," said Elston Howard, the first black member of the New York Yankees, who is now on the coaching staff. "I don't think the young players would go through what he did. He did it for all of us, for Willie Mays, Henry Aaron, Maury Wills, myself.

"Jack said he hoped someday to see a black manager in baseball. Now I hope some of the owners will see how important that would be as the next step."

Elected to Hall of Fame

After a versatile career as a clutch hitter and daring baserunner while playing first base, second base, third base and left field at various stages of his 10 seasons with the Brooklyn Dodgers, he was elected to baseball's Hall of Fame in 1962, his first year of eligibility for the Cooperstown, N.Y., shrine.

Despite his success, he minimized himself as an "instrument, a tool." He credited Branch Rickey, the Brooklyn Dodger owner who broke professional baseball's color line. Mr. Rickey signed him for the 1946 season, which he spent with the Dodgers' leading farm, the Montreal Royals of the International League.

"I think the Rickey Experiment, as I call it, the original idea, would not have come about as successfully with anybody other than Mr. Rickey," he often said. "The most important results of it are that it produced understanding among whites and it gave black people the idea that if I could do it, they could do it, too, that blackness wasn't subservient to anything."

Among his disappointments was the fact that he never was afforded an opportunity to be a major-league manager.

"I had no future with the Dodgers because I was too closely identified with Branch Rickey," he once said. "After the club was taken over by Walter O'Malley, you couldn't even mention Mr. Rickey's name in front of him. I considered Mr. Rickey the greatest human being I had ever known."

Robinson kept baseball in perspective. Ebbets Field, the Brooklyn ballpark that was the stage for his drama, was leveled shortly after Mr. O'Malley moved the Dodger franchise to Los Angeles in 1958. Apartment houses replaced it. Years later, asked what he felt about Ebbets Field, he replied:

"I don't feel anything. They need those apartments more than they need a monument to the memory of baseball. I've had my thrills."

He also had his heartbreak His older son, Jackie Jr., died in 1971 at the age of 24 in an automobile accident on the Merritt Parkway, not far from the family's home in Stamford.

Son Became Drug Addict

Three years earlier, Jackie Jr. had been arrested for heroin possession. His addiction had begun while he served in the Army in Vietnam, where he was wounded. He was convicted and ordered to undergo treatment at the Daytop drug abuse center in Seymour, Conn. Cured, he worked at Daytop, helping other addicts, until his fatal accident.

Robinson and his wife, Rachel, had two other children —David and Sharon.

"You don't know what it's like," Robinson said at the time, "to lose a son, find him, and lose him again. My problem was my inability to spend much time at home. I thought my family was secure, so I went running around everyplace else. I guess I had more of an effect on other people's kids than I did on my own."

With the Dodgers, he had other problems. His arrival in 1947 prompted racial insults from some opponents, an aborted strike by the St. Louis Cardinals, an alleged deliberate spiking by Enos Slaughter of the Cardinals and stiffness from a few teammates, notably Fred (Dixie) Walker, a popular star from Georgia.

"Dixie was very difficult at the start," Robinson acknowledged, "but he was the first guy on the ballclub to come to me with advice and help for my hitting. I knew why—if I helped the ballclub, it put money in his pocket. I knew he didn't like me any more in

(continued)

Robinson hookslides into home against the Giants.

(continued)

those few short months, but he did come forward."

A Cautioning by Rickey

As a rookie, Robinson had been warned by Mr. Rickey of the insults that would occur. He also was urged by Mr. Rickey to hold his temper. He complied. But the following season, as an established player, he began to argue with the umpires and duel verbally with opponents in the traditional give-and-take of baseball.

As the years passed, Robinson developed a close relationship with many teammates.

"After the game we went our separate ways," he explained. "But on the field, there was that understanding. No one can convince me that the things that happened on the ballclub didn't affect people. The old Dodgers were something special but of my teammates, overall, there was nobody like Pee Wee Reese for me."

In Boston once, some Braves' players were taunting Robinson during infield practice. Reese, the popular shortstop, who came from Louisville, moved to the rescue.

"Pee Wee walked over and put his arm on my shoulder, as if to say, 'This is my teammate, whether you like it or not,'" Robinson said. "Another time, all our white players got letters, saying if they don't do something, the whole team will be black and they'll lose their jobs. On the bus to the ballpark that night, Pee Wee brought it up and we discussed it. Pretty soon, we were all laughing about it."

In clubhouse debates, Robinson's voice had a sharp, angry tone that rose with his emotional involvement.

"Robinson," he once was told by Don Newcombe, a star pitcher, who was also black, "not only are you wrong, you're loud wrong."

As a competitor, Robinson was the Dodgers' leader. In his 10 seasons, they won six National League pennants—1947, 1949, 1952, 1953, 1955 and 1956. They lost another in the 1951 playoff with the New York Giants, and another to the Philadelphia Phillies on the last day of the 1950 season.

Jackie Robinson came to the Dodgers from their Montreal farm club in 1947.

In 1949, when he batted .342 to win the league title and drove in 124 runs, he was voted the league's Most Valuable Player Award. In 1947, he had been voted the rookie of the year.

Batted .311 Lifetime

"The only way to beat the Dodgers," said Warren Giles, then the president of the Cincinnati Reds, later the National League president, "is to keep Robinson off the bases."

He had a career batting average of .311. Primarily a line-drive hitter, he accumulated only 137 home runs, with a high of 19 in both 1951 and 1952.

But on a team with such famous sluggers as Duke Snider, Gil Hodges and Roy Campanella, who was also black, he was the cleanup hitter, fourth in the batting order, a tribute to his ability to move along teammates on base.

But his personality flared best as a baserunner. He had a total of 197 stolen bases. He stole home 11 times, the most by any player in the post-World War II era.

Ran Like Football Player

"I think the most symbolic part of Jackie Robinson, ballplayer," he once reflected, "was making the pitcher believe he was going to the next base. I think he enjoyed that the most, too. I think my value to the Dodgers was disruption — making the pitcher concentrate on me instead of on my teammate who was at bat at the time."

In the 1955 World Series, he stole home against the New York Yankees in the opening game of Brooklyn's only World Series triumph.

Pigeon-toed and muscular, wearing No. 42, he ran aggressively, typical of his college football training as a star runner and passer at the University of California at Los Angeles in 1939 and 1940. He ranked second in the Pacific Coast Conference in total offense in 1940 with 875 yards—440 rushing and 435 passing.

Born in Cairo, Ga., on Jan. 31, 1919, he was soon taken to Pasadena, Calif., by his mother with her four other children after his father had deserted them. He developed into an all-round athlete, competing in basketball and track in addition to baseball and football. After attending U.C.L.A., he entered the Army.

He was commissioned a second lieutenant. After his discharge, he joined the Kansas City Monarchs of the Negro National League as a shortstop.

"But if Mr. Rickey hadn't signed me, I wouldn't have played another year in the black league," he said. "It was too difficult. The travel was brutal. Financially, there was no reward. It took everything you made to live off."

If he had quit the black leagues without having been signed by Mr. Rickey, what would he have done?

"I more than likely would have gone to coach baseball at Sam Houston College. My minister had gone down there to Texas as president of the college. That was about the only thing a black athlete had left then, a chance to coach somewhere at a small black college."

Instead, his presence turned the Dodgers into the favorite of black people throughout the nation.

"They picked up 20 million fans instantly," said Bill Russell, the famous center of the Boston

Jackie Robinson's Career Record

By The Associated Press

Year	Team	G.	AB.	R.	H.	2B.	3B.	H.R.	R.B.I.	Avg.
1947	—Brooklyn	151	590	125	175	31	5	12	48	.297
1948	—Brooklyn	147	574	108	170	38	8	12	85	.296
1949	—Brooklyn	156	593	122	203	38	12	16	124	.342
1950	—Brooklyn	144	518	99	170	39	4	14	81	.328
1951	—Brooklyn	153	548	106	185	33	7	19	88	.338
1952	—Brooklyn	149	510	104	157	17	3	19	75	.308
1953	—Brooklyn	136	484	109	159	34	7	12	95	.329
1954	—Brooklyn	124	386	62	120	22	4	15	59	.311
1955	—Brooklyn	105	317	51	81	6	2	8	36	.256
1956	—Brooklyn	117	357	61	98	15	2	10	43	.275
Total.......		1,382	4,877	947	1,518	273	54	137	734	.311

(continued)

Celtics who was professional basketball's first black coach. "But to most black people, Jackie was a man, not a ballplayer. He did more for baseball than baseball did for him. He was someone that young black athletes could look up to."

As the Dodgers toured the National League, they set attendance records. But the essence of Robinson's competitive fury occurred in a 1954 game at Ebbets Field with the rival Giants.

Sal Maglie, the Giants' ace who was known as "The Barber" because of his tendency to "shave" a batter's head with his fast ball and sharp-breaking curve, was intimidating the Dodger hitters. In the Dodger dugout, Reese, the team captain, spoke to the 6-foot, 195-pound Robinson.

"Jack," said Reese "we got to do something about this."

Robinson soon was kneeling in the on-deck circle as the next Dodger batter. With him was Charlie DiGiovanna, the team's adult batboy who was a confidant of the players.

"Let somebody else do it, Jack," DiGiovanna implored. "Everytime something comes up they call on you."

Robinson agreed, but once in the batter's box, he changed his mind. Hoping to draw Maglie toward the first-base line, Robinson bunted. The ball was fielded by Whitey Lockman, the first baseman, but Maglie didn't move off the mound. Davey Williams, the second baseman, covered the base for Lockman's throw.

Knocked Over Williams

"Maglie wouldn't cover," Robinson recalled. "Williams got in the way. He had a chance to get out of the way but he just stood there right on the base. It was just too bad, but I knocked him over. He had a Giant uniform on. That's what happens."

In the collision, Williams suffered a spinal injury that virtually ended his career. Two innings later, Alvin Dark, the Giants' captain and shortstop, retaliated by trying to stretch a double into a third-base collision with Robinson.

Realizing that Dark hoped to avenge the Williams incident, Robinson stepped aside and tagged him in the face. But his grip on the ball wasn't secure. The ball bounced away. Dark was safe.

"I would've torn his face up," Robinson once recalled. "But as it turned out, I'm glad it didn't happen that way. I admired Al for what he did after I had run down Williams. I've always admired Al, despite his racial stands. I think he really believed that white people were put on this earth to take care of black people."

Ironically, after the 1956 season, Robinson was traded to the rival Giants, but he announced his retirement in Look magazine. Any chance of his changing his mind ended when Emil (Buzzy) Bavasi, then a Dodger vice president, implied that after Robinson had been paid for the by-line article, he would accept the Giants' offer.

Succession of Executive Posts

"After Buzzy said that," Robinson later acknowledged, "there was no way I'd ever play again."

He joined Chock Full O'Nuts, the lunch-counter chain, as an executive. He later had a succession of executive posts with an insurance firm, a food-franchising firm and an interracial construction firm. He also was chairman of the board of the Freedom National Bank in Harlem and a member of the New York State Athletic Commission.

In politics Mr. Robinson remained outspoken. He supported Richard M. Nixon in the 1960 Presidential election. When Mr. Nixon and Spiro T. Agnew formed the 1968 Presidential ticket, however, he resigned from Governor Rockefeller's staff where he was a Special Assistant for Community Affairs to campaign for Hubert H. Humphrey, the Democratic nominee.

Mr. Robinson described Mr. Nixon's stand on civil rights in 1960 as "forthright" but denounced the Nixon-Agnew ticket as "racist."

Mr. Robinson's niche American history is secure — his struggle predated the emergence of "the first black who" in many areas of the American society. Even though he understandably needed a Branch Rickey to open the door for him, Branch Rickey needed a Jackie Robinson to lead other blacks through that door.

In addition to his wife, a fellow-student at U.C.L.A. whom he married in 1946, Mr. Robinson leaves a son, David; a daughter, Mrs. Sharon Mitchell of Washington; a sister, Mrs. Willie Mae Walker, and two brothers, Mack and Edgar, all of Pasadena, Calif.

A funeral service will be held Friday at noon at the Riverside Church, Riverside Drive and 122d Street. Visiting hours will be from noon to 9 P.M. at the church tomorrow.

Baseball's revolutionaries—Jackie Robinson and Branch Rickey. Robinson later said of Rickey, "I considered Mr. Rickey the greatest human being I had ever known."

"All the News That's Fit to Print."

The New York Times.

Copyright, 1931, by The New York Times Company.

LATE CITY EDITION

THE WEATHER—Rain today; tomorrow fair, not much change in temperature. Temperature yesterday—Max. 49, min. 37. U. S. Weather Forecast—For details see Page 54.

VOL. LXXX....No. 26,730. ****+ NEW YORK, WEDNESDAY, APRIL 1, 1931. TWO CENTS In Greater New York | THREE CENTS Within 200 Miles | FOUR CENTS Elsewhere Except 7th and 8th Postal Zones

... IS DESTROYED, 1,100 REPORTED KILLED, ...S INJURED IN EARTHQUAKE AND FIRE; ...ERICAN CASUALTIES; HOOVER RUSHES AID

KNUTE ROCKNE DIES WITH SEVEN OTHERS IN MAIL PLANE DIVE

Ship's Engine Fails Above the Clouds, Wing Rips Off, Craft Falls on Kansas Farm.

ALL OCCUPANTS FOUND DEAD

Football Leaders of the Country Pay Tribute to Great Coach's Qualities.

CONSUMMATE IN STRATEGY

His Skill Raised Football Technique to Great Heights in His Notre Dame Teams.

Special to The New York Times.

WICHITA, Kan., March 31.—Knute Rockne, Notre Dame football coach, and seven others, were killed at 11 o'clock this morning when a ten-passenger Trans-Continental & Western Airways plane dived into a pasture in the Flint Hills cattle country near Bazaar in Southeastern Kansas.

Besides Rockne the dead were:

CHRISTEN, H. J., Chicago.
HAPPER, J. H., Chicago.
MILLER, W. B., Hartford, Conn.
GOLDTHWAITE, SPENCER G., New York City.
ROBRECHE, C. A., Wheeling, W. Va.
FRYE, ROBERT, pilot.
MATHIAS, JESS, pilot.

Radio Communication Ceases.

In a hazy drizzle which gave poor flying visibility the tri-motored Fokker left Kansas City at 9:15, three-quarters of an hour late after waiting for mail connections. It was due in Wichita at 10:25 under the regular schedule.

Flying above the clouds the big transport maintained radio communications with the Kansas City Airport until it sighted Cassoday, southwest of Bazaar. It asked for weather conditions at Wichita and then radio communication ceased, appa... about the scene of the cras...

Witnesses heard the drone ... motors above the clouds, hear... sputter and stop and soon sa... big craft flash down through ... cloud bank with a trail of smoke ... tering out behind.

A wing tore loose and swirled ... like a falling leaf, to land half a ... from where the plane plowed its ... into the soft earth of the pasture ... S. H. Baker. One of the three mo... tors was completely buried by the impact. All on board the plane were dead when witnesses arrived.

Four bodies were thrown clear, Baker said. He was feeding cattle when he heard the plane strike the earth. He telephoned to Cottonwood Falls, fifteen miles north, for ambulances.

Flying in a Dangerous District.

Bazaar is an isolated village in a section particularly treacherous for aviators. The hills provide bumpy air conditions.

Clarence McCracken, a farmhand on the Seward ranch, who also saw the plane fall, helped Baker and others to free the bodies. All were taken to a morgue at Cottonwood Falls over fifteen miles of muddy road, which impeded progress.

Identification was difficult, but was finally established by means of bill folds and luggage. W. L. White, son of William Allen White of The Emporia Gazette, confirmed the identification of Rockne's body, although for a time there was doubt whether he had been aboard the plane. Four of the eight bodies were identified at the scene of the crash and the others later at Cottonwood Falls.

Two hours after the accident Department of Commerce officials from Wichita and Kansas City were on their way to Bazaar to conduct an

Continued on Page Twenty-four.

PRESIDENT DECLARES AGAINST A TAX RISE; ASKS PEOPLE TO AID

Increase Can Be Avoided if Congress Will Follow Budget Figures, He Asserts.

GROUP DEMANDS TO WAIT

Restraint by the Public Is Called For to Make the Economy Program Effective.

HELP PLEDGED BY WATSON

Senator Favors Short-Term Borrowing to Meet Deficit—Collections Continue to Decline.

Special to The New York Times.

WASHINGTON, March 31.—President Hoover declared today that there would be no increase in taxes next year if Congress would keep appropriations within budget recommendations and sectional and group demands for Federal assistance were postponed.

Republican Senators, including Senator Watson, the floor leader, and Senator Jones of Washington, chairman of the Appropriations Committee, immediately pledged their efforts to keep taxes down, and declared that by cooperation between Congress and the President new taxation can be avoided. Short-term borrowing can be resorted to to tide over in an emergency, the Senators said.

After a Cabinet discussion of fiscal conditions and a conference with Senator Watson, President Hoover issued an appeal for the cooperation of the people in withholding sectional and group demands. The President's statement follows:

"There will be no increase in taxes if the next Congress imposes no increases upon the budget or other expenditure proposals which the administration will present. But for Congress to do this, the people must cooperate to effectively discourage and postpone consideration of the demands of sectional and group interests."

Tax Collections Still Decline.

The deficit this year is likely to be greater than estimated, because of the great decline in income tax collections, which for twenty-eight days in March have amounted only to $330,741,000, a reduction of $222,000,000 from the same period last year.

The President's statement, in the opinion of Republican leaders, defines the policy that the party will follow in Congress, and sets at rest predictions that new taxation will be imposed to meet the deficit.

Democratic Congressional leaders are reported to be disposed to accept the administration's fiscal plans, and indications are that no attempts will be made to pass new revenue measures in the next Congress, in which the Republicans will have only nominal control.

The administration, in deciding that the deficit can be handled without imposing new taxes, did so in the belief that an upturn in business will increase revenues. Treasury experts have reported that the government can carry on without any embarrassment by borrowing, and by reducing the amount applied to reduction of the national debt.

Rely on Pick-up in Business.

At the treasury it was pointed out that during a period when business is slack it would appear to be better policy to increase the public debt than to raise taxes. While another deficit is probable in 1932, it is generally believed that business will have recovered so much that government receipts again will start upward, permitting the usual reductions in the public debt as required by statute.

Senator Borah said that, of course, there would be no increase in taxation until after the Presidential election.

"Congress kept below the budget estimates in the two last sessions," he said, "and yet the deficits increased, due, among other things, to a reduction in the taxes last year."

Since taxes were reduced when a surplus existed, they should be increased when the necessity arises for additional revenues, Senator Borah added. The surtaxes should be raised, he declared.

During March the government has suffered the severest drop in revenue in any year since the World War. For the fiscal year, through March 28, income tax collections were $1,502,272,000, a decline of $[illegible] from the same period a year ago.

Final figures for March will be available Thursday. They will show losses in all receipts for the nine months of the fiscal year of more than $[illegible], including, besides income taxes, a drop of more than $120,000,000 in customs revenue and $40,000,000 in miscellaneous internal revenue receipts.

For the nine months total expendi-

Continued on Page Seventeen.

Single, Widowed and Divorced Must Pay Heavy Rumanian Tax

Wireless to The New ...

BUCHAREST, ... was introduced ... Parliament yeste... heavy taxation fo... sons.

The bill, contrary ... posals of the same ... tax merely on bachel... vides for complete ... sexes. All unmarried ... tween the ages of 30 an... have to pay an additional ... cent on his or her income ta... a further charge varying fro... to 500 lei.

Those who have lost their sp... by death or in the divorce c... will have to pay the same ... unless they remedy the loss w... two years.

INQUIRY COMMITTEE TO BE NAMED AT ONCE

Macy Goes to Albany to Speed Action After Seabury Objects to Waiting Until April 10.

MAYOR RETURNING TO FIGHT

Clark Prepares for First Crain Hearing Wednesday—Bastress Indicted for Bribery.

Developments yesterday in the investigations into city affairs were;

W. Kingsland Macy left for Albany to speed the naming of the legislative committee.

Mayor Walker started home to reply to charges.

Samuel Seabury, pushing Crain inquiry, won access to Federal grand jury records.

Rollin C. Bastress, former Building Inspector for Manhattan, was indicted on bribe charges.

COMMITTEE TO BE SPEEDED.

Speedy appointment of the legislative committee to investigate the city administration was expected yesterday as Mayor Walker started back from California to answer his accusers and rally his followers for the stiffest fight Tammany has faced in more than three decades.

W. Kingsland Macy, Republican State Chairman, went to Albany to advise legislative leaders that they must lose no time in setting up the machinery of the investigation which he was successful in obtaining after a long and bitter fight. He was to tell them also that Samuel Seabury, who now is investigating magistrate's courts and the District Attorney's office would serve them as counsel provided he got a free hand.

Macy and Seabury Confer.

Mr. Macy, who conferred with Mr. Seabury before starting for Albany, ascertained that the prospective counsel was not interested in the personnel of the committee so long as it agreed in advance not to hamper his inquiry with political considerations. Mr. Macy, on the other hand, promised there would be no interference.

As a consequence it was predicted that the committee would be named within a few days with Senator Samuel H. Hofstadter, sponsor of the empowering resolution in the upper house, as chairman. Three of the committee's members are to be named by Senator John Knight, president pro tem of the Senate, and four by Speaker Joseph A. McGinnies of the Assembly. Before the Legislature adjourns April 10, it was said, the committee would hold its first meeting to offer the post of counsel formally to Mr. Seabury, and promise him it would not interfere with the investigation.

It had been understood that the committee would not be appointed or hold a meeting until after the adjournment of the Legislature. The decision to speed up the program was attributed to Mr. Seabury's belief that the investigation, to be effective must start with as little delay as possible.

Fund Feared Inadequate.

As preparations were made for beginning the inquiry into city scandals in all five boroughs, fear was expressed in some quarters that the $250,000 appropriation in the resolution authorizing the investigation would prove inadequate for the task ahead of Mr. Seabury. One eminent member of the bar familiar with investigations predicted that unless Mr. Seabury obtained many volunteers to serve without pay on his legal staff, the funds would be exhausted within a few months.

Meanwhile Mr. Seabury, in his dual capacity of investigator of the lower courts for the Appellate Division and of District Attorney Crain as Commissioner for Governor Roosevelt, hastened to conclude those tasks before assuming the larger one ahead. He is to preside today at a public hearing on magistrates while John

Continued on Page Twenty-two.

The Map Shows the Location of Managua, Stricken Capital of Nicaragua, and the Proposed Route of the Nicaragua Canal.

2,500 AMERICANS ARE IN NICARAGUA

Of These, 900 Are Estimated to Be in the Vicinity of Managua Alone.

MARINES PLACED AT 1,440

...t of Them Camp in Tents ...n Outskirts of Capital—845 Civilians.

...l to The New York Times.

...NGTON, March 31.—The ... Americans in the earth...ken area of Managua and ...ate vicinity was estimated ... today as more than 900. ...umber in all Nicaragua ... more than 2,500.

... included 1,440 ma... ...ive navy medical offi... engineers, ten diplo...d 845 civilians in the ...nagua and its en... ...ts showed 550 ma... ...c officers and 355 ...

... conducting the ... Canal survey, shows ... three officers and 125 enlisted men on duty.

The roster of the officers is as follows:

Lieut. Col. Dan I. Sultan, commanding officer.

Major Charles P. Gross, Corps of Engineers.

Continued on Page Two.

AVIATOR DESCRIBES HORROR AT MANAGUA

Marine Says Buildings Fell on the Dead and Injured, Causing Panic.

PRISON TRAPS ITS INMATES

Flier Gets Aid in Corinto—American Women and Children to Be Evacuated by Air.

From the radio operator on Motor Ship City of Panama, at Corinto.

Wireless to The New York Times.

ABOARD MOTOR SHIP CITY OF PANAMA, AT CORINTO, Nicaragua, March 31.—Hoke Palmer, an aviator of the United States Marine Corps at Managua, was the first eyewitness to reach here today from the stricken capital. He came to obtain medical supplies from this ship. Mr. Palmer said:

"The entire town of Managua is in ruins. There is not a building left standing. Hundreds of bodies are entombed in the ruins, including many Americans. Fire is raging among the wreckage.

The greatest number of deaths occurred in the penitentiary, which crumbled to powder. Panic followed the earthquake and martial law was immediately declared.

"We shall evacuate all surviving American women and children as soon as possible by air. The railroad is destroyed, all wires are down, and there is no way at present to communicate with the outside world except by airplane to Corinto and then by radio from the motor ship City of Panama.

Rescue Work Well Under Way.

"Rescue work in charge of the United States marines was well under way when I left Managua.

"Among the dead are Lieut. Commander Baske, U. S. N.; Mrs. Murray, wife of Major Murray."

A special train has left Corinto for Managua, but it is believed it will ... unable to reach Managua, due to ... railroad tracks being torn up ...hin a radius of ten miles around ... city.

...rtial law is enforced by the ma... as it is feared the bandits who ...een causing so much trouble ... past will make a raid on the ... city.

...al supplies of all kinds are ...shed to Managua from other ... towns in the vicinity.

...thquake was entirely cen... ...n a ten-mile radius around ... Every effort is being ...cue those buried by fall... Rescue parties have ...d, and the marines are ...

...ing Plane Down.

...New York Times.

... March 31.—A ... plane, probably ...ant Christian F. ... Congressional ...ravery in Nica... ... the Philadel... ...ow for Mana...

...re received ...hington and ...mediately. Lieu... ..., who recently flew to ...aragua with Captain Ralph D. Weyerbacher, former commandant of the naval aircraft factory here, expects to complete the flight in two days if he is assigned as pilot.

Plane Line Helps in Emergency.

Emergency measures were taken yesterday afternoon by Pan-American Airways, it was announced at its offices in New York, to establish adequate communication facili-

Continued on Page Three.

CITY RAZED IN SIX SECONDS

Flames Start at Market, Where 35 Burn to Death —Water Cut Off.

MARTIAL LAW IS DECLARED

Marines Fight Holocaust With Dynamite—Snatch Bodies From Menaced Ruins.

REFUGEES AT MARINE CAMP

Roads Cleared for Ambulances —Only One Hospital Left— Loss Put at $30,000,000.

DEAD MAY TOTAL 2,500.

Special Cable to The New York Times.

BALBOA, C. Z., March 31.—Eleven hundred dead already have been located in Managua and the toll of dead may reach 2,500, according to radio reports received here.

By S. H. MOORE.

Special Correspondent of The New York Times. Via Tropical Radio to The New York Times.

MANAGUA, Nicaragua, March 31.—An earthquake destroyed Managua at 10:10 A. M. today (11:10 in New York).

The dead were estimated tonight at 1,000 and the injured at several thousand.

The tremor lasted only six seconds, but it razed nearly every building in the business district. Fire which started in the central market raged through the section, completing the devastation. Marines are fighting the fire, dynamiting where possible to check its spread.

The market was crowded with women and children, and thirty-five of them were burned to death when its walls collapsed.

Martial law has been declared and United States Marines and Nicaraguan National Guardsmen are enforcing it.

The first contingent of marines had expected to leave Managua tomorrow in accordance with the recently announced withdrwal plan, but because of the emergency the order for embarkation has been cancelled and the marines will remain to aid.

Among the known American casualties are:

THE DEAD.

Lieut. Commander HUGO F. A. BASKE, a doctor in the Nicaraguan National Guard.

Mrs. JOSEPH D. MURRAY, wife of Captain Murray, U. S. M. C.

Two United States officers in the Nicaraguan National Guard.

Two wives of National Guard officers.

Chauffeur for Irving W. Lindberg, Collector General of Customs.

THE INJURED.

IRVING W. LINDBERG, Collector General of Customs; leg injury.

Lieut. Col. FREDERIC BRADMAN, commander of the marines; slight head injury.

Chief Quartermaster Clerk JAMES F. DICKEY of Vallejo, Cal.; severe internal injuries, buried debris national penitentiary. Nearest relative, Lillian F. Dickey, wife, same address.

Gunnery Sergeant LOUIS ROSSICK of Detroit; severe scalp wounds and internal injuries. Nearest relative, B. N. Rossick, brother, same address.

Mrs. LOUIS ROSSICK, Sergeant Rossick's wife; fractured skull, eyes possibly destroyed.

First Sergeant ROBERT G. CRAWFORD of Summerville, Ga.; severe internal injuries. Father, George H. Crawford, same address.

Mrs. R. G. CRAWFORD, Sergeant Crawford's wife, slightly injured.

Major ROBERT L. DENIG of Sandusky, Ohio; fractured right leg below knee. Mother, Mrs. Robert G. Denig, same address.

Gunnery Sergeant GEORGE OCCHIONERO of Brainerd, Minn.; severe scalp wounds, severe injury right hip. Wife, Mrs. Gertrude Occhionero, same address.

First Lieut. JAMES L. DENHAM of Chevy Chase, Md.; scalp wound, not serious. Wife, same address.

Sergeant HUGO A. MAKUS of Peru, Ind.; bad body bruises. Wife, same address.

First Sergeant CHARLES DAVIS of Buffalo; contusions left foot. Wife, Mrs. Marie A. Davis, same address.

Mrs. BUCKNER, wife of Gunnery Sergeant Buckner; slightly injured.

Line Sergeant HODSKIN, scalp and face injuries.

The marine camp is a place of refuge for all injured and as many

Thousands See Two Geysers in Times Squa... As 20-Inch High-Pressure Steam Main Bu...

A huge steam conduit of the New York Steam Corporation burst in two places in Forty-third Street, between Sixth Avenue and Broadway, early this morning, blowing manhole covers high into the air, sending up two geysers of steam more than five stories high and attracting an early morning crowd of 2,000 spectators. No one was injured. Several passing taxicabs escaped undamaged.

The two pillars of steam showered a heavy mist and rain for more than a block in all directions, soaking policemen, firemen and onlookers. A leakage from a cold water pipe, causing cold water to flow to the twenty-inch steam conduit, which had a steam pressure of eighty pounds per square inch, was blamed for both explosions.

The conduit first broke at a point about ten feet east of Times Square about 2 A. M. Before the arrival of emergency crews from the steam company with tools for shutting off the conduit another explosion occurred in the same pipe about fifty feet further east on Forty-third Street.

As soon as the first explosion occurred, calls were sent in for police and fire crews and for emergency crews from the steam company. The crowd of spectators, thinking at first that an explosion had occurred in the Times Square subway station, gathered quickly, but they were kept at a distance of more than 200 feet from the scene, fascinated by the spectacle.

With the second explosion tongues of steam began shooting out of other manholes, the covers of which were hastily removed to relieve the pressure underground. Cracks in the street paving added to the weirdness of the scene.

The main that exploded furnished heat and power for hotels and other buildings in the Times Square area.

Telephone service on the Medallion exchange was disrupted, presumably because of water flooding into the telephone conduits. The water also flowed into the cellars of near-by buildings and into the Times Square subway station.

ROCKNE DIES WITH 7 IN MAIL PLANE FALL

Continued from Page One.

communication ceased, apparently at about the scene of the crash.

Witnesses heard the drone of the motors above the clouds, heard them sputter and stop and soon saw the big craft flash down through the cloud bank with a trail of smoke fluttering out behind.

A wing tore loose and swirled away like a falling leaf, to land half a mile from where the plane plowed itself into the soft earth of the pasture of S. H. Baker. One of the three motors was completely buried by the impact. All on board the plane were dead when witnesses arrived.

Four bodies were thrown clear, Baker said. He was feeding cattle when he heard the plane strike the earth. He telephoned to Cottonwood Falls, fifteen miles north, for ambulances.

Flying in a Dangerous District.

Bazaar is an isolated village in a section particularly treacherous for aviators. The hills provide bumpy air conditions.

Clarence McCracken, a farmhand on the Seward ranch, who also saw the plane fall, helped Baker and others to free the bodies. All were taken to a morgue at Cottonwood Falls over fifteen miles of muddy road, which impeded progress.

Identification was difficult, but was finally established by means of bill folds and luggage. W. L. White, son of William Allen White of The Emporia Gazette, confirmed the identification of Rockne's body, although for a time there was doubt whether he had been aboard the plane. Four of the eight bodies were identified at the scene of the crash and the others later at Cottonwood Falls.

Two hours after the accident Department of Commerce officials from Wichita and Kansas City were on their way to Bazaar to conduct an investigation. Reports as to what happened were indefinite. All actual witnesses agreed that a wing ripped loose before the plane hit the ground. Baker said he heard only the noise of the fall. McCracken said the only warning came from the sputter of the engine. Both said the plane was above the clouds, probably at about 2,000 feet.

Rockne was on his way to Los Angeles, where he was to make a talking picture at Hollywood. He had waited at Kansas City for a chat with his sons, Billy Rockne, 11 years old, and Knute Rockne Jr., 14 years old, but missed them by minutes because he had to leave the railroad station before they arrived in order to get to the airport on time. Then the plane delayed its departure. They arrived twenty minutes after their father had left.

The boys, who had been visiting their mother at Coral Gables, Fla., were returning to Pembroke School, Kansas City. When news of the accident came, Dr. D. M. Nigro got into telephone communication with Mrs. Rockne, who remained at Coral Gables, and she asked him to take charge of the body. He brought the sons here by automobile tonight. The news was told to them only after their arrival. They showed the

Knute Rockne

strength of their father in bearing the blow.

Dr. Jacob Hinden, coroner at Cottonwood Falls, inspected the wreckage of the airplane. He said that, contrary to early reports, there had been no fire, indicating that the pilot, fighting to control the ship, had foreseen the crash and cut his ignition before it hit.

A theory was put forward to the Coroner by H. G. Edgerton of Wichita, district passenger agent of the line, that ice had formed on the wing of the plane and broken it. The temperature on the ground was above the freezing point.

Some witnesses told of a gust of wind coming down sharply on a nearby hilltop soon after the plane fell.

Rockne's Sons "Take It Like Sports."

COTTONWOOD FALLS, Kan., March 31 (AP).—Dr. D. M. Nigro, president of the Notre Dame Club of Kansas City, and a close friend of Knute Rockne, broke the news of the coach's death to his two young sons here tonight. He had brought them from Kansas City. After identifying the body and calling up Mrs. Rockne in Florida, he told the boys.

They sobbed for a few minutes on his shoulder, but he comforted them, and they fought back the tears and became more composed when asked to "take it like sports—the sons of a great man."

"I'm going to be a coach like my father," Knute, Jr., said.

Rockne Had Double Mission.

Special to The New York Times.

LOS ANGELES, March 31.—Knute Rockne was en route to Los Angeles on combined business with motion picture interests and the Studebaker Corporation, according to General Manager Earl R. Carpenter of the Paul G. Hoffman Company, Studebaker agents here. Dut to arrive tonight, he was to have appeared at the Los Angeles Breakfast Club tomorrow and to have spent Wednesday and Thursday at Universal studios in connection with a football picture in which he was to appear.

He was expected to hold a sales promotion meeting for local Studebaker salesmen Friday, as he recently signed a contract as sales promotion manager of that concern, agreeing to devote available time outside his football work to it.

"Just a moment after hearing of the fatal air crash," Carpenter said, "I received a telegram from the head office asking me to get in touch with Rockne here and arrange a sales meeting Friday."

Horace M. Hanshue, president of Transcontinental and Western Airways, late today issued this statement:

"Until we have obtained and analyzed accurate reports on the conditions of the wrecked plane and all of the provable circumstances incidental to the crash it is useless to speculate on the cause of the tragedy. Needless to say every one connected with Transcontinental and Western, Inc., grieves with those bereaved by the accident."

WORKED SIX YEARS TO GET TO COLLEGE

Rockne While at Notre Dame Was an Instructor in Chemistry —Native of Norway.

When Knute Rockne first went to Notre Dame as a freshman in 1910, he explained later, he was "looking only for an education—to my mind, college players were supermen to whose heights I could never aspire."

He had been about six years getting to the college at South Bend, Ind., after he was graduated from the Northwestern Division High School (now Tully) in Chicago. He had to earn the money first. By working as a railroad brakeman and later as a mail clerk in Chicago he accumulated $1,000 and reached the age of 22.

His original intention was to go to the University of Illinois when he had saved this much, but two of his friends were going to Notre Dame at the time and they urged him to go with them. According to his own explanation of his decision, the chief inducement was the possibility of living more cheaply at South Bend.

Since his father brought him to this country at the age of 6 from Voss, Norway, where he was born, the cost of living was the chief thing that affected Knute Rockne's life.

Notre Dame made him a chemist, good enough to be an instructor during his last undergraduate year, and it also made him an end and captain of the football team who made forward-passing history in the combination of Dorais to Rockne on the plains of West Point.

After his graduation in 1914 Rockne remained at Notre Dame to teach the young men, not chemistry, but football. He did it with such success that the public in Chicago has paid as much as $400,000 at the gate in recent years to see Notre Dame in one of its big games. Last year, as a physical indication of Rockne's influence on the corporate fortunes of the college, Notre Dame opened a $750,000 stadium in South Bend, Ind.

After he was graduated from Notre Dame in 1914, Rockne returned there that Fall as assistant football coach. He became head coach in the Fall, 1918, succeeding Jesse C. Harper.

His tenure at South Bend was uncertain only once, in 1925, when J. R. Knapp, chairman of the Columbia football committee, obtained his agreement to come to New York if a release could be secured from Notre Dame on a ten-year contract which Rockne had signed the previous year. His salary would have gone from $10,000 a year to $25,000.

Premature publicity disturbed the negotiations, and Rockne traveled back from New York to South Bend, wondering publicly if he still had a job. In testimonial of the undiminished esteem of Notre Dame, a group of alumni in Chicago collected $2,000 and bought him a new automobile.

Rockne was born in 1889. He is survived by his wife, Bonnie Skiles Rockne of Kenton, Ohio, whom he married in 1914, and by their four children.

Notre Dame's Complete Record Under Rockne

1918.

26—Case	6	26—Purdue	6
66—Wabash	7	0—Nebraska	0
7—Great Lakes N. T. S.	7	132	39
7—Michigan Ags.	13		

1919.

14—Kalamazoo	0	13—Michigan Ags.	0
60—Mt. Union	7	33—Purdue	13
14—Nebraska	9	14—Morningside	6
53—West. Normal.	0		
16—Indiana	3	229	47
12—Army	9		

1920.

39—Kalamazoo	0	13—Indiana	10
42—West. State N.	0	33—Northwestern	7
16—Nebraska	7	25—Michigan Ags.	0
28—Valparaiso	3		
27—Army	17	251	44
28—Purdue	0		

1921.

56—Kalamazoo	0	48—Rutgers	0
57—De Pauw	0	42—Haskell	7
7—Iowa	10	21—Marquette	7
33—Purdue	0	48—Mich. Aggies.	9
7—Nebraska	0		
28—Indiana	7	375	40
28—Army	0		

1922.

46—Kalamazoo	0	0—Army	0
46—St. Louis	0	38—Butler	3
20—Purdue	0	19—Carnegie Tech.	0
34—De Pauw	7	6—Nebraska	14
13—Georgia Tech.	3		
27—Indiana	0	249	27

1923.

74—Kalamazoo	0	7—Nebraska	14
14—Lombard	0	34—Butler	7
13—Army	0	26—Carnegie Tech.	0
25—Princeton	2	13—St. Louis U.	0
35—Georgia Tech.	7		
34—Purdue	7	275	37

1924.

40—Lombard	0	34—Nebraska	6
34—Wabash	0	13—Northwestern.	6
13—Army	7	40—Carnegie Tech.	19
12—Princeton	0	27—Stanford	10
34—Georgia Tech.	3		
38—Wisconsin	3	285	54

1925.

41—Baylor	0	0—Penn State	0
69—Lombard	0	26—Carnegie Tech.	0
19—Beloit	3	13—Northwestern.	10
0—Army	27	0—Nebraska	17
19—Minnesota	7		
13—Georgia Tech.	0	200	64

1926.

77—Beloit	0	7—Army	0
20—Minnesota	7	21—Drake	0
28—Penn State	0	0—Carnegie Tech.	19
6—Northwestern.	0	13—So. California.	12
12—Georgia Tech.	0		
26—Indiana	0	210	38

1927.

28—Coe	7	0—Army	18
20—Detroit	0	32—Drake	0
19—Navy	6	7—So. California	6
19—Indiana	6		
26—Georgia Tech.	7	158	57
7—Minnesota	7		

1928.

12—Loyola (La.).	6	12—Army	6
6—Wisconsin	22	7—Carnegie Tech	27
7—Navy	0	14—So. California	27
0—Georgia Tech.	13		
32—Drake	6	99	107
9—Penn State	0		

1929.

14—Indiana	0	13—So. California	12
14—Navy	7	26—Northwestern.	6
19—Wisconsin	0	7—Army	0
26—Georgia Tech.	6		
7—Carnegie Tech.	0	145	38
19—Drake	7		

1930.

20—So. Methodist	14	28—Drake	7
26—Navy	2	14—Northwestern.	0
21—Carnegie Tech	6	7—Army	6
35—Pittsburgh	19	27—So. California	0
27—Indiana	0		
60—Pennsylvania.	20	265	74

RECAPITULATION.

	W.	L.	T.		W.	L.	T.
1918	3	1	2	1926	9	1	0
1919	9	0	0	1927	7	1	1
1920	9	0	0	1928	5	4	0
1921	10	1	0	1929	9	0	0
1922	8	1	1	1930	10	0	0
1923	9	1	0				
1924	10	0	0	Total	105	12	5
1925	7	2	1				

ROCKNE A PIONEER ON FOOTBALL FIELD

Perfected Forward Pass and Shift Play and Taught Scoring From Any Position.

HAD FIVE UNBEATEN TEAMS

Made Them Work Closely Together on Simple Lines and Frowned on Tricks.

DEVELOPED MANY COACHES

A Keen Student of Psychology, He Knew When to Keep His Sharp Tongue in Leash.

By ROBERT F. KELLEY.

From his days as a player Knute Rockne made his influence felt on the trend of football. As captain of the 1913 Notre Dame team, he figured at end in the most successful exhibition of forward passing the game had seen up to that time; and from that date on the forward pass grew steadily to its present importance in the game.

As a coach he brought the shift play to its highest state of perfection and made it such an important factor in offensive football that the rules committee finally passed legislation designed to take some of its power away.

That shift development, the back field hop, was the most important of his contributions to the coaching of the game, but he added others, notably the reshaping of the line. Prior to Rockne, linemen were big men inevitably. Rockne brought the idea of using linemen, particularly guards, in intereference, and demonstrated that the small, fast lineman could hold his own with the big man and outplay him where the big man was not as fast

Changed Strategy of Touchdown.

He worked for the perfection of a team as a whole and his last two teams won game after game through the successful application of what came to be called "the perfect plays." In these every individual carried out a part of the blocking, and when no man failed to carry out his job the play often went for a touchdown.

This perfect play did a great deal to wipe away the idea of aiming first for scoring territory and then the score. Rockne always said that every play, if perfectly carried out, would go for a touchdown from wherever it was started. His last two teams usually started their scoring with long runs from scrimmage.

In coaching he tried always for perfection and spent hours in teaching the art of blocking. Simple plays, well executed, were his idea of the way to win football games. He had small use for any so-called trick plays. There were only seven places in a line to send a man with a ball, he said, and there ought not to be many more than seven plays.

Hard work was another of his slogans. "The best thing I ever learned in life," he said last June during a visit to Poughkeepsie for the intercollegiate boat race there, "was that things have to be worked for. A lot of people seem to think there is some sort of magic in making a winning football team. There isn't, but there's plenty of work."

Suddenly Developed the Pass.

As a player and captain of the 1913 Notre Dame team, the first to ever beat the Army, Rockne began his shaping of football's destinies by bringing the forward pass suddenly and dramatically into the front of the game. Army that season had scheduled Notre Dame as a "breather" game on its schedule. Only a small crowd turned out, and they stood amazed as Notre Dame defeated Army, 35 to 13. Gus Dorais, now coach at Detroit, threw seventeen passes in that game and thirteen were completed, and a great majority of these went to the short, chunky end, Knute Rockne.

The forward pass had been more or less of a haphazard thing until that time. The success of this Western team with it amazed the football world. Dorais and Rockne remained behind at West Point for a few days after that game to show the Army how its was done. One of the results of that was the famous Pritchard to Merrillat combination of Army teams.

In that first success was an indication of the capacity for taking pains which Rockne owned. That game was the direct result of the Summer before. Dorais and Rockne had obtained vacation jobs together at a mid-West beach and included a football in their baggage. All that Summer they got out on the beach and threw passes. The success against Army was no accident. It had been carefully planned.

Remarkable Record as Coach.

As a coach, of course, Rockne's record is one of the most remarkable that any coach of any sport has ever piled up. Nearly all of his teams have been in the front rank of the game, despite the fact that they always played hard schedules. Five of them were undefeated. Taking over the head coach job, after helping instruct in the chemistry department of Notre Dame, in 1918, Rockne had almost immediate success. His 1919 team was undefeated and his 1920 team was one of the greatest that he had.

To the game in general Rockne brought the high development of the backfield shift and a new conception of line play. He never claimed the invention of the shift play. But there can be small argument with the idea that under him Notre Dame's players brought it to its highest perfection.

So successful were his teams with the shift that three years ago the football rules committee, fearing the offense of the game would overbalance the defense, began ruling against it and this last year finally insisted that a full second, in which an official might count five, must come between the close of the shift and the start of the ball.

Rockne never was reconciled to this and never lost an opportunity to defend his favorite style of play. Legislating against the shift, he said, was like taking the feinting out of boxing and leaving in only the slugging.

Rockne organized coaching schools in which coaches might gather during the off seasons and study the methods of others. He assisted with Summer schools all over the country and in 1928 even conducted one at sea when he chartered a ship and took a party of coaches and athletes to the Olympic Games of that year.

Developed Famous Players.

Perhaps his greatest teams came in 1920, 1924, 1929 and 1930. On the first was George Gipp, who was named by Rockne as the greatest player he ever had. The coach told the story of seeing Gipp, who was not trying for the team, throwing a ball and kicking on the campus and of inducing him to join the squad. Gipp died a few weeks after the close of the 1920 season of a throat infection, with Rockne at his bedside.

The 1924 team was the one of the famous Four Horsemen, Harry Stuhldreher, Jimmy Crowley, Don Miller and Elmer Layden. As a combination, they have not been excelled in modern back fields and they had a great line in front of them, led by the famous Adam Walsh at centre, who is now assisting with the coaching at Yale. That team of the Four Horsemen won all over the country, beating Princeton at Princeton with a temperature of 10 above zero, and several weeks later journeying to the Coast to defeat Stanford in a temperature of 70 degrees.

The records and names of the members of the two recent teams are still fresh in memory, Frank Carideo, Marchmont Schwartz, Marty Brill, Joe Savoldi, Bucky O'Connor, Moon Mullins. And the 1930 team came very near to being the best. Northwestern, Army and Southern California were played on successive Saturdays. One Saturday, in Chicago, Army was turned back in ice and cold rain and the following week the highly regarded Southern California team was badly beaten on the Coast.

Provided Coaches for Nation.

If there were any doubt of the influence of Rockne on football, the list of head coaches for the past year might remove it. There were, throughout the country, North, South, East and West, twenty-three head coaches of football from Notre Dame without naming the assistants here and there. Notable among them are Walsh and Rip Miller, who has this year been elevated to head coach at Navy.

The mere record of his work fails to bring out for those who did not know him the biting, incisive, clear-cut character and personality of the man. Dramatic in everything he did, even to his death, Rockne became a sort of god to the boys who played for him. A great talker, a keen wit, he had a balanced, sane philosophy of life and a keen knowledge of psychology.

There are numerous instances in the near legends which have sprung up about him of his use of the latter element in dealing with his boys. The year that Army and Navy played in Chicago, in 1926, he went to Chicago to watch the game, confident his strong team would beat Carnegie Tech without too much trouble in his absence. They did not.

Used the Delayed Criticism.

The coach returned to South Bend. The next week the team was to play on the Pacific Coast. All week, Rockne coached without mentioning the defeat. The players kept waiting for him to say something. He did not. But when they boarded the train and opened their baggage, each player found a carefully clipped account of the lost game in his baggage. They won on the Coast.

This year, before the Army game, Rockne sat in the dressing room with his players, waiting for the time to go out on the field. The players sat silently, waiting for him to say something. The minutes ticked off in the quiet room, and finally an official came to tell them to come out. Rockne nodded, stood up and said, "Come on, boys." That was all.

He has given words to the vocabulary of the sport as well, some of which fit exactly the army of people who criticize the players and coaches after a defeat, waiting until the day after to display their wisdom. "Sunday morning coaches" was Rockne's name for this class.

A polished story-teller and a constantly interesting companion, Rockne made friends wherever he went, and was almost as much at home at the colleges he played against on his numerous visits as he was at his own. At these places he will be greatly missed as a friend.

MRS. ROCKNE TOLD OF DEATH.

At First Refuses to Believe It, Then Prepares for Journey.

CORAL GABLES, Fla., March 31 (AP).—Shocked by news of the death of her husband, Mrs. Knute Rockne bravely helped members of her household here pack for their departure for South Bend tonight.

She was with Mr. and Mrs. Thomas O'Neil of Akron, old friends of the family, on a shopping tour today when a filling-station attendant called Mr. O'Neil aside and told him of the accident.

Mr. O'Neil immediately took Mrs. Rockne to his Miami Beach home and summoned the Rev. Father David Garry of Miami Beach. They then informed Mrs. Rockne of her husband's death. Mrs. Rockne at first refused to believe it, but when she was convinced asked to be taken home in order to prepare for her trip North.

NEWS OF ROCKNE'S END STUNS NOTRE DAME

University to Hold Mass Today—Group Will Bring the Body There Tomorrow.

Special to The New York Times.

SOUTH BEND, Ind., March 31.—News of the death of Knute Rockne came as a stunning blow to Notre Dame University and to all of South Bend. Flags throughout the city are at half staff. Men, women and children who knew the famous coach seem to be dazed by the sudden passing.

A solemn requiem mass will be said for the noted coach at the Sacred Heart Church on Notre Dame campus tomorrow morning. The entire university is in mourning; but semester examinations will be completed, as the Easter recess starts tomorrow noon.

The Rev. Michael Mulcaire, vice president of the university; Heartly Anderson and Jack Chevigny, assistant coaches, and Howard Edward, South Bend manufacturer, a close friend of Rockne and captain of the Notre Dame football team in 1910, left in the afternoon for Kansas City to bring the body of Rockne back to this city.

At the same time the Rev. Charles L. O'Donnell, C. S. C., president of the university, talked with Mrs. Bonnie Rockne, widow, at Miami, Fla., over the telephone and was informed that she was leaving at once with their two youngest children, Jackie and Mary Jean, for South Bend.

Harper to Return With Body.

When the Notre Dame group arrives in Kansas City it will be met by Dr. Michael Nigro, a Notre Dame graduate and friend of the coach, who will accompany the body to South Bend. It is probable that Jesse Harper, former coach and tutor of Rockne in football, also will return with the body. He was located by telephone at his ranch at Sitka, Kan.

The party will reach here Thursday morning. Final funeral arrangements will be made then with Mrs. Rockne, who is expected at about the same time. She will be met in Chicago by the Rev. John O'Hara, pre-

Knute Rockne showing a Notre Dame player how to block an opponent.

fect of religion at the university. The services may be deferred to Monday owing to the intervention of the Easter season.

"I want him buried from the church at Notre Dame amid the surroundings and boys he loved so well," Mrs. Rockne told Father O'Donnell briefly over the telephone.

Father O'Donnell's Tribute.

Father O'Donnell, friend of Rockne for more than two decades, spoke for the university in paying tribute.

"Nothing has ever happened at Notre Dame that has so shocked the faculty and student body as the tragic news that came at noon today of the accident which took the life of Knute K. Rockne," he said. "To every person at Notre Dame this is as personal a grief as it would be if a member of his family had died.

"Everybody was proud of Rockne. Everybody admired him. But far more than that, we loved him. Apart from the unique and deserved success which he achieved as director of athletics and football coach, he was a great personality, with the attributes of genius. His loss is in many ways irreparable.

"My own friendship for him extends over the last twenty-one years. When I was first assigned to Notre Dame, before my ordination, Rockne was then a student in Corby Hall, where I was prefect. The friendship then formed has remained unbroken and will always be for me one of the fairest memories of life.

"Our hearts go out in loving sympathy to Mrs. Rockne and to his children. Pending completion of arrangements for his funeral the university will hold a solemn requiem service in Sacred Heart Church, Notre Dame, tomorrow. All the students will receive holy communion for the repose of his soul."

FOOTBALL'S HERO MOURNED IN PASSING

Football coaches who admired Knute Rockne's genius and idealism, many of them mentors of rival teams and some of them former players under him, were joined by administrators of college athletics and civic leaders yesterday in eulogizing him for his contribution to American intercollegiate sportsmanship.

Among the tributes were the following:

John F. (Chick) Meehan, New York University football coach and president of the American College Football Coaches Association—Knute Rockne was the finest character and the greatest leader football ever knew. He was so considerate of every one, so great a man, football will never know another like him. The boys he taught and the generations he should have been spared to teach have lost the greatest influence that could have come into their lives.

Lou Little, Columbia football coach—He was the greatest football coach and the finest fellow I ever knew. The game of football will be put back by his death.

John Law, Manhattan College coach, captain of 1929 Notre Dame eleven—It hits me very hard. To me he was like one of the family. He always put up a fight. This time he didn't have a chance.

Major Frank Cavanaugh, Fordham Coach—News of the death of my old friend Knute Rockne affects me almost as deeply as if it was a member of my own family. I can't believe it. Notre Dame and football have lost a great coach and a good leader.

John F. Coffey, graduate manager at Fordham—In the passing of Rockne Notre Dame in particular and the football world in general suffer an irreparable loss.

Dr. **Harold J. Parker**, City College Coach—Football can ill afford to lose a man of Rockne's stature. The sports world, amateur and professional, intercollegiate or otherwise, suffers a deep, lasting hurt through his death.

Professor **Walter Williamson**, Manager of Athletics at City College—Rockne's death is a blow to football throughout the country. The Notre Dame coach was undoubtedly the greatest force for good the game had.

Reynolds Benson, Columbia Graduate Manager of Athletics—We are very shocked and terribly sorry to hear of Mr. Rockne's death. The college and athletic world loses a great man and we send our condolence to Notre Dame and his family.

Professor **Phillip O. Badger**, Chairman of the Board of Athletic Control, New York University—Mr. Rockne was probably the greatest football genius this country has ever seen, but aside from that he was known and admired for his sterling qualities as a gentleman and a leader.

Albert B. Nixon, Graduate Manager of Athletics, New York University—Knute Rockne was dearly loved and respected by every one throughout the college world. Football especially has lost its outstanding leader and greatest friend.

Acting Mayor **Joseph V. McKee**—The people of New York City sincerely mourn the sudden death of Knute Rockne. He was held in great esteem by all our citizens for his manly character, his high sense of sportsmanship and his splendid influence on the youth of our country.

Dr. **Marvin A. Stevens**, Head Coach at Yale—Unquestionably the greatest of football teachers, his delightful sense of humor, his quick sympathy for a fallen adversary and his indomitable spirit are more than a legend and he will carry on as an inspiration to all who love the game of football.

Adam Walsh of the Yale Coaching Staff, Captain of 1924 Notre Dame Eleven—Rock was like a father to me at Notre Dame. He was one of the best friends a man ever had.

John M. Cates, Director of Athletics at Yale—I believe that the whole country will mourn the passing of the great coach. His qualities of lofty sportsmanship endeared him to all who knew him.

Edward L. Casey, Head Coach at Harvard—What a pity that the smartest coach in the game should lose his life at the height of his career! His wit will be missed by all the coaches, because he was the greatest humorist of all in the profession. But the wonderful records of his teams and the steadfast loyalty of his players will be recalled as long as football is played. Rockne was the Napoleon of football.

President Thomas S. Gates, University of Pennsylvania—His passing removes from the field of intercollegiate athletics a man whose ability, high ideals, capacity for leadership and influence for good served to justly earn for him the respect and affection of all.

The New York Times MONDAY, MARCH 8, 1976

Maxie Rosenbloom Dead; Boxer and Actor Was 71

By ROBERT E. TOMASSON

Maxie Rosenbloom, the former world light-heavyweight boxing champion whose unorthodox style in the ring earned him the nick name "Slapsie Maxie" and who went on to a movie career portraying punchdrunk fighters and thugs, died Saturday in the Braewood Convalescent Hospital in South Pasadena, Calif. He was 71 years old.

Rosenbloom had been in the hospital for several years, apparently suffering from the debilitating effects of his 16-year career as a boxer, which ended in 1939.

In 1972, the year he was elected to the Boxing Hall of Fame, Dr. Russell Jones, director of medicine for the Motion Picture and Television Fund, which paid for much of Rosenbloom's medical treatment, said that tests had indicated that the fighter's condition was due to the cumulative effects of head blows in 289 professional bouts.

Had Paget's Disease

He had been ill with Paget's disease, an often progressive bone disease of unknown cause.

Rosenbloom was born in Harlem, and, according to early newspaper accounts, left school in the fifth grade and spent some time in a reformatory.

His first professional fight, at the age of 19, resulted in a third-round knockout of his opponent.

By the time he won a 15-round decision over Jimmy Slattery on June 25, 1930, to win the New York light-heavyweight title, his unusual style in the ring and his flamboyant antics outside provided a steady flow of colorful copy for gossip columnists and sports writers.

Analysis of Style

"Anyone who gets into the ring with Rosenbloom is slapped with great froquency and a moderate amount of vigor," wrote John Kieran, a former sports columnist for The New York Times. "Whether or not this furious slapping is to be regarded as a high form of pugilistic artistry ish another question."

The fighter's roadwork for his fights was done on the dance floor, The Times columnist wrote.

Rosenbloom's 15-round decision over Adolph Heuser, Germany's light-heavyweight champion, in Madison Square Garden in 1933 was considered a factor in Germany's decision to ban its athletes from competing with Jewish athletes to avoid contradictions of the Nazi claim of superiority over "non-Aryans."

Defeated Scozza for Title

On July 14, 1932, Rosenbloom was recognized as the world champion after beating Lou Scozza in a 15-round decision.

He lost the title to Bob Olin on Nov. 16, 1934, in a lackluster decision fight that was booed by fans in Madison Square Garden. The fight was held under rules of the state's Athletic Commission restricting hitting with an open hand.

While he continued to fight for a few more years, Rosenbloom spent more time in Hollywood, where he was to play character roles in numerous movies, including "The Kid Comes Back," 1938; "Each Dawn I Die," 1939; "The Boogie Man Will Get You," 1942; "Louisiana Purchase," 1942, and "Irish Eyes Are Smiling," 1944.

His acting career, characterized by a pronounced New York accent, hesitant but threatening, failed to impress the critics, as had his fighting career.

In his 289 professional fights as a light-heavyweight, generally weighing in around 170 pounds, Rosenbloom won 210 bouts and lost 35, the others being draws or no decisions. He knocked out 18 opponents and was twice knocked out.

"I always hated to hit hard," the fighter said after more than one bout when asked why he hit his opponents with an open glove. It was an opening line he used later in nightclub appearances at the time he began making movies.

In one of many stories he liked to tell, where the apocryphal was not always distinguishable from fact, he said he got into acting after Carole Lombard asked him to teach her to box to help her in fights with her husband, Clark Gable.

He had also operated nightclubs in Los Angeles and San Francisco.

Rosenbloom's marriage to the former Muriel Faeder ended in divorce in 1945.

He is survived by three brothers, Herman, Sam and Sol, and two sisters, Ann Moskowitz and Sylvia Rosenbloom.

Burial will be tomorrow in the Valhalla Memorial Park in North Hollywood.

Maxie Rosenbloom, Claire Trevor and Humphrey Bogart starred in *The Amazing Dr. Clitterhouse.*

Maxie Rosenbloom's 1933 victory over German Adolph Heuser was probably a factor in Germany's decision not to let its athletes compete with Jewish athletes.

The New York Times THURSDAY, JANUARY 19, 1967.

Ross, Ring Champion and War Hero, Is Dead

Stricken by Cancer at 57—Chicagoan Won 2 Titles

Special to The New York Times

CHICAGO, Jan. 18 — Barney Ross, the former lightweight and welterweight boxing champion, died today of throat cancer at the age of 57 in his apartment on Lake Shore Drive.

He is survived by his widow, the former Catherine Howlett; four brothers, Ben, Sam and George Rasof of Chicago, and Maurice Rasof of Los Angeles, and a sister, Mrs. Ida Kaplan of Chicago.

Funeral services will be held Friday at 1 P.M. at the Original Weinstein & Sons Chapel on the North Side. Burial will be in Rosemont Park cemetery.

Tough and a Hero

A student of the Talmud who turned to prize-fighting after his father's murder, Barney Ross was regarded as one of the toughest champions. Outside the ring, moreover, his heroism on Guadalcanal and his victory over a narcotics habit brought him further recognition as a man who had never been knocked out and had never quit.

In recent years Ross was frequently present at major fights as a promotion aide. But he never lost his quality of independence. He would sit for hours, a small, round man with gray hair, chain-smoking cigarettes and softly talking of the years when boxing was more important and its heroes were hungrier.

At a championship fight, Ross once asked the promoter for "walking-around money."

"But, Barney," said the promoter, "your room, your food, your drinks, your cabs are all paid for. What do you need 20 bucks for?"

"I am a big tipper," said Ross coolly.

Barnet David Rosofsky was born Dec. 23, 1909, on Rivington Street on New York's lower East Side. His father, Isidore Rosofsky, a Talmudic scholar from Brest-Litovsk in Russia, moved the family to Chicago and opened a tiny grocery store on Jefferson Street. They lived in two and a half rooms on the other side of the street.

In his autobiography, "No Man Stands Alone," Ross remembered the gangland killings and spirit of lawlessness in the Chicago of the 20's, and

Barney Ross was never knocked down in his 78-bout, nine-year career.

how his father had tried to insulate his family from those conditions with his orthodox Judaism.

Once, when Barney and some friends stole socks from a pushcart peddler, his father whipped him to his knees. Barney complained that other parents did not make such a fuss over petty thieving.

"These people are not us!" shouted his father. "They do not have our traditions to live up to."

Small and skinny, Ross seldom participated in sports while in high school. He concentrated on religious studies, thinking of a carreer as a Hebrew teacher. He was not a particular boxing fan.

A week before Ross's 15th birthday, in 1924, his father was shot by two young hoodlums attempting to rob the grocery. He died several days later, and his death broke up the family.

Mrs. Rosofsky suffered an emotional breakdown and was sent out of town to live with a relative. The three youngest children were sent to an orphanage. Ross and an older brother, Morrie, were taken in by a cousin.

The killers were arrested, but set free when a neighborhood woman, a eyewitness, refused to testify against them out of fear.

Ross, bitter, rebelled against his father's religion, dropping his studies. He became a troublemaker, seeking his vengeance in fierce street fights against neighborhood punks.

He and Morrie worked to support the family, hoping to bring the younger children out of the orphanage. He began running a dice game in the back of a luncheonette and eventually went to Al Capone for a job.

According to the autobiography, the gangster was sympathetic to the youngster and indignant at the murder. But Capone refused to take Ross into his mob because he said it was not proper for a rabbi's son.

To augment an income drained by his mother's medical bills, he began fighting as an amateur. He was an immediate success, overpowering opponents with fury and recklessness, rather than skill. He pawned the gold medals he won at $3 each.

Soon he was fighting as often as six times a week. He won the amateur intercity Golden Gloves lightweight title in 1929, and turned professional just before his 19th birthday. He took the name of Barney Ross to keep his mother from finding out.

Ross's professional career lasted less than nine years. But when it was over, he had earned a place in boxing's Hall of Fame, a rating in the top 10 welterweights of all time, and about $500,000. The money, however, didn't last long.

In his early club fights, the purses were small and Ross was restless. He did not begin to develop until taken over by Sam Pian and Art Winch. They forced him into a strict training regimen, and brought him up slowly.

In June, 1933, Ross got his big chance. He beat Tony Canzoneri for the world's lightweight title. The decision, a narrow one, was booed. On Sept. 13 he beat Canzoneri again, and there were only cheers.

Writing of that fight at the Yankee Stadium, James P. Dawson of The New York Times described Ross as a "cagey boxer, a smashing body puncher, the possessor of an effective left hook, and with the physical equipment to withstand assault and keep coming in; he is no fluke champion."

Ross rediscovered spiritual life that year. He found "peace," he said, in returning to religious study during training periods, and "came to terms with myself about Pa's death, for I'd learned that God has a reason for everything He does."

He also discovered the high life, the pleasure of being "cock of the walk" in Chicago. He was a soft touch for instant buddies, and found a new hole in which to throw money when Al Jolson took him to the racetrack for the first time. He was to become a compulsive gambler, saying the track gave him "emotional release."

In 1934 he stepped up in class and upset the hard-hitting Jimmy McLarnin for the welterweight title. McLarnin won the title back later that year, and Ross regained it from him in 1935. Those fights were long remembered by the fans as classics.

Ross held the crown until May 31, 1938, when Henry Armstrong gave him a savage beating over 15 rounds. Ross felt slow and sluggish that night, but when his managers wanted to stop the fight, Ross told them:

"You do that and I'll never talk to you again. I want to go out like a champion."

Winch and Pian persuaded Ross to retire after that bout, his 82d as a pro. It was only his fourth defeat, and he had had three draws. He was 28 years old. Despite the many big purses he had earned, all he had was $62,000 for having fought Armstrong.

Vigil in the Jungle

He invested successfully in a cocktail lounge. However, the late hours broke up his brief marriage to the former Pearl Spiegel.

When Pearl Harbor was attacked, Ross got an age waiver and joined the Marines. After boot camp, he married Cathy Howlett, a show girl, who had a young daughter by a previous marriage.

Refusing an assignment as boxing instructor, Ross hit Guadalcanal with the Second Division. He won a Silver Star for an all-night vigil, alone, in defending three men who had been badly wounded.

Later he was stricken with malaria. He became more and more dependent on morphine to ease his pain. On his medical discharge, he was a national hero — and a drug addict.

Scrounging syrettes of morphine from doctors, turning his friends into "runners," Ross found himself spending $500 a week on drugs. An old fight doctor who examined him suggested he enter the Public Health Service hospital in Lexington, Ky., for treatment.

His pain and suffering in Lexington were later depicted in a movie based on his life, "Monkey on My Back." As he emerged from the agony of withdrawal, he was handed hundreds of letters from well-wishers, former Marine buddies and fighters.

Ross became a crusader against narcotics dealers. He testified before a Senate investigating committee, saying that "smugglers and all peddlers of narcotics, except addicts, should be hung immediately."

"He was a man of fine character," said boxing's Boswell, Nat Fleischer, "and fear was no part of his make-up."

The New York Times FRIDAY, JULY 6, 1979

MENDY RUDOLPH, 53, DIES; N.B.A. REFEREE

Officiated a Record 2,112 Games in 22 Years in Pro Basketball League—Retired in '75

"I used to kid him a lot about how dapper he looked" said Mr. Auerbach yesterday from his home in Washington. "I used to tell him if he would spend more time running and less time worrying about his looks and his hair, he would work a better ball game. But he knew I was kidding him. When Mendy worked a game, he had complete control. He was as good as anybody who ever blew a whistle."

Marvin (Mendy) Rudolph, who refereed 2,112 games during his flamboyant 22-year career in the National Basketball Association, died yesterday of a heart attack in his home in Manhattan. He was 53 years old.

Mr. Ruldoph, whose trademarks were a loud whistle and an emphatic way of making calls, was dubbed "Mr. Hollywood" by the players because of his dapper offcourt dress and his theatrical manner. In his time running up and down hardwood courts, he presided over more games that any other N.B.A. referee.

Red Auerbach of the Boston Celtics, noted as a referee-baiter, had many run-ins with Mr. Rudolph.

A Father-and-Son Team

Mr. Rudolph was raised in Wilkes-Barre, Pa. He became an official when he was 20 years old and worked his first professional game in the old Eastern League, teaming with his father, the late Harry Rudolph. They operated as a father-and-son team in more than 125 games. Mr. Rudolph officiated his first N.B.A. game, between the Knicks and the Baltimore Bullets, in February 1953.

"It's style and there's no substitute for it," Mr. Rudolph said of his officiating. "I was fortunate enough to have it from the beginning. I've got this pet philosophy about this business. My theory is, don't get 'em to like you, get 'em to respect you."

Mr. Rudolph, when he was the league's chief referee, was forced into retirement after suffering a pulmonary embolism in a playoff game between the Buffalo Braves and the Washington Bullets at the Capital Centre in Landover, Md., on April 25, 1975. He left the N.B.A. two months later to become a television commentator. In his earlier days, he worked as a salesman in the offseason.

"We are deeply saddened to learn of the death of Mendy Rudolph," said Lawrence F. O'Brien, the N.B.A. commissioner, yesterday. "He was one of the great basketball officials of all time. He symbolized the fine qualities and knowledge of the game all officials should possess. Mendy's contributions to the integrity of pro basketball are legendary. His passing is not only a personal loss to his family, but to all basketball and sports."

Mr. Rudolph is survived by his mother, Rose; his wife, Susan; two daughters, Jennifer and Pamela; two sons, Jim and Ted, and a granddaughter, Lauren.

Funeral services will be held at noon today at the Riverside Memorial Chapel, 76th Street and Amsterdam Avenue.

Colorful Mendy Rudolph (dubbed "Mr. Hollywood" by the players) officiated more N.B.A. games than any other referee.

"All the News That's Fit to Print"

The New York Times.

LATE CITY EDITION
Partly cloudy and warm today. Scattered showers tomorrow.
Temperature Range Today—Max.,84; Min.,70
Temperatures Yesterday—Max.,82; Min.,70
Full U. S. Weather Bureau Report, Page 43

VOL. XCVII...No. 33,078. Entered as Second-Class Matter, Postoffice, New York, N. Y. NEW YORK, TUESDAY, AUGUST 17, 1948. Times Square, New York 18, N. Y. Telephone Lackawanna 4-1000 THREE CENTS IN NEW YORK CITY

CITY POLICE REJECT RUSSIANS' VERSION IN KOSENKINA CASE

State Department Gets Report Holding Their Kidnapping Charge Is 'Unfounded'

LOMAKIN RENEWS ATTACK

Consulate Statement Admits Leap Was Suicide Attempt, Laying It to U. S. Harassing

Text of the statement by Consul General Lomakin, Page 3.

By ALEXANDER FEINBERG

An exhaustive report by the Police Department, made to Mayor O'Dwyer and turned over by him to prosecuting agencies, says flatly that the Soviet charges that Mrs. Oksana Stepanova Kosenkina was kidnapped are "unfounded."

This was learned last night from trustworthy sources as Consul General Jacob M. Lomakin was restating these charges and giving to the American press the official Soviet version of the Russian teacher's leap from a window of the Soviet consulate last Thursday.

For the first time Soviet officials admitted in a formal statement that Mrs. Kosenkina's fall was not an accident but that she had jumped from a third-story window in an attempt at suicide. He attributed the attempt to a breakdown brought on by harassment from American sources.

The police report, the contents of which have been kept secret, has been in the offices of District Attorney Frank Hogan and United States Attorney John F. X. McGohey since late Saturday. A copy has been forwarded to Attorney General Tom Clark in Washington and a copy of the confidential document was received yesterday by the State Department.

It is on this that the State Department will rely for the answer of the United States Government to the formal protests made in Moscow by Soviet Foreign Minister Molotov and in Washington by Ambassador Alexander S. Panyushkin.

Teacher's Statement Included

It contains, it was learned, a complete stenographic statement from Mrs. Kosenkina, given to police in question and answer form through a competent interpreter. In her story she denies to ranking police officials that she was kidnapped and declares that she jumped from the consulate window to effect her escape from confinement in the building.

Mrs. Kosenkina refutes in her statement the declaration by the consul that she had jumped after listening to radio accounts of her "drugging" and "kidnapping" by "White Russian bandits" and her subsequent "rescue," by Mr. Lomakin and members of his staff, from the Reed Farm at Valley Cottage, N. Y., operated by the Tolstoy Foundation, Inc.

The Soviet teacher, who sought a haven here after determining not to be sent back to Russia with the other teachers of a now closed Soviet school for children in New York, says that she had a radio in her room at the consulate but that she heard her case discussed only once. That was on Wednesday, the day before her leap.

At that time, she says, she heard her name mentioned along with that of Mikhail Ivanovitch Samarin, the other teacher who refused to return to Russia and who is now in hiding, but she told her questioners that she was unable to understand the broadcast because of her imperfect knowledge of the English language.

The day she jumped, she says, she did not have the radio turned on.

Investigation Termed Thorough

The report, which originated from a complaint by the Consul General addressed to Police Commissioner Arthur W. Wallander, who is now recovering from an operation, closes with the considered police opinion that "the charge of kidnapping is unfounded." The investigation was said to be one of the most thorough and exhaustive ever made by the department.

At no time has the complaint by Mr. Lomakin been listed as a kidnapping. It was placed in the classification of "investigation." Completion of the investigation, it was pointed out, does not automatically place the case in the category of those listed as "case

Continued on Page 3, Column 2

4 More Olympic Men Refuse to Go Home

By The Associated Press.

LONDON, Aug. 16 — Four more Czech Olympic athletes decided today against returning to Communist-ruled Czechoslovakia.

Their decision brought to at least eight the number of Olympic competitors refusing to go back to Communist homelands. Two Czechs and three Hungarians disclosed yesterday that they intended to stay in England, but one of the Hungarians later went back to Budapest.

The Czech Committee for Political Refugees, which announced the action of the athletes, withheld the names. A spokesman said:

"Six Czech athletes who came here for the Olympic Games definitely have decided against returning. Two of the athletes are swimmers. The other four were on the rowing team."

ALGER HISS TO FACE CHAMBERS AUG. 25

'Confront... Inqu...

WAS... hours of ... of Alge... partment ... Mr. Chambers ... ities admit ... determine w... er Chambers, ... leadership in ... Communist "un... telling the truth.

At the committe... ings Mr. Hiss had ... ingly and categ... charges by Mr. Cham... editor of Time magaz... an opportunity to co... cuser, declaring that ... known him and never h...

Mr Chambers swore ... serving as a courier for ... "underground," he had k... Hiss well and went to ... later and urged him to b... from the Communists.

Mr. Hiss repeated today ... vious denials and made ne... als, it was reported, as ne... tions were flung at him. ... new questions arose, it was ... stood, from a second questi... of Mr. Chambers behind c... doors in New York last week.

"Confrontation Day" Set

After today's session the committee set "a confrontation day," Aug. 25, when Mr. Hiss and Mr. Chambers will face each other before the investigating body.

Mr. Hiss left the committee room this evening refusing to comment on his long session with the committee. Representative J. Parnell Thomas, committee chairman, issued a statement in which he said:

"From the testimony of the two witnesses it is impossible at this point to tell which one is telling the truth. The committee is taking every step to determine the true facts."

Mr. Thomas declared that transcripts of the closed session interrogations of Mr. Hiss and Mr. Chambers would be sent to George Morris Fay, United States attorney for the District of Columbia. Last week Mr. Fay asked for complete record of the committee's investigation into spy rings. He indicated

Continued on Page 3, Column 8

3 WESTERN ENVOYS AND MOLOTOV MEET IN LONGEST PARLEY

Sixth Kremlin Session Lasts 3 Hours 40 Minutes—Word on Further Talks Lacking

NEW BERLIN RULE LOOMS

Three-Power Kommandatura Studied—2 Russian Fighters Buzz British Passenger Plane

By The Associated Press.

MOSCOW, Aug. 16—Envoys of the United States, Great Britain and France met with Soviet Foreign Minister Molotov again tonight in the negotiations seeking to settle East-West differences over Berlin and Germany.

The ...

six... Fore... ing ... is ... Mr. Mo... and Au... The ... met an... British E... for the Krem... There has b... Moscow as to ... going: the We... have been silent ... Most Moscow o... the opinion, how... talks were crucia...

Continued on Pag...

Babe Ruth, Baseball Idol, Dies At 53 After Lingering Illness

BIG CAMPAIGN ROLE SET UP FOR WARREN AT DEWEY MEETING

Brownell Reveals Conference Assigns California Governor to Coast to Coast Tours

SENATE VOTES AT STAKE

Candidates and Managers Will ... Attention to Contests ... Seats Appear Close

By LEO EGAN

Special to THE NEW YORK TIMES.

...Aug. 16—Gov. Earl ...fornia, the Repub... Vice President, ...ajor role in the ... votes for the ...icket headed by ...Dewey of New ...e for President. ...ed this after... Brownell Jr., ... the Dewey... top level ...ference in ... in which ...red. ...rs, Mr. ... candi... anagers ... ention" ... ts for ... ap... in ... are ... our

...repub... ...ably weak ... President Roosevelt first elected in 1932.

Hickman Powell, free lance writer and a researcher and political adviser of Governor Dewey for the last six years, may be assigned to accompany Governor Warren

Continued on Page 12, Column 2

5,792 Miles Flown By Loaded Bomber

By The United Press.

WASHINGTON, Aug. 16—The Strategic Air Command announced today that a B-29 carrying a simulated bomb load of more than 10,000 pounds set a record last week-end by flying 5,792 miles non-stop from Florida to the West Coast and back in 23 hours and 30 minutes.

Leaving MacDill Air Force Base at Tampa, the B-29 flew to the West Coast, dropped its "bombs" in the Pacific and returned to its base with 327 gallons of gasoline left in its tanks—enough for about another hour of flying

The Strategic Air Command said the return flight was made at an altitude of more than 25,000 feet. The plane and crew are from the Eighth Air Force 509th Bomb Group, stationed at Walker Air Force Base, N. M.

CUT RATES PLANNED AT BATTERY GARAGE

Ground Is Broken for Building to Park 1,500 Autos—First in City Publicly Owned

As ground was broken yesterday for the city's first publicly owned garage at the Manhattan approach to the Brooklyn-Battery Tunnel it was made known that the rates would be substantially under the tariffs exacted by private garages and parking lots.

The ceremony, at the site of what is to be a 1,050 or 1,500 car facility, was brief. At a signal from Mayor O'Dwyer, a huge crane ...erated by Ben Griff dropped its ...m-shell scoop into the stony ... soon after noon and construc... of the $3,500,000 project ... officially.

...king on were Robert Moses, ...an of the Triborough Bridge ...unnel Authority, the agency ... building the structure; ...ller, president of Thompson-...t Company, Inc., the con... and several high city ... involved in the undertak...

...age will rise seven stories ...vided by the city. The ...essed at $800,000 and ...demnation at $1,000,... will be construct... concrete and cars ... floor to floor by a ... There also will be ... on the roof.

...ign was copied ...t by a private ...t, Mr. Moses ...rage has been ...s on the basis ... elevators for ...wa vehicles. ...ncreased to ...ts do the ...determined ...peration ...ic feasi... ...ease the ...ator who ...meet all amortization and interest charges as well as reimburse the Authority for its supervisory expenses. In addition, the Authority has agreed to pay the city $23,600 a year in lieu of taxes out of any net earnings from the garage in excess of all operating expenses. Mr. Moses reported.

Provision also is being made for servicing cars and the sale of automobile accessories. The first floor

Continued on Page 23, Column 2

SIGNING CREDIT BILL, TRUMAN DENOUNCES 'AID TO PRIVILEGED'

He Deplores Fighting Inflation 'by Putting Average Family Through the Wringer'

ECONOMIC CRASH FEARED

Congress Failed U.S. as Whole, He Says, Comparing Aid to Aged With Business Profits

Text of President's statement on anti-inflation bill, Page 11.

By FELIX BELAIR Jr.

Special to THE NEW YORK TIMES.

WASHINGTON, Aug. 16—President Truman signed today the extra-session measure tightening consumer and bank credit and in doing so asserted that Republican leaders of the Eightieth Congress had served the ends of special privilege rather than the welfare of the whole nation.

The final proof of this, the President maintained, was the refusal of the Republican leaders to consider his anti-inflation program.

He termed the enacted measure a "tiny fraction of what we need" and "feeble response" from Congress to the popular demand for relief from exorbitant prices and for strong safeguards against inflationary threats to our prosperity.

He did not believe the nation should fight inflation by putting the average American family "through the wringer," he declared.

All Credit Affected

In addition to reviving wartime consumer-credit controls, the new law will tighten bank credit by authorizing increased reserve requirements behind bank notes and deposits. Both moves were intended to make it more difficult for individuals and business to get credit and thus to lessen the amount of money available for spending on short supplies.

President Truman's allegations brought a quick response from Senator Eugene D. Millikin, Republican, of Colorado, chairman of the Finance Committee and president of the Senate Republican Conference.

"The Congress did not give the President the right to reimpose allocations, rationing, inventory and price control and excess-profits taxes," Senator Millikin said. "This parcel of egregious error was misdirected to a peacetime America devoted to its economic and political freedom. Therefore it was rejected by the special session of the Congress.

"Even if said controls were solutions, the administration of them could not be entrusted to the present Executive Department."

President Truman asserted that while the Republican majority had no anti-inflation program of its own, it had turned a deaf ear to his proposals.

Fears Worse Conditions

"Unless inflation is checked, the situation will get even worse, and we shall invite economic collapse," he added.

The President said that the nation had the resources and the ingenuity to maintain good farm prices, good wages, full employment and maximum production and that all these could be accomplished "if we have faith and act together."

But he said it could not be done by turning our backs on common problems and ignoring the lessons of our recent economic history.

"Unfortunately for all of us, this Congress has failed to heed those lessons of the immediate past," he said.

Mr. Truman noted that the same people who opposed as inflationary his proposals for a higher minimum wage, increased Social Security benefits and Federal aid to education "refuse to do anything about the excessive profits of giant corporations."

He assailed "these same men" who protested as inflationary a $19.50-a-month increase in old-age benefits while remaining silent about the inflationary consequences of reducing the taxes of a couple with an income of $100,000 so that they had $16,725 more a year to spend.

Still directing his remarks to Republican Congressional leaders, the President recalled how "these same men" argued that we could afford to let wages fall behind prices, withdrawing farm price supports, creating large-scale unemployment and bring on a recession.

The President said there was a

Continued on Page 11, Column 5

Babe Ruth, Baseball Idol, Dies At 53 After Lingering Illness

Famous Diamond Star Fought Losing Battle Against Cancer for 2 Years—End Comes Suddenly After Encouraging Rally

By MURRAY SCHUMACH

Babe Ruth died last night. The 53-year-old baseball idol succumbed to cancer of the throat at Memorial Hospital at 8 o'clock, less than two hours after a special bulletin had announced he was "sinking rapidly."

The home-run king's death came five days after he had been placed on the critical list. It ended nearly two years of fighting against a disease that had sent him repeatedly to hospitals.

About a half hour before his death the famous Yankee slugger said a prayer. Last rites of the Roman Catholic Church had been administered on July 21.

After his death, the Rev. Thomas H. Kaufman of Providence College, Providence, R. I., who had blessed him shortly before death, said: "The Babe died a beautiful death. He said his prayers and lapsed into a sleep. He died in his sleep."

At the deathbed, besides the priest, were the Babe's wife, Claire, his two adopted daughters, Mrs. Daniel Sullivan and Mrs. Richard Flanders; his sister, Mrs. Wilbur Moberly; his doctor, his lawyer, and a few of his closest friends.

There was a hush around the hospital when the end came. The groups of youngsters who had gathered about the red-brick hospital since Wednesday when the name of George Herman Ruth first

Continued on Page 15, Column 3

Israel Issues Own Currency T... New Pound Is Convertible at $4

By GENE CURRIVAN

Special to THE NEW YORK TIMES.

TEL AVIV, Israel, Aug. 16—The Provisional Government of Israel issued tonight a declaration of monetary independence. Beginning tomorrow, there will be Israeli currency completely divorced from British sterling or Palestinian pounds.

The notes will be backed up to 60 per cent with dollars, gold and sterling balances for the main part, and their convertibility will be at the present rate of a trifle over $4 to the pound. There will be exceptions as there are now, with pounds being exchanged for $3 in foreign trade with dollar countries and at that rate for gift dollars such as those received by the Jewish Agency for Palestine.

[An Israeli communiqué said that Arab riflemen had resumed sniping at highway traffic.]

The announcement was made by Eliezer Kaplan, Israeli Finance Minister and treasurer of the Jewish National Council, who said that the Council would effect necessary legislation tonight.

He declared that about £75,000,000 ($300,000,000) of Palestinian funds was held in Britain. He added that he was not worried about it because "Great Britain had clearly undertaken the legal obligation to make funds available in sterling on the basis of one pound sterling for one pound Palestinian." He declared: "It is clearly impossible that an independent state should leave control of its currency in the hands of a foreign government."

"The Israeli pound," Mr. Kaplan said, "which will take the place of the Palestinian pound, will be equal to it and to the pound sterling. Bank notes in Israeli pound denominations will be issued by the Anglo-Palestine Bank of Tel Aviv, which has at all times served as the Jewish national bank and at present acts as banker to the Government.

"The bank will for this purpose open an issue department. This

Continued on Page 6, Column 3

...the Roosevelt-... Administrations as the ... for the Democrats' campaign [11:1], it was agreed in the Republican camp that Governor Warren would be used extensively in campaigning and that both he and Governor Dewey would make coast-to-coast trips. [1:6.]

The House Committee on Un-American Activities questioned Alger Hiss, former State Department official, in a three-hour closed session, but reached no conclusion. Mr. Hiss will confront his accuser Whittaker Chambers, on Aug. 25. [1:2.]

Five days after Mrs. Kosenkina's leap from a window of the Soviet Consulate in New York, the Consulate reversed its version of the incident and said that she had attempted suicide. An official police report on the case, which has been sent to the State Department, rejects the Russian story of the kidnapping of the teacher. [1:1.]

Attorney General Clark announced that an American-born Japanese girl, known as Tokyo Rose, would be brought to this country to face a treason charge. [1:6-7.]

In Moscow, the three Western envoys again conferred with Foreign Minister Molotov. It was

...Rus... authority ... [2:2.]

...the Soviet sector of the city and in the Soviet occupation zone, a vigorous purge of the Socialist Unity party was being carried out to reduce it to purely Communist elements. [2:4.]

General Clay stated that he did not expect to resign as Military Governor even if United States policy on Western Germany were changed, which he thought unlikely. [2:6.]

Russian occupation authorities in Austria banned from the Soviet zone, on the charge of warmongering, seven newspapers published in the Western zones. [4:5.]

The Government of Israel announced that it would begin the circulation of new currency today and that the currency would become the sole legal tender in the country on Sept. 15. [1:2-3.] An Israeli communiqué said that Arab riflemen had resumed highway sniping. Israeli forces and Arabs engaged in a pre-dawn artillery duel. [6:6.]

Count Bernadotte reported to the United Nations that 330,000 Arab and Israeli refugees were in grave danger and need. [6:3.] The United Nations Children's Emergency Fund will spend $400,000 to feed displaced Arab mothers and children. [6:4-5.]

Babe Ruth died in a New York hospital at 8 o'clock last night. [1:4-5.]

Arrest of 'Tokyo Rose' Ordered; San Francisco Jury to Sift Case

By JAY WALZ

Special to THE NEW YORK TIMES.

WASHINGTON, Aug. 16—The only American-born girl to whom American troops in the Pacific are believed to have applied the name "Tokyo Rose" will be brought to this country to face a treason charge. Attorney General Tom Clark announced today.

The Department of Justice chief asked the Army to arrest Iva Toguri d'Aquino and transport her as quickly as possible to San Francisco where a grand jury will be convened to determine if she should be tried.

Mrs. d'Aquino is only one of a half dozen women who took part in Tokyo broadcasts beamed to United States soldiers while they were stationed on islands across the Pacific. The idea of the programs was to instill war-weariness in our fighting men. In sweet-toned chit-chat the various Tokyo Roses talked to their American listeners as "forgotten men," and made frequent mention of wayward wives and sweethearts back home.

It is in connection with such broadcasts that Mrs. d'Aquino, a native of Los Angeles who once attended the University of California, will be prosecuted. When first seized by the Army shortly after the war, Mrs. d'Aquino explained that her part in the wartime Tokyo broadcasts was simply to announce phonograph recordings. She said she never attempted propaganda for American fighting men.

She also contended that her marriage a few months before the end of the war to Philip d'Aquino, a Portuguese employe of Domei, Japanese news agency, made her a citizen of Portugal as well as of the United States.

She was arrested after the Japanese surrender, but was released a year ago when no charge was made. She said she applied for a passport to return to the United

Continued on Page 9, Column 5

Among his other achievements, Babe Ruth was also baseball's all-time greatest right fielder.

BABE RUTH, 53, DIES AFTER LONG ILLNESS

Continued From Page 1

appeared on the critical list, were home having dinner.

In the marble lobby, where late last week groups of boys had occasionally tarried, sometimes leaving flowers for the great right fielder, there were just a handful of adults, all of them waiting to see other patients.

On the ninth floor, where the Babe had spent his final illness, nurses and doctors talked in whispers. Those who had seen him had been shocked at the change since the days of his baseball prime.

The powerful six-footer who had once electrified Americans with sixty homers in a season, had wasted away. The famous round face had become so hollowed that his snub nose looked long. The once black hair so often seen when the Babe doffed his cap rounding the bases, was almost white.

Deeply moved, Father Kaufman said little as he left after having been with the Babe most of the day. Others in the party were just as uncommunicative and hastened past the dozens of youngsters who quickly gathered in East Sixty-eighth Street outside the hospital.

The Babe's death brought tributes from men equally famous in other fields. Among those who sent messages were President Truman and former President Herbert Hoover. Included in the many tributes from baseball figures were those from Will Harridge, president of the American League, and Ford Frick, head of the National League.

Members of the Ruth family said that although funeral plans had not yet been completed, it had been arranged tentatively that a mass would be sung in St. Patrick's Cathedral at 11 A. M. Thursday. Meanwhile the body was to be taken to the Universal Funeral Chapel, 595 Lexington Avenue.

Relapse Comes Suddenly

Though the public had been aware for several days of the baseball idol's grave condition, his relapse yesterday was surprising because he had shown steady improvement over the week-end. On Sunday he had left his bed for twenty minutes.

Even yesterday morning, the first bulletin, issued at 10:20 o'clock, showed a continuation of this trend. It said the former Yankee slugger had spent a comfortable night and was "holding his own." "There has been no significant change," the announcement said.

In the next few hours, however, the patient's temperature began to rise. Early in the afternoon his condition was obviously worse. At 2:20 P. M. the second hospital bulletin noted that pulmonary complications that had not been present the previous day had returned in "moderate" degree. At the same time the Babe showed difficulty in taking nourishment.

But the full extent of his relapse did not become evident until nearly three hours later. In a special bulletin at 5:10 P. M.—ordinarily hospital authorities would have waited until 9 P. M. for the next report—it was announced:

"Pulmonary complications have become worse since this morning. Condition considered more critical."

Even then, however, visitors to the hospital were unaware that anything unusual was taking place. The groups of youngsters that on previous days had gathered outside the twelve-story building were missing. There was no excitement in the lobby, and most of the green chairs were unoccupied.

At 6:25 o'clock the second special bulletin was issued. As the word passed down from the patient's room on the ninth floor to the lobby, photographers began testing their equipment.

Within five minutes, a flurry of telephone calls that set switchboard lights flashing made it apparent that news of the Babe's extremely critical condition had spread beyond the hospital.

From the moment it became known last Wednesday that Babe Ruth was critically ill, his condition became a matter of nation-wide concern exceeding that usually accorded to the country's most important public officials, industrialists and princes of the church.

Headed by President Truman and Cardinal Spellman, American leaders in many fields inquired about his health and wished him recovery. By last night more than 15,000 messages had been received at the hospital from all over the United States and Canada.

The range of greetings to the ailing man, who was more famous in his heyday than Presidents, showed how strong a hold he still had on the people.

On the one hand, Mayor James M Curley of Boston set aside Friday in his city as "Babe Ruth Day," thus following the precedent established in New York on July 26. At the other extreme, hundreds of youngsters huddled outside the hospital or drifted into the lobby for a few moments.

Though many persons had long been aware that the famous slugger was very ill, the first announcement of his critical condition on Wednesday came as a shock. He had entered Memorial Hospital on June 24, presumably for observation and rest.

Last Monday, when it became known that he had a cold, the situation was not considered alarming by the public, particularly when, the next day, his condition was reported improved. The Babe had been in and out of hospitals since Nov. 26, 1946, when he was admitted to French Hospital.

On Wednesday, however, it was obvious that this illness might be Ruth's last. Only his wife, immediate relatives and closest friends were allowed to see him. He was running a high temperature, hospital officials said then, and there were pulmonary complications. Police Headquarters added telephone operators because of the surge of public interest.

The next day, though the Babe improved slightly, his condition was still critical. That evening, his personal physician conferred with Dr. George Baehr, president of the New York Academy of Medicine.

By Friday, the hospital was issuing its reports only three times a day and the patient was reported to be continuing his recovery. His temperature went down and he began taking nourishment. However, he was still on the critical list.

That night, at the Yankee Stadium, more than 60,000 fans stood for a minute in silent prayer for the man whose bat had furnished so much baseball drama.

George Herman "Babe" Ruth

Throng at Yankees-Giants Game Stands At Polo Grounds for a Moment of Silence

News of Babe Ruth's death came last night to the Polo Grounds a few minutes before the New York Yankees—the team on which he starred for so many years—was about to take the field against the New York Giants in their annual game for possession of the Mayor O'Dwyer Trophy.

Over the public address system, announcer Jim Gorey told the huge gathering of Ruth's passing and asked the crowd to stand for a moment of silent prayer. Men, women and children rose, the men with heads bared, while the members of the two teams doffed their caps and stood in front of the dugouts.

The moment of silence over, the Giants trotted out on the field to defend their territory against the "alien" Yankees—and the crowd roared. It was just as the Babe would have it, a game he would have been watching.

Mayor O'Dwyer, scheduled to hurl the first ball, arrived too late for the ceremony but not too late to express his regret.

"All I have to say," he declared, "is what the whole town and the whole nation has to say—God bless him and may he have a happy landing."

Before Col. Jake Ruppert and Col. Til Huston erected the Yankee Stadium—the house that Ruth built—the Babe was hitting home runs in the Polo Grounds. His passing was in the tradition, for the Yankees were playing the Giants before a gathering of about 18,000 to raise funds for the city's agencies devoted to sandlot baseball.

The players in the opposing dugouts, the Giants in the "home" team cubicle to the first base side of the plate, and the Yanks in the "visitors'" quarters to the third base side of home, were sobered and saddened by the news. They shuffled about on the benches silently.

SLUGGER STARRED IN 10 WORLD SERIES

Ruth Set Major League Homer Mark on Total of 714—Hit Over 40 Eleven Se[illegible]sons

HAD MOST WALKS IN 1923

All-Time Batting Great Also Struck Out Most Times in Career Lasting 22 Years

Babe Ruth held fifty-four major league records and was tied for four others. In addition, he had ten strictly American League records to his credit and was tied for five more. His outstanding performances follow:

Regular Season

Highest slugging percentage (extra base hits) season 100 or more games—.847, New York, 142 games, 1920 (major league record).

Highest slugging percentage, American League—.692, Boston and New York, 21 years, 1914-1934 inclusive (major league record).

Most years leading American League in slugging percentage, 100 or more games—13, Boston and New York, 1918-1931, except 1925 (major league record).

Most runs, season (American League)—177, New York, 152 games, 1921.

Most years leading American League in runs—8, Boston and New York, 1919, 1920, 1921, 1923, 1924, 1926, 1927, 1928 (major league record).

Most home runs—714, Boston (A.), New York (A.) and Boston (N.), 22 years, 1914 to 1935 inclusive. 708 in A. L. and 6 in N. L. (major league record).

Most home runs, league—708, Boston and New York, 21 years, 1914-1934 inclusive (American League).

Most home runs, season—60, New York, 151 games, 1927 (major league record).

Most home runs, two consecutive seasons—114, New York, 60 in 1927, 54 in 1928 (major league record).

Most years leading American League in home runs—12, Boston and New York, 1918 (tied), 1919, 1920, 1921, 1923, 1924, 1926, 1927, 1928, 1929, 1930, 1931 (tied)—(major league record).

Most consecutive years leading American League in home runs—6, New York, 1926 to 1931 (tied in 1931).

Most home runs, season, on road—32, New York, 1927 (major league record).

Most years, 50 or more home runs, American League—4, New York, 1920, 1921, 1927, 1928 (major league record).

Most consecutive years, 50 or more home runs, season, American League—2, New York, 1920-1921; 1927-1928 (major league record).

Most years, 40 or more home runs, American League—11, New York, 1920, 1921, 1923, 1924, 1926, 1927, 1928, 1929, 1930, 1931, 1932 (major league record).

Most consecutive years, 40 or more home runs, American League—7, New York, 1926-1932 inclusive, (major league record).

Most years, 30 or more home runs, American League—13, New York, 1920 to 1933, excepting 1925 (major league record).

Most times, two or more home runs in one game—72, Boston (A.), New York (A.) and Boston (N.), 22 years, 1914-1935; 71 in American League, 1 in National League (major league record).

Most times, three home runs in a double-header—7, New York, 1920 to 1933 (major league record).

Most home runs with bases filled in one season—4, Boston, 130 games, 1919 (tied American and major league records).

Most home runs with bases filled in two consecutive games—2, New York, Sept. 27, 29, 1927, also Aug. 6, second game, Aug. 7 first game, 1929 (tied American League record).

Most home runs, 5 consecutive games—7, New York, June 10, 11, 12, 13, 14, 1921 (American League record and tied major league record).

Most home runs, two consecutive days—6, New York, May 21, 21, 22, 22, 1930, 4 games (American League record).

Most home runs, one week—9, New York, May 18 to 24, second game, 1930, 8 games (tied American League record).

Most total bases, season—457, New York, 152 games, 1921 (major league record).

Most years leading American League in total bases—6, Boston and New York, 1919, 1921, 1923, 1924, 1926, 1928 (tied American League record).

Most extra-base hits—1,356, Boston (A.), New York (A.) and Boston (N.), 22 years, 1914 to 1935 inclusive (major league record); 506 doubles, 136 triples, 714 home runs.

Most long hits, American League—1,350, Boston and New York, 21 years, 1914-1934 inclusive (major league record for one league); 506 doubles, 136 triples, 708 home runs.

Most extra-base hits in one season—119, New York, 152 games, 1921 (major league record); 44 doubles, 16 triples, 59 home runs.

Most years leading American League in extra-base hits—7, Boston and New York, 1918, 1919, 1920, 1921, 1923, 1924, 1928.

Most consecutive years leading American League in extra-base hits—4, Boston and New York, 1918, 1919, 1920, 1921 (major league record).

Most extra bases on long hits—2, 1920, Boston (A.), New York (A.) and Boston (N.), 22 years, 1914-1935 inclusive (major league record).

Most extra bases on long hits, American League—2, 902, Boston and New York, 21 years, 1914-1934 inclusive (major league record).

Most extra bases on long hits, in one season—253, New York, 152 games, 1921 (major league record).

Most years leading American League in extra bases on long hits—9, Boston and New York, 1918, 1919, 1920, 1921, 1923, 1924, 1926, 1928, 1929 (major league record).

Most consecutive years leading American League in extra bases on long hits—4, Boston and New York, 1918, 1919, 1920, 1921 (major league record).

Most years 200 or more extra bases on long hits—4, New York 1920, 1921, 1927, 1928 (major league record).

Most years, 100 or more extra bases on long hits—14, Boston and New York, 1919-1933 inclusive, except 1925 (tied American League record).

Most runs batted in—2,209, Boston (A.), New York (A.) and Boston (N.), 22 years, 1914-1935 inclusive (major league record).

Most runs batted in, American League—2,197, Boston and New York, 21 years, 1914-1934 inclusive.

Most years leading American League, runs batted in—6, Boston and New York, 1919, 1920, 1921, 1023 (tied), 1926, 1928 (tied).

Most consecutive years leading American League, runs batted in—3, Boston and New York, 1919, 1920, 1921.

Most years, 100 or more runs batted in—13, Boston and New York, 1919-1933 except 1922 and 1925 (tied American and major league records).

Most consecutive years, 150 or more runs batted in, league—3, New York, 1929, 1930, 1931 (tied American and major league records).

Most bases on balls—2,056, Boston (A.), New York (A.) and Boston (N.), 22 years, 1914-1935 inclusive (major league record).

Most bases on balls, American League—2,036, Boston and New York, 21 years, 1914-1934 inclusive.

Most bases on balls in one season—170, New York, 152 games, 1923 (major league record).

Most years leading American League in bases on balls—11, New York, 1920, 1921, 1923, 1924, 1926, 1927, 1928, 1930, 1931, 1932, 1933 (major league record).

Most consecutive years leading American League in bases on balls—4, New York, 1930, 1931, 1932, 1933 (major league record).

Most years 100 or more bases on balls, American League—13, Boston and New York, 1919, 1920, 1921, 1923, 1924, 1926, 1927, 1928, 1930, 1931, 1932, 1933, 1934 (major league record).

Most consecutive years, 100 or more bases on balls, league—5, New York, 1930-1934 inclusive (tied American League record).

Most strikeouts, 1,330, Boston (A.), New York (A.) and Boston (N.), 22 years, 1914-1935 inclusive (major league record).

Most strikeouts, American League, 1,306, Boston and New York, 21 years, 1914-1934 inclusive.

World Series

Most series played, 10, Boston (1915, 1916, 1918); New York (1921, 1922, 1923, 1926, 1927, 1928, 1932).

Most series batting .300 or better—6, New York (1921, 1923, 1926, 1927, 1928, 1932).

Highest batting percentage, four or more games, one series—.625, New York, 1928.

Most runs, total series—37, New York (A.).

Most runs, one series—Nine (four-game series)—New York, 1928; eight (six-game series), New York, 1923; eight (six-game series), New York (1923).

Most runs, one game—4, New York, 1926 (tie).

Most consecutive games, one or more runs, one or more series—9, New York.

Most hits, one series—10 (four-game series), New York (1928).

Most two-base hits, one series—3 (four-game series), New York, 1928.

Most home runs, total series—15, New York, 1921, 1923, 1926, 1927, 1932.

Most home runs, one series—3 (six-game series), New York, 1923; 4 (seven-game series), New York, 1926.

Most home runs, one game—3, New York, 1928.

Three home runs in one game—New York, 1932.

Most total bases, one series—22 (four-game series), New York, 1928; 19 (six-game series), New York, 1923.

Most total bases, one game—12, New York, 1926, 1928.

Most extra-base hits, one series—6 (four-game series), New York, 1928; five (six-game series), New York, 1923 (tied).

Most extra-base hits, total series—22, Boston and New York.

Most extra bases on long hits, total series—54, Boston and New York.

Most extra bases on long hits, one game—9, New York, 1926, 1928.

Most times player batting in three runs on long hit—2, New York, 1927, 1932 (tied).

Most bases on balls, total series—33. Boston and New York.

Most bases on balls, one series—8 (six-game series), New York, 1923; 11 (7-game series), New York, 1926.

Most bases on balls, one game—4, New York, 1926 (tied).

Most strike-outs, total series—30, Boston and New York.

7TH OF '27 YANKEES TO DIE

Six Who Preceded Ruth Were Members of Famous Team

Babe Ruth became the seventh member of the famous Yankee team of 1927 to die. This was the team that swept easily to a pennant with its "Murderers Row" and fine pitching.

Among those who played prominent roles with that club and have since died were Lou Gehrig, first baseman; Tony Lazzeri, second baseman; Herb Pennock, pitcher; Urban Shocker, pitcher; John Grabowski, catcher, and Miller Huggins, manager.

Shocker died in 1928, after he

(continued)

had passed his prime. A year later, Huggins, who had fined the Babe $5,000, died at his peak. Gehrig's death came in 1940, and last year Lazzeri died.

Grabowski was killed in a fire the next month, and early this year Pennock, one of the great southpaws of his day, died of a cerebral hemorrhage.

RUTH NEVER KNEW OF CANCER MALADY

Operation, Latest Drug Tried —Babe Was in Great Pain, Could Not Eat Solids

By WILLIAM L. LAURENCE

Babe Ruth was the latest victim of cancer, the scourge that kills more than 170,000 Americans every year and is responsible for one out of every eight deaths.

He was operated on in the spring of 1947 for a malignant tumor on the left side of the neck. By that time, however, the cancer had spread to the point at which it could be removed only partly. The operation necessitated the ligation of the external carotid artery, which supplies the face, tongue and external parts of the head, as the cancer had straddled that vital organ.

As is unfortunately the case in such surgical procedures where part of the cancer cannot be removed, the remaining part continued growing. Subsequent X-ray treatment failed to stop the continued growth of the mass.

The case reached the desperate stage by the middle of June, 1947. The pains were most severe, so much so that Ruth could not sleep, or eat solid foods. The mass became so tender that even the slightest touch caused excruciating pain. The patient required large doses of morphine. He had lost about ten pounds in weight. The left vocal cord and the left side of the soft palate were immobile.

It was at that stage, when all standard medical procedures are of no help and the patient is given up as hopelessly incurable, that a new drug, known as pteroyl tri-glutamic acid, or teropterin, which had shown some promise in checking cancer in certain species of mice, was tried on Ruth as a desperate last resort. Teropterin is a synthetic relative of folic acid, a vitamin of the B-complex family.

Treatment with the teropterin was started on June 29, 1947, with daily doses of five milligrams injected intramuscularly. He also received a blood transfusion during the course of treatment.

After six weeks with the new drug, the patient appeared greatly improved, so much so that it was made the subject of a special report before the International Cancer Congress at St. Louis in September, 1947, without, of course, the use of the patient's name. Examination on Aug. 14, the report said, showed the following:

"The mass in the neck had disappeared completely. His pain has practically gone. He eats solid food without any difficulty in swallowing. The tenderness on palpation is gone. The voice has improved a great deal. The soft palate on the left side now moves as well as on the right side. The left vocal cord is still immobile. He has gained twelve pounds in weight."

The report added, however: "We are naturally aware of the possibility that the excellent results in this one case may be only temporary. It seems most opportune to warn against exaggerated hopes as to the results in patients suffering from cancer."

Ruth never knew that he had cancer, and although millions of his fans learned about it through word of mouth, it was one of the best kept secrets in modern times.

Lou Gehrig shakes hands with Babe Ruth as Ruth crosses the plate after hitting a home run in a World Series game against Chicago.

Mize Quits Game as Ruth Dies

Johnny Mize, home-run hitter of the Giants, a cousin of Babe Ruth by marriage, left the game against the Yankees last night after hitting a home-run in the fourth inning. After dressing hurriedly, he left the Polo Grounds to join Ruth's family.

Ruth's Pay by Seasons During Baseball Career

Babe Ruth's salary by seasons for his professional baseball career follows:

Year.	Team.	Salary.
1914	Baltimore (I. L.)	$600
*1914	Boston (A. L.)	1,300
1915	Boston (A. L.)	3,500
1916	Boston (A. L.)	3,500
1917	Boston (A. L.)	5,000
1918	Boston (A. L.)	7,000
1919	Boston (A. L.)	10,000
1920	New York (A. L.)	20,000
1921	New York (A. L.)	30,000
1922	New York (A. L.)	52,000
1923	New York (A. L.)	52,000
1924	New York (A. L.)	52,000
1925	New York (A. L.)	52,000
1926	New York (A. L.)	52,000
1927	New York (A. L.)	70,000
1928	New York (A. L.)	70,000
1929	New York (A. L.)	70,000
1930	New York (A. L.)	80,000
1931	New York (A. L.)	80,000
1932	New York (A. L.)	75,000
1933	New York (A. L.)	50,000
1934	New York (A. L.)	35,000
1935	Boston (N. L.)	40,000
1938	Brooklyn (N. L.)	15,000
	Total	$925,900

*Bought by Red Sox from Baltimore and farmed to Providence (I. L.).

31,432 Boston Fans Stand In Silent Prayer for Ruth

Special to THE NEW YORK TIMES.

BOSTON, Aug. 16—A singularly subdued crowd of 31,432 Boston fans stood for one minute in silent prayer at Braves Field tonight just before the Dodgers and Braves faced each other.

They paid this tribute to Babe Ruth immediately after it was announced over the public address system that baseball's most famous player was dead.

It was an impressive moment, and when the Braves ran out to take the field a moment later there was not the usual rising roar of applause.

"All the News That's Fit to Print"

The New York Times

LATE CITY EDITION

Weather: Partly sunny, warm today; Partly cloudy tonight, tomorrow. Temp. range: today 85-63; Sunday 81-55. Full U.S. report on Page 70.

VOL. CXIX ... No. 41,036 © 1970 The New York Times Company. NEW YORK, MONDAY, JUNE 1, 1970 15 CENTS

OPERATING BUDGET OF CITY IS SEEN UP AN 'ALARMING' 17%

Citizens' Group Says the New Taxes Entailed Are 'Economically Harmful'

ANALYSIS HELD 'NAIVE'

Lindsay Aides Put Rise at 15.9% and Cite Shift to State Revenue-Sharing

By PETER KIHSS

The Citizens Budget Commission charged yesterday that Mayor Lindsay's new operating budget involved "an alarming one-year rise of 17.6 per cent" and called for "economically harmful new city taxes and charges."

In an analysis that drew an immediate counter-attack from the Lindsay administration, the watchdog civic group charged that the Mayor's proposals would "adversely affect all those who live and work in the city by increasing both residential and business rent bills directly or indirectly."

Mr. Lindsay has proposed a budget for the 1970-71 fiscal year beginning July 1 of $7.8-billion, $1.1-billion more than the current year's budget.

Criticizing the city's h[...] for vast increases in state [...] Federal aid for the future, th[...] civic body asserted that "fiscal fantasies are no substitutes for hard fiscal planning."

Mayor's Aides Hit Back

In turn, Thomas Morgan, the Mayor's press secretary, and James A. Cavanagh, assistant budget director, declared that "a combination of naivete, insentivitiy and error make the report of the Citizens Budget Commission nonconstructive and misleading."

"In its charge that city residents would pay 47 per cent of any added state taxes next year," the two Lindsay aides said in a statement, "it ignores the critical fact that this would be far better than paying 100 per cent of taxes now that would have had to be raised locally to meet the city's need for revenue this year."

Mr. Morgan said the Mayor had led a six-city campaign that won state sharing of the income tax this year when no one expected this, making New

Continued on Page 39, Column 1

Sluggish S.E.C. Is Facing A Pile of Unsettled Issues

Many of Critics in Securities Industry Blame Chairman Budge — Defenders Cite Complexity of Problems

By EILEEN SHANAHAN

Special to The New York Times

WASHINGTON, May 31—The Securities and Exchange Commission, long noted as one of the most vigorous and effective agencies in the entire Federal Government, has lost its zest.

This is the firm opinion of many knowledgeable individuals who regularly follow the commission's activities.

The opinion is shared by many—perhaps a majority—of the most experienced and valued members of the commission's own staff.

It is also shared by a striking number of those in the securities business who, in the past, have complained that the commission was doing too much, rather than too little, in its role as overseer of the honesty and fairness of the nation's securities markets.

The dispirited atmosphere at the S.E.C., and its apparent inability to reach decision[...] a host of issues th[...] ing before it, [...] cent dram[...] prices[...]

However, there are some people in the securities industry (they are a minority) who do believe that if the S.E.C. had been on its toes, the market break might have been smaller and less precipitous.

Even those who reject completely the idea that the commission is in any way responsible for the market slump tend to fear that the S.E.C., with its present staff and leadership, will prove unable to cope with the stock markets that will exist after the great bear market of 1969-70 is history.

This severely critical view of the commission is, of course, not unanimously held.

Those who defend the agency point out that it curren[...] before it proble[...] precedented [...] potent[...] tha[...]

Go[...] thoug[...] paging[...] crossing[...] making in[...] and afflicti[...] proportion o[...]

The alarm [...] officials over [...] as a nationwi[...] gonorrhea is p[...] what by an inc[...] number of report[...] syphilis in all but [...] of the country durin[...] four months of t[...] Syphilis has been on[...] cline for the last fi[...] and many officials ex[...] this decline to continue.

With more than one a[...] half million new cases [...] year, venereal disease is [...] nation's most common co[...] municable disease, except for the common cold. The re-[...]

TO OUR READERS

Effective today, June 1, the regular newsstand price of the weekday issues of The New York Times will be 15 cents. (Higher in air delivery cities.)

Effective Sunday, June 7, outside the 50-mile New York metropolitan area and all of Long Island, the new price of the Sunday Times will be 75 cents (where the price is now 60 cents).

There is no change in the price of the Sunday New York Times within the 50-mile New York metropolitan area where the price will remain at 50 cents.

CANADIAN DOLLAR TO FLOAT IN VAL[...]

United Press International

[...]eeting with Gen. Creighton W. Abrams, [...]curity, at the Western White House.

[...]riefing on War

[...] tary of Defense Melvin R. Laird, Deputy Secretary of Defense David Packard, Gen. [Ea]rle G. Wheeler, retiring [Cha]irman of the Joint Chiefs [of] Staff, Adm. Thomas H. [...] the next chairman of [...] Chiefs, and Henry A. [...] Mr. Nixon's adviser [...]l security.

[...] reporters later, Mr. [...] that the President [...]ouraged" by the [...] been receiving [...]ne in the last [...] was equally [...]he accounts [...] General Moorer. [...]is advis[...]paneled Pres[...]pound [...]

ENEMY UNITS QUIT VIETNAM RESORT, AVOIDING A FIGHT

Reds Elude Saigon's Troops After Holding Buildings in Dalat for 24 Hours

AREA WAS SURROUNDED

U.S. Official Voices Dismay —Foe's Losses Are Put at 47 Dead, 4 Captured

By The Associated Press

SAIGON, South Vietnam, May 31—About 75 Vietcong and North Vietnamese soldiers, who seized part of the resort city of Dalat yesterday, slipped past hundreds of encircling Government troops today and escaped into the surrounding hills.

They fled under cover of predawn darkness, reportedly meeting no resistance from the South Vietnamese infantry, armored and militia forces that had surrounded a Roman Catholic seminary, a convent and university buildings that the invaders held for 24 hours.

"How did they get out without being caught or pursued—that's what we are trying to find out," an exasperated United States official said. "We don't know that the Government troops didn't just stick their heads in the sand and hope that the enemy went away."

Enemy Dead Put at 47

Military officials said that 47 enemy soldiers had been killed, most of them early yesterday when the attackers struck with mortars and ground assaults against 13 installations in and around Dalat. Four enemy soldiers were captured. Government losses were put at 16 killed and two wounded.

A 21-year-old Catholic novice was killed at the convent of St. Demaine de Marie, when Government troops fired into the building.

Dalat, situated at an elevation of almost 5,000 feet in mountains 145 miles northeast of Saigon, is the capital of Tuyenduc Province. It is South Vietnam's ninth largest city, with a population of about [...]7,000.

Lieut. Gen. Arthur S. Collins [...] commander of United States [...]s in the 12-province area [...]orms the II Corps tactical [...]timated that 200 enemy [...]ad participated in the [...]ack on the mountain

[...] on Page 6, Column 4

Democratic 'Bosses': [...]

The New York Times — Albert Guida

Three important county leaders in the Democratic party, from the left: Joseph F. Crangle from Erie County (Buffalo), Meade H. Esposito from Kings County (Brooklyn), and Patrick J. Cunningham, the organization head in the Bronx.

By MARTIN TOLCHIN

A Brooklyn Democratic leader telephoned his Congressman last month and set in motion the events that brought Pvt. Joseph C. Caruso halfway around the world, from a line company in Vietnam to his ailing mother in Red Hook.

The same week, James V. Mangano, the leader, telephoned his Councilman and Assemblyman and obtained school crossing guards for Our Lady of Peace parochial school, arranged for the admission of a retarded child into a specialized school, and managed an inter-departmental transfer of an employe of Merrill Lynch, Pierce, Fenner and Smith, a stock brokerage concern.

"I take care of the neighbors' children," the 64-year-old Mr. Mangano said in a quiet, steely voice. "If the constituents are satisfied with the service they receive, I assume they'd want the service to continue."

Mr. Mangano, Red Hook's district leader since 1934 and the $27,000-a-year general clerk of State Supreme Court in Brooklyn, is one of the 46 elected leaders (there is a leader and a co-leader in each district) in the borough. Their power and that of their counterparts in the Bronx and Buffalo have prompted charges of "bossism" in the June 23 primary for the Democratic nomination for Governor.

This has become one of the principal issues of the campaign in which Howard J. Samuels has accused his primary opponent, Arthur J. Goldberg, of being the "handpicked" candidate of the "bosses."

Who are the men called "bosses?"

What is their power and how do they use it?

What keeps their "machines" intact?

"We're keeping this organization together with spit," said Meade H. Esposito, the rapsy-voiced, 61-year-old leader of the Brooklyn Democrats. "There's no patronage."

"Respect, loyalty and honor holds our organization together," said Patrick J. Cunningham, the 42-year-old Bronx leader. "Patronage today is greater than ever, but it's not with the Democratic party, it's with John Lindsay and Nelson Rockefeller."

"No political party can operate without an organization," said Joseph F. Crangle, the 37-year-old Erie County (Buffalo)

Continued on Page 27, Column 1

[...]ording [...] com[...] [...]d two tanks [...]mored vehicles, kill[...] [...]ll the occupants except one, who was taken prisoner.

[...] military [...]ported that two [...] planes had been shot [d]own by antiaircraft fire along the northern sector of the canal. The Egyptian fighter-bombers attacked Israeli positions oppo-

The second ambush was directed against an Israeli relief column moving northward along the canal. Two armored vehicles and a tank were destroyed and all but one of the

Continued on Page 12, Column 4

Earthquake Rocks Half of Peru; Nearly 200 Are Reported Killed

By United Press International

LIMA, Peru, May 31 — An earthquake rocked Peru this afternoon, bringing down homes and buildings and leaving dead and injured in an area spanning half the country. Some towns were reported to be in rubble.

The worst hit city was Huarás, 180 miles northeast of Lima. Amateur radio operators reported that the town "has been destroyed."

[The Associated Press reported that Lima newspapers had received reports indicating that nearly 200 people had been killed in the quake. Radio Panamerica reported that 140 had died in Huaras.]

One of the radio operators said "maybe 95 per cent of the houses" had collapsed. He said that several persons had been killed, including policemen who were trapped when the police station collapsed.

All power and telephone lines to the area were cut by the quake.

The National Geophysics Institute in Lima said the quake measured 7.75 on the Richter scale, considered very intense and damaging. The institute said the epicenter was located 210 miles northwest of Lima, in the Pacific. The quake shook parts of Peru well into the night, but its peak was reached in the first few minutes.

Another city hard hit by the quake was Chimbote, 260 miles north of Lima facing the Pacific. Radio reports said the fishing city of 80,000 also suffered heavy damage and casualties.

Because of the lack of com-

Continued on Page 17, Column 1

[Sawchuk of R]angers Dies Here [Following] 'Horseplaying' Injury

By GERALD ESKENAZI

Terry Sawchuk of the New York Rangers, the holder of many National Hockey League records for goaltenders and considered by many to be the sport's finest goalie, died yesterday at the age of 40 after being hospitalized for more than a month.

Sawchuk was admitted to Long Beach (L.I.) Memorial Hospital on April 29 at 10:45 P.M. after reportedly "horseplaying" on the lawn of his rented house with his teammate, Ron Stewart.

In an early account of the incident, a source close to the Rangers said the fracas and resulting injury had occurred just after the two players returned from a bar.

Sawchuk underwent two operations at the Long Beach hospital. In the first, his gall bladder was removed. A second operation was performed to correct a bleeding liver condition.

Last Friday, he was moved to New York Hospital in Manhattan, and another operation was performed on his liver on Saturday.

The preliminary findings of an autopsy, which determined that he died of a pulmonary embolism—a clot on one of the arterial branches—have been forwarded to the Nassau County District Attorney, according to Dr. Elliott Gross, Deputy Chief Medical Examiner of New York City.

A detective in the Nassau

Continued on Page 46, Column 5

The New York Times

Terry Sawchuk

NEWS INDEX

Sawchuk of Rangers Dies Here Following 'Horseplaying' Injury

By GERALD ESKENAZI

Terry Sawchuk of the New York Rangers, the holder of many National Hockey League records for goaltenders and considered by many to be the sport's finest goalie, died yesterday at the age of 40 after being hospitalized for more than a month.

Sawchuk was admitted to Long Beach (L.I.) Memorial Hospital on April 29 at 10:45 P.M. after reportedly "horseplaying" on the lawn of his rented house with his teammate, Ron Stewart.

In an early account of the incident, a source close to the Rangers said the fracas and resulting injury had occurred just after the two players returned from a bar.

Sawchuk underwent two operations at the Long Beach hospital. In the first, his gall bladder was removed. A second operation was performed to correct a bleeding liver condition.

Last Friday, he was moved to New York Hospital in Manhattan, and another operation was performed on his liver on Saturday.

The preliminary findings of an autopsy, which determined that he died of a pulmonary embolism—a clot on one of the arterial branches—have been forwarded to the Nassau County District Attorney, according to Dr. Elliott Gross, Deputy Chief Medical Examiner of New York City.

A detective in the Nassau

Continued on Page 46, Column 5

Sawchuk Dies After 'Horseplay' Injury

Continued From Page 1, Col. 7

County homicide bureau said yesterday an investigation would begin today into the cause of death.

Sawchuk shared his winter home at 58 Bay Street in East Atlantic Beach, L.I., with Stewart. Both men had been separated from their wives.

Sawchuk had been hospitalized for three weeks before the public learned of his injury. At the time he was admitted to the Long Beach hospital, the police in that South Shore city went to the players' home and took a statement from Stewart. But East Atlantic Beach, a part of the Town of Hempstead, is not in the Long Beach police jurisdiction, and no formal report was made by the Long Beach police.

Roughhousing Reported

A detective at the Long Beach stationhouse reported at the time that Sawchuk said he had "tripped" over Stewart while the two were roughhousing.

Most of the Rangers, whose season extends from October through April, live during that time in East Atlantic Beach, a summer resort that has homes for rent during those months. The players form a winter enclave in the area. A resident characterized the enclave yesterday as "a quiet place where everyone minds his own business."

Emile Francis, the Rangers' general manager and coach, said he had been with Sawchuk "day and night" for the four days before the player's death. Himself a former big-league goalie, Francis called Sawchuk "the best I ever saw, no doubt about it."

"We only had him for one year," Francis said, "and he didn't let us down one bit."

Sawchuk was acquired last summer from the Los Angeles Kings. By then, the reflexes that enabled him to be a seven-time all-star had diminished. His job with the Rangers, he knew, was to be the back-up goalie for Ed Giacomin.

"That's fine," he said at the time of his trade, when informed of his duties. "I'm old and I'm tired. I don't want to be—I can't be—No. 1 any more."

Next-door neighbors of Sawchuk and Stewart didn't even know the two were hockey players until they read about Sawchuk's injury.

Stewart, 37, is believed to be at his home in Barrie, Ontario, at present. Attempts by the Rangers to reach him in the last few days were unsuccessful.

Stewart had known Sawchuk since the nineteen-sixties, when they shared a home in Toronto while both were playing there. They were not roommates on the road, however. Stewart preferred to have his own hotel room.

Stewart, a laconic person known as one of the game's cleanest players, had only 14 minutes in penalties last season—a low total for the fast, often brutal game of hockey.

In his first full season in the National Hockey League, Terrence Gordon Sawchuk, who was born in Winnipeg, Manitoba, on Dec. 28, 1929, became the outstanding goaltender in the sport. That season was the 1950-51 campaign, and the team was the Detroit Red Wings.

For five straight seasons, he posted a goals-against average of less than 2 a game, and over the years he four times captured the Vezina Trophy for posting the lowest average. He set a National Hockey League record of 103 regular season shutouts.

The Wings traded him to the Boston Bruins in 1955, after they found another goaltender, Glenn Hall, whom they considered to be potentially better. At Boston, Sawchuk contracted mononucleosis. He tried to return too soon and often played poorly.

The crowds taunted him for his poor play. He left the team without permission and had what he was to describe later as a nervous breakdown.

He returned to the Red Wings in 1957, and was traded to the Toronto Maples Leafs in 1964. Most people expected him to end his career there.

Outstanding in 1967

But in his final season with the Leafs, in 1967, he reached back to his former greatness and helped lift the Leafs to victory in the Stanley Cup playoffs, hockey's World Series.

Because of his age he was considered expendable, and the Leafs made him available in the expansion draft, which took place a month later to stock six new teams that were entering the leagues. Sawchuk, drafted by the Los Angeles Kings, was the first player chosen.

This past season, he played at 175 pounds, 25 pounds lighter than his weight during his glory years. He had a perpetual stoop from his 20 seasons of stopping flying rubber disks at 100 miles an hour.

During his career the goalie required more than 400 stitches to close facial wounds received in games. In later years he took to wearing a fiberglass mask—a skin-colored protector with slits for sight and breathing.

Last year, when he turned in a good performance for the Rangers, he would often seek reassurance from reporters after a game. "Do you really think I played well?" he might ask. Or: "I didn't embarrass anyone out there, did I?"

The next day, however, he often would be surly and unapproachable. Many times he would sit in the lobby of a hotel doing The Times crossword puzzle in ink and motioning questioners away.

Ron Stewart

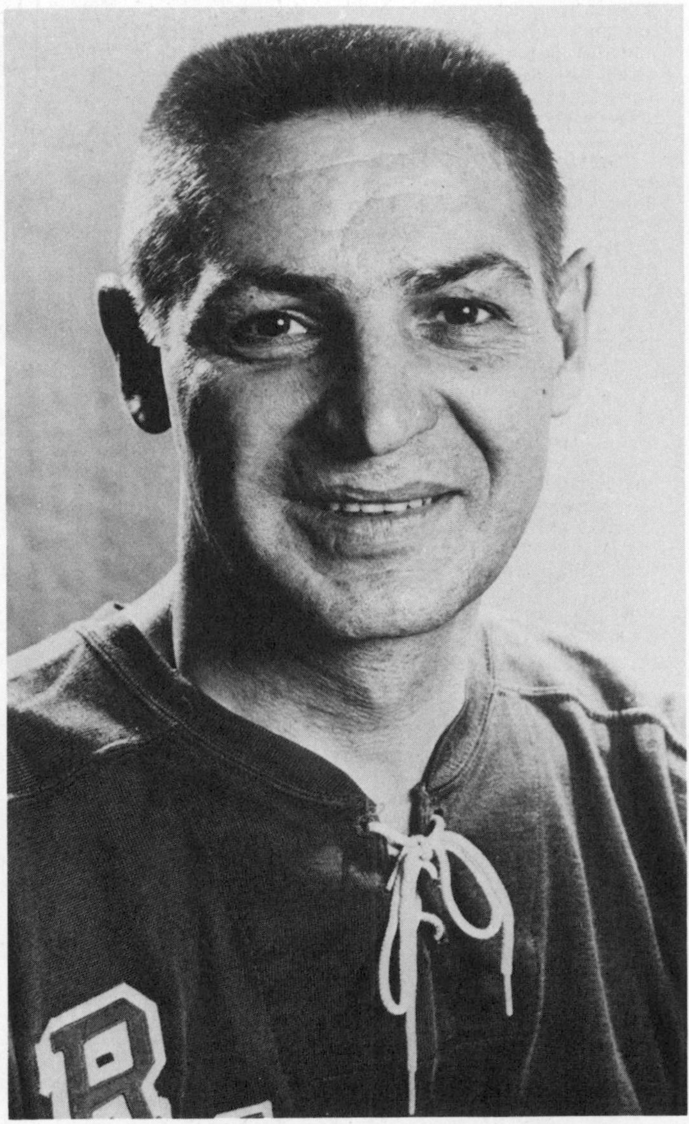

One of hockey's greatest goalies—Terry Sawchuk.

Sawchuk, Once Called 'the Best,' Fell Victim of His Own Despair

Terry Sawchuk, who died yesterday at the age of 40, had a dual attitude in recent years toward the game of hockey that he played probably better than any other goaltender.

Images of him in training camp with the Rangers last fall come back—how he was always the last to finish his exercises, how he didn't bother lunging for pucks during the scrimmages.

But in some games during the National Hockey League season, a child's exhuberance returned. After one contest he remarked: "Not bad for an old man eh? I felt I could have played four periods tonight. I was really stopping them."

Sawchuk was a transcendent athlete, but one wonders how much greater his horizons would have been had he not succumbed so often to personal despair. The record he was proudest of was his 103 career shutouts.

"Greatest angle goalie I ever saw," once said Boom Boom Geoffrion, who possessed one of the game's hardest shots. "You think you can find an opening past him, but he's got all the angles covered. I tell you, he was the best."

Feud Is Recalled

Sawchuk, at best, had a difficult relationship with the press, reminiscent of the feud between Ted Williams and Boston newspapermen. Some say Sawchuk's feud started when he was with the Detroit Red Wings in the late 1950's shortly after suffering a nervous breakdown.

A story appeared quoting a Ranger player, Bill Gadsby, as saying, "If Terry has a few more bad games, he might go tweet, tweet, tweet again." Sawchuk saw the story—and that night shut out the Rangers. For more than 10 years afterward he refused to talk to New York reporters.

It was ironic that he returned to New York to close out his career. Coach Emile Francis acquired him last summer from the Los Angeles Kings, merely to spell the Rangers' No. 1 goalie, Ed Giacomin.

Sawchuk was erratic and only once—when he turned in a shutout in Madison Square Garden—did he hear the cheers as he once had. But he was a popular player with his teammates.

After the shutout, Brad Park, the young all-star defenceman, said: "We like Terry. We wanted to show the fans he wasn't washed up. He's the kind of guy you liked to play for. He's always encouraging the younger guys."

Sawchuk has a record that will never be equaled, especially under the present conditions of the two-goalie system. For five straight seasons with Detroit he posted an average of under two goals a game.

A goalie who rarely left his feet, Sawchuk made the crouch famous and was probably the best goaltender on screen shots and tip-in attempts.

In 1952, his second season in the league, Detroit won the Stanley Cup in eight straight games in which Sawchuk posted four shutouts. During the entire eight games he allowed only five goals.

Francis, who spent many hours with Sawchuk since the goalie was hospitalized, was too upset to indicate yesterday what effect the goalie's death would have on the team's plans.

GERALD ESKENAZI

Sawchuk's Record

REGULAR SEASON

Season	Club	GP.	GA.	SO.	GAPG.
1949-50	Detroit	7	16	1	2.28
1950-51	Detroit	70	139	11	1.98
1951-52	Detroit	70	133	12	1.90
1952-53	Detroit	63	120	9	1.90
1953-54	Detroit	66⅔	129	12	1.92
1954-55	Detroit	68	132	12	1.94
1955-56	Boston	68	181	9	2.66
1956-57	Boston	34	81	2	2.38
1957-58	Detroit	70	207	3	2.96
1958-59	Detroit	67	209	5	3.12
1959-60	Detroit	58	156	5	2.69
1960-61	Detroit	35⅔	113	2	3.17
1961-62	Detroit	43	143	5	3.32
1962-63	Detroit	46	119	3	2.48
1963-64	Detroit	52⅓	138	5	2.70
1964-65	Toronto	36	92	1	2.56
1965-66	Toronto	25⅓	80	1	3.16
1966-67	Toronto	23⅓	66	2	2.81
1967-68	Los Angeles	32⅓	99	2	3.07
1968-69	Detroit	10⅔	28	0	2.62
1969-70	Rangers	7	20	1	2.86
Totals		953⅓	2,401	103	2.52

G.P.—Games played. G.A.—Goals against. SO—Shutouts. G.A.P.A. — Goals-against-per-game average.

Terry Sawchuk's hockey career spanned four decades and five teams. He is shown here when he was with the New York Rangers—the last team he was to play for.

"All the News That's Fit to Print"

The New York Times.

LATE CITY EDITION
Considerable cloudiness and cold today. Some cloudiness tomorrow.

NEWS SUMMARY AND INDEX, PAGE 95 — SECTION ONE

VOL. CIV. No. 35,344. — NEW YORK, SUNDAY, OCTOBER 31, 1954. — TWENTY CENTS

Wilbur Shaw Dies in Air Crash, Won Top Auto Race Three Times

By The Associated Press.

DECATUR, Ind., Oct. 30—Wilbur Shaw, president of the Indianapolis motor speedway and three-time winner of the 500-mile race, was killed with two companions in a plane crash near here late today.

The great racing figure, who had survived serious accidents on the tracks and a severe heart attack, would have been 52 years old tomorrow. He was returning home from Detroit after a test run in a new car to get information for a magazine article.

"This is safer than flying an airplane," Mr. Shaw had remarked after the test run at Detroit.

Killed with Mr. Shaw were Ernest R. Roose, 41, Indianapolis artist who painted the portrait of the 500-mile race winner each year, and Ray Grimes, 40, a pilot from Greenfield, Ind.

The light plane crashed and broke to pieces in a field as a farmer watched. It tore up a spot where he had been picking corn thirty seconds before. The bodies were ground to bits in the wreckage, which was scattered over a distance of several hundred feet.

Identification of the bodies was impossible. Mr. Shaw and Mr. Grimes were identified by their pilot's licenses and Mr. Roose by a wallet.

A representative of the advertising firm of McCann-Erickson said the three men were in Detroit today testing a new Chrysler car on the Chrysler proving grounds.

Mr. Shaw flew the plane to Detroit and Mr. Roose was to have flown it back, the advertising man said. The plane left Ann Arbor Airport at 4 P. M.

The state police said the plane exploded on striking the ground on a farm near Peterson, five miles southwest of Decatur.

Homer Ginter, owner of the farm, who was working on his tractor, said he heard a roar, looked up and saw the plane in pieces, twenty to thirty feet from the ground.

Gordon Lackey, manager of Sky Harbor Airport at Indianapolis, said the plane with three men left Indianapolis at 9:05 A. M. for Detroit.

Peterson is twenty miles south of Fort Wayne, in Adams County.

Mr. Shaw won the big race at Indianapolis in 1937, 1939 and

Continued on Page 35, Column 1

FOREIGN LEADERS JOIN IN HONORING COLUMBIA AT FETE

Queen Mother Brings Greeting of Britain—Asia, Europe, Americas Represented

2 RUSSIANS IN AUDIENCE

Hammarskjold Stresses Need of Free Use of Knowledge to Fight New 'Dark Ages'

Texts of the addresses at the Columbia dinner, Page 72.

By PETER KIHSS

Led by a Queen, leaders of many nations joined last night to hail Columbia University for 200 years of international service since King George II of England granted its charter on Oct. 31, 1754.

One after another took up the bicentennial theme of the free use of knowledge, describing it as vital for peace in a ...

A picture of royalty, with her diamond tiara and a blue sash of the Order of the Garter across her jeweled pink satin gown, she read a message from her sovereign daughter, Queen Elizabeth II. The message felicitated the university for fulfilling its charter injunction to uphold religious principles and "equal liberties and the advantage of education for all."

Unity in Ideals Foreseen

In a message from a country whose heart was pierced by "the borderline between freedom and suppression," West German Chancellor Konrad Adenauer foresaw common ideals uniting peoples in the struggle for peace and liberty. Dr. Adenauer was kept away from the dinner by mourning for one of his chief lieutenants, and his statement was read by his State Secretary for Foreign Affairs, Walter Hallstein.

In the audience were two Soviet scholars, eleventh-hour official delegates. Other speakers included the Vice President of India, the Foreign Minister of Belgium and representatives of the French and Italian Ministries of Education and the universities of Latin America.

Dr. Grayson Kirk, Columbia's president, found it encouraging but also "disquieting" that more than 500 institutions throughout the world had joined the year-long celebration. He interpreted this as evidencing a widespread belief that forces threatening independence of the human spirit were "still on the march."

By precept and example, he said, the university will continue to be "one of the most powerful forces known to man to bring

Continued on Page 73, Column 2

Major Sports News

FOOTBALL

Notre Dame beat Navy and Yale halted Dartmouth in major Eastern contests. Scores of leading games:

Alabama	0	Georgia	0
Arkansas	14	Texas A. & M.	7
Army	21	Virginia	20
Brown	34	Lehigh	6
Colgate	6	Princeton	6
Cornell	26	Columbia	0
Duke	21	Georgia Tech	20
Harvard	27	Ohio Univ.	13
Indiana	13	Michigan	9
Iowa	13	Wisconsin	7
Kentucky	28	Villanova	3
Maryland	20	So. Carolina	0
Minnesota	19	Mich. State	13
Nebraska	25	Missouri	19
Notre Dame	6	Navy	0
Ohio State	14	Northw'n	7
Oklahoma	13	Colorado	6
Penn State	35	Pennsylvania	13
Pittsburgh	13	W. Virginia	10
Purdue	28	Illinois	14
Rutgers	25	Temple	0
Syracuse	28	Holy Cross	20
U. C. L. A.	27	California	6
Yale	13	Dartmouth	7

HORSE RACING

Summer Tan won the $260,965 Garden State Stakes.

(Details in Section 5)

Grau Quits Race in Cuba, Charging Vote Is Rigged

Calls on Public Not to Go to Polls—Batista Alone in Tomorrow's Election

By R. HART PHILLIPS

Special to The New York Times.

HAVANA, Oct. 30—The Cuban people, preparing to go to the polls Monday to choose a President and Congress, were stunned today when Dr. Ramón Grau San Martín, the only opponent of the Government candidate Gen. Fulgencio Batista, declared he would not run because of the lack of guarantees for impartial elections.

In a statement to the public, Dr. Grau accused the Government of rigging the elections and asked the people not to go to the polls.

"We have become convinced there exists a well directed plan to convert the coming elections into a common farce in order to perpetuate the present usurpers in power," Dr. Grau declared.

General Batista said ...

By DREW MIDDLETON

Special to The New York Times.

LONDON, Oct. 30 — ... striking dock workers ... day by overwhelming ... to return to work Monday ... eight ports.

The biggest dock strike ... twenty-eight years will end ... twenty-eight days after it began, with its leaders claiming a "glorious victory" that has established the principle of voluntary overtime and revealed the solidarity of the labor forces in the nation's ports.

The strike immobilized 240 ships and entailed delay in shipments of imports and exports valued at £200,000,000 ($560,000,000). The British automobile industry reported a loss of £15,000,000 ($42,000,000) worth of exports.

D. F. MacDonald, general manager of the National Association of Port Employers, explained that some strike losses could never be recovered.

"Irretrievable damage has been done," he said, "schedules missed, cargoes possibly lost and damage to the flow of import and export trade."

44,000 Out at Peak

Two weeks ago the employers offered almost exactly the same terms that the strikers accepted today.

The strike, which involved at its peak 44,000 dockers also shook the structure of British trades unionism and disarranged the system of employer-union negotiation. For the stoppage was led, in many instances, not by responsible union officials but by unofficial strike committees, many of whose leaders were under Communist influence.

The unofficial leaders today defied Arthur Deakin, who, with his Transport and General Workers Union, opposed the strike, and promised continuation of their efforts to overthrow Mr. Deakin, the most powerful figure in the union movement.

Urging greater union activity upon his followers, Vic Marney declared "that is the only way we can defeat Arthur Deakin and the leadership of the T. G. W. U."

Martin Lindsay, Conservative member of Parliament, will ask Sir Walter Monckton, Minister of Labor, to publish a White Paper with details of the support given to the dock strike by the Communist party.

The Government faces other

Continued on Page 3, Column 2

PRESIDENT TO RUSH PACTS TO SENATE AT NOV. 8 SESSION

Seeks Ratification Early in '55 for European Security and Asian Defense Treaties

By WALTER H. WAGGONER

Special to The New York Times.

WASHINGTON, Oct. 30—The White House announced today that President Eisenhower will submit the European and Southeast Asian ... agreements to ...

Wilbur Shaw Dies in Air Crash, Won Top Auto Race Three Times

By The Associated Press.

DECATUR, Ind., Oct. 30—Wilbur Shaw, president of the Indianapolis motor speedway and three-time winner of the 500-mile race, was killed with two companions in a plane crash near here late today.

The great racing figure, who had survived serious accidents on the tracks and a severe heart attack, would have been 52 years old tomorrow. He was returning home from Detroit after a test run in a new car to get information for a magazine article.

"This is safer than flying an airplane," Mr. Shaw had remarked after the test run at Detroit.

Killed with Mr. Shaw were Ernest R. Roose, 41, Indianapolis artist who painted the portrait of the 500-mile race winner each year, and Ray Grimes, 40, a pilot from Greenfield, Ind.

The light plane crashed and broke to pieces in a field as a farmer watched. It tore up a spot where he had been picking corn thirty seconds before. The bodies were ground to bits in the wreckage, which was scattered over a distance of several hundred feet.

Identification of the bodies

As the President's 'Chain Calls' Got Under Way

... Elaine Anderson, retired teacher in ... Calif., begins calling ten neighbors after getting President's message.

Associated Press Wirephotos

... Bids the Country ... G. O. P. for 'Smears'

... on voters last night to rebuke ... what he described as a ... innuendo, and misrepresenta-...

The Republican candidate re-

Continued on Page 69, Column 1

... Warns Nixon of Poison Plot; Seattle Police Quiz 2 in Mystery

Special to The New York Times.

SEATTLE, Oct. 30—The Seattle police were called at 7:30 tonight to investigate a reported attempt to poison Vice President Richard M. Nixon in his hotel here.

An elevator boy said by the police to have discussed the relative merits of cyanide and arsenic poison with the hotel cook yesterday was being questioned. The cook also was undergoing questioning.

Mr. Nixon was staying in the Hawaiian Suite, 1217, in the Benjamin Franklin Hotel and, as was his custom before making an address, called room service at 7 o'clock to order a light meal of tomato soup, a sandwich, ice cream and tea.

Just as the food arrived, at 7:22 o'clock, a person with a young voice that could have belonged to a man or a woman called the hotel switchboard and asked for Room 1219, the room next to Mr. Nixon's. It was occupied by security officers, though only the official party knew this.

The voice warned: "Don't let him eat that food! The night elevator operator poisoned it!" The security officer who took the call rushed next door and stopped Mr. Nixon as he was about to begin eating. The caller disconnected while this was going on.

Mr. Nixon's personal reaction to the incident was that it was the work of a crank. He promptly put in a new order for the same meal, which was prepared under supervision of Secret Service men, and left the hotel at about 8:35 o'clock to make a speech at the Palomar Theatre on schedule.

The suspected food was taken by the Seattle police to their laboratory for analysis. But efforts to reach toxicologists tonight were unavailing and no laboratory report was expected until tomorrow. Meanwhile, both

Continued on Page 76, Column 7

EISENHOWER OPENS CHAIN PHONE DRIVE TO GET OUT VOTE

Calls Ten Supporters in All Parts of Country and Asks Each to Call Ten More

DEMOCRATS ACT AT ONCE

Mitchell Wires Chiefs Urging They Walk to Ten Homes—'Walkathon' vs. 'Talkathon'

By CHARLES E. EGAN

Special to The New York Times.

WASHINGTON, Oct. 30—President Eisenhower set a political precedent here today by using the White House telephone to ask ten stanch Republicans to get out and vote next Tuesday. He asked each of the ten to do the same for ten others, and so on.

The President's personal appeals were intended by Republican party leaders to set off a nation-wide chain telephone drive to win control of the new Congress. The names of the ten to whom the President talked, the White House explained, had been taken from among several thousand who had written to the President recently expressing their support.

He started out by calling a cook in the Pi Beta Phi sorority house at Bradley University in Peoria, Ill.

The President opened each telephone conversation with the salutation:

"This is the President speaking. I have your letter and I want to thank you for writing me and for the sentiments you express."

He then asked the listener to do him a favor by getting out and voting for party candidates on Tuesday and further to call ten friends repeating the request to get out and vote and urge them in turn to call ten others.

Governors Pick Up Idea

Republican Governors, members of the Republican National Committee and representatives of Citizens-for-Eisenhower picked up the "telephone your neighbor" idea in an effort to overcome the election "apathy" that has been worrying Republican leaders lately.

Stephen A. Mitchell, Democratic National Chairman, immediately called the Republican efforts a "talkathon." He telegraphed party leaders and candidates to go the Republicans one better by organizing a "walkathon."

G. O. P. to Pay for Calls

White House aides said that because of the political nature of the telephoning, the Republican National Committee would pay the long distance tolls. They were made to people in Illinois, Ohio, Pennsylvania, California, North Carolina, Michigan, Texas, Missouri and Oregon. All the states except Pennsylvania and Missouri have Senatorial contests.

Republican National Committee headquarters here are elated over the response President Eisenhower's personal calls had stirred through the nation. They said that telephone checks with party leaders and workers in states to which the President phoned indicated that interest in getting out the vote and party morale had been given a "tremendous boost" by the campaign. The state workers and leaders said they expected enthusiasm for the telephone campaign to carry up to election day.

From party headquarters in all parts of the country, it was added, messages of approval for the chain telephone idea had been enthusiastic in tone. The state workers predicted a record turn-

Continued on Page 76, Column 5

WILBUR SHAW DIES IN A PLANE CRASH

Continued From Page 1

1940. World War II ended his career as a driver, but when Anton Hulman Jr. of Terre Haute, Ind., bought the big two and one-half mile track at the west edge of Indianapolis in 1945 he gave Mr. Shaw the job of running it.

The track was full of holes and the grandstand was going to pieces. Cynics said auto racing was an anachronism in a day of supersonic air speeds. But under Mr. Shaw's direction the Memorial Day event boomed again, drawing crowds estimated at more than 150,000.

Besides his three victories, Mr. Shaw finished second in the "500" in 1933, 1935 and 1938, fourth in 1927 and seventh in 1936.

He was the leading money winner at the track, with a total of $91,300 in winnings, until Bill Vukovich won his second straight victory last May 31.

Mr. Shaw survived several racing accidents and a severe heart attack. In 1941, in his last Memorial Day race, he hit the wall and spent the summer in a cast with three smashed vertebrae. In 1923 he suffered a skull fracture at Paris, Ill., and he broke some ribs in two crack-ups at Ascot, Calif.

The heart attack felled him in 1951 as he ran up a hill at the Soap Box Derby in Akron, Ohio. He was in critical condition for several days but made it back to his office before the 1952 race.

He was married and had one son, Warren Wilbur Jr.

Both the drivers and the public benefited when the Hulman-Shaw regime took over the historic but delapidated speedway after World War II. Millions of dollars were poured into construction of new steel and concrete stands and the prize money soared.

While Mr. Vukovich won $164,-431.80 in winning just two races, Mr. Shaw had to capture three firsts, three seconds, a fourth and a seventh to win $91,300 in the pre-war era.

Mr. Shaw couldn't race as a track executive, but every May he itched to compete again and was boyishly grateful when racing teams let him drive a few laps.

Only a few weeks ago he asserted he would drive the powerful Novi special in an attempt on a new closed-course record at Chrysler's proving ground track at Chelsea, Mich. This was the car in which noted drivers Ralph Hepburn and Chet Miller were killed—but Mr. Shaw wasn't afraid of anything.

Associated Press

Wilbur Shaw was president of the Indianapolis Speedway Corporation when he was killed at Decatur, Maryland. He was 51 years old.

He told a newsman recently: "Auto race drivers are like boxers, or pit bull dogs. Once one gives ground to another, the other fellow will be the boss forever after that. I never was about to back off and let somebody pass me in a jam!"

He drove some of his greatest races at the old Ascot Speedway, Los Angeles, where, he said, "You just counted on spending a certain amount of time in the hospital."

Warren Wilbur Shaw, born Oct. 31, 1902, spent most of his life in Indianapolis. The shrewd, combative ex-champion who ran the famed Indianapolis Motor Speedway, was weaned on the roar of racing cars.

From boyhood Mr. Shaw wanted to be an automobile race driver. Once termed "one of the nation's most pleasing examples of success," he began racing on dirt tracks in his late teens. In 1927, at the age of 25, he made his debut on the Indianapolis brick oval.

His idol was Tommy Milton, "speed king" of the Twenties, the first man to win the 500-mile classic twice. Mr. Shaw eventually eclipsed Milton's feats by capturing the Memorial Day grind three times. A new auto-racing star appeared on the horizon when Mr. Shaw finished fourth in the 1927 race.

Few persons in that 1927 crowd ever had heard of Wilbur Shaw. When he quit racing after the 1941 event, there were few Americans, or for that matter few motorists, who were not familiar with his name.

He was always a crowd pleaser, but there was nothing spectacular about him. He entered racing as a business, and when it was necessary to take a chance, he took it. However, he never took unnecessary chances. He knew cars and he also knew how to get the most out of them.

Mr. Shaw experienced a streak of bad luck at Indianapolis after his brilliant debut. A broken timing gear, an oil leak and similar mechanical breakdowns handicapped him until 1932. That year he appeared to have won the race with only forty-three laps to go. But a ring gear was shattered and his pit crew was unable to get the car moving again. At that time he had a five-minute lead over the field.

In 1933, he was a close second, but in the next year an oil leak forced him out. In 1935, he was overhauling the pace - setting Kelly Petillo when it began raining, and the cars couldn't change their positions for the last 100 miles.

The next year Mr. Shaw led most of the way. Again victory appeared within sight. But the hood of his car came loose, and it took his crew seventeen minutes to make repairs. Mr. Shaw finished seventh.

In 1937 he made his first trip to the winner's circle. That same year he added the national championship to his honors. He again got the checkered flag in 1939, repeated as national titleholder and won his third race in 1940.

In the 1941 race, with a few laps to go, Mr. Shaw appeared to be an easy winner. He had made his final pit stop, and was far in front. Then disaster struck. A rear wheel broke, hurling the car at 117 miles per hour into a retaining wall. Mr. Shaw wasn't too badly injured, but he never drove another race. It was not long after the mishap that he became president of the speedway.

Mr. Shaw miraculously escaped death when he went "over the wall" in the 1931 race. Many a driver will swear Wilbur Shaw died in that crash. Nobody had ever walked away from a trip over the wall, but he did. Patched up in the field hospital, he walked back to the pit to watch the finish of the race.

One of the first racers to use a crash helmet, Mr. Shaw set other racing styles. One of them was to attach a tube to a thermos bottle so he could drink while racing. Another was custom-fitting his car so that the steering wheel had to be taken out before he could get in.

Racing was not the only sport at which he excelled. Mr. Shaw took up golf and was able to shoot occasionally in the 60's. He piloted airplanes of every type, raced speed boats in Cuba and ice boats in Detroit and was a motorcyclist and tobogganist.

As a hunter, he once shot twenty running rabbits with twenty-three shots and a groundhog at 430 yards. He was also expert with bow and arrow. Among his other expert accomplishments were as a bowler, fencer, fisherman and a rider in horse shows.

Wilbur Shaw on his way to the winner's circle after the 1939 Indianappolis 500.

"All the News That's Fit to Print"

The New York Times.

LATE CITY EDITION
U.S. Weather Bureau Report (Page 83) forecasts: Snow ending this morning followed by some clearing. Fair tomorrow. Temp. range: 32—24. Yesterday: 31.8—23.2.

VOL. CVIII..No. 36,844. © 1958, by The New York Times Company. Times Square, New York 36, N. Y. NEW YORK, TUESDAY, DECEMBER 9, 1958. 30c beyond 100-mile zone from New York City. Higher in air delivery cities. FIVE CENTS

Tris Speaker, Outfielder, Dies; Ex-Star for Red Sox and Indians

'GrayEagle,' Who Batted .344, Was Cleveland Manager—Elected to Hall of Fame

By United Press International.

WHITNEY, Tex., Dec. 8—Tris Speaker, the former great "Gray Eagle" of American League outfields, died of a heart attack. He was 70 years old.

The baseball Hall of Fame member was on a fishing trip with a friend, Charles Vaughan, of near-by Hubbard, Speaker's birthplace.

Besides his widow, Frances, Speaker is survived by two sisters. They are Mrs. Pearl Scott of Hubbard and Mrs. Alma Lindsey of Abilene.

Associated Press

Tris Speaker

When Tris Speaker was a young cowboy in Texas, he suffered a broken right arm in a fall from a horse and became a left-handed pitcher. Then his left arm was injured in a football accident. Surgeons advised amputation, but he refused. He recovered to become one of baseball's great hitters and outfielders, a manager of a world's championship team and seventh member of the game's Hall of Fame.

The indomitable will of young Speaker attracted a discerning baseball man, Doak Roberts, then owner of the Houston club of the Texas League, in the town of Cleburne in 1906.

The boy, 17, was the sensation of his town after two years at Fort Worth Polytechnic Institute. Not only was he a winning pitcher, but he was a battler. He wanted to be a professional ballplayer, but his mother opposed his being "sold into slavery." She said she would never give her consent to her son's going to the Red Sox, even

Continued on Page 41, Column 2

HIGH COURT BACKS QUICK RATE RISES BY GAS PIPELINES

5-to-3 Reversal of Lower Bench Clears Way for Increases in 6 Months

DISTRIBUTORS JUBILANT

They Can Lift Their Prices Without Dealing With the Customer Companies

By ANTHONY LEWIS
Special to The New York Times.

WASHINGTON, Dec. ... Supreme Court cleared ... today for natural-gas ... companies to raise th... without first going th... rate proceeding at the F... Power Commission.

By a vote of 5 to 3, the h... court held that companies usin... the most common form of contract might use a short-cut rate provision of the Natural Gas Act. Under this provision gas prices go up six months after filing of new rate schedules, subject to later revision by the F. P. C.

The decision reversed the District of Columbia Court of Appeals in the so-called Memphis case. It was a solid victory for the pipeline companies in their most important legal fight in years—one they said could make or break them. Under this decision the pipelines were required to obtain consent of their customers before any proposed rate increase could go into effect.

Ruling Is Far-Reaching

The probable effect of the ruling will be to cut sharply the lag in the time required under the lower court decision for a rate rise to reach the ultimate consumer, whether a household or a big industrial user. However, local distributors still must obtain approval of state regulatory authorities in order to pass such increases on to their customers.

Justice John Marshall Harlan wrote the opinion for the court. With him in the majority were Justices Felix Frankfurter, William J. Brennan Jr., Charles Evans Whittaker and Potter Stewart. Justice Tom C. Clark took no part in the case.

Justice Frankfurter, who has been in the hospital for two weeks with a heart ailment, was not on the bench today. He participated in the Memphis case and another decided by written opinion today but not in the list of summary orders without opinion.

For the dissenters Justice William O. Douglas predicted "dire consequences" from today's decision. He said it reduced the natural gas act to "a shambles * * * so far as consumer interests are concerned, and they are the ones the act was designed to protect."

Joining him were Chief Jus-

Continued on Page 47, Column 1

BI-STATE RAIL BILL KILLED IN JERSEY

Proposal for Transit Area Will Be Offered Again

By GEORGE CABLE WRIGHT
Special to The New York Times.

TRENTON, Dec. 8.—Legislation to establish a New York-New Jersey transit district died tonight in an Assembly committee after being completely rewritten.

Thus it finally became clear that there will be no bi-state action to solve the serious commuter rail transit problem for many months. The New Jersey Legislature will not meet again until Jan. 13, while the New York Legislature will convene on Jan. 7.

The transit legislation was approved by the New York lawmakers last March and signed by Governor Harriman in April. It was subsequently adopted by the New Jersey Senate.

The measure was then buried in an Assembly committee here, primarily because of widespread local opposition to it in northern New Jersey.

Rewritten today to meet some of these objections, the bill was immediately brought to the floor of the lower house and moved to second reading. A lack of votes to assure its passage, however, caused it to be pigeon-

Continued on Page 33, Column 4

ELEVAT... STUDIE...

Homicide Aid... on Boy—Rec... Bomb Threat...

By BILL BE...

The District Attorn... moved yesterday into ... tigation of the elevator ... death of a Morningside ... boy as the city's anti-slum ... picked up momentum.

The day's developments included:

¶An anonymous threat ... blow up the West Side chur... of an Episcopal rector who ha... charged that slum landlords bribe city inspectors.

¶A pledge of cooperation by the City Investigation Commissioner in following up the accusations of the rector, the Rev. James A. Gusweller, of the Protestant Episcopal Church of St. Matthew and St. Timothy, 26 West Eighty-fourth Street.

¶A meeting of city officials with Deputy Mayor Paul T. O'Keefe to discuss ways of prosecuting housing violators.

Homicide Chief Called In

District Attorney Frank S. Hogan named Alexander Herman, chief of his homicide bureau, to head the inquiry into the death of 14-year-old Stanley Gunn at 380 Riverside Drive.

The boy was crushed Saturday as he saved the life of a 2-year-old child. The plunging elevator was one that had been found faulty and repaired at least twice this year.

Peter J. Reedy, the city's Buildings Commissioner, agreed to turn over to the District Attorney all records concerning the building. Commissioner Reedy said that the two elevators in the building had been inspected and found wanting in January and June. In July they were satisfactorily repaired, he said.

In October, however, two complaints were received from tenants of the building—the once-fashionable Hendrik Hudson Apartments at the corner of 110th Street. An inspector pronounced the elevators operable early in November, Mr. Reedy added.

Yet a group of visitors a week ago yesterday went down when an "up" button was pushed.

Commissioner Reedy said a comment on the elevator was contained in an over-all report on the building—but the report was not turned in until yesterday morning.

The building—which has 301 single rooms and fifty-eight apartments—had forty-seven violations pending against it several months ago. In 1957 fines totaling $110 were levied against the owner, the Estpearl Realty Corporation.

The building was one of

Continued on Page 48, Column 3

... closed the ... Service Co... fourth floo... Tenth Stree...

Fourteen sc... been shut dur... city-wide inspe... the department ... following a Chica... that caused ninety-...

The department ... schools had reopene... four yesterday—the ... Industrial Arts and C... cational High School ... hattan; the Rafield Pla... in Jamaica, Queens, an...

Continued on Page 45, C...

Snowstorm Co... Upstate Repo...

New York was caught last night in a snowstorm that stretched across a wide belt of northern states.

Snow began to fall here at 7:30 P. M. and was not expected to end until this morning. The Weather Bureau did not forecast an accumulation for the storm, which is the first of the season. It did concede, however, that "there was a chance of more than two inches."

More than an inch of snow had fallen on the city by midnight.

The snow was still falling steadily in the city at 3 A. M.

The police reported that streets and highways here were icy and slippery.

Sanitation Commissioner Paul R. Screvane sent the first sanding and salting units out to critical points at 8:30 P. M. Snow removal was handled by ... sanding and salting units were in operation.

The Port of New York Authority reported that traffic was moving freely over all approaches to its tunnels and bridges. An authority spokesman said that salt spreaders were covering the approaches and bridges every half hour.

Record-breaking snow fell in upstate New York. In Oswego, Mayor Vincent Corsall declared a state of emergency as snow on the ground mounted to five feet. The declaration placed all city employes on a twenty-four-hour stand-by basis.

The worst snowstorm in Oswego's history forced schools,

Continued on Page 22, Column 2

ALABAMANS DEFY U.S. RIGHTS BOARD AT FIRST HEARING

Registrars Withhol... Data—...

... Vaughan, ... Hubbard, Speaker's birthplace.

Besides his widow, Frances, Speaker is survived by two sisters. They are Mrs. Pearl Scott of Hubbard and Mrs. Alma Lindsey of Abilene.

Associated Press
Tris Speaker

When Tris Speaker was a young cowboy in Texas, he suffered a broken right arm in a fall from a horse and became a left-handed pitcher. Then his left arm was injured in a football accident. Surgeons advised amputation, but he refused. He recovered to become one of baseball's great hitters and outfielders, a manager of a world's championship team and seventh member of the game's Hall of Fame.

The indomitable will of young Speaker attracted a discerning baseball man, Doak Roberts, then owner of the Houston club of the Texas League, in the town of Cleburne in 1906.

The boy, 17, was the sensation of his town after two years at Fort Worth Polytechnic Institute. Not only was he a winning pitcher, but he was a battler. He wanted to be a professional ballplayer, but his mother opposed his being "sold into slavery." She said she would never give her consent to her son's going to the Red Sox, even

Continued on Page 41, Column 2

Humphrey Says 'Cold War' Will Persist for Long Time

Senator Home to Report on His Talk in Moscow With Khrushchev

By ALLEN DRURY
Special to The New York Times.

WASHINGTON, Dec. 8—Senator Hubert H. Humphrey predicted today that there would be no settlement of political differences between the Soviet ... and the United States ... long time."

He told a crowded news ... that he did not fore... between the two ... in the "cold war" ... seven years, the ... newly announced ... plan.

..., he said, could ... United States ... people-to-people" ... with the Rus... as medical ... might prevent ... added.

... Democrat met ... from a ... during ... -hour con... Nikita S. ... accom-

Associated Press

Senator Hubert H. Humphrey and his wife, Muriel, at Idlewild yesterday on their way to Washington.

... in Caracas ... urt Victory

... —Riots protesting the ... court as President of ... day. They continued

... EES AGREE ... MIC POLICE

... tes Reach ... rticle of ... eaty

... drafting group

Continued on Page 4, Column 4

Africa Is Warned Of New Colonialism

By KENNETT LOVE
Special to The New York Times.

ACCRA, Ghana, Dec. 8—Prime Minister Kwame Nkrumah of Ghana warned African nationalists today to beware of new forms of colonialism and imperialism carried out by non-European powers.

Addressing the opening session of the first All-African People's Conference, Dr. Nkrumah also endorsed nonviolence in the struggle for African independence. This was in blunt opposition to the policy championed in preliminary sessions by the United Arab Republic and the Algerian National Liberation Front.

"Do not let us also forget that colonialism and imperialism may come to us yet in a different guise, not necessarily from Europe" Dr. Nkrumah

Continued on Page 15, Column 1

SOVIET RELIEVES SEROV AS CHIEF OF SECURITY UNIT

Official Statement Is Silent on Future Duties of Head of the Secret Police

NO SUCCESSOR IS NAMED

Russian Succeeded Beria in 1954—Accompanied Khrushchev on Trips

By MAX FRANKEL
Special to The New York Times.

MOSCOW, Tuesday, Dec. 9—Army Gen. Ivan A. Serov, chief of the Soviet internal security apparatus, was relieved of his post this morning.

There was no indication whether the experienced security officer was being moved up or down in the Soviet hierarchy. He was released from his duties as chairman of the State Security Committee "in connection with his transfer to other duties," the Government announced.

General Serov's next job was not listed, nor was there any clue to his successor as chief of the secret police.

As is customary here, the announcement was made in a terse paragraph on the back pages of the major newspapers. A phrase to the effect that a relieved official is in line for other work usually means that he is not in disgrace.

There was no suggestion in the announcement that the security apparatus was being formally altered. Frequently, in simple personnel changes, a successor is announced at the same time, but this procedure was not followed this morning.

Arranged Leaders' Safety

General Serov, 53 years old, a small, wiry man with receding reddish hair and alert eyes, has often accompanied Premier Nikita S. Khrushchev and other Soviet leaders on trips abroad to arrange for their security. In recent years, he was also seen often at diplomatic receptions both in and out of uniform. He was last seen at a Kremlin party a month ago.

General Serov became chief of the newly created State Security Committee in 1954, just a few months after Mr. Khrushchev's election as First Secretary of the Communist party. General Serov was associated with Mr. Khrushchev before World War II when he served as security chief of the Ukraine while Mr. Khrushchev was the party leader there.

Little is known about the nature of the security apparatus established by Stalin's successors after the execution of the former security chief, Lavrenti P. Beria.

The State Security Committee was made administratively

Continued on Page 6, Column 1

...TER BY DULLES ... BERLIN AID

... ent to Adenauer ... Soviet Proposal

By SYDNEY GRUSON
Special to The New York Times.

BONN, Germany, Dec. 8—Secretary of State Dulles has sent a personal letter to Chancellor Konrad Adenauer reaffirming United States support for West Berlin. The letter is understood to express unqualified rejection of the Soviet proposal to make West Berlin a demilitarized free city.

[In East Germany, Premier Otto Grotewohl said it was not for the West Berliners to decide their own fate. He declared that under no circumstances could the outcome of Sunday's West Berlin elections be taken as a decision on the Soviet proposal to make West Berlin a demilitarized free city.]

Unity on rejecting the free city plan apparently has been reached by West Germany, the United States, Britain and France. But it seems clear that there is disagreement on what should follow from this.

Bonn wants the West not to weaken the rejection by clothing it in counter-proposals for a Big Four conference on the whole German problem.

It is on this point that cur-

Continued on Page 2, Column 3

Tris Speaker, Outfielder, Dies; Ex-Star for Red Sox and Indians

Continued From Page 1, Col. 6

after he had made a success at Houston.

His mother was won over. Mr. Roberts had faith that young Speaker would make the grade, and he sold the youngster to the Sox for $800—the Boston scout beating the Browns of St. Louis by a mere half-hour.

And in seven years Mrs. Speaker's boy became the highest-paid player in the American League when he signed a contract with Joseph J. Lannin of the Red Sox for $16,000 a year and a $5,000 bonus on a two-year contract. He later received $40,000, highest until the advent of Babe Ruth.

The Texas youngster played most of 1908 at Little Rock, Ark., where he had been "farmed" for development. But in 1909 he got his first real start. He batted .309 in 143 games for Boston and the team finished third. They bowed to the Athletics of Coombs, Bender and Plank fame in 1910 and 1911, but in 1912 they won the pennant—Speaker batting .383—and they took the world's championship from the Giants on the memorable "$30,000 muff" of Fred Snodgrass.

Competed With Cobb

But always in front of Speaker in his striving for the top was another Southerner, Tyrus Raymond Cobb. Two years ahead of the Texan in coming to the majors, the fiery Georgian was the idol of the fans, and it took years of wearing work for the sheer merit of the newcomer to show.

But for the batting prowess of Cobb, who reigned supreme in the years when Speaker was at his best with the Red Sox, the graceful Texan might have been acknowledged the greatest all-around outfielder of his time. Beginning with 1910, he always gave the Georgia Peach a battle for batting honors, finishing second on many occasions with averages that would have been good for titles in other years. Speaker lost with .383 to the Tiger star's .410 in 1912 and with .365 to .390 in 1913.

That was when he was the pivot man in what is often referred to as the greatest outfield of all time—the Speaker-Duffy Lewis-Harry Hooper combination in Boston. He batted .338 in 1914 and .322 in 1915, the year he led the Red Sox to a world series victory over the Phillies.

Caught Up With Cobb

It was not until 1916 that Speaker caught up with Cobb. He had been traded that winter

Tris Speaker when he played for the Boston Red Sox. He led the Red Sox to a World Series victory over the Philadelphia Phillies in 1915.

to the Indians. He came through the season with .386 and stopped Cobb's incredible consecutive winning streak at nine seasons to take the American League batting title.

Speaker never won it again, but his lifetime average of .344 attests to his worth on the offense. He reached .388 in 1920 only to fall before Sisler's .407; .378 in 1922 to find Sisler ahead again with .420 and in 1923 and 1925 he reached .380 and .389 only to come up against Harry Heilmann in his best years with .403 and .393.

But as a defensive outfielder neither Cobb, Heilmann, Mostil, Felsch of the tarnished Black Sox, Hofmann, Carey nor Roush of the National League—stars of his time, to name only a few—ever excelled Speaker in covering ground, throwing prowess, canniness as to "playing" hitters and general all-round grace in action. He was remarkable in his ability to go back after a far-driven ball. It was often said that only the fence stopped him. Sometimes it didn't do even that, for he once jumped over a fence in Washington to make a remarkable catch.

So great was Speaker's ability at covering ground in center that for years before the lively ball came into play he would anchor himself for many batsmen not more than forty feet behind second base. It is almost legend how he would come in and cover the bag on infield plays. Many times he would slip behind a runner watching the shortstop and second baseman, take the throw from the pitcher or catcher and tag the amazed victim.

Speaker became the manager of the Indians on July 19, 1919, succeeding Lee Fohl. They finished second in 1919 and first the next year. The Indians went on to capture the world championship from the Dodgers under Wilbert Robinson, with manager Speaker showing fine judgment in handling his pitchers, and leading his team with hard hitting—he batted .324—and fine fielding.

That was his only pennant and the only pennant Cleveland was to win until 1948. The star of Miller Huggins was rising in the East and the Yankees won in 1921, 1922 and 1923. In 1921 Speaker finished second, in 1922 he was fourth, in 1923 he was third and then sixth in 1924 and 1925. After he had brought his team home second in 1926—again trailing the Huggins-trained Yankees—he resigned as manager.

The next season Speaker was in the outfield for the Senators and Cobb was with the Athletics. The great rivals, curiously enough, closed their big league careers on the same team—playing with Connie Mack on the Athletics in 1928. Then Cobb retired and Speaker became the manager of the Newark Bears, a post he held for two years.

Speaker had been associated with baseball in different capacities during later seasons. He turned to broadcasting games and his knowledge of the diamond made him a favorite. He also became a part owner of the Kansas City team of the American Association.

The announcement of Speaker's election to baseball's Hall of Fame was made in January, 1937. At the time he was in the wholesale liquor business in Cleveland and was chairman of the city's Boxing Commission.

Additional honors were accorded to Speaker in 1952, when he was named to an all-star team of baseball's greatest performers from 1900 to 1950. The other outfielders on the team were Ty Cobb, the late Babe Ruth and Joe DiMaggio.

Tris Speaker—one of baseball's greatest defensive outfielders of his time—also achieved a lifetime batting averag of .344.

STAGG DIES AT 102; DEAN OF COACHES

76 Years in College Football —On First All-America

By The Associated Press

STOCKTON, Calif., March 17 —Amos Alonzo Stagg, patriarch of American athletics, died in a rest home today at the age of 102.

Mr. Stagg, who was called the grand old man of football, had been in fragile health for several years but only last night developed a fever. Death was attributed to uremic poisoning.

Mr. Stagg's last birthday was observed quietly, in contrast to the celebration of his 100th birthday. On that occasion, sports figures and admirers from all over the nation attended a huge civic dinner in his honor.

Against the advice of his doctors, the bent, white-haired Mr. Stagg left the rest home with his wife and was driven

Continued on Page 30, Column 1

"All the News That's F.. to Print"

The New York Times.

LATE CITY EDITION

U.S. Weather Bureau Report (Page 65) forecasts: Rain ending, then cloudy and windy today and tonight. Cloudy tomorrow. Temp. range: 43—39; yesterday: 46—35.

VOL. CXIV. No. 39,135. © 1965 by The New York Times Company. Times Square, New York, N. Y. 10036 NEW YORK, THURSDAY, MARCH 18, 1965. TEN CENTS

M'KEON EXPECTED TO YIELD HIS POST TO UPSTATE CHIEF

Van Lengen of Syracuse Is Backed by Wagner for Democratic Leader

QUIET OUSTER SOUGHT

Party Is Reported Ready to Give Present Chairman Another Good Job

By RONALD SULLIVAN
Special to The New York Times

ALBANY, March 17—George H. Van Lengen, the Democratic leader in Syracuse and the Secretary of the Senate, is expected to replace William H. McKeon soon as Democratic State Chairman.

Mr. Van Lengen has Mayor Wagner's full support, virtually assuring his election by the 300-member Democratic State Committee. Mr. McKeon's resignation and Mr. Van Lengen's election would be another victory for the Mayor over the Democratic forces in the state opposed to him.

The only question, according to high Democratic sources, is how Mr. McKeon's removal can be carried out painlessly and without the bloodletting that marked the recent Democratic legislative leadership fight. Mr. McKeon backed the losing anti-Wagner candidates in that battle, and the Mayor has called for his resignation.

Several influential Democrats reported tonight that Mr. McKeon probably would step aside peacefully, provided that he received another good job. The Mayor was said to have agreed that Mr. McKeon "should be taken care of."

Liquor Vacancy Due

But the process of finding something suitable for Mr. McKeon has been difficult, and this could delay his resignation for weeks or possibly one or two months. One job mentioned was the imminent Democratic vacancy on the State Liquor Authority. Oddly enough, the outgoing Democrat on the authority, William H. Morgan of Cortland, is contending for the party's state leadership himself.

Mr. Van Lengen, the 50-year-old son of a physician and grandson of a Lutheran minister in Syracuse, was reported today to have more than enough support on the state committee to be elected, even if the anti-Wagner Democratic leaders across the state oppose him.

Several Van Lengen supporters have counted at least 174 votes for him thus far; he needs 151.

Among those who would be expected to oppose his election are Peter J. Crotty, Democratic

Continued on Page 23, Column 6

Attack by Israelis On Water Project Charged by Syria

LEBANON Saida Hazzani Spring Sur Dan R. Baniyas R. TEL DAN DEMILITARIZED ZONE SYRIA Acre Sea of Galilee Haifa Yarmuk R. ISRAEL Mokeibe Jordan JORDAN

The New York Times March 18, 1965

Area of new clash (cross)

By DANA ADAMS SCHMIDT
Special to The New York Times

BEIRUT, Lebanon, March 17—The Damascus radio reported that Israeli troops and tanks attacked a Syrian project for diversion of the Jordan River headwaters today "in the Dan and Doka areas."

A Syrian bulldozer driver was killed and two bulldozers were destroyed, the broadcast said.

[At the United Nations, an Israeli spokesman said that Israel had not initiated an attack in the Dan area but had returned Syrian fire. Page 3.]

A Syrian spokesman said,

Continued on Page 3, Column 1

LEGISLATURE GETS AN OFF-TRACK BILL

Betting Measure in Senate Would Let Referendum Here Decide Issue

Special to The New York Times

ALBANY, March 17 — The long-awaited bill to make off-track betting legal in New York City was introduced today in the Legislature.

Drafted by Mayor Wagner's office, it had been expected for weeks. One reason for the delay, it was understood, was that changes were being made to improve its chances of passage.

A major revision provides that before the plan could go into effect it would have to be approved by the voters of New York City at a referendum in November, or sooner, if the City Council chooses.

Similar bills have been presented in previous years and defeated by Republican majorities. This is the first time the measure has been submitted to a Democratic-controlled Legislature.

Nevertheless, its prospects are far from certain. Senate Majority Leader Joseph Zaretzki conceded that there would be opposition in the Democratic party, but he predicted the bill would pass.

Under the measure a New York City Racing Authority would be formed to run betting shops. About 50 shops—well-lighted offices similar to banks in appearance and atmosphere —would be opened eventually.

All money wagered in the shops would be taxed 15 per cent. On races at tracks in the state, 1 per cent of the gross betting handle would go to the tracks, with the city and state

Continued on Page 23, Column 1

LEGISLATORS PASS 10C CIGARETTE TAX EFFECTIVE APRIL 1

Republican Minority Enables Both Houses to Clear Bill Sought by Governor

By R. W. APPLE Jr.
Special to The New York Times

ALBANY, March 17 — The Legislature voted this afternoon to double the state's 5-cent-a-pack tax on cigarettes.

Governor Rockefeller, who had proposed the increase in the executive budget, is expected to sign it into law tomorrow. The new rate will go into effect on April 1 and is expected to produce about $11[...] million in the fiscal year [...]ginning on that date.

Althoug[...]

[...]

"My Democrat[...] upstate New Yor[...] selves off the ho[...] dour Senator went[...] serving notice now [...] won't let you off the h[...] it comes to the rest [...] budget."

Tax Fight Promised

In rebuttal, Senator [...] Glinski of Erie County a[...] Mr. Brydges of "taking t[...]ernor off the hook." He p[...]ised that upstate Democra[...] and those from Buffalo in p[...]ticular, would fight every o[...] of the Governor's tax bills.

The cigarette tax, first revenue measure to come to the floor of the Legislature, was the least controversial part of the Rockefeller program. The Governor has also proposed increased auto registration fees and a state sales tax to help balance his record $3.48 billion budget for next year.

In another action, the Senate passed unanimously a revised version of a bill that would allow the New York City Council

Continued on Page 22, Column 4

Soviet Space Craft Carrying Two Men Is Placed in Orbit

By Reuters

MOSCOW, Thursday, March 18—The spaceship Voskhod II with two cosmonauts on board was launched this morning, the Soviet press agency Tass announced.

Tass said at 10 A.M. today that the new spaceship, Voskhod II, had been orbited.

It named the men on board as Col. Pavel Belyaev, the commander, and Lieut. Col. Alexei Leonov, co-pilot.

There was speculation in Moscow that the flight would last between one and two weeks.

Russia's last manned space shot — its seventh — was Oct. 12 last year.

[...]

BILL TO REINFORCE THE RIGHT TO VOTE GOES TO CONGRESS

Measure Gives U.S. Power to Appoint Registrars in Six Southern States

Texts of Johnson letter and proposed bill, Page 20.

By CHARLES MOHR
Special to The New York Times

WASHINGTON, March 17—President Johnson submitted to C[...]day a bipartisan bill [...]criminatory prac[...]e prevented Ne[...]gistering and vot[...]outhern states. [...]es the Attorney [...]ower to appoint [...]ation examiners [...] states in which [...] voter qualifi[...] used and in [...]50 per cent of [...]ed in 1964. [...] Alabama, [...], Georgia, [...] Virginia. [...]ply to [...]isions"

[...]

[...] this legislation [...]enact it promptly."

To newsmen in his office he said, with obvious pleasure, that Representative Emanuel Cel-

Continued on Page 20, Column 1

Associated Press Wirephoto

SIGNS LETTER TO CONGRESS: President Johnson at the White House with Attorney General Nicholas deB. Katzenbach. Mr. Johnson sent letter accompanying his voter rights bill, urging Congress to pass the legislation.

Selma Arrests Ministers Picketing Home of Mayor

By JOHN HERBERS
Special to The New York Times

SELMA, Ala., March 17—Thirty-six white adults, most of them ministers, were arrested today for picketing the home of Mayor Joseph T. Smitherman. The arrests were ordered by Wilson Baker, the city's Public Safety Director, who apparently was angered by what he considered a [v]iolation of an agreement.

"This is stupid," Mr. Baker [sh]outed at Harry Boyte, a [st]aff member of the Southern [C]hristian Leadership Confer[en]ce. "You told me if you went [to] the courthouse there would [be] no further demonstrations [...]. You ought to call your [...]ation the Southern [...]eadership Conference."

[...] ordered the demon[...] [p]laced under arrest for [pic]keting in a residential [...]od.

[...]veness Offered

[...] forgive you," said [...] soft-spoken man [...]ustache.

[...]'t forgive you," [...]t back. "Chris[...]ed a new low." [...]trators were [...]ellow school[...] Smitherman's [...]ors flocked [...] prisoners [...]d ordered [...]n recog[...]aring. [...]he group, [...] sign the [...]nd and [...]second[...] po[...] jail [...]hey [...]he

ACCORD REACHED IN MONTGOMERY

Sheriff Gives Public Apology for Violence—Marchers Agree to Get Permits

By ROY REED
Special to The New York Times

MONTGOMERY, Ala., March 17—Civil rights leaders won a public apology from the sheriff of Montgomery County tonight for the routing of 600 demonstrators with horses and clubs here yesterday.

The sheriff in turn won an agreement from civil rights leaders that in the future they would apply for official parade permits for all public marches in Montgomery.

The agreement was reached after the Rev. Dr. Martin Luther King Jr. and other civil rights leaders led a mass march on the Montgomery County Courthouse today, and then spent seven hours in private conference with Sheriff Mac Sim Butler.

The 600 demonstrators who were chased off the streets yesterday by mounted state troopers and sheriff's officers added 1,000 persons to their ranks today and marched to the courthouse to protest yesterday's violence.

After the conference with the sheriff, Dr. King and James Forman, executive secretary of the Student Nonviolent Coordinating Committee, told reporters that the conference and the resulting agreement were an "historic occasion." They said it was the first time that any Southern city had made such an agreement.

A statement setting out the agreement was signed by Sheriff Butler, Dr. King, Mr. For-

Continued on Page 21, Column 2

U.S. COURT ALLOWS ALABAMA MARCH; ENJOINS WALLACE

Officials Ordered to Protect Demonstrators in Journey to the State Capital

SHERIFF CLARK ASSAILED

Judge Says Selma Negroes Have Been Intimidated— 'Brutal' Acts Found

By BEN A. FRANKLIN
Special to The New York Times

MONTGOMERY, Ala., March 17—A Federal district judge authorized Negroes today to hold a mass march from Selma, Ala., to Montgomery, the state capital.

In an injunction and opinion released tonight, Judge Frank M. Johnson Jr. ordered Gov. George C. Wallace and other Alabama officials to refrain from "harassing or threatening" the protest marchers on the 50-mile trip, and to extend them full police protection from hostile whites.

Judge Johnson specifically enjoined Governor Wallace, Col. Al J. Lingo, director of the Alabama Highway Patrol, Sheriff James G. Clark Jr. of Dallas County (Selma), and all law enforcement officers under their command from arresting "or in any way interfering with the effort to march" along U.S. 80 from Selma to Montgomery.

Governor Wallace said after hearing of the order that he would address a joint session of the Legislature at 6:30 P.M. tomorrow. The Governor's press secretary, Bill Jones, said tonight that it would be "safe to assume" the state would appeal Judge Johnson's order.

Full Approval Given

The judge said he was giving his full approval to the plan for the march, which was presented in court here yesterday by attorneys for the Selma voter-registration movement.

The court order gave President Johnson legal grounds for the use of Federal troops to protect the marchers if Governor Wallace or any other Alabama official refuses to comply. President Johnson said at his news conference last Saturday that he would dispatch Federal troops to Alabama if necessary to enforce a Federal court order.

Judge Johnson noted, in his opinion, that the marchers would be "entitled to be protected by the law enforcement agencies of the state of Alabama against traffic and other hazards." He said further:

"This court, after inquiry, has been informed by the attorneys representing the United States in this case that the United States Government stands ready, if requested by the Gov-

Continued on Page 20, Column 6

110,000 CONQUER 5TH AVE. FOR ERIN

Everything, Even Girl's Hair, Turns Green for Parade

By WILLIAM E. FARRELL

To the skirl of hundreds of bagpipes and the echoing thud of thousands of drums, 110,000 Irish-Americans and their green-bedizened sympathizers laid siege yesterday to two miles of Fifth Avenue to honor one Patricius Magonus Sucatus.

From 44th Street to 86th Street, the elegant boulevard was awash in green, white and orange (Irishmen prefer to call it gold), the colors of the Irish flag. The crowd that lined the St. Patrick's Day Parade route—estimated at a million —dazzled the eye with a proliferation of green derbies, green dresses, green buttons, green kerchiefs, green ties and green hair.

The pale, lime-colored locks belonged to Miss Barbara Caffrey, a 16-year-old from Bayside, Queens, who said, "I think it's rather subdued." Patting the elaborately teased, bouffant hairdo, she said the color was from a vegetable dye that would be washed out today.

The annual parade began promptly at noon and the last of the 235 marching units and 230 pipe, brass and fife-drum-and-bugle bands dispersed at 86th Street and Third Avenue almost six hours later. As al-

Continued on Page 29, Column 6

Crime Inquiry Jury Indicts Rao as Liar

By EDWARD RANZAL

Vincent John Rao, 67-year-old millionaire Mafia underboss, was indicted yesterday on five counts of perjury in testimony before a Federal grand jury.

The indictment was the culmination of the "most extensive investigation of organized criminal activities by a Federal grand jury," United States Attorney Robert M. Morgenthau said.

The special rackets grand jury was sworn in 18 months ago and returned the indictment on the last day of its term. Mr. Morgenthau said the investigation would be continued by a new rackets grand jury to be impaneled soon.

In discharging the grand jury, Judge Irving Ben Cooper said: "Without you this city would be a jungle." The panel's un-

Continued on Page 34, Column 1

Suspect Gives Up in IN[...] Sister Calls Him Black[...]

The New York Times (by Neal Boenzi)

Christopher Lynch outside Police Headquarters yesterday

By EMANUEL PERLMUTTER

A taciturn, 17-year-old youth sought in the subway slaying of a Brooklyn schoolboy surrendered to the police early yesterday and was immediately charged with homicide.

The suspect, Christopher Lynch, a 210-pound, 6-foot-4 unemployed Negro with a police record, was booked on charges of having stabbed to death 17-year-old Andrew Mormile, a white high school student, last Friday night in an IND subway train.

Detectives at the Gates Avenue station described Lynch as a frequenter of black extremist meetings. One detective asserted that the suspect hated white persons.

A similar description of Lynch was given by his sister, Mrs. Patricia Harris. "He believed in something like black nationalists," she remarked in a taped interview for radio station WNEW.

"That's what got him in

Continued on Page 24, Column 6

Computers to Land Jetliners Next Year

By FREDRIC C. APPEL

Sometime next January a four-engine Boeing jetliner will probably land with a full load of passengers at a major airport in this country and the pilot will then announce "Ladies and gentlemen, this aircraft was just landed by a computer. I didn't touch the controls until we taxied off the runway."

That is the likely result of a decision by the Federal Aviation Agency yesterday to grant an airworthiness certificate for an automatic landing system developed jointly by the Boeing Company and the Bendix Corporation. According to a Boeing engineer, it is the first system in the world to be so certified by the F.A.A., for operation in the United States.

The first Boeing 707 or 720 jetliners equipped with the sys-

Continued on Page 22, Column 2

[...] Qualifications

By C. P. TRUSSELL
Special to The New York Times

WASHINGTON, March 17—The House of Representatives refused today to give the Chief Justice and his associates on the Supreme Court $3,000 pay increases.

A bill last year gave $7,500 increases to lesser judges and to members of Congress but only $4,500 to the Supreme Court.

The vote today was 203 to 177.

One hundred fifty-four Democrats and 23 Republicans voted for the $3,000 increase. They were outvoted by 99 Democrats and 104 Republicans.

The vote followed an earlier roll-call by which the leadership was enabled by a margin of only 19 votes to get the House to consider the question at all.

The storm of disagreement that greeted the pay-rise proposal came from every geographical direction. It was largely from the South and many Republican areas. But it also came from Border States and the West and Midwest.

Representative Emanuel Celler, the Brooklyn Democrat who heads the Judiciary Committee and who handled the proposed increases, denounced his colleagues for "petty criticisms"

Continued on Page 18, Column 5

Farouk Dead at 45; Egypt's Exiled King

By Reuters

ROME, Thursday, March 18—Former King Farouk of Egypt died in a hospital here early today after collapsing over the dinner table at a fashionable restaurant on Via Cassia, north of Rome. He was 45 years old.

The former monarch was dining with a woman whom the police declined to identify. He had ended his meal when he collapsed. There was no immediate word on the cause of death.

Farouk, who was deposed in 1952 by an Egyptian officers' coup, lived a comparatively quiet life in recent years in a villa outside Rome.

The reign of King Farouk began in an auspicious atmosphere of hope and popular admiration when a handsome, slender, seemingly energetic

Continued on Page 30, Column 5

STAGG DIES AT 102; DEAN OF COACHES

76 Years in College Football —On First All-America

By The Associated Press

STOCKTON, Calif., March 17 —Amos Alonzo Stagg, patriarch of American athletics, died in a rest home today at the age of 102.

Mr. Stagg, who was called the grand old man of football, had been in fragile health for several years but only last night developed a fever. Death was attributed to uremic poisoning.

Mr. Stagg's last birthday was observed quietly, in contrast to the celebration of his 100th birthday. On that occasion, sports figures and admirers from all over the nation attended a huge civic dinner in his honor.

Against the advice of his doctors, the bent, white-haired Mr. Stagg left the rest home with his wife and was driven

Continued on Page 30, Column 1

NEWS INDEX

STAGG DIES AT 102; DEAN OF COACHES

Continued From Page 1, Col. 8

to an auditorium to personally acknowledge the acclaim.

His death was not altogether unexpected, although his long-time physician, Dr. Langley Collis, said at his last birthday, "He is in better condition than most 90-year-olds."

Nurses said that "Mr. Stagg couldn't see a thing." He spent half of his waking hours sitting in a chair. He was unable to walk and had to be assisted by nurses.

Mrs. Stagg died last July 22 at the age of 88. The old coach was not told of her death.

Survivors include two sons, Paul, athletic director at the University of the Pacific, and Amos Alonzo Stagg Jr., and a daughter, Mrs. Ruth S. Lauren.

A funeral service will be held Sunday at 2 P. M. at the Central Methodist Church in Stockton.

Aimed for Ministry

In the spring of 1888, as a slender Yale University undergraduate, Mr. Stagg pitched its baseball team to a 2-1 victory over the Boston Braves. Within a week the young pitcher was offered six professional contracts. He turned them down. He disliked the character of the professional game, he explained, and, besides, in several years he expected to enter the ministry.

In time, Mr. Stagg abandoned both of his early loves—pitching and preaching. But, in 70 years as a college football coach, he was the most compelling single force for the tactical growth and ethical elevation of the game.

He pioneered the forward pass and the T-formation as it is played today. He molded 13 charter students of the University of Chicago into the first of a long line of football powerhouses. He developed such great coaches as Fritz Crisler and Jesse Harper. And before each game he gathered his players about him for a moment of silent prayer — not a prayer for victory, he often said, but a supplication that they might do their very best.

Mr. Stagg was older than college football. He was born on Aug. 16, 1862, in West Orange, N. J., seven years before the first collegiate game. The fifth of eight children of an impoverished cobbler, Lon Stagg did odd jobs by the hour after classes at Orange High School and helped his father to mow and cradle hay in the summer.

Physical conditioning was a by-product of his life. He ran the mile between home and school each day because he was always either coming from a job or going to one. He once said that he was particularly fascinated by the tale of the Spartan lad who made no outcry while a fox, which he had hidden in his shirt, began to chew on his flesh.

In lieu of foxes, Mr. Stagg led a Spartan life of his own. He gave up coffee in high school, never drank and never tasted nicotine. He chewed one-quarter of a stick of gum at a time—even when he could afford a whole piece. His only indulgence was sourballs and other hard candies.

At 21, Lon Stagg entered Phillips Exeter Academy. He pitched its team to victory while living on soda crackers and waiting on tables. Offered a baseball scholarship at Dartmouth, Mr. Stagg turned it down so that so that he might enter Yale as a predivinity student.

Pitched Yale to 5 Titles

A year leater, with $32 and no overcoat, Mr. Stagg arrived in New Haven. He continued his soda-cracker diet until he was hospitalized with malnutrition, then, more substantially nourished, pitched the Yale baseball team to five championships. He played end on the football team for five years and was named to Walter Camp's first All-America squad in 1889.

By the spring of 1890, after six years of athletic fame, Mr. Stagg was convinced that he lacked the ability to talk easily before a group. He quit the Yale Divinity School and became a faculty member at the Young Men's Christian Association training school at Springfield, Mass. One of his colleagues there was James Naismith, the inventor of basketball.

While at Springfield, he coached the local college football team with such success that in 1892 he was invited to coach at the as yet uncompleted University of Chicago. The response to the football call at Chicago was not overwhelming. Thirteen boys showed up. Mr. Stagg suited up, placed himself on the roster as No. 14, and began the first of 41 years of coaching there.

His teams won six Big Ten Conference titles and were unbeaten in five seasons. He became the first football coach to have a field named for him, the first athletic director to achieve faculty status and, to thousands of students and fans, was as much a part of the university as its imposing Gothic buildings.

The university remembered him as a short, well-knit figure (he maintained his playing weight of 160 into his 90's) walking briskly about campus without an overcoat in winter, playing tennis with his son Paul or driving in a vintage electric runabout; a man who scorned the cold winds whipping in from Lake Michigan, the stiffening muscles of middle age or the easy temptations of a materialistic era.

His influence and importance reached far beyond the Midway. He was selected to the Football Hall of Fame both as a player and as a coach. He was instrumental in the formation of the Western Conference. He was a member of five Olympic Games committees, one of the original members of the Intercollegiate Football Rules Committee and he staged some of the first national collegiate track and baseball contests. Through trying moments on and off the field, the strongest word he ever used was "jackass."

If a player made a series of mistakes, Mr. Stagg would call him a "double jackass" or even a "triple jackass." His players at the University of Chicago formed a "jackass club" and the coach's son, Paul, the Maroon quarterback from 1929 to 1931, became a member. "He called me a double jackass once," Paul said.

Mr. Stagg was revered as the "grand old man," but in 1932, at the age of 70, the university asked him to retire and accept an honorary position as supervisor of athletics. He refused.

"I could not and would not accept a job without work," he later said.

So, at a time when most men would be ready to call it a career, Alonzo Stagg went West.

"I went West when I was a young man," he said. "I'm going West again, and I'm still a young man."

For 14 years, at the College of the Pacific in Stockton, Mr. Stagg turned out big-time teams in a small school. At 84, again asked to take an advisory role, Mr. Stagg moved on. He joined his son, Amos Alonzo Jr., at Susquehanna College in Pennsylvania. There he took charge of the offensive platoon and actively coached on the field for six years.

In 1953, when his wife, the former Stella Robertson of Albion, N. Y., become unable to travel between California and Pennsylvania, Mr. Stagg took an advisory job at Stockton Junior College.

Mrs. Stagg not only had an avid interest in her husband's teams but she also served as an aide on more than one occasion.

When Mr. Stagg was coaching at Susquehanna, Mrs. Stagg went off on a Saturday to scout Dickinson College, the next week's opponent. When she came back she reported, "You can pass on their left halfback. He's slow."

Susquehanna beat Dickinson by the margin of one touchdown, achieved late in the game. It came on a pass, over the losers' left halfback.

On Sept. 16, 1960, Mr. Stagg sent this note to Coach Larry Kentera of Stockton:

"For the past 70 years I have been a coach. At 98 years of age it seems like a good time to stop."

Wrote 'Stagg of Yale'

CHICAGO, March 17 (AP)—According to Amos Alonzo Stagg Jr., Mr. Stagg left an unpublished autobiography entitled "Stagg of Yale."

"I know after all those years at Chicago that title may sound strange," said his eldest son, who is 65. "But dad and I decided that he came from Yale, where he was a great athlete, and that was the best title.

He added:

"Dad had written about two-thirds of his autobiography and I have nearly finished it for possible publication by the end of May. Perhaps, however, the publishers will change the name of the book."

Hall of Fame member, Amos Alonzo Stagg was one of football's greatest coaches ever. He is shown here with Pat O'Dea, the famous punter and drop-kicker.

"The Ol' Professor"—Charles Dillon Stengel.

"All the News That's Fit to Print"

The New York Times

LATE CITY EDITION

Weather: Partly sunny today; cool tonight. Chance of rain tomorrow. Temperature range: today 60-76; Tuesday 56-73. Details on Page 89.

VOL. CXXV . . No. 42,984 — © 1975 The New York Times Company — NEW YORK, WEDNESDAY, OCTOBER 1, 1975 — 20 CENTS

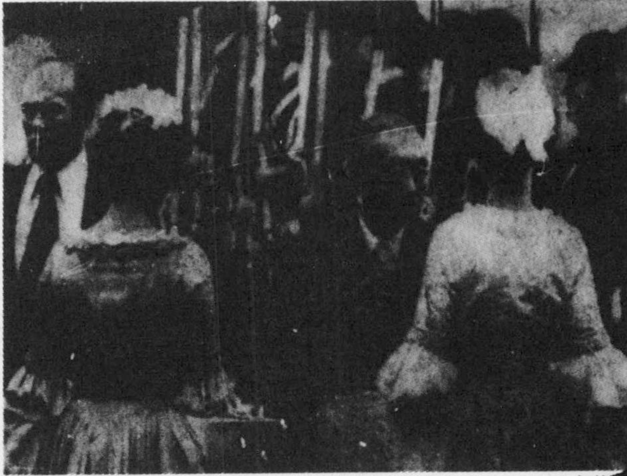

EMPEROR HIROHITO GREETED IN VIRGINIA: The Emperor being welcomed by women in colonial costu[me] ... port News yesterday. It is the first time a reigning Japanese monarch has made official visit to United ...

PRESIDENT ASKS $13-MILLION MORE FOR PROTECTION

Tells Chicago Audience That He Will Continue Travel by 'Every Prudent Means'

By JAMES M. NAUGHTON

Special to The New York Times

CHICAGO, Sept. 30—President Ford, after asking Congress today for $13.5-million more this year for Secret Service protection, said tonight that he would continue traveling across the country "not in any foolhardy spirit, but by every prudent and practical means."

Mr. Ford told a Republican fund-raising dinner at the Conrad Hilton Hotel here that his travels were intended to help him "talk straight to the American people."

"I have also done ... listening." ...

A State Financing Agency Finds Loan Market Is Shut

With $69-Million Needed in the Next 2 Weeks, Banks' Position Perils Many Kinds of Construction

By FRANCIS X. CLINES

Officials of the state's Housing Finance Agency, facing the need to raise $69-million in the next two weeks, have been told by bankers that the borrowing market is closed to it for the foreseeable future.

The situation, which is even more critical in time than the threatened default by the city, is now at an impasse, according to officials of the huge agency, who said yesterday that they were hoping the Governor and Legislature could come up with some sort of em...

Default would ... pin... the borrowing agency would strike at the credit rating of the state itself and precisely when it is hoping its healthier status can be used to prop up the city.

The difficulty at the Housing Finance Agency, which must borrow at the rate of about $100-million a month, represents the entwinement of the state and city credit problems, in the view of harried state offi...

... ncy has a good credit ... revenue flow, but ... caught in what ... ller Arthur Levitt ... rational emotion... f potential inves... ll offerings from ... ardless of rela...

BANKS RESISTING NEW STATE ISSUE OF NOTES FOR CITY

Stand Further Jeopardizes Legislative Package Aimed at Staving Off Default

CAREY ASKS LEVITT AID

Fails to Persuade Controller to Invest Pension Funds Despite Court Ruling

By LINDA GREENHOUSE

A second crucial element in the financial package for staving off a New York City default appeared jeopardized yesterday by a growing unwillingness of bankers to buy the $500-million in short-term notes the state is due to issue over the next two months on the city's behalf.

"The marketability of that state paper is problematic at this point," Felix G. Rohatyn, chairman of the Municipal Assistance Corporation, said after a long meeting with Governor Carey and other members of the M.A.C. board here.

On Monday, the State Court of Appeals threw out a section of the emergency plan that required State Controller Arthur Levitt to invest $125-million from two state pension funds in M.A.C. bonds. The Governor met with Mr. Levitt for more than two hours yesterday, but failed to persuade him to make the investment voluntarily.

Rescue in Doubt

With these rapid consecutive ...ws—the loss of $125-million ...pension investments and the ...spect of failure of the $500-...ion note sale—the intricate ...billion rescue package that ...egislature patched to... in a special session three ... ago appeared close to ...part.

...backs for the city ...et another drop in ... New York State... and notes, and ...ity was virtually ...bonds of the Mu... ...nce Corporation ... low as 75 cents ...while general... ...onds sold at ... up to 9 per ...

... of Federal Funds

The only cheerful news for the city was the announcement by President Ford that, at the request of Senator James L. Buckley, he had ordered two Cabinet officers to review Federal allocations to the city and make sure that they were being given fairly. [Page 29.]

The meeting in the Governor's office yesterday afternoon ended with no public statements and apparently without a decision on what to do next. Mr. Carey will fly to Washington this morning to brief members of the state's Congressional delegation on

Continued on Page 28, Column 4

MADRID REJECTS FOREIGN PROTESTS

Premier Defends Executions and Accuses Critics of 'Intole...

By H...

Special to ...

MADRID, ... Carlos Arias ... angrily denoun... protests against ... execution of five ... called on the S... to unite behind ... Francisco Franco... Government.

In his first public a... since Saturday when ... rorists, two of them B... aratists, were put to d... Premier attacked the ... protests from abroad ... intolerable aggression ... Spanish sovereignty."

[In London, the organiza... tion Amnesty International issued a report asserting that it had evidence that Spanish authorities used torture on Basque detainees on a large scale. Page 5.]

Speaking of the expressions of hostility from many countries, the Premier said, "We do not desire to be alone but the possibility of isolation does not intimidate us."

Mass Rally Planned

The Premier's 15-minute address was preceded through the day by numerous official and semiofficial calls for a mass rally tomorrow in Madrid in support of General Franco's regime. It will be the fourth such rally since World War II, each held when the regime felt itself in danger from internal and external sources.

The various appeals pictured

Continued on Page 4, Column 4

U.S. Will Let Vietnamese Who Ask to Go ...

for ... Reve... embro... over ... of an ... R. Ford ... unusual ... of the Nat... around 196...

The pros... Goldstein, ... whether the I... sue the allega... made, apparen... by a former lea... At the same ti... says it acted "appropriately." And some officials of the tax agency contend that the United States Attorney's office had known of the charge by the fall of 1974 and had dismissed it out of hand.

Neither Mr. Goldstein's office nor the I.R.S. is believed to have any evidence at this stage

... ve ... -up. ... of their conflict, ... comes during a period of heightened public and Congressional interest in the integrity and techniques of Federal investigative agencies, illustrates how two major law-enforcement agencies—ostensibly working together—can come to challenge each other's motives, actions and memory.

The story has two threads

Continued on Page 90, Column 1

... Ford's ... sources said that the chairman, Representative Otis G. Pike, personally took possession of the documents late today. The material delivered represents pre-Tet reports by the C.I.A., the defense intelligence agency, and the national security agency. Committee sources said, however, that this did not include information from the Department of State and that that controversy would be handled separately.

A source close to the com-

Continued on Page 21, Column 1

...oops

...emier removed ...upying leftist-con...olled radio and television stations. In reversing the step he took two days ago to prevent the suspension of civil liberties, the Premier said he was "confident that it would not be necessary to reimpose emergency measures." Page 3.

... that the calls ... the fact that they had been made—were not relayed to the agents who questioned Miss Moore and that her attempts to telephone them were not discovered until after the shooting incident in front of the St. Francis Hotel about 3:30 P.M.

The two agents and other Federal law enforcement chiefs who testified today said that

Continued on Page 19, Column 1

... L. ... Attorney General in charge of the Criminal Division, to Senator William Proxmire, Democrat of Wisconsin, who made the letter public.

Mr. Thornburgh wrote that "insufficient evidence has been developed to date to support criminal charges." But Senator Proxmire said he was "flabbergasted" by that conclusion and asked Attorney General Edward H. Levi to overturn "the outrageous decision."

While declining to press criminal charges, Mr. Thornburgh did say that "it would appear

Continued on Page 21, Column 1

Yale Sets Up School Of Administration With Dual Purpose

By MICHAEL KNIGHT

Yale University will announce today the establishment of a Graduate School of Organization and Management to train leaders for both business and government service.

Named to head the school, which is expected to open next fall, will be William H. Donaldson, former Under Secretary of State and Wall Street "whiz kid." In the nineteen-sixties, as a partner in Donaldson, Lufkin, Jenrette, Inc., he helped transform institutional investors into a major force in the securities market and he amassed a personal fortune in excess of $10-million.

The new graduate school is expected to combine the study of business administration and public management techniques—increasingly needed by the growing corps of executives who shuttle between jobs in industry and government.

"I think the lines between the private and public sectors are blurring more and more,"

Continued on Page 57, Column 1

Stengel's Death at 85 Widely Mourned

By JOSEPH DURSO

Casey Stengel, who died Monday night in California at the age of 85, was mourned yesterday by a public that had marveled for more than 60 years at his antics and achievements as a baseball player, coach, manager and nonstop showman.

Tributes poured in during the hours after "the Ol' Professor" died in Glendale Memorial Hospital from around the country—from public officials like Governor Carey and Mayor Beame, who recalled that he had worked for all four of New York's major league teams in this century, to former players like Yogi Berra, who remembered him as "a great man."

Mr. Stengel died at 10:58 P.M., Pacific Time, only a few hours after a family spokesman disclosed that he was suffering from cancer of the lymph glands. He had entered the hospital two weeks earlier for tests, not far from the home he had shared for half a century with his wife, Edna, who was in a nursing home nearby.

The legends that he had created continued long after his retirement 10 years ago and, as recently as June, he enlivened the Mets' annual old-timers' reunion by riding into Shea Stadium in a Roman chariot dressed in a toga and gladiator's helmet.

"Casey Stengel had the baseball mind of a genius," Governor Carey said yesterday, "the heart of Santa Claus and St. Francis, and the face of a clown, and something very good has gone from our lives.

"Casey Stengel will be ranked in the history of baseball with such great managers as John McGraw, Connie Mack and Joe McCarthy. And New Yorkers will always hold him in their hearts, with warm memory, because he is the only baseball figure who wore the uniforms

Continued on Page 30, Column 1

ALI RETAINS TITLE: Joe Frazier recoiling from a blow to the head by Muhammad Ali in heavyweight championship bout in Manila. Ali won on a technical knockout after 14 rounds. Details, Page 31.

Stengel's Death at 85 Widely Mourned

By JOSEPH DURSO

Casey Stengel, who died Monday night in California at the age of 85, was mourned yesterday by a public that had marveled for more than 60 years at his antics and achievements as a baseball player, coach, manager and nonstop showman.

Tributes poured in during the hours after "the Ol' Professor" died in Glendale Memorial Hospital from around the country—from public officials like Governor Carey and Mayor Beame, who recalled that he had worked for all four of New York's major league teams in this century, to former players like Yogi Berra, who remembered him as "a great man."

Mr. Stengel died at 10:58 P.M., Pacific Time, only a few hours after a family spokesman disclosed that he was suffering from cancer of the lymph glands. He had entered the hospital two weeks earlier for tests, not far from the home he had shared for half a century with his wife, Edna, who was in a nursing home nearby.

The legends that he had created continued long after his retirement 10 years ago and, as recently as June, he enlivened the Mets' annual old-timers' reunion by riding into Shea Stadium in a Roman chariot dressed in a toga and gladiator's helmet.

"Casey Stengel had the baseball mind of a genius," Governor Carey said yesterday, "the heart of Santa Claus and St. Francis, and the face of a clown, and something very good has gone from our lives.

"Casey Stengel will be ranked in the history of baseball with such great managers as John McGraw, Connie Mack and Joe McCarthy. And New Yorkers will always hold him in their hearts, with warm memory, because he is the only baseball figure who wore the uniforms

Continued on Page 30, Column 1

Casey Stengel: Baseball and the Nation Mourn the Death of an Amazing Man

Continued From Page 1, Col. 4

of the Dodgers, Giants, Yankees and Mets.

"He made a unique contribution, too, to American letters with his inimitablet 'Stenglese,' a language for which he invented his own prose and syntax. He was a joy in more ways than anyone in public life. We shall not see his like again."

The man behind the legend—Charles Dillon Stengel of Kansas City, the man from K.C.—owned oil wells in Texas, was vice president of a bank in California and controlled real estate that made him a millionaire. But for all his status, he was best known as a baseball man with a wrinkled, expressive face and a guttural voice.

He was transported to his early baseball games as a boy in Missouri in horse-drawn surreys and wound up flying coast to coast in jetliners. He reached the major leagues in 1912 when William Howard Taft was President and retired in 1965 during the Administration of Lyndon B. Johnson.

He was a player, coach or manager on 17 professional teams. He was traded four times as a left-handed outfielder in the major leagues. He was dropped or relieved three times as a manager in the big leagues. He was even paid twice for not managing.

From 1910 to 1931, he played on four teams in the minors, then five in the majors and finally two more in the minors. Then, as a manager, he lived through 25 years of frustration at both levels, finishing no higher than fifth in an eight-team league during one decade.

Then he suddenly graduated to the New York Yankees in 1948 as the 15th manager in their 46-year history of dominating the sport and won 10 pennants and 7 world championships in 12 years.

Finally, at the age of 72, he wound up as the first manager of the New York Mets where he had started—at the bottom of the ladder.

Through it all, he was one of the busiest characters on the American scene — and one of the most theatrical. His pantomime, monologues and storytelling defied description, until he was accused (with some reason) of carrying on to distract the public from the less effectual performances of his teams.

Casey at bat.

He spoke in a nonstop style that came to be known as Stengelese — a kind of circuitous doubletalk laced with ambiguous antecedents, dangling participles, a lack of proper names and a liberal use of adjectives like "amazing" and "terrific."

He drew on baseball lore back to the days of John J. McGraw, his idol as a manager, and would clinch points in rhetoric by saying with finality: "You could look it up." When a listener's attention waned, he would recapture it by suddenly exclaiming, "Now, let me ask you," and would be off and running again.

The perpetrator of this commotion was born in Kansas City, Mo., on July 30, 1890. His father had emigrated from Germany in 1851 and had settled in the farm country across the Mississippi River from Davenport, Iowa. A first child, Louise, was born in 1886; a son, Grant, in 1887, and Charles three years later.

Charles became an all-around athlete at Kansas City Central High School and pitched (and won) against Joplin for the state championship in 1909. He turned professional the following year with the Kansas City Blues, who farmed him out to Kankakee, Ill., in the Northern Association.

Baseball was a means to an end: Stengel was working his way through the Western Dental College in Kansas City. But two things swerved him from his course. He was left-handed, which raised some problems for his instructors. And left-handed dentists had a less riotous future than left-handed baseball players.

The dental college, Stengel recalled, also did not have the daring to turn him loose on society with a "weapon" in his hand.

Called Up by Dodgers

For whatever reasons, he became a fulltime ballplayer and was discovered by Larry Sutton, a scout for the Brooklyn Dodgers. In September of 1912, the Dodgers—then known as the Trolley Dodgers and Superbas—called him up from Birmingham, and he was in the big leagues.

For the next 14 seasons, Stengel played the outfield in the National League — with Brooklyn until 1917, Pittsburgh until 1920, Philadelphia until the middle of 1921, New York until 1924 and Boston until 1925.

He batted .284 and hit 60 home runs in 1,277 games. His best year was 1922, when he hit .368 in 84 games with McGraw's Giants. His best moments came in the World Series of 1923, when he hit two home runs and won two games —only to be upstaged by the young Babe Ruth, who hit three home runs as the Yankees won the Series.

After the 1923 Series, Stengel was traded to the Boston Braves and two years later began his career as a manager

(continued)

The great Stengel once led the New York Yankees to five consecutive world championships—1949 through 1953.

with Boston's farm club at Worcester, Mass.

He already had gained a sizable reputation as a brawler and clown, and promptly increased it when the Boston club installed him as a one-man triumvirate at Worcester — president, manager and right fielder.

Casey fretted until the final day of the season, then hatched a monumental triple play to escape. As manager, he released Stengel the player; as president, he dismissed Stengel the manager; and as Stengel, he resigned as president.

The owner of the Boston team, Judge Emil Fuchs, was outraged by this impertinence, but nobody was too surprised. After all, Stengel had long since become famous as "the king of the grumblers," a locker - room clique whose chief talent was trouble.

He had been the bane of umpires and of managers like Wilbert Robinson of Brooklyn, who became the butt of one Stengel prank at Daytona Beach, Fla., in the spring of 1915. On that occasion, Casey was inspired by the recent feat of Gabby Street, who had caught a baseball dropped from the Washington Monument. The question now became: Could a man catch a baseball dropped from an airplane?

The airplane was supplied by Ruth Law, the pioneer woman flier, and the baseball was supplied by C. D. Stengel, except that somehow it became a grapefruit by the time it was dropped.

"Uncle Robbie," Stengel recalled, "was warming up this pitcher on the sidelines — we didn't have six coaches in those days. And this aviatorix—it was the first one they had — she flew over and dropped it. And Uncle Robbie saw it coming and waved everybody away like an outfielder and said, 'I've got it, I've got it.'

"Robbie got under this grapefruit, thinking it was a baseball, which hit him right on this pitcher's glove he put on and the insides of it flew all over, seeds on his face and uniform, and flipped him right over on his back. Everybody came running up and commenced laughing, all except Robbie."

In one of his most fabled escapades, Stengel returned to Ebbets Field in 1918 with the Pittsburgh Pirates, who had just acquired him from Brooklyn. He was greeted by a rousing round of catcalls from the fans. In reply, he marched to home plate, bowed with courtliness to the grandstand, doffed his cap — and out flew a sparrow. He had given them the bird.

On another occasion, he went to right field, found a drainage hole and simply disappeared from sight. A moment later he rose majestically, the manhole cover under his arm, just in time to catch a fly ball.

Later, when he became a manager, Stengel looked back on his wayward years and said: "Now that I am a manager, I see the error of my youthful ways. If any player ever pulled that stuff on me now, I would probably fine his ears off."

Stengel's success as a manager, meanwhile, was lean. In seven years in the minor leagues from 1925 to 1931, his teams won only one pennant. But he was developing skills that became his trademark in later years: He was thriving as a buffoon who could draw attention away from inept players to himself, and he was learning the business side of baseball — buying players low, selling them high and converting farm clubs into pools of

(continued)

talent for the major leagues.

He also was branching out in his personal life. In 1924 he had married Edna Lawson, a tall, lively brunette from California who once had acted in silent films with Hoot Gibson and who later was an accountant with a shrewd business sense.

They settled in a two-story house at the foothills of the Sierras in Glendale, Calif. And for the next 40 years it was their base as both roamed the country on Casey's travels.

Investment in Oil

They had no children, but had hordes of relatives who lived nearby, plus young ballplayers who often stayed with them. They also had interests in real estate, established the Valley National Bank with Mrs. Stengel's family, and literally struck oil in Texas on a chance investment Casey had made with some baseball friends.

With all this going for him, Stengel was hardly considered the type of man who would flower late in life into a baseball manager of renown—not even when he was called to the Brooklyn Dodgers as a coach in 1932 and became manager two years later.

From 1934 until 1943, his teams at Brooklyn and Boston never finished higher than fifth in an eight-team league. Then in 1943, when he was struck by a taxi in Boston and suffered a broken leg, it appeared that his career was finally ended.

However, the following year he agreed to leave his swimming pool and patio in Glendale to take over the Milwaukee club in the American Association. He did it as a favor for a friend, but it proved to be a turning point. After one season as manager at Milwaukee and another at Kansas City, he spent three at Oakland in the Pacific Coast League, won 321 games and suddenly at the age of 58 was offered the job as manager of the lordly Yankees.

His selection as the replacement for Bucky Harris evoked surprise. It was widely thought that the Yankees had hired "Professor" Stengel to throw a screen of hilarity around the club for a season or two while rebuilding. But the "interim" manager, who had never spent a day in the American League, stayed 12 years and the Yankees reached spectacular heights.

In 1949, his first season, the Yankees suffered 72 injuries. Joe DiMaggio even missed half the season. But Stengel kept juggling lineups and the Yankees defeated the Boston Red Sox in the last two games, won the pennant and defeated the Dodgers in the World Series.

A year later they won again and they kept on winning until they had taken five straight pennants and world championships. It was a record streak for a team and a manager. In a rash moment Stengel remarked that if the Yankees didn't make it six in a row in 1954, the manager should be dismissed. They didn't, but he wasn't.

In 1955, they won the pennant again and also took it in 1956, 1957, 1958 and 1960. But they won only two World Series during that time, and in 1959 even slipped to third place.

Stengel was earning $85,000 a year by now and was the foremost manager in baseball. He was surrounded by stars like Yogi Berra, Whitey Ford, Phil Rizzuto, Mickey Mantle and Roger Maris. But the second half of his administration was a somewhat troubled time, and he grew increasingly arbitrary with players and bitter to suggestions that he was "too old."

His bitterness reached a peak on Oct. 18, 1960, five days after the Yankees had lost the series to Pittsburgh.

In an acrimonious press conference at the Savoy Hilton Hotel, the Yankee brass — led by Dan Topping — announced that Stengel had "retired." A short time later George M. Weiss, Stengel's friend and sponsor, was released as general manager.

"I was fired," Casey commented.

After a year in the California sunshine, though, he was hired again — by Weiss, who now was organizing the Mets, the successors to the Giants and the Dodgers, who had left New York in 1957 for the West Coast.

So, at the age of 72, Stengel began a new career, one that crystallized all his talents for teaching, acting and enchanting the public. The Mets needed such talents, too, since they lost 452 games while winning 194 during the next four years, finishing dead last each time

They were as downtrodden as the Yankees had been exalted. But they were cast in the image of the stumpy, waddling old man who directed them, a team whose sins were pardoned by an adoring public, whose life was surrounded by legend. whose bank account grew with the legend.

In 1965, Stengel's last year in a baseball suit, 1,768,389 persons paid up to $3.50 each to watch the Old Man and his celebrated Youth of America in their new Shea Stadium on Flushing Bay; and 1,075,431 paid to see them on the road.

Casey Stengel was the only man to be associated with all four of New York's baseball teams.

The partnership began to fold on July 25, 1965, when Stengel fractured his left hip —somewhere between an old-timers' party at Toots Shor's restaurant, where he slipped and fell, and a house in Queens, where he slipped and fell again while getting out of an automobile.

Missed Birthday Fete

In any event, he was in Roosevelt Hospital that afternoon while 39,288 persons celebrated his 75th birthday at Shea Stadium. Two days later he underwent an operation on his hip and one month later he retired to the side of his swimming pool as titular vice president of the Mets.

One year later, however, leaning on a crooked black cane, he limped into baseball's Hall of Fame at Cooperstown, N.Y., alongside Ted Williams. Stengel, the 104th person inducted into the shrine, told the crowd in valedictorian Stengelese:

"I want to thank my parents for letting me play baseball, and I'm thankful I had baseball knuckles and couldn't become a dentist. . . . I got $2,100 a year when I started in the big league, and they get more money now. . . . I chased the balls that Babe Ruth hit."

Funeral services will be held next Monday at 1 P.M., Pacific Time, at the Church of the Recessional in Forest Lawn Memorial Park, Glendale. In lieu of flowers, the family requested donations in his name be made to the Association of Professional Baseball Players of America, 630 East Wardlow Road, Long Beach, Calif. The association helps men formerly associated with baseball.

The body will lie in state on Sunday from 9 A.M. until 9 P.M. at Scovern Mortuary in Glendale.

The New York Times TUESDAY, APRIL 7, 1970

STOKES DIES AT 36; BASKETBALL STAR

Player Stricken With Rare Illness at Peak of Career

CINCINNATI, April 6 (AP) —Maurice Stokes, the former basketball star with the Cincinnati Royals, died today after suffering a heart attack March 30. He was 36 years old.

Stokes suffered the heart attack at Good Samaritan Hospital here, where he has been hospitalized since March, 1958.

Jack Twyman, a former Royals' star, has served as Stokes's guardian and has sponsored numerous benefit games to help pay his hospital bills.

Stokes is survived by his mother, a brother and a twin sister, Mrs. Clarice Washington.

Heroic Off the Court

By STEVE CADY

They called Maurice Stokes "Mighty Mo" in college, but his efforts on the basketball court dimmed in comparison to the heroics he performed in hospital therapy rooms during a 12-year struggle to regain the use of his body.

"Anybody else would have been dead long ago," a friend remarked as Stokes painfully fought his way back, year by year, from total paralysis.

Eventually, he was able to talk in slow, guttural speech that close friends could understand. The use of his body was improving in other areas, too, but he never made it out of the wheelchair, as he kept insisting he would.

Before the injury that ended his basketball career, Stokes had been one of the game's top young professionals: an all-America center at St. Francis College of Loretto, Pa., in 1955; most valuable player in the 1955 National Invitation Tournament at Madison Square Garden, and rookie of the year in the National Basketball Association the following season with the Rochester Royals.

In his three seasons of pro ball with the Royals—one at Rochester and two at Cincinnati after the franchise was shifted—Stokes was a member of the N.B.A. all-star squad every time. In his final season, the 6-foot-7-inch, 240-pound center was second in the league in rebounds (18.1 a game), third in assists (6.4) and among the top 15 scorers with an average of 16.9 points a game.

That was where he stood, at the age of 24, on the night of March 15, 1958, the night his career and life came toppling down.

The Royals had just lost to Detroit in the opening game of the Western Division playoffs, and were returning by plane to Cincinnati for the second game. Three days earlier, against the Mineapolis Lakers, Stokes had taken a hard bump on the head when he fell to the floor during a scramble for a rebound. It had knocked him unconscious, but he had revived and continued to play.

No. 1 Brother's Keeper

Stokes collapsed on the plane ride to Cincinnati and was in such critical condition that a teammate, aware of Stokes's desire to become a Roman Catholic, had baptized him. At the hospital, doctors cut an opening in his throat and inserted a tube into his windpipe. He received the last rites of the Catholic Church the following day, and remained in a coma for six months.

Finally, he moved his eyelids —and began the long struggle that was to become a symbol of individual courage, as well as a means for others to prove that a man could still be his brother's keeper.

The No. 1 brother's keeper was Jack Twyman, now a Cincinnati insurance executive and broadcaster, then a teammate on the Royals. Twyman visited Stokes daily in the hospital, and began arranging means of paying what eventually became enormous medical costs.

The major fund-raising device was the annual Maurice Stokes Benefit Game at Kutsher's Country Club in Monticello, N. Y., which was staged each summer for 11 years.

When Stokes was stricken, doctors thought he was suffering from encephalitis (sometimes called sleeping sickness), an inflammation of the brain caused by a virus. Later, when no virus could be found, they diagnosed the trouble as post-traumatic encephalopathy: paralysis and unconsciousness brought on by swelling of the brain caused by the bump on the head.

The rehabilitation process was agonizingly slow. From the time he regained consciousness, Stokes could understand everything said to him. His mind was always clear and sharp, and he could laugh. But in every other function, he was helpless.

At first, in replying to questions, he had to spell out words by having the person conversing with him recite the alphabet letter by letter. Each time the person would come to the right letter, Stokes would nod his head.

He spent most of his days chewing carrots or celery for speech therapy, immersed in whirlpool baths or other physical-therapy devices, pushing against objects in resistive exercises trying to coax life back into paralyzed muscles.

Later, when he learned to use an electric typewrite, he wrote: "I always tried to bear down in competition, but I never had to put out quite as hard as I do in this exercising."

Maurice Stokes was one of the N.B.A.'s greatest players when his career was cut short by an injury.

The New York Times SATURDAY, OCTOBER 6, 1979

KEN STRONG, STAR OF FOOTBALL GIANTS

N.Y.U. Graduate, 73, Gained Fame as N.F.L. Place-Kicker

By GERALD ESKENAZI

Ken Strong, one of the first place-kicking specialists in the National Football League while playing with the New York Giants, died of an apparent heart attack on a West Side street yesterday. He was 73 years old.

Mr. Strong, who lived in Bayside, Queens, was found dead outside 25 West 54th Street at about 11:45 A.M., police said. He was brought to the medical examiner's office, where an autopsy will be performed today.

Strong, a running back in addition to being a place-kicker, scored 319 points in a 12-year professional career.

Strong was the product of a time that demanded heroes and legends. His name in the 1920's was prominent with those of Bobby Jones, Jack Dempsey and Babe Ruth. In mentioning football stars, the experts would talk of Johnny Blood, Cliff Battles and Ken Strong.

Graduate of N.Y.U.

He was, perhaps, the most famous graduate of New York University who went on to a career in sports. In an often turbulent career that included baseball, Strong established himself as one of the better athletes of his time, a true triple-threat who could run, pass and kick the football.

His full name was Elmer Kenneth Strong Jr., and he was born in the Savin Rock section of West Haven, Conn., on April 21, 1906. N.Y.U. and the Giants' , however, were to be the institutions with which most people associated him. He entered college in 1925 and made the freshman team as a halfback. In his second year he did not attract attention, being used as a blocking back. Coach Chick Meehan let Strong run with the ball as a junior, and when he was a senior, he led the East in scoring with 160 points, none on field goals.

In his senior year he secretly married a showgirl, Amelia Hunneman, known professionally as Rella Harrison. Although the marriage was stormy and the couple lived apart as soon as the honeymoon ended, Strong was still able to concentrate on football. He was a unanimous all-America selection after gaining 2,100 yards, then acollegiate record.

Strong joined the Staten Island Stapes of the National Football League in 1929 and quickly became the team's star. In one game against the Giants he was tackled on the sidelines by Ray Flaherty, who continued to apply a stranglehold to Strong after the whistle blew.

Ken Strong in fine kicking form. Had it not been for a surgical error, Strong might have become a baseball star.

"Let go," said Strong.

"As soon as you stop kicking me," replied Flaherty.

But Strong was not doing the kicking. Instead, a little old lady had left the stands and was beating Flaherty for halting her hero.

The Stapes, playing in a handbox park, were dissolved in 1930 and Strong tried professional baseball. He set a New York-Penn League record of 41 home runs. The Detroit Tigers signed him and sent him to their Toronto farm team. At that point, when a bright major league baseball career seemed likely, Strong underwent a wrist operation, and a surgeon removed the wrong bone. Unable to throw a baseball, he sued for $275,000, and eventually collected $75,000. The award, however, was turned down following an appeal by the surgeon.

In 1931, Strong married Mabel Anderson, and joined the Giants in 1933, beginning a strange career with the New Yorkers. He played for three seasons and established himself as one of the pro's top performers. But he jumped to the fledging American League in 1936. When he tried to rejoin the Giants, he was banned from the National Football League for three seasons.

However, the Giants took him back in 1939. He underwent an operation for a bleeding ulcer in 1940, and "retired" after the 1940 campaign. At the time, he had scored more points than anyone in league history.

The Giants called on Strong in 1943, when he was 37 years old, to help them through the war years. He responded, but played only as a kicker because of his age.

When he retired in 1947, at the age of 41, he had led the league in scoring three times and was the Giants' leading career scorer.

He worked in public relations and as a liquor salesman until he returned to the Giants as kicking coach in 1962. In the periods between his associations with the Giants he was not forgotten. He was elected to the National Football Hall of Fame and the Pro Football Hall of Fame.

He remained with the Giants as a coach until 1965. In 1966 the Giants acquired Pete Gogolak, the N.F.L.'s first soccer-style place-kicker.

"All the News That's Fit to Print"

The New York Times.

LATE CITY EDITION

U. S. Weather Bureau Report (Page 70) forecasts: Variable cloudiness and cold today; clear tonight. Fair tomorrow. Temp. range: 40—25; yesterday: 43—30

VOL. CXIV. No. 39,085. NEW YORK, WEDNESDAY, JANUARY 27, 1965. TEN CENTS

BASIC G.O.P. PLAN FOR LEGISLATURE UPHELD BY COURT

3 VERSIONS VOIDED

Redistricting Is Based on 1960 Census—2 Houses to Grow

By HOMER BIGART

A special three-man Federal Court upheld yesterday the basic Republican plan for the legislative reapportionment of New York State.

Whether the plan is valid under the New York State Constitution awaits the outcome of a test brought by New York City, Radio Station WMCA and other plaintiffs in the state courts.

The panel held that Plan A—one of four plans enacted by the Republican majority at a lame-duck special session of the Legislature of 1964—complied with the order issued by the court last July 27. The order stipulated that the state be reapportioned to implement the Supreme Court's historic "one-man, one-vote" ruling of last June.

Plans B, C and D were ruled invalid. The court said that these plans did not comply with the order of the Court and were in conflict with the 14th Amendment of the United States Constitution.

Based on Census Figures

Plan A was the one most acceptable to the Democrats and the least palatable to the Republicans, who had been forewarned by their lawyers that Plans B, C and D had scant chance in the courts.

A straight reapportionment based on the 1960 Census figures, Plan A provides for a Senate enlarged from 58 to 65 members and an Assembly enlarged from 150 to 165. Each legislator would have one vote. Two of the rejected plans provided fractional votes for some legislators.

The decision was handed down just before 5 P.M. yesterday by Judge Sterry R. Waterman of the United States Court of Appeals and Federal District Judges Sylvester J. Ryan and Richard H. Levet. The court said that an "explanatory" opinion would be filed shortly.

Democrats had contended that all four plans involved gerrymandering by the Republicans.

But last week the plaintiffs in the case—New York City, Radio Station WMCA, Nassau County and others—were sharply rebuffed. The court declined

Continued on Page 21, Column 4

Bronston's Hopes Fading in Albany; Mackell Also Out

By R. W. APPLE Jr.
Special to The New York Times

ALBANY, Jan. 26—Senator Jack E. Bronston, who has been the front-running candidate for Senate majority leader, has concluded that he no longer has any real chance of election.

A source in a position to know the Queens Senator's thinking said today that he had no plans to withdraw from the contest. The source added, however, that Mr. Bronston's prospects of amassing the 30 votes needed for victory appeared remote.

Mr. Bronston's principal opponent, Senator Thomas J. Mackell, also of Queens, seemed to have dropped from serious contention.

These developments, together with the increasing restlessness of the Republican legislators, gave rise to a fragile hope that a settlement of the leadership deadlock might be within sight. The deadlock will be three weeks old tomorrow.

The Senate took one futile ballot this afternoon, its 23d, and the Assembly took five, making the total in that house

Continued on Page 21, Column 5

$598 MILLION RISE IN STATE COST DUE

Record Increases Planned by Rockefeller—Budget of $3.48 Billion Likely

By THOMAS P. RONAN
Special to The New York Times

ALBANY, Jan. 26—Governor Rockefeller announced today that the major appropriation increases he would recommend in his 1965-66 budget would total $598 million.

That will be the biggest increase for one year in the history of the state and will lift the budget to $3.48 billion, the first above the $3-billion mark. Spending under the current budget is an estimated $2.90 billion. The largest previous increase was $306 million in 1957 under Gov. W. Averell Harriman.

The largest part of the increase, nearly $200 million, would go for education.

Mr. Rockefeller will present his budget to the Legislature on Friday. It must be approved by April 1, the beginning of the new fiscal year. Initial consideration of it may be delayed, however, because the inability of the Democrats to elect leaders of the Assembly and Senate has stalled legislative procedure.

The Governor did not discuss the tax proposals he would make to cover much of the increased spending, but there was an indication that the gasoline tax of 6 cents a gallon

Continued on Page 21, Column 7

U.S. AGENCY SPURS CAR SAFETY DRIVE

Seeks 17 Devices for Autos It Will Buy Next Year

By DAVID R. JONES
Special to The New York Times

DETROIT, Jan. 26—The General Services Administration, the Government's purchasing agent, published today in the Federal Register a list of 17 safety features that it would like to see included in the new automobiles it buys.

This might appear at first glance to be merely another business deal between the Government agency and some of its big suppliers. However, its influence may eventually be felt by millions of new-car buyers.

The agency's move is an important symptom of the mounting pressures on the nation's automobile companies to build safer cars. Its significance, therefore, is not so much that it may lead to setting safety standards for Government-purchased cars, but that it is expected to hasten efforts by the Federal Government and the states to impose stricter safety standards on privately purchased autos.

The General Services Administration will allow 30 days for public comment on today's list of safety proposals and then will settle down to select standards by June 30 for the 1967 models it will buy in 1966.

The G.S.A. alone buys about

Continued on Page 15, Column 1

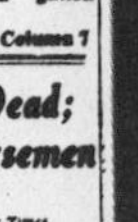

Stuhldreher Dead; One of 4 Horsemen

Special to The New York Times

PITTSBURGH, Jan. 26—Harry A. Stuhldreher, the quarterback of the famous Four Horsemen of Notre Dame, died today in West Penn Hospital. He was 63 years old.

He entered the hospital Dec. 29 and underwent major surgery Jan. 14. The nature of his illness was not disclosed.

Mr. Stuhldreher, who was football coach at Villanova University and the University of Wisconsin following graduation from Notre Dame, was director of community relations and recreational programs for the United States Steel Corporation at his death. He joined United States Steel in 1950 and moved to Pittsburgh.

In addition to his widow, Mary, Mr. Stuhldreher is survived by four sons, Harry Jr. of Detroit, Michael of Pittsburgh,

Continued on Page 38, Column 5

United Press International Telephoto

LEAVE HOSPITAL: ... States Naval Hospital at Bethesda, Md.

... Whitmore, a 20 ... er, was indicted ... police said he had ... the Wylie and Hoffert ... during a questioning ... he also allegedly ad... Brooklyn murder and ... tempted rape.

Whitmore has since ... ated all three confessions, ... taining that he was coerced ... making them.

Convicted of Rape Attempt

Presumably, the office ... District Attorney Frank ... Hogan will move to dismiss the Manhattan indictment. However, Whitmore would remain under indictment in the Brooklyn murder of Mrs. Minnie Edmonds, a charwoman. He has been convicted, but not sentenced, in the attempted Brooklyn rape.

Robles was understood to have appeared voluntarily for questioning a number of times at Mr. Hogan's office. He was said to have denied that he was involved in the Wylie-Hoffert murders, which took place on Aug. 28, 1963.

He had been free on parole in a felonious assault case.

He was booked at 11:40 last night, nearly five hours after

Continued on Page 16, Column 2

Stuhldreher Dead; One of 4 Horsemen

Special to The New York Times

PITTSBURGH, Jan. 26—Harry A. Stuhldreher, the quarterback of the famous Four Horsemen of Notre Dame, died today in West Penn Hospital. He was 63 years old.

He entered the hospital Dec. 29 and underwent major surgery Jan. 14. The nature of his illness was not disclosed.

Mr. Stuhldreher, who was football coach at Villanova University and the University of Wisconsin following graduation from Notre Dame, was director of community relations and recreational programs for the United States Steel Corporation at his death. He joined United States Steel in 1950 and moved to Pittsburgh.

In addition to his widow, Mary, Mr. Stuhldreher is survived by four sons, Harry Jr. of Detroit, Michael of Pittsburgh,

Continued on Page 38, Column 5

JOHNSONS RETURN TO WHITE HOUSE

President Still Has a Cough—His Plans for Churchill Rites Remain in Doubt

By CHARLES MOHR
Special to The New York Times

WASHINGTON, Jan. 26—President Johnson, who entered the Naval Hospital at Bethesda, Md., with a cold three and a half days ago, returned to the White House today.

Mrs. Johnson, who was also ...ted for a cold at the same ...al, returned with him.

...ough it was said he still ... slight cough, Mr. Johnson ...ed otherwise to be re... from his illness.

...ver, there was still no ... announcement as to ...e would head a United ...gation to the state ... Sir Winston Church... Saturday.

...d States thus re... the only nation ...amed such a dele...

...ic Alarm

...id he wants ... to the fu... depends on ...

...said today ... not want ...ntention. ...rce said ...pse or ... him ... an ...ght ...

...rters ... felt.

...resident winked but ... nothing.

He was dressed in a dark blue suit and a black overcoat. As he stepped out into the sunny, mild air, he put on a gray fedora and snapped down

Continued on Page 18, Column 3

Celler Split a Fee With Baker's Firm

By CABELL PHILLIPS
Special to The New York Times

WASHINGTON, Jan. 26—Senator John J. Williams, the Delaware Republican who initiated the investigation of Robert G. Baker 15 months ago, said today that Representative Emanuel Celler, Brooklyn Democrat, split a legal fee with Mr. Baker's law firm in 1961.

Mr. Celler acknowledged the payment of a fee to Mr. Baker's law firm, but said that the transaction had had no connection with any Government business.

The fee originated, Mr. Williams said, with the Sweetwater Development Company of Dallas, which has a contract with the Interior Department to construct a pilot desalinization plant at Wrightsville Beach, N. C. It was learned

Continued on Page 14, Column 4

DISCUSS WORLD'S FAIR: Deputy Mayor Edward F. Cavanagh Jr., left, Robert Moses and Thomas J. Deegan Jr., right, at meeting of directors of the fair at Terrace Club on grounds in Queens. Mr. Moses is president and Mr. Deegan heads executive committee.

SAIGON GENERALS ASSUME CONTROL AND BACK KHANH

Nixon Asserts U.S. Risks Defeat Soon In Vietnam Conflict

By EARL MAZO

Former Vice President Richard M. Nixon said yesterday that "we are losing the war in Vietnam." He added, "If our strategy is not changed, we will be thrown out in a matter of months—certainly within the year."

Security requires the United States to "end the war in Vietnam by winning it," or all of Asia will be lost to the Communists, Mr. Nixon declared.

He proposed that the United States commit the Navy and Air Force to "quarantine" the war by cutting Communist supply lines to South Vietnam and destroying Communist staging areas in North Vietnam and Laos.

It would not be necessary to employ either nuclear weapons or American ground troops, he said.

The former Vice President spoke at a luncheon of the Sales Executive Club of New York at the Hotel Roosevelt. He conceded that the stepped-up direct action he advocated would be unpopular and that it might risk war with Com-

Continued on Page 2, Column 1

DISORDER IS CITED

Council to Be Formed—Buddhist Girl, 17, a Suicide by Fire

By SEYMOUR TOPPING
Special to The New York Times

SAIGON, South Vietnam, Wednesday, Jan. 27—The military leaders of South Vietnam ousted the civilian Government of Premier Tran Van Huong today.

Lieut. Gen. Nguyen Khanh was appointed to deal with the crisis caused by current anti-Government demonstrations.

[In the central coastal city of Nhatrang Tuesday, a 17-year-old Buddhist girl burned herself to death in protest against the Huong regime. Page 3.]

A statement by the Armed Forces Council declared that the Huong Government had shown itself "unable to cope with the present critical situation." It asserted that the armed forces had therefore withdrawn their support from the Premier and the chief of state, Phan Khac Suu.

The Council pledged to stand by those clauses of the October charter that called for convening a national congress to act as an interim legislature and draft a new constitution.

March Congress Accepted

The statement said that the Council would accept the terms of an electoral law proclaimed this week that provides for elections and the meeting of the national congress on March 21.

The terms of the statement made it clear that the military had once more seized power in what appeared to be a bloodless coup d'état.

The legal position of the Government was not immediately known in the hours shortly before noon when the statement was issued. However, without military support in the face of the Buddhist agitation sweeping the country, the Government was powerless.

The statement said that General Khanh "would immediately convene an Army-Peoples Council consisting of 20 representatives of the religions, of the armed forces and personalities from various parts of the country."

"The Army-Peoples Council will advise the Government in all its important decisions," the statement said.

The statement, which was broadcast by General Khanh

Continued on Page 3, Column 5

HOUSE ACTS TO BAR FOOD AID TO U.A.R.

Votes, 204-177, to Stop Sale of Surpluses—Action Is Rebuff to Administration

By JOSEPH A. LOFTUS
Special to The New York Times

WASHINGTON, Jan. 26—The House voted today to stop sales of surplus food to the United Arab Republic.

The roll-call, first of the year on substantive legislation, showed 204 favoring the ban and 177 opposed.

The decision struck at least a glancing blow at President Johnson's foreign policy. For some members, however, the objective was a direct slap at President Gamal Abdel Nasser of the U.A.R.

House leaders, including Speaker John W. McCormack, pleaded with their fellow Democrats not to tie the President's hands, but 76 refused to go along.

Among them were all the Democrats from New York City except for two who did not vote, and several from upstate New York. They joined 128 Republicans in adding the restrictive amendment to a supplemental appropriation for the Commodity Credit Corporation.

G.O.P. Discipline

Representative Robert H. Michel, Republican of Illinois, led the fight. No Republican crossed the party line to vote against the Michel amendment.

Republicans also criticized the appropriation of $1.6 billion for the Commodity Credit Corporation, which administers the disposal of surplus foods.

They said the fund request was the consequence of a "phony" budget sent by President Johnson to Congress last year to help keep the budget total below $100 billion.

Since the appropriation is a supplement to the budget adopted in the last Congress, it does not raise the total of the new budget sent to Congress this week.

The Republicans made no serious attempt to block the appropriation, however. It carried by a voice vote and was sent to the Senate.

The anti-Nasser amendment

Continued on Page 14, Column 3

NEWS INDEX

U.S. EMBASSY AIDE OUSTED BY SOVIET

Americans Term Espionage Charges 'Unfounded'

By HENRY TANNER
Special to The New York Times

MOSCOW, Jan. 26—The Soviet Union ordered today the expulsion of Richard F. Stolz, 39-year-old first secretary at the United States Embassy, on charges of espionage.

The expulsion was made known in a note to Malcolm Toon, the embassy's political counselor, at the Foreign Ministry. The note was later made public without comment by Tass, the official press agency.

It is said that a Soviet citizen was arrested here last December "for espionage and criminal connection" with foreign intelligence agents.

An investigation showed, the note said, that the citizen, identified only as "B," had been in contact with Kenneth A. Kerst, first secretary at the American Embassy. Mr. Kerst left the Soviet Union last November on normal rotation.

The note charged that Mr. Stolz had participated in Mr. Kerst's "espionage" activity.

Mr. Toon told V. I. Obereenko, the Soviet official who handed him the note, that he felt the charges were "unfounded," according to an embassy statement.

The statement called the So-

Continued on Page 4, Column 5

STUHLDREHER, 63; A FOUR HORSEMAN

Continued From Page 1, Col. 2

John of Washington and Peter of New York City, and four grandchildren.

A high mass of requiem will be sung in St. Paul's Cathedral at 1 P.M. Saturday. Interment will be in Calvary Cemetery.

Harry Stuhldreher's career in college football began in 1922, and for the next three years, as the Notre Dame quarterback, he heard his name shouted in adulation.

His career ended in 1948, as football coach at the University of Wisconsin, with another generation of football fans shouting—for his removal.

But no one ever forgot that Stuhldreher had been one of Notre Dame's Four Horsemen together with Don Miller, Jim Crowley and Elmer Layden.

The late Grantland Rice gave the Notre Dame backfield its name after the team defeated Army in 1924. Rice began his story:

"Outlined against a blue-gray October sky, the Four Horsemen rode again. In dramatic lore they are known as Famine, Pestilence, Destruction and Death. These are only aliases. Their real names are Stuhldreher, Miller, Crowley and Layden."

The Four Horsemen—(L. to R.) Don Miller, Harry Stuhldreher, Jim Crowley and Elmer Layden.

Undefeated in 1924

Knute Rockne's fabulous backfield, playing behind the Seven Mules—as the line was called—starred in 29 games from 1922 through 1924. In that span the Irish won 26 games, tied one and lost only two—both to Nebraska and both by a single touchdown. Notre Dame was undefeated in 1924 and won the national championship.

The Four Horsemen ended their college careers by beating Pop Warner's fine Stanford team, 27-10, in the Rose Bowl game on New Year's Day, 1925—the only time Notre Dame has played in a bowl game.

Few, if any, football experts are willing to rate any one of the Horsemen above the others in ability; but if they were the engine of the team, Stuhldreher was the engine inside the engine.

Harry A. Stuhldreher was the quarterback of the Four Horsemen of Notre Dame.

Like the others, Stuhldreher was light by modern standards: he weighed 152 pounds, while the other three were only a few pounds heavier. He was also the shortest of the four.

Even then, however, Stuhldreher was full of authority, which some say later developed into occasional pontification. "He sounded like a leader the first time I heard him," Rockne said. "And he was. It was like having another coach on the field to direct play."

None of the four, however, had particularly impressed Rockne when they were freshmen. And although Stuhldreher was a superb play-caller, passer and blocker, he was the last of the four to make the varsity.

Stuhldreher's classic performances included that most classic of situations: playing with a broken ankle in the Rose Bowl game.

Stuhldreher was named to Walter Camp's all-America team in 1924—the only Four Horseman so honored—and later was elected to the National Football Hall of Fame and the Helms Foundation Hall of Fame.

Stuhldreher was born in Massilon, Ohio, a town that has produced an inordinate share of athletes. He drove a delivery wagon for his father, a grocer, and played football in high school.

After he was graduated from Notre Dame with an A.B. degree, he became head football coach at Villanova University. In 11 years he turned Villanova—once described as a school without a locker room"—into a major football college.

Under his tutelage Villanova won 65 games, lost 24 and tied 10. While at Villanova, Stuhldreher met and married Mary McEnery, then a movie columnist for the Philadelphia Ledger.

In 1935 Stuhldreher was appointed football coach and athletic director at the University of Wisconsin, which had been going through a reappraisal of its athletic department.

Stuhldreher's Wisconsin teams never won a Western Conference (Big Ten) title, although they came close in 1942 before losing to Iowa late in the season. During his 13 seasons as coach, the Badgers won 45 games, lost 62 and tied 6.

After World War II, Stuhldreher began to come under attack from students and alumni. At the Yale-Wisconsin game in October, 1958—which Wisconsin lost, 17—7 — students unfurled a banner that said, "Good-by, Harry." There were angry telephone calls and letters to the coach.

The bitter dispute was detailed in an article by Mrs. Stuhldreher in an October, 1948, issue of The Saturday Evening Post. It was called "Football Fans Aren't Human."

In December, 1948, Stuhldreher resigned as coach, but stayed on as athletic director. In 1950 he left Wisconsin to join the United States Steel Corporation.

Once, at a meeting of the American Football Coaches Association, he remarked, with a sigh: "Sons of coaches have to learn to box very well. My boys did because they were forever defending the honor of the old man."

Stuhldreher, who always kept his interest in football, was president of the football coaches association in 1938. Two weeks ago he received the Stagg Award for 1965 from the association in recognition of his contributions to the sport, but he was too ill to attend the meeting in Chicago.

The New York Times SUNDAY, FEBRUARY 3, 1918.

JOHN L. SULLIVAN FATALLY STRICKEN

World's Most Popular Ring Gladiator Dies Suddenly from Heart Attack.

BATTLES UNTIL THE END

Romantic Career of Picturesque Boxing Character Ends at His Home on Massachusetts Farm.

John L. Sullivan is dead. The former heavyweight champion of the world and the most picturesque figure the prize ring ever knew passed away yesterday at his home, Donelee Ross Farm, at West Abington, Mass. He was taken ill with heart trouble three weeks ago, but his health improved and he was able to go to Boston Friday. Yesterday he fainted and did not recover consciousness for ten minutes. George Bush, a friend who lived with him, applied ice bags to the former champion's head and he rallied.

Sullivan's game fighting spirit was with him to the end. When Bush sent for a doctor, John L. said: "I don't want any doctor. I've listened to a lot of them in my life and I know I am all right and I can doctor myself." Sullivan protested when his doctor ordered him to go to bed. "Is the bathroom warm?" asked Sullivan. "Well, that's fine. I want to take a bath." Ten minutes later the white-haired old pugilist was dead. At his bedside when the end came were Dr. Rann, his friend, George Bush, and Willie Kelley, the 15-year-old boy who was adopted by Sullivan.

The prize ring never brought fame to any man as it did to John L. Sullivan. For a period of more than ten years, from the time he defeated Paddy Ryan in 1882, in a bareknuckle fight under the London prize ring rules, until he was defeated by Jim Corbett in 1892, his personality and methods of fighting dominated sporting circles in this country.

Sullivan was born in Boston on Oct. 15, 1858. His father, Michael Sullivan, was a native of Tralee, County Kerry, Ireland, and his mother was born at Athlone. Sullivan was a rough and tumble fighter in his early days and a terror among the lads of his generation.

Knocks Out First Opponent.

The first time he ever took part in a boxing match was when he was 19 years old. A strapping young fighter named Scannell appeared on the stage of a Boston theatre and offered to fight any one in the house. Sullivan, who was in the gallery, accepted the challenge and, in the fight which followed, Sullivan knocked out his opponent. Then Sullivan realized that he possessed a remarkable punch in his famous right fist and took up prizefighting as a livelihood. He was known as the Boston Strong Boy, for he could lift heavy weights and juggle beer kegs, and one time he is said to have lifted a piano in a test of strength.

John L.'s first fight as a professional was against a scrapper named Cockey Woods. In 1878 Sullivan knocked out Woods with his terrific right. His fame as a fighter spread to other cities, and in that same year he boxed Mike Donovan in Boston and, after Sullivan had knocked him down two or three times, Donovan had a hard time saving himself from being knocked out.

Sullivan's greatest fights were with Paddy Ryan in 1882, a 39-round bareknuckle draw with Charley Mitchell of England in 1888, and his famous fight with Jake Kilrain in 1889. It was largely through Sullivan's achievements in the ring that the championship title became a great money prize. In the early days of his career $1,000 a side was considered a heavy purse. Sullivan received only $53 for his fight which gave him the right to challenge Paddy Ryan for the championship.

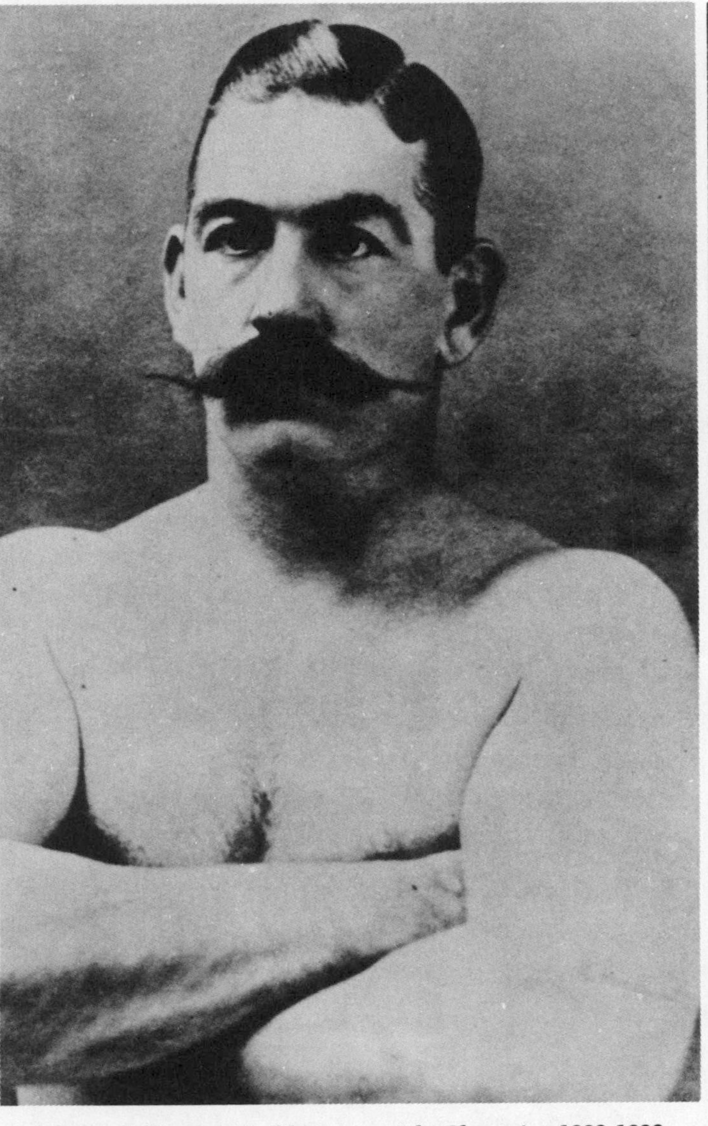

John L. Sullivan—World Heavyweight Champion 1882-1892.

Won Title From Ryan.

Sullivan knocked out Paddy Ryan at Mississippi City, Feb. 7, 1882. It was a bare-knuckle fight for $5,000 a side and the championship of America. At this fight the expression "knockout" was coined by Billy Madden, Sullivan's trainer. On March 10, 1888, Sullivan fought a 39-round draw with bare knuckles against Charley Mitchell at Chantilly, France. Sullivan's hardest fight was with Jake Kilrain at Richburg, Miss., on July 8, 1889. This fight lasted 75 rounds, and was the last championship fight held in this country under London Prize Ring rules.

That fight practically decided the uselessness of trying to beat Sullivan at his own sledgehammer style of fighting. A 39-round fight with Charley Mitchell, a wary, skillful boxer, showed fight managers that John L. would be vulnerable to a man who could box and stay away from him long enough to wear him down.

This opportunity fell to the lot of Jim Corbett, the pompadoured bank clerk of San Francisco. The famous fight was held at New Orleans before the Olympic Club. For twenty rounds the agile, youthful Corbett danced and pranced around the great John L., who became so infuriated that he threw all caution to the winds and made frantic efforts to flatten the youngster with his sledgehammer right, only to so tire himself he was easy prey for Corbett, who won the championship in the twenty-first round.

In his day Sullivan made more than a million dollars at prizefighting and he admitted that most of it was spent for whisky. After his defeat by Corbett Sullivan changed from the gruff, rough-and-tumble fighter. In spite of his dissipation, Sullivan's remarkably strong physical constitution withstood the ravages of drink. In later years John L. became a mild-mannered, jovial old gentleman. He settled down on his farm in Massachusetts and became a country squire.

Wrote of Boxing Matches.

Sullivan left his farm a few years ago to go to Reno to write the Jeffries-Johnson fight for THE NEW YORK TIMES. His last public appearance in this city was at the ringside at Madison Square Garden when Jess Willard boxed ten rounds with Frank Moran. On that occasion Sullivan was with Moran heart and soul and jeered at the cautious boxing tactics of the big champion. When Sullivan was introduced in the ring at the Garden that night he got a reception which brought tears to his eyes, and he said afterward that it was the happiest moment of his life.

No fighter ever lived about whom so much has been written as John L. Sullivan. He always had a fund of interesting yarns and delighted to tell about the rough, unchecked, wild career of his early days. They tell about Sullivan knocking down a horse with one punch in Boston. They tell of how he used to clean out barrooms and subdue bullies by the dozen. He wrecked saloons by throwing chairs and tables through the windows and mirrors, and when John L. was at large everybody ran to cover. It was then his delight to pay for the damage with a lavish hand. Sullivan was a terror for policemen, hackmen, and bartenders, and they all gave him a free road when he was out on an expedition to paint the town red.

For all his trouble-making, Sullivan was always forgiven because he was champion. He was a ready spender and scattered money right and left. When it became necessary to place Sullivan in the clutches of the law, the Magistrates always let him off with a reprimand and a promise never to do it again.

When news came that Corbett had challenged Sullivan, John L. laughed and said, "He wants to fight me, eh? Well, all the training I need is a hair cut and a shave to beat his head off in one round." Sullivan would not listen to the advice of his friends to train faithfully for Corbett, so he only went through the motions of training for the fight which marked the end of his pugilistic career. Sullivan never allowed any man to dictate to him. When he left this city on a special train for New Orleans before the fight, Sullivan yelled from the car platform to the crowd of friends who were there to cheer him on his way, "I'll knock this young dub out in a punch."

Everywhere that Sullivan went he was hailed as a hero. Everywhere his train stopped there were great throngs to cheer him. Men fought with each other to reach him and shake his hand.

Becomes Temperance Lecturer.

When Sullivan reformed in later years he became a rabid prohibitionist and toured the country as a temperance lecturer. In 1905, while in a saloon in Terre Haute, Ind., he suddenly got up and said to the crowded barroom of men that he was going to give his greatest enemy, the Black Bottle, a knockout punch.

It was an impressive scene, Sullivan with a whisky bottle in his hand then and there took an oath that he was through with drink. "If I take another drink I hope I choke, so help me God," said Sullivan. He never took another, and from that day to the day he died he kept up his fight for temperance.

For the last ten years Sullivan has lived on his little Massachusetts farm. John L. was first married in 1882 to Annie Bates of Centreville, R. I., but she left him after a few months, and finally got a divorce on the ground of desertion after twenty-six years. When he was 51 John L. married Kate Harkins of Roxbury, Mass., a girl friend of his boyhood days. They were happy on their farm for several years, and it was a heavy shock to old John L. when she died several months ago.

The white-haired old man of Donelee Ross Farm, jovial, kind, and smiling, was quite a different character from the young rowdy who used to go on the wild rampages in Boston in his youthful days. "I have anchored here," said John L. at West Abington a few years ago, "until my time comes. There is no place like home. My greatest battle was with the Black Bottle and I won."

His later years were peaceful and serene. Occasionally he would run into Boston, but most of the time he was looking after his live stock and his farm. The famous John L., whose name was known all over the world after that famous fight with Charley Mitchell at Chantilly, changed into a lovable, patriarchal old sage, with a kind word for every one on his lips, and with always a word of advice to young men to follow the straight and narrow path. Never has the American prize ring had such a character as Sullivan, and never again will the fighting game produce another man who will stamp his personality on the world of pugilism as the blunt, gray, old philosopher of Donelee Farm.

JOHN L. HAD CIRCUS PLANS.

Negotiations Completed for Next Summer Just Before His Death.

That the death of John L. Sullivan was totally unexpected by even his close advisers and friends was substantiated by Darcy O'Connor, who just returned from Abington, Mass., where he had a long business talk with the once-famous fighter. O'Connor went to Abington to get the signature of John L. to a contract for a circus act which was to be the feature of Ringling Brothers circus next Summer. O'Connor, who managed the last stage appearance and tour of

(continued)

John L., had completed arrangements with the circus whereby John L. was to receive $1,000 a week for appearing in an old Irish jaunting car act. The venerable ring hero was to be used to offset the circus influence of Jess Willard, the present heavyweight cahmpion, who now wears the crown once belonging to John L.

O'Connor felt deeply the passing of the "old man of the ring," as he termed his former employer. He made plans to hurry back to Abington for the burial services.

It was hard to convince O'Connor that John L. finally had been knocked out for the last time. he said that the famous Irish fighter had appeared in sound health, although he acknowledged he was not as strong as usual. This did not worry O'Connor, since John L. used to measure his strength by lifting a piano or knocking down a horse, and O'Connor said it was not be be considered unusual that John L. should complain of losing strength.

He Earned a Place in History.

Not only was John L. Sullivan the best known of all American pugilists, but it cannot be denied that the great majority of his fellow-countrymen, no matter how much they disapproved of prizefighters and prizefighting, had for this particular product of the squared 'ring a feeling in which there were appreciable elements of pride and affection.

He was, of course, for many years the idol of all to whom such prowess as his appeals, and there seems to have been no doubt that the man had likable qualities in addition to his courage—which is a quality that earns and wins respect, no matter by whom displayed or how.

A tale used to be told of somebody who ventured to converse in the presence of the Archbishop of Canterbury about an approaching battle between the then heavyweight champions of Great Britain and the United States. According to the legend, the prelate professed is proper ignorance of such matters, but could not refrain from adding that nevertheless it seemed to him probable that the Englishman would win. So Sullivan, even in his most roisterous days, was expected to win by the whole American public, and when at last he fell there was more sorrow for his defeat than acclaim for the victor.

No other pugilist ever has gained in America the position Sullivan held, and probably no other representative of his class ever will do so. There was something amiable even in his follies and weaknesses, and he was picturesque and quotable long after his inevitable fate overtook him.

ANTICS OF JOHN L. AMUSED THE WORLD

Sullivan Supplied Happiness for Prince and Pauper During His Career.

HIS LAST FIGHT RECALLED

John L. Sullivan's last stand, in the twenty-first round, against his conqueror, Gentleman Jim Corbett, at New Orleans, was one of the most dramatic moments in the history of pugilism. Here is one newspaper account of that short twenty-first round, when the mighty John L. was crushed in defeat:

"In regard to this trifling minute and a half, which decided the heavyweight championship of the world, a great deal might be said. That the contest would end in that round no man present believed. Sullivan came from his corner in the same shape that he had shown for a half dozen rounds before. The same cross expression was on his face and he seemed as strong as at any time during the fight. He continued to do the edging in, and Corbett followed his original tactics of edging away. This sort of trade was not going on more than ten seconds when Corbett jumped back, rushed forward, and hit John L. on the nose. John was dazed. Corbett went after him further and the same old nose was again smashed and more blood came out.

"John looked astounded and Corbett jumped back with the merry smile of a schoolboy with a big apple. Suddenly he returned to the fray, and before Sullivan knew what was the meaning of the Californian's happy look, he got a crack on the side of the head which made him close his eyes. With that, Corbett was on top of him and in no time, with a left hander on the side of the head and a right hander on the other, poor John L. became an unconscious, beaten man. He staggered about on his pins for a second or so and, while displaying his fatal weakness, Corbett was on him again, as a crow lights on corn where there is no dummy in the middle of the field. A right on the ear and a left on the jaw settled the business and the championsnip. The last blow sent the great John L. Sullivan to the floor with a thump, the second time in all his career as a fighter that he had ever been knocked down. But he was down this time, fair and finally. It was a clean and clever knockout blow.

"Sullivan doubled up his legs as though in pain, but in another instant seemed to collect his senses and made an effort to rise. He failed in that and tried a second time, with the same result. He was knocked out, sure and simple. His seconds had to come and assist him to his corner. even then, John L. was out and did not know what was going on. It was not for more than two minutes that John L. recovered himself."

When John L. was in England and boxed before the prince of Wales, later King Edward, the Prince was so impressed with the American fighter that he sent him a gold-headed cane. A mild, meek-mannered gentleman in waiting delivered the present to Sullivan at his hotel.

John L. opened the box, and when he saw what it was he threw it back at the Prince's messenger and roared at him as he hastily retreated from the room: "Take this back to his nobs and tell him I'm no cripple."

Sullivan had a great admirer in Chicago in an Irishman named Colonel Thomas Jefferson Dolan. When Sullivan was fighting Corbett at New Orleans a large crowd gathered in a Chicago armory and heard the returns over a private wire. Dolan's witty remarks on that day formed the basis of one of the first Irish dialect stories written by Finley P. Dunne, (Mr. Dooley.) Lou Houseman, now a theatrical man, was at the wire in New Orleans, and sent over the returns. Houseman flashed:

"Sullivan knocked out in the twenty-first round."

Colonel Dolan yelled out, "On whose authority?"

John L. Sullivan was the last of the bareknuckle champions.

"On the authority of the Western Union and Lou Houseman!" was the answer of Paddy Carroll, the announcer.

"They're both d—— liars!" yelled back Colonel Dolan.

If there was anything that John L. hated more than anything else, it was cigarettes. A few years ago, Billy Birch, a boyish looking Chicago reporter, went to interview the former champion. Birch walked into John L.'s presence with a cigarette hanging from his lips. John L. let out a roar which shook the building.

The only interview that Birch got was this:"Young man, you're a sap. Don't you know that cigarette smoking will take 20 years off your life? That's the reason most of you newspapermen have a complexion like a banana. you haven't many brains or you wouldn't be smoking those things, but you have an awful nerve coming to me with one of those things in your mouth. Now, beat it." Of course all this conversation was prettily decorated with expressions which would make a pirate blush.

One day, Sullivan went up to Bridgeport to see Terry McGovern, who was then at Cap Bond's training camp at Stratford. It was a cold, wintry day, and Sullivan hired a sleigh in Bridgeport and started to drive to Stratford, a few miles away. The harness broke and the horse tore away from the sleigh. Sullivan held the reins and was dragged out of the sleigh along the street for some distance until he finally landed in a snow bank.

When the spectaors came running up one of them remarked: "Why didn't you let go?"

"Oh go to ——" yelled John L., "I never let go."

John L. had a fund of slang expressions many of which are heard even today. It was Sullivan who first used "To the woods with ya" when he wanted to get rid of anybody. His slang was rough but timely.

Sullivan's honest mistakes in his speeches were widely quoted throughout the country. One time in a speech in Washington Sullivan said:

"The greatest guy this country ever produced was Daniel Webster, the guy who wrote the dictionary."

Most of the yarns about the famous Boston gladiator have grown in the telling, and there are many versions about his first meeting with the Prince of Wales, when King Edward held that title. Sullivan didn't believe there was any fighting blood in the world unless it was in Ireland, and he had a great contempt for the English champion.

When John L. first went to England he expected to fight Jem Smith, champion of England, for the world's title. He met Smith during a boxing show at the National Sporting Club, where he sparred a few rounds for the Prince. He was taken to the royal box after the bout and introduced to the Prince, Sullivan honestly believed that it was up to him to make the Prince feel at ease. He didn't wish royalty to feel any embarrassment over meeting such a celebrity as himself.

"Glad to meet you, Prince," growled John L. "I think I've heard of you before. If you're ever in Boston look me up."

After that Jem Smith was brought up and introduced to Sullivan. The Prince remarked the he would like to see the English champion fight the American champion. Sullivan, who didn't care much for ceremony, scowled at Smith and roared, "I'll fight you right now in the ring down there, and you can take the purse and side stakes if I don't knock you out in four rounds.

Then another version of Sullivan's meeting with the Prince of Wales is that Sullivan said, "Prince, I'm glad you met me."

Sullivan was as rough in his charity as he was in everything else. His generosity, however, was so frank and open-hearted that the roar of his voice and the glare of his eye were forgiven. One wintry night John L. was going past a Sixth Avenue elevated station and saw an old lady selling papers. Sullivan frightened the woman half to death by grabbing her armful of papers and throwing them out into the street.

Then he turned around and handed the woman a roll of bills, a yelled at her: "Go home. This is no kind of a night for you to be out."

In the heyday of his popularity, Sullivan always had from $10 to $20 worth of change in his pockets before sallying out on his daily promenade, and at every corner where he saw the newsboys congregated waiting for him, he would toss a handful of silver into the air and then roar with delight as they fought, scratched, and scrambled for the coins.

"All the News That's Fit to Print"

The New York Times.

LATE CITY EDITION
Partly cloudy today. Fair and mild tomorrow.
Temperature Range Today—Max., 53; Min., 41
Temperature Yesterday—Max., 53; Min., 40
Full U. S. Weather Bureau Report, Page 95

Section 1

NEWS SUMMARY AND INDEX, PAGE 95

Copyright, 1953, by The New York Times Company.

VOL. CII. No. 34,763. Entered as Second-Class Matter, Post Office, New York, N. Y. NEW YORK, SUNDAY, MARCH 29, 1953. Including Magazine and Book Review. TWENTY CENTS New York City & 50 Mile Zone | Elsewhere Twenty-five Cents

REDS AGREE TO TRADE ILL AND WOUNDED IN KOREA AS FIRST STEP TOWARD TRUCE; U. S. CAUTIOUS ON BID TO RENEW TALKS

TRAIN TOLL STANDS AT 22 DEAD, 62 HURT IN 3-WAY SMASH-UP

Only One Is Injured Seriously but Rescuers Fear List of Ohio Victims May Rise

2D WRECK BLASTS TOWN

Ammunition Cars Blow Up—Fires, Explosion Raze Fourth of Indiana Community

By The Associated Press.

CONNEAUT, Ohio, March 28—A weary band of rescue workers dug deeper today into the twisted hulks of nineteen railroad coaches in search of more victims of last night's three-train wreck here. Twenty-two bodies were found, and the coroner said he believed at least one more might be found under one car dug far into the ground.

Sixty-two persons were injured, only one critically. They were being treated in hospitals here and in Ashtabula, Ohio, and Erie, Pa.

[In another railroad accident, on Saturday, an ammunition train was derailed and blew up, scattering shells over the town of Lewis, Ind. Fires spread over a radius of a mile and the state police estimated that at least one-quarter of the town was destroyed. Five of the 275 residents were hurt. No one was killed. Lewis is twenty miles southeast of Terre Haute.]

Railroad men said the odds against the Ohio accident were 1,000,000 to 1. The trains — one freight and two passenger flyers — happened to pass almost exactly at the same spot just before 10 o'clock.

The scene was a desolate section of the New York Central main line in western Pennsylvania, half a mile from the Ohio border. There are four tracks, the inner ones used by passenger trains, the outer ones by freights.

An 18-inch pipe 35 feet long fell from an eastbound freight, bending a rail on the westbound passenger tracks. At that instant a westbound Buffalo-to-Chicago express came past at eighty miles an hour and hit the bent rail. Its locomotive derailed fifteen freight cars, which in turn piled up the flyer.

400 Persons Involved

Seconds later the headlight of the second passenger train—the St. Louis-to-New York Southwestern Limited, flashed across the wreckage in its eastbound path and the train, also at about eighty miles an hour, rammed into the derailed cars.

There were 400 persons involved in the series of crashes.

The wrecked cars sheared telegraph poles, cutting off communications, so a railroad man ran three miles to carry word of the accident and to get help.

Meanwhile, passengers and trainmen pitched into rescue efforts long before outside help could come. About 150 passengers needed some kind of assistance.

The work then went on for hours, as professional rescue men pried with crowbars and cut through metal with acetylene torches.

Scores of survivors, including many of the injured, milled around in the chilly night. The more seriously injured were taken to hospitals. Later, passengers whose destinations had been east of the wreck scene were put on makeshift trains east of the 1,000-foot stretch of torn track and similar

Continued on Page 62, Column 3

Jim Thorpe Is Dead On West Coast at 64

Special to The New York Times.

LOS ANGELES, March 28—Jim Thorpe, the Indian whose exploits in football, baseball and track and field won him acclaim as one of the greatest athletes of all time, died today in his trailer home in suburban Lomita. His age was 64.

Thorpe was eating dinner with his wife when he suffered a heart attack. Mrs. Thorpe's screams attracted a neighbor, Colby Bradshaw, who administered artificial respiration for nearly half an hour.

A county fire rescue squad took over and was momentarily successful. Thorpe revived, recognized persons around him and spoke to them. He was conscious for only a brief time before he suffered a relapse and died.

Hero of the 1912 Olympic Games at Stockholm and a towering football figure, Jim Thorpe was prob-

Continued on Page 92, Column 4

Year's Study of Draft Begun To Set Long-Term Program

Defense Heads Seek to Close All Loopholes and Map a Clear Plan to Let Every Young Man Know How He Stands

By A. H. RASKIN

Convinced that all physically fit young men are going to have to give at least two years of their lives to military service for a long time to come, defense officials have begun a year-long study intended to take the guesswork out of the draft and close the loopholes that enable some youths to duck service altogether.

Unless the world situation gets worse, there will be few major changes in draft policy this year, but Washington planners feel that the manpower pinch will be so tight from 1954 on that they had better start now drawing up a program that will enable every young man to know exactly where he stands on going into the armed forces and when he is likely to be called.

The worry about the nation's long-term ability to fulfill its need for soldiers, sailors and fliers will continue even if the Korean War ends soon, military leaders say.

They feel our manpower plans must be sufficiently stable to guarantee that there will be no gaps in the ranks if the Soviet threat lasts until "1960 or beyond."

The expectation that the military departments will be able to squeeze through the next twelve or fifteen months without draining the Selective Service pool of available manpower has caused the Pentagon to abandon any hope that it can persuade Congress in this session to extend the draft term from twenty-four months to thirty-six months.

Congressional leaders have made it clear that any discussion of how long men should serve was more likely to produce a shorter term than a longer one, and the Defense Department is disposed to let the whole issue ride unless the advocates of a cut in the service period take the initiative in bringing the

Continued on Page 44, Column 1

Kenny Ex-Aide Reveals Role As Anti-Crime Spy on Pi[...]

By CHARLES GR[...]
Special to The New [York Times.]

WASHINGTON, March 28—[...] John V. Kenny of Jersey City [...] hearing of a Senate subcommi[ttee ...]

an[...]

Th[...] said h[...] year a[...] the New[...] Committ[...] bothered [...] year since [...] Mayor Ken[ny ...]

The Anti-C[rime ...] privately fin[anced ...] headed by Spru[ille ...] Ambassador to [...] Mr. Napolitano'[s ...] available to the N[ew York] Crime Commission, [...] ed him in private bu[t ...] him on the stand at [...] hearings. Mr. Napolitan[o ...] day he had kept his un[...] work, for which he recei[ved ...] pay, a secret from Mayor [...] until last week. He said Mr. K[enny] in some way had learned o[f ...] trip to Washington for a clo[sed] session in preparation for toda[y's] hearing.

Mr. Napolitano, black-haired and heavy-set, was one of two witnesses appearing today before the Senate Foreign and Interstate Commerce subcommittee investigating waterfront conditions. The other was Bernard Patrick Joyce of 47-15 Twenty-eighth Avenue, Astoria, Queens. He is a former supervisor of longshoremen for Dade Brothers, which processed

Continued on Page 69, Column 4

2 BROTHERS SEIZED IN DOCKER SLAYING

22-Month Hunt for Murphys, Fugitives From Hoboken, Ends in Florida Cottage

Special to The New York Times.

HOBOKEN, N. J., March 28—A twenty-two-month manhunt following the waterfront slaying of a dock boss in a longshoreman's union office here ended last last night when Federal Bureau of Investigation agents captured Francis and Michael Murphy, formerly local pier workers, in a tourist cottage at Madeira Beach, Fla.

Francis, 26 years old, and Michael Murphy, 29, were indicted in 1951 with a third brother, William Murphy, by a special Hudson County grand jury on a charge of murdering Nunzio (Wally) Aluotto, who was shot on May 21, 1951. William, who surrendered on June 11, 1951, is awaitng trial under $40,000 bail.

When arrested at the cottage in which they had been living since last September, Francis Murphy was using the alias Knute Miller and his brother was known as

Continued on Page 64, Column 3

DEWEY APPROVES CITY MANAGER BILL; PROMPT ACTION DUE

Commission's Study of Plan to Be Sped to Have Report Ready for Special Session

FOR LONG-RANGE REFORM

Governor Seeks a Way to End Budget 'Crises'—State Fiscal Inquiry Also Authorized

By WARREN WEAVER Jr.
Special to The New York Times.

ALBANY, March 28—Creation of a temporary state commission to study the possibility of setting up a city manager system in New York City and to seek ways to "wipe out the grim toll of years of mismanagement and waste" in the city's government was approved today by Governor Dewey.

In signing the last of the twelve measures he ordered to me[et the] city's financial crisis, M[r. Dewey] said he was "hopeful[...] sion establish[...] point the w[...] overdu[e ...]

[...] r[...] b[...] deci[...] agen[...] mana[...] anything [...] under the [...] of conduc[t ...]

The Go[...]

Continued [...]

ISSUES SEPARATED

Capital Wants to Keep Prisoner Plan Apart From Armistice

DULLES HOPES FOR SPEED

Communists' Action Termed 'Unconditional Acceptance' of Proposal by Clark

By WALTER H. WAGGONER
Special to The New York Times.

[WASH]INGTON, March 28—The [State De]partment, exercising cau[tion and ur]ging restraint, today de[...] Communist offer for [...] of sick and wounded [...] war in Korea as "an [...] acceptance" of a vol[...] tion proposal last [...] [Uni]ted Nations Com[...]

[...] made it clear [...] [Nati]ons Command, [...] Clark, would [...] to explore [...] ders their [...] oner ex[...] tements [...] ch be[...] es: [...]

U. S. and France Warn Reds On New Far East Aggression

Agree Free World Relies on Strong West—Aid in Indo-China Backed in Principle—Saar Accord Put Before Army Unity

By FELIX BELAIR Jr.
Special to The New York Times.

WASHINGTON, March 28—The United States and France warned the Chinese Communist regime today that violation of any Korean armistice by aggressive warfare anywhere in the Far East "would have the most serious consequences for efforts to bring about peace in the world."

A joint communiqué covering political and economic discussions between the two Governments also said that they were in "full agreement on the necessity of concerting their efforts so as to defeat Communist aggression in the Far East and to strengthen the defenses of the free countries in the West."

Washington and Paris "remain convinced," the statement said, "that true peace can be achieved and maintained only by constructive efforts of all free nations."

The warning to the Chinese Communists came on the heels of Communist acceptance of a United Nations proposal for an exchange of wounded war prisoners in Korea, and Communist suggestions for renewed peace talks.

Preliminary to their joint warning, the United States and France agreed as a matter of policy that, in the absence of any tangible proof to the contrary, there was no reason to suppose that the recent change of personalities in the Kremlin had changed the basic nature of the threat confronting the free world.

It was agreed further that, since separate Communist aggressions in the Far East were parts of the same pattern, the successful outcome of operations in Korea and Indo-China demanded full recognition of their interdependence and continued diplomatic and military consultation between the two Governments.

At a final plenary meeting at

Continued on Page 13, Column 1

Text of the United States-French communiqué is on Page 12.

BURMA TO REFUSE U.S. AID AFTER JUNE

[...] Follows Protests in [...] Chiang Guerrillas—[...] Soviet Help Seen

[By The] Associated Press.

[RANGOON,] Burma, March 28 [...] e Government, in[...] rilla warfare with [...] who claim alle[...] [Gener]alissimo Chiang [...] tonight it was [...] [Uni]ted States aid next [...]

[...] $12,000,000 [...] since June, [...] each $31,[...] [...] r present [...]

[...] n Of[...] [...] assy [...] the [...] d a [...]

[...] 1953."

[...] sistance

[...] essed appreciation [...] titude for materials and [ser]vices received by the Burmese Government under the Economic Cooperation Administration, "which have been of great help in implementing rehabilitation programs." It added:

"The Government of Burma wishes to make it clear that this action is not intended in any way to cast a reflection on existing programs nor on the activties of E. C. A. personnel in Burma."

There has been some rise in anti-American feeling here recently. The chief issue in Burma today is the presence of 12,000 Nationalist Chinese guerrillas within her borders. Burma charged in a note to the United Nations this week that these survivors of the war against Communist China are aggressors against Burma. Help was asked to oust them.

Despite United States protestations of innocence, the Burmese charge that the irregulars are supplied with United States weapons. And they dislike the American policy of equipping Generalissimo Chiang's forces on Formosa

[In Washington, a United States spokesman said there was no indication that a growth of anti-United States feeling had anything to do with the cancellation of aid.]

Premier U Nu, who left Rangoon by plane today for the Indian bor-

Continued on Page 18, Column 1

MARINES WIN BACK EMBATTLED HEIGHT

Foe in Korea Driven Off 'Vegas' After Heavy Artillery Duel—Toll of Chinese Is Heavy

By LINDESAY PARROTT
Special to The New York Times.

TOKYO, Sunday, March 29 — United States Marines recaptured today their "Vegas" outpost north of Munsan, on the western Korean front, after a seesaw two-day battle during which the crest of the battered hillock repeatedly changed hands.

The Leathernecks pushed to the top this morning after a night attack by 500 Chinese Communist infantry had forced them down the southern slope. By an hour after dawn the fighting had ceased at least temporarily.

Front-line dispatches said the Marines had found the hilltop strewn with enemy dead. The Chinese apparently pulled back hurriedly, for they usually are careful to remove killed and wounded from the battlefield.

The Marines said the Chinese [app]eared for the moment to have [aban]doned the hill, though the[y] previously had shown every [ind]ication of making a grim fight and might attack again. The ground below "Vegas" was covered by mist and smoke that could conceal further enemy movement. United Nations guns fired sporadically at the approaches to the outpost from the north.

During the night the Chinese made three probing attacks on the

Continued on Page 4, Column 1

CLARK WEIGHS PLAN

Enemy Assents to Offer the U. N. Commander Made on Feb. 22

QUICK EXCHANGE IS HINTED

Allied Headquarters Is Wary on Move to Resume Armistice Parley, Off Since Fall

Text of exchange of letters is printed on Page 4.

By WILLIAM J. JORDEN
Special to The New York Times.

TOKYO, March 28—The Chinese and North Korean Communist commanders accepted today a long-standing United Nations proposal for an immediate exchange of sick and wounded prisoners of war by both sides in Korea.

The Communists also suggested that settlement of this problem should be "made to lead" to a Korean armistice, and they proposed immediate resumption of the suspended truce talks.

The enemy's acceptance of the offer made Feb. 22 by Gen. Mark W. Clark, United Nations commander, was contained in a letter to General Clark delivered to a United Nations liaison officer at Panmunjom, Korea, this afternoon. The message, signed by Kim Il Sung, North Korean Premier and supreme commander of the North Korean Army, and Peng Teh-huai, commander of the Chinese "volunteers" in Korea, also was broadcast tonight by the Peiping and Pyongyang radios.

Allies 'Making Preparations'

Acknowledging receipt of the unexpected Communist acceptance of the United Nations offer, a spokesman for the United Nations Command said that the headquarters here was "already making preparations" for the exchange of wounded and ill prisoners. The United Nations Command said it would be ready to begin transfer of the prisoners "within a matter of days."

However, General Clark's headquarters reserved judgment on the Communist suggestion that the truce delegates immediately go back to the conference site at Panmunjom to resume the armistice talks, which broke down last October.

General Clark and other United Nations officers said the proposal to resume the talks would be taken under consideration immediately, but General Clark himself said he wanted to make sure the Communist offer was sound and not merely another propaganda move.

In a message to the Communist commanders after the talks were suspended in October General Clark informed the enemy leaders that the United Nations would "never agree to or negotiate further on the basis of any proposal that would require the United Nations Command to use force to repatriate prisoners" to the Communist side.

It was noted here that the Com-

Continued on Page 3, Column 1

G. O. P. Committee Meets April 10 To Elect a Successor to Roberts

By PAUL P. KENNEDY
Special to The New York Times.

WASHINGTON, March 28—C. Wesley Roberts, chairman of the Republican National Committee, today called a meeting of the committee for April 10 in Washington for the purpose of accepting the resignation he tendered yesterday and electing his successor.

Mr. Roberts, in a telegram to all committee members, noted that rules of the Republican party called for a convention of the entire committee to act upon the resignation. He said the call for the meeting had been delayed until hotel facilities could be assured.

The chairman, who assumed his $32,500-a-year position Jan. 18, two days before President Eisenhower was inaugurated, resigned yesterday afternoon after a visit to the White House. His resignation followed a report of a joint investigating committee of the Kansas Legislature in which he was censured for "deliberately and intentionally" violating the "spirit" of the Kansas Lobbyist Act.

The report was signed by seven Republicans and two Democrats. It charged that Mr. Roberts had not registered as a lobbyist during the 1951 Legislature session. It was at this time that he received $11,000 for his part in the sale to the state for $110,000 of an insurance company's sanitarium that the company had built on state property.

There was widespread speculation here as to Mr. Roberts' successor. Most of the reports, all of them vague, centered primarily on two persons: Surrogate Leonard W. Hall of New York, a former member of Congress, and Mc-

Continued on Page 54, Column 1

Associated Press Wirephoto

SCENE OF RAIL DISASTER: This is the wreckage left by a freakish collision of three New York Central trains Friday night near Conneaut, Ohio. Two passenger trains, coming fast from opposite directions, and a freight were involved.

Jim Thorpe Is Dead On West Coast at 64

Special to The New York Times.

LOS ANGELES, March 28—Jim Thorpe, the Indian whose exploits in football, baseball and track and field won him acclaim as one of the greatest athletes of all time, died today in his trailer home in suburban Lomita. His age was 64.

Thorpe was eating dinner with his wife when he suffered a heart attack. Mrs. Thorpe's screams attracted a neighbor, Colby Bradshaw, who administered artificial respiration for nearly half an hour.

A county fire rescue squad took over and was momentarily successful. Thorpe revived, recognized persons around him and spoke to them. He was conscious for only a brief time before he suffered a relapse and died.

Hero of the 1912 Olympic Games at Stockholm and a towering football figure, Jim Thorpe was prob-

Continued on Page 92, Column 4

JIM THORPE DEAD ON THE COAST AT 64

Continued From Page 1

ably the greatest natural athlete the world had seen in modern times.

King Gustaf V of Sweden said to the black-haired Sac and Fox Indian as he stood before the royal box, "Sir, you are the greatest athlete in the world." That was after Thorpe almost single-handedly gained the Olympic honors for the United States, setting a point-total record never before approached and dominating the games as no other figure.

Thorpe came back from Stockholm with $50,000 worth of trophies. They included a Viking ship presented to him by the Czar of Russia, and gifts from King Gustaf.

A month later the new American sports idol was toppled from his high pedestal when the Amateur Athletic Union filed charges of professionalism against him, accusing him of receiving pay for playing summer baseball with the Rocky Mount Club in the Eastern Carolina League. The amount of money was negligible, helping to tide him over at school, but the American Olympic Committee offered its apologies and sent back the gifts and medals lavished upon the young man to whom President Theodore Roosevelt had cabled long messages of congratulation.

The medals were forwarded to the runners-up in the pentathlon and decathlon events at Stockholm. Thorpe had won four of the five events in the Pentathlon and finished third in the other, a record unequaled to this day, and in the decathlon he scored 8,412 out of a possible 10,000 points, also unequaled.

Thorpe's decathlon feats in the Olympics have since been surpassed by Bob Mathias, who won the event for the second straight time last year. However, another Olympic great — Finland's Paavo Nurmi—declared that "Jim Thorpe could still beat them all."

Even if Thorpe never could beat Mathias in his prime, most experts still place the Indian ahead as an all around athlete.

In 1950 Thorpe's athletic prowess won for him selection as the greatest athlete of the twentieth century and the greatest football player in an Associated Press poll of sports writers and broadcasters.

Before leaping into world-wide fame as the star of the Olympics Thorpe had become a national sports figure through his deeds on the gridiron as a member of the famous Carlisle Indians football teams coached by Glenn S. (Pop) Warner. In 1911 and 1912 he was chosen as halfback on Walter Camp's All-America teams.

Thorpe played professional football for almost fifteen years and in his prime at Carlisle and as a pro he never had to leave the field because of an injury, such was his courage and stamina. In his last year at the Indian school he won letters in five major sports, and he was proficient in others. His activities included running, jumping, football, lacrosse, boxing, rough-and-tumble, basketball, hockey, archery, rifle shooting, canoeing, handball, swimming and skating.

His Record as Track Athlete

He could run the 100-yard dash in 10 seconds flat, the 220 in 21.8, the 440 in 50.8, the 880 in 1:57, the mile in 4:35, the 120-yard high hurdles in 15 seconds and the 220-yard low hurdles in 24 seconds. He broad-jumped 23 feet 6 inches and high-jumped 6 feet 5 inches. He pole-vaulted 11 feet, put the shot 47 feet 9 inches, threw the javelin 163 feet, the hammer 140 feet and the discus 136 feet.

Thorpe was born on a farm at Prague, Okla., the son of Hiram Thorpe, a ranchman. Dutch, Welsh and Irish blood were understood to flow in his veins, but he was predominantly Indian. As might have been expected he learned to ride swim and shoot almost as soon as he could walk, and he was punching cattle at the age of 10. His favorite diversion was following his hunting dogs in the forest, which helped to develop his magnificent body.

His mother gave him the Indian tribal name of Wa-Tho-Huck, or Bright Path. Official records, however, list him as James Francis Thorpe.

Young Jim was sent to the Haskell Indian School at Lawrence, Kan., and then to the Carlisle School at Carlisle, Pa. He showed no particular interest in college athletics until Warner persuaded him to come out for football. That was in the fall of 1907 and he played as a substitute. The next year he became a regular and attracted attention as a ball-carrier and kicker. He weighed around 178 pounds.

Career at Carlisle

In the spring of 1908 Jim made the track team. Jumping and hurdling were his specialties. By the time he finished his five-year term at Carlisle in the spring of 1909 he had developed into a track star.

Thorpe returned to his home and played baseball in North Carolina. In the fall of 1911 he came back to Carlisle. Warner thought he would have a better chance of making the Olympic team if he returned and persuaded him to do so. That year he won All-America honors in football, as he did in 1912 also, performing sensationally against Harvard, Penn, Princeton, Army, Syracuse and Penn State. Against Harvard in 1911 Thorpe ran 70 yards in nine plays for a touchdown and kicked three

(continued)

Jim Thorpe

Jim Thorpe during the peak of his career in 1911-12

field goals from back of the 40-yard line.

President Eisenhower can attest to Thorpe's hitting power. When the general was a cadet at the United States Military Academy, the Army team played Carlisle, the Indians winning, 27—6. Thorpe stopped General Eisenhower time after time, and in the process the general injured his knee and never played again.

In his track days Carlisle was booked to meet the Lafayette team at Easton. A welcoming committee was puzzled when only two Indians got off the train.

"Where's your team?" they asked.

"This is the team," replied Thorpe.

"Only two of you?"

"Only one," Jim said with a smile. "This fellow's the manager."

In the spring of 1912 he started training for the Olympics. He had confined his efforts to the jumps, the hurdles and the shot-put but now he undertook the pole vault, the javelin, discus, the hammer and the fifty-six-pound weight. In the Olympic trials held at Celtic Park in New York, his all-round ability stood out in all these events and so he riveted a claim to a place on the team that went to Sweden.

After his suspension as an amateur athlete, following his return from Stockholm, Thorpe left Carlisle in 1913 and signed with the New York Giants. He was optioned out to the Milwaukee club of the American Association and remained there until 1916, when he came back to the Giants for two seasons. After that he went to the Boston Braves and then it was back to the minors.

Enters "Pro" Football

Although he never could be considered a star in the major leagues having trouble hitting a curve ball, Thorpe was good enough to last for seven seasons. In his last year, 1919, he batted a highly creditable .327 in sixty games, playing first base and the outfield for the Boston Braves.

Meanwhile, he went into the game he loved best—football—as a professional.

In 1915 he organized the famous Canton (Ohio) Bulldogs, which beat most of the good teams. Later he played with the Cleveland Tigers, the LaRue (Ohio) Indians and the Rock Island Independents. Jim got heavier and found it more difficult to keep in shape and he was appearing in New York at the Polo Grounds in a drop-kicking contest with Charley Brickley as an extra attraction to the game. He played with other teams in Hammond, Ind., and Portsmouth, Ohio, and finally his competitive days ended.

After his retirement, Thorpe fell upon hard days. He went to California in 1930 as master of ceremonies for C. C. Pyle's cross-country marathon, known as the bunion derby. He settled down in Hawthorne, Calif., and got work as an extra in motion pictures, appearing in Western serials and in short football features, but things got worse for him.

Thorpe was back in the news in 1943, when the Oklahoma Legislature adopted a resolution that the A. A. U. be petitioned to reinstate the Sac and Fox" Olympic records, but no action was taken.

In February, 1952, a group in Congress made another unsuccessful attempt to have the medals restored. After an operation for cancer of the lip in the preceding November, he had been discovered to be nearly penniless and groups throughout the country raised thousands of dollars for him.

Although past the age for acceptance by the Army or Navy in World War II, he joined the merchant marine in 1945 and served on an ammunition ship before the conflict ended.

In the summer of 1949, Warner Brothers started work on a motion picture entitled "Jim Thorpe—All American," with Burt Lancaster in the athlete's role. The picture reached Broadway in the summer of 1951.

Thorpe married three times. His first wife was the former Iva Miller, whom he wed in 1913 and was the mother of his three daughters, Gale, Charlotte and Frances, and his first son, the late James Francis Jr. He married Freeda Kirkpatrick in 1926 and they had four sons, Phillip, William, Richard and John. On June 2, 1945, Thorpe wed Patricia Gladys Askew of Louisville, Ky.

Jim Thorpe is considered to be the world's greatest all-around athlete, although football was always his greatest love.

Bill Tilden

"All the News That's Fit to Print"

The New York Times.

LATE CITY EDITION
Warm, thunderstorms late today. Showers, slightly cooler tomorrow.
Temperature Range Today—Max., 86; Min., 70
Temperature Yesterday—Max., 87.1; Min., 69.3
Full U. S. Weather Bureau Report, Page 21

Copyright, 1953, by The New York Times Company.

VOL. CII..No. 34,832. Entered as Second-Class Matter, Post Office, New York, N. Y. NEW YORK, SATURDAY, JUNE 6, 1953. Times Square, New York 36, N. Y. Telephone Lackawanna 4-1000 FIVE CENTS

STATE'S HIGH COURT BACKS TRANSIT ACT; TOKEN HUNT PUSHED

Ruling, However, Leaves Door Open for New Attack After Authority Takes Over

DYE SEES HOME-RULE LOSS

His Dissent Says Constitution Was Ignored in Passing Law —Mint to Get New Plea

Texts of court opinion and of Dye dissent are on Page 32.

By LEO EGAN

The Court of Appeals, highest judicial tribunal in the state, upheld yesterday the constitutionality of Governor Dewey's fiscal program for New York City in a six-to-one decision handed down in Albany.

It thereby removed the last obstacle to the transfer of the deficit-burdened city-owned transit system to the newly created City Transit Authority, which was vested by the Legislature with power to raise fares on rapid transit and surface lines to make the lines self-sustaining.

The decision left the door open to a subsequent attack on the validity of the legislation after the transfer is made on June 15. However, concessions made by the authority in negotiating a lease with the Board of Estimate, if ratified at a special session of the Legislature, appeared to have removed the main grounds on which the city had depended to upset the program.

Legislation creating the authority and granting additional taxing powers to the city contingent on the transfer of the transit system to the authority had been attacked by the city administration and a taxpayer as invasions of the city's home rule powers.

Moreover, Corporation Counsel Denis M. Hurley and Assistant Corporation Counsel Bernard Richland had contended in a three-hour hearing before the court that city acceptance of the transit authority would force it to exceed its constitutional debt limit.

Taxing Powers Involved

The statutes upheld by the court provided for the creation of the authority and gave to the city, if it transferred the transit system to the authority, the right to increase real estate taxes by $50,000,000 a year and to impose a one-half of 1 per cent payroll tax, payable in equal parts by employes and employers. It was estimated the two levies would raise $60,000,000. If the city, which contended it needed additional revenue to balance its budget for the fiscal year starting July 1, refused to make the transfer to the authority, none of the additional taxing powers would become available to it.

Upholding decisions of Supreme Court Justice Benjamin F. Schreiber and the Appellate Division, First Department, in overruling the city's arguments, the Court of Appeals majority said yesterday:

"The statutes in question are permissive only, in a field in which the state is concerned. Under these circumstances, and assuming that any transfer will not be absolute conveyance but by a lease of limited term with reversion to the city, we cannot say that the legislation is on its face unconstitutional.

"Whether it would be constitutional without those concomitants

Continued on Page 32, Column 2

Two Tankers Afire; 40 Feared Missing

Special to The New York Times.

PHILADELPHIA, Saturday, June 6—Two tankers were ablaze off Reedy Point early this morning after colliding in the Delaware River near the east entrance of the Chesapeake and Delaware Canal. The Coast Guard here said about forty survivors had been picked up by an unidentified tug.

A Coast Guard patrol vessel at the scene radioed an estimate that another forty crew members were missing. It said in a message shortly before 3 A. M. that it based the estimate on the normal complement carried by the tankers.

[The vessels were identified as the tankers Massachusetts and Phoenix, The Associated Press reported. A survivor of the Phoenix said she was a bulk carrier of the Sinclair Oil Company. A dispatcher at the Chesapeake, Md., Coast Guard station said he knew only that one ship was

Continued on Page 31, Column 3

Letters Found by Dog Bring U. S. Ex-Aide Before Inquiry

Former Justice Department Lawyer Testifies He Threw 'Personal' Files in River— Denies Trying to Hide Anything

By LUTHER A. HUSTON
Special to The New York Times.

WASHINGTON, June 5—A tale of a mongrel dog whose beachcombings along the shores of the Patuxent River turned up b... Department of Justice ... told today to a House ... sentatives Judiciary sub...

Lieut. (j.g.) Roy L. B... the Naval Air Force told ... fished the letters from t... after his dog had brought ... of them from the beac... dropped them in his yard.

Turner L. Smith, a former ... tice Department lawyer, ack... edged that he had dumped ... letters in the river near its con... ence with the Chesapeake Bay. ... said that they were not offici... letters and that he was not trying to protect the department or himself when he threw them away.

"There couldn't be anything in there to indicate that Turner Smith is a crook," he told the subcommittee. "I've never done anything crooked or dishonest. I was not

doing anything to prot... partment...

'Affluent' City A... In a $600 Tax ...

A $4,700-a-year accountant in the ... who had acquired properties here and up... $75,000, was arrested yesterday with a sc... alleged $6... Columbus A...

The accu... custody in a... Avenue, near... by detectives ... trict Attorney ... after they alle... from the victim... a payment of si...

The prosecuto... suspects as John ... old, of 1190 Shake... the Bronx, a senior ... the audit control d... Bureau of Excise Tax... troller's office, and T... Grath, 42, a public acc... 201-10 Thirty-second Ave... side, Queens.

Cascell Called Affluen...

Cascell, the District At... said, has been a city employe... 1936 and in his present job ... 1942. Assistant District Atto... James J. Fitzpatrick, who rece... Mr. McGlade's complaint of ... extortion, said an investigati... had showed that in the last seve... years Cascell had developed "int... a person of affluent means."

He said that in 1946 Cascell had purchased for $24,000—$10,000 of it in cash—a building at 25 Division Street; had acquired the White Cat Inn, near Monroe, N. Y., for $40,000, and was attempting to sell a house, valued at $10,500 at Walton Lake, near Monroe.

Informed of Cascell's arrest, Controller Lazarus Joseph announced his immediate suspension. Mr. Hogan said that his office would conduct an extensive inves-

Continued on Page 32, Column 3

BILL TILDEN IS DEAD; TENNIS STAR WAS 60

Former Davis Cup Ace Held Amateur Title 7 Years Before Turning Pro in 1930

By The Associated Press.

HOLLYWOOD, Calif., June 5—William Tatum (Big Bill) Tilden 2d, former world tennis champion, died late today, apparently of a heart attack, in his Hollywood apartment. He was 60 years old.

The manager of the apartment, where Mr. Tilden had lived for the last few months, said the player and coach had been suffering from a cold and went out for medicine this afternoon. He died some time after returning to his apartment.

Mr. Tilden was to have left tomorrow for Cleveland, where he was to have taken part in a tournament.

Hero of United States Sports

William T. Tilden 2d won a place among the great American heroes of sport. At the height of his remarkable career, in sport's golden age of the Twenties, his name was a national and international byword, along with Jack Dempsey, Bobby Jones, Babe Ruth and Tommy Hitchcock.

Mr. Tilden was an amateur in those days and, great as was his fame, he won even more superlatives as a professional at an age when tennis players and athletes in other fields of endeavor had long since closed their competitive careers. His victories, in his forties, over the world's foremost professionals established him as one of the real miracle men of sport, and he continued to be a headline attraction almost until he had reached the half-century mark.

Mr. Tilden's record shows that:

¶He won the national amateur championship seven times, from 1920 through 1925, inclusive, and in 1930, thus equaling the record of William Larned and Richard Sears.

¶He was the first American to win the men's championship of Great Britain at Wimbledon, in 1920, and that he triumphed there twice again, in 1921 and 1930.

¶He won thirty-one national crowns as an amateur indoors and outdoors in singles, doubles and mixed doubles.

¶He was ranked as the No. 1 player of his country as an amateur ten times from 1920 through 1929.

¶He played on the Davis Cup team eleven years from 1920 through 1930 and that from 1920 through 1925 he was unbeaten in singles and lost only one match in doubles of a total of twenty-two cup matches.

It was as the ace of the American Davis Cup team that Mr. Tilden gained his greatest prestige, though from 1920 through 1925 he was so invincible that no player in the world ever stood a chance against him in any competition. A member of the team that went

Continued on Page 17, Column 4

BILL TILDEN IS DEAD; TENNIS STAR WAS 60

Former Davis Cup Ace Held Amateur Title 7 Years Before Turning Pro in 1930

By The Associated Press.

HOLLYWOOD, Calif., June 5—William Tatum (Big Bill) Tilden 2d, former world tennis champion, died late today, apparently of a heart attack, in his Hollywood apartment. He was 60 years old.

The manager of the apartment, where Mr. Tilden had lived for the last few months, said the player and coach had been suffering from a cold and went out for medicine this afternoon. He died some time after returning to his apartment.

Mr. Tilden was to have left tomorrow for Cleveland, where he was to have taken part in a tournament.

Hero of United States Sports

William T. Tilden 2d won a place among the great American heroes of sport. At the height of his remarkable career, in sport's golden age of the Twenties, his name was a national and international byword, along with Jack Dempsey, Bobby Jones, Babe Ruth and Tommy Hitchcock.

Mr. Tilden was an amateur in those days and, great as was his fame, he won even more superlatives as a professional at an age when tennis players and athletes in other fields of endeavor had long since closed their competitive careers. His victories, in his forties,

Continued on Page 17, Column 4

LEMAY OPPOSES CUT IN GLOBAL BOMBERS AS TOO GREAT A RISK

His Views Are... Unit by V...

KOREA PEACE HOPE SEEN CASTING DOUBT ON TAX EXTENSION

...t Folsom Tells House Unit ...e Doubts Armistice Would Bring Program Revision

By JOHN D. MORRIS
Special to The New York Times.

...SHINGTON, June 5—The ...ty of an early truce in ...st new doubt today on ... for favorable Congres... ...on on President Eisen... ...quest for a six-month ...f the excess profits

...e demands in the ... and Means Committee ...ate halt to the cur... ...n the proposal, but ...om, Under Secre... ...ury, voiced strong ...rmistice would ...ation to revise

...ts in the tax ...llowing: ...oard of the ... Organiza... ...ion of the ...s needed ...ration of ...gency." ...embers ...mmittee ...airman, ...ed, Re... ...ork, to ...xten... ...rade ...ires ...one ...tion

President Stars at Whit...

President Eisenhower jovially fends off a blow from heavyweight champion Rocky Marciano, right, as Joe DiMaggio, retired Yankee star, approves the horseplay. Behind the President is swimmer Mary Freeman (dark hair). The occasion was a White House luncheon for forty-three outstanding sports figures, which was prelude to annual Congressional baseball game for charity.

Associated Press Wirephoto

By CHARLES E. EGAN
Special to The New York Times.

WASHINGTON, June 5—President Eisenhower, a devotee of the golf ball, ended a day largely devoted to sports matters tonight by tossing out the first ball at the annual baseball game between Republican and Democratic members of Congress.

The sixth annual meeting of the teams attracted a crowd that packed the grandstands of Griffith Stadium, creating a large "purse" for The Washington Star's Children's Camp Fund.

Earlier, the President had forty-three noted sports figures as his luncheon guests and took the group on a tour of the White House. Included in the gathering were Rocky Marciano, the heavy-

Continued on Page 8, Column 3

TRUCE TEAMS MEET BRIEFLY; CAPTIVES ACCORD EXPECTED, WITH CEASE-FIRE TO FOLLOW

Associated Press Wirephoto via Radio from Tokyo

...TIRS HOPE FOR TRUCE: Lieut. Gen. Nam Il of North ...orea, senior Communist negotiator, arriving at Panmunjom ...hursday for armistice talks with United Nations delegates.

SECRECY PERSISTS

Enemy Requests Day's Recess After Session of Only 19 Minutes

By LINDESAY PARROTT
Special to The New York Times.

TOKYO, Saturday, June 6—United Nations and Communist delegates met for nineteen minutes at Panmunjom today amid a belief widely expressed here that a quick agreement now might result for an armistice in the three-year-old war. The delegates then scheduled a new session for 11 A. M. tomorrow [10 P. M. Saturday, Eastern daylight time].

The recess was requested by the Communists, it was announced, but no reason for the new adjournment was made public. The session —the twenty-second held since the conferences resumed after a six-month breakdown—was secret, like the two that had preceded it.

Lieut. Col. Milton Herr, official spokesman at Allied advance headquarters, said no comment could be made under the secrecy agreement. It was assumed, however, that the Chinese and North Koreans had listened to a reply from the United Nations delegates to a long commentary made at Thursday's session by North Korean Lieut. Gen. Nam Il, senior enemy representative.

After that meeting, it was reported unofficially that the views of the two sides were fairly close together. The brevity of today's session suggested the Allied delegates had little to say regarding General Nam's statement.

The continued secrecy on the discussion of the vexing question of disposition of war prisoners who refuse to return behind the Iron Curtain after a truce might be an indication that some progress was being made that might be imperiled by a public announcement.

South Korean Again Absent

Only American and Communist delegates attended today's conference. Maj. Gen. Choi Duk Shin, South Korean delegate, again boycotted the session. His Government is bitterly opposed to any armistice that would leave Korea divided and Chinese troops on the peninsula.

Although both the United Nations plan and the Communist commentary on it were still officially secret, South Korean officials said the Chinese and North Koreans appeared to have one major objection to the Allied plan.

This was that, if an international political conference after an armistice failed to agree on what should be done with the 48,500 anti-Communist North Korean and Chinese prisoners, the General Assembly of the United Nations should be the final arbiter.

This proposal, General Nam is understood to have stated, is unacceptable because the United Nations itself is a belligerent in Korea. But the suggestion for Assembly intervention in the prisoner dispute was a new one introduced by the Allied command for the first time last month. It previously had not been one of the firm demands by the United Nations delegation and therefore presumably could be withdrawn, as General

Continued on Page 2, Column 6

...SENHOWER GIVES ...URANCE TO BONN

...ars Bermuda Parley ... Germany Without ...ing Adenauer

...HANDLER ...w York Times.

..., June 5—Sam... States Deputy ...r for Germany, ...ncellor Konrad ...h a cable mes... Eisenhower ...nce that no Germany ...forthcoming the Presi... Winston Premier ...th the ...ssur... ...hed in ...anken... ...epart... Of... ...with ...s...

...ments reassert their interest in integration and take concrete steps to achieve unity the isolationist trend, which he sees rising in the United States, will force a change in American policy.

The speech by Senator Robert A. Taft in Cincinnati May 26 was interpreted in that sense by Dr. Adenauer and his advisers. As a measure of reinsurance against what he fears may develop into a political disaster, Dr. Adenauer tried to convince the United States Government that the policy of Western European integration must be given precedence over all other possible European solutions at the Bermuda conference.

It was obvious that President Eisenhower could not grant such an assurance without British and

Continued on Page 6, Column 6

RHEE BIDS CHINESE AND U. N. WITHDRAW

Asks U. S. Guarantees of Korea as Condition of Armistice in Appeal to Eisenhower

By ROBERT ALDEN
Special to The New York Times.

SEOUL, Korea, Saturday, June 6—In a last-ditch appeal to President Eisenhower, President Syngman Rhee of the Republic of Korea has asked either that a specific military defense pact be concluded between South Korea and the United States or that South Korean forces be allowed to continue the war against the Communists alone.

The defense pact would be a condition under which Dr. Rhee's Government would agree to a truce that would provide for withdrawal of both United Nations and Communist Chinese forces from the Korean peninsula.

[South Korea's Ambassador to Washington, Dr. You Chan Yang, warned that "unless the United States accepts our counter-proposals" South Korea would not sign a truce agreement.]

Dr. Rhee wrote to General Eisen...ower: "Our preference is still to ...ve United States forces by our ...e to help us out. But if that ... longer possible, Korea should ...ercise its innate right of self-...ermination to decide the na-

Continued on Page 2, Column 2

...Carthy Asks State Department ...Keep Coe From Leaving Country

Special to The New York Times.

...ASHINGTON, June 5—Senator Joseph R. McCarthy, Republican of Wisconsin, publicly called upon the State Department today to keep Frank Coe, an American citizen who formerly was secretary of the International Monetary Fund, from leaving the United States.

This was one of the high spots of a televised hearing before the Senate Investigations subcommittee, of which Mr. McCarthy is chairman, that wound up in disorder and bitterness with the words "lie," "persecution" and "intimidation" being hurled about the room.

Mr. Coe had just refused, by invoking the constitutional right not to give testimony that might incriminate him, to say whether he was or had been a Communist or whether he had been involved in espionage while an official of the fund.

He said that he was not engaged in espionage now and was not so engaged last Dec. 2. He would not answer, however, the question as it applied to Dec. 1, his last day with the fund.

Mr. Coe appeared at the hearing with a written statement dealing with what he contended was the stated purpose of the inquiry, that is, to discover whether as a fund official he had attempted to block a devaluation of Austrian currency that had been opposed by Communist Czechoslovakia.

He never was able to read this statement, however, though he handed it out to the press.

In this statement Mr. Coe accused the subcommittee of having "gratuitously released to the press the fantastic misinformation that I was involved in an imaginary subversive plot to obstruct the devaluation of Austrian currency in 1949."

As the session was adjourned to

Continued on Page 7, Column 3

BILL TILDEN DIES OF A HEART ATTACK

Continued From Page 1

over the world's foremost professionals established him as one of the real miracle men of sport, and he continued to be a headline attraction almost until he had reached the half-century mark.

Mr. Tilden's record shows that:

¶He won the national amateur championship seven times, from 1920 through 1925, inclusive, and in 1930, thus equaling the record of William Larned and Richard Sears.

¶He was the first American to win the men's championship of Great Britain at Wimbledon, in 1920, and that he triumphed there twice again, in 1921 and 1930.

¶He won thirty-one national crowns as an amateur indoors and outdoors in singles, doubles and mixed doubles.

¶He was ranked as the No. 1 player of his country as an amateur ten times from 1920 through 1929.

¶He played on the Davis Cup team eleven years from 1920 through 1930 and that from 1920 through 1925 he was unbeaten in singles and lost only one match in doubles of a total of twenty-two cup matches.

It was as the ace of the American Davis Cup team that Mr. Tilden gained his greatest prestige, though from 1920 through 1925 he was so invincible that no player the world over stood a chance against him in any competition. A member of the team that went to Australasia in 1920 to bring back the international team trophy to the United States, he stood as the bulwark of its defense until the Four Musketeers of France—Rene Lacoste, Henri Cochet, Jean Borotra and Jacques Brugnon—broke America's long hold on the trophy in 1927, marking France's first victory in a Davis Cup challenge round.

In 1928, Mr. Tilden was the captain of the team that went to Europe seeking to win back the cup. Out of that trip arose the most celebrated of the many dramatic episodes in his career.

While in France he was removed as captain of the team and declared ineligible to play for his country because of his violation of the player-writer provision of the amateur rule. That provision had been written into the rule as the aftermath of the controversies between Mr. Tilden and the United States Lawn Tennis Association over his writing activities.

The United States defeated Italy without his services and qualified to meet France in the challenge round. When the French realized that he was not to be allowed to play against their team, their indignation knew no bounds.

This was the first time they were to have the honor of staging a Davis Cup challenge round. For the occasion, they had built a beautiful new stadium at Auteuil, indirectly a monument to the drawing power of Tilden, just as is the stadium of the West Side Tennis Club at Forest Hills, Queens. To put on the show without Big Bill was unthinkable to them. It was like putting on Hamlet without the Melancholy Dane.

Reinstated for Matches

The outcry was so great, feeling ran so high, that Ambassador Myron T. Herrick found it necessary to intercede for the sake of international unity. Upon his request, the United States Lawn Tennis Association restored Tilden to the team at the eleventh hour.

To add to the drama, Tilden threw a scare into the French by defeating the great Lacoste. Upon his return home with the team, which was beaten by the French, Tilden was brought up on charges of violating the amateur rule and was barred from competing in the national championships that year, 1928.

Except for that year and 1926, when he was beaten in the quarter finals by Cochet, Mr. Tilden was in every national championship final from 1918 through 1929. He was runner-up to R. Lindley Murray in 1918, to William Johnston in 1919 and to Lacoste in 1927. In 1930, his last year as an amateur, he was beaten in the semi-finals by John Doeg, the first American to conquer him in the championship since 1919.

It was on the private court of the family country home at Ontcora that Bill Tilden had his introduction to tennis. There and at Germantown, Philadelphia, where he was born on Feb. 10, 1893, he was playing the game when he was barely able to hold a racquet.

By 1910, young Tilden was widely known in competition around Philadelphia.

In 1920 Tilden was named on the Davis Cup team that went to England for the qualifying rounds, and with his victory at Wimbledon began the most absolute sway tennis has known. From the age of 27 to 33 he bestrode the court like a colossus. In the autumn of 1922, he suffered the amputation of the upper joint of his right middle finger as the result of an infection.

Regained Crown in 1930

That might have ended the career of some, but Mr. Tilden overcame it, as he did physical frailties in his boyhood days and a knee injury later in his career. If anything, he was even more the master in 1923, 1924 and 1925. Then Lacoste and Cochet caught up with him in 1926 and 1927. He came back in 1929 to regain the championship and in 1930, at the age of 37, he thrilled the tennis world by triumphing at Wimbledon on the same stretch of turf where he was victorious ten years earlier.

In December, 1930, Tilden said good bye to amateur tennis. Like Bobby Jones, he made his exit by way of the motion pictures. He signed a contract to appear in a series of short films devoted to tennis, automatically disqualifying himself for amateur competition.

The next February, Mr. Tilden launched his career as a professional player at the age of 38 at Madison Square Garden. He defeated Karel Kozeluh of Czechoslovakia. In May, he defeated Vincent Richards and again in 1932.

On Feb. 3, 1950, he was named the greatest tennis player of the first half of the Twentieth Century by an overwhelming vote in a poll taken by The Associated Press. He got 310 votes, with Jack Kramer, receiving thirty-two votes, in second place.

In 1947, Mr. Tilden was sentenced to the county jail in Los Angeles for contributing to the delinquency of a minor. He was released after seven and one-half months. Arrested again in 1949 for violation of his probation, he remained in jail from February until December of that year.

One of the great players of the 1920s, Bill Tilden was voted the greatest tennis player of the first half of the twentieth century, in an Associated Press poll.

Bill Tilden developed spins, chops, and slices—he was a true tactician of the game of tennis.

The New York Times WEDNESDAY, JULY 28, 1948.

JOE TINKER IS DEAD; A BASEBALL GREAT

End Comes to Cubs' Shortstop in Famous Double-Play Trio on His 68th Birthday

ORLANDO, Fla., July 27 (AP)—Joe Tinker, one of baseball's greats, died today on his sixty-eighth birthday. He was cheerful to the last hour of his life, although he died in an oxygen tent where he had been placed because of a respiratory ailment which no one considered serious.

Ten days ago the last surviving member of the Chicago Cubs' Tinker-to-Evers-to-Chance double play combination was taken to Orange Memorial Hospital for treatment for his indisposition and to have his diet straightened out.

A brief while before his death the hospital issued a bulletin saying, "Mr. Tinker's condition today is better than it has been at any time since he entered the hospital. He ate a hearty breakfast and appears in excellent spirits."

Surviving are three sons, Joe Jr. of Tallahassee, Fla.; William of Baltimore and Rowland of Orlando, and a daughter, Mrs. Charles Clapp of Boulder, Col.

Joined the Cubs in 1902

When the late Frank Selee reorganized the Chicago Cubs in 1902 he shocked the baseball world by placing two youngsters at shortstop and second base—Joe Tinker and Johnny Evers—who had had no major league experience, had no records as batsmen and didn't weigh 135 pounds apiece.

They went on to become one of the greatest—and undoubtedly the best known—second-base combination of all time. With Frank Chance, who later became manager, they made up the "Tinker-to-Evers-to-Chance" double play array, carried on to win four National League pennants — 1906, 1907, 1908 and 1910—and two world championships.

It would be unfair to Evers to say that Tinker was the sparkplug of that machine. They were both full of dynamite and despite their lack of stature they became known as desperate battlers. Tinker developed into somewhat of a distance hitter. Veteran Polo Grounds fans recall him as the man whose long two-bagger sailed over Cy Seymour's head and decided the great play-off game between the Giants and Cubs in 1908 after the teams had finished the season in a tie caused by the Merkle "bone play" a few weeks before.

The scrappy shortstop, one of the great advocates of hit-and-run baseball of the most aggressive sort, remained spirited throughout his life. Thus, earlier this year, while recuperating from the amputation of his left leg, the Hall of Fame shortstop remarked:

"Guess I won't be able to pitch for a couple of weeks."

Not even from Evers would Tinker take any nonsense. At the height of their fame when Evers took a hack to the ball park one day, forcing Tinker and other players to wait until it returned, the shortstop had a fight with Evers and the two did not speak for nearly three years.

When his playing days had ended, Tinker managed minor and major league clubs without too much success. But while heading Columbus, he pulled a stunt that led to the abolition of the spitball. His men seemed unable to hit this pitch, then commonplace in baseball. So he ordered one of them to get a file and work on the baseball. The end of that season the spitball was banned in the American Association and the majors followed them.

Tinker became the manager of the Cubs after the retirement of Chance. He never had much luck with them. He was manager of the Reds and quit in disgust. He was sold to the Dodgers for $25,000, of which he was supposed to get $10,000 for signing. The Cincinnati club refused to sanction the deal without getting some players from Brooklyn and Tinker never got the $10,000. That was in 1913.

Managed in Federal League

He went to the Federal League as manager of the Chicago club for Charles F. Weeghman in 1914, played shortstop in addition and in 1915 won the pennant. But the league was swallowed up in the peace agreement the following season.

Tinker became a minor league manager at Columbus and had a long term with Derby Bill Clymer at Buffalo. He also managed Jersey City and worked for several years as a scout for the Cubs. Many years ago he went to Florida, invested in a baseball plant, Tinker Field, at Orlando, and prospered during the years that his firm friend, Jack Hendricks, long manager of the Reds, took that big league team to his park to train.

The 1929 depression smashed the Florida boom and Tinker returned to baseball for a brief spell, becoming manager at Jersey City, where he succeeded Nick Allen in 1930. For a short time in 1937 he was manager of the Orlando Gulls in the Florida State League. He was in the real estate business there in his late years.

In 1946, Tinker, Evers and Chance were selected to join baseball's other immortals in the Hall of Fame at Cooperstown, N. Y.

Tinker had suffered a serious illness in 1936, and at one time hope for his recovery was virtually abandoned. But his sturdy constitution pulled him through. He also had several serious illnesses in the last decade. He was taken to the Orange Memorial Hospital in Orlando in 1944, suffering from influenza. A heart condition and diabetes caused his condition to take a turn for the worse. He rallied and apparently had regained his health only to enter the hospital again in December, 1944, suffering from nasal hemorrhages.

Joe Tinker (left) and Johnny Evers who, along with Frank Chance, made up baseball's most famous double-play combination with the Chicago Cubs..

The New York Times SATURDAY, MARCH 31, 1951.

JEROME D. TRAVERS, GOLF STAR, 64, DIES

Four-Time Amateur Champion Captured National Open in '15—Famed as Putter

Special to THE NEW YORK TIMES.

EAST HARTFORD, Conn., March 30—Jerome D. Travers, who won five national golf titles between 1907 and 1915, died in his home here late last night at the age of 64.

Travers won the national amateur golf championship in 1907, 1908, 1912 and 1913. He won the national open in 1915, the second amateur in history to win the open title up to that time.

For the last ten years, Travers had been an inspector at the Pratt & Whitney Aircraft Company. He frequently taught golf to employes of the concern. In 1949, he was elected to the Helm's Golf Hall of Fame in California, an honor given to only five golfers up to that time.

His widow, a daughter, Miss Gerry-Anne Travers of Central Islip, L. I., and two sons, Jerome A. Travers of Meriden and David B. Travers of New Haven, survive.

One of the Game's "Greats"

Jerome Dunstan Travers, known as Jerry during his tournament days, was one of the nation's most celebrated golfers. Before the era dominated by Bobby Jones, Travers won four national amateur golf championships and one United States Open championship.

Of slight physique, he was regarded as a keen putt. and a sterling iron player. A pupil of the late Alex Smith, one of the famous Carnoustie brothers, Travers said he made his golf debut at the age of 9 on Long Island.

Travers won his first metropolitan amateur championship in 1906, when he was 19, at the Garden City (L. I.) Golf Club course, where he had many matches with Walter J. Travis. His triumph over Eben Byers for this title and subsequent victories in 1907, 1911, 1912 and 1913 established a record that was exceeded only last summer, when Frank Strafaci won the honors for the sixth time.

In 1907, Travers captured the national amateur title for the first time at the Euclid Club in Cleveland by defeating Archibald Graham. The next year, at the Garden City course, he retained the crown by winning from Max Behr.

He held the amateur title on two more occasions. In 1912, he turned back Charles (Chick) Evans at Wheaton, Ill., and the next year won from John G. Anderson at Garden City.

Although Travers had used the orthodox wooden club as a driver, he found later that he could be more accurate with a driving iron from the tee and gradually developed his game around the irons. He was also a superb putter, adopting the Schenectady-style center-shaft club that Travis had wielded so well at Garden City.

The four national amateur crowns won by Travers remained a record until Bobby Jones won five between 1924 and 1930.

Travers lost in the final of the 1914 national amateur to Francis Ouimet. But in 1915 he achieved what only one other amateur—the same Ouimet in 1913—previously had done, the winning of the United States open golf championship at the Baltusrol Golf Club in Short Hills, N. J. Since then, only Chick Evans, Bobby Jones and Johnny Goodman have won this honor as amateurs.

In later years, Travers played most of his golf in New Jersey. He became president of the New Jersey Golf Association, relinquishing the post in 1932, when he decided to quit the amateur ranks and become, as he described it, a "business man golfer." In this capacity he chiefly played exhibition matches.

Between the years 1906 and 1915, Jerome D. Travers won five major and five semi-major championships, including four U.S. Amateur titles.

The New York Times THURSDAY, JULY 24, 1975

Emlen Tunnell, 50, Dies; Star of Football Giants

By NEIL AMDUR
Special to The New York Times

PLEASANTVILLE, N.Y., July 23—Emlen Tunnell, who talked the New York Giants into giving him a tryout and became one of professional football's greatest defensive backs, died here early this morning, apparently of a heart attack. He was 50 years old.

Mr. Tunnell, who played 14 seasons in the National Football League, including 11 with the Giants, was the first black named to the Pro Football Hall of Fame. At his death, he was assistant director of pro personnel for the Giants.

As a player, the 6-foot 3-inch 210-pound Mr. Tunnell was acknowledged as a trend-setter for the modern-day defensive back in pro football.

"Emlen changed the theory of defensive safeties," said Jim Lee Howell, a current member of the Giants staff, who coached Mr. Tunnell in the latter part of his career. "He would have been too big for the job earlier, and they'd have made him a lineman. But he had such strength, such speed and such quickness I'm convinced he was the best safety ever to play."

'Never Heard of Man'

In a book entitled "The New York Giants: Yesterday, Today and Tomorrow," Dave Klein recalled how Mr. Tunnell, who had not been drafted by the pros after his college class graduated from Iowa State in 1943, traveled to New York showed up at the Giants offices and asked for a tryout.

"Never heard of you," Steve Owen, then the coach, said.

However, Ray Walsh, the general manager, remembered that Mr. Tunnell had played at Iowa State and suggested that Mr. Owen give him a chance.

Before his career ended in 1961 with the Green Bay Packers, Mr. Tunnell set 16 Giant records and four National Football League records that still stand—most career interceptions (79), most punt returns (258) and most yardage on both interceptions and punt returns. He was named to the All-Pro Team seven times, was inducted into the Hall of Fame at Canton, Ohio, in 1967 and was named to the first team 50th anniversary all-N.F.L. all-time team.

Mr. Tunnell, a Giant scout from 1962 through 1964, joined the staff as an assistant coach in 1965. This year, he asked to return to personnel and scouting "because I like going to colleges and spending time with young people instead of being bottled up in all those meetings."

Casual and Easy-Going

Mr. Tunnell, who was born March 25, 1925, in Bryn Mawr, Pa., was known for a casual, easy-going demeanor. Andy Robustelli, director of operations for the Giants and a former teammate, described him as "very loose and confident . . Em didn't get shaken by things that weren't going right."

Mr. Robustelli also noted that the civil rights movement during the fifties had produced problems on many pro football teams. "One of the reasons we never had problems was because of Em Tunnell," Mr. Robustelli said. "Emlen was good to all people. He was a hell of a decent person who meant a lot to young ballplayers."

Mr. Tunnell was the first black player on the Giants and the first black hired to a coaching position in the modern era of the N.F.L.

During his early years in New York, Mr. Tunnell joined three other defensive backs, Tom Landry, Otto Schellenbacher and Harmon Rowe, as key figures in the Giants' "umbrella," defense, a tactic that revolutionized pro football.

The umbrella defense was designed to counter such pass-oriented quarterbacks of the time as Sammy Baugh and Otto Graham. Its principle was to shift from the traditional six-man defensive line and drop off two linemen for pass coverage, a move that defined the role of linemen, linebackers and defensive backs in the modern system.

"He was very quiet during the scouting meetings on personnel," Mr. Robustelli recalled of Mr. Tunnell's post-playing career. "He would just say 'I just don't think the kid can play.' He never tried to put a kid down for something he couldn't do."

Mr. Tunnell's biggest adjustments, according to friends, came after his playing days, as pro football entered its era of big business.

"It was a terrific adjustment for him," Mr. Robustelli said. "Em was very frustrated by things he couldn't control. I think he became very sensitive."

Others felt that Mr. Tunnell's sensitivity on such issues as the failure of pro teams to hire black head coaches or more black management executives was justified.

The talented and innovative Emlen Tunnell was one of football's greatest defensive players.

The New York Times WEDNESDAY, NOVEMBER 8, 1978

Tunney, Boxing Champion Who Beat Dempsey, Dies

Gene Tunney, the former heavyweight boxing champion who twice defeated Jack Dempsey, died yesterday at the Greenwich Hospital in Connecticut. He was 80 years old and had been suffering from a circulation ailment.

Mr. Tunney, who won the title by scoring a 10-round decision over Jack Dempsey in 1926, retired undefeated as champion two years later after just two more bouts—one of them a return match with Dempsey that produced the famous "long count" of 1927.

His retirement the next year at the age of 30 stunned the boxing world, but the champion, who had won $2 million, had no regrets. In contrast to other fighters whose earnings slipped away, Mr. Tunney managed to hold onto much of his winnings and enjoyed a later career as a successful executive and officer of several corporations and banks.

The father of former Senator John V. Tunney of California, Mr. Tunney is survived also by his wife, the former Polly Lauder; two other sons, Gene L. and Jonathon R. Tunney, and a daughter, Joan Tunney Cook.

Mr. Tunney, who earned $990,445 for his first bout with Dempsey, collected his first paycheck of $5 as an office boy in New York. Educated only in the public schools, he rose to an eminence that saw him lecture on Shakespeare at Yale.

Mr. Tunney was born in New York, at 416 West 52d Street, on May 25, 1898. He was the son of a longshoreman and had three brothers and a sister. Mr. Tunney acquired the name of Gene because of his baby sister's inability to pronounce "Jim" properly.

His family moved to Greenwich Village when he was three months old. There Gene attended school until he was 16, when he went to work. In his leisure time he engaged in a variety of athletic activities but showed a preference for boxing.

Mr. Tunney engaged in two professional fights as a middleweight before joining the United States Marines in 1917. During his service in France, he participated in boxing programs, showing a skill and strength that enabled him to rise to the light-heavyweight championship of the American Expeditionary Force in 1918.

After returning home, Mr. Tunney resumed his professional career, and in 1922 he captured the light-heavyweight championship of the United States from Battling Levinsky.

Mr. Tunney lost the title the same year to Harry Greb in a one-sided 15-rounder. It was the only setback ever experienced by Mr. Tunney in a professional ring career of 65 fights.

The defeat by Greb was only a temporary setback, however, and Mr. Tunney soon engaged Greb again, this time winning easily.

After a 15-round defeat of Georges Carpentier on July 24, 1924, and a 12-round knockout of Tommy Gibbons on June 5, 1925, Mr. Tunney emerged as one of the challengers for the heavyweight championship, then held by Dempsey. A title fight was arranged for Sept. 23, 1926, in Philadelphia, and turned out to be one of the most successful promotions in the history of boxing.

Gene Tunney—World Heavyweight Champion 1926–1928.

A crowd of 118,736 paid a total of $1,895,723 to watch the methodical Tunney win a decisive victory over the defending champion, who was the 4-to-1 favorite.

A rematch was widely demanded by fight fans who refused to believe the Manassa Mauler could be beaten, and was arranged by Tex Rickard, the promoter, in Chicago.

This fight, staged on Sept. 22, 1927, was even more successful than the Philadelphia one. As a promotion it drew a crowd of 102,450 and receipts of $2,658,660 at Soldier Field. Its climax was the matter of the "long count."

Tunney won the decision, again in 10 rounds, but before he did he suffered a knockdown that thousands of witnesses swore was a proper knockdown. It occurred in the seventh round when Dempsey landed six punches to the jaw to floor the ex-marine in a neutral corner.

Tunney dropped, his legs crumpled under him, his eyes dull, his mouth agape and his right arm groping for a ring strand that escaped his feeble clutch.

The knockdown timekeeper, Paul Beeler, started counting from his post outside the ring as soon as Tunney fell. Referee Dave Barry, however, motioned Dempsey to a corner opposite his fallen foe. Dempsey stood, defiantly, in the corner almost immediately above Tunney, and it was not until Beeler's count had gone to four that Dempsey moved. Then Barry started counting at "one."

With a great effort, Tunney regained his feet at "nine" on the referee's count. He gave an exhibition of superb defensive boxing and back-pedalling to survive the round. He came out strong for the eighth, in which he sent Dempsey to one knee with a right to the jaw, and remained the master to the end.

It was for this fight that Mr. Tunney was paid $990,445. He engaged in only one more contest after that, defeating Tom Heeney of New Zealand at Yankee Stadium on July 26, 1928.

Mr. Tunney had enjoyed little popularity among fight fans. He was a boxer in a time when punchers like Jack Dempsey were idolized. After his retirement the fans resented his blandness, his literacy, his wealth and his decision to retire undefeated.

Mr. Tunney had a genuine love for learning, and read extensively. He was a Shakespeare enthusiast in his fighting days, and while he held the title he lectured on the Bard before 200 students at Yale, where he was made an honorary member of Pundits, society of wits and scholars.

A dazed Gene Tunney grabs one of the ropes as the referee begins the famous "long count." The respite may have been crucial for Tunney.

The New York Times SUNDAY, MARCH 21, 1937.

HARRY VARDON, 66, NOTED GOLFER, DIES

British Star's Record of Six Open Championships in Own Country Never Equaled

Wireless to THE NEW YORK TIMES.

LONDON, March 20.—Harry Vardon, generally regarded as one of the greatest of all golfers, died at his home in Totteridge, Hertfordshire, today of pleurisy at the age of 66. He had suffered from chest trouble for many years.

Never Took Lesson

LONDON, March 20 (AP).—Harry Vardon, who never took a golf lesson in his life, ranked jointly with Bobby Jones as one of the two greatest masters the game ever produced.

Death resulted from a chill he contracted Wednesday evening while walking around the South Herts golf course, which only six years ago he shot in 67 strokes.

His passing removed the only player whom English and Scottish adherents of the game ever were willing to mention in the same breath with Jones. They still are undecided which was the greater. Vardon, a member of the Ryder Cup team in 1921, had won sixty-two first-class championships.

While his game was well-rounded, Vardon will remain famous principally for his beautiful iron shots, which those who watched him during his best years say never will be equaled. He gained the reputation of being an indifferent putter, but his admirers declare this was exaggerated.

His clubs were almost the lightest used by a ranking player. His favorite was the cleek, which he used almost to the exclusion of the brassie. He was one of the first golfers to wear plus fours.

One of his last recorded appearances in championship play was in the 1927 open at St. Andrews, which Jones won with what then was a record total of 285.

The fickle public—even at St. Andrews—had forgotten Vardon as 5,000 of them followed Jones onto the rambling fifth green. Vardon, all alone with his caddy, was playing onto the fourteenth, a few yards away. As the crowd threatened to overrun his ball, the veteran was seen standing over it valiantly fighting them off. Nobody recognized him.

HELPED POPULARIZE GOLF

Played Large Role in Making the Game One for Millions

By WILLIAM D. RICHARDSON

The death of Harry Vardon will be mourned wherever the game of golf is played, especially by linksmen who were in the game up to the early 1920's.

No man played a greater part in building up this game, which is now the recreation of millions in almost every nation on earth, than this product of the little village of Grouville on the Isle of Jersey in the English Channel.

Not only will he be remembered for the prodigious feats he performed on the links but for his influence as a master stylist. He won the British open on six occasions, the years being 1896, 1898, 1899, 1903, 1911 and 1914; he was runner-up in 1900, 1901, 1902 and 1912, twice finished third, once fourth and four times fifth—a record of consistency.

He also played a large rôle in the development of golf in America, focusing attention on the game, which was then in its infancy here by his triumph in the national open at the Chicago Golf Club in 1900.

On the occasion of Vardon's first trip here he made a tour of the country playing exhibition matches during which he was on the winning end of fifty, halved two and lost only thirteen, eleven of his losses coming when he played the best ball of two opponents.

That tour, made thirty-seven years ago, marked the beginning of golf exhibitions in this country. It was the first serious missionary effort American golf had ever enjoyed and following it golf stocks of manufacturers became rapidly depleted and golf, then confined almost solely to men of means, was here to stay.

Thirteen years later Vardon returned to America, accompanied by Ted Ray, rollicking, pipe-smoking Englishman. That year the open championship was held at the Brookline course and at the end of the seventy-two-hole journey Vardon and Ray had been tied by a mere stripling of a youth whose name was Francis Ouimet.

On the day following this 19-year-old ex-caddie wrote America's emancipation proclamation in so far as golf was concerned when he beat his two noted adversaries. The news of that triumph went all over the world, but its effect was principally on America. Not only did it bring golf into the headlines of newspapers, but it stirred the imaginations of thousands of boys and lifted the game out of the category of a "sissy" pastime, limited in scope to a few old but wealthy individuals.

Vardon returned to America in 1920 and, at Inverness, Toledo, finished second, one stroke behind his traveling companion, Ray.

How Vardon came to learn the game is an interesting story in itself. It appears that on a certain Sabbath morning a party of English gentlemen arrived from the mainland and proceded to lay out a course on the common. This intrusion was resented until it was learned that permission had been duly granted.

Was a Caddy at 7

Within a few weeks the course was in operation and among the lads who carried clubs was the boy Vardon, then 7 years old, son of a gardener and one of a family of eight.

Vardon, his brother Tom, now a professional at the White Bear Club in St Paul, and some of the other youngsters were not content merely carrying clubs for others. They laid out a course of their own. Each hole measured fifty yards, their clubs were crude affairs fashioned out of blackthorn shafts driven into lady oak heads. The balls were marbles.

Observing others for whom he caddied and playing on this course was the only instruction Vardon ever had.

Caddying failed to meet all the necessities of the Vardon family and at 13 Harry became a gardener, to a man named Major Spofford who, being a golfer himself, gave young Harry a set of clubs and often took him with him to play.

His encouragement, plus the fact that brother Tom had left home to learn the art of club-making at St. Anne's, finally led Vardon into a field in which he was to become outstanding.

His first golfing job was as pro and greenkeeper at the Studley Royal Club at Ripon. Later he went to the Bury Club and it was from there he registered when he played in the British open for the first time at Prestwick in 1893.

The following year he finished fifth in the event, but two years later he won the first of six championships—an unequaled record. In that one he and Taylor tied with a total of 316 at Muirfield and Vardon won in a play-off. He scored at Prestwick in 1898 with a total of 307, won at Sandwich in 1899 with 310, registered 300 to win at Prestwick in 1903, scored 303 to win at Sandwich in 1911 and finished first at Prestwick in 1914 with 306.

Took Part in Big Money Matches

At the time Vardon came along, the era of big money matches in which the professionals played either for their own money or money put up by their followers was just coming to an end, but he did participate in many, once beating Willie Park over North Berwick and Ganton for £100 a side (roughly $500). He and Taylor played as partners in many, often opposing the two Scots, J. H. Braid and Alex Herd.

Three of those men, Vardon, Braid and Taylor, formed what was known as the "Great Triumvirate" and dominated British professional golf. There was a period from 1894, when Taylor won his first crown, to 1914, when Vardon won his last, that the open was almost their joint property. Only five times during those twenty-one years did it happen that one of the three did not win the title.

Harry Vardon—winner of six British Open championships—is considered by many to be the greatest golfer ever.

The New York Times TUESDAY, MAY 31, 1955.

Vukovich Is Killed Seeking Third Straight Indianapolis Auto Race Victory

Fatal Speedway Accident Occurs On Driver's 5th 500 Appearance

Vukovich, Twice Coast Midget Champion, Started Big-Car Competition in 1950

Special to The New York Times.

INDIANAPOLIS, May 30—Bill Vukovich was killed today attempting to accomplish what no others had been able to do—win the 500-mile auto race here three times in a row. Only two others, Mauri Rose and Wilbur Shaw, had taken two successive 500's.

Before his victories in 1953 and 1954, Vukovich had shown his tailpipe to the field through most of the 1952 race before a steering gear failure caused him to hit the wall on the 192d lap. His car was out, but he was unhurt.

Vukovich's successes in those three years were achieved in the Fuel Injection Special entered by Howard Keck of Los Angeles. This year Keck failed to get his new car ready in time for the race.

Car Seventh Last Year

Bill switched to a Hopkins Special entered by Lindsey Hopkins of Miami, Fla. The car was driven by Pat O'Connor last year and finished seventh.

The $57,750 Vukovich won in lap-prize money in his three big years made him the leader in lap-prize earnings.

The 1,000 points Vukovich earned for winning the 500 last year tied Bill with Jimmy Reece for fourth place in the American Automobile Association national standings. In 1953 he ranked third.

This was his fifth appearance at the Indianapolis track. His first appearance was in 1951 when his Central Excavating Special dropped from the running after twenty-nine laps with an oil leak.

Although he had been racing since 1938, Vukovich started driving big cars only in 1950. He was the national midget champion in 1950 and he won the Pacific Coast midget crowns in 1946 and 1947.

Since confining his racing to the 500, Bill spent most of his time managing two service stations in his home town of Fresno, Calif. He was 36 years old, 5 feet 8 inches tall and weighed 155 pounds.

Vukovich had iron nerves. He was a soft-spoken man of few words. He was loved by the men who worked on his cars and in the pits. He was admired by every driver in the land for his great skill at the wheel. Only a few in the history of the 500 could match his endurance.

Only yesterday Ralph De Palma, now 72, who had won the classic in 1915 and had driven in the race eleven times without relief, had congratulated Vukie for his three "unrelieved" races here. "I think," said De Palma, "that you can do it again."

Pit Signals 'Way Ahead'

The last time Vukovich flashed by his pit, his "boys" signalled him that he was well ahead. Vukie could see the disabled car of his chief rival, Jack McGrath, in the pit that adjoined his own. His own car was running perfectly. He had planned to go many more laps before going in for tires and fuel.

That was the last time his wife, Esther, saw him. She was sitting in the stands at the finish line. When the yellow flags and the yellow lights went on, she sat tense.

The slowed-down cars passed three times. Car No. 4 was not among them. She then sensed that something had gone wrong. She was escorted to the hospital area. It was there that she received the news.

The Vukovich's two children, Marlene, 13, and William, Jr., 11, are back in Fresno.

Bill Vukovich was America's foremost auto racing driver at the time of his death.

The New York Times TUESDAY, DECEMBER 6, 1955.

HONUS WAGNER DIES AT AGE OF 81

Shortstop, One of Baseball Immortals, Made Mark With Pittsburgh Club

MANY RECORDS STAND

Played Most Games, 2,785, and Led League 8 Times—Lifetime Average of .328

PITTSBURGH, Tuesday, Dec. 6 (AP)—John (Honus) Wagner, one of baseball's greatest shortstops, died today at his home in near-by Carnegie. He was 81 years old.

The bandy-legged, barrel-chested star of the early part of the century, had been in ill health for the last several years.

Ranked Among the Immortals

Baseball can be as controversial a topic as politics, especially when it comes to ranking the great players of the past and present. But, as with Babe Ruth, Ty Cobb, Christy Mathewson and a select few other outstanding performers, there has been almost perfect unanimity among the experts that Honus Wagner belonged among the immortals of the game.

In fact, there are many who will argue that the "Flying Dutchman" should be placed at the top of the list. Be this as it may, there have been or are now no serious challengers to Mr. Wagner in his generally accepted designation as baseball's greatest shortstop.

It was at this position that Mr. Wagner performed for the greater part of his twenty-one consecutive years of major league service, from 1897 through 1917. In various emergencies, he filled in at other spots, in fact, playing every position except catcher. He still is regarded as the yardstick of excellence for shortstops.

Mr. Wagner also was one of the most noted batsmen of his day, and many of the records he set are still on the books. He had a lifetime mark of .328, hitting more than .300 in seventeen successive seasons. He led the National League eight times, 1900, 1903, 1904, 1906, 1907, 1908, 1909 and 1911.

His lifetime fielding mark was .945, and he was first among the National League shortstops in 1912, 1914 and 1915. In addition, he led his league in stolen bases in 1902, 1904, 1907 and 1908.

Some of Mr. Wagner's records that still are on the books are the National League marks for playing the most games, 2,785; leading the league the most times in batting, eight; hitting more than .300 the most times, seventeen, and making the most hits, 3,430; the most runs, 1,740, and most total bases, 4,878. His batting feats were all the more remarkable since he had to contend with such obstacles as trick pitches, long outfields and a "dead" ball.

Mr. Wagner was modest and good natured. He avoided disputes with the umpires and had no salary wrangles with his employers. He never was a holdout. In fact, it is said that he often signed blank contracts, leaving it to the late Barney Dreyfuss, president of the Pirates, to fill in a figure he considered fair.

His love for baseball went far deeper than the money he made in the game. He played for the love of playing and his interest in baseball survived his playing days and he retained his active connections until the very end.

Mr. Wagner was born in Carnegie, Pa., on Feb. 24, 1874. He was christened John Peter, but during his baseball career he was familiarly known as Honus or Hans. The "Flying Dutchman" sobriquet, fastened on him by the fans, was indicative of the dash and speed he displayed in the field and on the baselines.

After gaining prominence on the sandlots while earning his livelihood as a barber, Mr. Wagner broke into professional baseball in 1895 with the Steubenville (Ohio) club. He received a trial at the insistence of his older brother, Albert, also a ballplayer, who refused to sign unless the club took Honus as well.

Mr. Wagner was an immediate success at Steubenville and the next year advanced to the Paterson, N. J., club of the old Atlantic League. His play at Paterson attracted the attention of the Louisville club, then a member of the National League and operated by Mr. Dreyfuss. Louisville purchased Mr. Wagner's release for $2,200, and he began his major league career with the Colonels in 1897, winning a regular position at the start.

In 1900 the National League circuit was reduced from twelve teams to eight and Mr. Dreyfuss bought the Pittsburgh franchise, taking Mr. Wagner with him. The shortstop remained with the Pirates until he retired from active play in 1917 at the age of 43. In his final season he was made manager of the team, but the task was not to his liking and he gave it up after less than a week.

After leaving the Pirates, Wagner continued to play semi-professional baseball in the Pittsburgh area until he was well past 50. During this period he served as manager of a sporting goods store and in other ways kept in contact with baseball. He was appointed an assistant sergeant-at-arms in the Pennsylvania State Legislature in 1929, and once was nominated for the office of Sheriff in Pittsburgh.

Mr. Wagner was brought back to his old team in an official capacity in 1933, when he was appointed a coach. He had served continuously with the Pirates ever since; the sight of his rugged, bow-legged figure on the field awakened nostalgic feelings among the old-timers in the stands.

Throughout his career one of the outstanding features about Mr. Wagner was his vitality. One of the strongest players in the game in his active days—he weighed 190 pounds and was 5 feet 11 inches tall—he possessed an amazing vigor, even after he had passed 60, and he often set the pace for his youthful charges in the pre-game workouts of the Pirates.

During his term as coach of Pittsburgh, Mr. Wagner also served for several years as commissioner for the National Semi-Pro Baseball Congress, in which capacity he had jurisdiction over 25,000 sandlot teams.

In 1936, he was among the first group of stars named to baseball's Hall of Fame. He retired on a Pirate pension in 1951, and two years later the locker he had used as player and coach was shipped to the baseball shrine at Cooperstown, N. Y.

At the turn of the century the bat-manufacturing concern of Hillerich & Bradsby conceived the idea of having major league ball players endorse their product, with the players autographing their particular models. Mr. Wagner was the first to have his autograph appear on one of these bats. This was in 1905.

Although in recent years Mr. Wagner remained confined to his home in Carnegie, honors continued to be showered upon him. On the occasion of his eightieth birthday in 1954, he was deluged with greetings, one of them from President Eisenhower.

With the opening of the 1954 season at Forbes Field in Pittsburgh, the Pirates, as part of the inaugural day ceremonies, presented a special plaque to Wagner as baseball's Mr. Shortstop. It was accepted by his daughter, Mrs. Harry Blair. His 3-year-old granddaughter, Leslie Ann Blair, then threw out the first ball.

A bronze statue of Mr. Wagner was unveiled in Schenley Park in Pittsburgh on April 30 of this year. A public campaign had provided the $30,000 needed for the statue. The great shortstop, weakened by age, saw the unveiling from an automobile parked near adjacent Forbes Field, where he had played for the Pirates half a century before.

John "Honus" Wagner, with a lifetime batting average of .328, was the greatest hitting shortstop of all time.

The New York Times — MONDAY, DECEMBER 16, 1968

Jess Willard, Boxing Champion, Dies at 86

Giant Fighter Beat Johnson and Lost to Dempsey

LOS ANGELES, Dec. 15 (AP) — Jess Willard, the former heavyweight boxing champion, who won the title from Jack Johnson and lost it to Jack Dempsey in two of the sport's most controversial fights, died here today of a cerebral hemorrhage. He was 86 years old. He was admitted to Pacoima Memorial Lutheran Hospital yesterday after suffering a heart attack.

Survivors include his widow, Hattie, and two sons, Jess Jr. and Alan.

Embroiled in Controversy

Willard lived in the shadow of another man's legend.

The moment of his greatest triumph, 53 years ago in Havana, was frozen in one of sport's most famous and controversial photographs: He towers over the supine Jack Johnson, whom he has just knocked down, waiting to be hailed as the new heavyweight champion of the world.

But Johnson's gloves seem to be shading his eyes from the boiling Cuban sun. Generations believed the loser, when he later said he had thrown the fight for $50,000 and the promise of relief from police persecution.

"If Johnson throwed that fight," Willard often said, "I wished he throwed it sooner. It was hotter than hell down there."

A current hit play, "The Great White Hope," embellished the Johnson legend, and assigned Willard a more grotesque and symbolic role in it. After the two men fought, the character based on Johnson was helped from the arena, but the character based on Willard was borne out in triumph, more dead than alive.

The tragedy of Willard's career was pointed up by the discovery in 1960 of a print of the film of his fight with Johnson, and later the assembly of other old movies of his ring appearances — the fight with Jack Dempsey and others.

Viewers of these films, most of them experts on boxing, agreed on two major factors: Willard was quite possibly the most underrated of all heavyweight champions.

Willard was an excellent

Jess Willard (center), the "White Hope," squared up to Jack Johnson on April 5, 1915.

boxer who could also punch; he was not the big awkward giant he had for so long been pictured.

"I'm glad some of these things finally came out, even if it was 45 years too late," Willard recently said.

Willard was born Dec. 29, 1881, in the Pottawatomie Indian land in Kansas. He was raised on a farm.

He had 36 fights, but the two that remain indelibly imprinted in boxing history are the championship bouts with Johnson and Dempsey.

The movie of the Johnson fight on a Havana race track April 5, 1915, showed that it was an even contest for 20 rounds. Willard amazed his erstwhile critics with his footwork, his long straight left jab —he had a reach of 84 inches —and his ability to take Johnson's best punches.

Willard knocked Johnson out in the 26th round of the scheduled 45-round match. The fight lasted one hour 44 minutes in weather well over 100 degrees.

Johnson Said He Threw It

It was not until five years later that Johnson, penniless and living in Paris, sold a magazine article in which he asserted he deliberately lost the fight at Havana.

Johnson was in trouble with the United States Government, which had forced him to flee the country, and a law had been passed prohibiting interstate shipment of prizefight films.

Therefore, as the years passed and the movie remained outlawed, the public was unable to determine what had happened at Havana.

As for the Dempsey fight, again, it was a broiling day, July 4, 1919, at Toledo, Ohio. Willard came in at 245 pounds and his 6-foot 7-inch frame towered over the shorter, compact 187-pound Dempsey.

Willard stabbed at the weaving Dempsey a few times and then the carnage began. Willard had never been knocked off his feet. Dempsey floored him seven times in the first round.

In moments, the right side of Willard's face was battered. His cheek and jaw bones were fractured. His right eye was shut and he floundered around the ring, gamely getting up after each knockdown.

Films show that Dempsey stood over the fallen Willard and hit him before he could get to his feet.

"I'd say," commented Willard, "the referee didn't exactly give me the best of it."

Cheers for Game Loser

Dempsey was unable to floor Willard again in either the second or third rounds. Willard was physically unable to answer the bell for the fourth.

Mrs. Willard recalled that on the way back to their home in California, news had drifted ahead of their train that Willard was aboard. At each station fans crowded the platform to cheer the old champion.

"I never thought people would want to see me again," he told his wife.

Willard contended all his life that Dempsey's gloves — or at least the left one that did all the damage — contained something other than the usual padding.

He blamed Dempsey's manager, the late Jack Kearns, and Kearns once, in joking, told The Associated Press: "Naw, I didn't use plaster of Paris on the bandages. It was cement."

Before becoming a fighter, Willard had been breaking horses, running a wagon train and farming.

"One day I saw some fellows straining to lift a bale of cotton," he said. "It must of weighed 500 pounds. I lifted it up on the wagon and they said, "With your size and strength, why don't you take up fighting?"

Willard sold his wagons and went to Oklahoma City to train. "I never had a glove on until I was 28," he said. This began his career in the ring, which also included a tour with the old Sells Floto Circus, another circus that he eventually bought, and a brief career in silent movies.

Willard's fights were all main events billed for 10 or more rounds. He scored 20 knockouts — a fighter named Bull Young, died in a hospital after being knocked out by Willard—won 4 decisions, lost 3 by decision, lost 1 on an unintentional foul, had 4 no-decision matches, 1 draw and was stopped twice — by Dempsey and Luis Firpo.

Willard eventually bought the 101 Ranch Circus, but misfortune stepped in. World War I came along and the Government, in need of his riding stock, bought him out, ending that source of revenue.

Willard never sought fame and was reluctant in later years to make public appearances. During World War II, however, he emerged from semiseclusion to join groups of boxing people on visits to military camps.

These were the last of the old champion's bows to the public.

The New York Times SATURDAY, NOVEMBER 5, 1955

CY YOUNG IS DEAD; FAMED PITCHER, 88

His Record of 511 Victories Has Never Been Surpassed —Hurled 3 No-Hit Games

NEWCOMERSTOWN, Ohio, Nov. 4 (AP)—Denton True (Cy) Young, one of baseball's great pitchers, died today at the age of 88.

A member of baseball's Hall of Fame, Mr. Young was stricken while sitting in a chair in the home of Mr. and Mrs. John Benedum, with whom he made his home near here.

His Feats Unequaled

Traded to the majors from the minors for a suit of clothing, Cy Young thrilled the baseball world from 1890 to 1911 with a blazing fast ball that set pitching records still unequaled.

Six feet two inches tall and weighing 210 pounds, this Ohio farmer pitched and won more games than any major leaguer. When he retired at the age of 45 because his legs had weakened, he had won 511 of 826 decisions in both leagues and for five teams. In all, he hurled in 906 games.

As the starting pitcher for the Boston Red Sox in 1903, Mr. Young threw the first pitch in a world series game. Fifty years later, as a guest at the opening game of the world series between the Brooklyn Dodgers and New York Yankees, he stood in the pitcher's box and threw a ceremonial strike to the Yankee catcher, Yogi Berra, to open the series. He was 86 at the time.

During his career, he was a thirty-game winner five seasons; a twenty-game victor sixteen times. He pitched one perfect game, two other no-hit shutouts and performed the "iron man" feat of hurling and winning complete games of a doubleheader.

One of the early members of the baseball Hall of Fame at Cooperstown, N. Y., Mr. Young pitched for the Cleveland Nationals, St. Louis Cardinals, Red Sox and Cleveland Indians and Boston Braves. He won 291 National League games and 220 in the American.

Had 36-10 Mark in 1892

For fourteen consecutive years, beginning in 1891, Mr. Young won twenty or more games. The 1892 season, when he posted a 36-10 record, was his best.

Mr. Young's feat of pitching twenty-three consecutive hitless innings over a four-game span early in 1904 still stands as a major league record. His total of 2,836 strikeouts was surpassed only by the late Walter Johnson's 3,497.

He was born on a farm in Gilmore, Ohio, on March 29, 1867. While pitching for the Canton (Ohio) club of the old Tri-State League in 1890, Mr. Young was nicknamed Cy. "I thought I had to show all my stuff," he recalled years later, "and I almost tore the boards off the grandstand with my fast ball. One of the fellows called me 'Cyclone,' but finally shortened it to 'Cy,' and it's been that ever since."

The league disbanded during the 1890 season and the pitcher joined the Cleveland Nationals early in August of that year.

Still a gawky country boy, he made his major league debut against Cap Anson's Chicago White Stockings and won the game. Mr. Young won 10 and lost 7 for Cleveland during the late stages of the season. Two of those victories were obtained on Oct. 4, when he captured both ends of a doubleheader against Philadelphia.

In his first complete major league campaign the next year, Mr. Young won 27 and lost 22 games. For the next thirteen seasons he stayed above the .500 mark. He pitched his first major league no-hit, no-run contest on Sept. 18, 1897, blanking Cincinnati, 6 to 0. His affiliation with Cleveland ended after the 1898 campaign and he played with the St. Louis Cardinals in 1899 and 1900.

Mr. Young began eight years with the Red Sox in 1901. While blanking Philadelphia on May 5, 1904, he did not permit an opposing runner to reach first base. It was the third perfect game in major league history. On June 30, 1908, he won his third no-hit, no-run decision in the majors by shutting out New York, 8 to 0.

He was traded to the Cleveland Indians in 1909, and in the middle of the 1911 campaign was traded to the Braves. He retired to his farm near Peoli, Ohio, after that season.

Denton "Cy" Young, the winningest pitcher in baseball history.

Babe Zaharias

"All the News That's Fit to Print"

The New York Times.

LATE CITY EDITION
Condensation of U. S. Weather Bureau forecast:
Rain, windy and cool today.
Rain ending, little milder tomorrow.
Temperature range today: 60—48.
Temperature range yesterday: 57.1—48.8
Full U. S. Weather Bureau Report, Page 54.

VOL. CVI..No. 36,042. Entered as Second-Class Matter, Post Office, New York, N. Y. NEW YORK, FRIDAY, SEPTEMBER 28, 1956. Times Square, New York 36, N. Y. Telephone Lackawanna 4-1000 FIVE CENTS

EISENHOWER HEEDS FRIENDS' APPEALS FOR MORE TALKS

Says Many Have Asked Him to Give Speeches in Their Areas—Declines Most

BALKS AT BARNSTORMING

But Adds '2 or 3' TV Dates—Asserts Health Is No Bar to Stepped-Up Drive

Transcript and summary of the news conference, Page 14.

By RUSSELL BAKER
Special to The New York Times.

WASHINGTON, Sept. 27—President Eisenhower took the relaxed view of the election race today, but explained that he would campaign a little harder to please his many "good friends."

Still, he told his news conference, he does not intend to do "one-tenth of what a lot of people" want him to do in the way of campaign activity.

He expects to make two or three television speeches in addition to the six originally planned, he said. He insisted again, however, that he would not go "barnstorming" or "whistle-stopping."

And excursions like his 150-mile drive through Iowa last week, he suggested, will be undertaken only when necessary to transport him from an airport to a speaking site.

Political Compass Boxed

Health, the President said, is no consideration against campaigning. Although he is now leading "a somewhat more ordered life" than before his heart attack, he reported, he has noticed no ill effects from his recently stepped-up golfing and campaigning.

The questions put to him this morning boxed the political compass from Adlai E. Stevenson and Dr. Milton S. Eisenhower to Senator Joseph R. McCarthy, Ezra Taft Benson and Dean Acheson.

The answers supplied little new information about the progress of the campaign. But they showed the President in a relatively mellow mood toward the enemy and less than frantic about the progress of the fight.

Only twice did he speak sharply: Once while defending his brother, Dr. Milton S. Eisenhower, from attack by Mr. Stevenson and again while deploring his own party's efforts to paint the Democrats as the "war party."

He had been asked about Republican campaign literature

Continued on Page 14, Column 3

PRESIDENT BACKS BROTHER ON PERON

Denies Appeasement Policy—Loans Truman's, He Says

Special to The New York Times.

WASHINGTON, Sept. 27—President Eisenhower mounted a counter-offensive today against a Democratic charge that his brother had been responsible for appeasing the dictatorship of Juan D. Perón in Argentina.

The President spoke to his news conference on the subject with considerable warmth. He said that the Truman Administration, not his, had been responsible for $130,000,000 in loans to the former Argentine dictator.

Hence, he argued, if Perón had used United States money to build a private bank balance of $100,000,000 in Switzerland, as charged by Adlai E. Stevenson, the fault was with the Truman Administration. Under his Administration, the President said, no money was lent to Perón.

The debate over United States relations with the deposed dictator was started Tuesday by Mr. Stevenson. The Democratic Presidential nominee charged then that Dr. Milton S. Eisenhower, the President's youngest brother, had fostered an appeasement policy toward Perón.

Mr. Stevenson contended that Dr. Eisenhower, assuming "informal responsibility," had kept a United States Ambassador in Buenos Aires "because Perón liked him." The Ambassador was Albert F. Nufer.

During this same period, he

Continued on Page 16, Column 6

Stevenson Asks Expansion Of Economy to Block Reds

Holds G.O.P. Offers 'Bread and Circuses' Rather Than Progressive Vision—Nominee Cheered in St. Louis

By HARRISON E. SALISBURY
Special to The New York Times.

ST. LOUIS, Sept. 27—Adlai E. Stevenson warned tonight that within twenty years the Communist nations might seize production leadership from the free world.

He called for a rational pro-

Text of the Stevenson address appears on Page 16.

gram of mobilizing America's unparalleled resources of raw materials, managerial genius and skilled labor to meet this and the other great challenges of the twentieth century.

Instead of facing the issues of the day, he charged, the Eisenhower Administration has embarked upon a program of "bread and circuses." It is giving the people, he said, "cant and slogans and streamers and balloons and ballyhoo" instead of clear thinking and progressive vision.

Mr. Stevenson's indictment of the Eisenhower Administration was presented to an audience of 3,300 persons in the Missouri Theatre. It was the Democratic nominee's second major address in Missouri within two days.

Mr. Stevenson is fighting hard to assure a Democratic victory in this key state with 13 electoral votes. He was told by leading Democrats that he held a substantial margin and should carry the state comfortably in November. But he is taking no chances in this Midwestern area.

Mr. Stevenson got the biggest demonstration of his current tour in downtown St. Louis. His motorcade passed through the center of the city just after 6 P. M. Crowds lined the streets and swarmed out to surround his car at several points. Someone had provided bags of confetti to many of the onlookers.

The nominee was...

Continued...

LINCOLN SQ. PLANS ADVANCED BY CITY DESPITE PROTESTS

Estimate Board Authorizes Negotiation—Pledges Aid to Displaced Residents

By PAUL CROWELL

The $175,000,000 Lincoln Square redevelopment project moved a step nearer realization yesterday.

By unanimous vote, the Board of Estimate authorized the city's Committee on Slum Clearance to negotiate contracts with the Federal Government and private sponsors for redevelopment of the eighteen-block area into an art and cultural center with modern housing facilities.

Before the board voted, Mayor Wagner read into the ... formal statement, ... the other members ... concurred ... sible ...

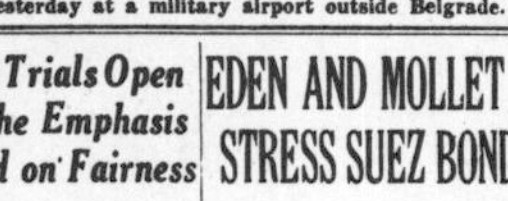

TO RUSSIA: Yugoslavia's President Tito, center, his wife and Nikita ... before boarding plane yesterday at a military airport outside Belgrade.
Associated Press Radiophoto

TITO VISITS SOVIET WITH KHRUSHCHEV IN PUZZLING MOVE

Sudden Trip Follows Talks on Undisclosed Topics With Moscow Leader

PARTY TIES HELD ISSUE

Journey Despite Marshal's Distaste for Flying Seen as Indication of Urgency

By ELIE ABEL
Special to The New York Times

BELGRADE, Yugoslavia, Sept. 27—President Tito of Yugoslavia flew off to the Soviet Union early today with Nikita S. Khrushchev on a mission whose nature was not disclosed.

Western Ambassadors and the Belgrade public were dumfounded by the news, which was published six hours after the two leaders had taken off from a military airport at Batajnica.

The circumstances of Marshal Tito's abrupt departure—without a word of explanation to the Yugoslav public or the Western powers—suggest that his secret talks on Brioni Island with Mr. Khrushchev over the past week had raised questions of highest importance and urgency.

The most straightforward line of speculation here was that the talks had reached a stage where Mr. Khrushchev, who is Soviet Communist party chief, was unwilling or unable to make a commitment without consulting his partners in the Soviet collective leadership.

No Word to U. S. Aide

Marshal Tito seemed oblivious to the effect of his trip on Western opinion. United States aid to Yugoslavia is to be terminated by act of Congress unless President Eisenhower certifies before Oct. 16 that its continuance would be in the national interest.

The Yugoslav Foreign Ministry did nothing before or after Marshal Tito's departure to cushion the shock. No effort was made to call in the United States Chargé d'Affaires, Robert Gay Hooker, to explain what President Tito hoped to achieve by rushing off to the Soviet Union so soon after his state visit last June. One high Yugoslav official remarked that he hoped the visit would not be misunderstood in the West but did not explain Marshal Tito's objectives.

Official Version Persists

The Yugoslav President was accompanied by two members of the Yugoslav Communist party's Politburo, Aleksander Rankovic and Djuro Pucar, as well as by his wife. M. Rankovic, one of Yugoslavia's four Vice Presidents, made a bitter enemy of Stalin during the events leading up to the 1948 break by his zeal as Minister of Internal Security in countering Soviet espionage. M. Pucar is president of the Assembly of Bosnia-Hercegovina.

The official explanation that Mr. Khrushchev had come to Yugoslavia for a rest was maintained until he left the country today. In the same spirit Tanjug, official news agency, announced that the Yugoslavs would "spend a few days' vacationing on the Black Sea."

The Tanjug bulletin published at 1 P. M. said Mr. Khrushchev's plane had left Batajnica Airport at 7 A. M. No effort was made to explain why Marshal Tito, whose dislike of planes is well

Continued on Page 9, Column 1

1,900-M.P... Crashes a...

Special to ...

WASHINGTON, Sept. ... fastest and highest-flying ... pilot. The Air Force annou...

... been ... its B...

The ... Capt. Mil... old, of Bu... on an indo... was the first ... the plane's ... was found in ...

There was n... on the cause o... investigation wa... diately.

The experimen... slender, swept-wing ... the first specifically ... lenge the so-called th... rier. This is the point o... speed where so much ... generated that conventi... craft materials lose stren... melt.

To help resist heat at ... speeds, the X-2 was made la... ly of stainless steel and a spec... nickel alloy, rather than con... ventional aluminum alloys. ... was said to have cost $3,000,000.

It was announced within the last two months that the plane had set both world speed and altitude records. The speed mark of about 1,900 miles an hour was made in a test in late July at the Edwards base with Lieut. Col. Frank K. Everest at the controls. This broke the previous record of 1,650 miles an

Continued on Page 12, Column 2

WAGNER ATTACKS JAVITS' POLICIES

Says Foe Backs Reactionary Economic Plans of G. O. P. —Opens Upstate Swing

Text of Mr. Wagner's talk will be found on Page 18.

By DOUGLAS DALES
Special to The New York Times.

BUFFALO, Sept. 27—Mayor Wagner assailed Attorney General Jacob K. Javits tonight as an extoller of reactionary economic policies and an apologist for "dangerous international blunders."

In his strongest attack on his Republican opponent in the race for the United States Senate, Mayor Wagner said Mr. Javits was no "Johnny-come-lately" Republican, but "a Republican by long conviction, a Republican by heart."

The Democratic nominee also hit hard tonight at the economic policies of the Eisenhower Administration, attacking particularly the Administration's hard money policy. He said this had been a boon to the money lenders and had cost the American people $10,000,000,000 in higher interest rates since the Republicans took over.

The Mayor made these charges in an address before an Erie County Democratic rally at the Lafayette Hotel, his first stop on a three-day upstate campaign tour. He spoke to an enthusiastic audience of 1,000 persons. It was his first foray above Westchester since his nomination Sept. 10.

Tomorrow the Mayor is scheduled to meet with labor leaders

Continued on Page 18, Column 4

Babe Zaharias Dies; Athlete Had Cancer

Special to The New York Times.

GALVESTON, Tex., Sept. 27—Mrs. Mildred (Babe) Didrikson Zaharias, famed woman athlete, died of cancer in John Sealy Hospital here this morning. She was 42 years old.

Mrs. Zaharias had been under treatment since 1953, when the malignant condition was discovered after she had won a golf tournament. The tournament was one named for her—the Babe Zaharias Open of Beaumont, Tex., where she was reared.

Mrs. Zaharias had fought valiantly against cancer for the last several months. She remained confident almost to the end that she would get well. Her final weeks were relatively free of pain, although the malignancy was general. Physicians here had performed a cordotomy—a severing of

Continued on Page 30, Column 2

Babe Zaharias Dies; Athlete Had Cancer

Special to The New York Times.
GALVESTON, Tex., Sept. 27—Mrs. Mildred (Babe) Didrikson Zaharias, famed woman athlete, died of cancer in John Sealy Hospital here this morning. She was 42 years old.

Mrs. Zaharias had been under treatment since 1953, when the malignant condition was discovered after she had won a golf tournament. The tournament was one named for her—the Babe Zaharias Open of Beaumont, Tex., where she was reared.

Mrs. Zaharias had fought valiantly against cancer for the last several months. She remained confident almost to the end that she would get well. Her final weeks were relatively free of pain, although the malignancy was general. Physicians here had performed a cordotomy—a severing of

Continued on Page 30, Column 2

X-2 and Flier It Carried to H...

Capt. Milburn G. Apt beside plane in which he was killed
Associated Press Wirephoto (U. S. Air Force)

The rocket plane had set speed and altitude records

...AFT; ... U. S.

...gton ...to ...

...month ... telephone ...tion resort at

Continued on Page 8, Column 5

Poznan Trials Open With the Emphasis Placed on Fairness

By SYDNEY GRUSON
Special to The New York Times.

POZNAN, Poland, Sept. 27—The Poznan trials began today in a klieg-lighted show of official fair play inside the courtroom and a show of police power in the streets.

A state prosecutor conceded the police had used "active ...e" against persons held ...ast June's riots, in which ...ree persons were killed ...veral hundred were ...or injured.

...secutor, Alfons Le... court trying three ...two of them 18 ...e other 20, that ...nt" had taken ... the "very be... ...estigation.

... quickly to ...M. Leman ...sible," he ...een put ...ill have ...s."

...g held ...ld the ...r in... top ...an ...ed,

...YMOND

...mobile driving ... here have been closed in a state-wide crackdown on driving license rackets.

In announcing this yesterday, George M. Bragalini, State Commissioner of Taxation and Finance, said that the licenses of two other schools under investigation had expired and they had not applied for new ones.

Twenty-two school operators or instructors have been arrested, three employes of the Bureau of Motor Vehicles have been dismissed, four others have resigned and 102 driving licenses have been revoked, Mr. Bragalini said.

The Commissioner told a news conference that he had advised Governor Harriman of these results of his eighteen-month investigation of auto driving schools. The report, he explained, is an interim one and the investigation will continue.

State investigators uncovered a case in which a license examiner had awarded passing grades to applicants after "testing" their eyesight in a bar. The applicants read whisky prices on bottle tags.

Mr. Bragalini said that two of the schools that were closed as a result of the inquiry had been "brazenly" carrying on their illegal operations in a building virtually across the street from the New York office of the Bureau of Motor Vehicles. The

Continued on Page 12, Column 2

Pay Rise Reported In Secret Coal Pact

By A. H. RASKIN

John L. Lewis was reported last night to have won another major wage victory without any flurry of strike threats in the nation's coal fields.

Responsible industry sources said the 76-year-old president of the United Mine Workers had initialed a memorandum of understanding with Edward G. Fox, newly appointed chief negotiator for the Northern soft-coal operators.

The pact was negotiated secretly in Washington. It is subject to revision by the full wage committee of the Bituminous Coal Operators Association at a meeting tentatively set for next Wednesday in Pittsburgh. But little fear was indicated on either side that a final accord would be hard to achieve.

Terms of the agreement were kept secret. However, it

Continued on Page 19, Column 5

EDEN AND MOLLET STRESS SUEZ BOND

Two-Day Parley Is Declared to Have Sealed Agreement—Queen Will Visit Paris

British-French communiqué is printed on Page 4.

By HAROLD CALLENDER
Special to The New York Times.

PARIS, Sept. 27—British and French leaders, after long talks today, announced they had agreed to work closely together in the Suez Canal crisis.

They said they would follow a common line on this question in the Security Council. They hoped the Council would recommend negotiation for international operation of the canal. Such operation was urged by the eighteen-nation London conference but rejected by Gamal Abdel Nasser, President of Egypt.

The assertion that the meetings here yesterday and today had "reinforced Franco-British solidarity in all domains" was the dominant theme of the communiqué at the end of the visit of Prime Minister Eden and his Foreign Secretary, Selwyn Lloyd, to Premier Guy Mollet and his Foreign Minister, Christian ...neau.

...lizabeth's Visit in April

...supplementary proof of ...British friendship," to ...erms employed by the ...rench news agency, ...d in a simultaneous ...nt that Queen Eliza... ...ad accepted an invita... ...visit Paris April 8 to 11, ...7.

It was reported on reliable authority that the French-British understanding reached today embraced the following:

¶Agreement to retain the two nations' armed forces in the state of readiness in which they were put just after Egypt's seizure of the Universal Suez Canal Company.

¶Agreement for close consultation on policy in the Middle East generally, where the British and French were rivals until united by what they believed the threat of President Nasser.

[In Washington the International Monetary Fund announced it had lent Egypt $15,000,000 to help meet the cost of needed imports.]

Baghdad Pact Discussed

France and Britain long have disagreed sharply on the Baghdad Pact, which Britain signed with Pakistan, Iran, Iraq and Turkey. This was discussed today. The French were reported to have modified their criticism and even to have considered joining the pact as part of the French-British solidarity they seek.

The test of the pact, in French eyes, will be the extent to which the members stand together on the Suez question.

Much time was spent discussing the United Nations debate on the Suez. The hope was that seven of the eleven members of the Security Council would approve the proposal of the eight

Continued on Page 4, Column 5

Captives Seize Plane In Air, Flee Bolivia

By EDWARD A. MORROW
Special to The New York Times.

LA PAZ, Bolivia, Sept. 27—Bolivian political prisoners seized control of a Government plane in midair today and escaped to Argentina.

The number of prisoners was not known here, but estimates ranged from thirty to fifty. [A United Press dispatch from Salta, Argentina, where the plane landed, said that there were forty-seven prisoners aboard and that they had asked for political asylum.]

The prisoners were to have been flown to La Paz from Santa Cruz, 370 miles southeast of here, by Lloyd Aereo Boliviano, the Government airline.

Radio messages reported that the prisoners had forced the pilot of the DC-4 cargo plane to fly 470 miles southward to Salta.

The political prisoners were

Continued on Page 16, Column 6

MRS. ZAHARIAS, 42, IS DEAD OF CANCER

Continued From Page 1

certain nerves—to relieve her of pain.

A funeral service is scheduled for tomorrow afternoon at the Bethlehem Lutheran Church in Beaumont.

'Greatest Female Athlete'

From the time she made the headlines during the 1932 Olympic Games at Los Angeles, winning the javelin throw and 80-meter hurdles, Mrs. Zaharias reigned as the world's top all-around woman athlete. In 1949 she was voted the greatest female athlete of the half century by The Associated Press, a selection that surprised no one.

The athletic career of Mrs. Zaharias was an unusual one. As a youngster—she was born on June 26, 1914, in Port Arthur, Tex.—she excelled at running, swimming, diving, high-jumping, baseball and basketball in addition to being adept with the javelin and at going over hurdles.

She was a success at any sport she undertook and gave conclusive proof of this with her prowess in golf—a game she began to play in 1935.

At least part of Mrs. Zaharias' success could be attributed to her powers of concentration and diligence. When she decided to center her attention on golf, she tightened up her game by driving as many as 1,000 golf balls a day and playing until her hands were so sore they had to be taped. She developed an aggressive, dramatic style, hitting down sharply and crisply on her iron shots like a man and averaging 240 yards off the tee with her woods.

She began winning golf titles in 1940. In that year she captured the Western and Texas Open Championships. These victories were forerunners of many to come. By the end of 1950 she had the distinction of having won every available golf title. Asked whether she had any idea of retiring, Mrs. Zaharias answered in characteristic style:

"As long as I am improving I will go on, and besides, there's too much money in the business to quit."

She turned professional in 1947, after her triumph in the British Amateur championship, a distinction that she was the first American to earn. In 1948 she won the world championship tournament and the National Open. She repeated her victory in the "world" event the next three years. She was the runner-up in the Nationals in 1949 and came back to win it in 1950.

Mrs. Zaharias was an athlete almost from the time she was strong enough to lift a baseball bat. She beat the boys at mumblety-peg, outsped them in foot races and outshone them in basketball and baseball. Her nickname of "Babe," after Babe Ruth, was acquired after she had hit five home runs in a baseball game. Instead of "wasting time with dolls," she conditioned herself by using a backyard weight-lifting machine built of broomsticks and her mother's flatirons.

The athlete from Texas was a constant source of colorful stories for newspaper men. She once pitched for the St. Louis Cardinals in an exhibition baseball game. She toured the United States giving billiard exhibitions and showed her true versatility with a demonstration of needlework and typing. She could type eighty-six words a minute.

She met her future husband on a golf course in 1937. They were married a year later and eventually set up house in Tampa, Fla., just off a golf course they had purchased in 1951. There Mrs. Zaharias designed a modern pushbutton kitchen and spent considerable time making chintz curtains.

In April, 1953, she underwent an operation for cancer in Beaumont, Tex. By July she had recovered—to play tournament golf again. Ten months after the surgery she won the $5,000 Serbin Women's Open Tournament at Miami Beach.

She regarded her comeback as complete when she won the 1954 Women's United States Open. Mrs. Zaharias' margin was twelve strokes at Peabody, Mass., as she recaptured the title she had held twice previously.

"It will show a lot of people that they need not be afraid of an operation and can go on and live a normal life," she commented shortly after this triumph.

Early in 1955, however, a hip pain sidelined Mrs. Zaharias. After an operation for a ruptured spinal disk, her physicians found that she was again suffering from cancer.

She was in and out of the hospital repeatedly after that, undergoing X-ray treatments for the disease, and early this year she successfully pulled through a siege of pneumonia.

But last July it became necessary to operate to relieve her pain from cancer, and the next month to operate again to by-pass an intestinal obstruction. Her condition steadily became worse.

Mrs. Zaharias accepted stoically the news that the disease had returned "Well, that's the rub of the greens," she told her husband. Together they established the Babe Didrikson Zaharias Fund to support cancer clinics and treatment centers

Her autobiography, "This Life I've Led," as told to Harry Paxton, was published late in 1955. And last July while critically ill, she established the Babe Didrikson Zaharias trophy, to be awarded annually to the American woman amateur athlete who had done the most during the year for women's sports.

Mrs. Zaharias won many golfing prizes. One of these was the Ben Hogan Trophy, named for another famous golfing Texan. This was awarded to her in 1953 by the Golf Writers of America for overcoming a physical handicap to play golf. She was the first winner of this trophy.

During the latter stages of her career as a golfer it was estimated she was earning more than $100,000 a year for exhibitions, endorsements and other activities connected with sports. She drew a considerable salary from a sporting goods company that manufactured equipment bearing her name. Mrs. Zaharias also dipped into the journalistic field, writing instructional articles and a book entitled "Championship Golf."

While she captivated many with her versatile stunts as a youngster, it was her achievements and deportment later in life that gained for her the most popularity. As a young girl she had disdained lipstick, plastered her hair back and talked out of the side of her mouth.

But as a top player and drawing power in golf, her attitude and demeanor changed. The once lonely tomboy became a social success. She developed into a graceful ballroom dancer and became the life of many a social gathering. She was too skillful at gin rummy for most and at times, to change the pace at a party, she would take out a harmonica and give a rendition of hillbilly tunes she had learned as a youngster.

Probably the greatest woman athlete of our day, Babe Zaharias was a master of many sports.

Bibliography

Abodaher, David J. *The Speedmakers: Great Race Drivers.* New York: Messner, 1979.

Allen, Maury. *You Could Look It Up: The Life of Casey Stengel.* New York: Times Books, 1979.

Betts, John R. *America's Sporting Heritage: 1850–1950.* Reading, Mass.: Addison-Wesley, 1974.

Blinn, William. *Brian's Song.* New York: Bantam, 1972.

Brondfield, Jerry. *Rockne: Football's Greatest Coach.* New York: Random, 1976.

Brown, Gene, ed. *The New York Times Encyclopedia of Sports.* 15 vols. New York: Arno Press, 1979.

Cohen, Richard M. et al. *The Notre Dame Football Scrapbook.* Indianapolis, Ind.: Bobbs-Merrill, 1977.

Creamer, Robert. *Babe.* New York: Simon & Schuster, 1974.

Danzig, Allison and Brandwein, Peter, eds. *Sport's Golden Age, a Closeup of the Fabulous Twenties.* facs. ed. New York: Arno Press, 1977.

Deford, Frank. *Big Bill Tilden.* New York: Simon & Schuster, 1976.

Devaney, John. *Superstars of Sports: Today and Yesterday.* New York: Manor Books, 1979.

Dowling, Tom. *Coach: A Season with Lombardi.* New York: Popular Library, 1977.

Durant, John. *The Heavyweight Champions.* 6th rev. ed. New York: Hastings, 1976.

Farr, Naunerle C. *Babe Ruth—Jackie Robinson.* West Haven, Conn.: Pendulum Press, 1979.

Frommer, Harvey. *Sports Roots: How Nicknames, Namesakes, Trophies, Competitions and Expressions Came to be in the World of Sports.* New York: Atheneum, 1979.

Gluck, Herb. *Baseball's Greatest Moments.* New York: Random House, 1975.

Goodner, Ross. *Golf's Greatest: The Legendary World Golf Hall of Famers.* Norwalk, Conn.: Golf Digest Books, 1978.

Grayson, Harry. *They Played the Game: The Story of Baseball Greats.* repr. of 1944 ed. New York: Arno Press, 1977.

Hollander, Zander and Schulz, Dave. *The Sports Nostalgia Quiz Book.* New York: New American Library, 1979.

Holway, John. *Voices from the Great Black Baseball Leagues.* New York: Dodd, Mead, 1975.

Johnson, William O. and Williamson, Nancy P. *Whatta-Gal! The Babe Diedrikson Story.* Boston: Little, Brown, 1977.

Kahn, Roger. *The Boys of Summer.* New York: New American Library, 1973.

Kieran, John and Daley, Arthur. *The Story of the Olympic Games: 776 B.C. to 1976.* New York: Lippincott, 1977.

Klein, Dave. *The Vince Lombardi Story.* New York: Lion Books, 1977.

McClure, Arthur F. and Young, James V. *Remembering Their Glory.* Cranbury, N.J.: A.S. Barnes, 1977.

McGraw, John J. *My Thirty Years in Baseball.* New York: Arno Press, 1975.

Marsh, Edwin T. and Ehre, Edward, eds. *Best Sports Stories 1944–1976.* 34 facs. vols. New York: Arno Press, 1980.

Mathewson, Christy. *Pitching in a Pinch.* New York: Stein and Day, 1977.

Morris, Jeannie. *Brian Piccolo: A Short Season.* New York: Dell, 1972.

Murray, Tom. *Sport Magazine's All-Time All Stars.* New York: New American Library, 1977.

Musick, Phil. *Who Was Roberto: A Biography of Roberto Clemente.* New York: Doubleday, 1974.

Owens, Jesse and Neimark, Paul. *Jesse: The Man Who Outran Hitler.* New York: Fawcett, 1979.

Ritter, L.S. *Glory of Their Times.* New York: Macmillan, 1971.

Rubin, Robert. *Lou Gehrig: Courageous Star.* New York: Putnam, 1975.

______________. *Ty Cobb: The Greatest.* New York: Putnam, 1978.

Schoor, Gene. *The Jim Thorpe Story: America's Greatest Athlete.* New York: Messner, 1951.

Smelser, Marshall. *The Life that Ruth Built: A Biography.* New York: Times Books, 1975.

Smith, Curt. *America's Dizzy Dean.* St. Louis: Bethany Press, 1978.

Smith, Ken. *Baseball's Hall of Fame.* rev., 9th ed. New York: Grosset & Dunlap, 1979.

Sodenberg, Paul and Washington, Helen, eds. *The Big Book of Halls of Fame in the United States and Canada.* New York: Bowker, 1977.

Sullivan, John L. *I Can Lick Any Sonofabitch in the House.* New York: Proteus, 1980.

Tollin, Mike. *Greatest Sports Legends.* New York: Ace Books, 1979.

Tuite, James, ed. *Sports of the Times: The Arthur Daley Years.* New York: Times Books, 1975.

Wells, Robert W. *Vince Lombardi: His Life & Times.* Canoga Park, Calif.: Major Books, 1977.

Wheeler, Robert W. *Jim Thorpe: World's Greatest Athlete.* Norman, Okla.: University of Oklahoma Press, 1979.

Zaharias, Babe D. *This Life I've Led.* Cranbury, N.J.: A.S. Barnes, 1955.